X-TREME parenting

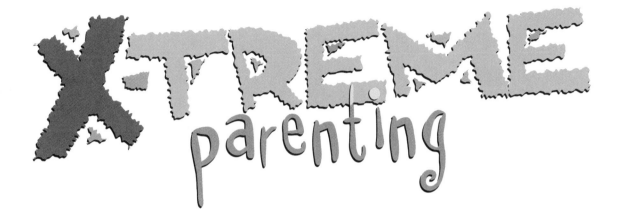

Other *Baby Blues®* Books from Andrews McMeel Publishing

Guess Who Didn't Take a Nap?
I Thought Labor Ended When the Baby Was Born
We Are Experiencing Parental Difficulties . . . Please Stand By
Night of the Living Dad
I Saw Elvis in My Ultrasound
One More and We're Outnumbered!
Check, Please . . .
threats, bribes & videotape
If I'm a Stay-At-Home Mom, Why Am I Always in the Car?
Lift and Separate
I Shouldn't Have to Scream More Than Once!
Motherhood Is Not for Wimps
Baby Blues®: Unplugged
Dad to the Bone
Never a Dry Moment
Two Plus One Is Enough
Playdate: Category 5
Our Server Is Down
Something Chocolate This Way Comes
Briefcase Full of Baby Blues
Night Shift

Treasuries

The Super-Absorbent Biodegradable Family-Size Baby Blues®
Baby Blues®: Ten Years and Still in Diapers
Butt-Naked Baby Blues®
Wall-to-Wall Baby Blues®
Driving Under the Influence of Children
Framed!

X-TREME parenting

A Baby Blues® Treasury by Rick Kirkman & Jerry Scott

**Andrews McMeel
Publishing, LLC**

Kansas City

Baby Blues is syndicated internationally by King Features Syndicate, Inc. For information, write King Features Syndicate, Inc., 300 West Fifty-Seventh Street, New York, New York 10019.

08 09 10 11 12 BAM 10 9 8 7 6 5 4 3 2 1

ISBN-13: 978-0-7407-7097-5
ISBN-10: 0-7407-7097-7

Library of Congress Control Number: 2007937786

www.andrewsmcmeel.com

Find *Baby Blues* on the Web at
www.babyblues.com.

─── **ATTENTION: SCHOOLS AND BUSINESSES** ───

Andrews McMeel books are available at quantity discounts with bulk purchase for educational, business, or sales promotional use. For information, please write to: Special Sales Department, Andrews McMeel Publishing, LLC, 4520 Main Street, Kansas City, Missouri 64111.

To Erin and Andrew, Niki and Corey and Kristin and Justin.
Congratulations . . . and watch out!

—J.S.

For Carol and (the other) Bill Keane, who have their own family
circus. Thanks for the laughs and friendship.

—R.K. and S.K.

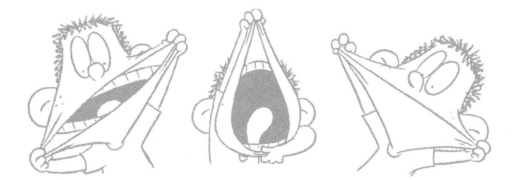

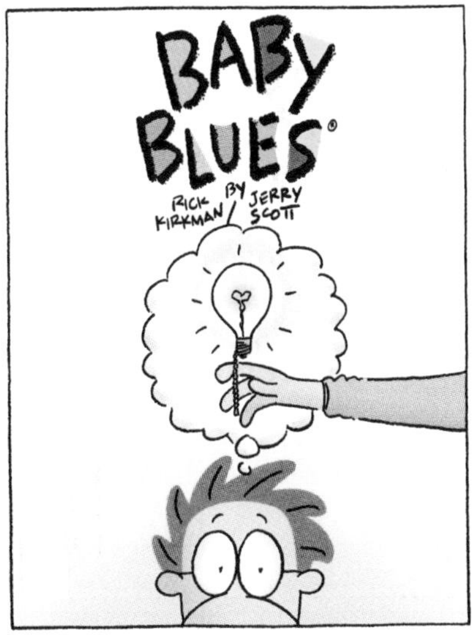
BABY BLUES®
BY RICK KIRKMAN / JERRY SCOTT

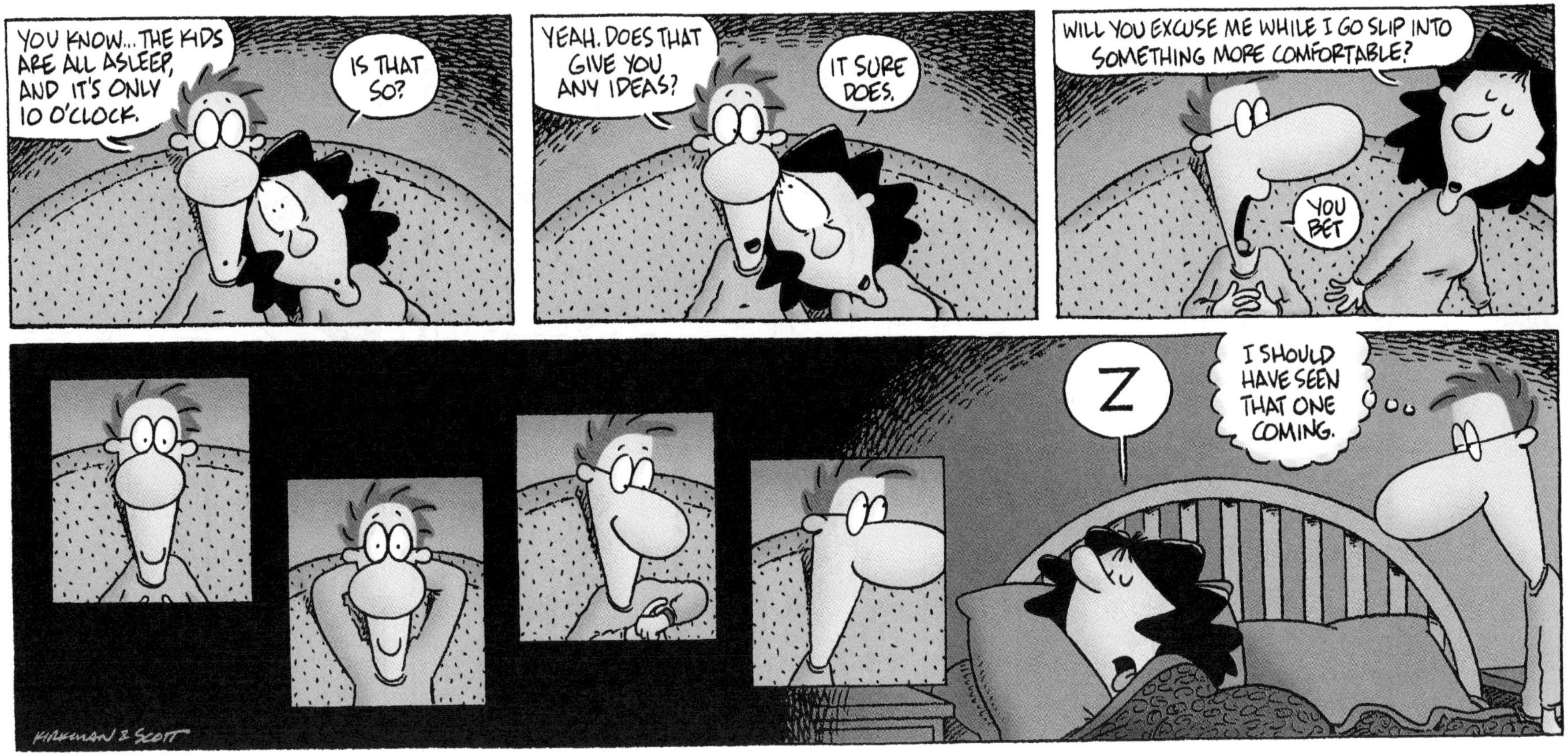
YOU KNOW... THE KIDS ARE ALL ASLEEP, AND IT'S ONLY 10 O'CLOCK.
IS THAT SO?
YEAH. DOES THAT GIVE YOU ANY IDEAS?
IT SURE DOES.
WILL YOU EXCUSE ME WHILE I GO SLIP INTO SOMETHING MORE COMFORTABLE?
YOU BET
Z
I SHOULD HAVE SEEN THAT ONE COMING.
KIRKMAN & SCOTT

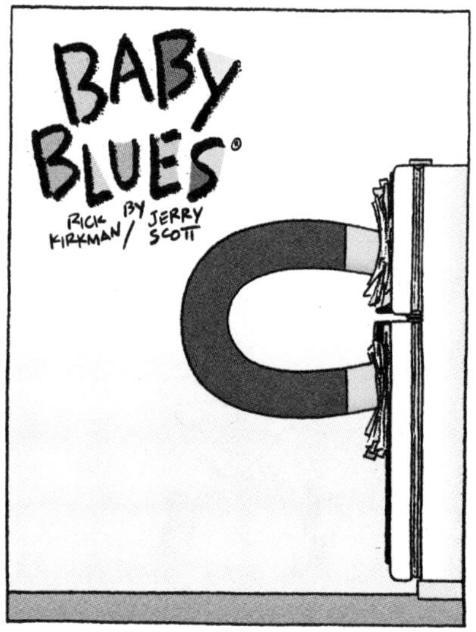
BABY BLUES®
BY RICK KIRKMAN / JERRY SCOTT

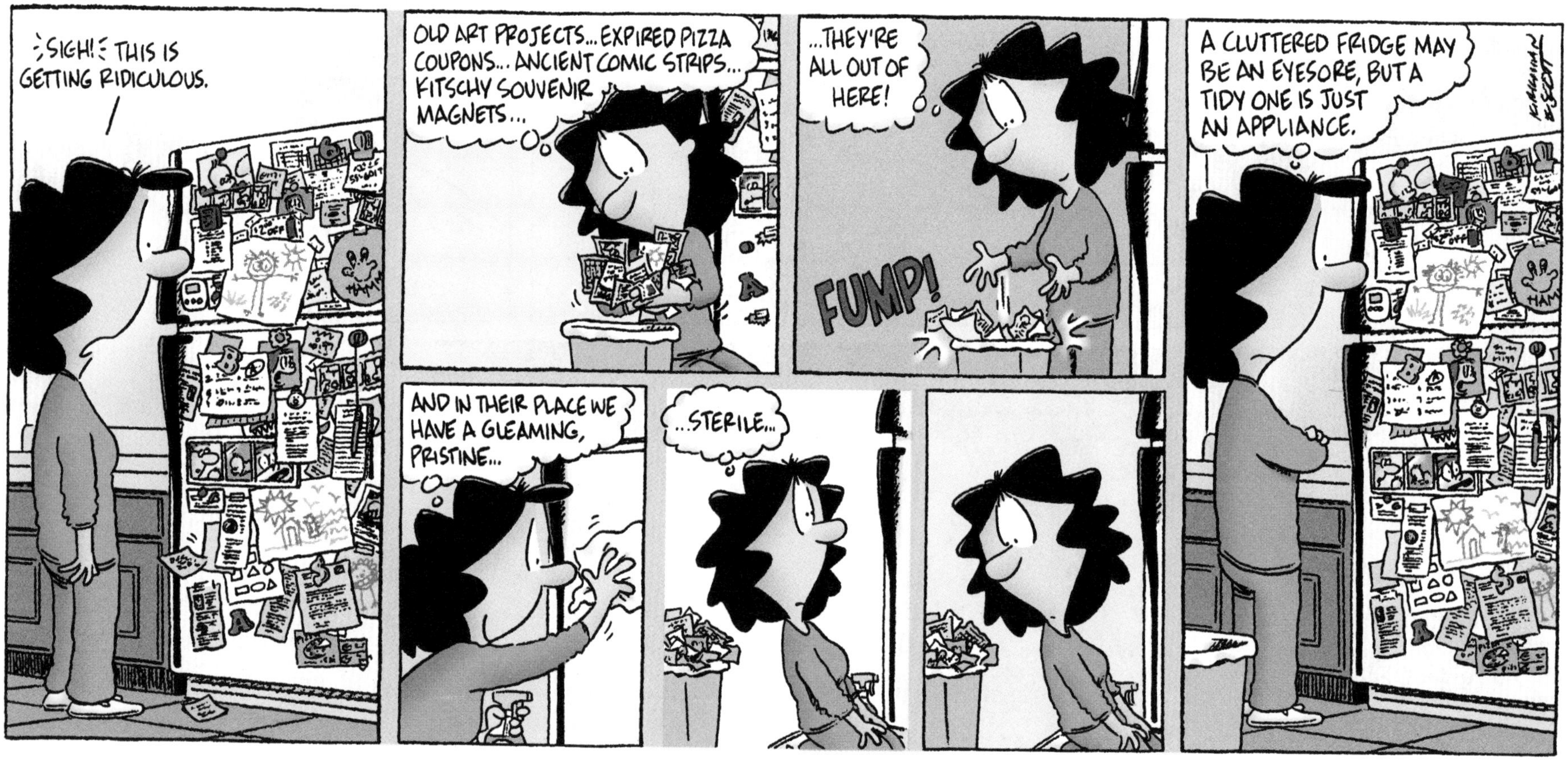
SIGH! THIS IS GETTING RIDICULOUS.
OLD ART PROJECTS... EXPIRED PIZZA COUPONS... ANCIENT COMIC STRIPS... KITSCHY SOUVENIR MAGNETS...
...THEY'RE ALL OUT OF HERE!
FUMP!
AND IN THEIR PLACE WE HAVE A GLEAMING, PRISTINE...
...STERILE...
A CLUTTERED FRIDGE MAY BE AN EYESORE, BUT A TIDY ONE IS JUST AN APPLIANCE.

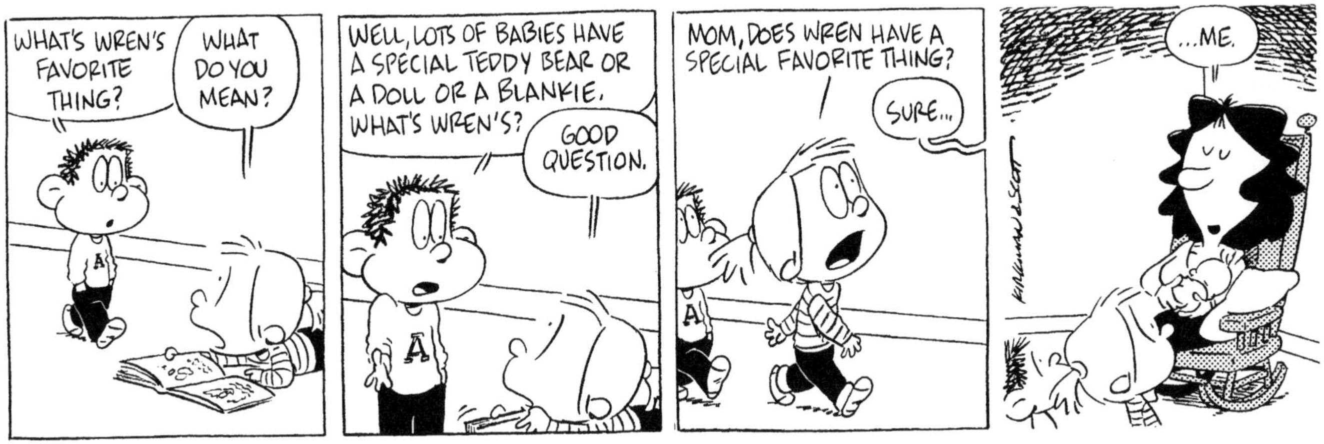
WHAT'S WREN'S FAVORITE THING?
WHAT DO YOU MEAN?
WELL, LOTS OF BABIES HAVE A SPECIAL TEDDY BEAR OR A DOLL OR A BLANKIE. WHAT'S WREN'S?
GOOD QUESTION.
MOM, DOES WREN HAVE A SPECIAL FAVORITE THING?
SURE...
...ME.
KIRKMAN & SCOTT

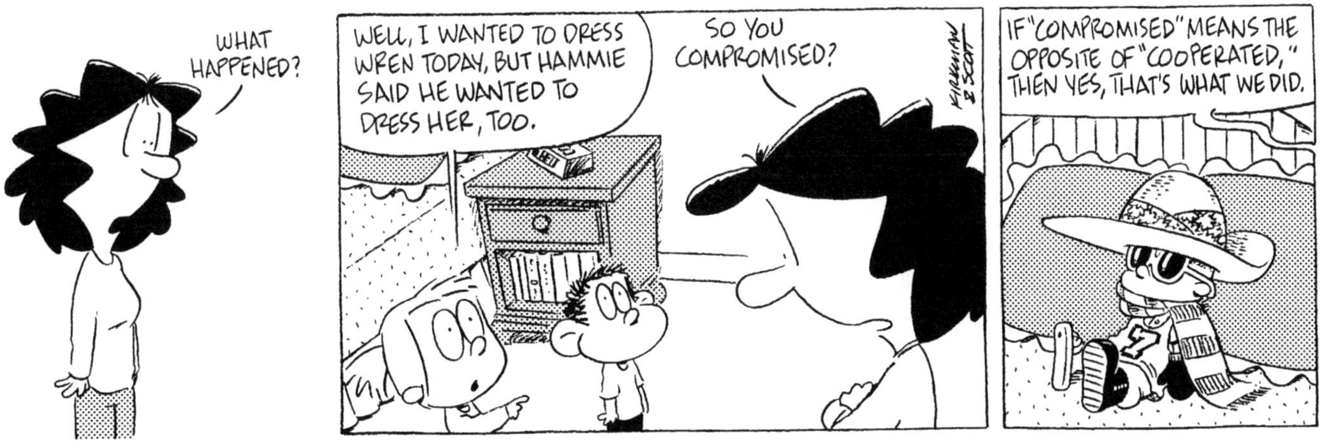
WHAT HAPPENED?
WELL, I WANTED TO DRESS WREN TODAY, BUT HAMMIE SAID HE WANTED TO DRESS HER, TOO.
SO YOU COMPROMISED?
KIRKMAN & SCOTT
IF "COMPROMISED" MEANS THE OPPOSITE OF "COOPERATED," THEN YES, THAT'S WHAT WE DID.

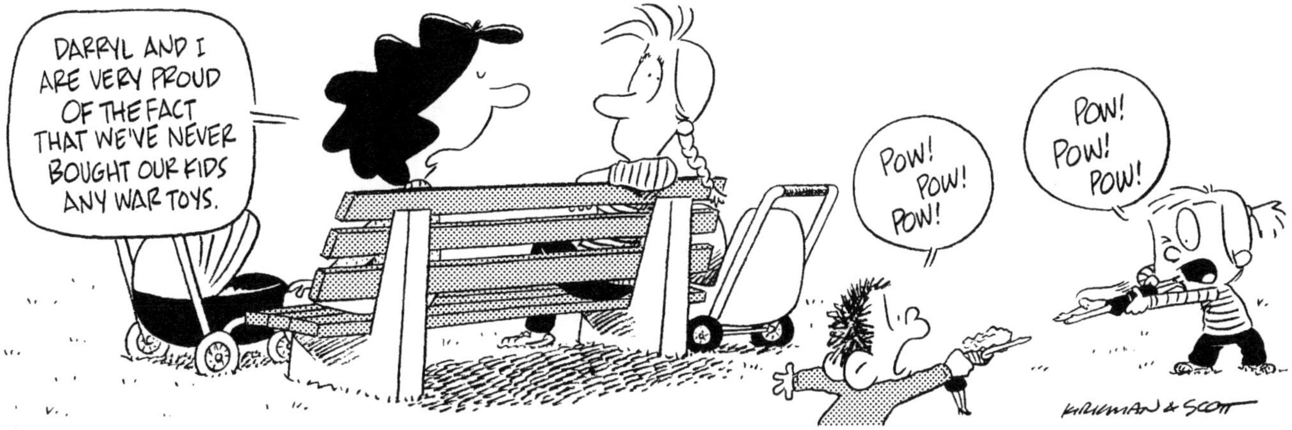
DARRYL AND I ARE VERY PROUD OF THE FACT THAT WE'VE NEVER BOUGHT OUR KIDS ANY WAR TOYS.
POW! POW! POW!
POW! POW! POW!
KIRKMAN & SCOTT

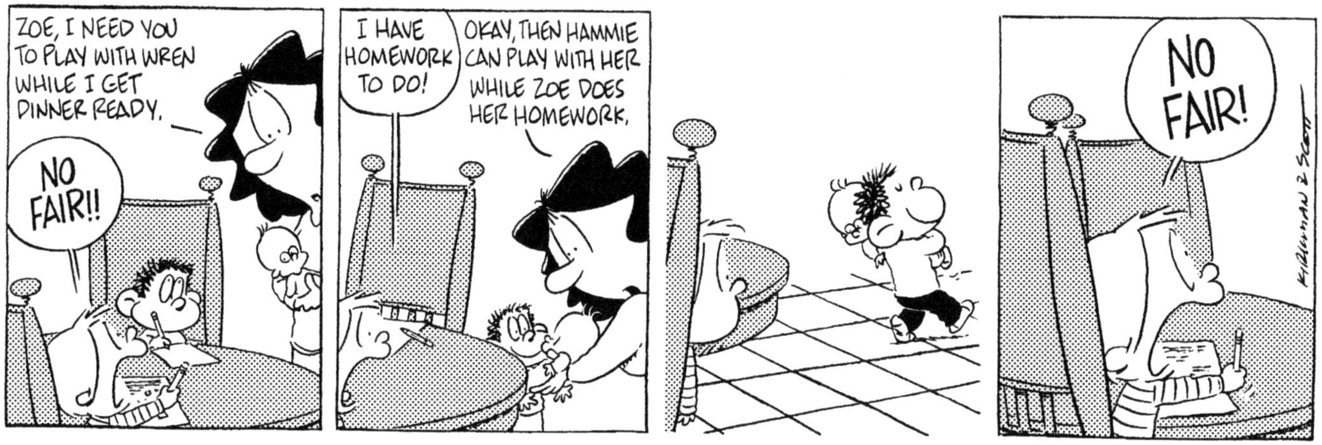
ZOE, I NEED YOU TO PLAY WITH WREN WHILE I GET DINNER READY.
NO FAIR!!
I HAVE HOMEWORK TO DO!
OKAY, THEN HAMMIE CAN PLAY WITH HER WHILE ZOE DOES HER HOMEWORK.
NO FAIR!
KIRKMAN & SCOTT

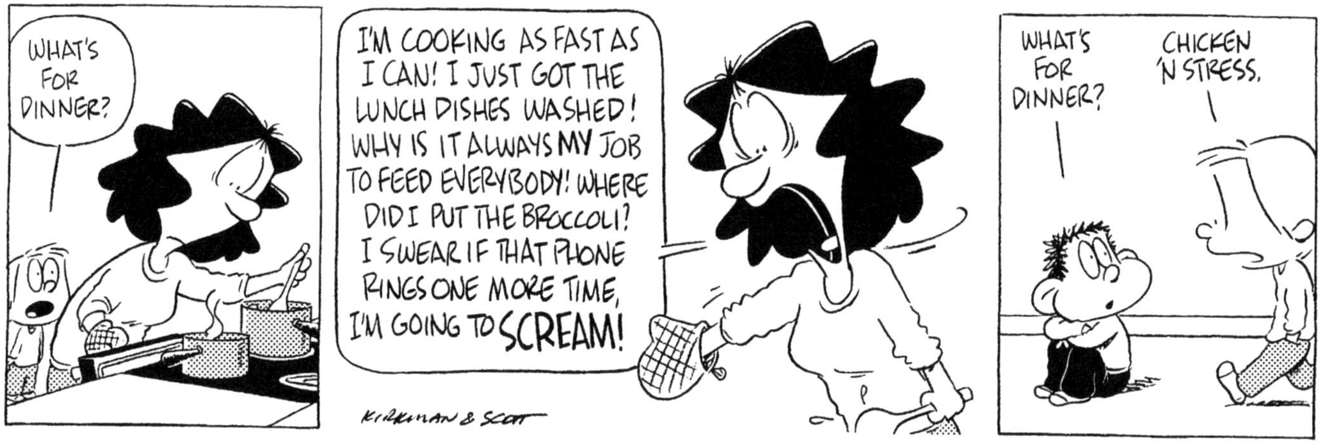
WHAT'S FOR DINNER?
I'M COOKING AS FAST AS I CAN! I JUST GOT THE LUNCH DISHES WASHED! WHY IS IT ALWAYS MY JOB TO FEED EVERYBODY! WHERE DID I PUT THE BROCCOLI? I SWEAR IF THAT PHONE RINGS ONE MORE TIME, I'M GOING TO SCREAM!
KIRKMAN & SCOTT
WHAT'S FOR DINNER?
CHICKEN 'N STRESS.

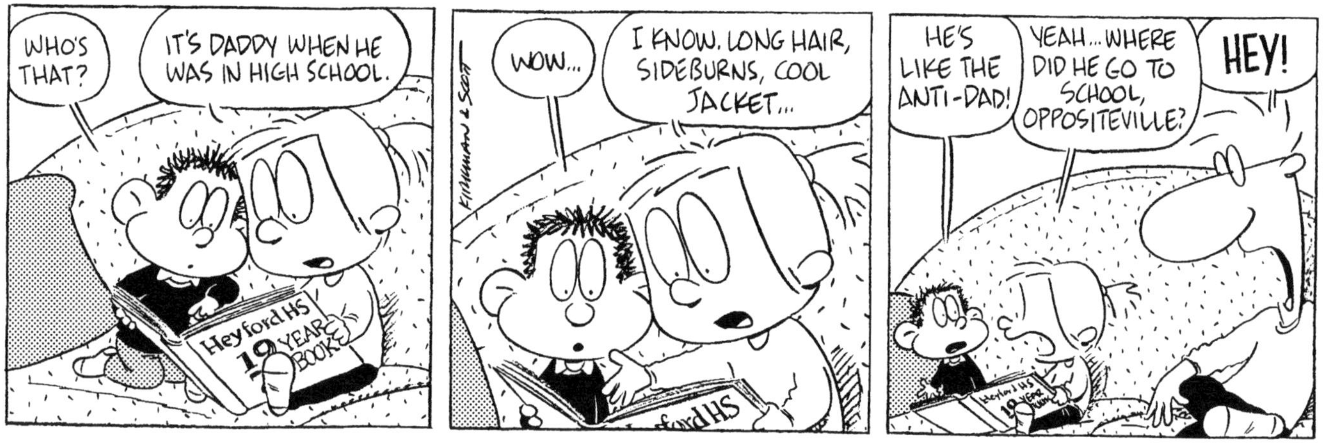
WHO'S THAT?
IT'S DADDY WHEN HE WAS IN HIGH SCHOOL.
Heyford HS 19 YEAR BOOK
KIRKMAN & SCOTT
WOW...
I KNOW. LONG HAIR, SIDEBURNS, COOL JACKET...
HE'S LIKE THE ANTI-DAD!
YEAH... WHERE DID HE GO TO SCHOOL, OPPOSITEVILLE?
HEY!

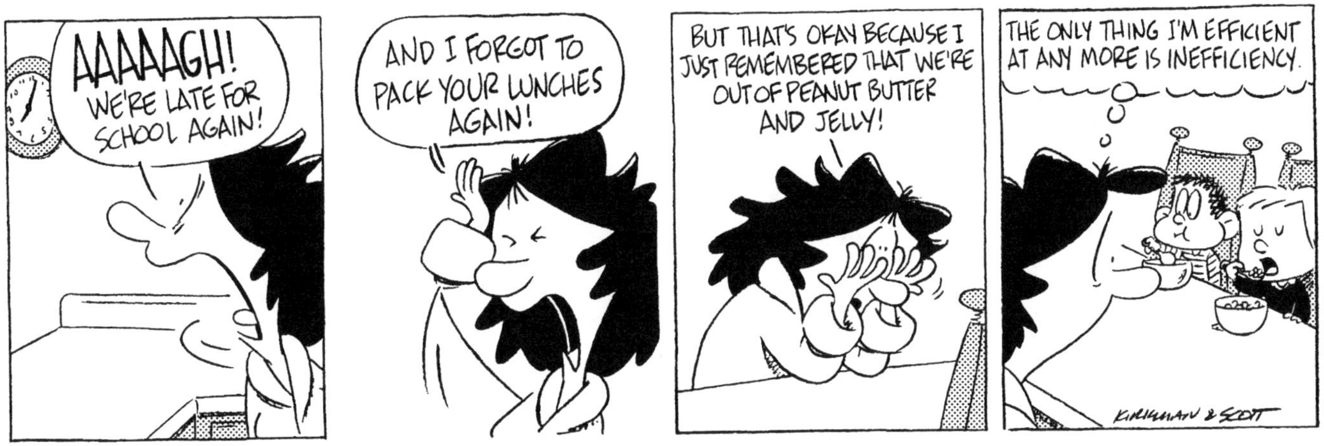
AAAAAGH! WE'RE LATE FOR SCHOOL AGAIN!
AND I FORGOT TO PACK YOUR LUNCHES AGAIN!
BUT THAT'S OKAY BECAUSE I JUST REMEMBERED THAT WE'RE OUT OF PEANUT BUTTER AND JELLY!
THE ONLY THING I'M EFFICIENT AT ANY MORE IS INEFFICIENCY.
KIRKMAN & SCOTT

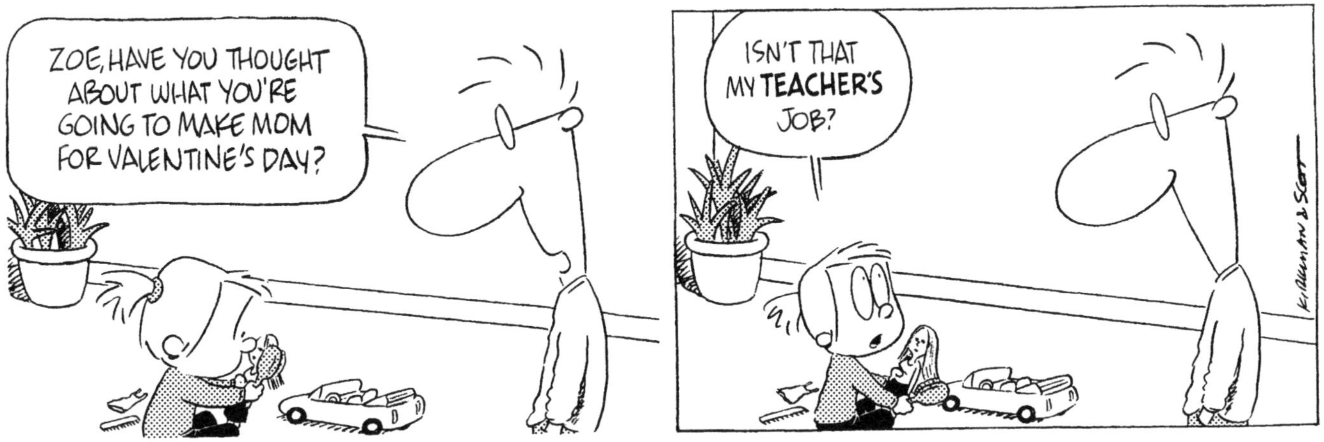
ZOE, HAVE YOU THOUGHT ABOUT WHAT YOU'RE GOING TO MAKE MOM FOR VALENTINE'S DAY?
ISN'T THAT MY **TEACHER'S** JOB?
KIRKMAN & SCOTT

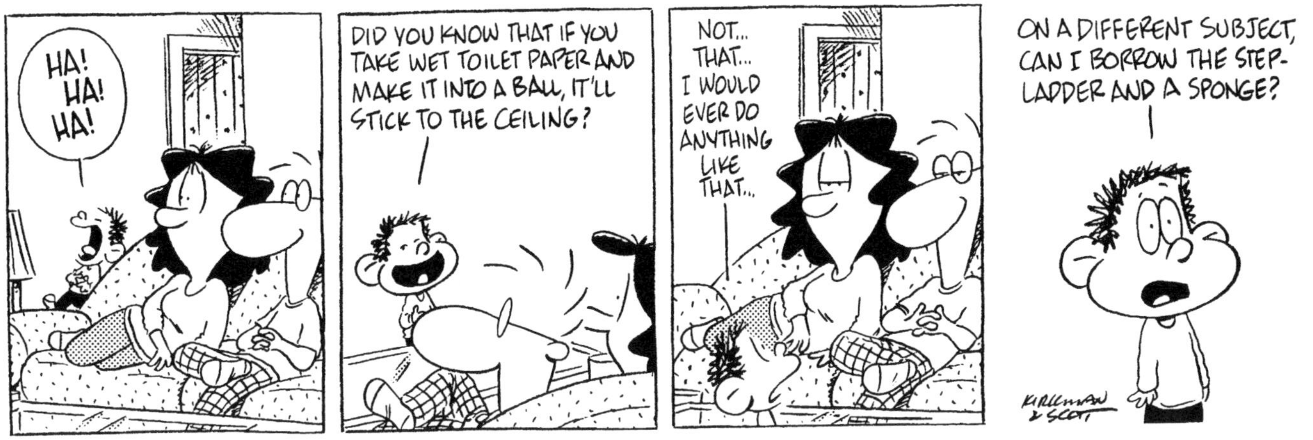
HA! HA! HA!
DID YOU KNOW THAT IF YOU TAKE WET TOILET PAPER AND MAKE IT INTO A BALL, IT'LL STICK TO THE CEILING?
NOT... THAT... I WOULD EVER DO ANYTHING LIKE THAT...
ON A DIFFERENT SUBJECT, CAN I BORROW THE STEP-LADDER AND A SPONGE?
KIRKMAN & SCOTT

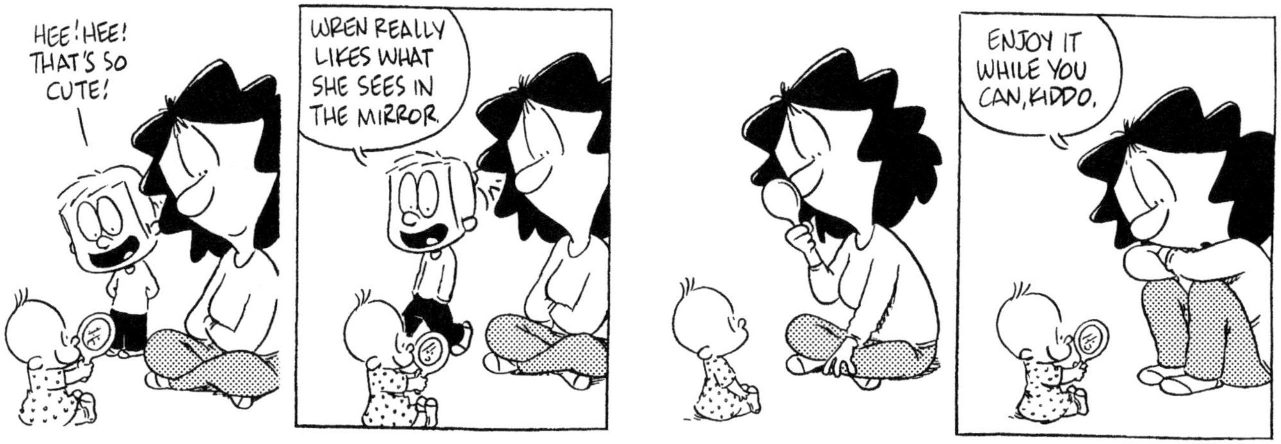
HEE! HEE! THAT'S SO CUTE!
WREN REALLY LIKES WHAT SHE SEES IN THE MIRROR.
ENJOY IT WHILE YOU CAN, KIDDO.

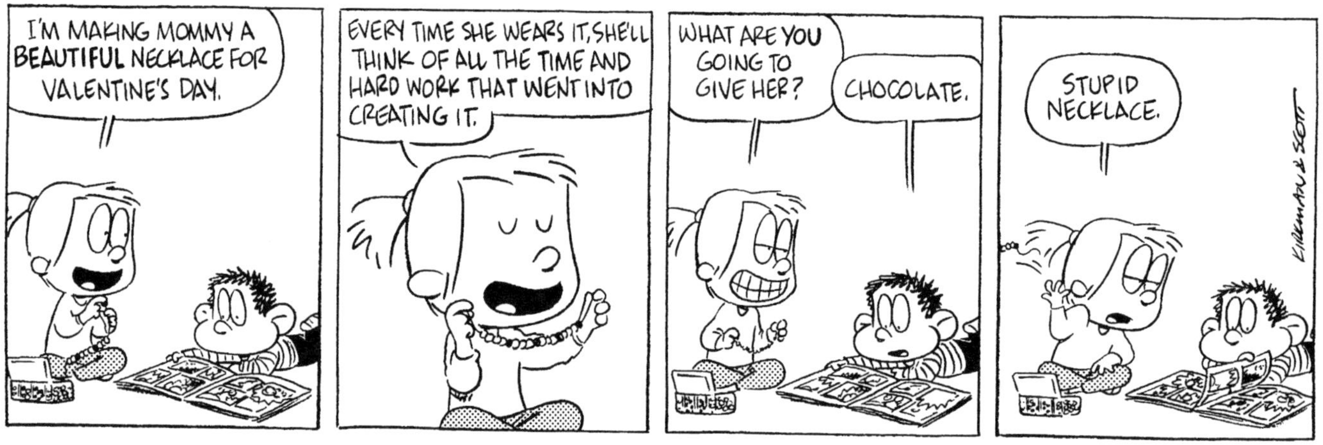
I'M MAKING MOMMY A BEAUTIFUL NECKLACE FOR VALENTINE'S DAY.
EVERY TIME SHE WEARS IT, SHE'LL THINK OF ALL THE TIME AND HARD WORK THAT WENT INTO CREATING IT.
WHAT ARE YOU GOING TO GIVE HER?
CHOCOLATE.
STUPID NECKLACE.

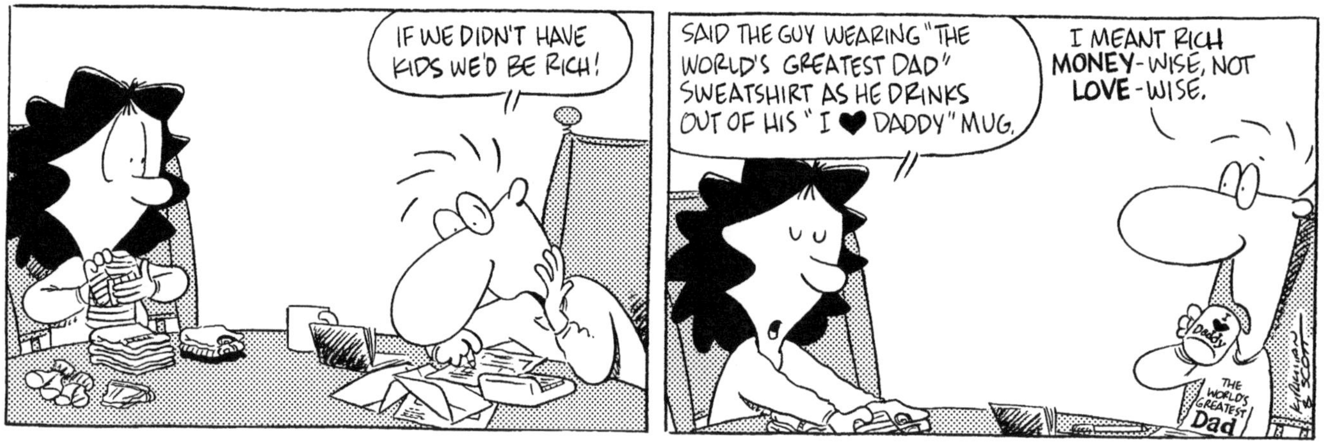
IF WE DIDN'T HAVE KIDS WE'D BE RICH!
SAID THE GUY WEARING "THE WORLD'S GREATEST DAD" SWEATSHIRT AS HE DRINKS OUT OF HIS "I ♥ DADDY" MUG.
I MEANT RICH MONEY-WISE, NOT LOVE-WISE.
THE WORLD'S GREATEST Dad

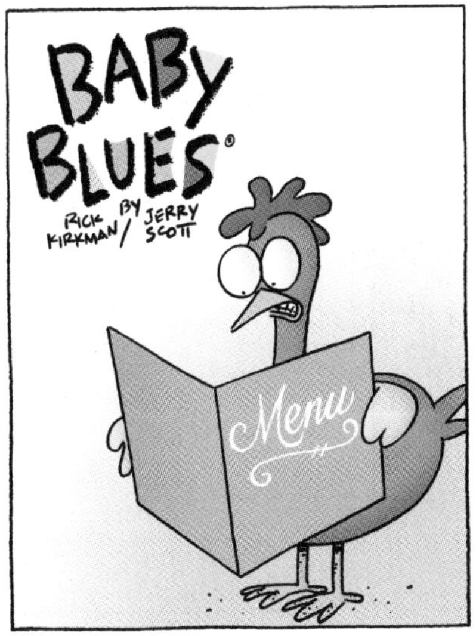
BABY BLUES®
BY RICK KIRKMAN / JERRY SCOTT
Menu

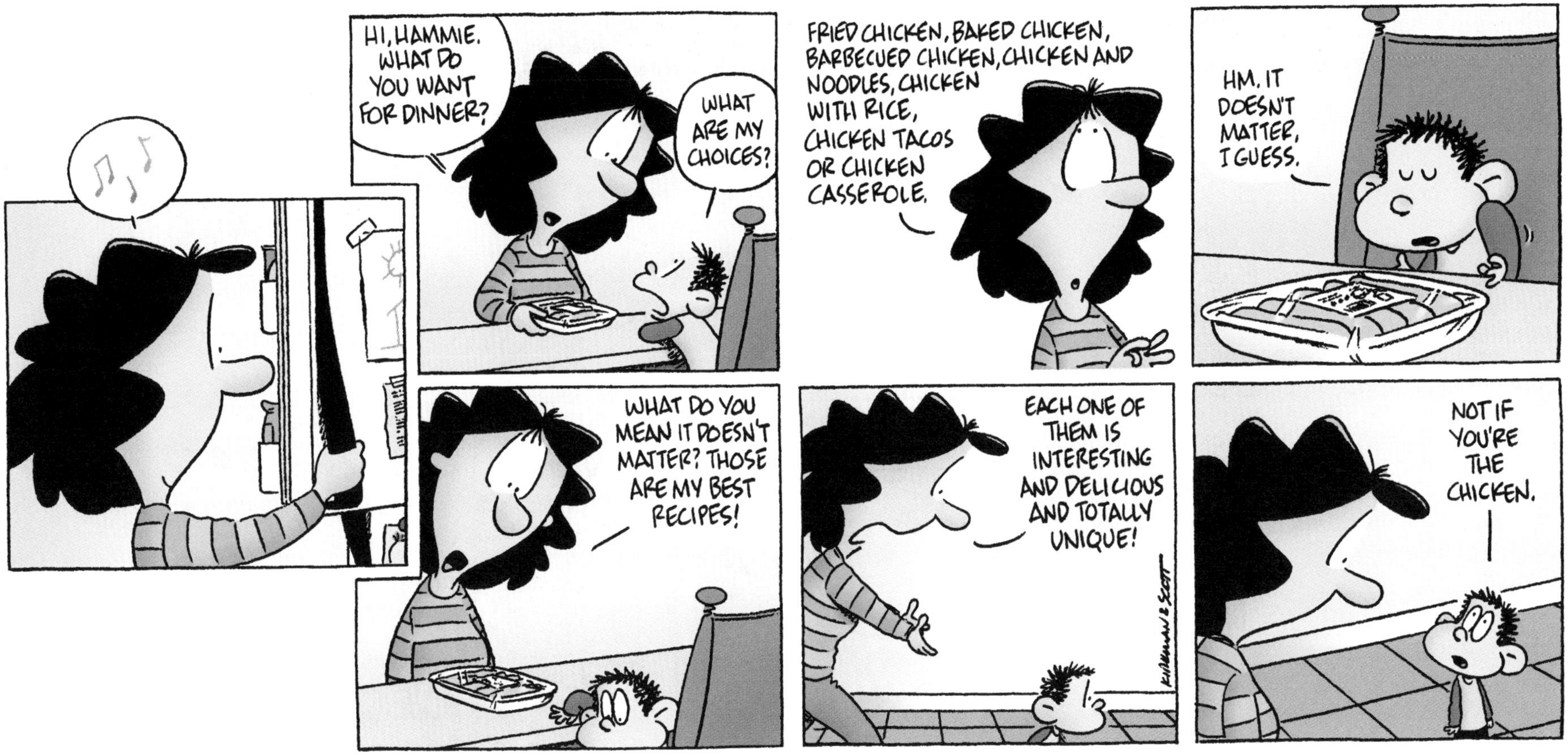
HI, HAMMIE. WHAT DO YOU WANT FOR DINNER?
WHAT ARE MY CHOICES?
FRIED CHICKEN, BAKED CHICKEN, BARBECUED CHICKEN, CHICKEN AND NOODLES, CHICKEN WITH RICE, CHICKEN TACOS OR CHICKEN CASSEROLE.
HM. IT DOESN'T MATTER, I GUESS.
WHAT DO YOU MEAN IT DOESN'T MATTER? THOSE ARE MY BEST RECIPES!
EACH ONE OF THEM IS INTERESTING AND DELICIOUS AND TOTALLY UNIQUE!
KIRKMAN & SCOTT
NOT IF YOU'RE THE CHICKEN.

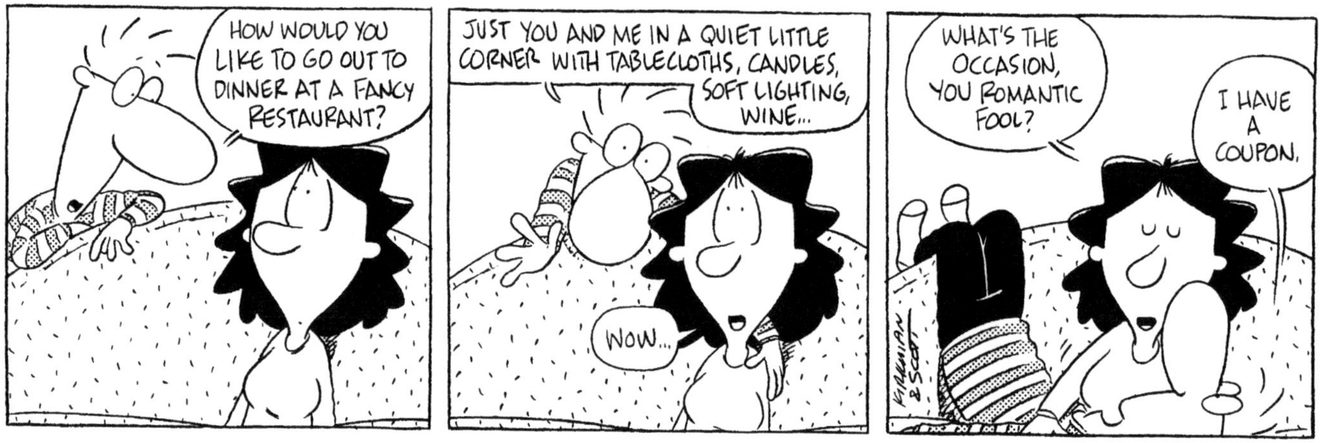
HOW WOULD YOU LIKE TO GO OUT TO DINNER AT A FANCY RESTAURANT?
JUST YOU AND ME IN A QUIET LITTLE CORNER WITH TABLECLOTHS, CANDLES, SOFT LIGHTING, WINE...
WOW...
WHAT'S THE OCCASION, YOU ROMANTIC FOOL?
I HAVE A COUPON.

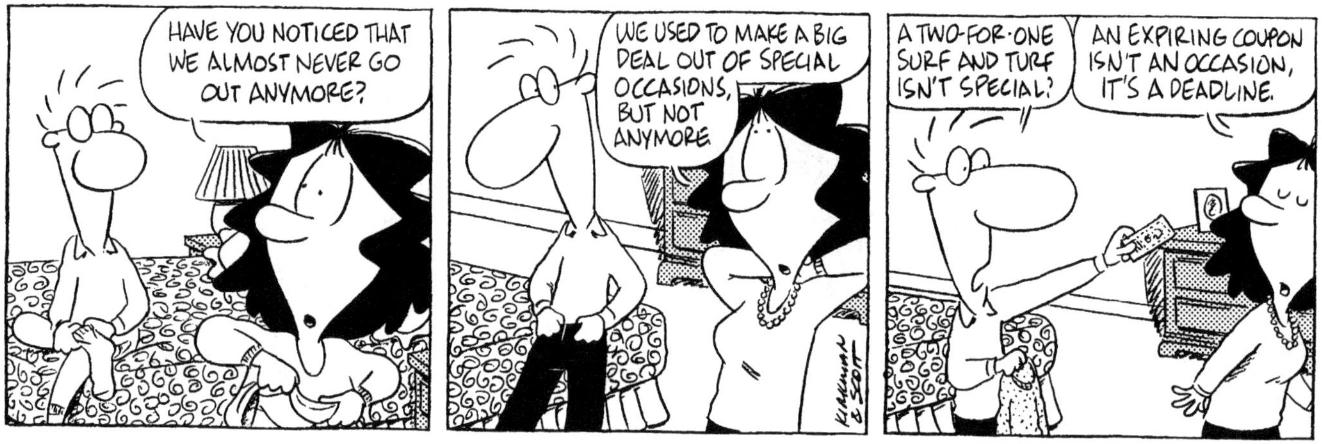
HAVE YOU NOTICED THAT WE ALMOST NEVER GO OUT ANYMORE?
WE USED TO MAKE A BIG DEAL OUT OF SPECIAL OCCASIONS, BUT NOT ANYMORE.
A TWO-FOR-ONE SURF AND TURF ISN'T SPECIAL?
AN EXPIRING COUPON ISN'T AN OCCASION, IT'S A DEADLINE.

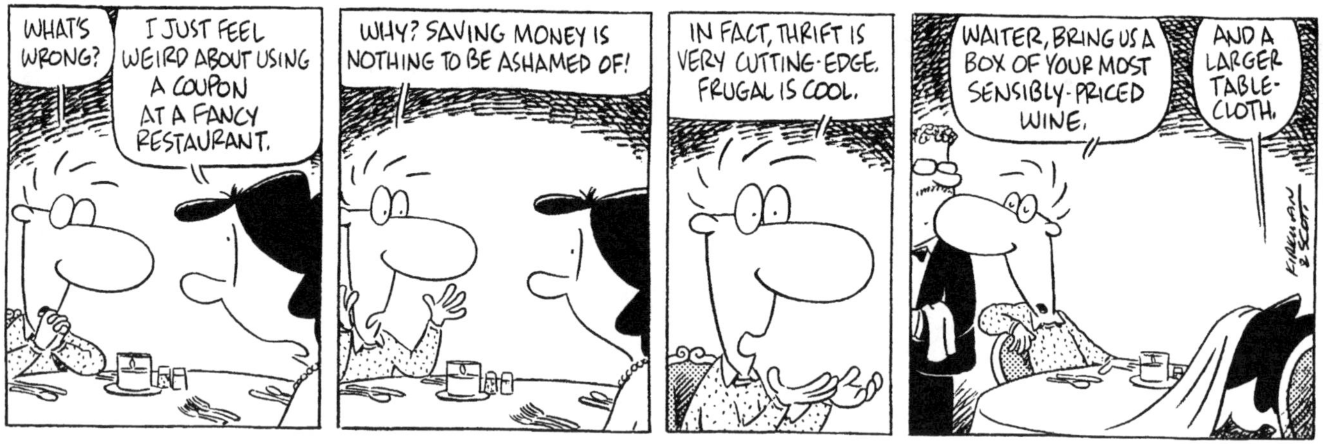
WHAT'S WRONG?
I JUST FEEL WEIRD ABOUT USING A COUPON AT A FANCY RESTAURANT.
WHY? SAVING MONEY IS NOTHING TO BE ASHAMED OF!
IN FACT, THRIFT IS VERY CUTTING-EDGE. FRUGAL IS COOL.
WAITER, BRING US A BOX OF YOUR MOST SENSIBLY-PRICED WINE.
AND A LARGER TABLECLOTH.

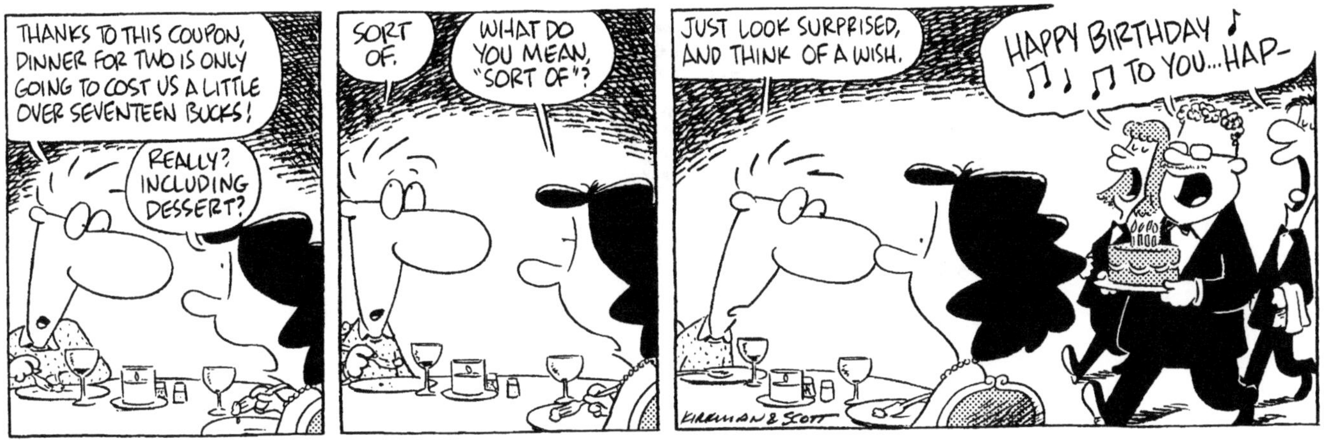
THANKS TO THIS COUPON, DINNER FOR TWO IS ONLY GOING TO COST US A LITTLE OVER SEVENTEEN BUCKS!
REALLY? INCLUDING DESSERT?
SORT OF.
WHAT DO YOU MEAN, "SORT OF"?
JUST LOOK SURPRISED, AND THINK OF A WISH.
HAPPY BIRTHDAY ♪ ♫ ♪ ♫ TO YOU...HAP-
KIRKMAN & SCOTT

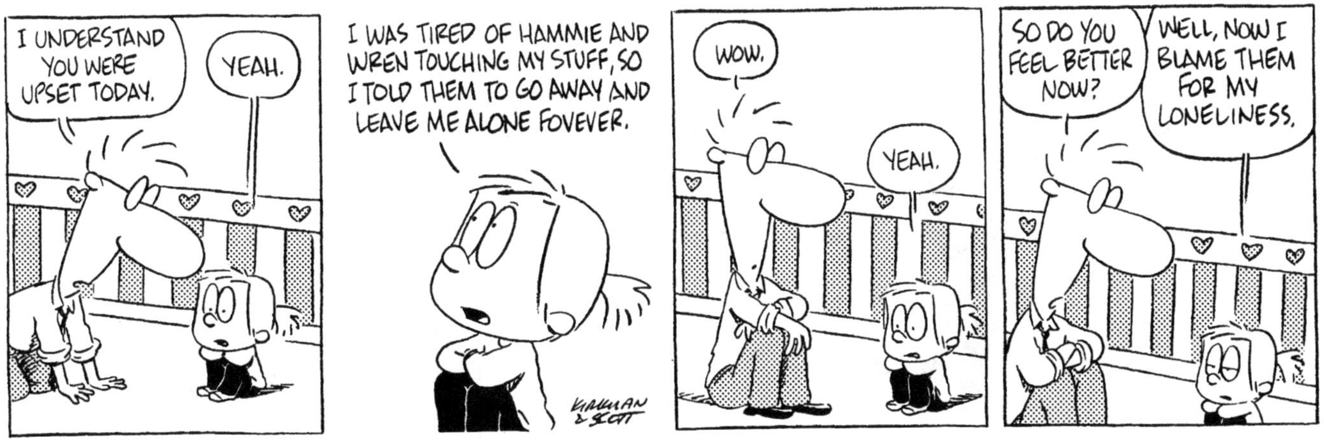
I UNDERSTAND YOU WERE UPSET TODAY.
YEAH.
I WAS TIRED OF HAMMIE AND WREN TOUCHING MY STUFF, SO I TOLD THEM TO GO AWAY AND LEAVE ME ALONE FOVEVER.
KIRKMAN & SCOTT
WOW.
YEAH.
SO DO YOU FEEL BETTER NOW?
WELL, NOW I BLAME THEM FOR MY LONELINESS.

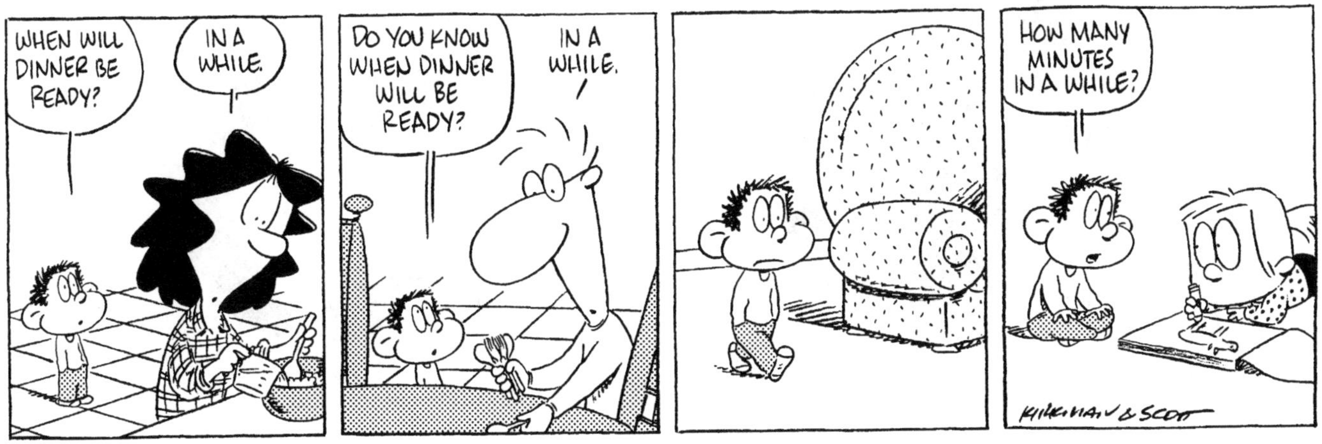
WHEN WILL DINNER BE READY?
IN A WHILE.
DO YOU KNOW WHEN DINNER WILL BE READY?
IN A WHILE.
HOW MANY MINUTES IN A WHILE?
KIRKMAN & SCOTT

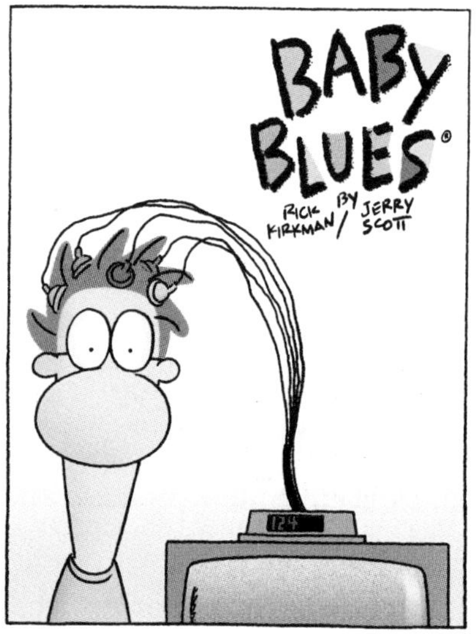
BABY BLUES®
BY RICK KIRKMAN / JERRY SCOTT

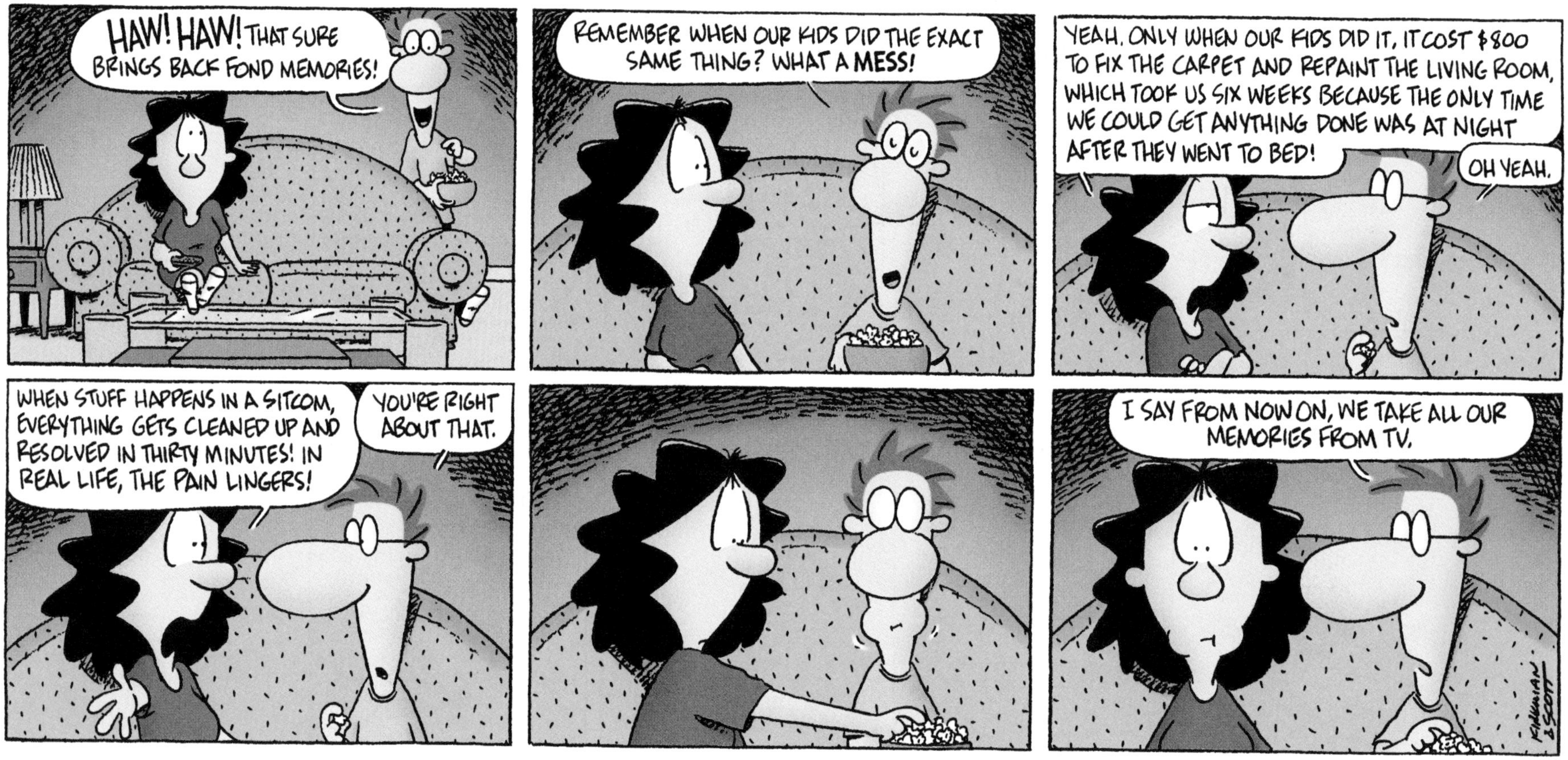
HAW! HAW! THAT SURE BRINGS BACK FOND MEMORIES!
REMEMBER WHEN OUR KIDS DID THE EXACT SAME THING? WHAT A MESS!
YEAH. ONLY WHEN OUR KIDS DID IT, IT COST $800 TO FIX THE CARPET AND REPAINT THE LIVING ROOM, WHICH TOOK US SIX WEEKS BECAUSE THE ONLY TIME WE COULD GET ANYTHING DONE WAS AT NIGHT AFTER THEY WENT TO BED!
OH YEAH.
WHEN STUFF HAPPENS IN A SITCOM, EVERYTHING GETS CLEANED UP AND RESOLVED IN THIRTY MINUTES! IN REAL LIFE, THE PAIN LINGERS!
YOU'RE RIGHT ABOUT THAT.
I SAY FROM NOW ON, WE TAKE ALL OUR MEMORIES FROM TV.
KIRKMAN & SCOTT

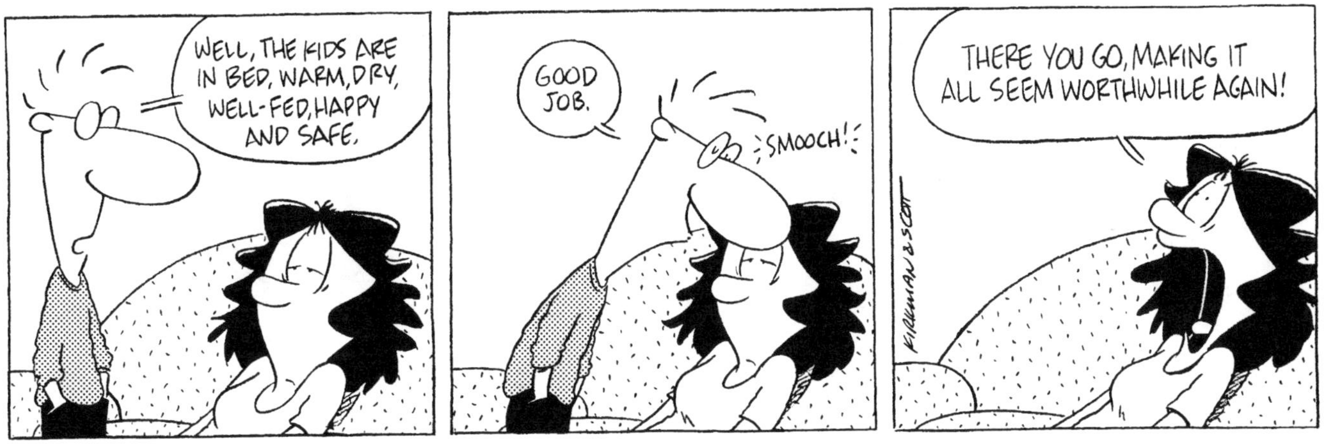
WELL, THE KIDS ARE IN BED, WARM, DRY, WELL-FED, HAPPY AND SAFE.
GOOD JOB.
SMOOCH!
THERE YOU GO, MAKING IT ALL SEEM WORTHWHILE AGAIN!
KIRKMAN & SCOTT

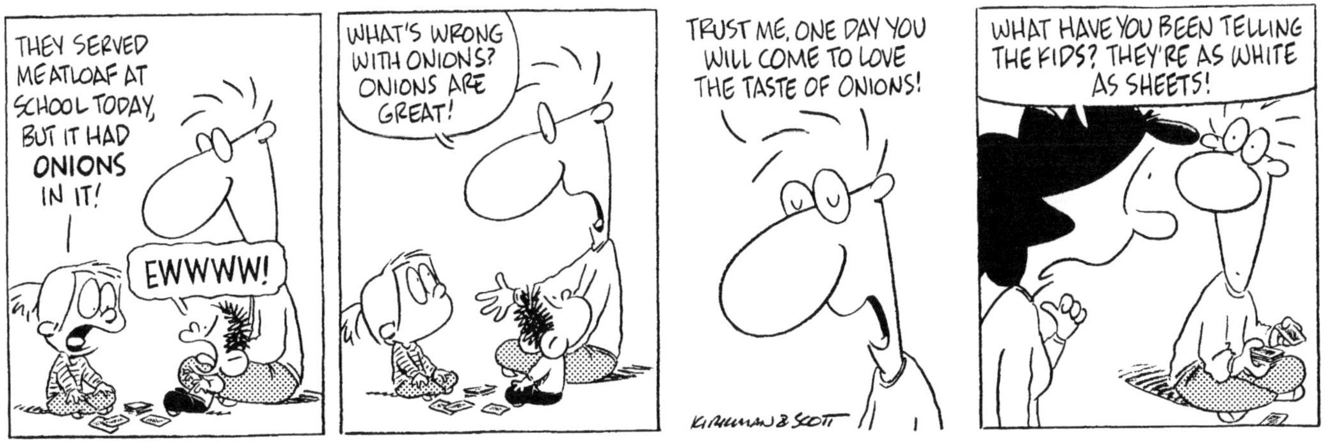
THEY SERVED MEATLOAF AT SCHOOL TODAY, BUT IT HAD **ONIONS** IN IT!
EWWWW!
WHAT'S WRONG WITH ONIONS? ONIONS ARE GREAT!
TRUST ME, ONE DAY YOU WILL COME TO LOVE THE TASTE OF ONIONS!
KIRKMAN & SCOTT
WHAT HAVE YOU BEEN TELLING THE KIDS? THEY'RE AS WHITE AS SHEETS!

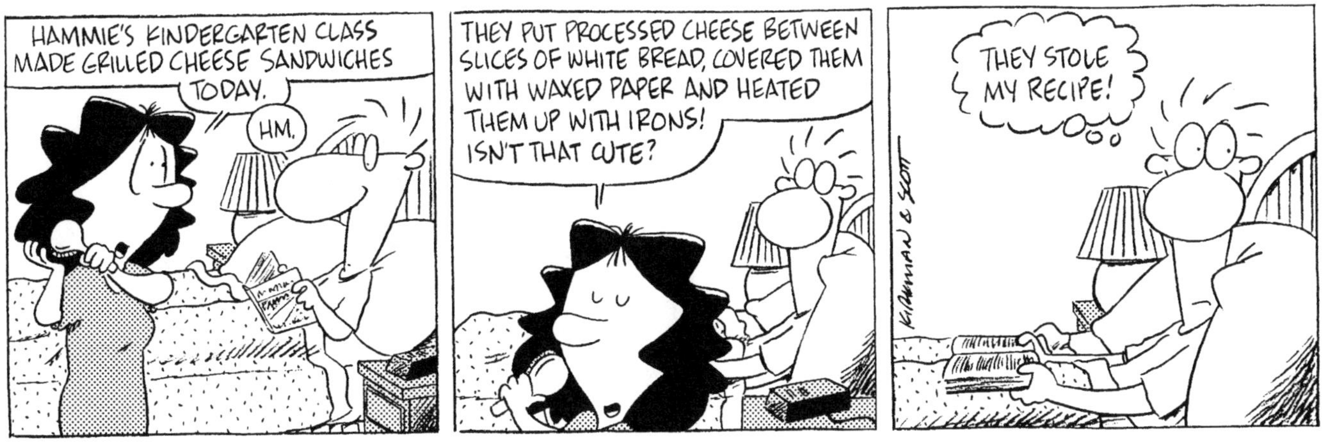
HAMMIE'S KINDERGARTEN CLASS MADE GRILLED CHEESE SANDWICHES TODAY.
HM.
THEY PUT PROCESSED CHEESE BETWEEN SLICES OF WHITE BREAD, COVERED THEM WITH WAXED PAPER AND HEATED THEM UP WITH IRONS! ISN'T THAT CUTE?
KIRKMAN & SCOTT
THEY STOLE MY RECIPE!

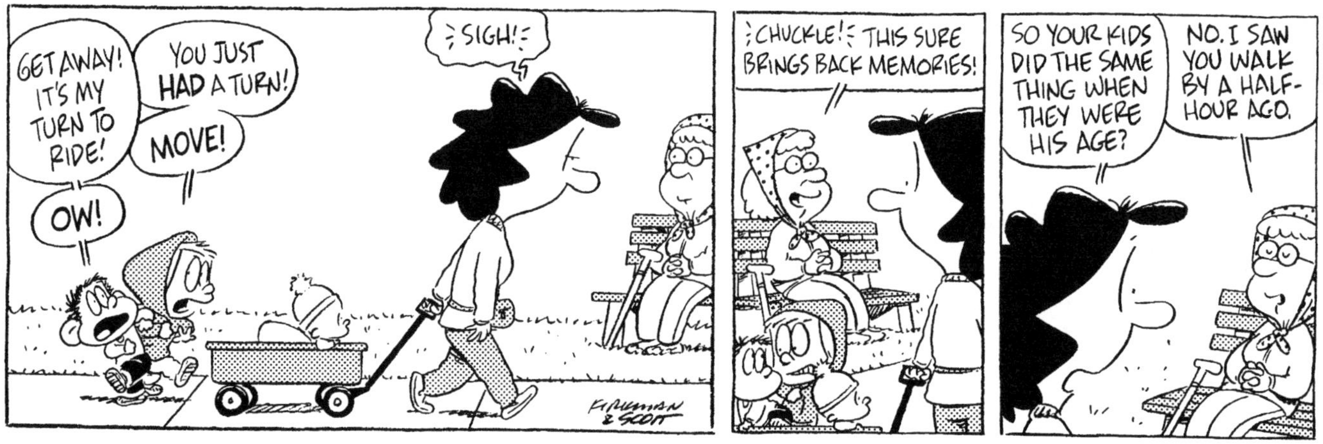
GET AWAY! IT'S MY TURN TO RIDE!
YOU JUST HAD A TURN!
MOVE!
OW!
SIGH!
KIRKMAN & SCOTT
CHUCKLE! THIS SURE BRINGS BACK MEMORIES!
SO YOUR KIDS DID THE SAME THING WHEN THEY WERE HIS AGE?
NO. I SAW YOU WALK BY A HALF-HOUR AGO.

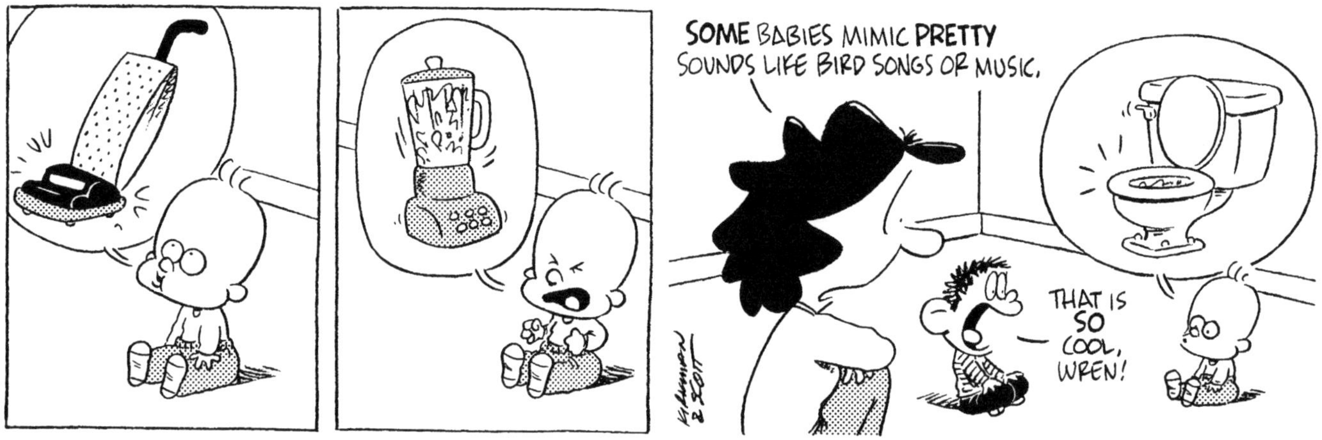
SOME BABIES MIMIC PRETTY SOUNDS LIKE BIRD SONGS OR MUSIC.
THAT IS SO COOL, WREN!
KIRKMAN & SCOTT

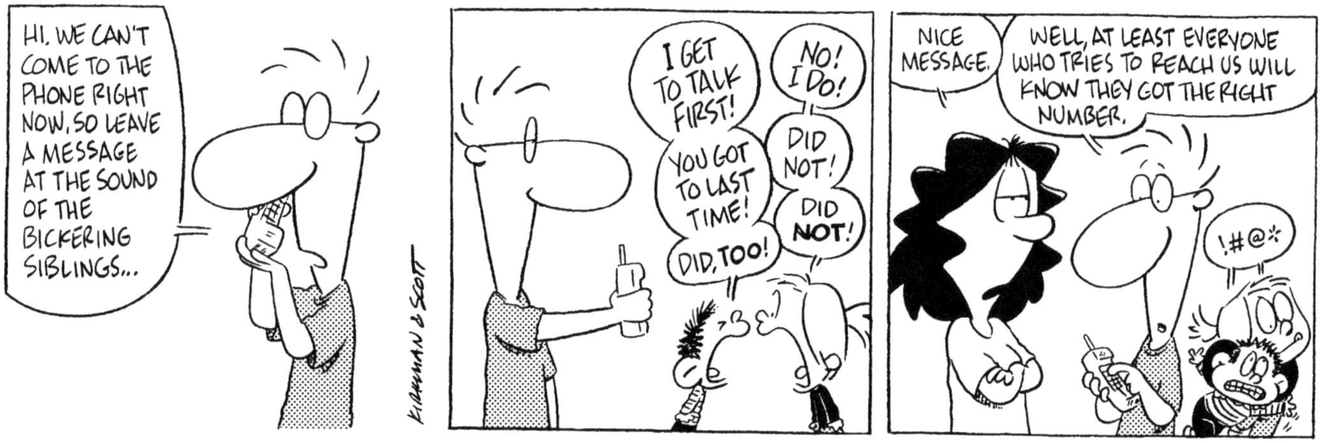
HI. WE CAN'T COME TO THE PHONE RIGHT NOW, SO LEAVE A MESSAGE AT THE SOUND OF THE BICKERING SIBLINGS...
KIRKMAN & SCOTT
I GET TO TALK FIRST!
NO! I DO!
YOU GOT TO LAST TIME!
DID NOT!
DID, TOO!
DID NOT!
NICE MESSAGE.
WELL, AT LEAST EVERYONE WHO TRIES TO REACH US WILL KNOW THEY GOT THE RIGHT NUMBER.
!#@*

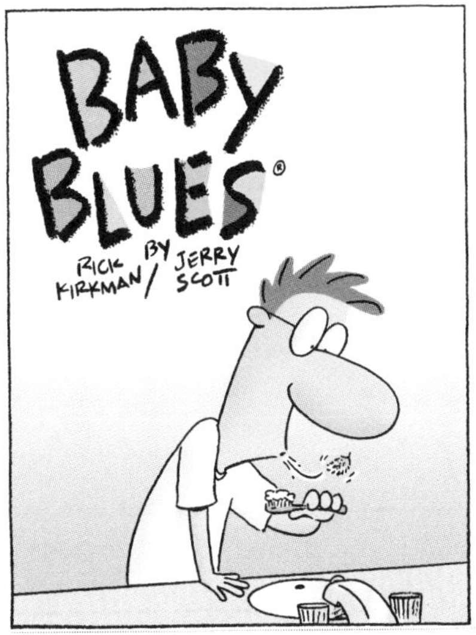
BABY BLUES®
BY RICK KIRKMAN / JERRY SCOTT

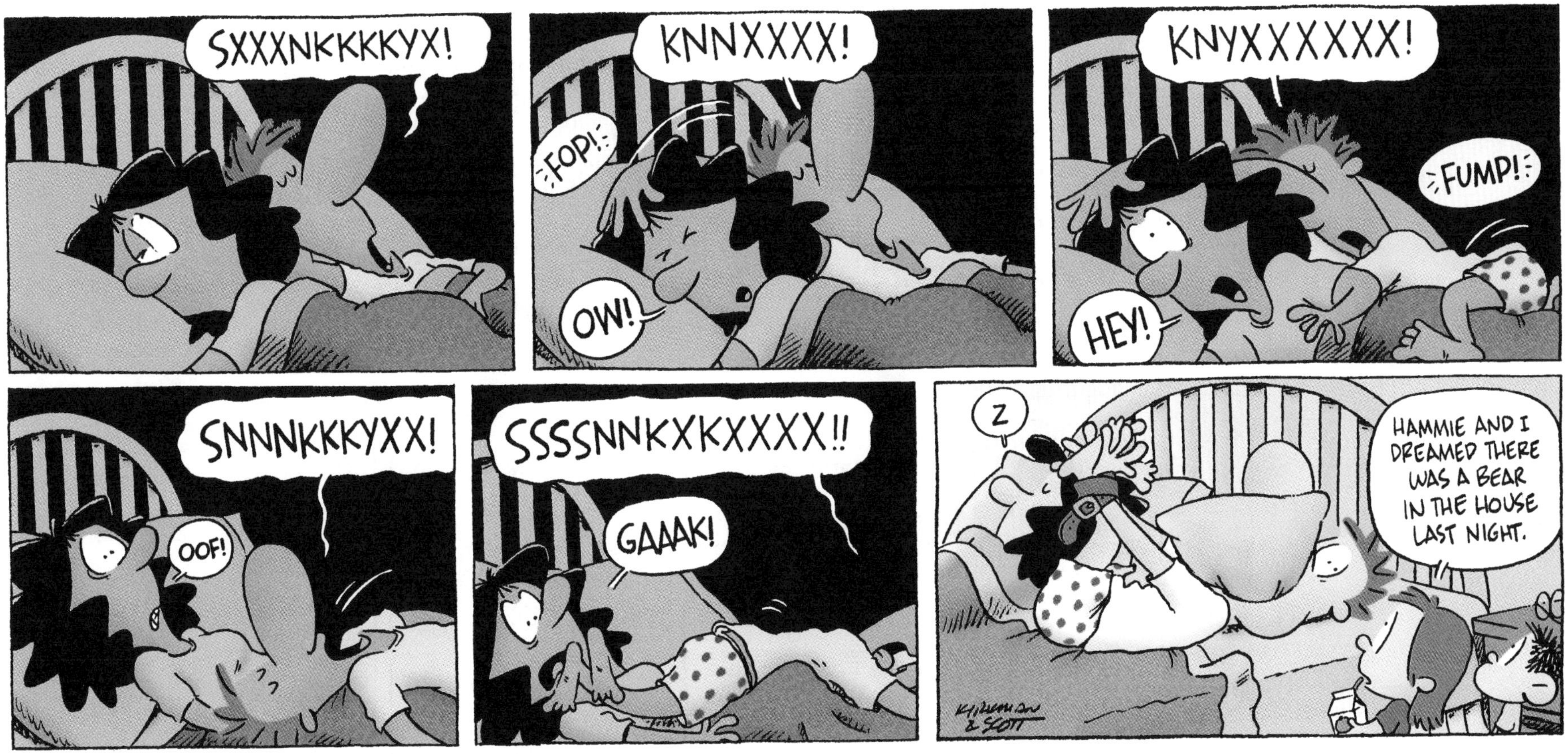
SXXXNKKKKYX!
KNNXXXX!
FOP!
OW!
KNYXXXXXX!
FUMP!
HEY!
SNNNKKKYXX!
OOF!
SSSSNNKXKXXXX!!
GAAAK!
Z
HAMMIE AND I DREAMED THERE WAS A BEAR IN THE HOUSE LAST NIGHT.
KIRKMAN & SCOTT

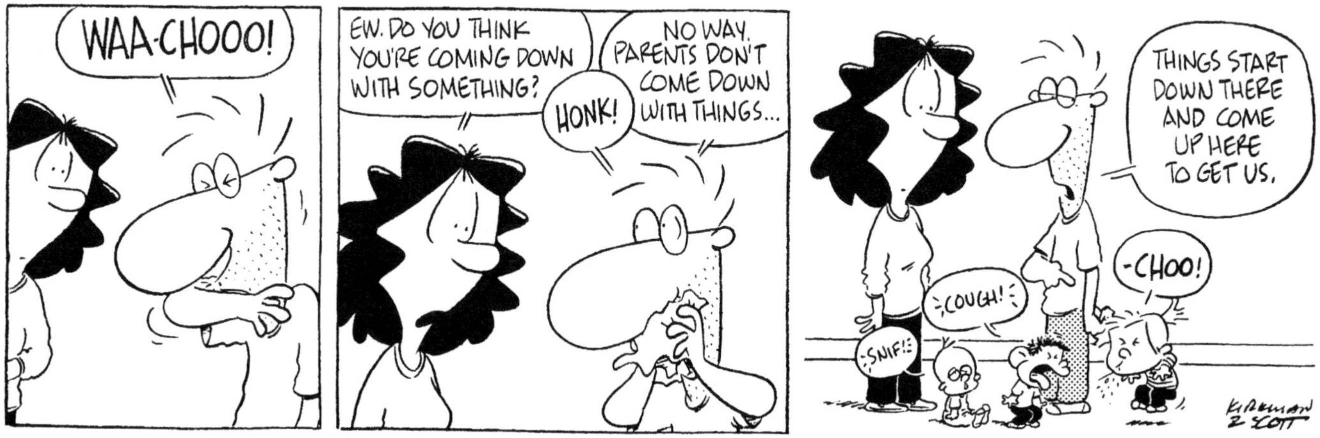
WAA-CHOOO!
EW. DO YOU THINK YOU'RE COMING DOWN WITH SOMETHING?
HONK!
NO WAY. PARENTS DON'T COME DOWN WITH THINGS...
THINGS START DOWN THERE AND COME UP HERE TO GET US.
SNIF!
COUGH!
-CHOO!
KIRKMAN & SCOTT

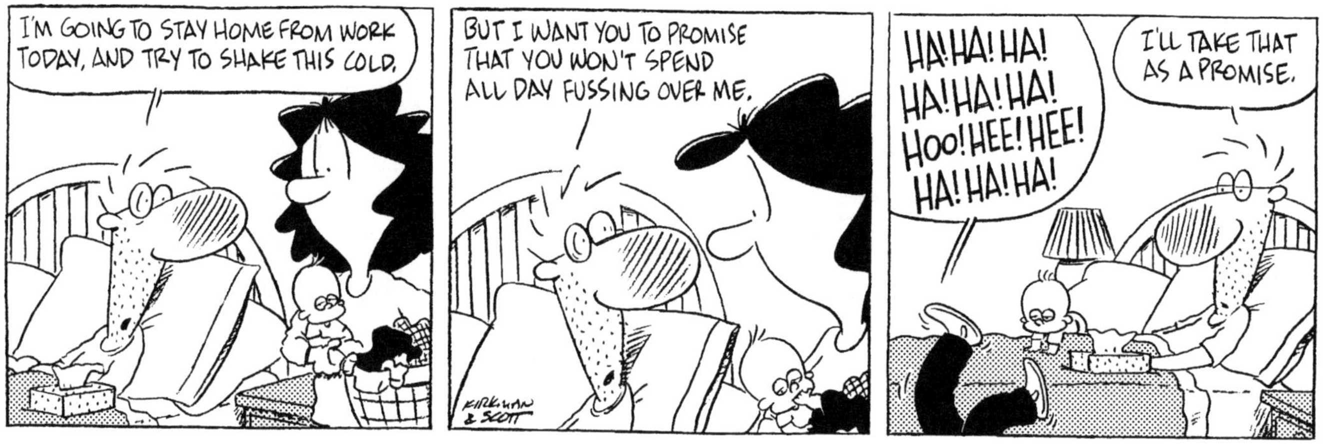
I'M GOING TO STAY HOME FROM WORK TODAY, AND TRY TO SHAKE THIS COLD.
BUT I WANT YOU TO PROMISE THAT YOU WON'T SPEND ALL DAY FUSSING OVER ME.
KIRKMAN & SCOTT
HA! HA! HA! HA! HA! HA! HOO! HEE! HEE! HA! HA! HA!
I'LL TAKE THAT AS A PROMISE.

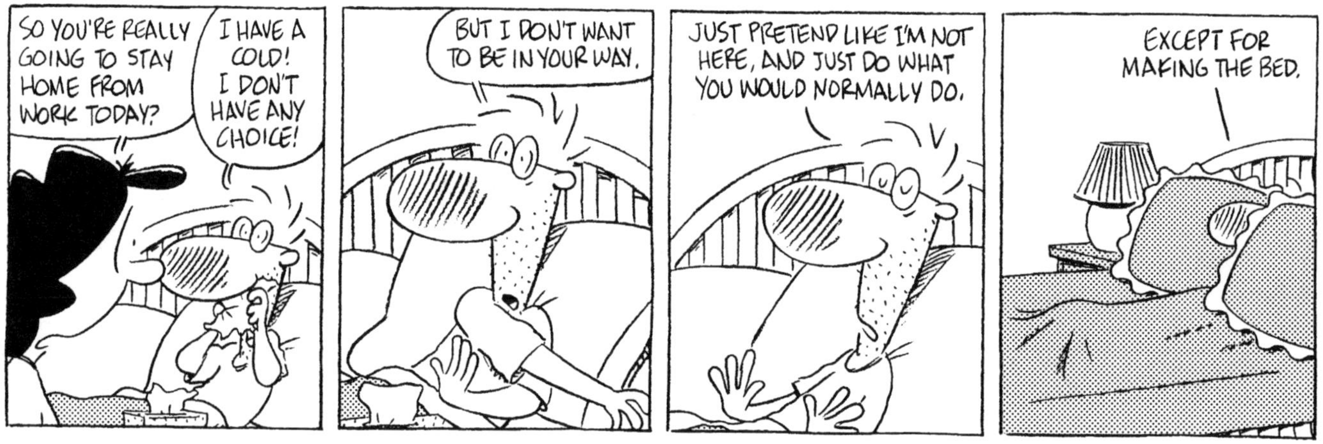
SO YOU'RE REALLY GOING TO STAY HOME FROM WORK TODAY?
I HAVE A COLD! I DON'T HAVE ANY CHOICE!
BUT I DON'T WANT TO BE IN YOUR WAY.
JUST PRETEND LIKE I'M NOT HERE, AND JUST DO WHAT YOU WOULD NORMALLY DO.
EXCEPT FOR MAKING THE BED.

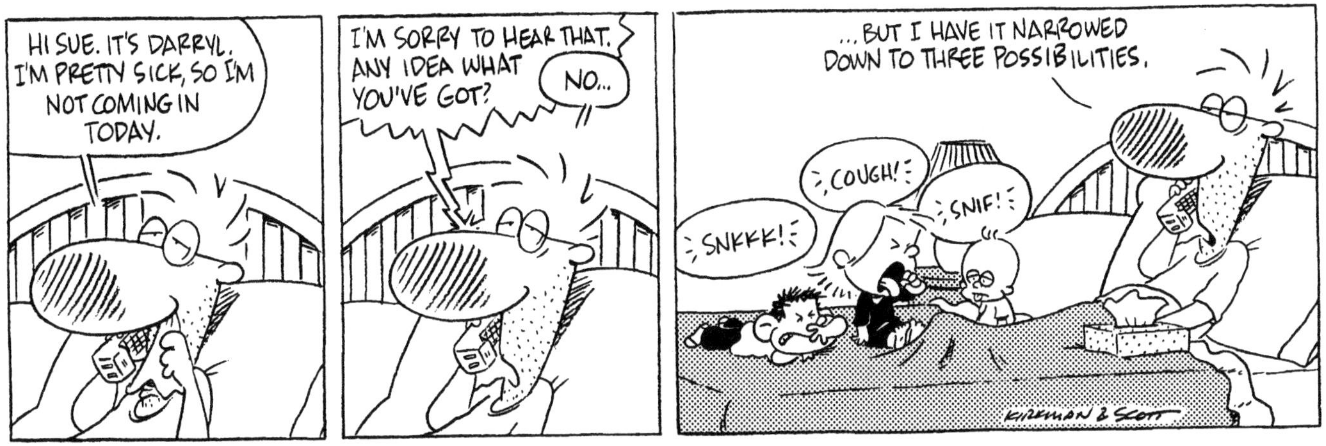
HI SUE. IT'S DARRYL. I'M PRETTY SICK, SO I'M NOT COMING IN TODAY.
I'M SORRY TO HEAR THAT. ANY IDEA WHAT YOU'VE GOT?
NO...
...BUT I HAVE IT NARROWED DOWN TO THREE POSSIBILITIES.
SNKKK!
COUGH!
SNIF!
KIRKMAN & SCOTT

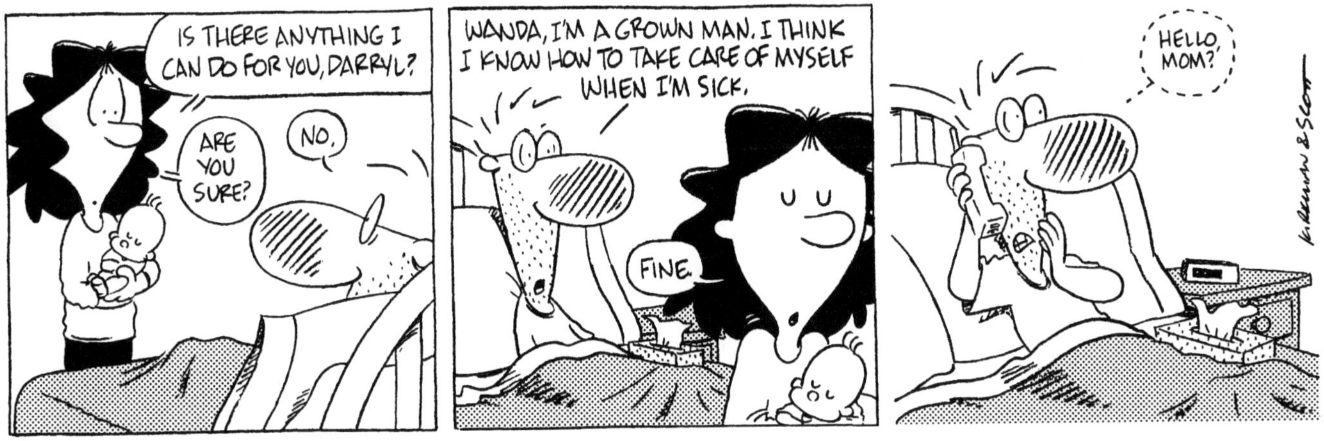
IS THERE ANYTHING I CAN DO FOR YOU, DARRYL?
NO.
ARE YOU SURE?
WANDA, I'M A GROWN MAN. I THINK I KNOW HOW TO TAKE CARE OF MYSELF WHEN I'M SICK.
FINE.
HELLO, MOM?
KIRKMAN & SCOTT

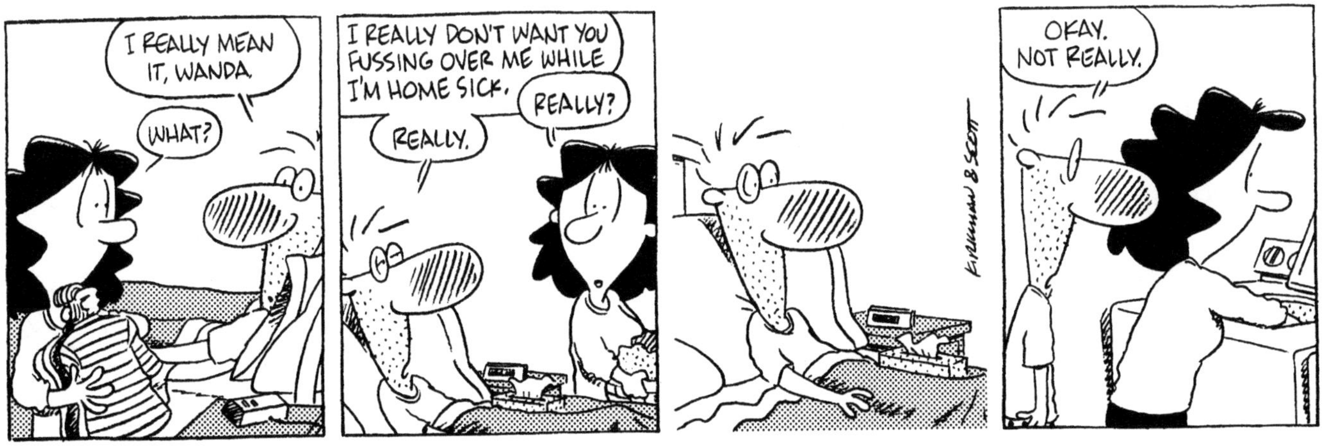
I REALLY MEAN IT, WANDA.
WHAT?
I REALLY DON'T WANT YOU FUSSING OVER ME WHILE I'M HOME SICK.
REALLY?
REALLY.
KIRKMAN & SCOTT
OKAY. NOT REALLY.

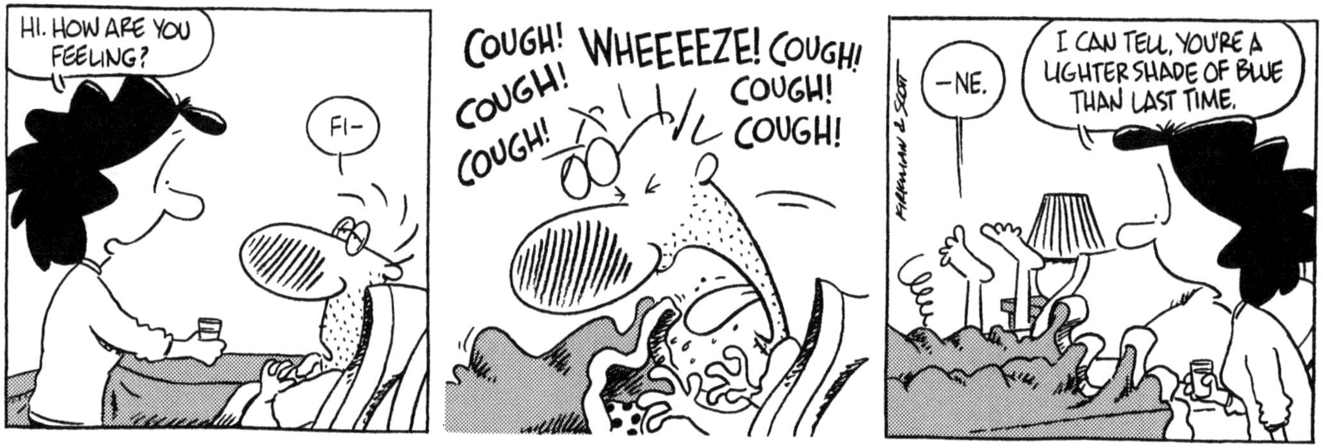
HI. HOW ARE YOU FEELING?
FI-
COUGH! COUGH! COUGH!
WHEEEEZE!
COUGH! COUGH! COUGH!
KIRKMAN & SCOTT
-NE.
I CAN TELL. YOU'RE A LIGHTER SHADE OF BLUE THAN LAST TIME.

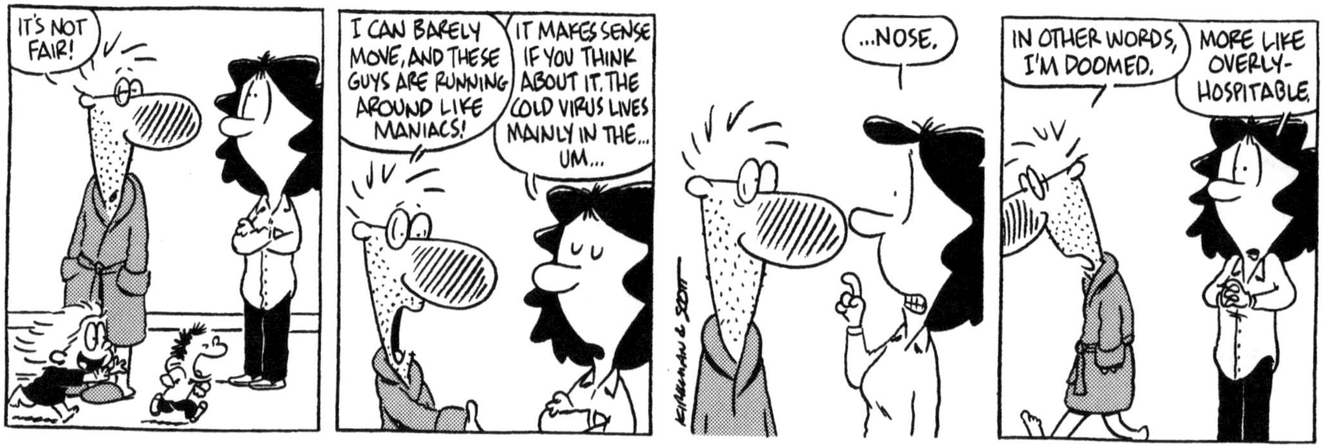
IT'S NOT FAIR!
I CAN BARELY MOVE, AND THESE GUYS ARE RUNNING AROUND LIKE MANIACS!
IT MAKES SENSE IF YOU THINK ABOUT IT. THE COLD VIRUS LIVES MAINLY IN THE... UM...
KIRKMAN & SCOTT
...NOSE.
IN OTHER WORDS, I'M DOOMED.
MORE LIKE OVERLY-HOSPITABLE.

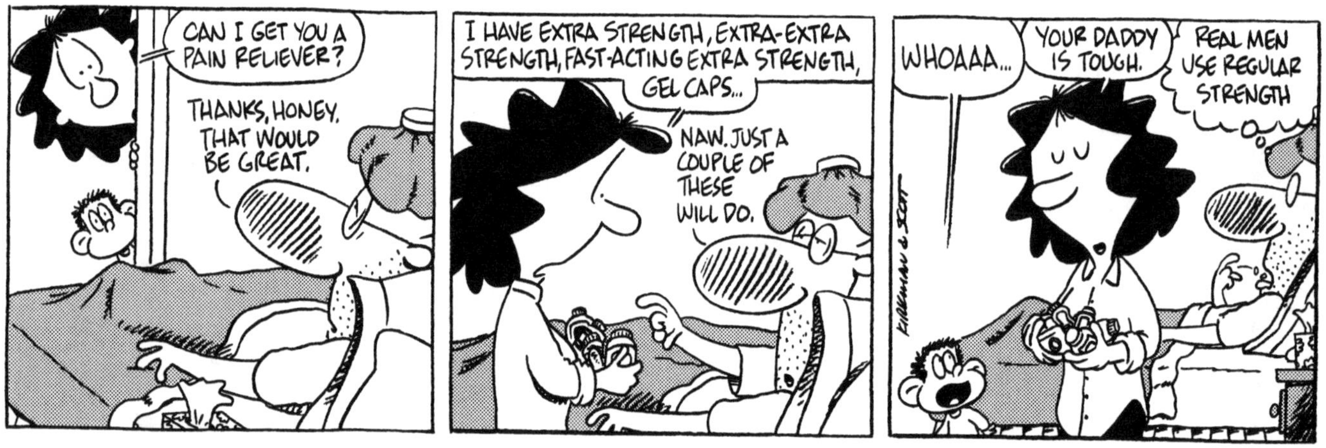
CAN I GET YOU A PAIN RELIEVER?
THANKS, HONEY. THAT WOULD BE GREAT.
I HAVE EXTRA STRENGTH, EXTRA-EXTRA STRENGTH, FAST-ACTING EXTRA STRENGTH, GEL CAPS...
NAW. JUST A COUPLE OF THESE WILL DO.
KIRKMAN & SCOTT
WHOAAA...
YOUR DADDY IS TOUGH.
REAL MEN USE REGULAR STRENGTH

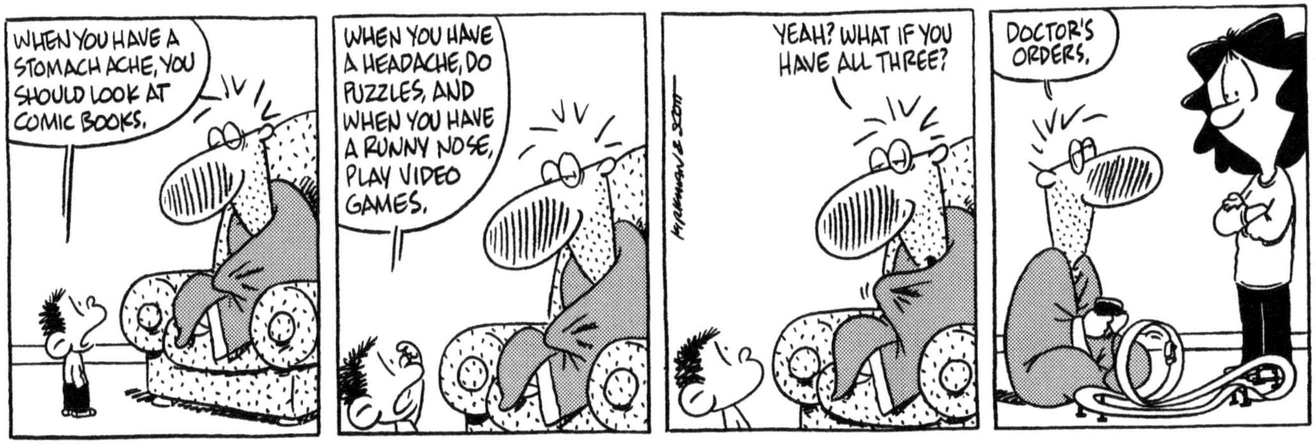
WHEN YOU HAVE A STOMACH ACHE, YOU SHOULD LOOK AT COMIC BOOKS.
WHEN YOU HAVE A HEADACHE, DO PUZZLES, AND WHEN YOU HAVE A RUNNY NOSE, PLAY VIDEO GAMES.
YEAH? WHAT IF YOU HAVE ALL THREE?
DOCTOR'S ORDERS.

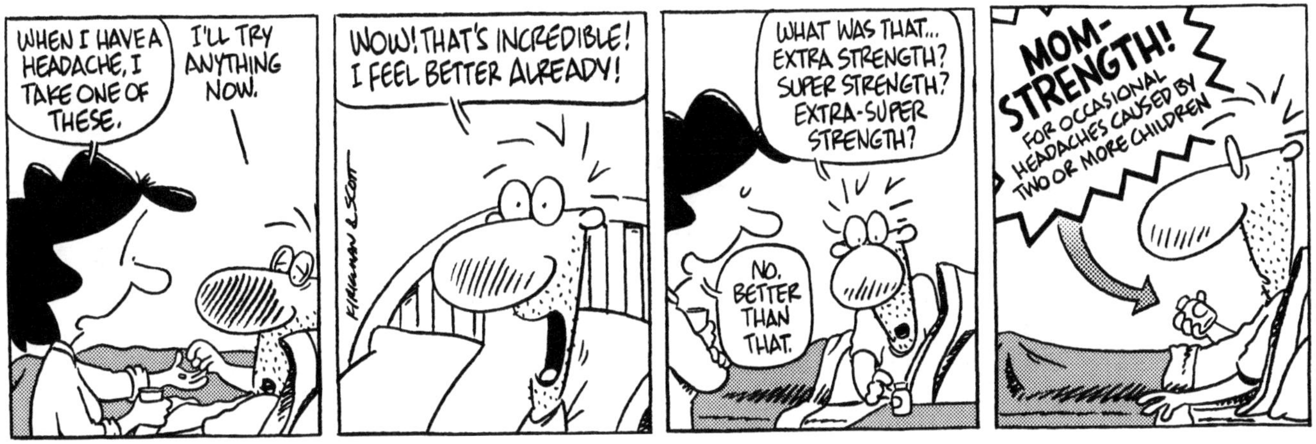
WHEN I HAVE A HEADACHE, I TAKE ONE OF THESE.
I'LL TRY ANYTHING NOW.
WOW! THAT'S INCREDIBLE! I FEEL BETTER ALREADY!
WHAT WAS THAT... EXTRA STRENGTH? SUPER STRENGTH? EXTRA-SUPER STRENGTH?
NO. BETTER THAN THAT.
MOM-STRENGTH!
FOR OCCASIONAL HEADACHES CAUSED BY TWO OR MORE CHILDREN

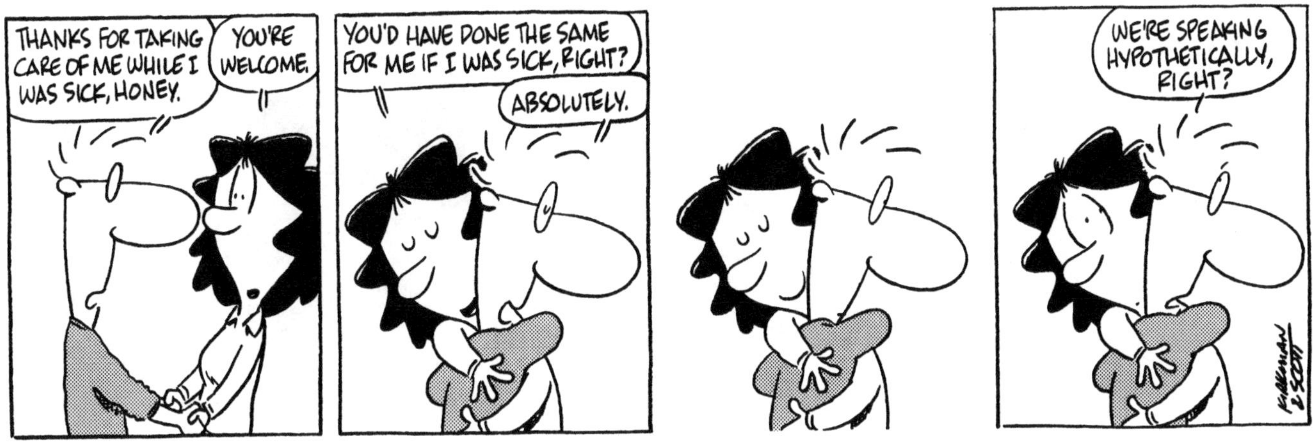
THANKS FOR TAKING CARE OF ME WHILE I WAS SICK, HONEY.
YOU'RE WELCOME.
YOU'D HAVE DONE THE SAME FOR ME IF I WAS SICK, RIGHT?
ABSOLUTELY.
WE'RE SPEAKING HYPOTHETICALLY, RIGHT?

BABY BLUES®
RICK KIRKMAN / BY JERRY SCOTT
~~ROAD TRIP~~
WH~~ERE'S ODYSSE~~US? MY LONG BORING POEM...
WITH APOLOGIES TO MATT GROENING
KIRKMAN & SCOTT
WHY IS IT WHEN I TAKE THE KIDS TO THE GROCERY STORE, IT'S JUST SHOPPING, BUT WHEN YOU DO IT, IT'S AN ODYSSEY?
GROAN!

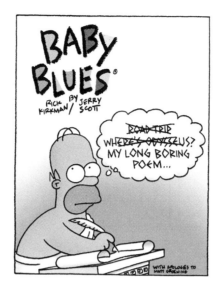

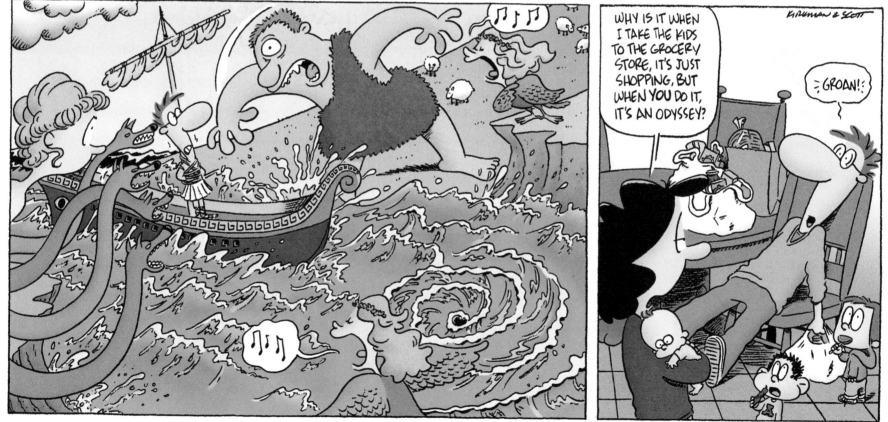

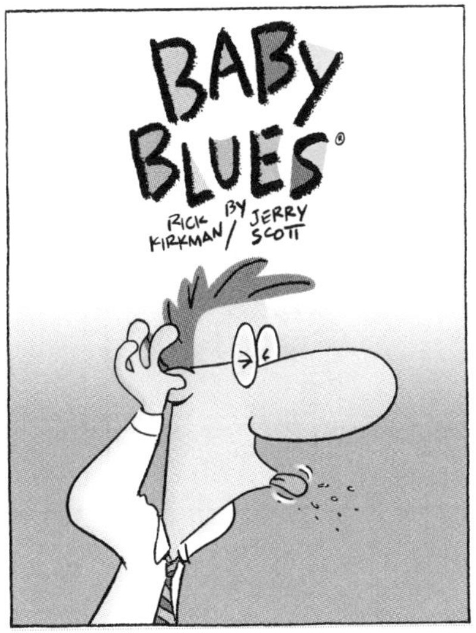
BABY BLUES®
BY RICK KIRKMAN / JERRY SCOTT

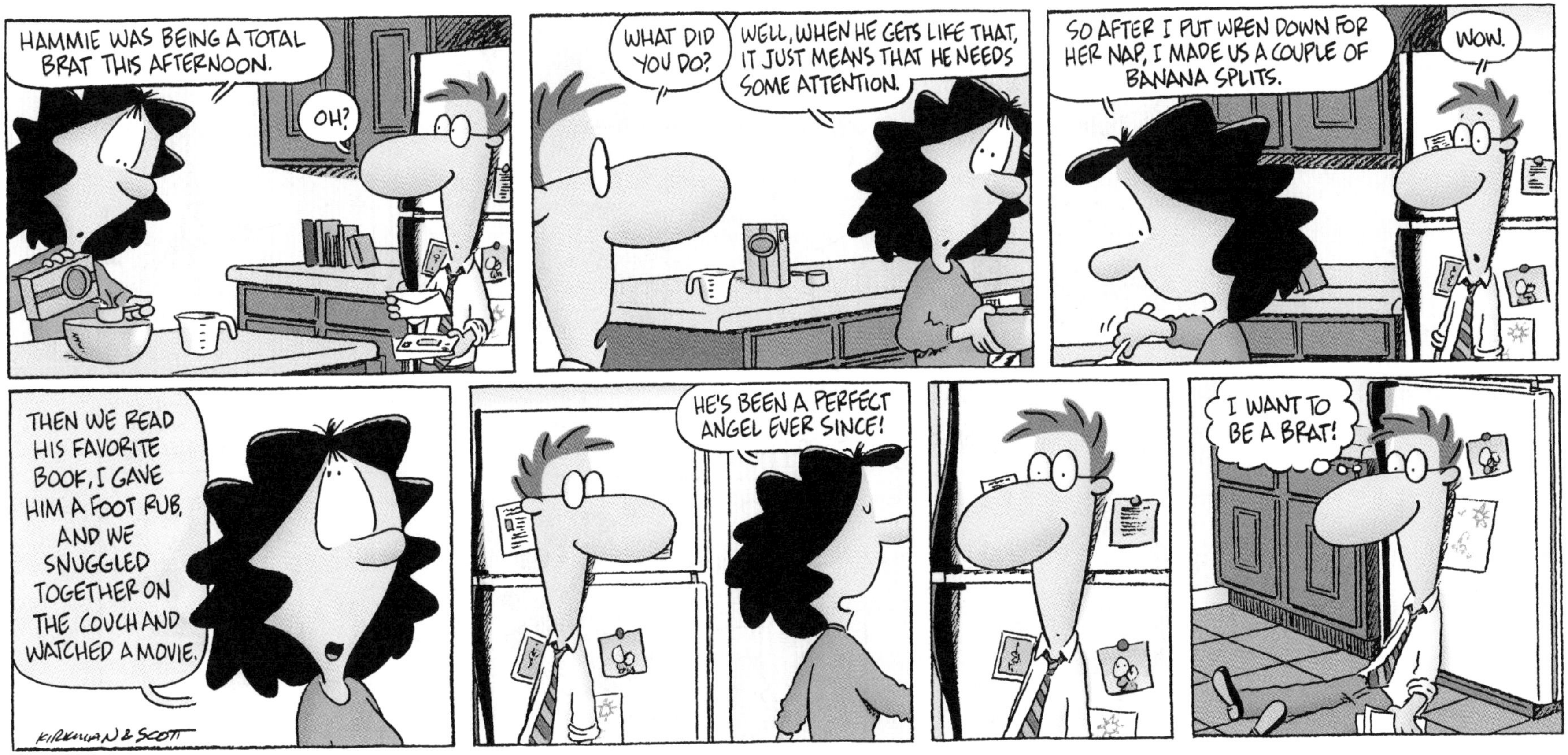
HAMMIE WAS BEING A TOTAL BRAT THIS AFTERNOON.
OH?
WHAT DID YOU DO?
WELL, WHEN HE GETS LIKE THAT, IT JUST MEANS THAT HE NEEDS SOME ATTENTION.
SO AFTER I PUT WREN DOWN FOR HER NAP, I MADE US A COUPLE OF BANANA SPLITS.
WOW.
THEN WE READ HIS FAVORITE BOOK, I GAVE HIM A FOOT RUB, AND WE SNUGGLED TOGETHER ON THE COUCH AND WATCHED A MOVIE.
KIRKMAN & SCOTT
HE'S BEEN A PERFECT ANGEL EVER SINCE!
I WANT TO BE A BRAT!

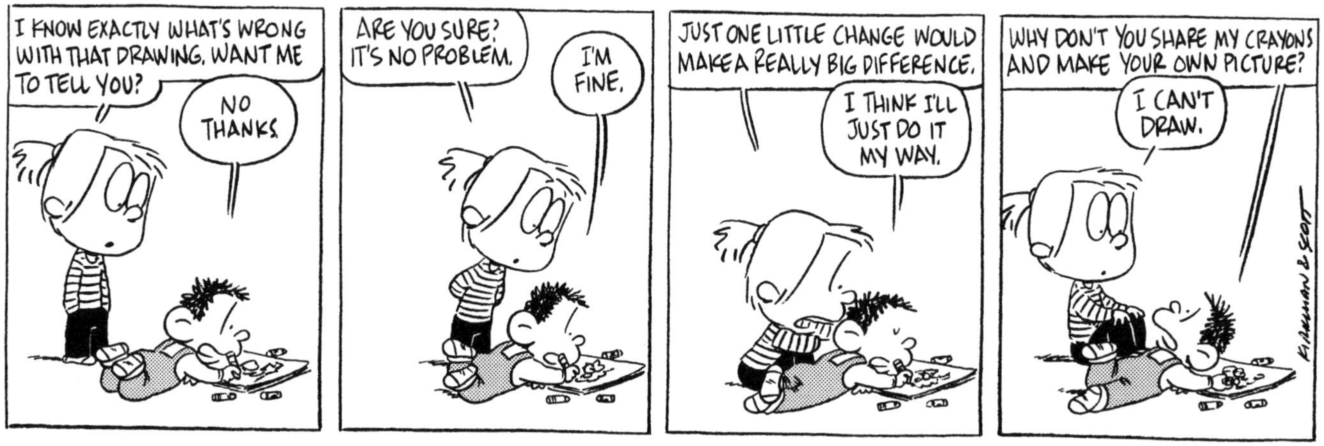
I KNOW EXACTLY WHAT'S WRONG WITH THAT DRAWING. WANT ME TO TELL YOU?
NO THANKS.
ARE YOU SURE? IT'S NO PROBLEM.
I'M FINE.
JUST ONE LITTLE CHANGE WOULD MAKE A REALLY BIG DIFFERENCE.
I THINK I'LL JUST DO IT MY WAY.
WHY DON'T YOU SHARE MY CRAYONS AND MAKE YOUR OWN PICTURE?
I CAN'T DRAW.
KIRKMAN & SCOTT

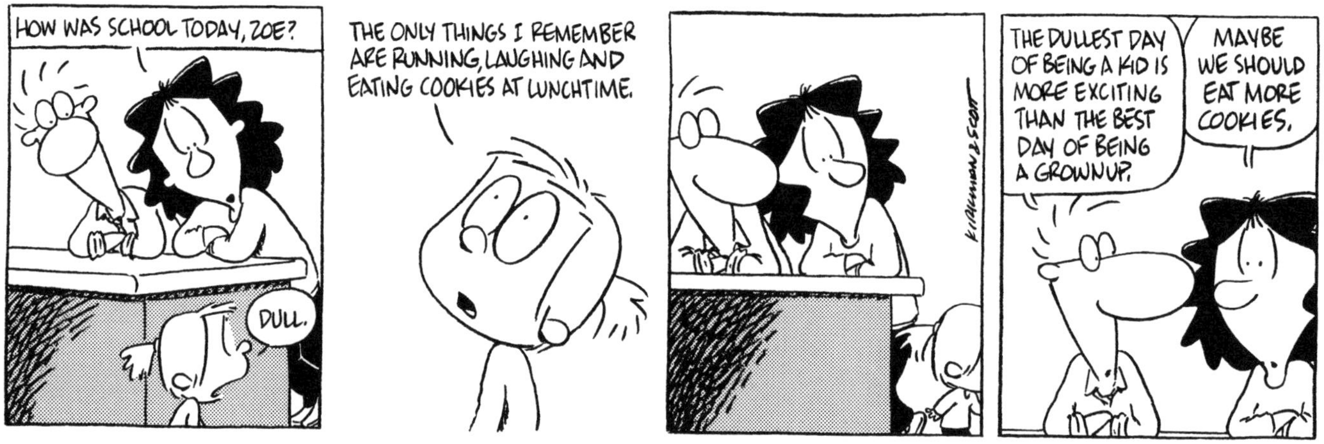
HOW WAS SCHOOL TODAY, ZOE?
DULL.
THE ONLY THINGS I REMEMBER ARE RUNNING, LAUGHING AND EATING COOKIES AT LUNCHTIME.
KIRKMAN & SCOTT
THE DULLEST DAY OF BEING A KID IS MORE EXCITING THAN THE BEST DAY OF BEING A GROWNUP.
MAYBE WE SHOULD EAT MORE COOKIES.

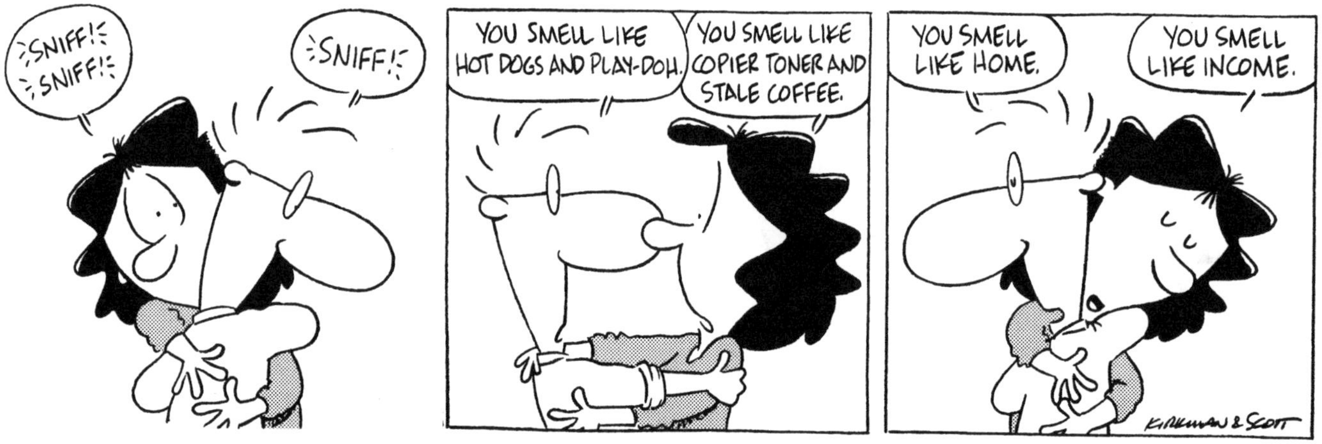
SNIFF! SNIFF!
SNIFF!
YOU SMELL LIKE HOT DOGS AND PLAY-DOH.
YOU SMELL LIKE COPIER TONER AND STALE COFFEE.
YOU SMELL LIKE HOME.
YOU SMELL LIKE INCOME.
KIRKMAN & SCOTT

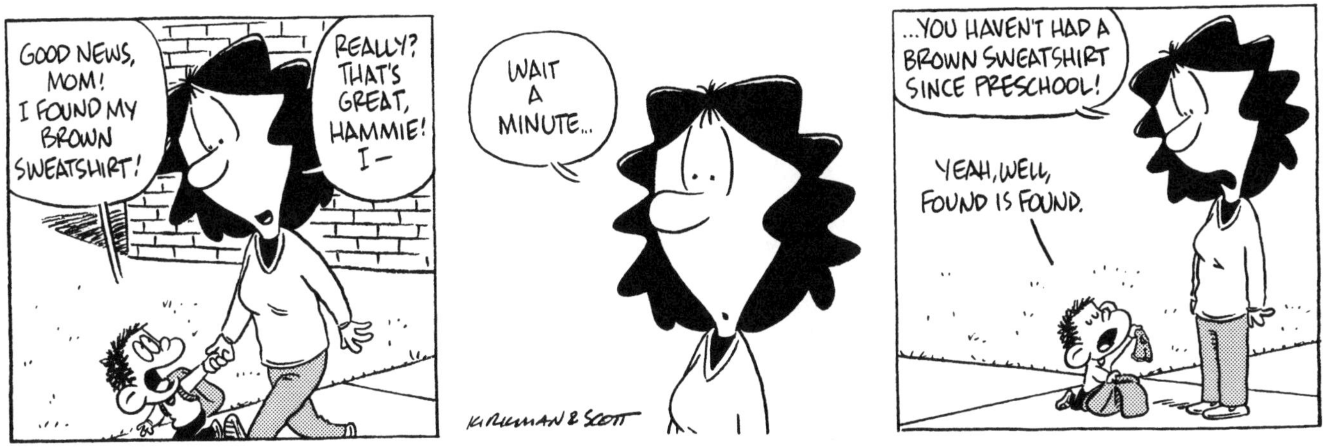
GOOD NEWS, MOM! I FOUND MY BROWN SWEATSHIRT!
REALLY? THAT'S GREAT, HAMMIE! I—
WAIT A MINUTE...
...YOU HAVEN'T HAD A BROWN SWEATSHIRT SINCE PRESCHOOL!
YEAH, WELL, FOUND IS FOUND.
KIRKMAN & SCOTT

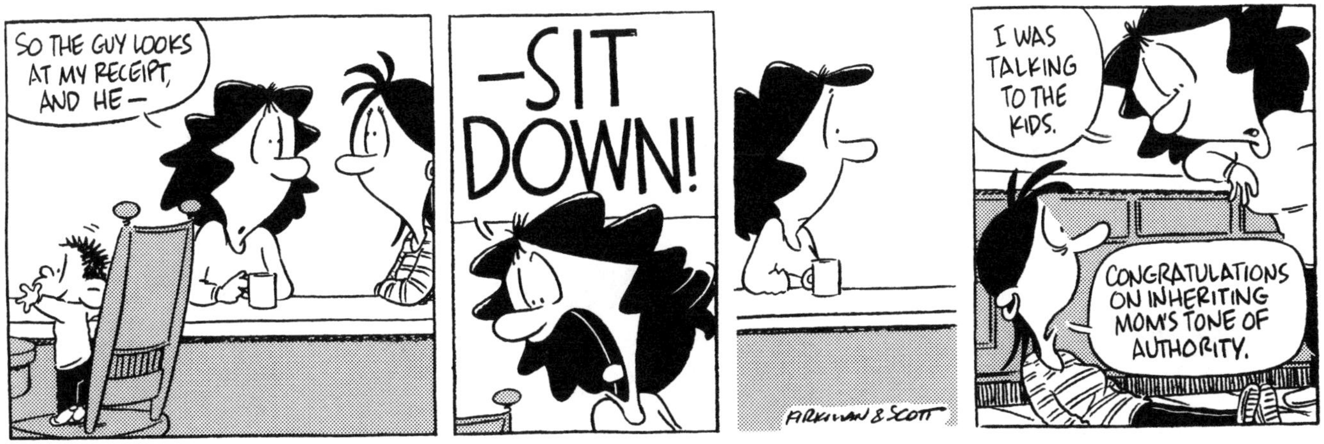
SO THE GUY LOOKS AT MY RECEIPT, AND HE—
—SIT DOWN!
I WAS TALKING TO THE KIDS.
CONGRATULATIONS ON INHERITING MOM'S TONE OF AUTHORITY.
KIRKMAN & SCOTT

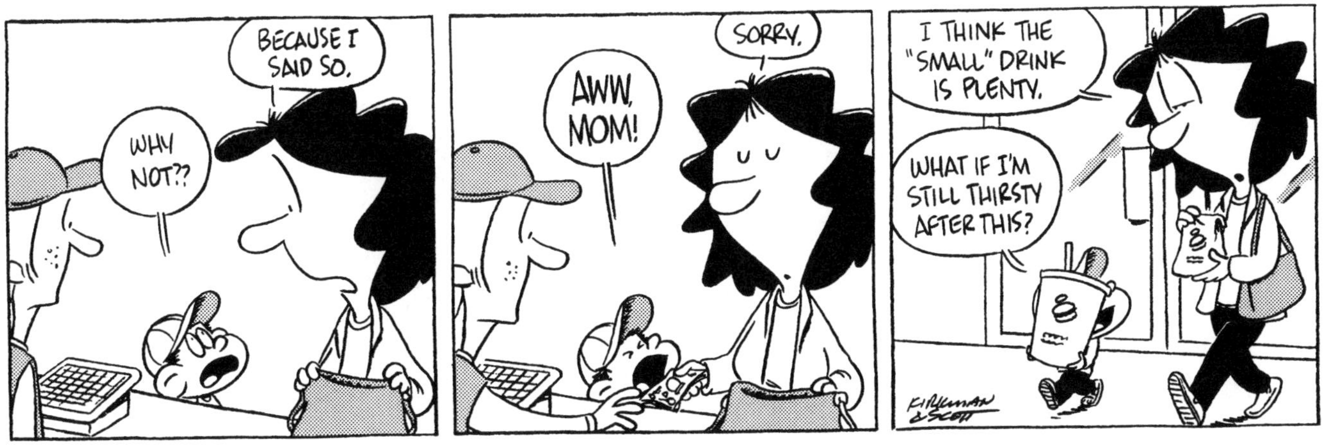
WHY NOT??
BECAUSE I SAID SO.
AWW, MOM!
SORRY.
I THINK THE "SMALL" DRINK IS PLENTY.
WHAT IF I'M STILL THIRSTY AFTER THIS?
KIRKMAN & SCOTT

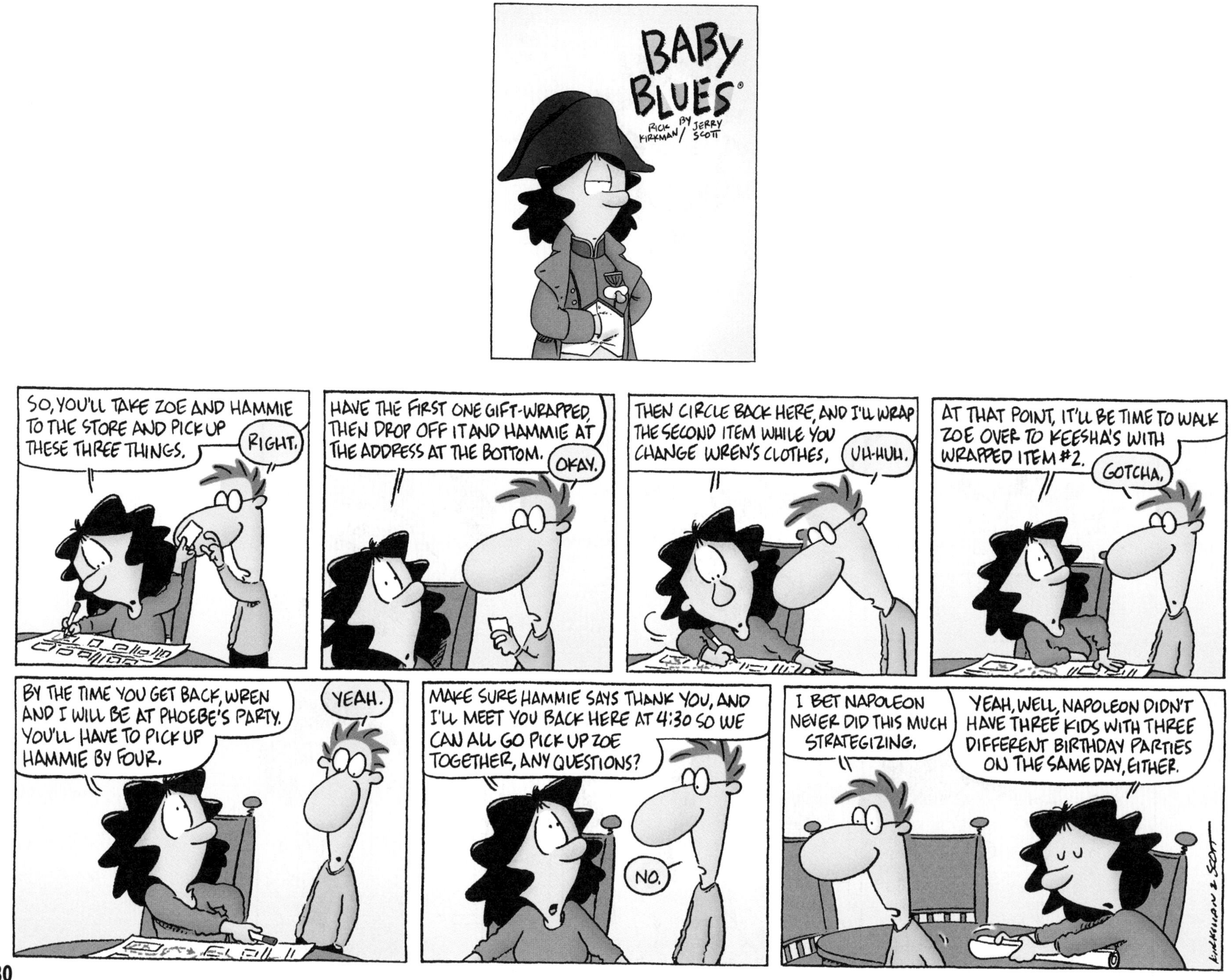
BABY BLUES®
BY RICK KIRKMAN / JERRY SCOTT
SO, YOU'LL TAKE ZOE AND HAMMIE TO THE STORE AND PICK UP THESE THREE THINGS.
RIGHT.
HAVE THE FIRST ONE GIFT-WRAPPED, THEN DROP OFF IT AND HAMMIE AT THE ADDRESS AT THE BOTTOM.
OKAY.
THEN CIRCLE BACK HERE, AND I'LL WRAP THE SECOND ITEM WHILE YOU CHANGE WREN'S CLOTHES.
UH-HUH.
AT THAT POINT, IT'LL BE TIME TO WALK ZOE OVER TO KEESHA'S WITH WRAPPED ITEM #2.
GOTCHA.
BY THE TIME YOU GET BACK, WREN AND I WILL BE AT PHOEBE'S PARTY. YOU'LL HAVE TO PICK UP HAMMIE BY FOUR.
YEAH.
MAKE SURE HAMMIE SAYS THANK YOU, AND I'LL MEET YOU BACK HERE AT 4:30 SO WE CAN ALL GO PICK UP ZOE TOGETHER. ANY QUESTIONS?
NO.
I BET NAPOLEON NEVER DID THIS MUCH STRATEGIZING.
YEAH, WELL, NAPOLEON DIDN'T HAVE THREE KIDS WITH THREE DIFFERENT BIRTHDAY PARTIES ON THE SAME DAY, EITHER.
KIRKMAN & SCOTT

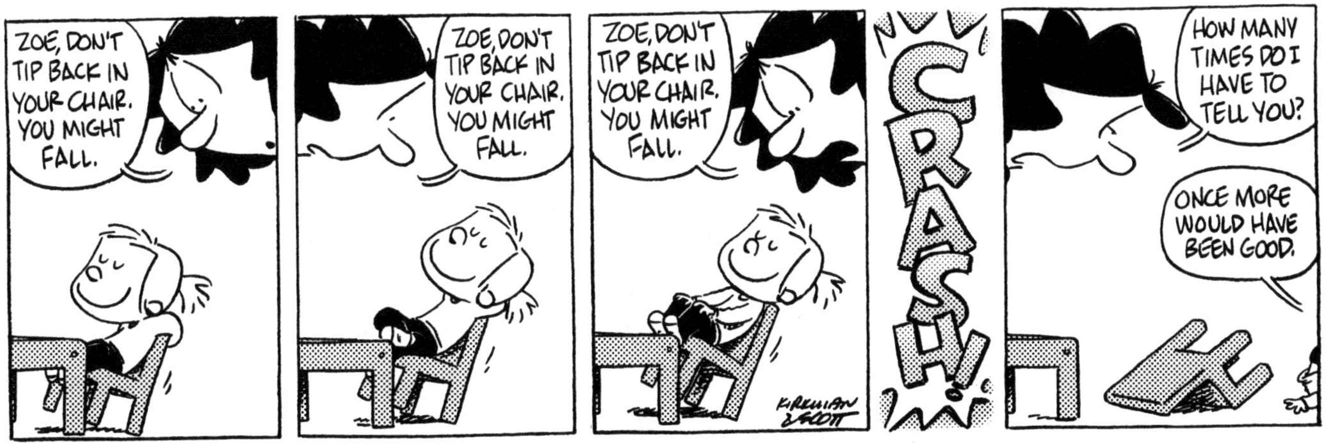
ZOE, DON'T TIP BACK IN YOUR CHAIR. YOU MIGHT FALL.
ZOE, DON'T TIP BACK IN YOUR CHAIR. YOU MIGHT FALL.
ZOE, DON'T TIP BACK IN YOUR CHAIR. YOU MIGHT FALL.
KIRKMAN & SCOTT
CRASH!
HOW MANY TIMES DO I HAVE TO TELL YOU?
ONCE MORE WOULD HAVE BEEN GOOD.

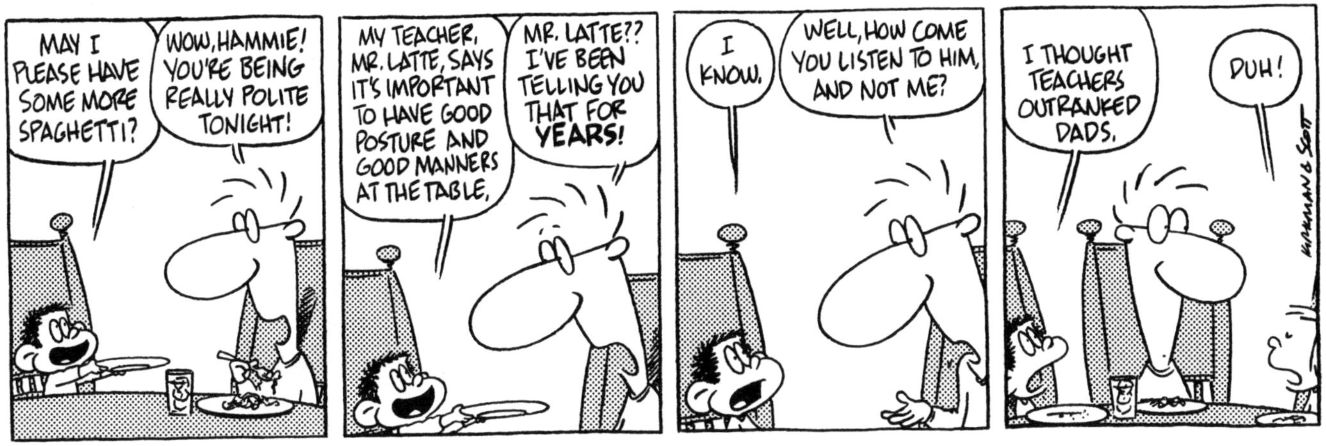
MAY I PLEASE HAVE SOME MORE SPAGHETTI?
WOW, HAMMIE! YOU'RE BEING REALLY POLITE TONIGHT!
MY TEACHER, MR. LATTE, SAYS IT'S IMPORTANT TO HAVE GOOD POSTURE AND GOOD MANNERS AT THE TABLE.
MR. LATTE?? I'VE BEEN TELLING YOU THAT FOR **YEARS!**
I KNOW.
WELL, HOW COME YOU LISTEN TO HIM, AND NOT ME?
I THOUGHT TEACHERS OUTRANKED DADS.
DUH!
KIRKMAN & SCOTT

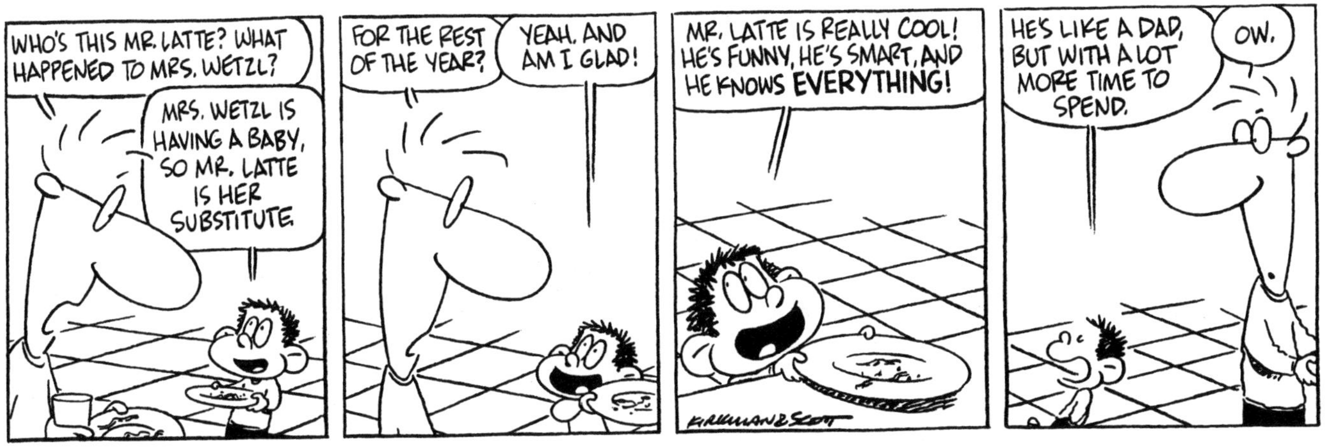
WHO'S THIS MR. LATTE? WHAT HAPPENED TO MRS. WETZL?
MRS. WETZL IS HAVING A BABY, SO MR. LATTE IS HER SUBSTITUTE.
FOR THE REST OF THE YEAR?
YEAH. AND AM I GLAD!
MR. LATTE IS REALLY COOL! HE'S FUNNY, HE'S SMART, AND HE KNOWS **EVERYTHING!**
KIRKMAN & SCOTT
HE'S LIKE A DAD, BUT WITH A LOT MORE TIME TO SPEND.
OW.

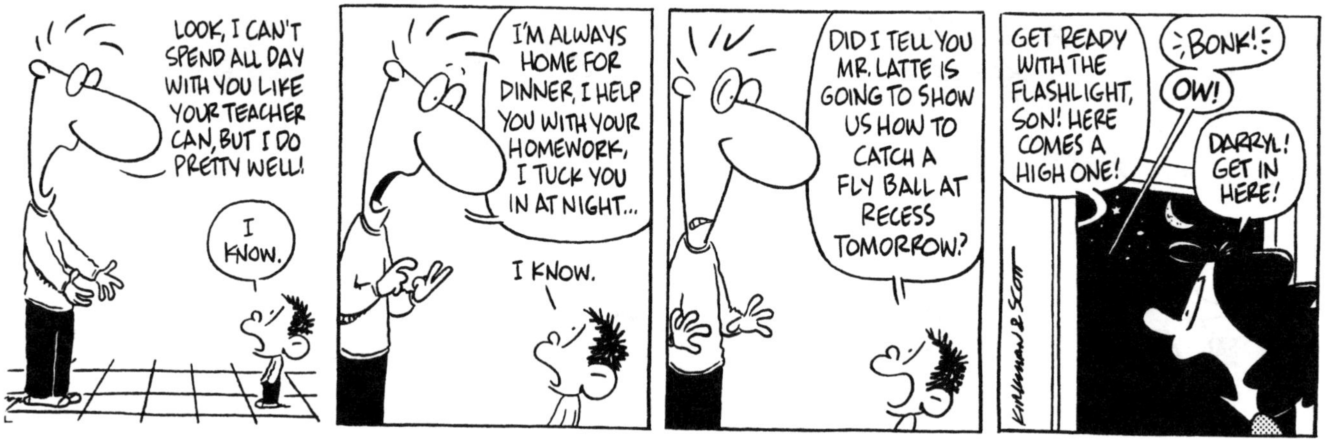
LOOK, I CAN'T SPEND ALL DAY WITH YOU LIKE YOUR TEACHER CAN, BUT I DO PRETTY WELL!
I KNOW.
I'M ALWAYS HOME FOR DINNER, I HELP YOU WITH YOUR HOMEWORK, I TUCK YOU IN AT NIGHT...
I KNOW.
DID I TELL YOU MR. LATTE IS GOING TO SHOW US HOW TO CATCH A FLY BALL AT RECESS TOMORROW?
GET READY WITH THE FLASHLIGHT, SON! HERE COMES A HIGH ONE!
BONK!
OW!
DARRYL! GET IN HERE!
KIRKMAN & SCOTT

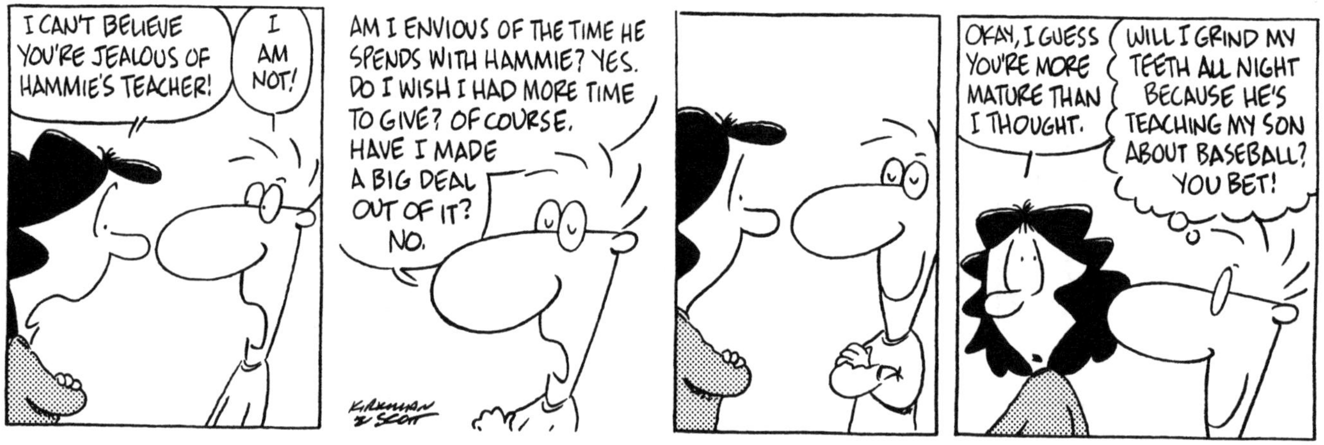
I CAN'T BELIEVE YOU'RE JEALOUS OF HAMMIE'S TEACHER!
I AM NOT!
AM I ENVIOUS OF THE TIME HE SPENDS WITH HAMMIE? YES. DO I WISH I HAD MORE TIME TO GIVE? OF COURSE. HAVE I MADE A BIG DEAL OUT OF IT? NO.
KIRKMAN & SCOTT
OKAY, I GUESS YOU'RE MORE MATURE THAN I THOUGHT.
WILL I GRIND MY TEETH ALL NIGHT BECAUSE HE'S TEACHING MY SON ABOUT BASEBALL? YOU BET!

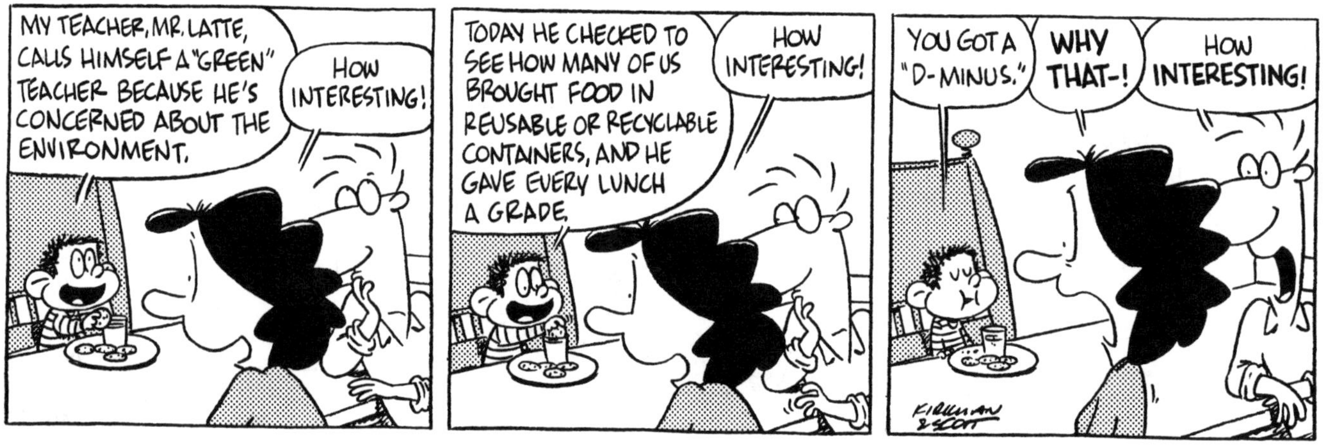
MY TEACHER, MR. LATTE, CALLS HIMSELF A "GREEN" TEACHER BECAUSE HE'S CONCERNED ABOUT THE ENVIRONMENT.
HOW INTERESTING!
TODAY HE CHECKED TO SEE HOW MANY OF US BROUGHT FOOD IN REUSABLE OR RECYCLABLE CONTAINERS, AND HE GAVE EVERY LUNCH A GRADE.
HOW INTERESTING!
YOU GOT A "D-MINUS."
WHY THAT-!
HOW INTERESTING!
KIRKMAN & SCOTT

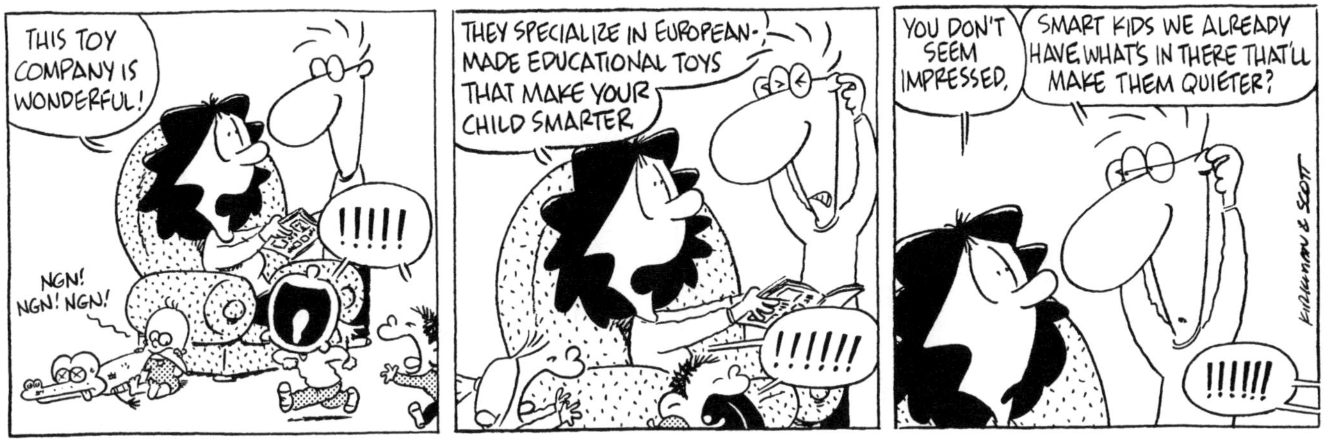
THIS TOY COMPANY IS WONDERFUL!
!!!!!
NGN! NGN! NGN! NGN!
THEY SPECIALIZE IN EUROPEAN-MADE EDUCATIONAL TOYS THAT MAKE YOUR CHILD SMARTER.
!!!!!!
YOU DON'T SEEM IMPRESSED.
SMART KIDS WE ALREADY HAVE. WHAT'S IN THERE THAT'LL MAKE THEM QUIETER?
!!!!!!
KIRKMAN & SCOTT

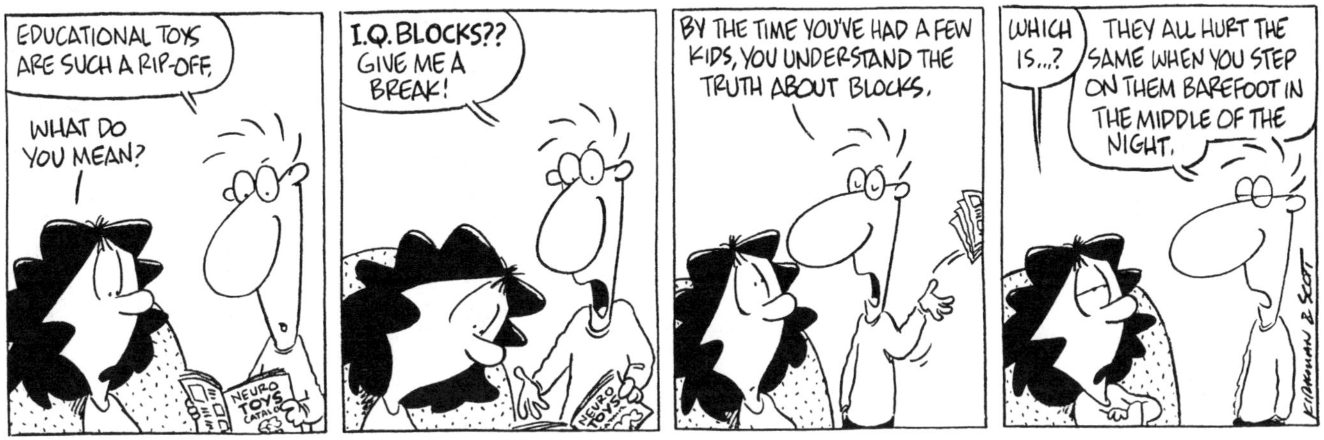
EDUCATIONAL TOYS ARE SUCH A RIP-OFF.
WHAT DO YOU MEAN?
NEURO TOYS CATALOG
I.Q. BLOCKS?? GIVE ME A BREAK!
BY THE TIME YOU'VE HAD A FEW KIDS, YOU UNDERSTAND THE TRUTH ABOUT BLOCKS.
WHICH IS...?
THEY ALL HURT THE SAME WHEN YOU STEP ON THEM BAREFOOT IN THE MIDDLE OF THE NIGHT.
KIRKMAN & SCOTT

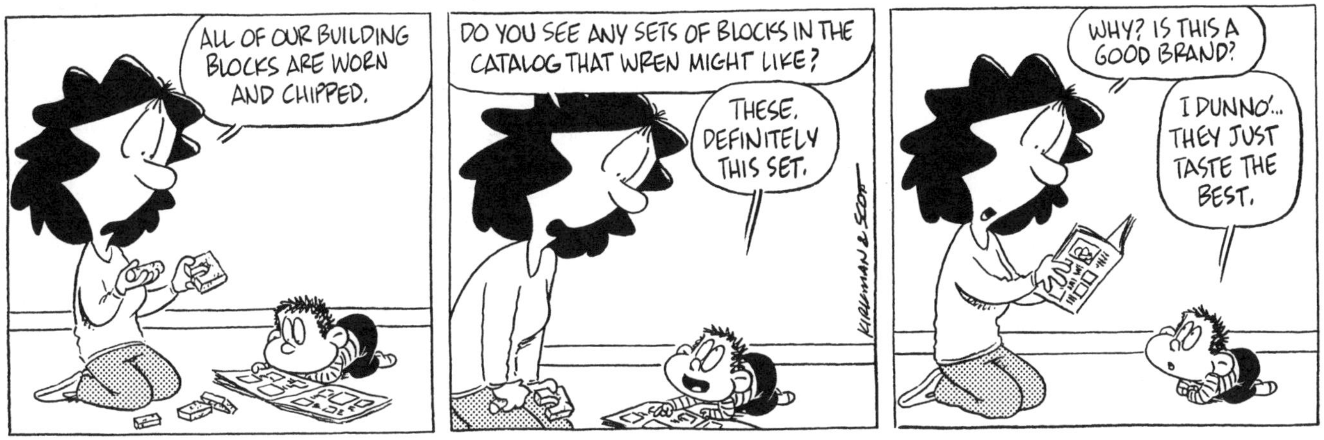
ALL OF OUR BUILDING BLOCKS ARE WORN AND CHIPPED.
DO YOU SEE ANY SETS OF BLOCKS IN THE CATALOG THAT WREN MIGHT LIKE?
THESE. DEFINITELY THIS SET.
KIRKMAN & SCOTT
WHY? IS THIS A GOOD BRAND?
I DUNNO... THEY JUST TASTE THE BEST.

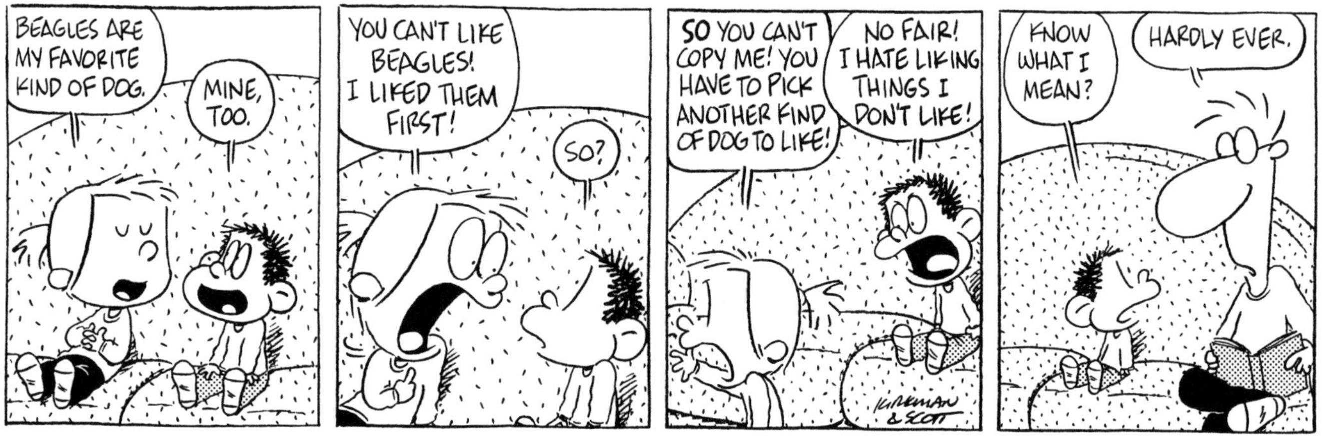
BEAGLES ARE MY FAVORITE KIND OF DOG.
MINE, TOO.
YOU CAN'T LIKE BEAGLES! I LIKED THEM FIRST!
SO?
SO YOU CAN'T COPY ME! YOU HAVE TO PICK ANOTHER KIND OF DOG TO LIKE!
NO FAIR! I HATE LIKING THINGS I DON'T LIKE!
KIRKMAN & SCOTT
KNOW WHAT I MEAN?
HARDLY EVER.

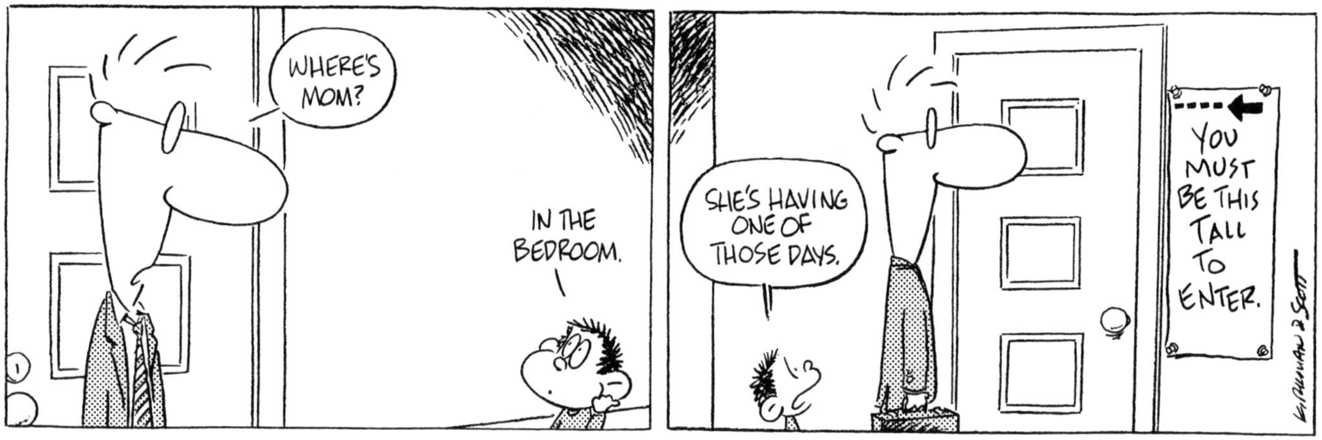
WHERE'S MOM?
IN THE BEDROOM.
SHE'S HAVING ONE OF THOSE DAYS.
YOU MUST BE THIS TALL TO ENTER.
KIRKMAN & SCOTT

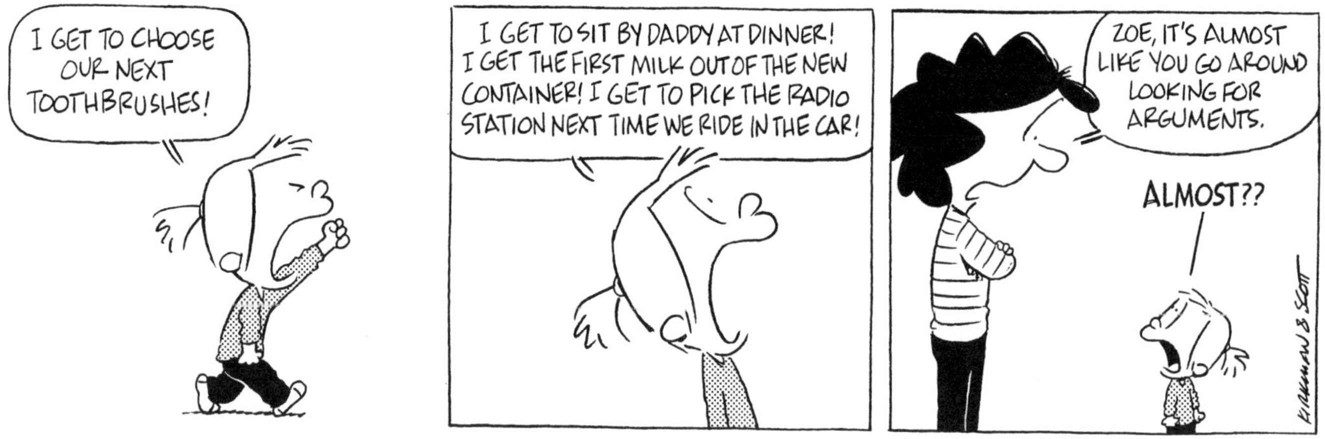
I GET TO CHOOSE OUR NEXT TOOTHBRUSHES!
I GET TO SIT BY DADDY AT DINNER! I GET THE FIRST MILK OUT OF THE NEW CONTAINER! I GET TO PICK THE RADIO STATION NEXT TIME WE RIDE IN THE CAR!
ZOE, IT'S ALMOST LIKE YOU GO AROUND LOOKING FOR ARGUMENTS.
ALMOST??
KIRKMAN & SCOTT

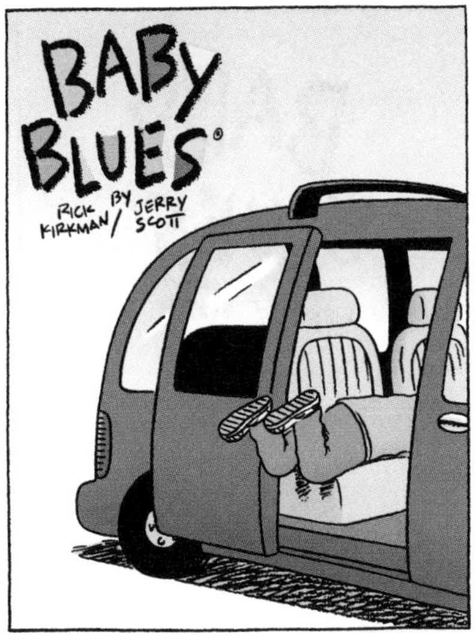
BABY BLUES®
BY RICK KIRKMAN / JERRY SCOTT

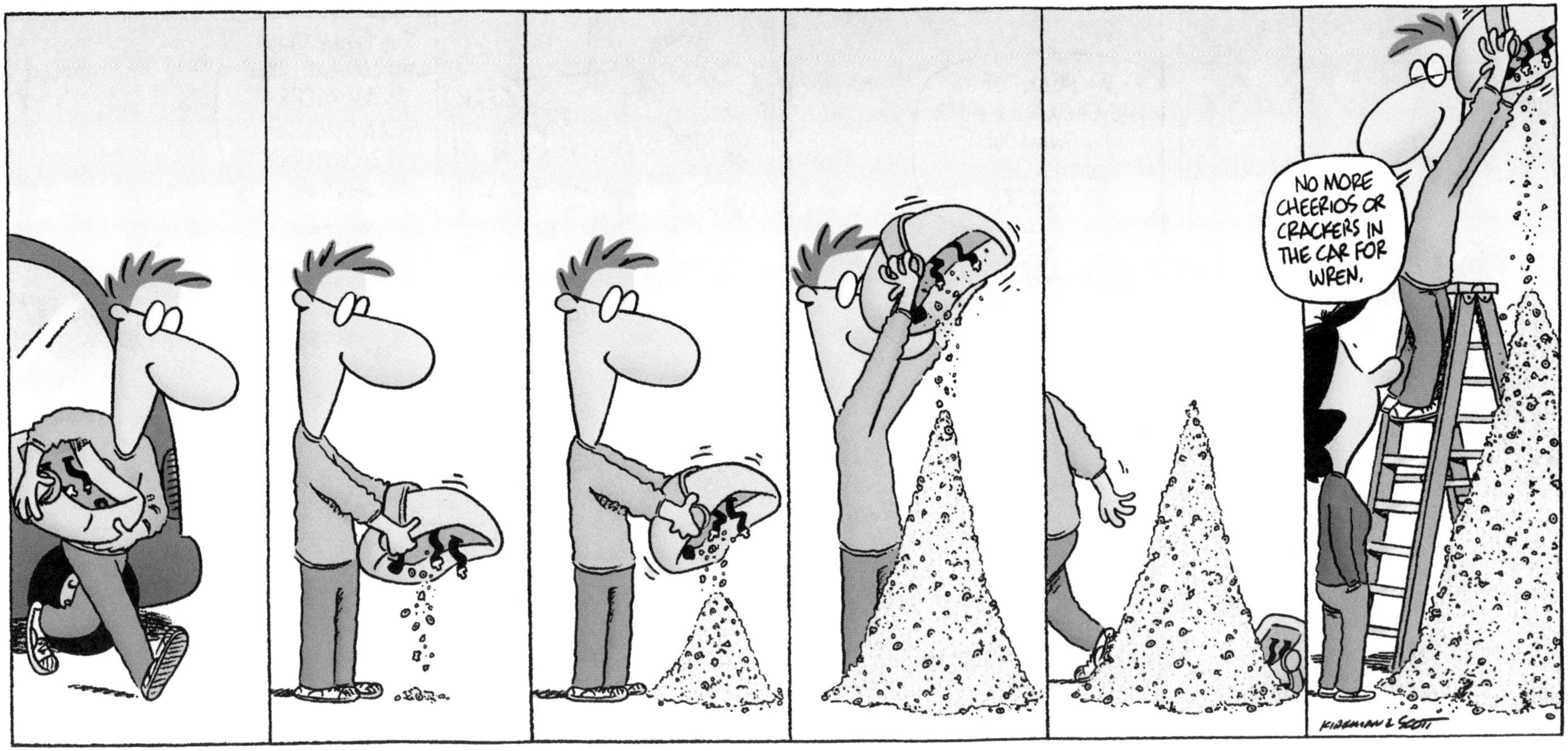
NO MORE CHEERIOS OR CRACKERS IN THE CAR FOR WREN.
KIRKMAN & SCOTT

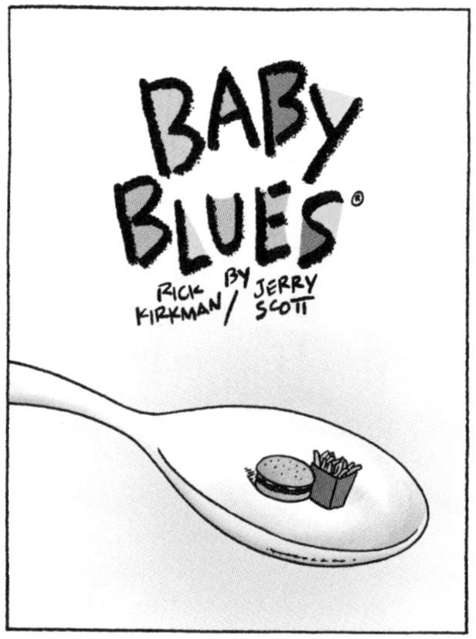
BABY BLUES®
BY RICK KIRKMAN / JERRY SCOTT

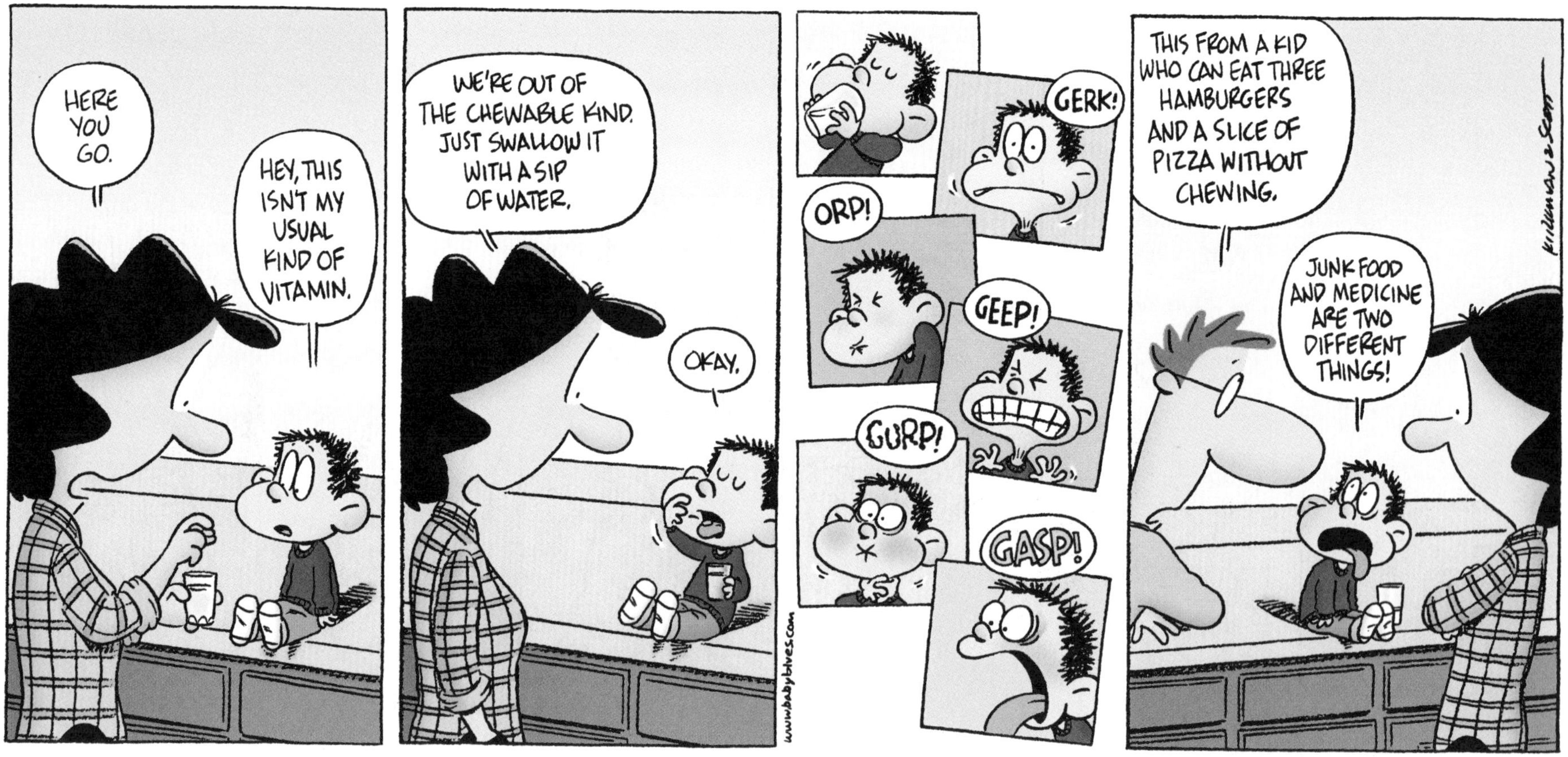
HERE YOU GO.
HEY, THIS ISN'T MY USUAL KIND OF VITAMIN.
WE'RE OUT OF THE CHEWABLE KIND. JUST SWALLOW IT WITH A SIP OF WATER.
OKAY.
GERK!
ORP!
GEEP!
GURP!
GASP!
THIS FROM A KID WHO CAN EAT THREE HAMBURGERS AND A SLICE OF PIZZA WITHOUT CHEWING.
JUNK FOOD AND MEDICINE ARE TWO DIFFERENT THINGS!
www.babyblues.com

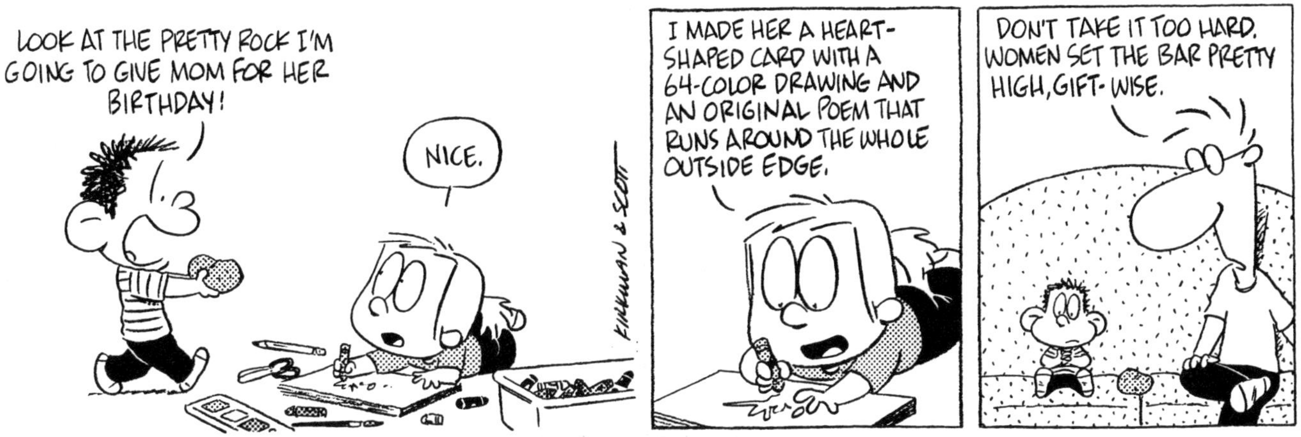
LOOK AT THE PRETTY ROCK I'M GOING TO GIVE MOM FOR HER BIRTHDAY!
NICE.
KIRKMAN & SCOTT
I MADE HER A HEART-SHAPED CARD WITH A 64-COLOR DRAWING AND AN ORIGINAL POEM THAT RUNS AROUND THE WHOLE OUTSIDE EDGE.
DON'T TAKE IT TOO HARD. WOMEN SET THE BAR PRETTY HIGH, GIFT-WISE.

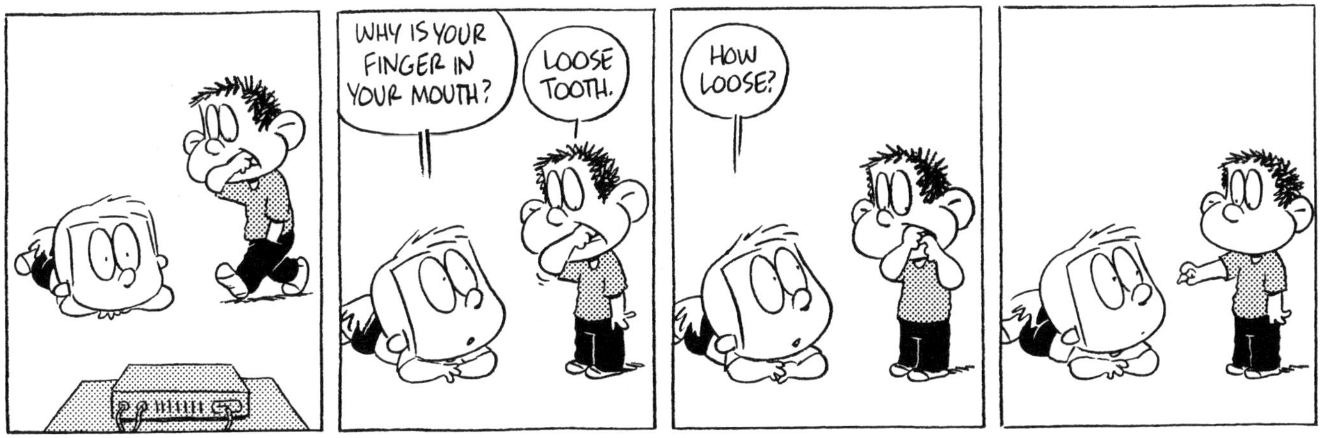
WHY IS YOUR FINGER IN YOUR MOUTH?
LOOSE TOOTH.
HOW LOOSE?

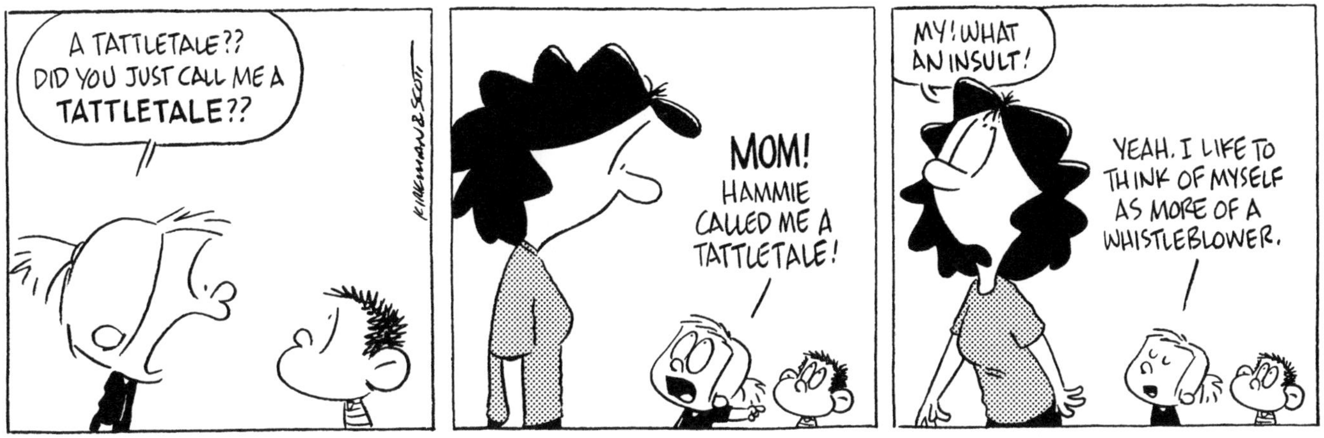
A TATTLETALE?? DID YOU JUST CALL ME A **TATTLETALE**??
KIRKMAN & SCOTT
MOM! HAMMIE CALLED ME A TATTLETALE!
MY! WHAT AN INSULT!
YEAH. I LIKE TO THINK OF MYSELF AS MORE OF A WHISTLEBLOWER.

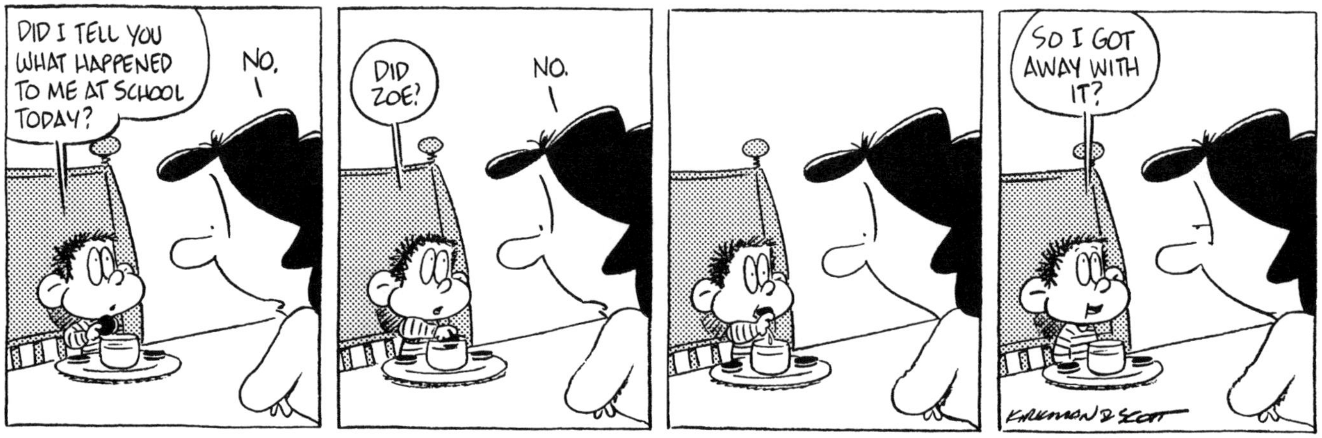
DID I TELL YOU WHAT HAPPENED TO ME AT SCHOOL TODAY?
NO.
DID ZOE?
NO.
SO I GOT AWAY WITH IT?
KIRKMAN & SCOTT

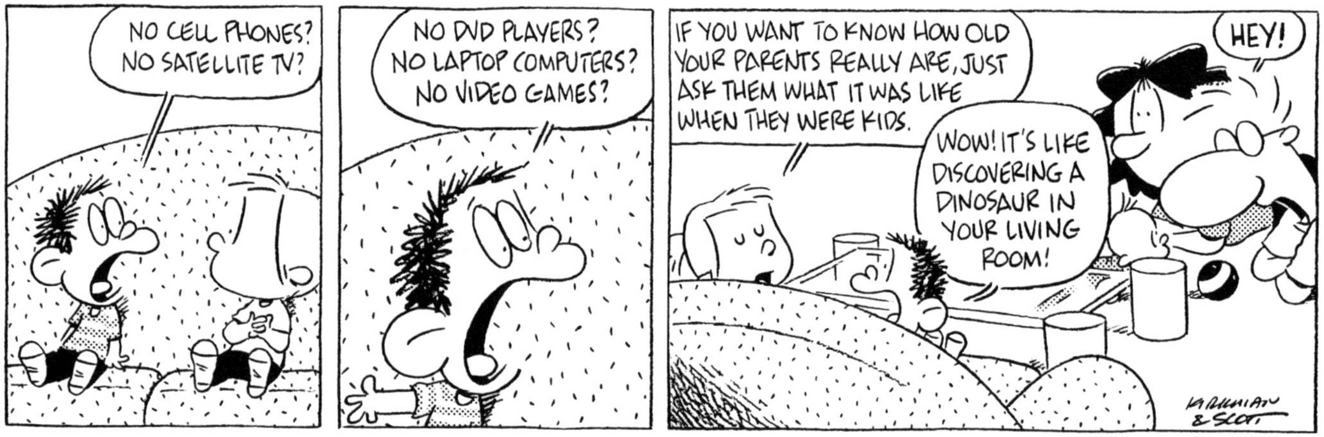
NO CELL PHONES? NO SATELLITE TV?
NO DVD PLAYERS? NO LAPTOP COMPUTERS? NO VIDEO GAMES?
IF YOU WANT TO KNOW HOW OLD YOUR PARENTS REALLY ARE, JUST ASK THEM WHAT IT WAS LIKE WHEN THEY WERE KIDS.
HEY!
WOW! IT'S LIKE DISCOVERING A DINOSAUR IN YOUR LIVING ROOM!
KIRKMAN & SCOTT

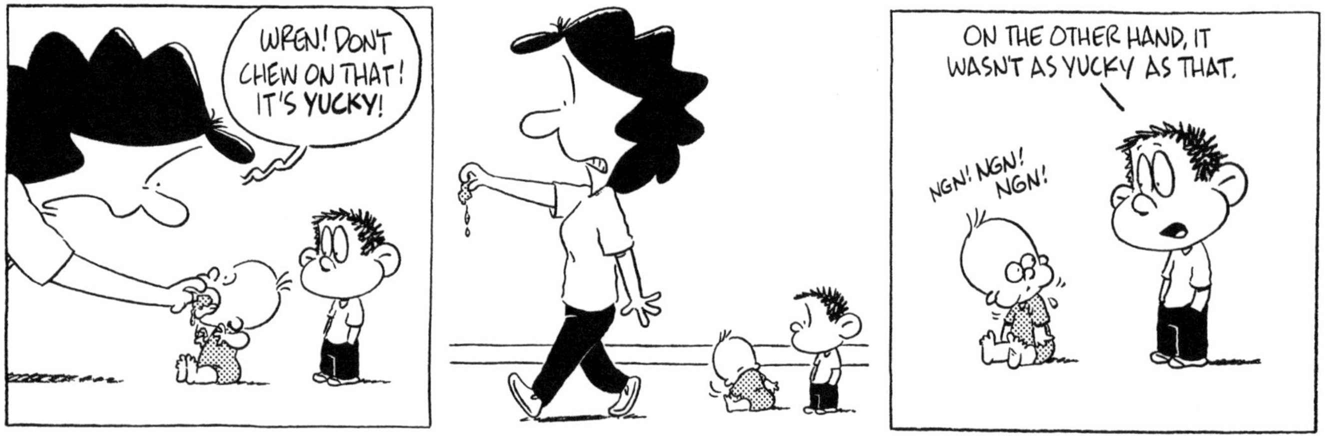
WREN! DON'T CHEW ON THAT! IT'S YUCKY!
ON THE OTHER HAND, IT WASN'T AS YUCKY AS THAT.
NGN! NGN! NGN!

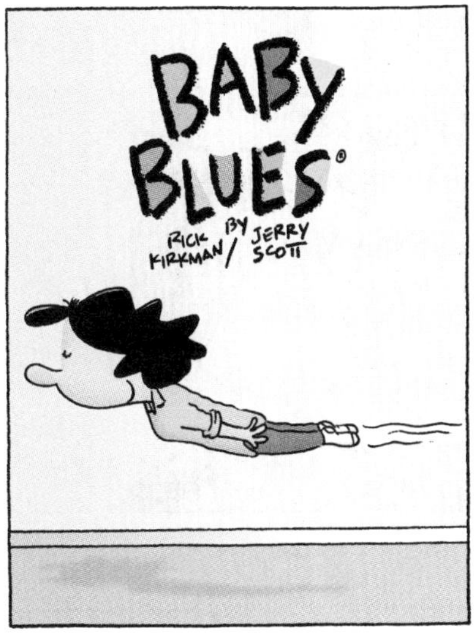
BABY BLUES®
BY RICK KIRKMAN / JERRY SCOTT

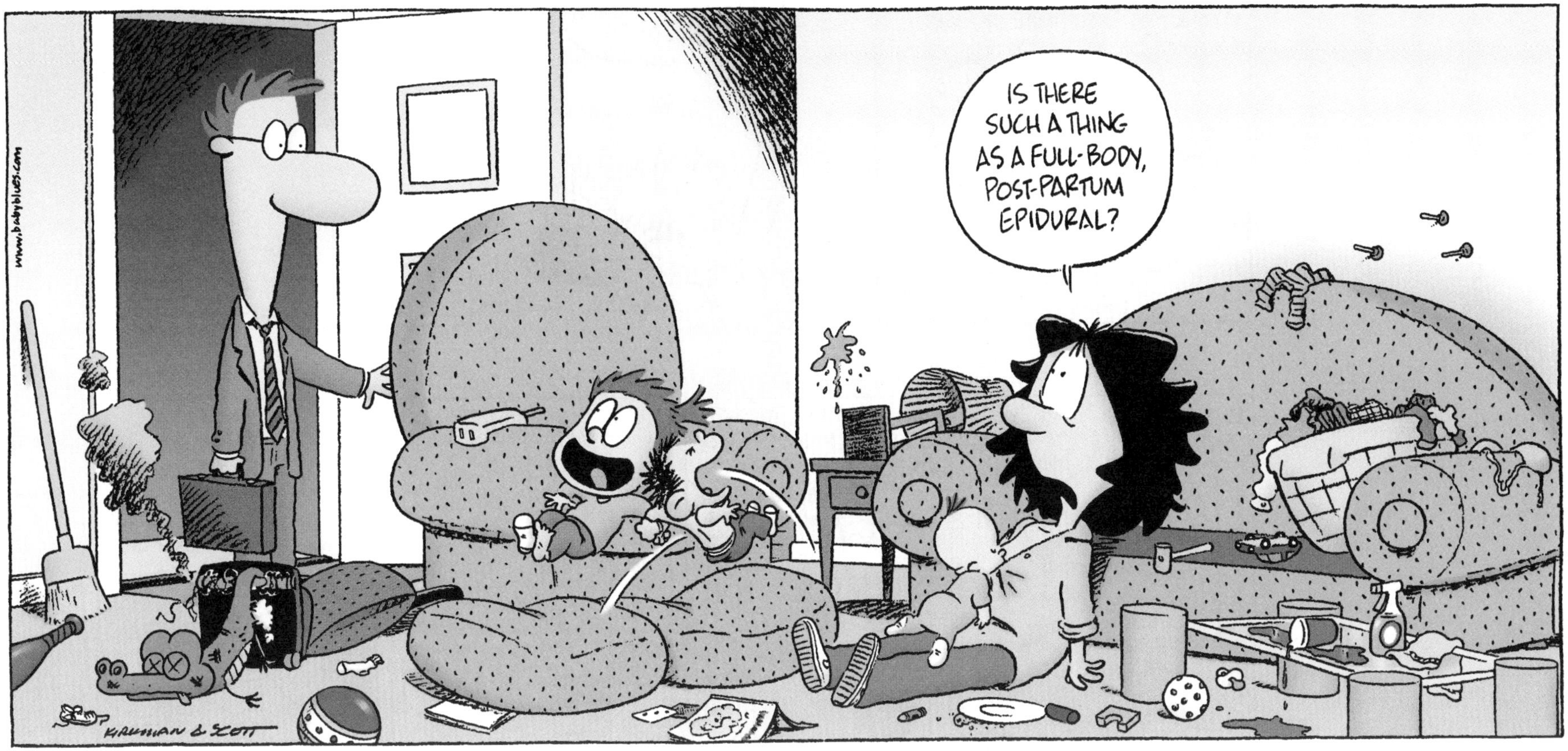
IS THERE SUCH A THING AS A FULL-BODY, POST-PARTUM EPIDURAL?
www.babyblues.com
KIRKMAN & SCOTT

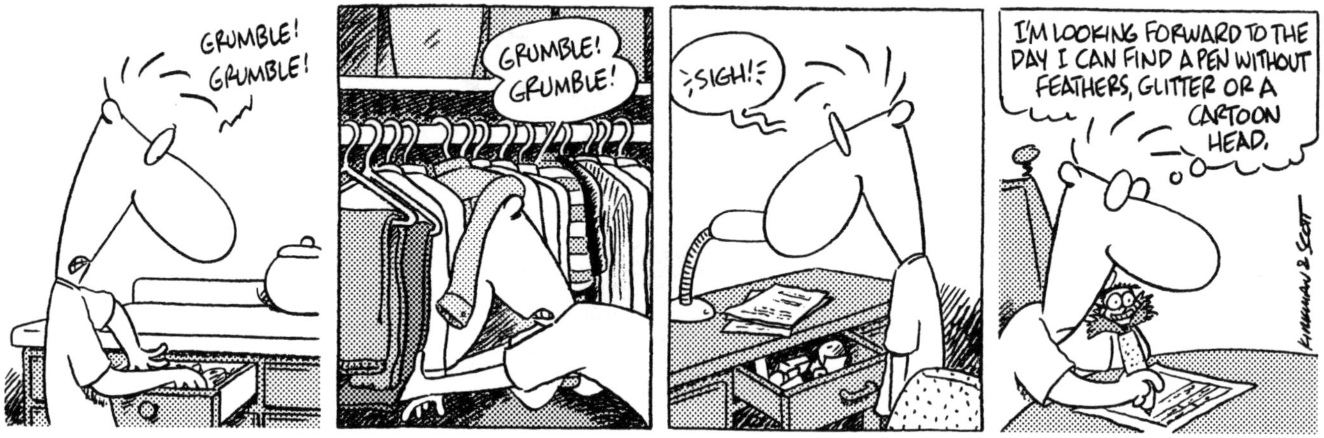
GRUMBLE! GRUMBLE!
GRUMBLE! GRUMBLE!
SIGH!
I'M LOOKING FORWARD TO THE DAY I CAN FIND A PEN WITHOUT FEATHERS, GLITTER OR A CARTOON HEAD.
KIRKMAN & SCOTT

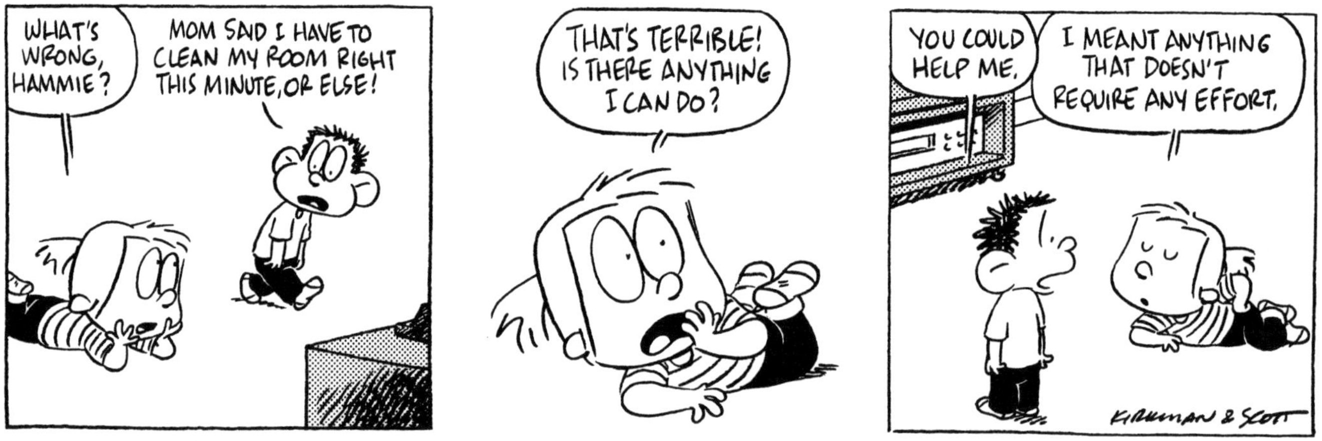
WHAT'S WRONG, HAMMIE?
MOM SAID I HAVE TO CLEAN MY ROOM RIGHT THIS MINUTE, OR ELSE!
THAT'S TERRIBLE! IS THERE ANYTHING I CAN DO?
YOU COULD HELP ME.
I MEANT ANYTHING THAT DOESN'T REQUIRE ANY EFFORT.
KIRKMAN & SCOTT

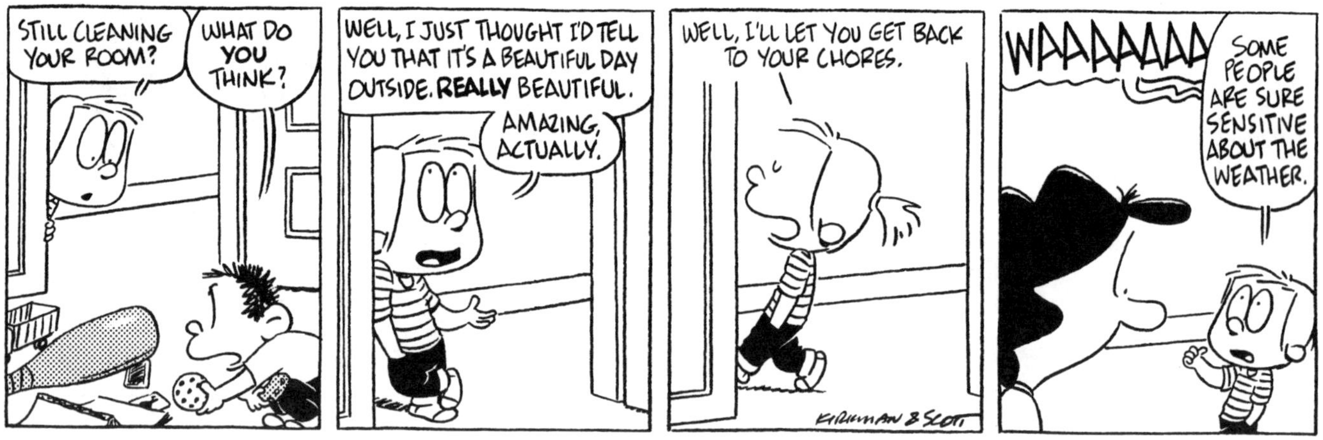
STILL CLEANING YOUR ROOM?
WHAT DO **YOU** THINK?
WELL, I JUST THOUGHT I'D TELL YOU THAT IT'S A BEAUTIFUL DAY OUTSIDE. **REALLY** BEAUTIFUL.
AMAZING, ACTUALLY.
WELL, I'LL LET YOU GET BACK TO YOUR CHORES.
KIRKMAN & SCOTT
WAAAAAAA
SOME PEOPLE ARE SURE SENSITIVE ABOUT THE WEATHER.

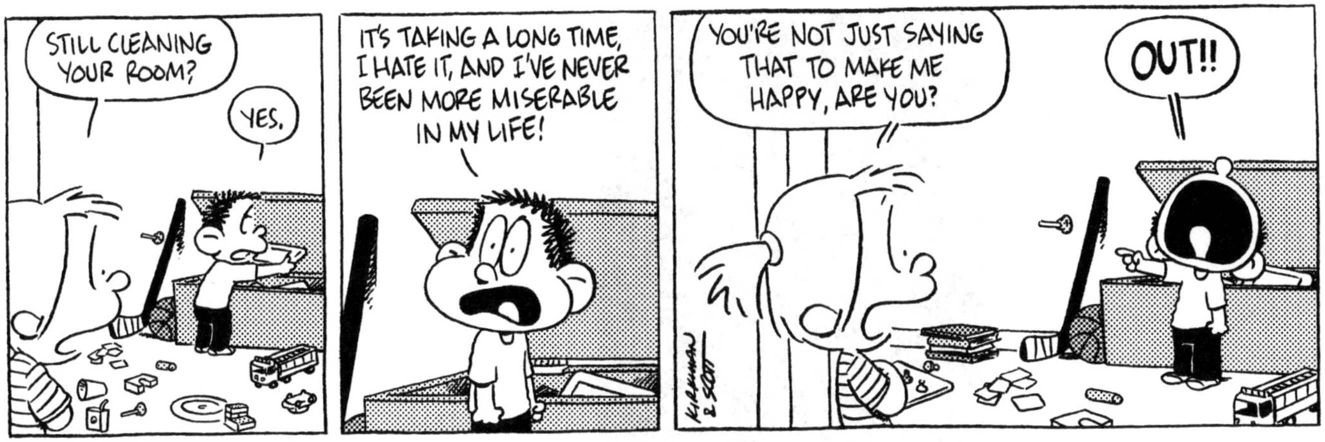
STILL CLEANING YOUR ROOM?
YES.
IT'S TAKING A LONG TIME, I HATE IT, AND I'VE NEVER BEEN MORE MISERABLE IN MY LIFE!
YOU'RE NOT JUST SAYING THAT TO MAKE ME HAPPY, ARE YOU?
OUT!!

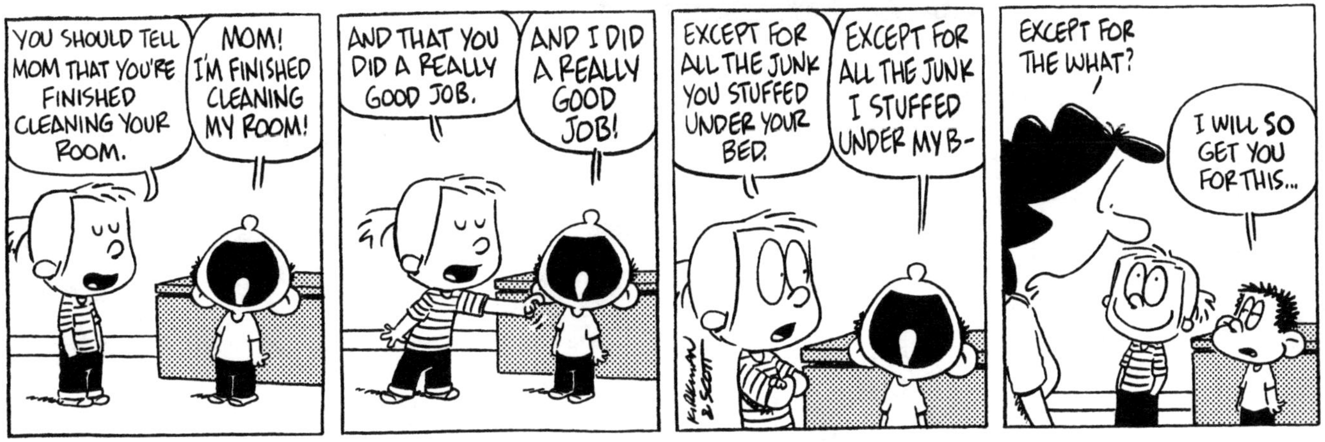
YOU SHOULD TELL MOM THAT YOU'RE FINISHED CLEANING YOUR ROOM.
MOM! I'M FINISHED CLEANING MY ROOM!
AND THAT YOU DID A REALLY GOOD JOB.
AND I DID A REALLY GOOD JOB!
EXCEPT FOR ALL THE JUNK YOU STUFFED UNDER YOUR BED.
EXCEPT FOR ALL THE JUNK I STUFFED UNDER MY B-
EXCEPT FOR THE WHAT?
I WILL SO GET YOU FOR THIS...

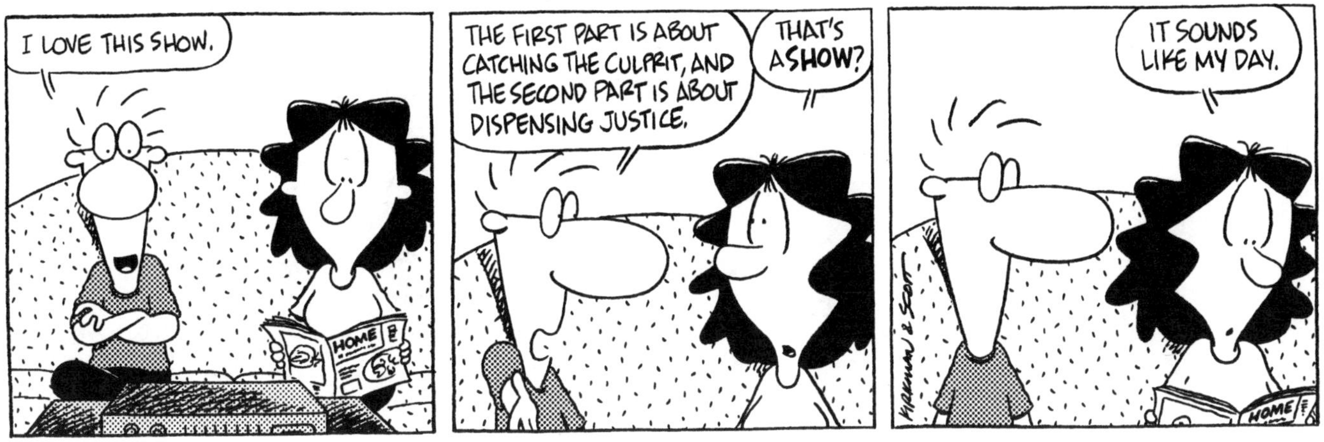
I LOVE THIS SHOW.
THE FIRST PART IS ABOUT CATCHING THE CULPRIT, AND THE SECOND PART IS ABOUT DISPENSING JUSTICE.
THAT'S A SHOW?
IT SOUNDS LIKE MY DAY.

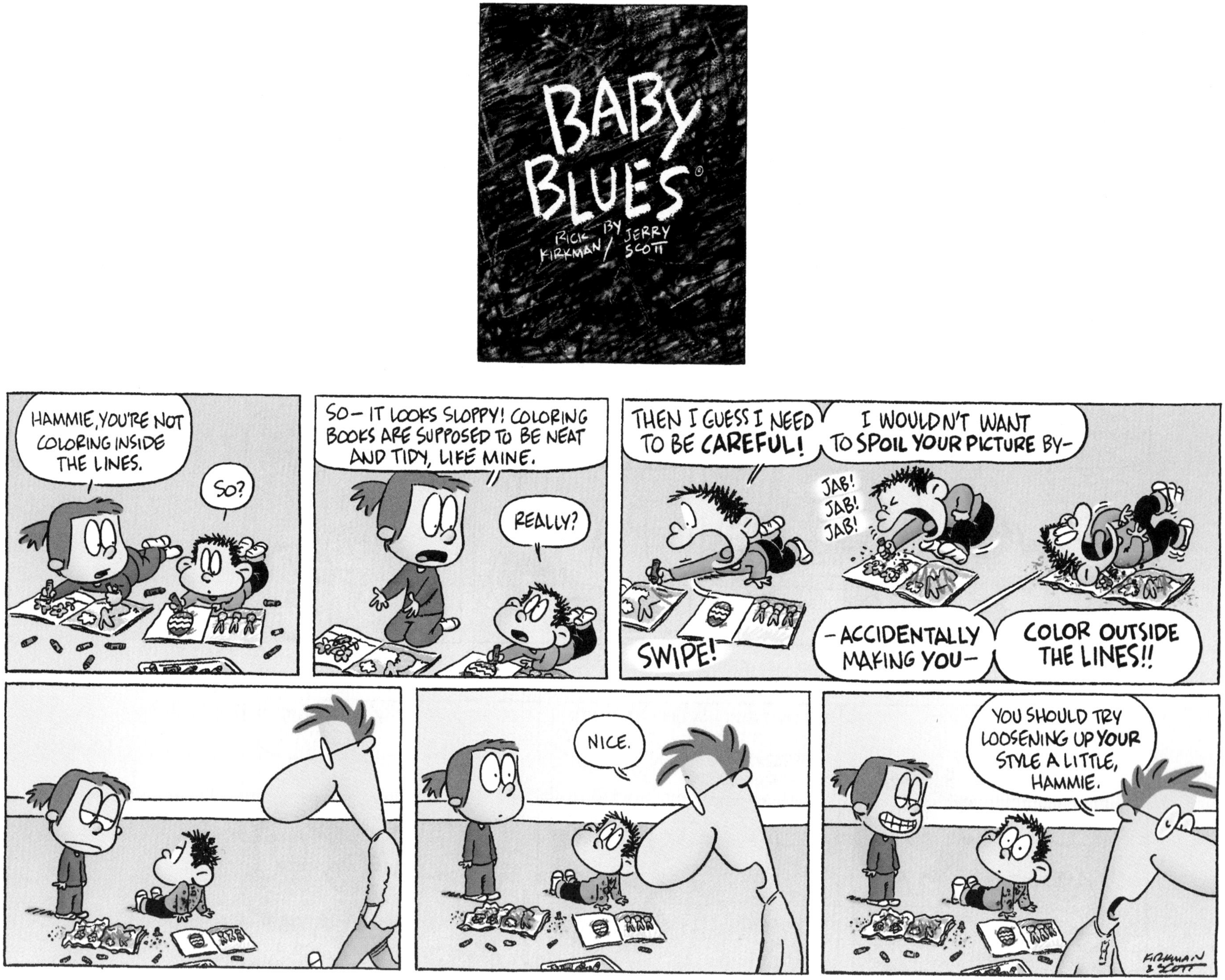
BABY BLUES®
BY RICK KIRKMAN / JERRY SCOTT
HAMMIE, YOU'RE NOT COLORING INSIDE THE LINES.
SO?
SO– IT LOOKS SLOPPY! COLORING BOOKS ARE SUPPOSED TO BE NEAT AND TIDY, LIKE MINE.
REALLY?
THEN I GUESS I NEED TO BE **CAREFUL!**
SWIPE!
I WOULDN'T WANT TO **SPOIL YOUR PICTURE** BY–
JAB! JAB! JAB!
–ACCIDENTALLY MAKING **YOU**–
COLOR OUTSIDE THE LINES!!
NICE.
YOU SHOULD TRY LOOSENING UP **YOUR** STYLE A LITTLE, HAMMIE.
KIRKMAN & SCOTT

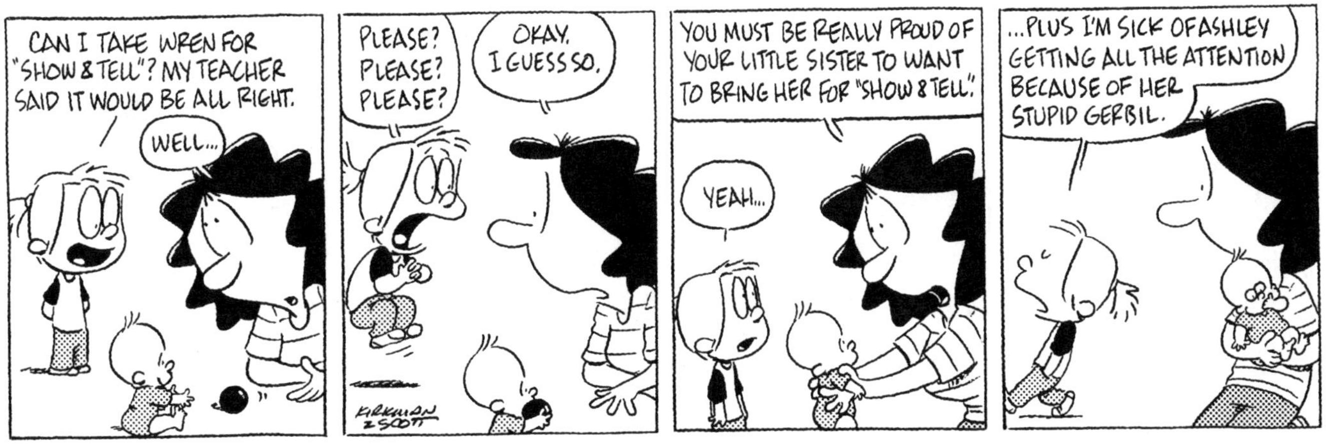
CAN I TAKE WREN FOR "SHOW & TELL"? MY TEACHER SAID IT WOULD BE ALL RIGHT.
WELL...
PLEASE? PLEASE? PLEASE?
OKAY. I GUESS SO.
KIRKMAN & SCOTT
YOU MUST BE REALLY PROUD OF YOUR LITTLE SISTER TO WANT TO BRING HER FOR "SHOW & TELL."
YEAH...
...PLUS I'M SICK OF ASHLEY GETTING ALL THE ATTENTION BECAUSE OF HER STUPID GERBIL.

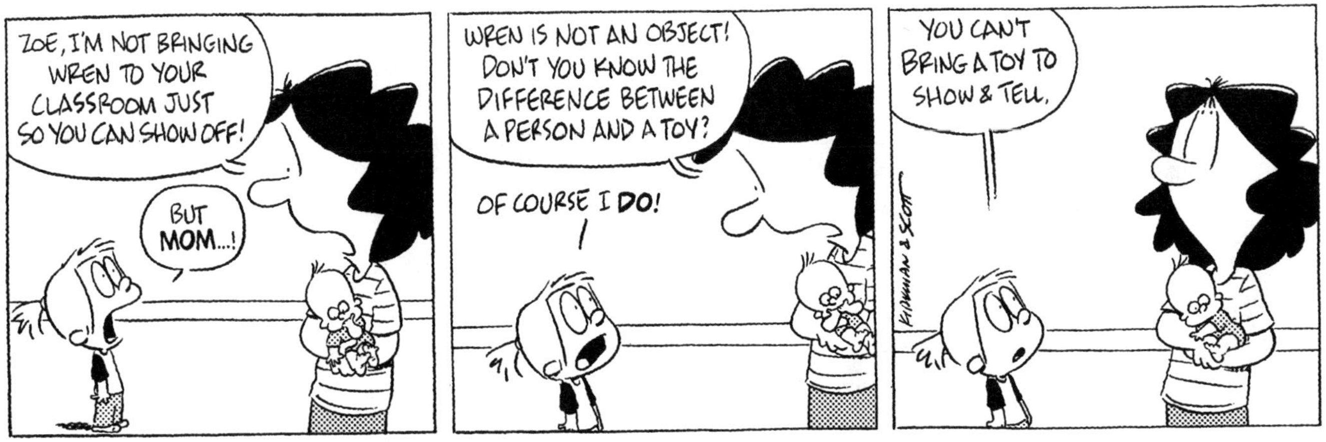
ZOE, I'M NOT BRINGING WREN TO YOUR CLASSROOM JUST SO YOU CAN SHOW OFF!
BUT MOM...!
WREN IS NOT AN OBJECT! DON'T YOU KNOW THE DIFFERENCE BETWEEN A PERSON AND A TOY?
OF COURSE I DO!
YOU CAN'T BRING A TOY TO SHOW & TELL.
KIRKMAN & SCOTT

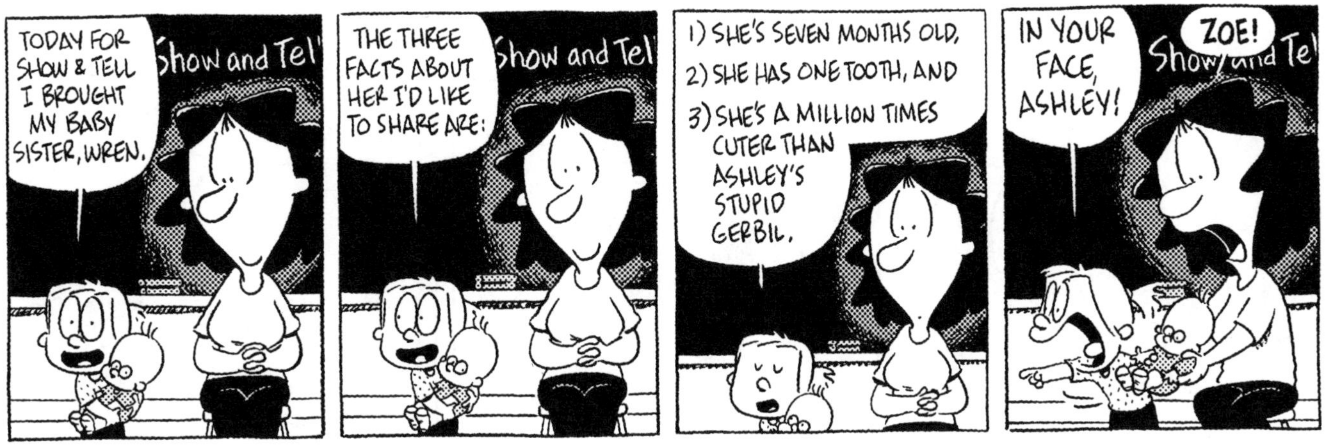
TODAY FOR SHOW & TELL I BROUGHT MY BABY SISTER, WREN.
Show and Tel
THE THREE FACTS ABOUT HER I'D LIKE TO SHARE ARE:
Show and Tel
1) SHE'S SEVEN MONTHS OLD,
2) SHE HAS ONE TOOTH, AND
3) SHE'S A MILLION TIMES CUTER THAN ASHLEY'S STUPID GERBIL.
IN YOUR FACE, ASHLEY!
ZOE!

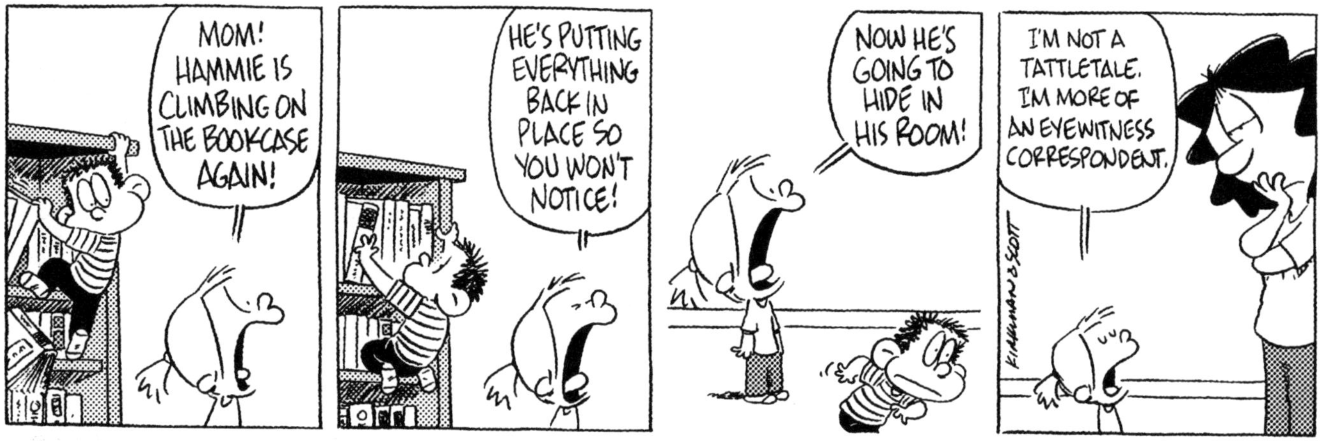
MOM! HAMMIE IS CLIMBING ON THE BOOKCASE AGAIN!
HE'S PUTTING EVERYTHING BACK IN PLACE SO YOU WON'T NOTICE!
NOW HE'S GOING TO HIDE IN HIS ROOM!
I'M NOT A TATTLETALE. I'M MORE OF AN EYEWITNESS CORRESPONDENT.
KIRKMAN & SCOTT

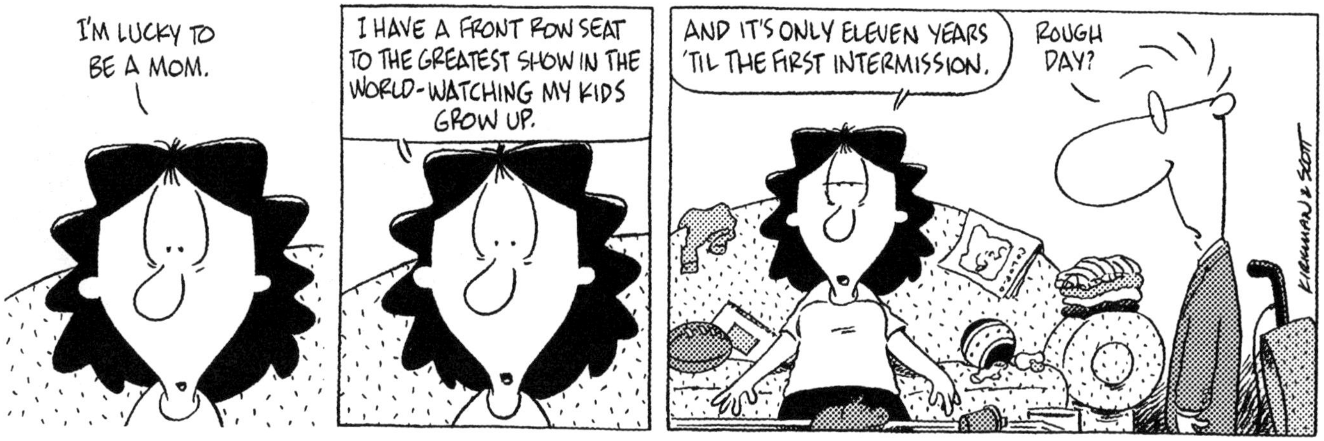
I'M LUCKY TO BE A MOM.
I HAVE A FRONT ROW SEAT TO THE GREATEST SHOW IN THE WORLD-WATCHING MY KIDS GROW UP.
AND IT'S ONLY ELEVEN YEARS 'TIL THE FIRST INTERMISSION.
ROUGH DAY?
KIRKMAN & SCOTT

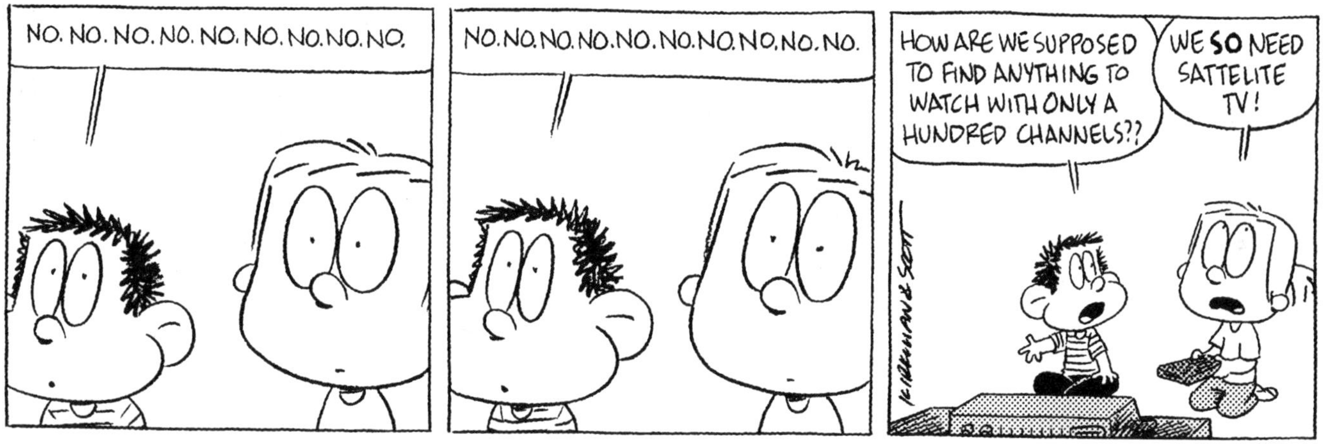
NO. NO. NO. NO. NO. NO. NO. NO. NO.
NO. NO. NO. NO. NO. NO. NO. NO. NO. NO.
HOW ARE WE SUPPOSED TO FIND ANYTHING TO WATCH WITH ONLY A HUNDRED CHANNELS??
WE **SO** NEED SATTELITE TV!
KIRKMAN & SCOTT

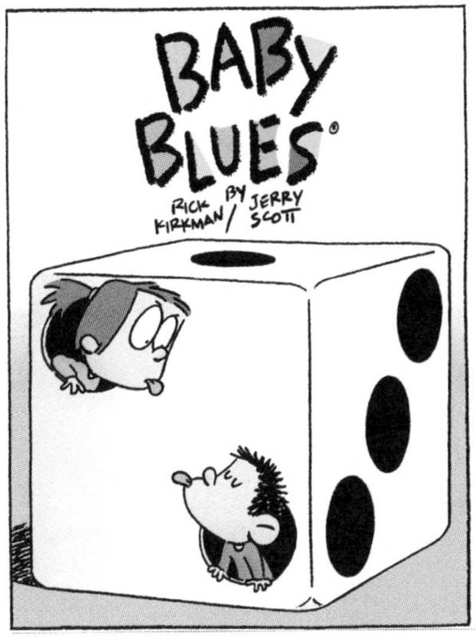
BABY BLUES®
RICK KIRKMAN / BY JERRY SCOTT

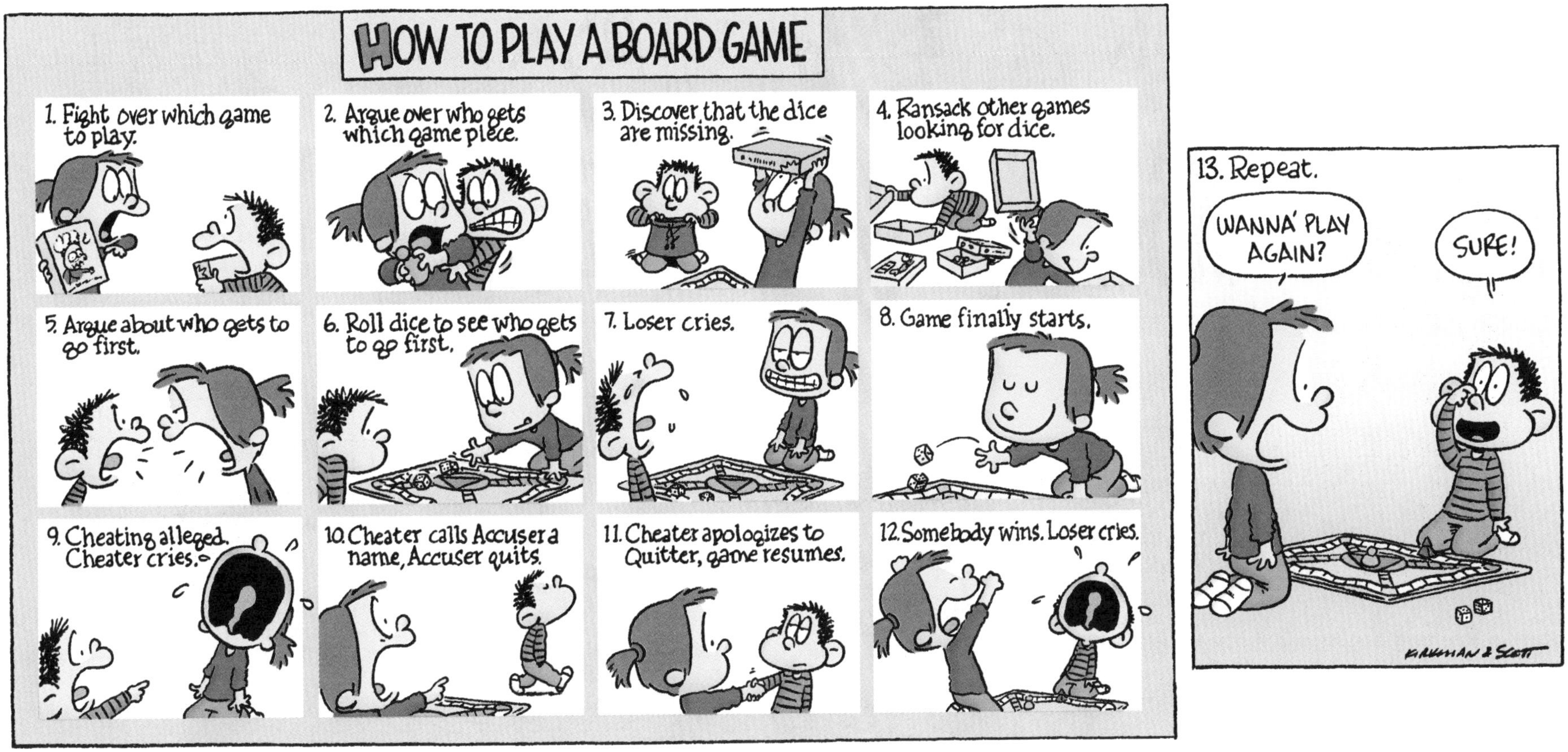
HOW TO PLAY A BOARD GAME
1. Fight over which game to play.
2. Argue over who gets which game piece.
3. Discover that the dice are missing.
4. Ransack other games looking for dice.
5. Argue about who gets to go first.
6. Roll dice to see who gets to go first.
7. Loser cries.
8. Game finally starts.
9. Cheating alleged. Cheater cries.
10. Cheater calls Accuser a name, Accuser quits.
11. Cheater apologizes to Quitter, game resumes.
12. Somebody wins. Loser cries.
13. Repeat.
WANNA' PLAY AGAIN?
SURE!
KIRKMAN & SCOTT

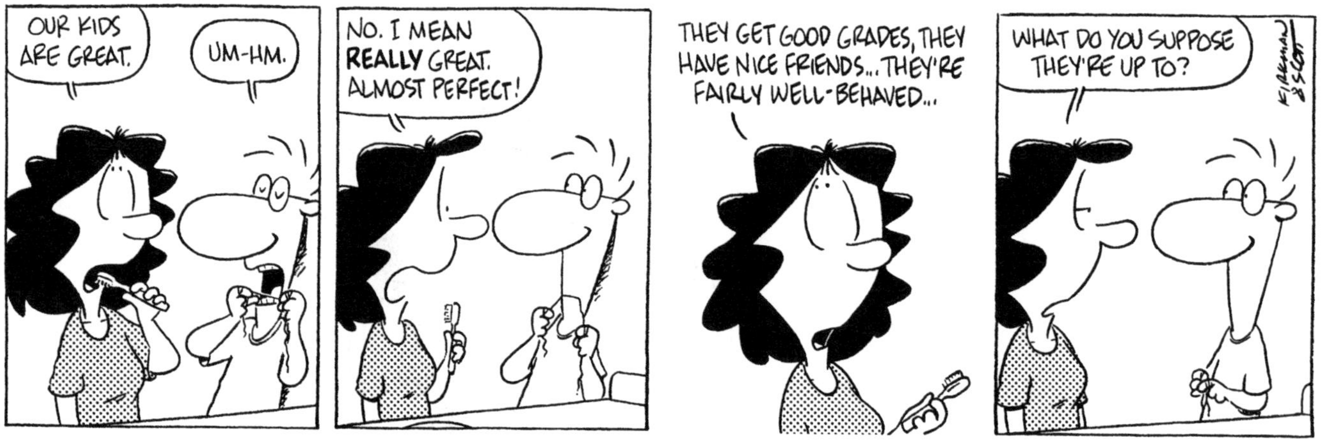
OUR KIDS ARE GREAT.
UM-HM.
NO. I MEAN **REALLY** GREAT. ALMOST PERFECT!
THEY GET GOOD GRADES, THEY HAVE NICE FRIENDS... THEY'RE FAIRLY WELL-BEHAVED...
WHAT DO YOU SUPPOSE THEY'RE UP TO?
KIRKMAN & SCOTT

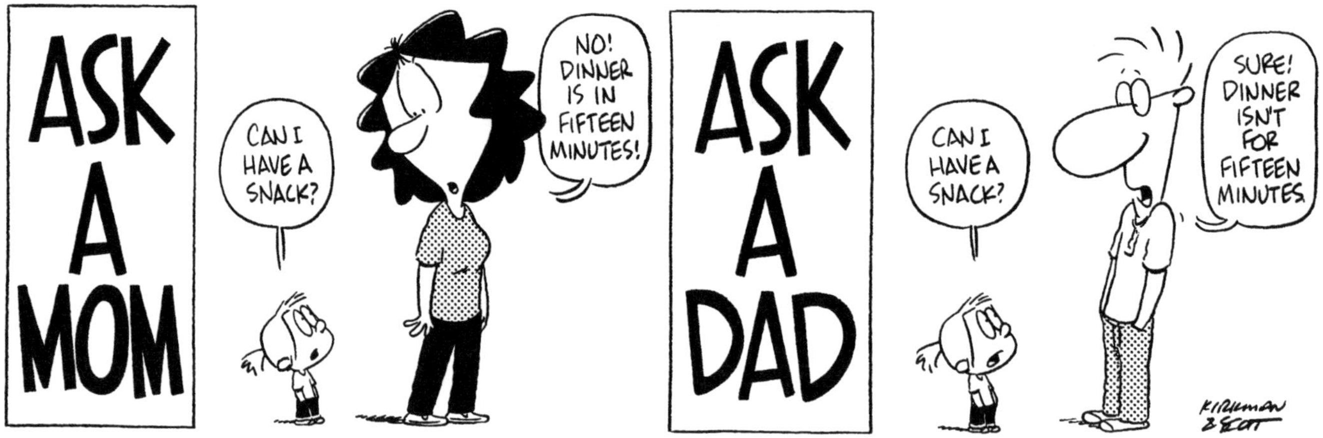
ASK A MOM
CAN I HAVE A SNACK?
NO! DINNER IS IN FIFTEEN MINUTES!
ASK A DAD
CAN I HAVE A SNACK?
SURE! DINNER ISN'T FOR FIFTEEN MINUTES.
KIRKMAN & SCOTT

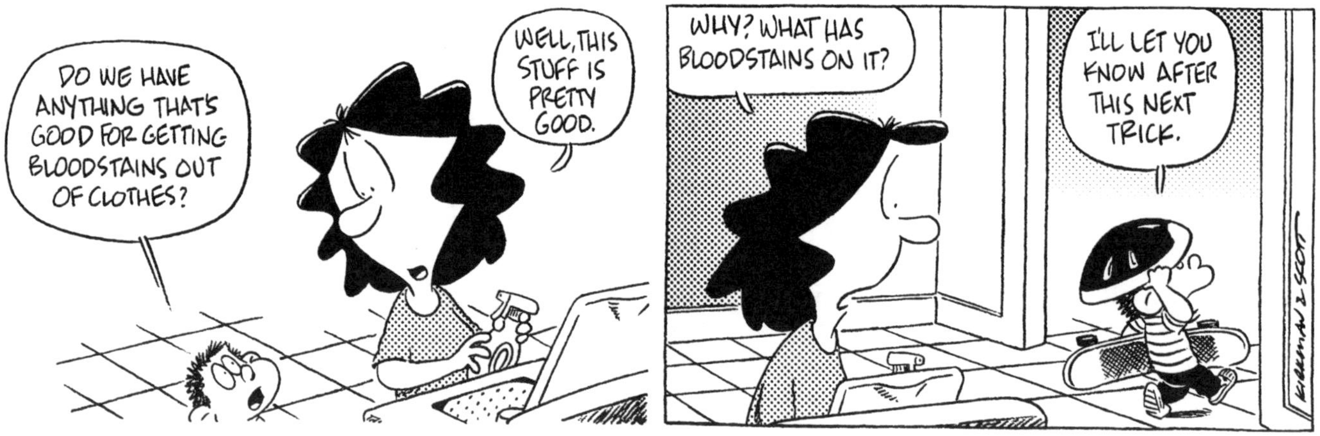
DO WE HAVE ANYTHING THAT'S GOOD FOR GETTING BLOODSTAINS OUT OF CLOTHES?
WELL, THIS STUFF IS PRETTY GOOD.
WHY? WHAT HAS BLOODSTAINS ON IT?
I'LL LET YOU KNOW AFTER THIS NEXT TRICK.
KIRKMAN & SCOTT

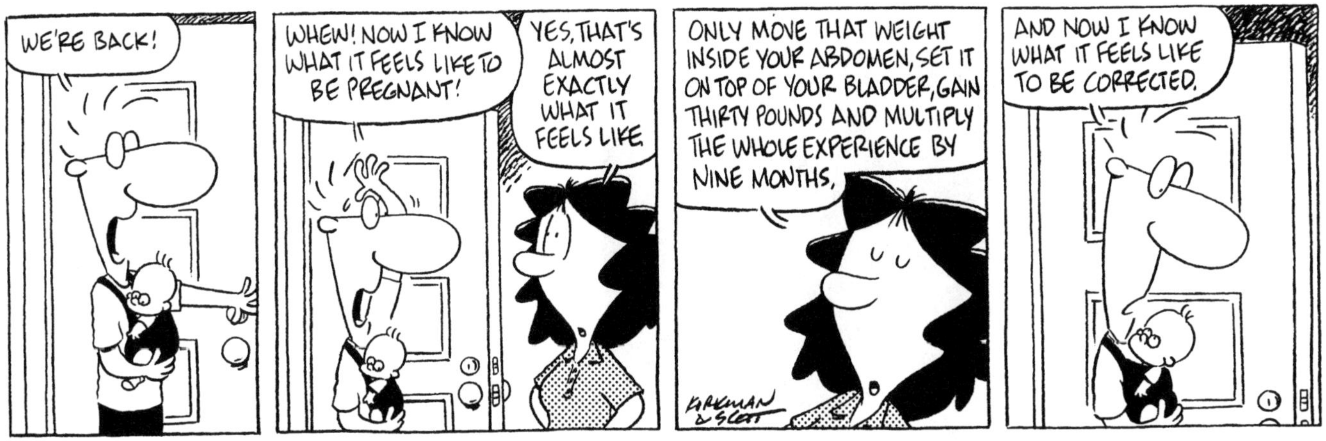
WE'RE BACK!
WHEW! NOW I KNOW WHAT IT FEELS LIKE TO BE PREGNANT!
YES, THAT'S ALMOST EXACTLY WHAT IT FEELS LIKE.
ONLY MOVE THAT WEIGHT INSIDE YOUR ABDOMEN, SET IT ON TOP OF YOUR BLADDER, GAIN THIRTY POUNDS AND MULTIPLY THE WHOLE EXPERIENCE BY NINE MONTHS.
KIRKMAN & SCOTT
AND NOW I KNOW WHAT IT FEELS LIKE TO BE CORRECTED.

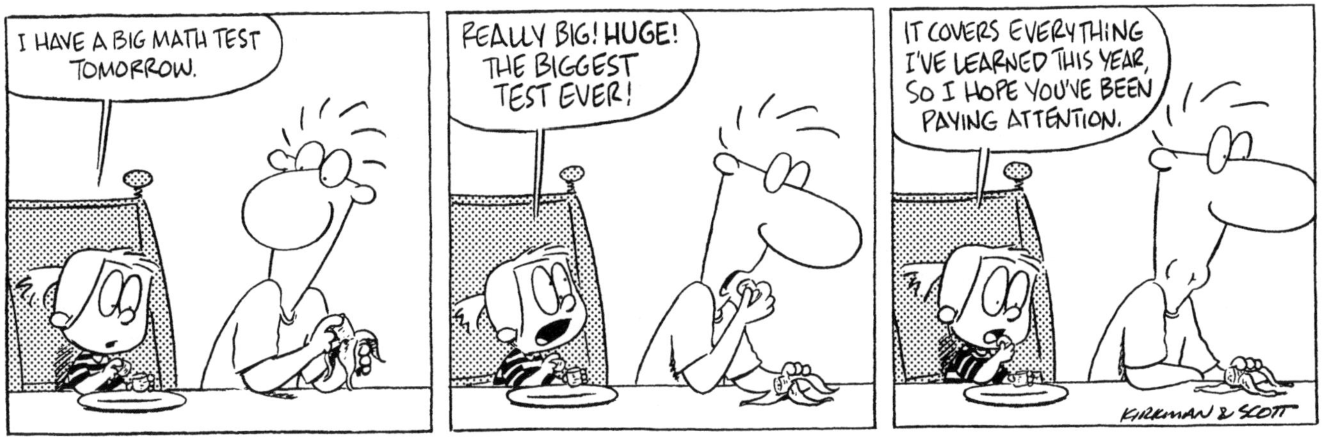
I HAVE A BIG MATH TEST TOMORROW.
REALLY BIG! HUGE! THE BIGGEST TEST EVER!
IT COVERS EVERYTHING I'VE LEARNED THIS YEAR, SO I HOPE YOU'VE BEEN PAYING ATTENTION.
KIRKMAN & SCOTT

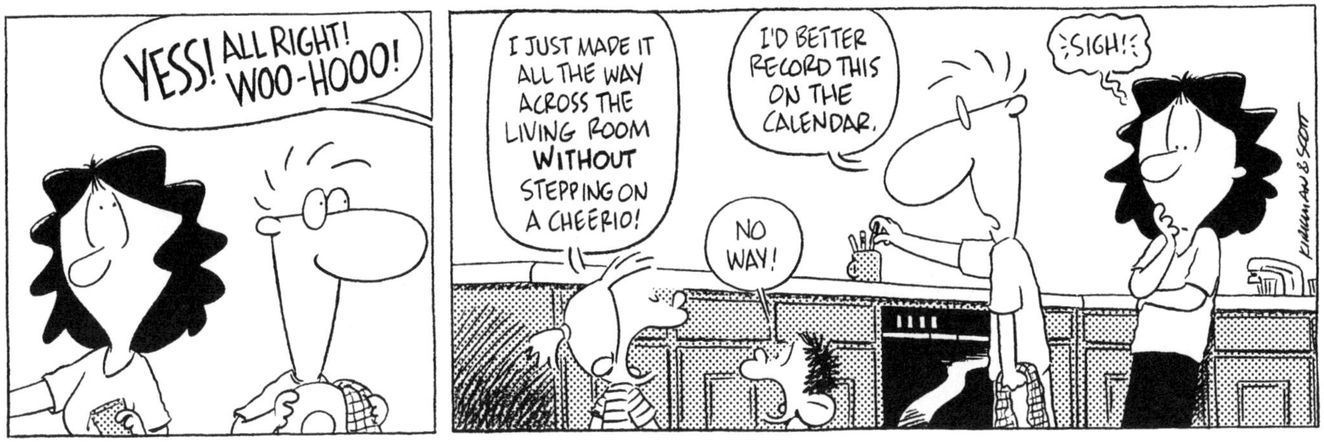
YESS! ALL RIGHT! WOO-HOOO!
I JUST MADE IT ALL THE WAY ACROSS THE LIVING ROOM WITHOUT STEPPING ON A CHEERIO!
I'D BETTER RECORD THIS ON THE CALENDAR.
NO WAY!
SIGH!
KIRKMAN & SCOTT

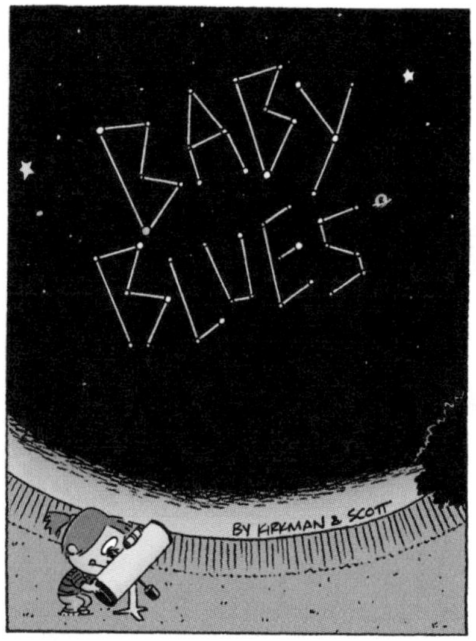

BABY BLUES
BY KIRKMAN & SCOTT

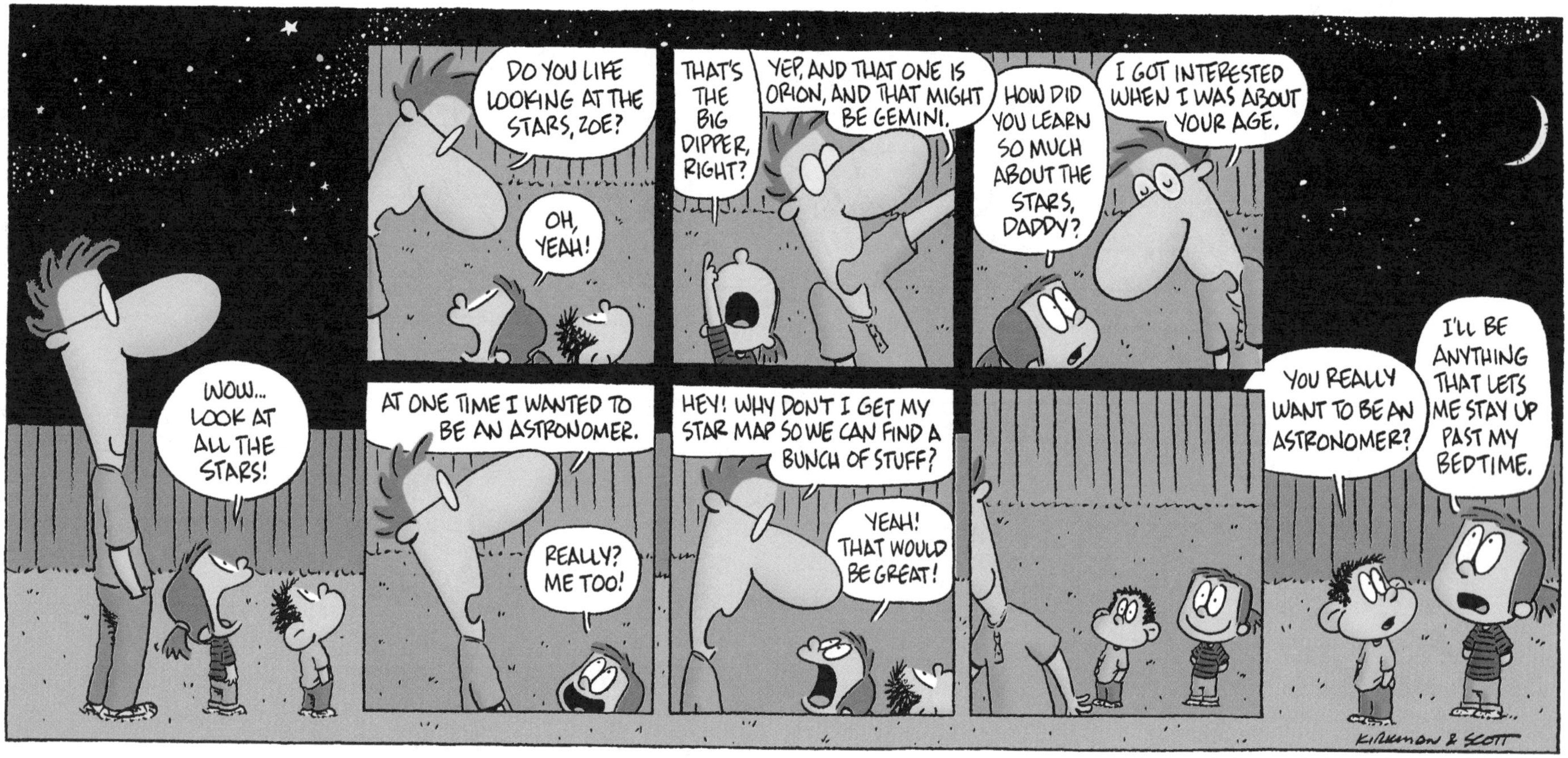

WOW... LOOK AT ALL THE STARS!
DO YOU LIKE LOOKING AT THE STARS, ZOE?
OH, YEAH!
THAT'S THE BIG DIPPER, RIGHT?
YEP, AND THAT ONE IS ORION, AND THAT MIGHT BE GEMINI.
HOW DID YOU LEARN SO MUCH ABOUT THE STARS, DADDY?
I GOT INTERESTED WHEN I WAS ABOUT YOUR AGE.
AT ONE TIME I WANTED TO BE AN ASTRONOMER.
REALLY? ME TOO!
HEY! WHY DON'T I GET MY STAR MAP SO WE CAN FIND A BUNCH OF STUFF?
YEAH! THAT WOULD BE GREAT!
YOU REALLY WANT TO BE AN ASTRONOMER?
I'LL BE ANYTHING THAT LETS ME STAY UP PAST MY BEDTIME.
KIRKMAN & SCOTT

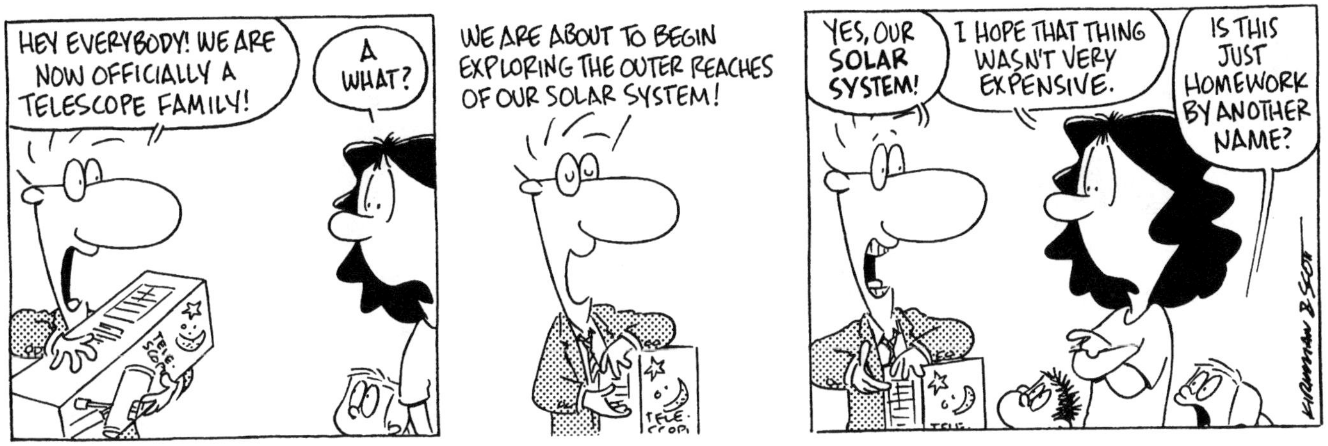
HEY EVERYBODY! WE ARE NOW OFFICIALLY A TELESCOPE FAMILY!
A WHAT?
WE ARE ABOUT TO BEGIN EXPLORING THE OUTER REACHES OF OUR SOLAR SYSTEM!
YES, OUR **SOLAR SYSTEM!**
I HOPE THAT THING WASN'T VERY EXPENSIVE.
IS THIS JUST HOMEWORK BY ANOTHER NAME?

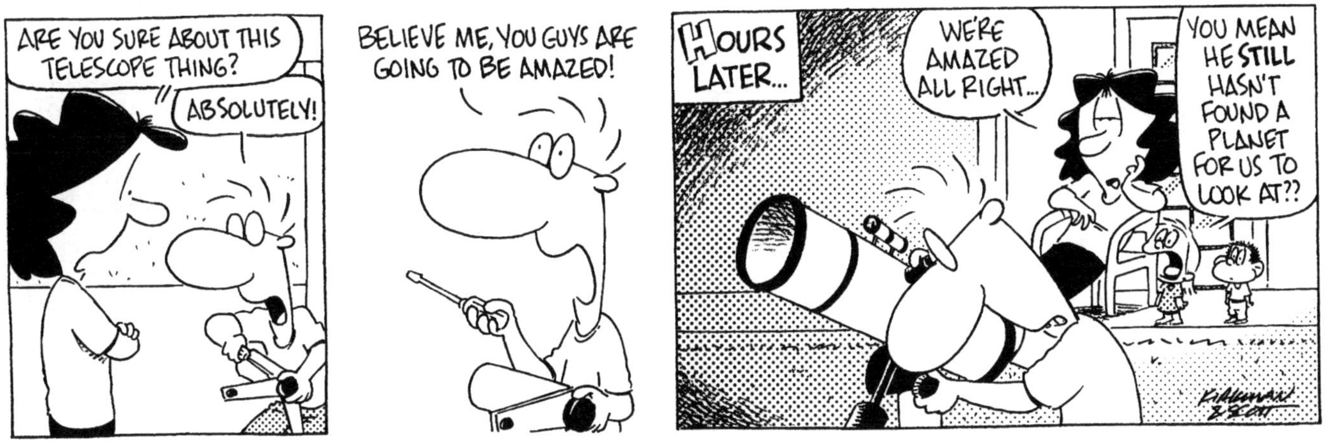
ARE YOU SURE ABOUT THIS TELESCOPE THING?
ABSOLUTELY!
BELIEVE ME, YOU GUYS ARE GOING TO BE AMAZED!
HOURS LATER...
WE'RE AMAZED ALL RIGHT...
YOU MEAN HE **STILL** HASN'T FOUND A PLANET FOR US TO LOOK AT??

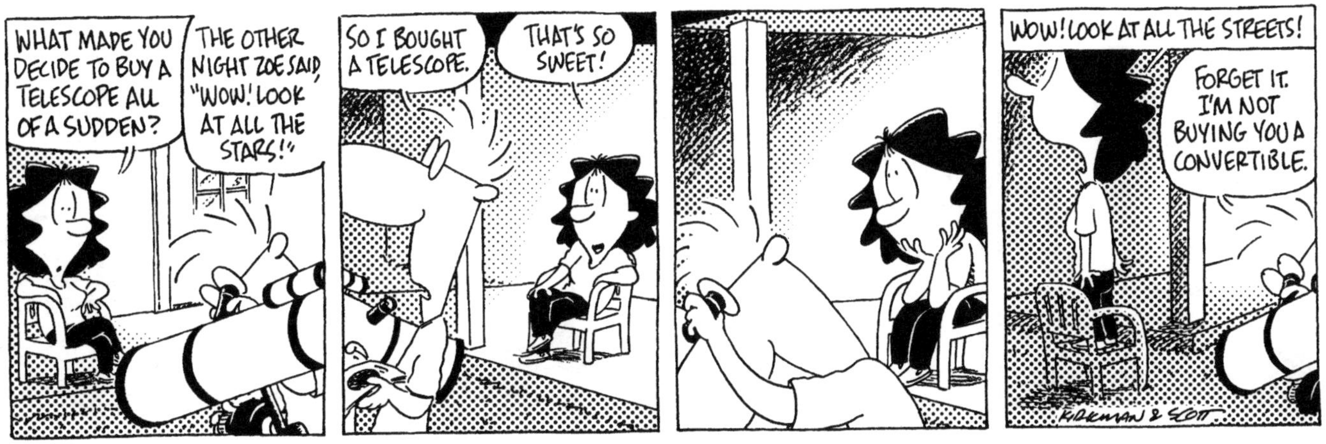
WHAT MADE YOU DECIDE TO BUY A TELESCOPE ALL OF A SUDDEN?
THE OTHER NIGHT ZOE SAID, "WOW! LOOK AT ALL THE STARS!"
SO I BOUGHT A TELESCOPE.
THAT'S SO SWEET!
WOW! LOOK AT ALL THE STREETS!
FORGET IT. I'M NOT BUYING YOU A CONVERTIBLE.

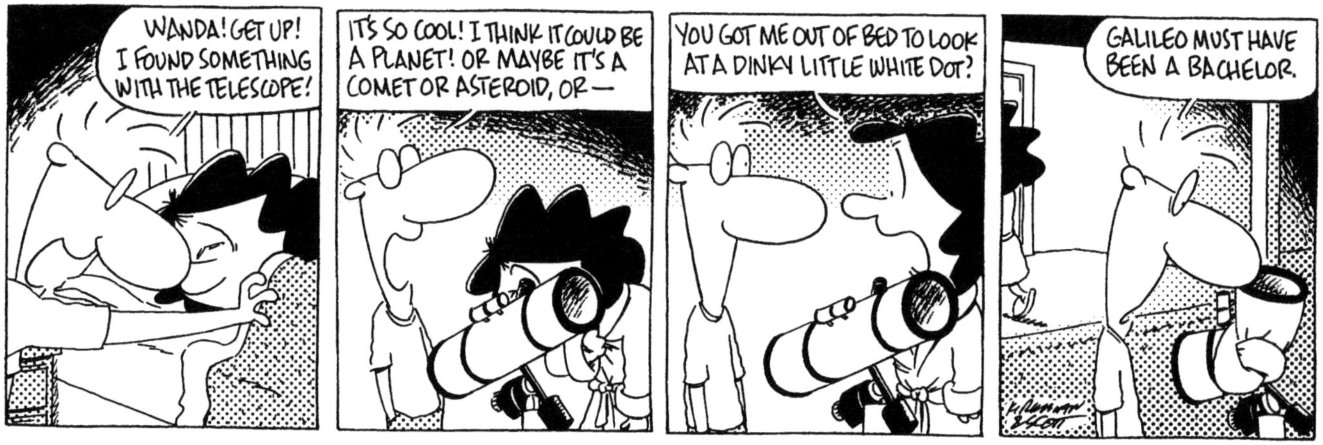
WANDA! GET UP! I FOUND SOMETHING WITH THE TELESCOPE!
IT'S SO COOL! I THINK IT COULD BE A PLANET! OR MAYBE IT'S A COMET OR ASTEROID, OR —
YOU GOT ME OUT OF BED TO LOOK AT A DINKY LITTLE WHITE DOT?
GALILEO MUST HAVE BEEN A BACHELOR.
KIRKMAN & SCOTT

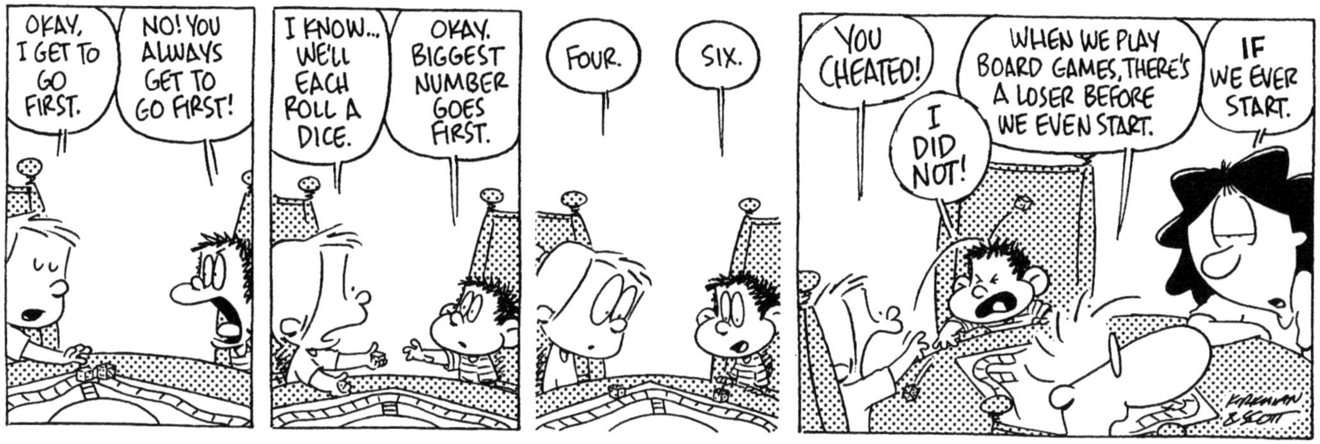
OKAY, I GET TO GO FIRST.
NO! YOU ALWAYS GET TO GO FIRST!
I KNOW... WE'LL EACH ROLL A DICE.
OKAY. BIGGEST NUMBER GOES FIRST.
FOUR.
SIX.
YOU CHEATED!
I DID NOT!
WHEN WE PLAY BOARD GAMES, THERE'S A LOSER BEFORE WE EVEN START.
IF WE EVER START.
KIRKMAN & SCOTT

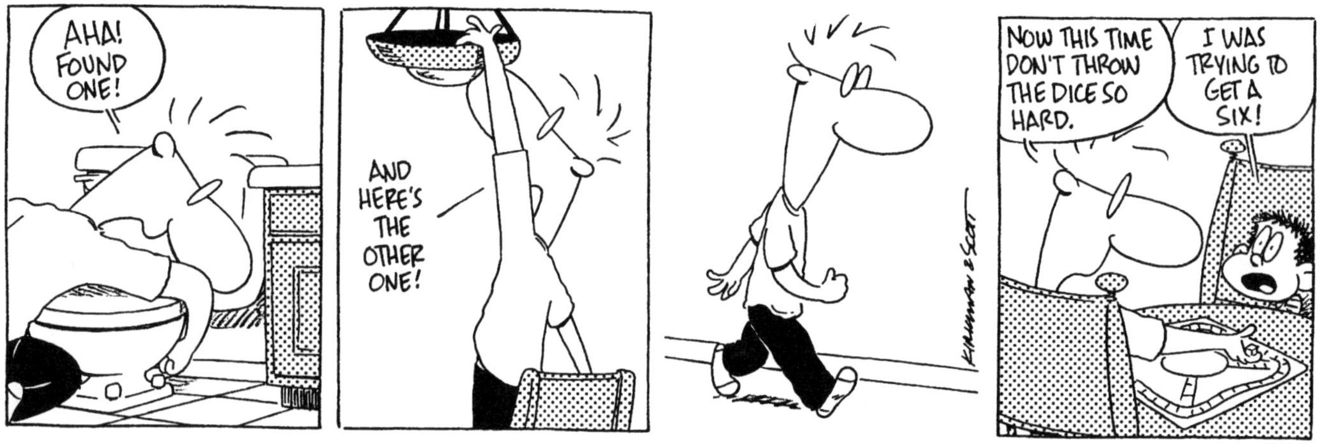
AHA! FOUND ONE!
AND HERE'S THE OTHER ONE!
KIRKMAN & SCOTT
NOW THIS TIME DON'T THROW THE DICE SO HARD.
I WAS TRYING TO GET A SIX!

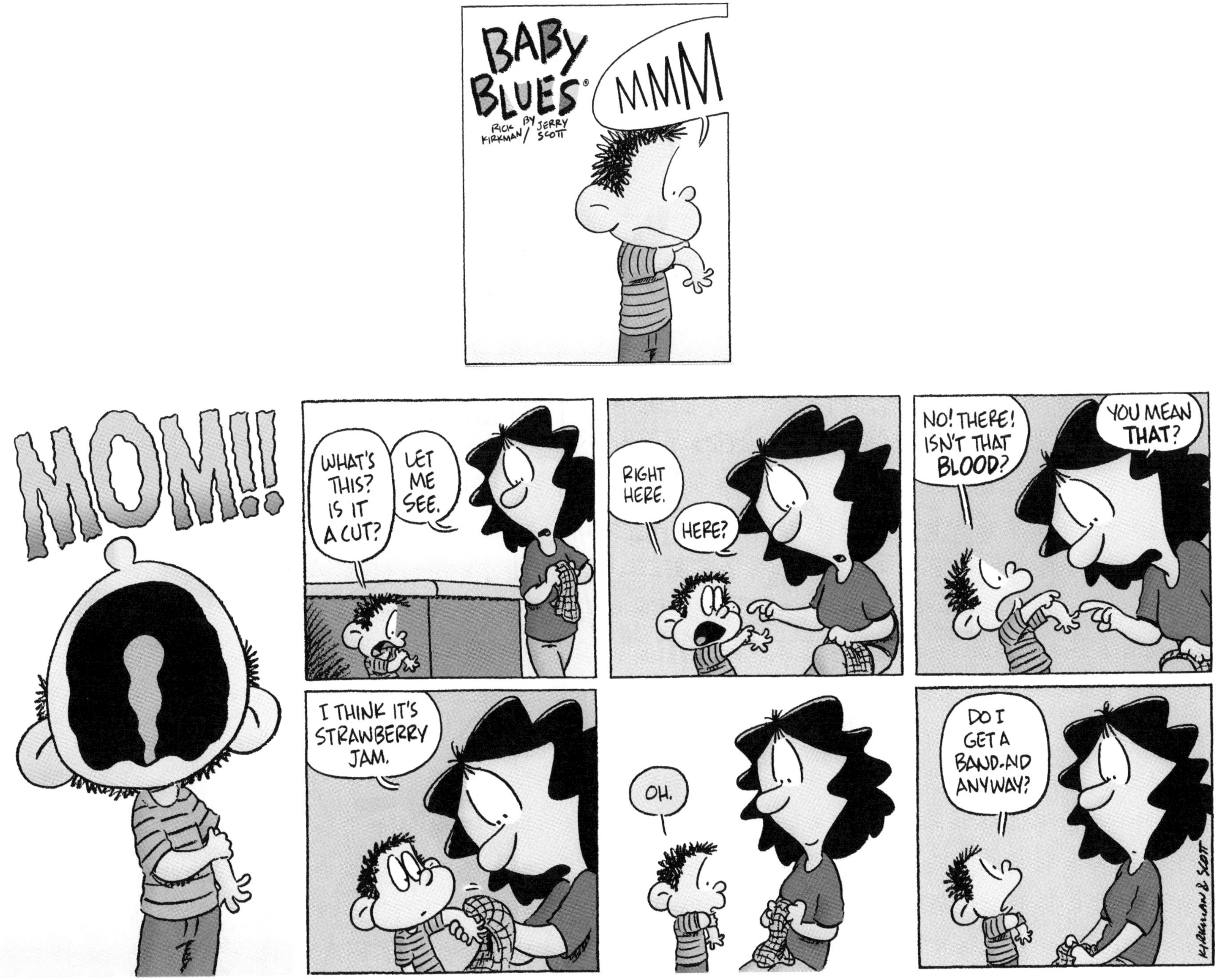
BABY BLUES®
RICK KIRKMAN / BY JERRY SCOTT
MMM
MOM!!
WHAT'S THIS? IS IT A CUT?
LET ME SEE.
RIGHT HERE.
HERE?
NO! THERE! ISN'T THAT BLOOD?
YOU MEAN THAT?
I THINK IT'S STRAWBERRY JAM.
OH.
DO I GET A BAND-AID ANYWAY?
KIRKMAN & SCOTT

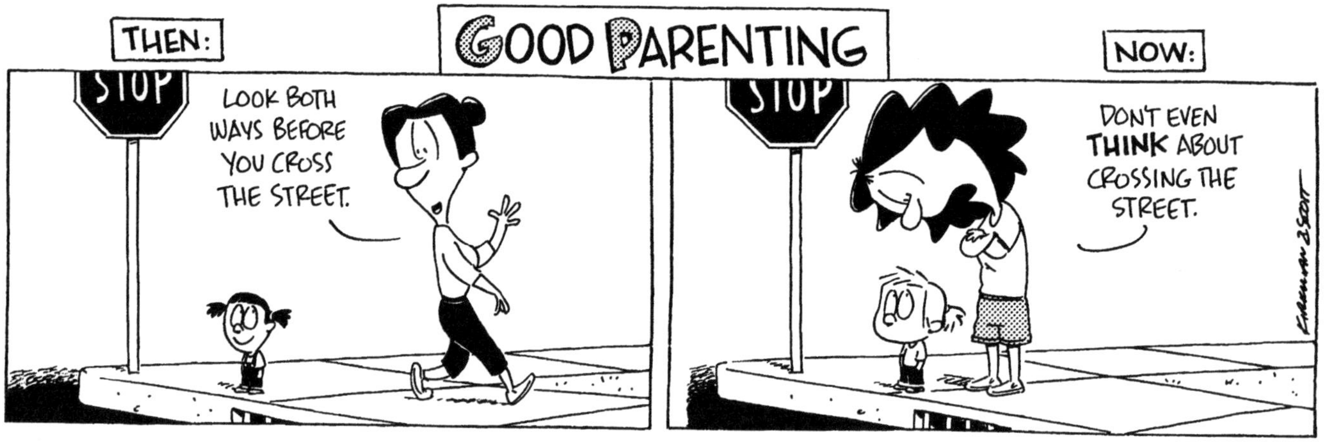
THEN:
GOOD PARENTING
NOW:
STOP
LOOK BOTH WAYS BEFORE YOU CROSS THE STREET.
STOP
DON'T EVEN **THINK** ABOUT CROSSING THE STREET.

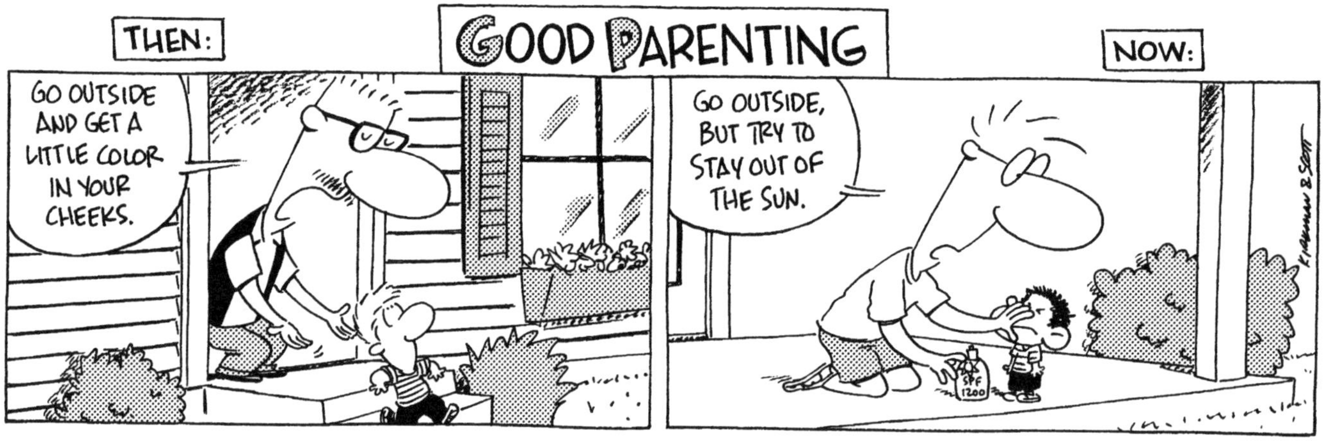
THEN:
GOOD PARENTING
NOW:
GO OUTSIDE AND GET A LITTLE COLOR IN YOUR CHEEKS.
GO OUTSIDE, BUT TRY TO STAY OUT OF THE SUN.
SPF 1200

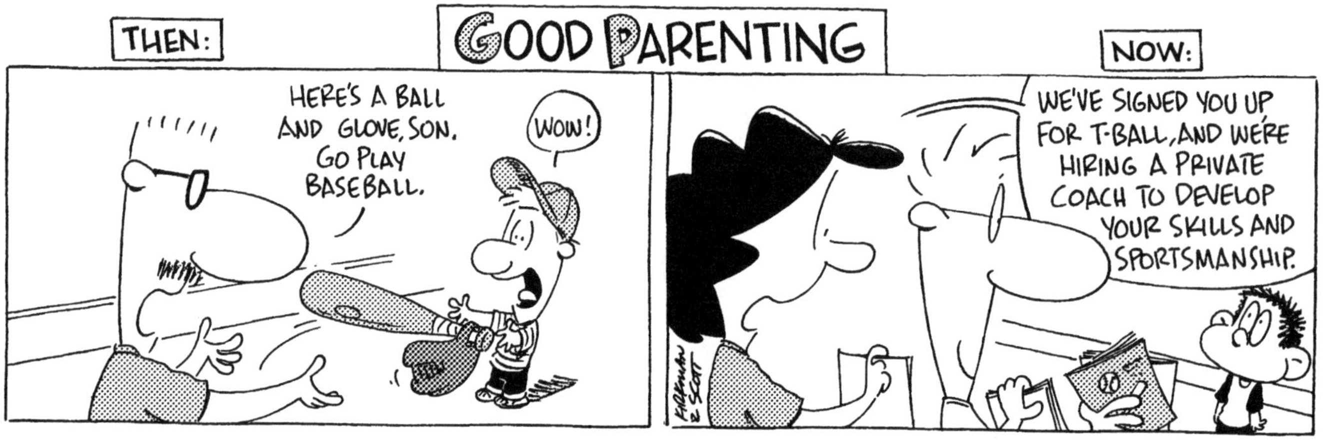
THEN:
GOOD PARENTING
NOW:
HERE'S A BALL AND GLOVE, SON. GO PLAY BASEBALL.
WOW!
WE'VE SIGNED YOU UP FOR T-BALL, AND WE'RE HIRING A PRIVATE COACH TO DEVELOP YOUR SKILLS AND SPORTSMANSHIP.

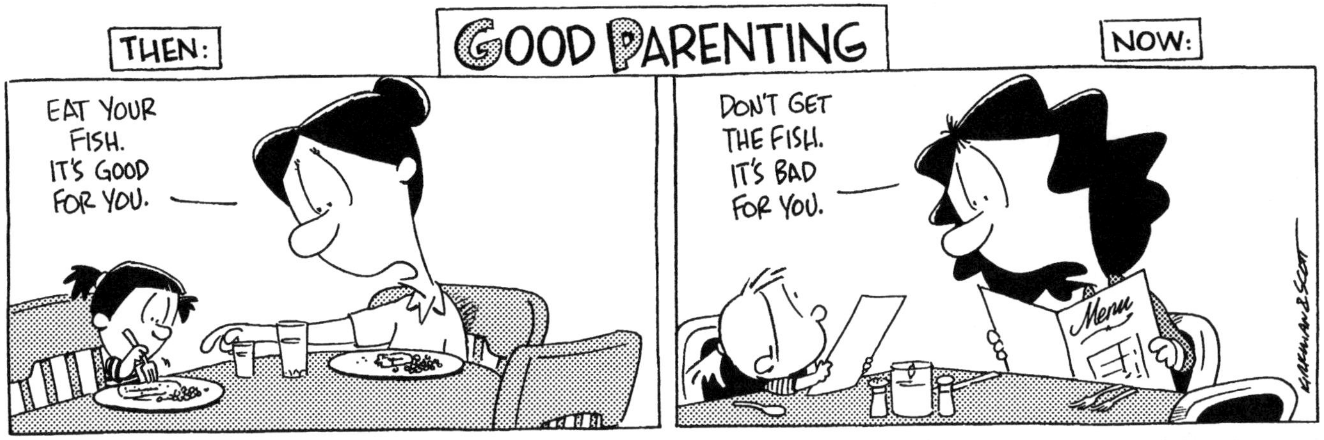
THEN:
GOOD PARENTING
NOW:
EAT YOUR FISH. IT'S GOOD FOR YOU.
DON'T GET THE FISH. IT'S BAD FOR YOU.
Menu
KIRKMAN & SCOTT

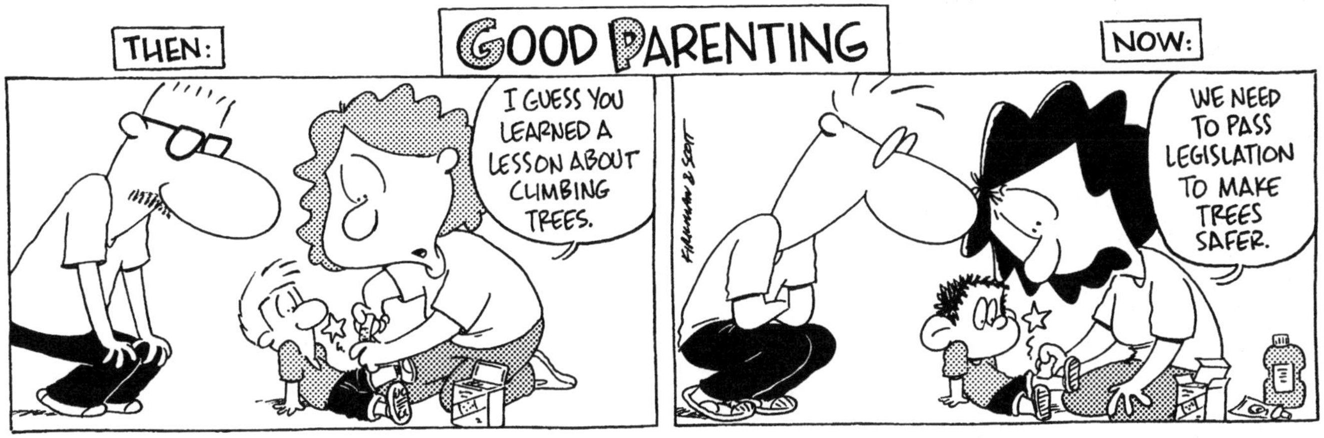
THEN:
GOOD PARENTING
NOW:
I GUESS YOU LEARNED A LESSON ABOUT CLIMBING TREES.
KIRKMAN & SCOTT
WE NEED TO PASS LEGISLATION TO MAKE TREES SAFER.

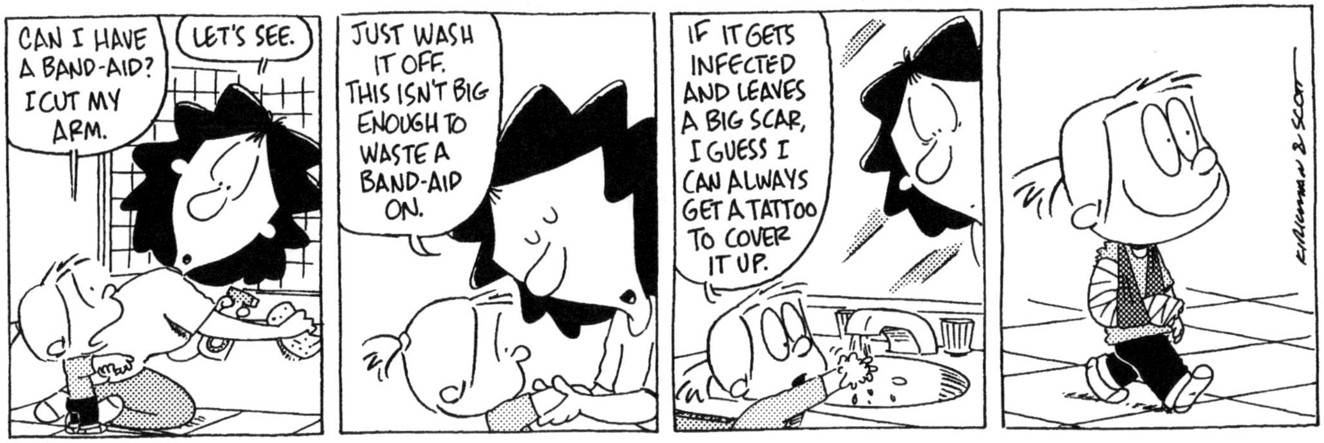
CAN I HAVE A BAND-AID? I CUT MY ARM.
LET'S SEE.
JUST WASH IT OFF. THIS ISN'T BIG ENOUGH TO WASTE A BAND-AID ON.
IF IT GETS INFECTED AND LEAVES A BIG SCAR, I GUESS I CAN ALWAYS GET A TATTOO TO COVER IT UP.
KIRKMAN & SCOTT

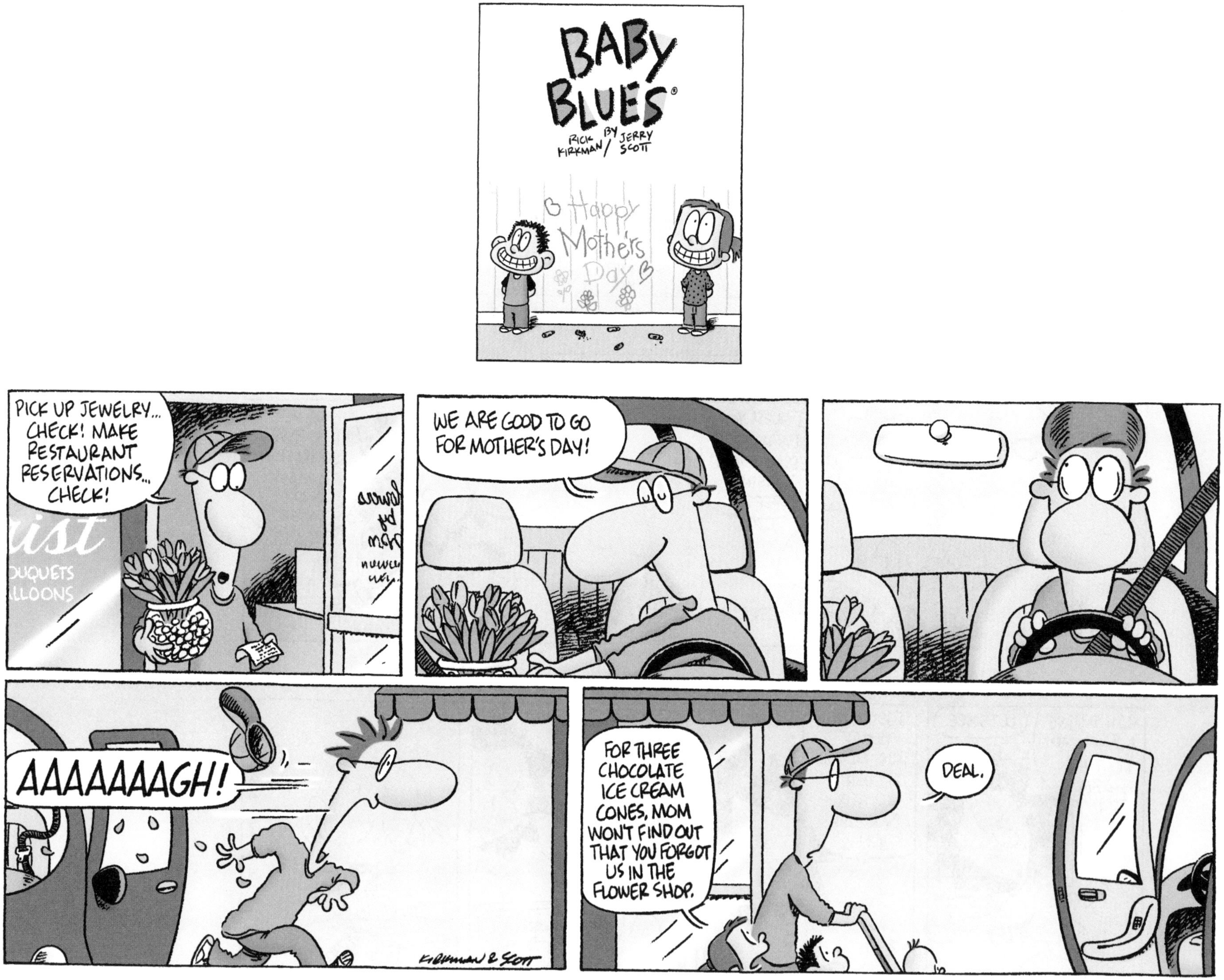
BABY BLUES®
BY RICK KIRKMAN / JERRY SCOTT
Happy Mother's Day
PICK UP JEWELRY... CHECK! MAKE RESTAURANT RESERVATIONS... CHECK!
WE ARE GOOD TO GO FOR MOTHER'S DAY!
AAAAAAAGH!
KIRKMAN & SCOTT
FOR THREE CHOCOLATE ICE CREAM CONES, MOM WON'T FIND OUT THAT YOU FORGOT US IN THE FLOWER SHOP.
DEAL.

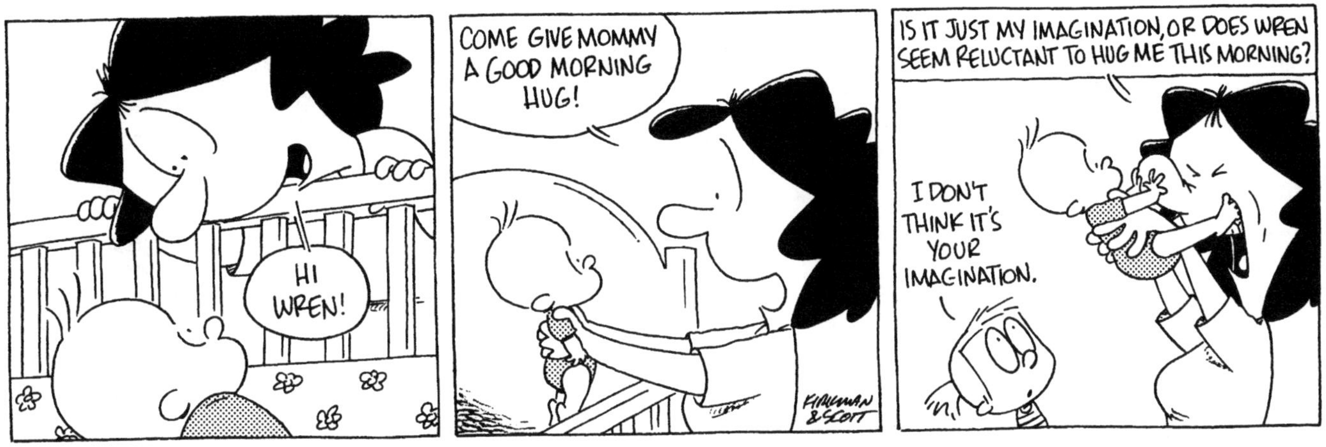
HI WREN!
COME GIVE MOMMY A GOOD MORNING HUG!
KIRKMAN & SCOTT
IS IT JUST MY IMAGINATION, OR DOES WREN SEEM RELUCTANT TO HUG ME THIS MORNING?
I DON'T THINK IT'S YOUR IMAGINATION.

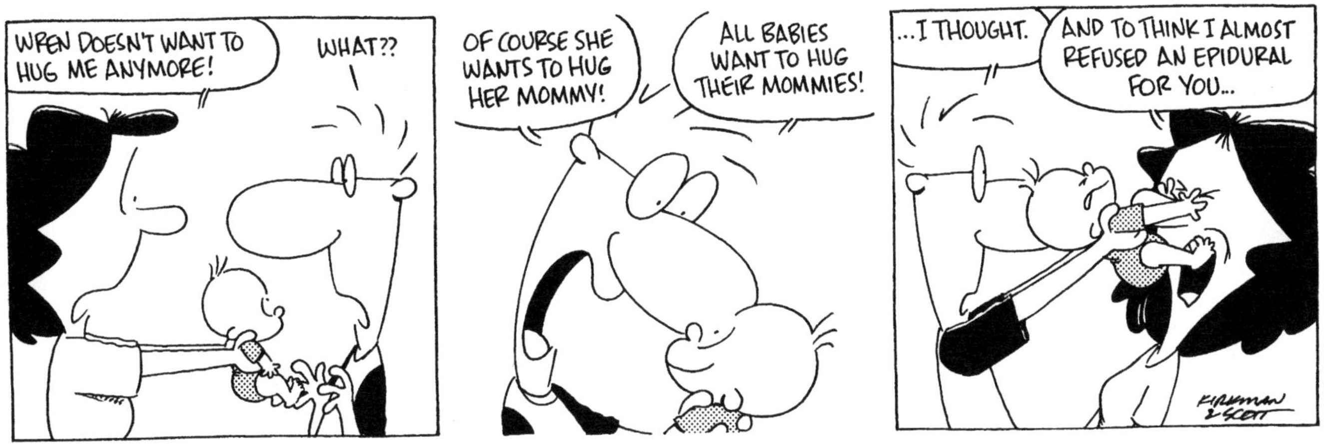
WREN DOESN'T WANT TO HUG ME ANYMORE!
WHAT??
OF COURSE SHE WANTS TO HUG HER MOMMY!
ALL BABIES WANT TO HUG THEIR MOMMIES!
...I THOUGHT.
AND TO THINK I ALMOST REFUSED AN EPIDURAL FOR YOU...
KIRKMAN & SCOTT

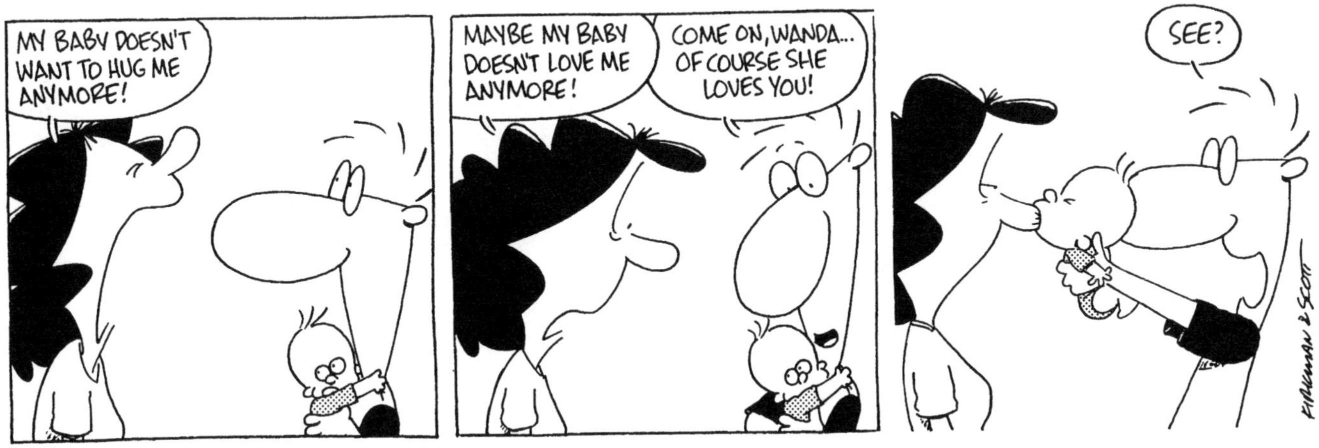
MY BABY DOESN'T WANT TO HUG ME ANYMORE!
MAYBE MY BABY DOESN'T LOVE ME ANYMORE!
COME ON, WANDA... OF COURSE SHE LOVES YOU!
SEE?
KIRKMAN & SCOTT

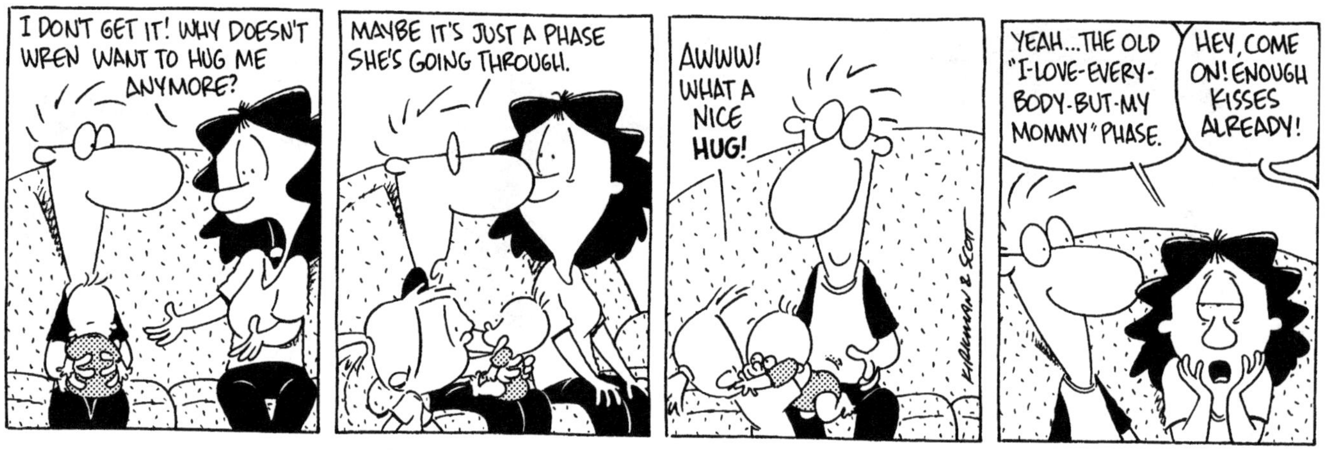
I DON'T GET IT! WHY DOESN'T WREN WANT TO HUG ME ANYMORE?
MAYBE IT'S JUST A PHASE SHE'S GOING THROUGH.
AWWW! WHAT A NICE HUG!
YEAH...THE OLD "I-LOVE-EVERY-BODY-BUT-MY MOMMY" PHASE.
HEY, COME ON! ENOUGH KISSES ALREADY!
KIRKMAN & SCOTT

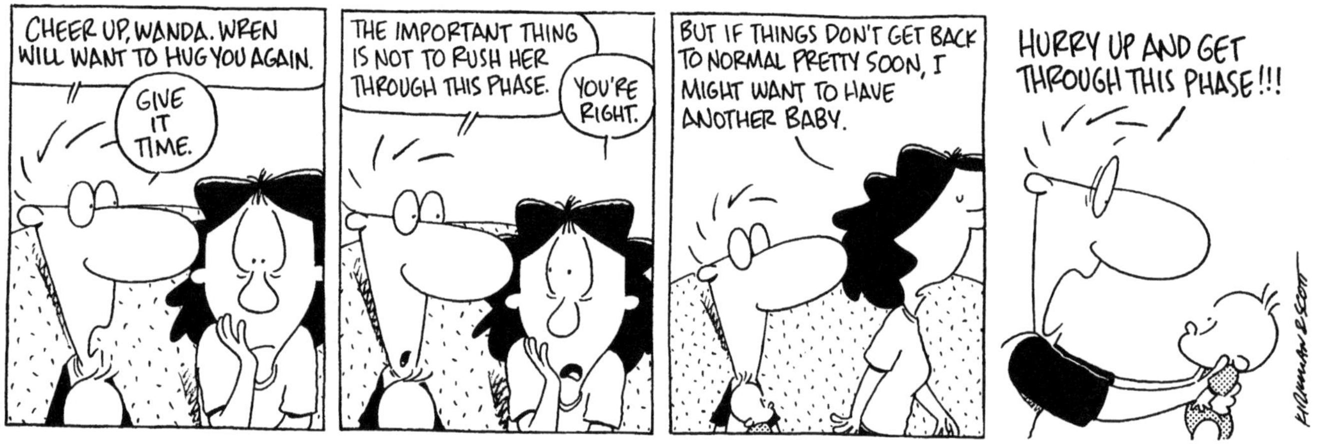
CHEER UP, WANDA. WREN WILL WANT TO HUG YOU AGAIN.
GIVE IT TIME.
THE IMPORTANT THING IS NOT TO RUSH HER THROUGH THIS PHASE.
YOU'RE RIGHT.
BUT IF THINGS DON'T GET BACK TO NORMAL PRETTY SOON, I MIGHT WANT TO HAVE ANOTHER BABY.
HURRY UP AND GET THROUGH THIS PHASE!!!
KIRKMAN & SCOTT

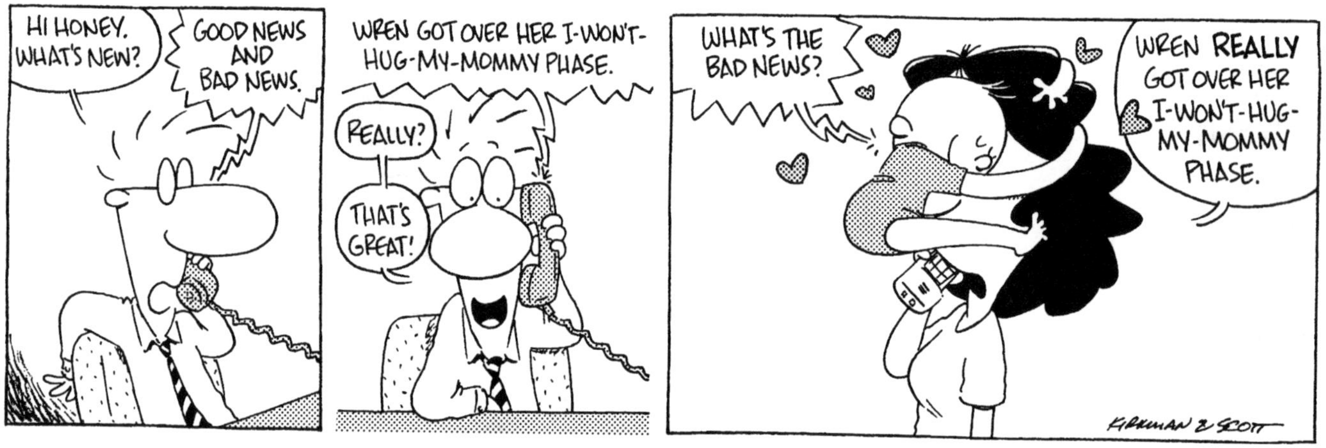
HI HONEY. WHAT'S NEW?
GOOD NEWS AND BAD NEWS.
WREN GOT OVER HER I-WON'T-HUG-MY-MOMMY PHASE.
REALLY?
THAT'S GREAT!
WHAT'S THE BAD NEWS?
WREN REALLY GOT OVER HER I-WON'T-HUG-MY-MOMMY PHASE.
KIRKMAN & SCOTT

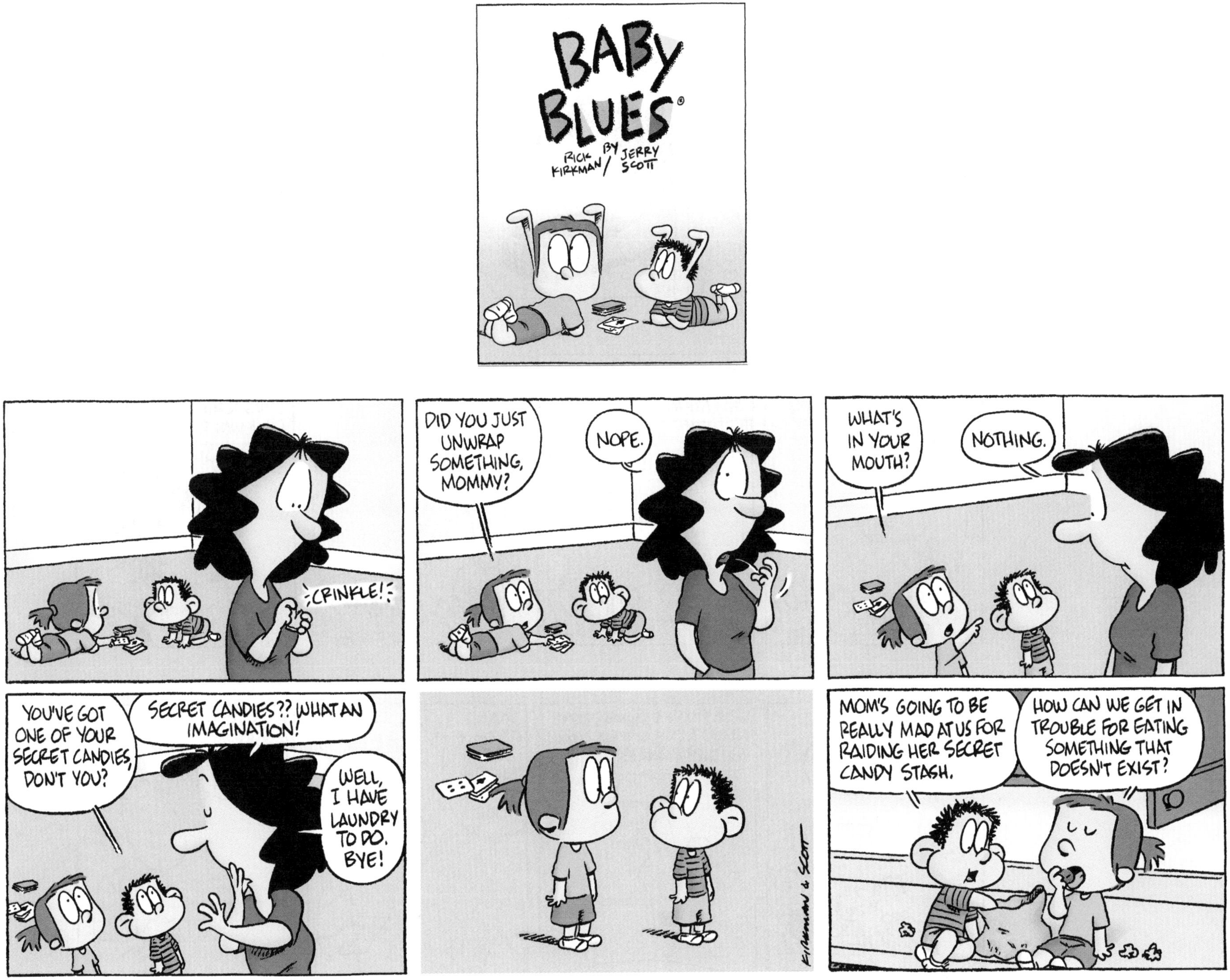
BABY BLUES®
BY RICK KIRKMAN / JERRY SCOTT
CRINKLE!
DID YOU JUST UNWRAP SOMETHING, MOMMY?
NOPE.
WHAT'S IN YOUR MOUTH?
NOTHING.
YOU'VE GOT ONE OF YOUR SECRET CANDIES, DON'T YOU?
SECRET CANDIES?? WHAT AN IMAGINATION!
WELL, I HAVE LAUNDRY TO DO. BYE!
KIRKMAN & SCOTT
MOM'S GOING TO BE REALLY MAD AT US FOR RAIDING HER SECRET CANDY STASH.
HOW CAN WE GET IN TROUBLE FOR EATING SOMETHING THAT DOESN'T EXIST?

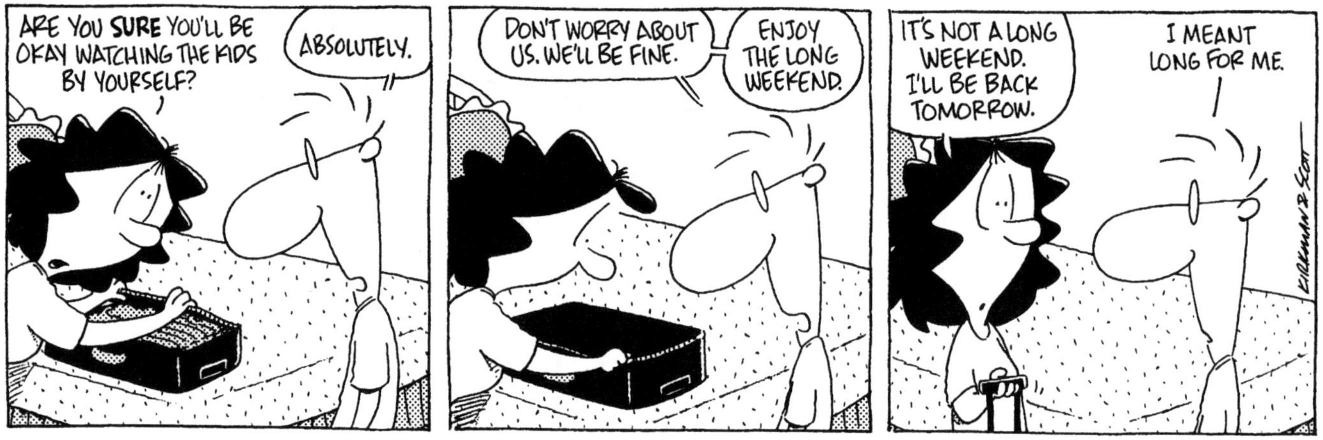
ARE YOU **SURE** YOU'LL BE OKAY WATCHING THE KIDS BY YOURSELF?
ABSOLUTELY.
DON'T WORRY ABOUT US. WE'LL BE FINE.
ENJOY THE LONG WEEKEND.
IT'S NOT A LONG WEEKEND. I'LL BE BACK TOMORROW.
I MEANT LONG FOR ME.
KIRKMAN & SCOTT

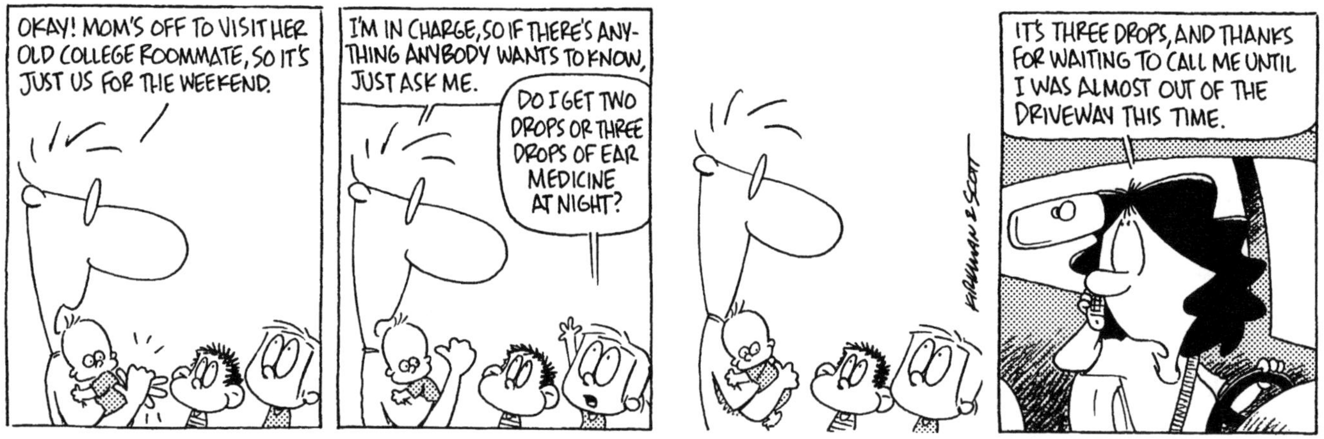
OKAY! MOM'S OFF TO VISIT HER OLD COLLEGE ROOMMATE, SO IT'S JUST US FOR THE WEEKEND.
I'M IN CHARGE, SO IF THERE'S ANYTHING ANYBODY WANTS TO KNOW, JUST ASK ME.
DO I GET TWO DROPS OR THREE DROPS OF EAR MEDICINE AT NIGHT?
KIRKMAN & SCOTT
IT'S THREE DROPS, AND THANKS FOR WAITING TO CALL ME UNTIL I WAS ALMOST OUT OF THE DRIVEWAY THIS TIME.

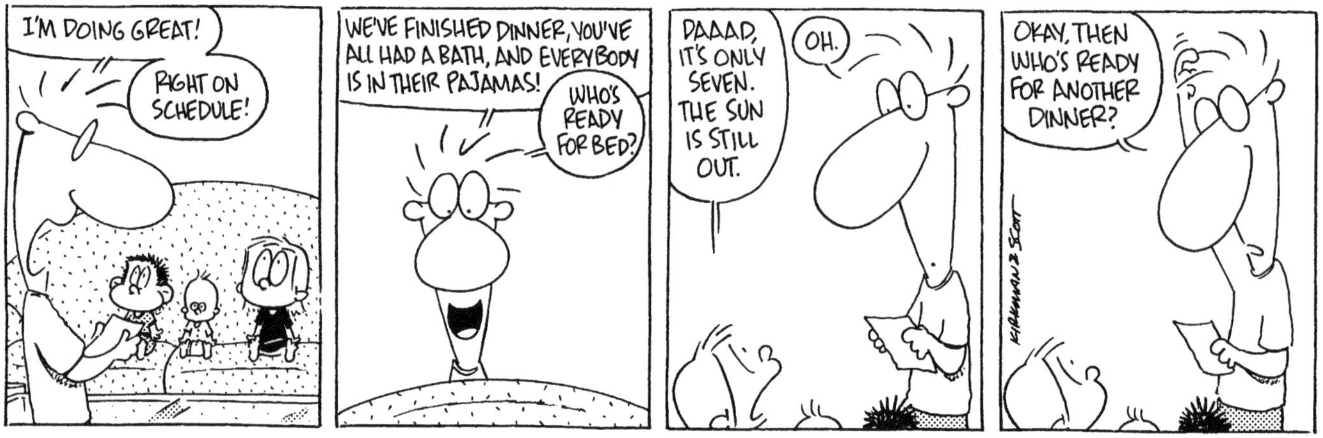
I'M DOING GREAT!
RIGHT ON SCHEDULE!
WE'VE FINISHED DINNER, YOU'VE ALL HAD A BATH, AND EVERYBODY IS IN THEIR PAJAMAS!
WHO'S READY FOR BED?
DAAAD, IT'S ONLY SEVEN. THE SUN IS STILL OUT.
OH.
KIRKMAN & SCOTT
OKAY, THEN WHO'S READY FOR ANOTHER DINNER?

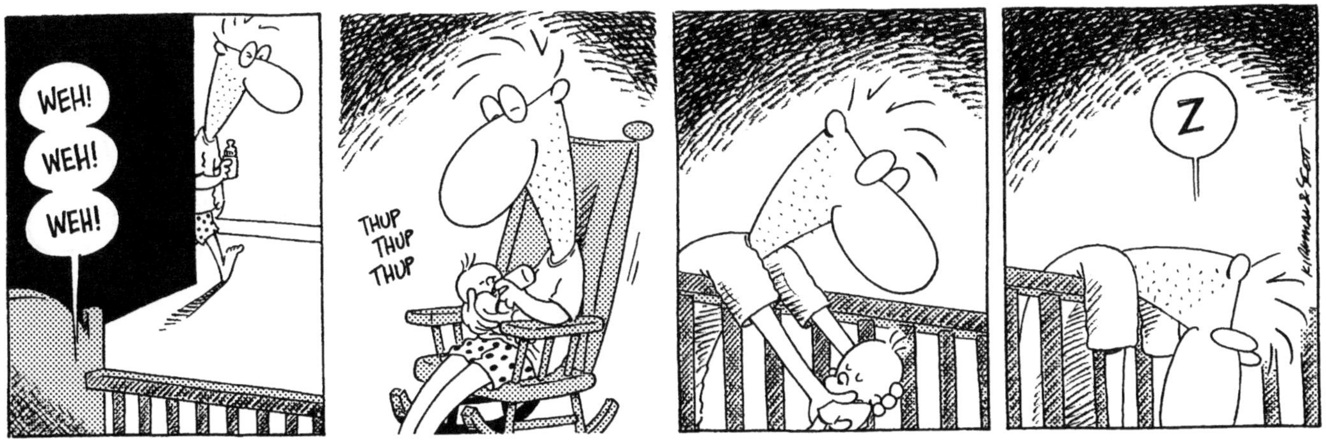
WEH!
WEH!
WEH!
THUP THUP THUP
Z
KIRKMAN & SCOTT

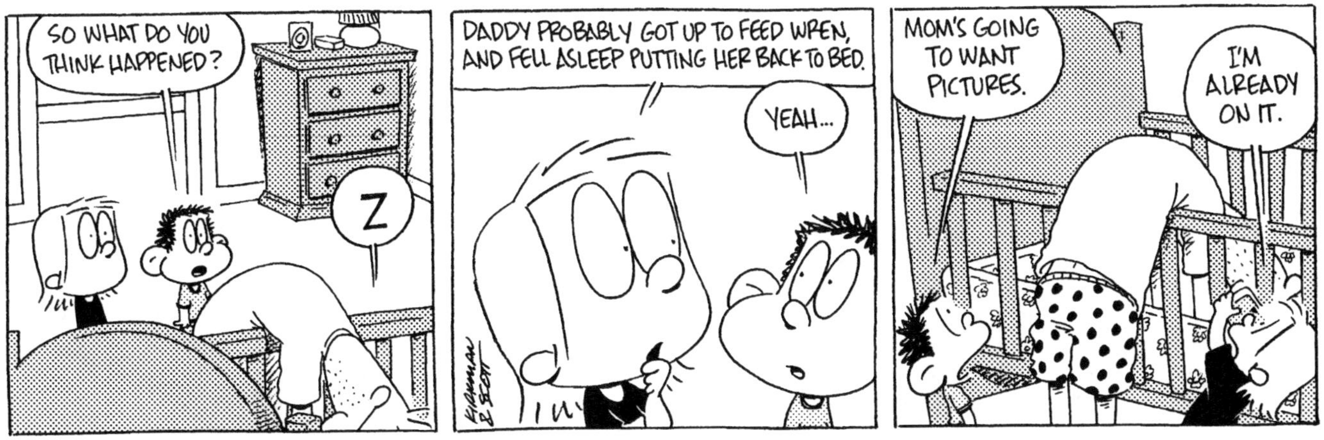
SO WHAT DO YOU THINK HAPPENED?
Z
DADDY PROBABLY GOT UP TO FEED WREN, AND FELL ASLEEP PUTTING HER BACK TO BED.
YEAH...
KIRKMAN & SCOTT
MOM'S GOING TO WANT PICTURES.
I'M ALREADY ON IT.

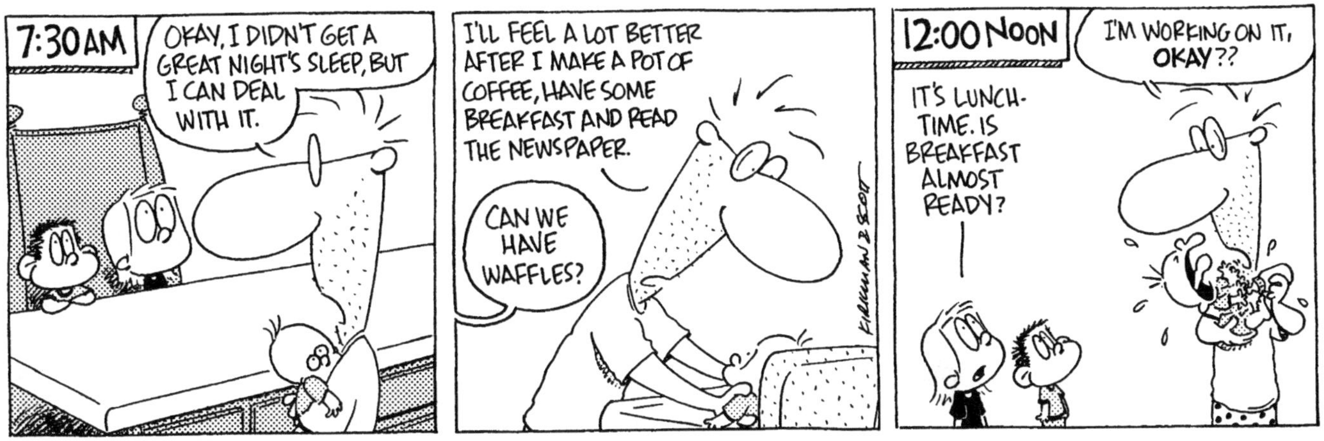
7:30 AM
OKAY, I DIDN'T GET A GREAT NIGHT'S SLEEP, BUT I CAN DEAL WITH IT.
I'LL FEEL A LOT BETTER AFTER I MAKE A POT OF COFFEE, HAVE SOME BREAKFAST AND READ THE NEWSPAPER.
CAN WE HAVE WAFFLES?
KIRKMAN & SCOTT
12:00 NOON
IT'S LUNCH-TIME. IS BREAKFAST ALMOST READY?
I'M WORKING ON IT, OKAY??

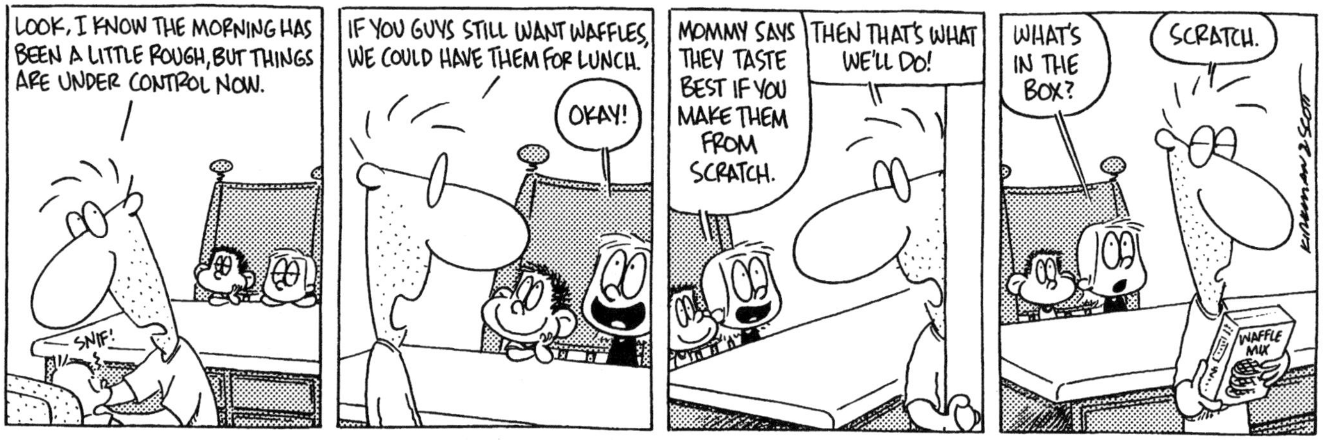
LOOK, I KNOW THE MORNING HAS BEEN A LITTLE ROUGH, BUT THINGS ARE UNDER CONTROL NOW.
SNIF!
IF YOU GUYS STILL WANT WAFFLES, WE COULD HAVE THEM FOR LUNCH.
OKAY!
MOMMY SAYS THEY TASTE BEST IF YOU MAKE THEM FROM SCRATCH.
THEN THAT'S WHAT WE'LL DO!
WHAT'S IN THE BOX?
SCRATCH.
WAFFLE MIX

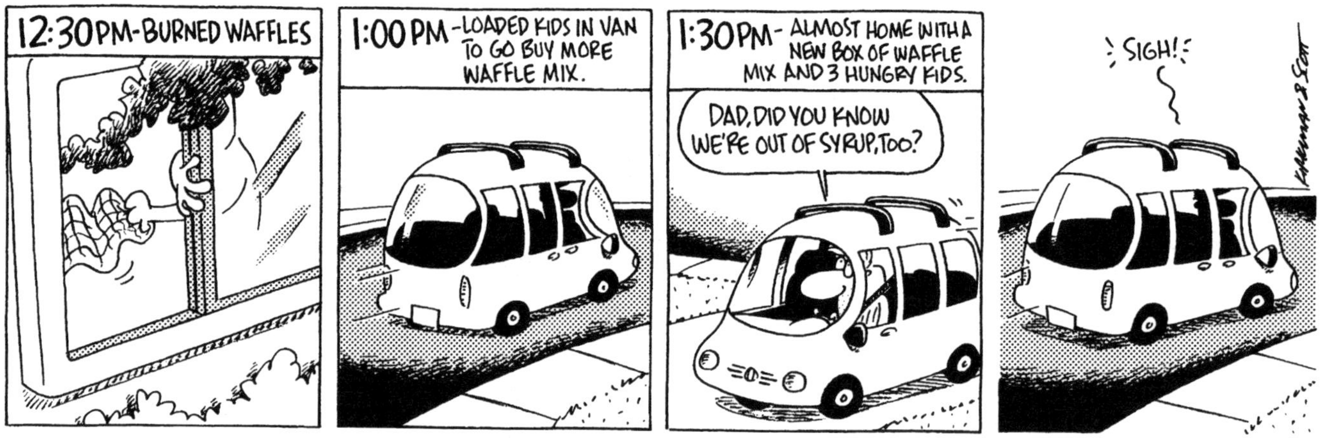
12:30 PM - BURNED WAFFLES
1:00 PM - LOADED KIDS IN VAN TO GO BUY MORE WAFFLE MIX.
1:30 PM - ALMOST HOME WITH A NEW BOX OF WAFFLE MIX AND 3 HUNGRY KIDS.
DAD, DID YOU KNOW WE'RE OUT OF SYRUP, TOO?
SIGH!

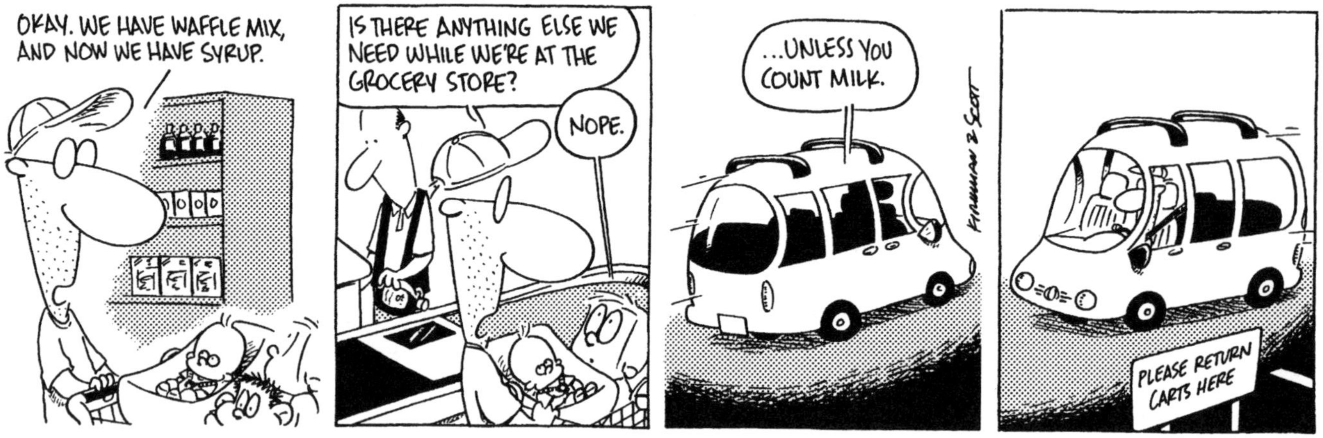
OKAY. WE HAVE WAFFLE MIX, AND NOW WE HAVE SYRUP.
IS THERE ANYTHING ELSE WE NEED WHILE WE'RE AT THE GROCERY STORE?
NOPE.
...UNLESS YOU COUNT MILK.
PLEASE RETURN CARTS HERE

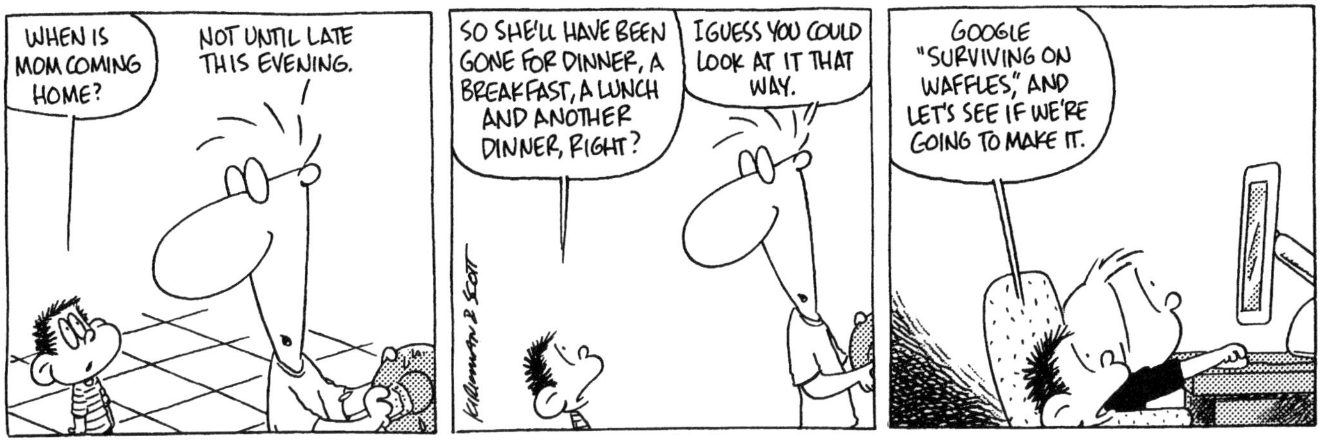
WHEN IS MOM COMING HOME?
NOT UNTIL LATE THIS EVENING.
SO SHE'LL HAVE BEEN GONE FOR DINNER, A BREAKFAST, A LUNCH AND ANOTHER DINNER, RIGHT?
I GUESS YOU COULD LOOK AT IT THAT WAY.
GOOGLE "SURVIVING ON WAFFLES," AND LET'S SEE IF WE'RE GOING TO MAKE IT.

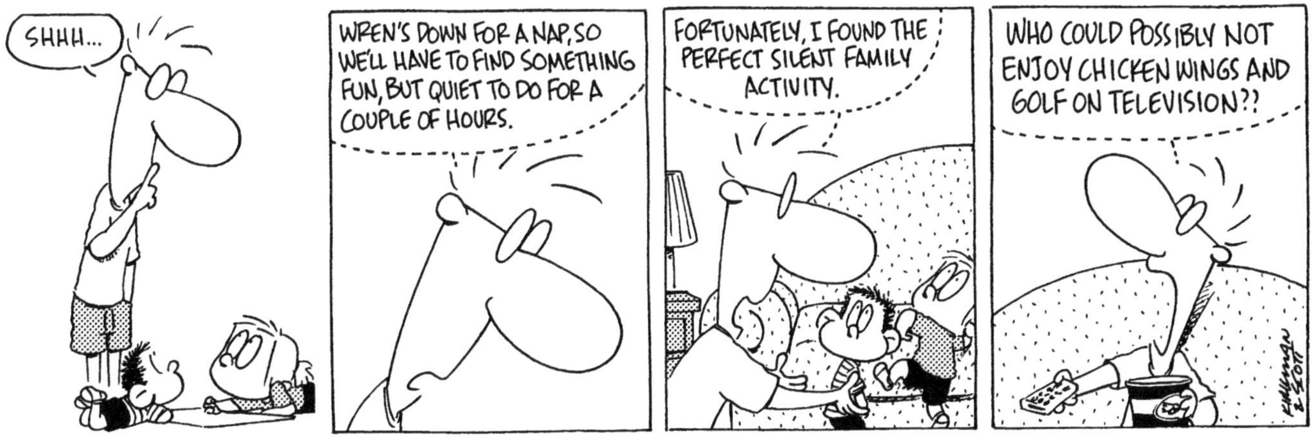
SHHH...
WREN'S DOWN FOR A NAP, SO WE'LL HAVE TO FIND SOMETHING FUN, BUT QUIET TO DO FOR A COUPLE OF HOURS.
FORTUNATELY, I FOUND THE PERFECT SILENT FAMILY ACTIVITY.
WHO COULD POSSIBLY NOT ENJOY CHICKEN WINGS AND GOLF ON TELEVISION??

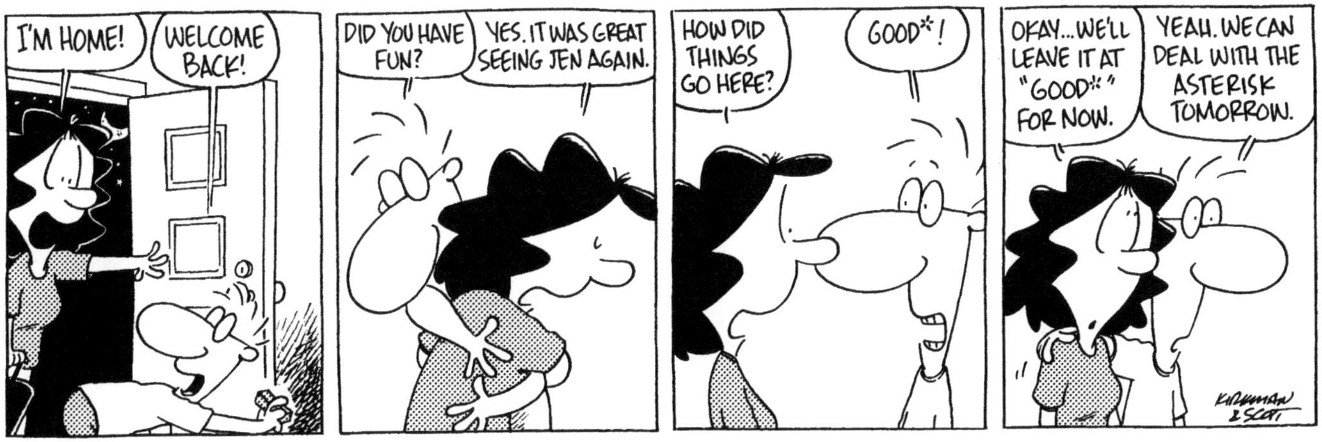
I'M HOME!
WELCOME BACK!
DID YOU HAVE FUN?
YES. IT WAS GREAT SEEING JEN AGAIN.
HOW DID THINGS GO HERE?
GOOD*!
OKAY... WE'LL LEAVE IT AT "GOOD*" FOR NOW.
YEAH. WE CAN DEAL WITH THE ASTERISK TOMORROW.

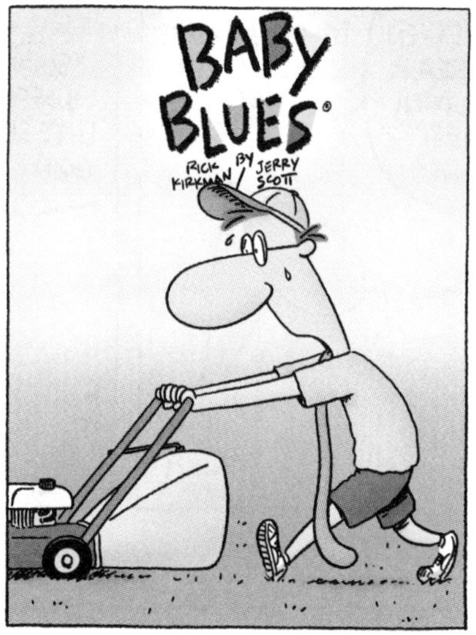
BABY BLUES®
RICK KIRKMAN BY JERRY SCOTT

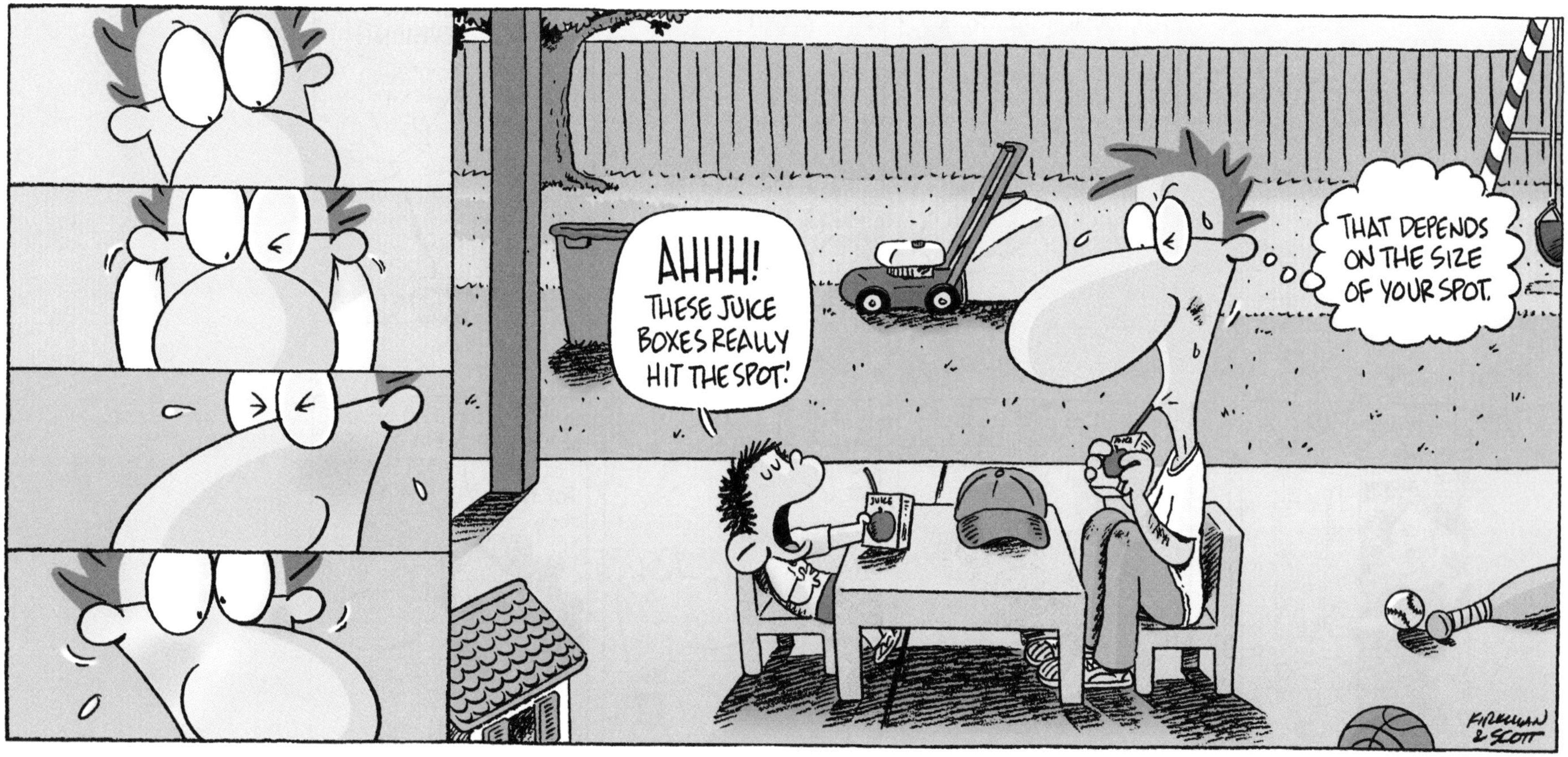
AHHH! THESE JUICE BOXES REALLY HIT THE SPOT!
THAT DEPENDS ON THE SIZE OF YOUR SPOT.
JUICE
KIRKMAN & SCOTT

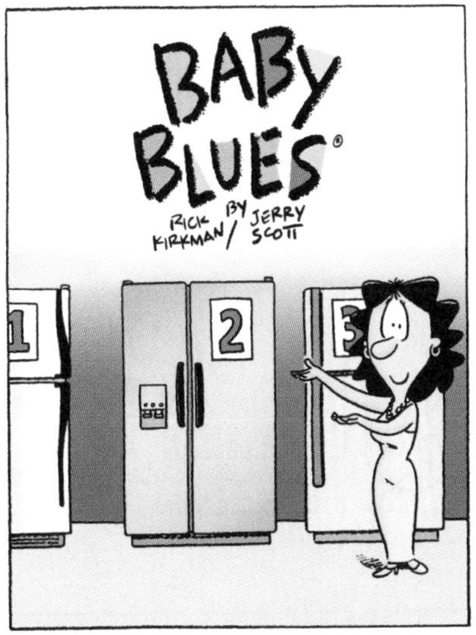

BABY BLUES®
BY RICK KIRKMAN/ JERRY SCOTT
1
2
3

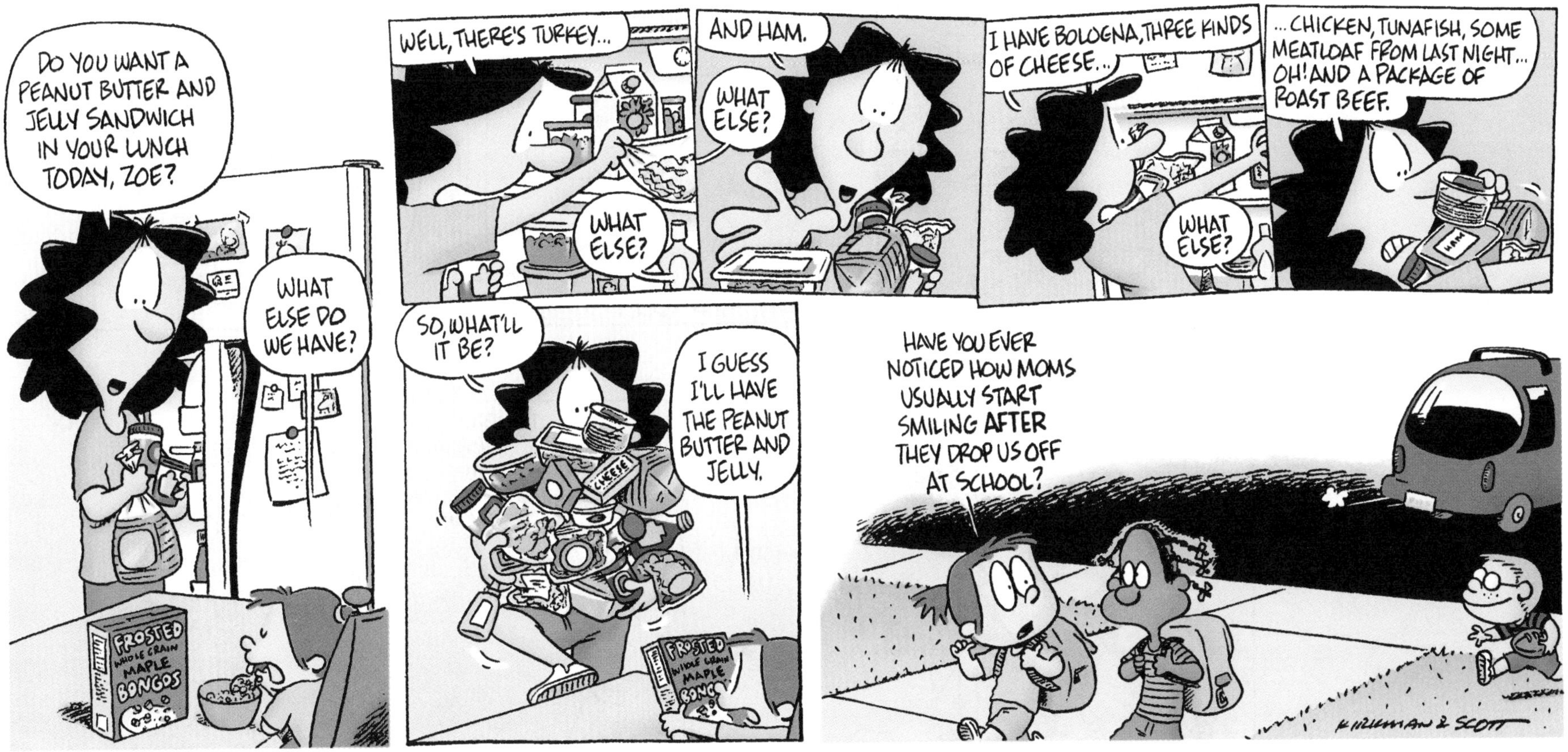

DO YOU WANT A PEANUT BUTTER AND JELLY SANDWICH IN YOUR LUNCH TODAY, ZOE?
WHAT ELSE DO WE HAVE?
FROSTED WHOLE GRAIN MAPLE BONGOS
WELL, THERE'S TURKEY...
WHAT ELSE?
AND HAM.
WHAT ELSE?
I HAVE BOLOGNA, THREE KINDS OF CHEESE...
WHAT ELSE?
...CHICKEN, TUNAFISH, SOME MEATLOAF FROM LAST NIGHT... OH! AND A PACKAGE OF ROAST BEEF.
HAM
SO, WHAT'LL IT BE?
I GUESS I'LL HAVE THE PEANUT BUTTER AND JELLY.
CHEESE
FROSTED WHOLE GRAIN MAPLE BONGOS
HAVE YOU EVER NOTICED HOW MOMS USUALLY START SMILING AFTER THEY DROP US OFF AT SCHOOL?
KIRKMAN & SCOTT

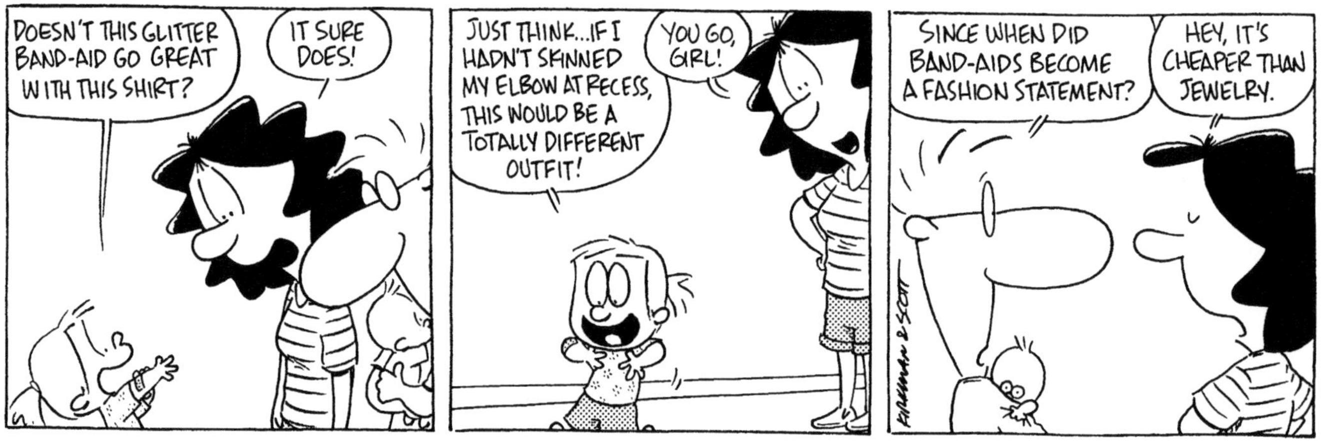
DOESN'T THIS GLITTER BAND-AID GO GREAT WITH THIS SHIRT?
IT SURE DOES!
JUST THINK...IF I HADN'T SKINNED MY ELBOW AT RECESS, THIS WOULD BE A TOTALLY DIFFERENT OUTFIT!
YOU GO, GIRL!
SINCE WHEN DID BAND-AIDS BECOME A FASHION STATEMENT?
HEY, IT'S CHEAPER THAN JEWELRY.
KIRKMAN & SCOTT

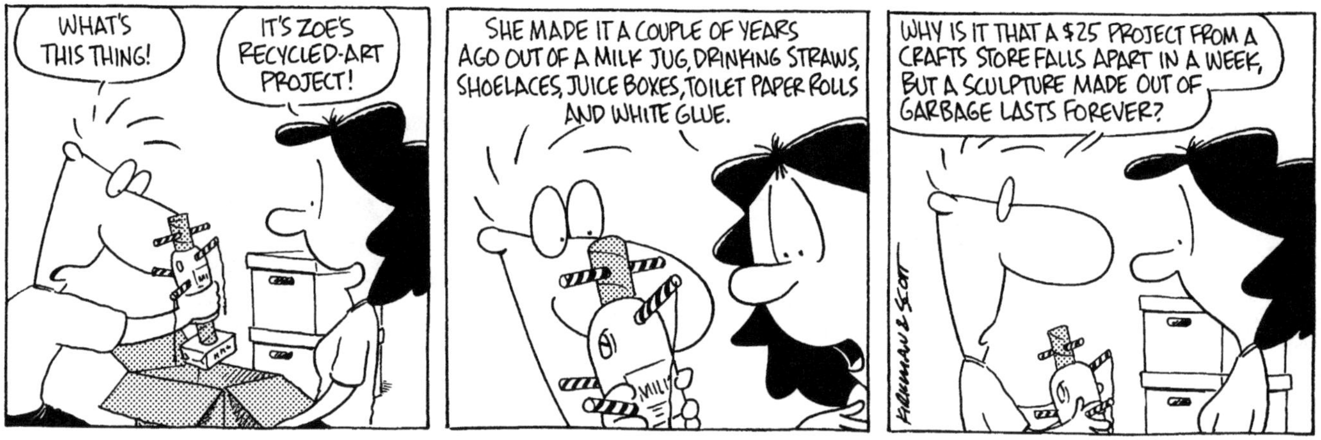
WHAT'S THIS THING!
IT'S ZOE'S RECYCLED-ART PROJECT!
SHE MADE IT A COUPLE OF YEARS AGO OUT OF A MILK JUG, DRINKING STRAWS, SHOELACES, JUICE BOXES, TOILET PAPER ROLLS AND WHITE GLUE.
WHY IS IT THAT A $25 PROJECT FROM A CRAFTS STORE FALLS APART IN A WEEK, BUT A SCULPTURE MADE OUT OF GARBAGE LASTS FOREVER?
KIRKMAN & SCOTT

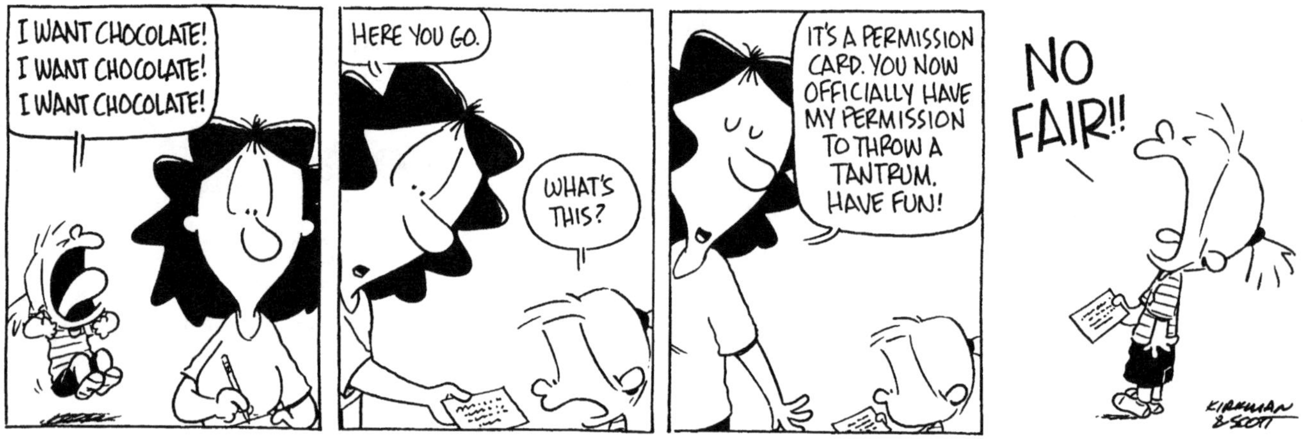
I WANT CHOCOLATE! I WANT CHOCOLATE! I WANT CHOCOLATE!
HERE YOU GO.
WHAT'S THIS?
IT'S A PERMISSION CARD. YOU NOW OFFICIALLY HAVE MY PERMISSION TO THROW A TANTRUM. HAVE FUN!
NO FAIR!!
KIRKMAN & SCOTT

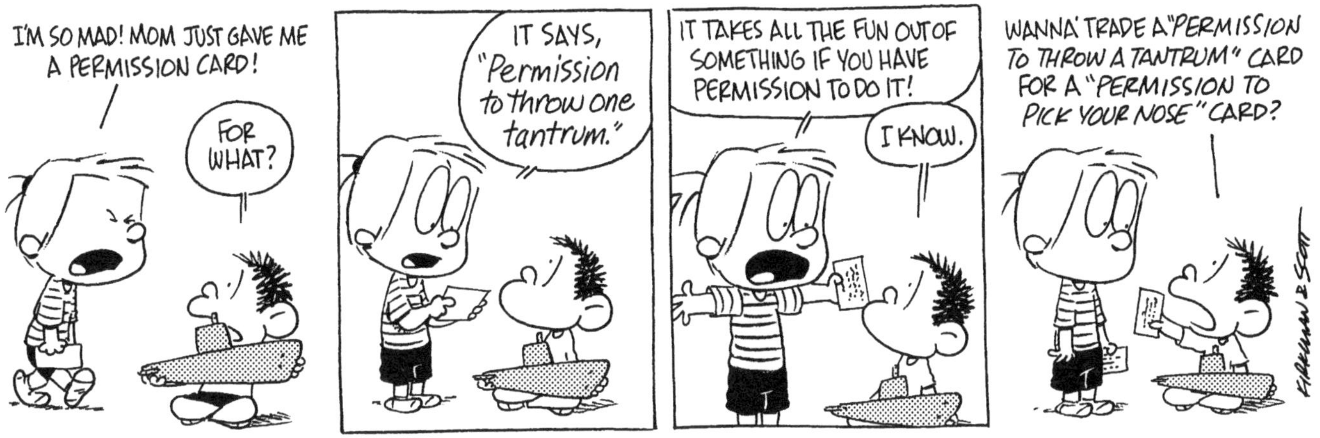
I'M SO MAD! MOM JUST GAVE ME A PERMISSION CARD!
FOR WHAT?
IT SAYS, "Permission to throw one tantrum."
IT TAKES ALL THE FUN OUT OF SOMETHING IF YOU HAVE PERMISSION TO DO IT!
I KNOW.
WANNA' TRADE A "PERMISSION TO THROW A TANTRUM" CARD FOR A "PERMISSION TO PICK YOUR NOSE" CARD?

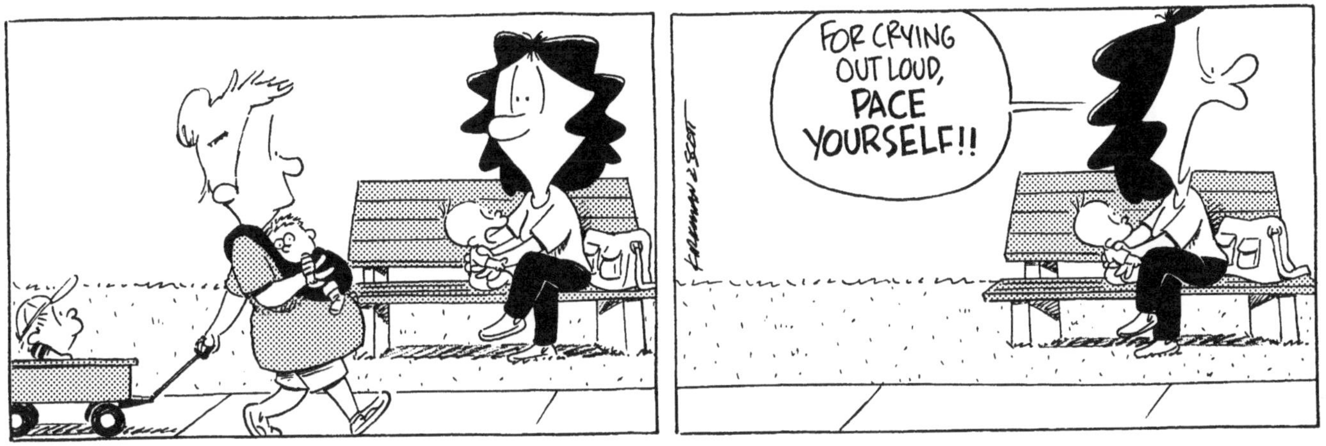
FOR CRYING OUT LOUD, PACE YOURSELF!!

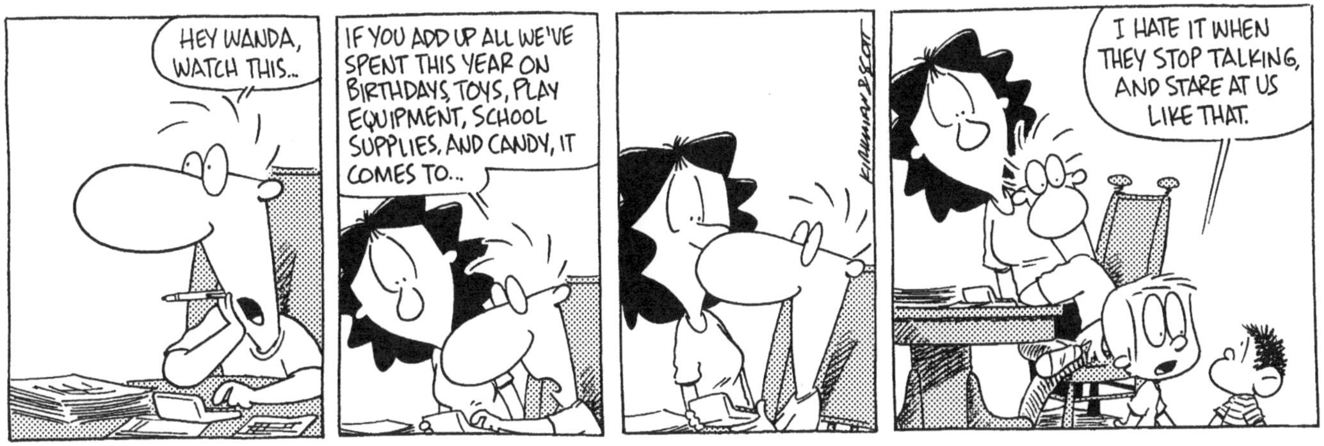
HEY WANDA, WATCH THIS...
IF YOU ADD UP ALL WE'VE SPENT THIS YEAR ON BIRTHDAYS, TOYS, PLAY EQUIPMENT, SCHOOL SUPPLIES, AND CANDY, IT COMES TO...
I HATE IT WHEN THEY STOP TALKING, AND STARE AT US LIKE THAT.

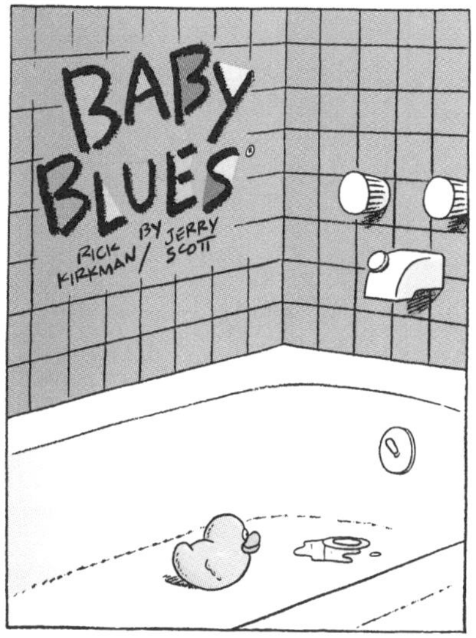
BABY BLUES®
BY RICK KIRKMAN / JERRY SCOTT

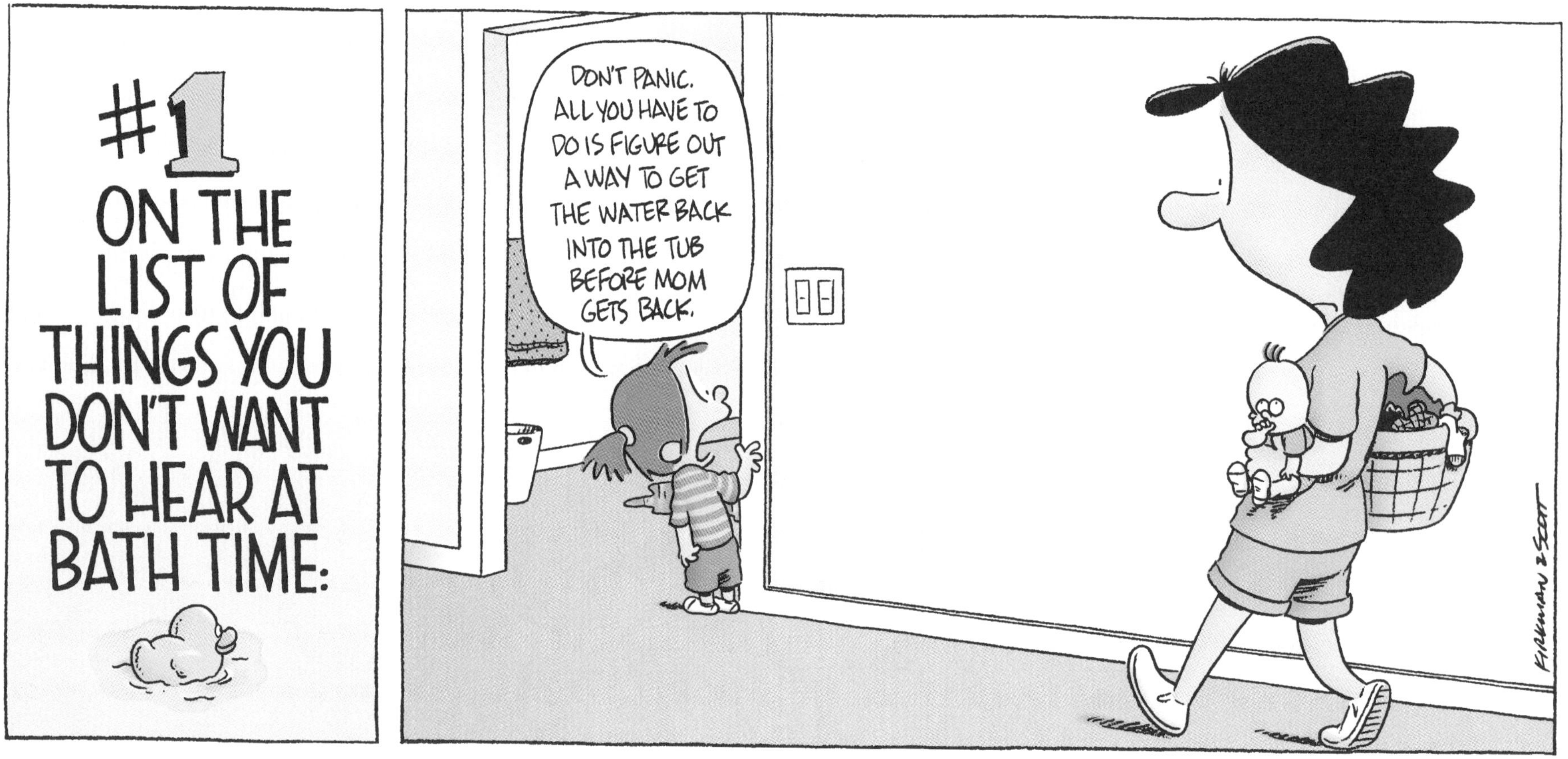
#1 ON THE LIST OF THINGS YOU DON'T WANT TO HEAR AT BATH TIME:
DON'T PANIC. ALL YOU HAVE TO DO IS FIGURE OUT A WAY TO GET THE WATER BACK INTO THE TUB BEFORE MOM GETS BACK.
KIRKMAN & SCOTT

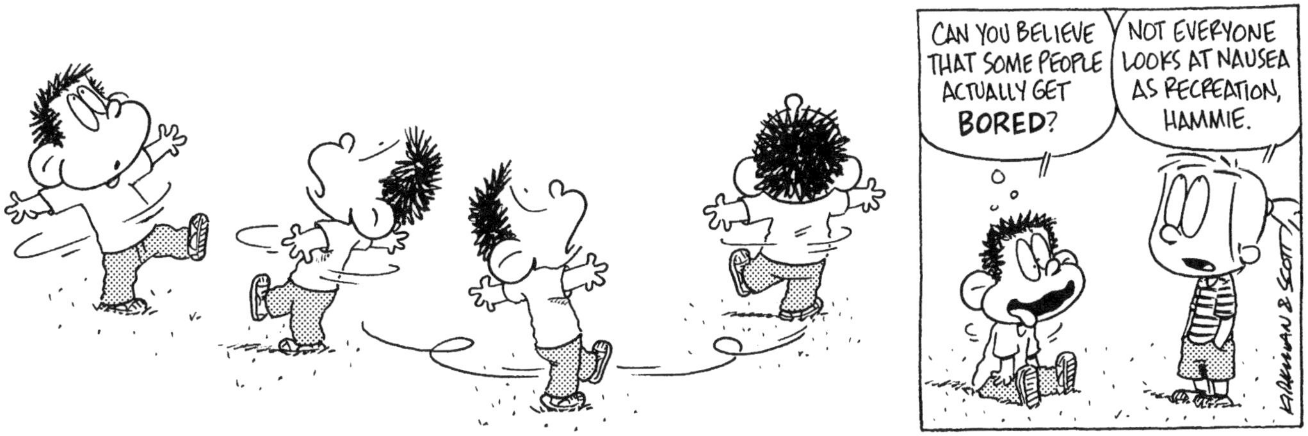

CAN YOU BELIEVE THAT SOME PEOPLE ACTUALLY GET BORED?
NOT EVERYONE LOOKS AT NAUSEA AS RECREATION, HAMMIE.
KIRKMAN & SCOTT

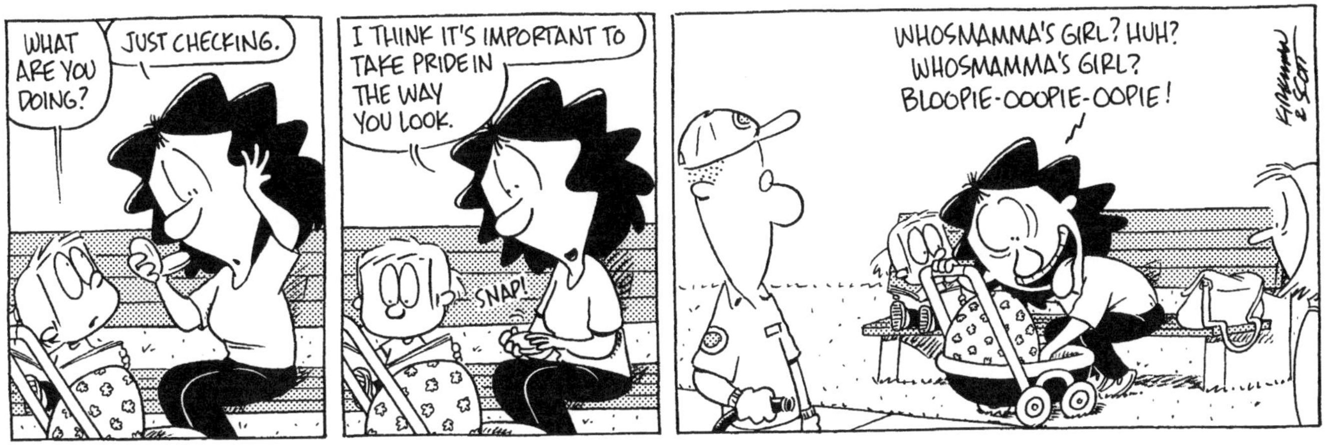

WHAT ARE YOU DOING?
JUST CHECKING.
I THINK IT'S IMPORTANT TO TAKE PRIDE IN THE WAY YOU LOOK.
SNAP!
WHOSMAMMA'S GIRL? HUH? WHOSMAMMA'S GIRL? BLOOPIE-OOOPIE-OOPIE!
KIRKMAN & SCOTT

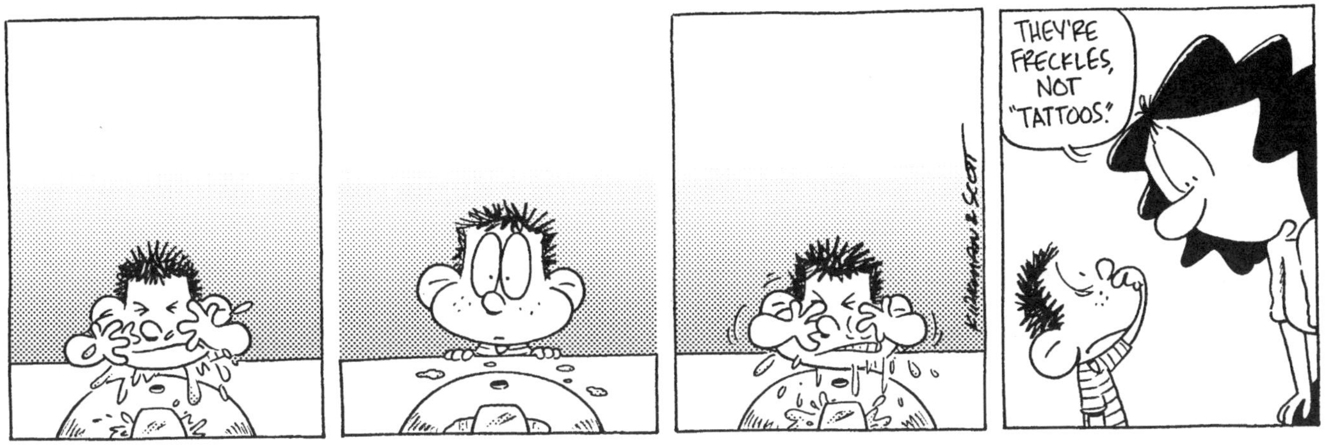

KIRKMAN & SCOTT
THEY'RE FRECKLES, NOT "TATTOOS."

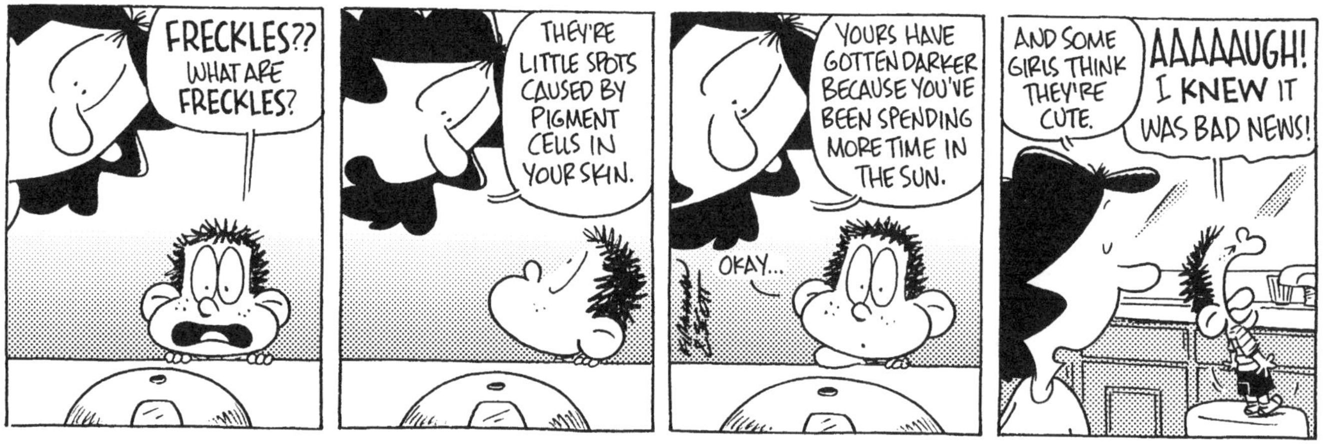
FRECKLES?? WHAT ARE FRECKLES?
THEY'RE LITTLE SPOTS CAUSED BY PIGMENT CELLS IN YOUR SKIN.
YOURS HAVE GOTTEN DARKER BECAUSE YOU'VE BEEN SPENDING MORE TIME IN THE SUN.
OKAY...
AND SOME GIRLS THINK THEY'RE CUTE.
AAAAAUGH! I KNEW IT WAS BAD NEWS!

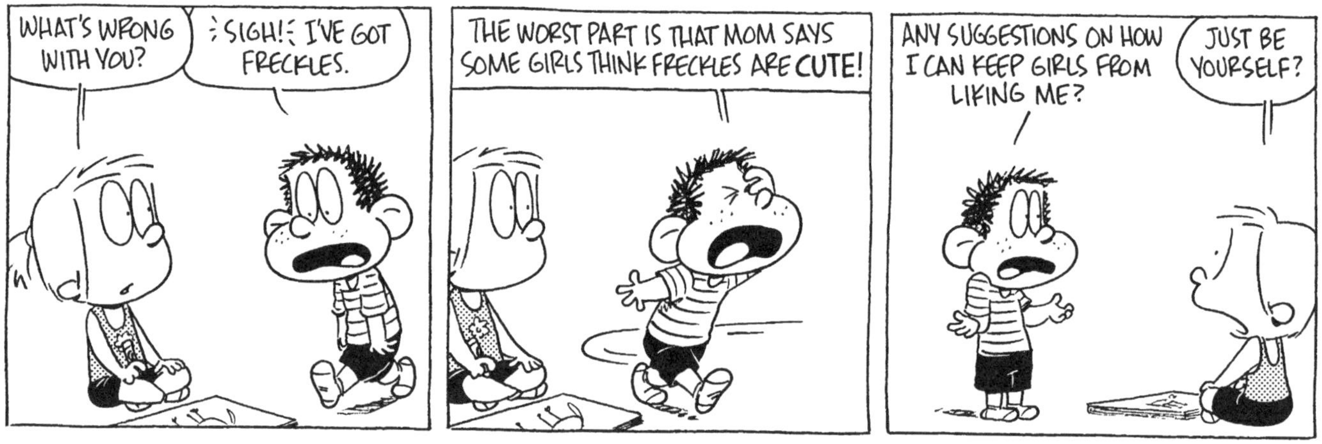
WHAT'S WRONG WITH YOU?
SIGH! I'VE GOT FRECKLES.
THE WORST PART IS THAT MOM SAYS SOME GIRLS THINK FRECKLES ARE CUTE!
ANY SUGGESTIONS ON HOW I CAN KEEP GIRLS FROM LIKING ME?
JUST BE YOURSELF?

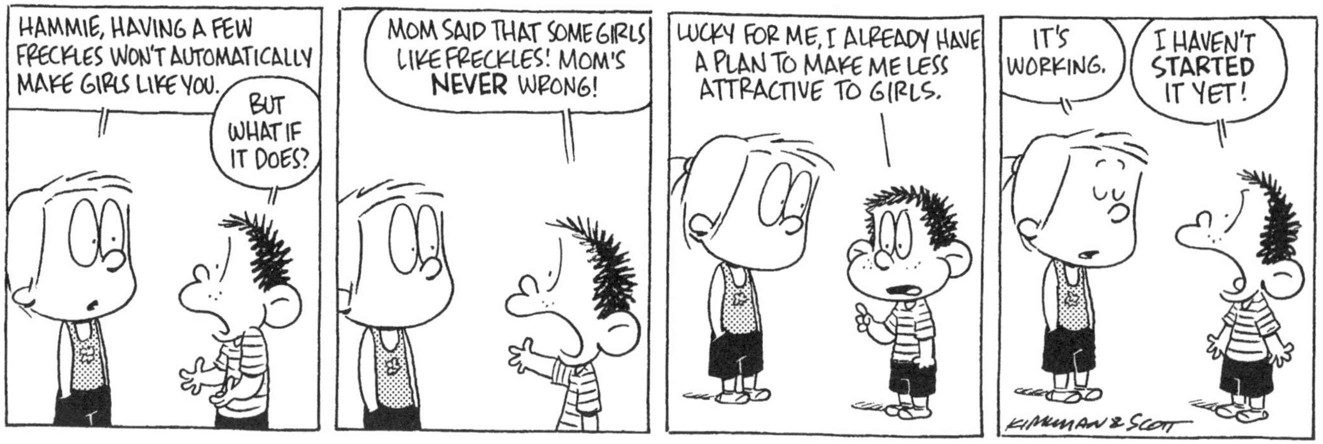
HAMMIE, HAVING A FEW FRECKLES WON'T AUTOMATICALLY MAKE GIRLS LIKE YOU.
BUT WHAT IF IT DOES?
MOM SAID THAT SOME GIRLS LIKE FRECKLES! MOM'S NEVER WRONG!
LUCKY FOR ME, I ALREADY HAVE A PLAN TO MAKE ME LESS ATTRACTIVE TO GIRLS.
IT'S WORKING.
I HAVEN'T STARTED IT YET!
KIRKMAN & SCOTT

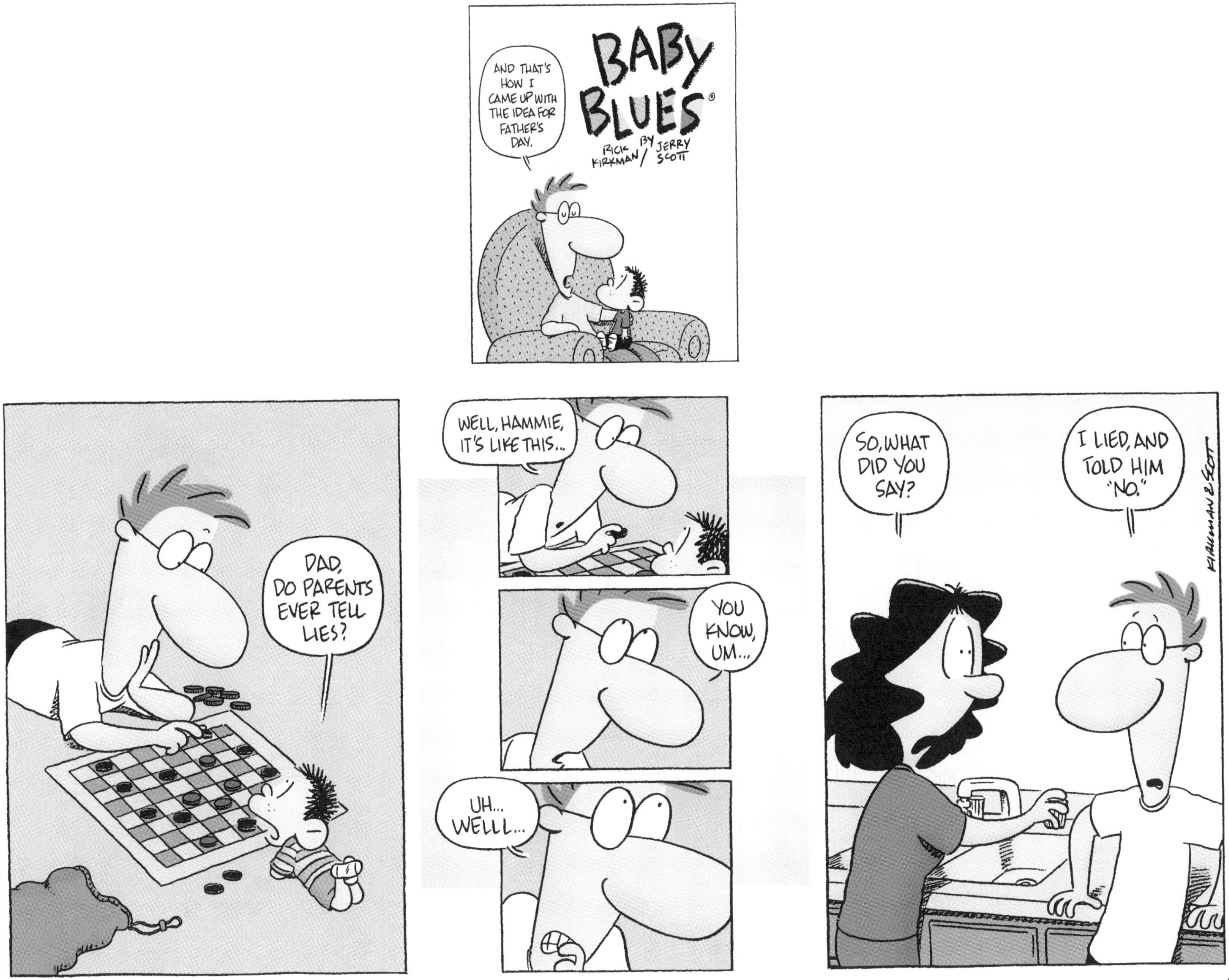
AND THAT'S HOW I CAME UP WITH THE IDEA FOR FATHER'S DAY.
BABY BLUES®
BY RICK KIRKMAN / JERRY SCOTT
DAD, DO PARENTS EVER TELL LIES?
WELL, HAMMIE, IT'S LIKE THIS...
YOU KNOW, UM...
UH... WELLL...
SO, WHAT DID YOU SAY?
I LIED, AND TOLD HIM "NO."
KIRKMAN & SCOTT

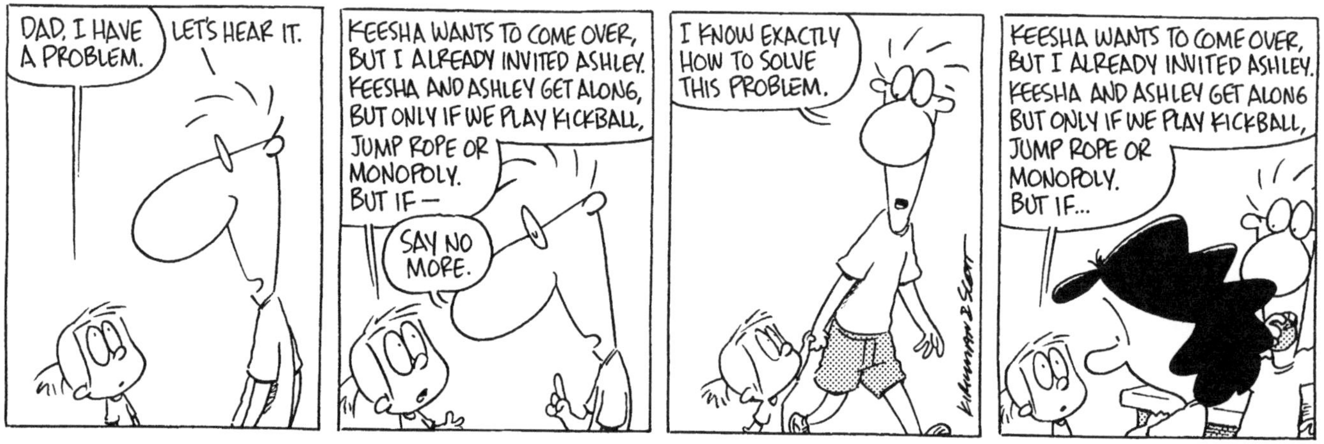
DAD, I HAVE A PROBLEM.
LET'S HEAR IT.
KEESHA WANTS TO COME OVER, BUT I ALREADY INVITED ASHLEY. KEESHA AND ASHLEY GET ALONG, BUT ONLY IF WE PLAY KICKBALL, JUMP ROPE OR MONOPOLY. BUT IF—
SAY NO MORE.
I KNOW EXACTLY HOW TO SOLVE THIS PROBLEM.
KEESHA WANTS TO COME OVER, BUT I ALREADY INVITED ASHLEY. KEESHA AND ASHLEY GET ALONG BUT ONLY IF WE PLAY KICKBALL, JUMP ROPE OR MONOPOLY. BUT IF...

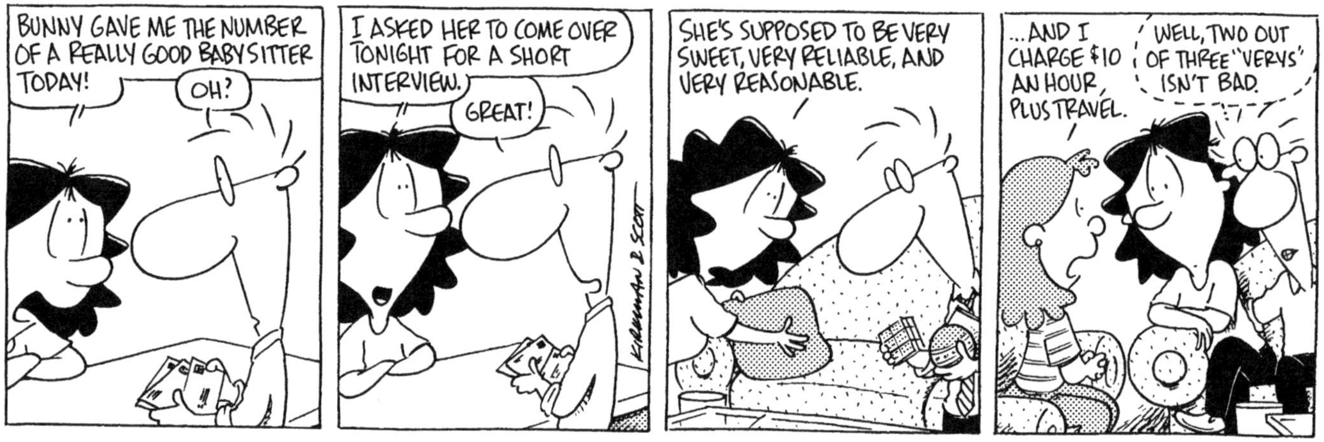
BUNNY GAVE ME THE NUMBER OF A REALLY GOOD BABYSITTER TODAY!
OH?
I ASKED HER TO COME OVER TONIGHT FOR A SHORT INTERVIEW.
GREAT!
SHE'S SUPPOSED TO BE VERY SWEET, VERY RELIABLE, AND VERY REASONABLE.
...AND I CHARGE $10 AN HOUR, PLUS TRAVEL.
WELL, TWO OUT OF THREE "VERYS" ISN'T BAD.

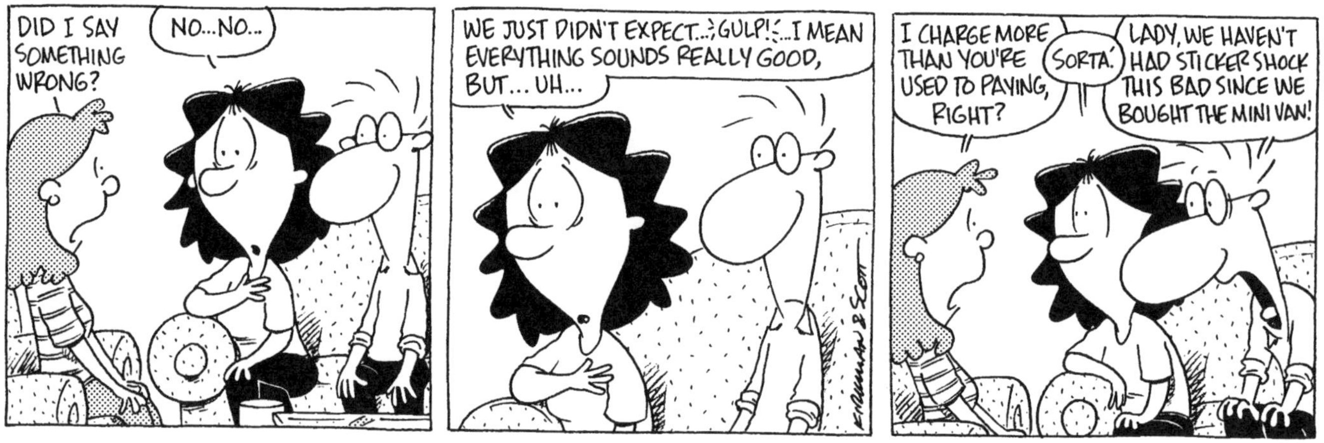
DID I SAY SOMETHING WRONG?
NO...NO...
WE JUST DIDN'T EXPECT...GULP!...I MEAN EVERYTHING SOUNDS REALLY GOOD, BUT... UH...
I CHARGE MORE THAN YOU'RE USED TO PAYING, RIGHT?
SORTA.
LADY, WE HAVEN'T HAD STICKER SHOCK THIS BAD SINCE WE BOUGHT THE MINIVAN!

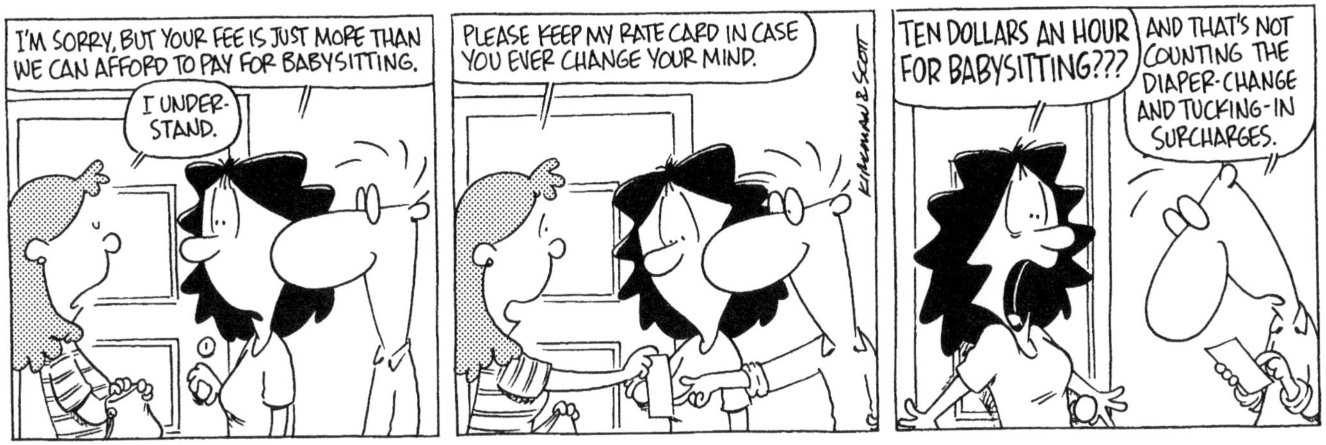
I'M SORRY, BUT YOUR FEE IS JUST MORE THAN WE CAN AFFORD TO PAY FOR BABYSITTING.
I UNDERSTAND.
PLEASE KEEP MY RATE CARD IN CASE YOU EVER CHANGE YOUR MIND.
KIRKMAN & SCOTT
TEN DOLLARS AN HOUR FOR BABYSITTING???
AND THAT'S NOT COUNTING THE DIAPER-CHANGE AND TUCKING-IN SURCHARGES.

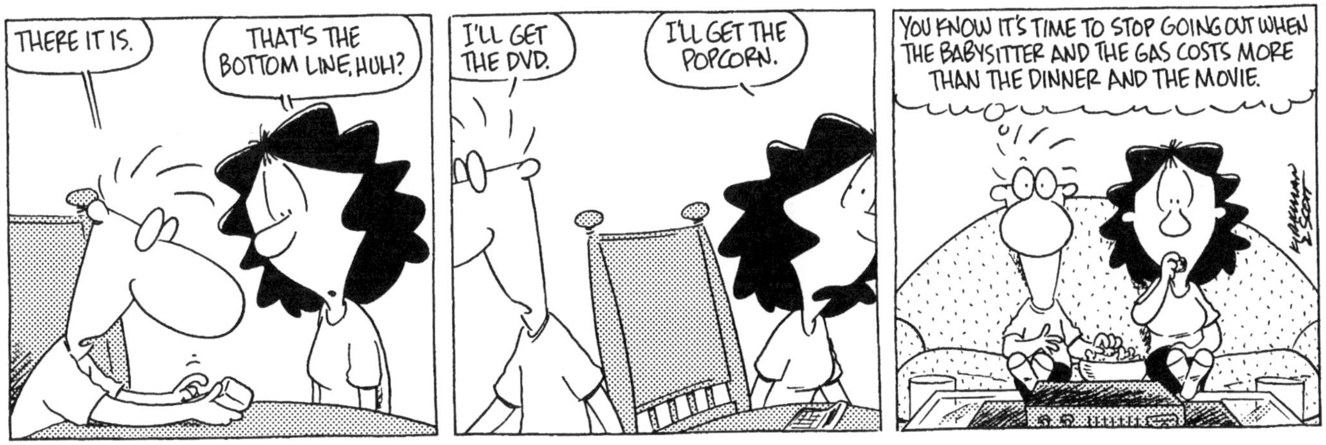
THERE IT IS.
THAT'S THE BOTTOM LINE, HUH?
I'LL GET THE DVD.
I'LL GET THE POPCORN.
YOU KNOW IT'S TIME TO STOP GOING OUT WHEN THE BABYSITTER AND THE GAS COSTS MORE THAN THE DINNER AND THE MOVIE.

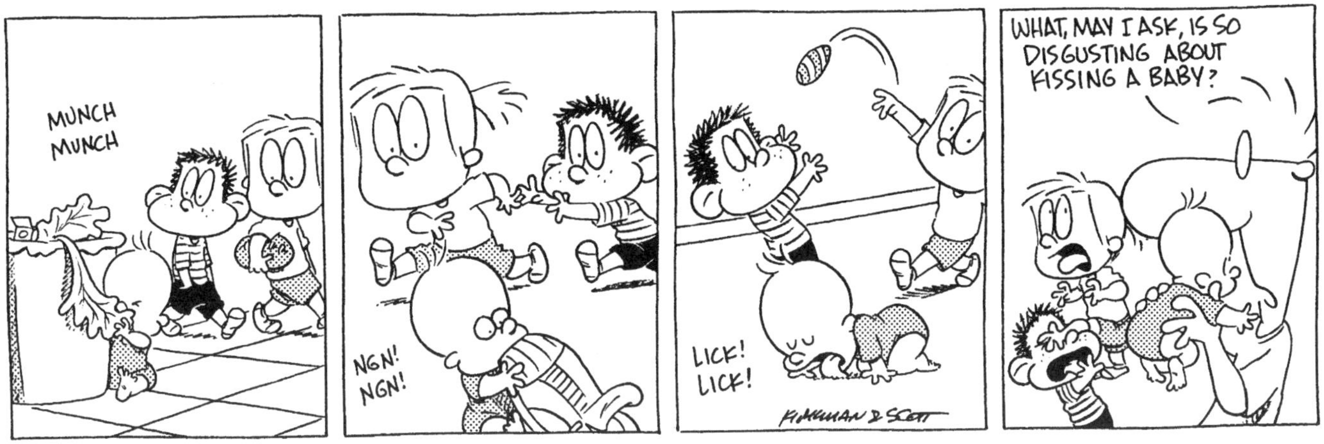
MUNCH MUNCH
NGN! NGN!
LICK! LICK!
KIRKMAN & SCOTT
WHAT, MAY I ASK, IS SO DISGUSTING ABOUT KISSING A BABY?

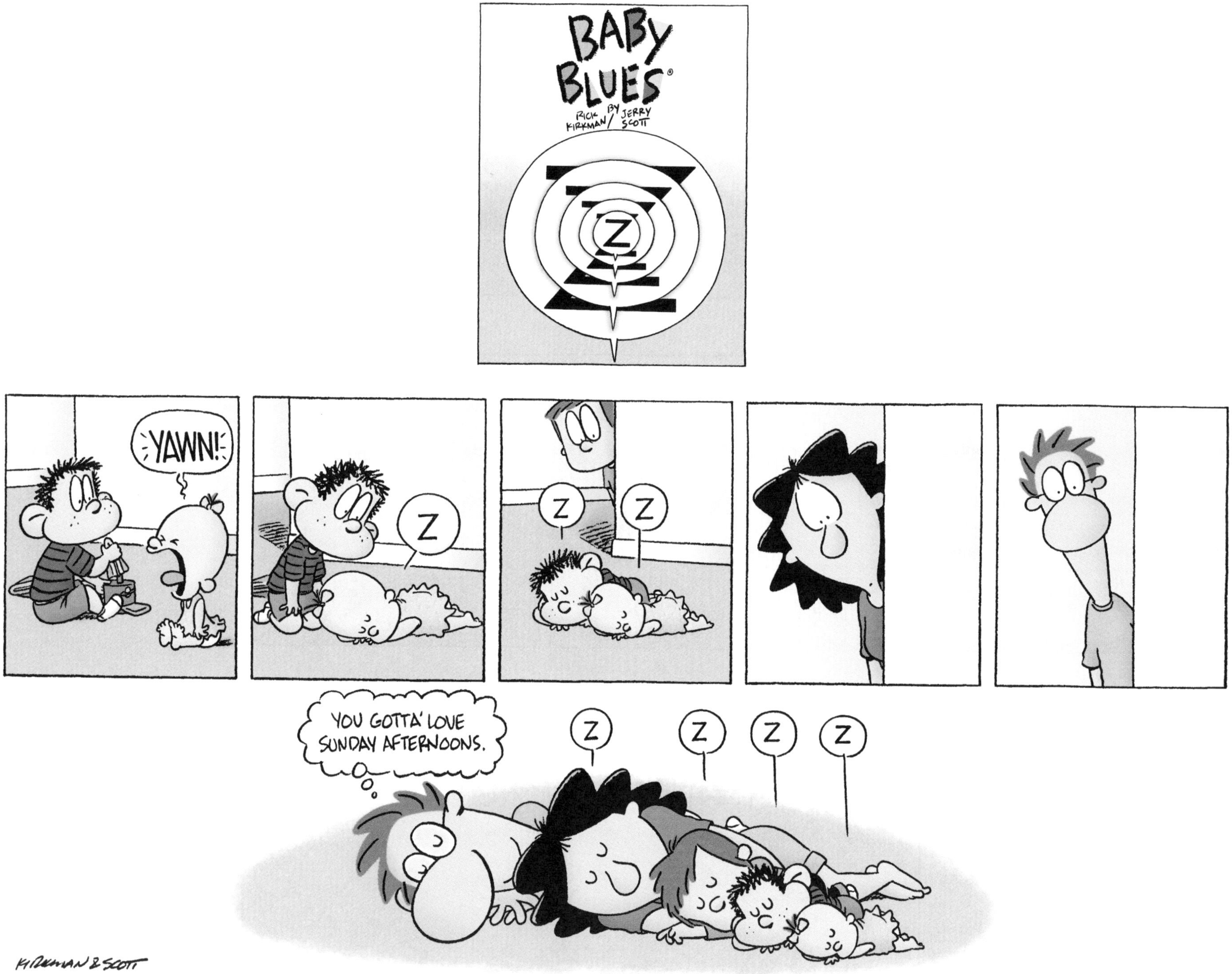
BABY BLUES®
BY RICK KIRKMAN / JERRY SCOTT
Z
YAWN!
Z
Z
Z
YOU GOTTA' LOVE SUNDAY AFTERNOONS.
Z
Z
Z
Z
KIRKMAN & SCOTT

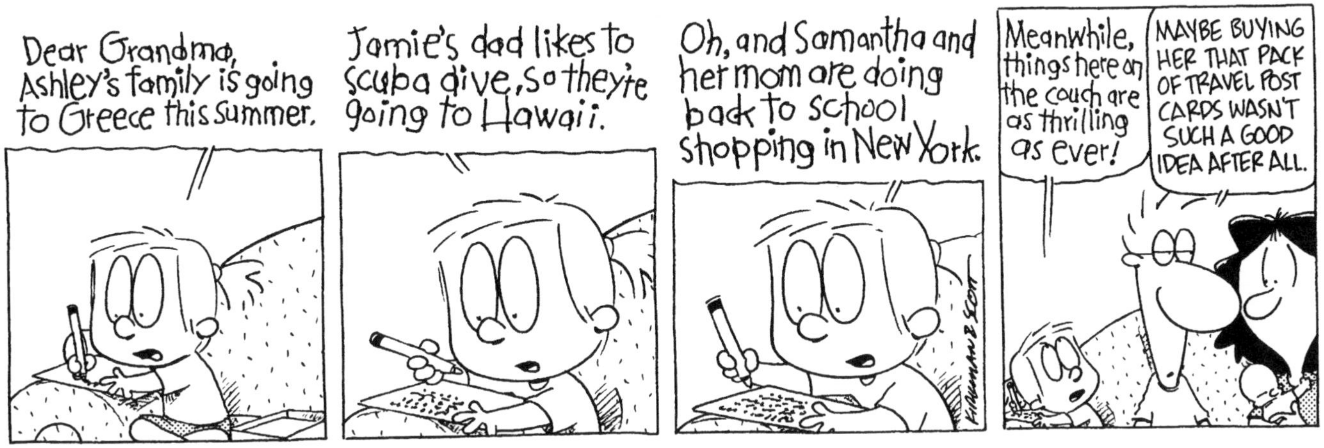
Dear Grandma,
Ashley's family is going to Greece this summer.
Jamie's dad likes to scuba dive, so they're going to Hawaii.
Oh, and Samantha and her mom are doing back to school shopping in New York.
Meanwhile, things here on the couch are as thrilling as ever!
MAYBE BUYING HER THAT PACK OF TRAVEL POST CARDS WASN'T SUCH A GOOD IDEA AFTER ALL.

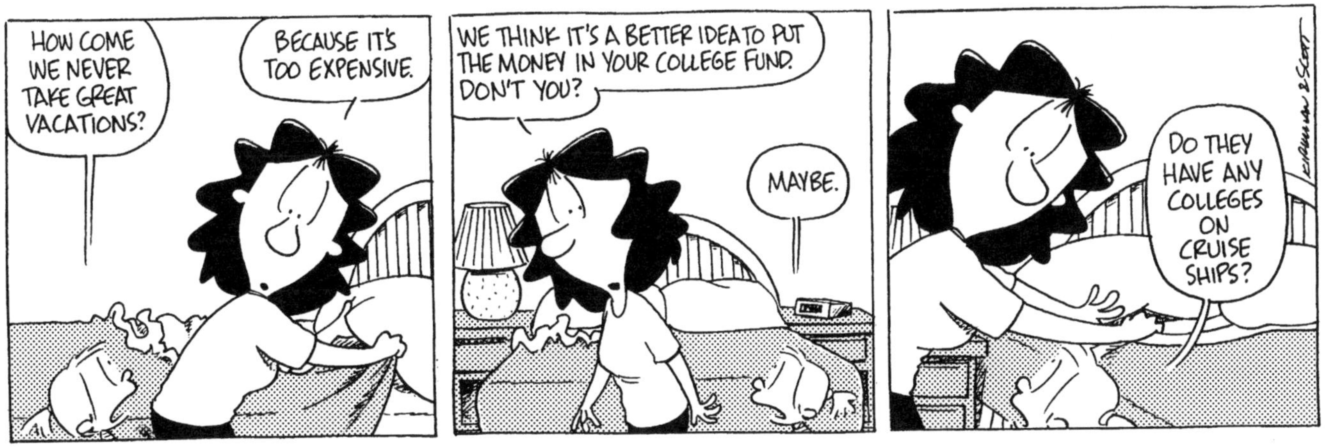
HOW COME WE NEVER TAKE GREAT VACATIONS?
BECAUSE IT'S TOO EXPENSIVE.
WE THINK IT'S A BETTER IDEA TO PUT THE MONEY IN YOUR COLLEGE FUND. DON'T YOU?
MAYBE.
DO THEY HAVE ANY COLLEGES ON CRUISE SHIPS?

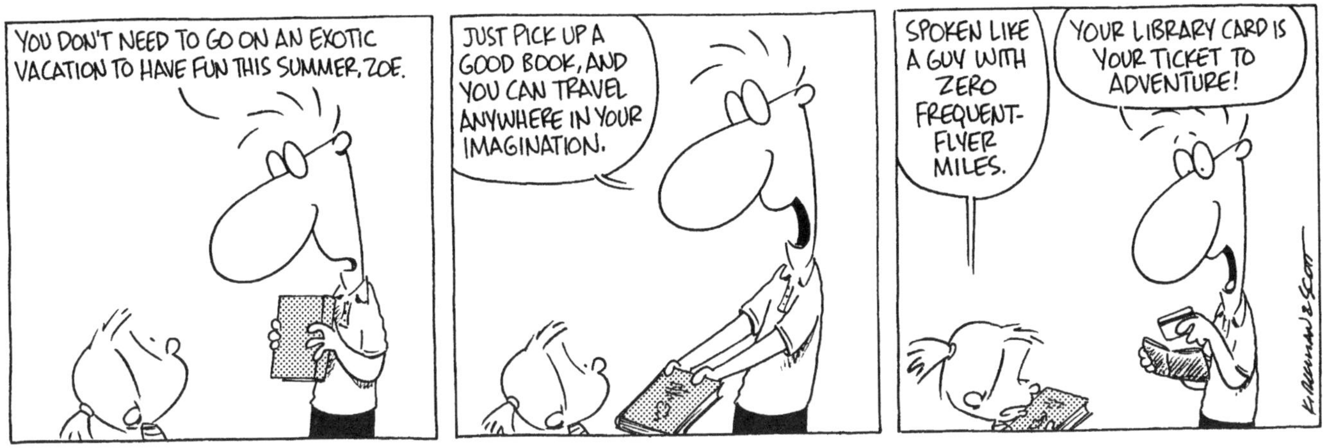
YOU DON'T NEED TO GO ON AN EXOTIC VACATION TO HAVE FUN THIS SUMMER, ZOE.
JUST PICK UP A GOOD BOOK, AND YOU CAN TRAVEL ANYWHERE IN YOUR IMAGINATION.
SPOKEN LIKE A GUY WITH ZERO FREQUENT-FLYER MILES.
YOUR LIBRARY CARD IS YOUR TICKET TO ADVENTURE!

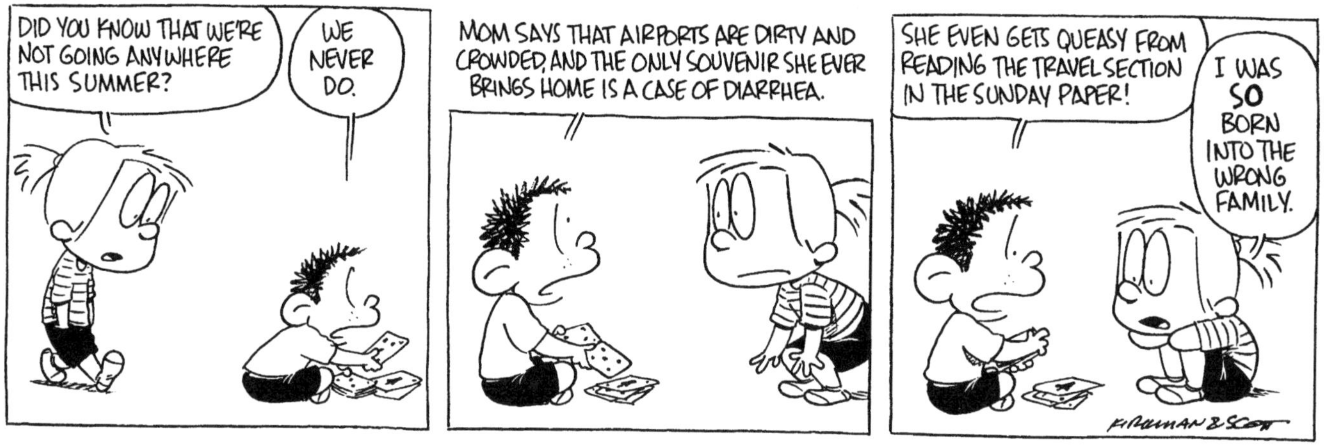
DID YOU KNOW THAT WE'RE NOT GOING ANYWHERE THIS SUMMER?
WE NEVER DO.
MOM SAYS THAT AIRPORTS ARE DIRTY AND CROWDED, AND THE ONLY SOUVENIR SHE EVER BRINGS HOME IS A CASE OF DIARRHEA.
SHE EVEN GETS QUEASY FROM READING THE TRAVEL SECTION IN THE SUNDAY PAPER!
I WAS **SO** BORN INTO THE WRONG FAMILY.

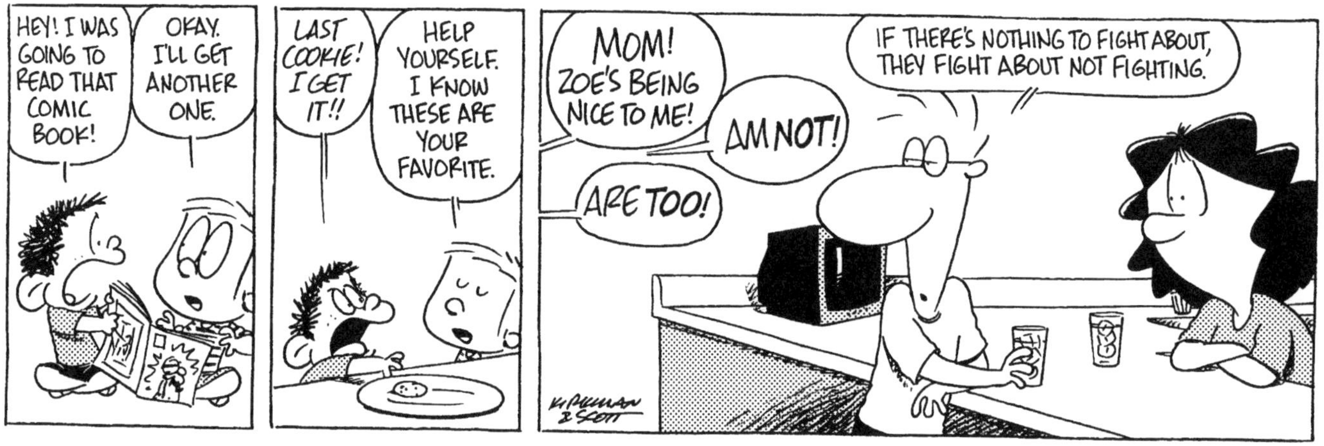
HEY! I WAS GOING TO READ THAT COMIC BOOK!
OKAY. I'LL GET ANOTHER ONE.
LAST COOKIE! I GET IT!!
HELP YOURSELF. I KNOW THESE ARE YOUR FAVORITE.
MOM! ZOE'S BEING NICE TO ME!
AM NOT!
ARE TOO!
IF THERE'S NOTHING TO FIGHT ABOUT, THEY FIGHT ABOUT NOT FIGHTING.

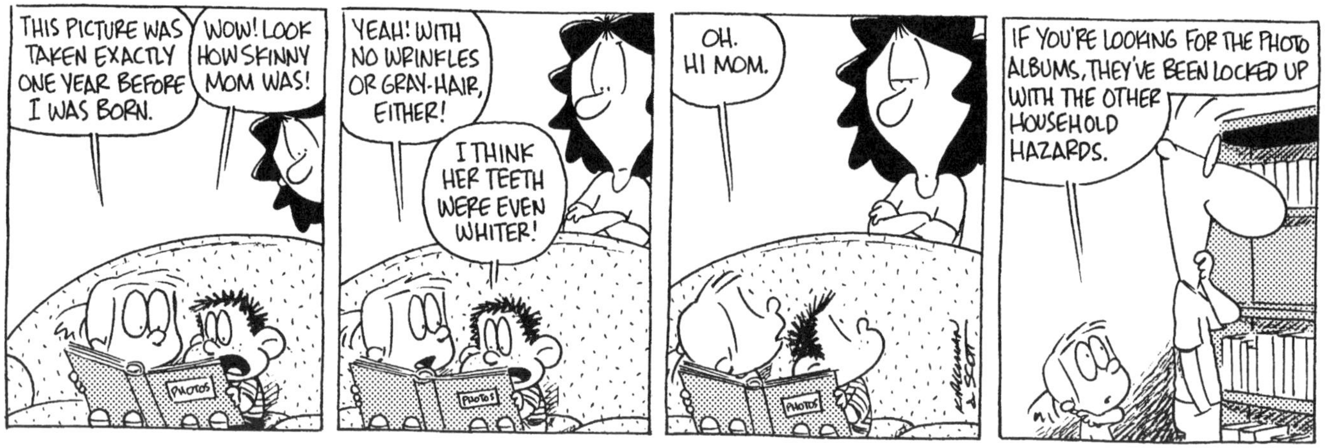
THIS PICTURE WAS TAKEN EXACTLY ONE YEAR BEFORE I WAS BORN.
WOW! LOOK HOW SKINNY MOM WAS!
YEAH! WITH NO WRINKLES OR GRAY-HAIR, EITHER!
I THINK HER TEETH WERE EVEN WHITER!
OH. HI MOM.
IF YOU'RE LOOKING FOR THE PHOTO ALBUMS, THEY'VE BEEN LOCKED UP WITH THE OTHER HOUSEHOLD HAZARDS.

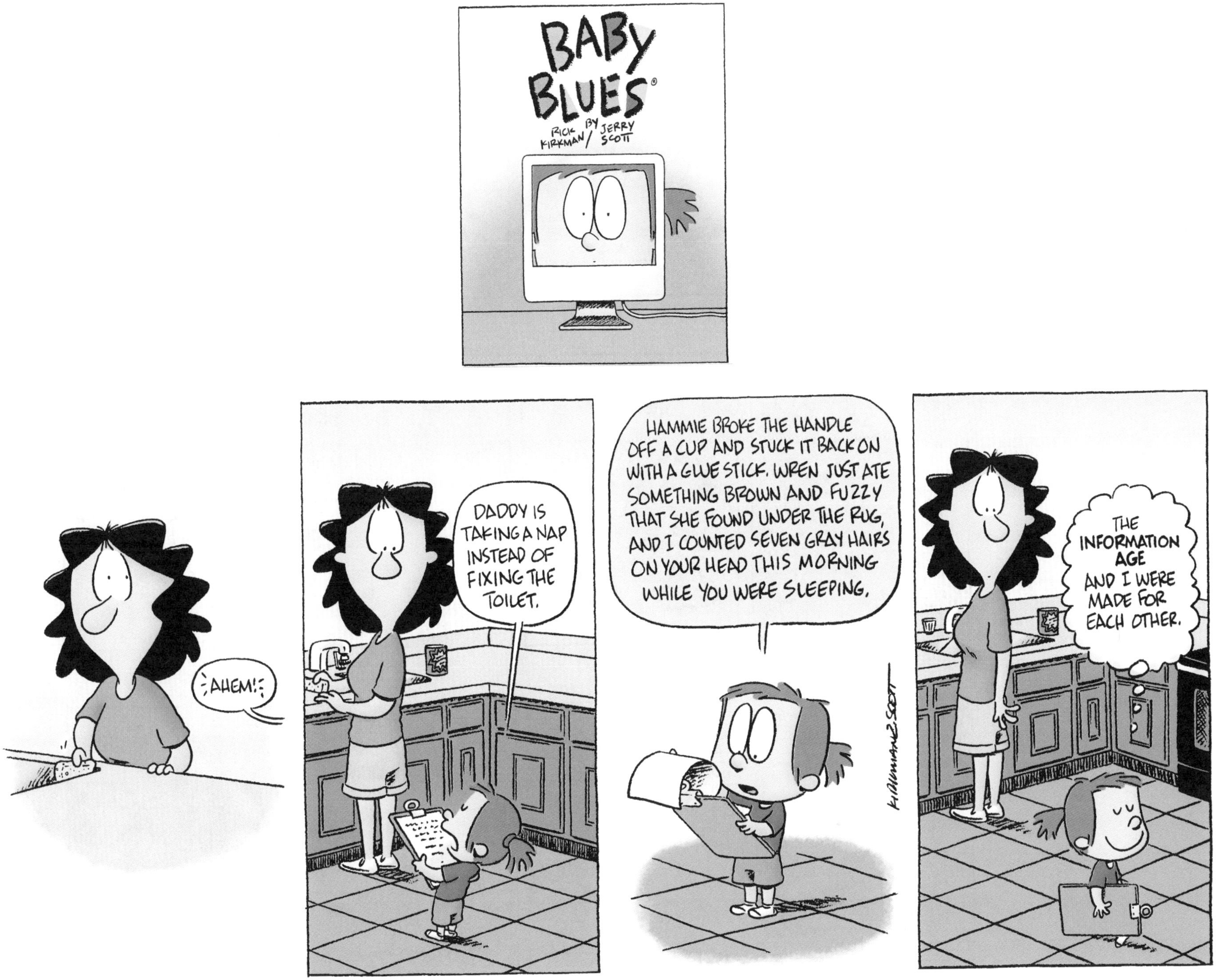
BABY BLUES®
BY RICK KIRKMAN / JERRY SCOTT
AHEM!
DADDY IS TAKING A NAP INSTEAD OF FIXING THE TOILET.
HAMMIE BROKE THE HANDLE OFF A CUP AND STUCK IT BACK ON WITH A GLUE STICK. WREN JUST ATE SOMETHING BROWN AND FUZZY THAT SHE FOUND UNDER THE RUG, AND I COUNTED SEVEN GRAY HAIRS ON YOUR HEAD THIS MORNING WHILE YOU WERE SLEEPING.
THE **INFORMATION AGE** AND I WERE MADE FOR EACH OTHER.

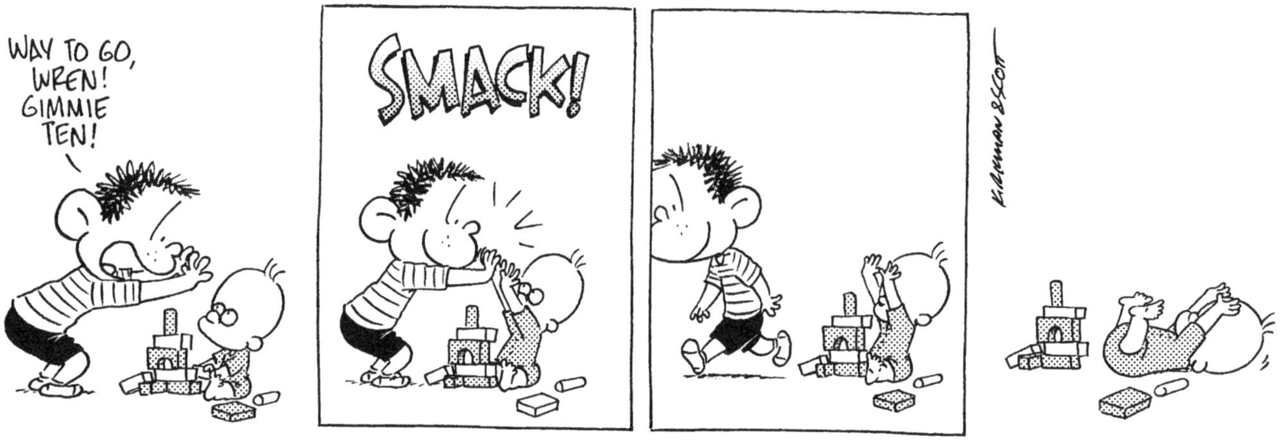
WAY TO GO, WREN! GIMMIE TEN!
SMACK!
KIRKMAN & SCOTT

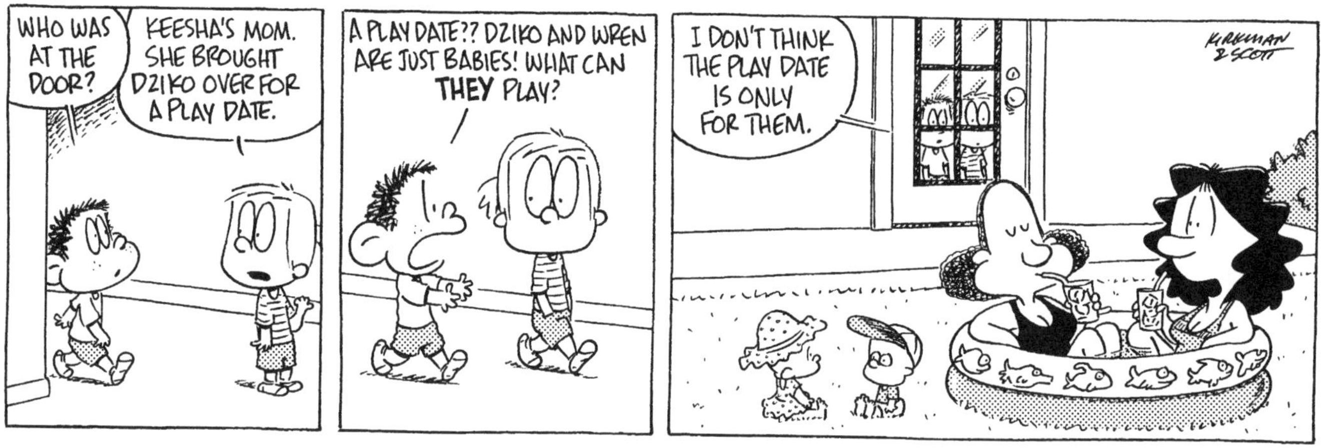
WHO WAS AT THE DOOR?
KEESHA'S MOM. SHE BROUGHT DZIKO OVER FOR A PLAY DATE.
A PLAY DATE?? DZIKO AND WREN ARE JUST BABIES! WHAT CAN THEY PLAY?
I DON'T THINK THE PLAY DATE IS ONLY FOR THEM.
KIRKMAN & SCOTT

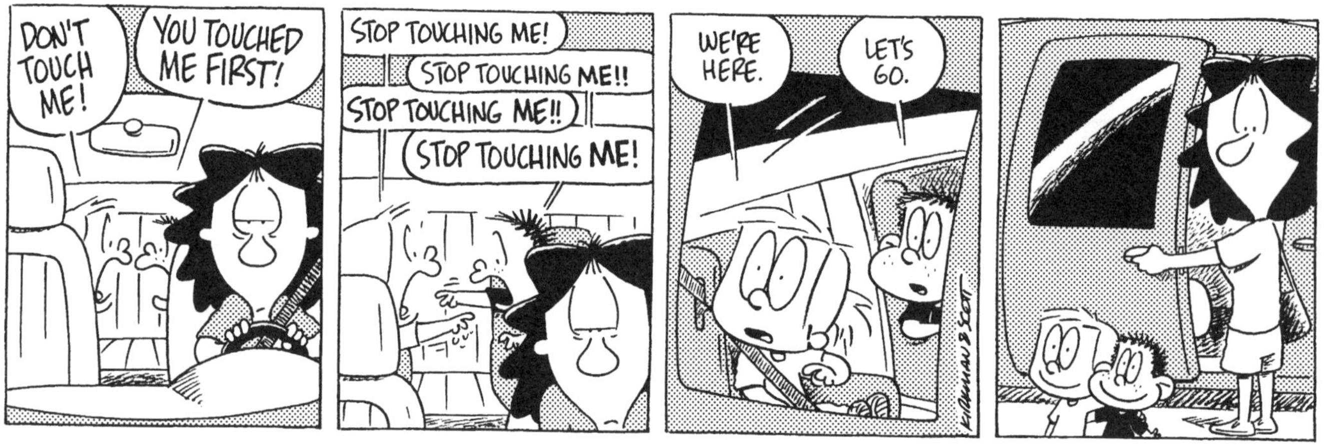
DON'T TOUCH ME!
YOU TOUCHED ME FIRST!
STOP TOUCHING ME!
STOP TOUCHING ME!!
STOP TOUCHING ME!!
STOP TOUCHING ME!
WE'RE HERE.
LET'S GO.
KIRKMAN & SCOTT

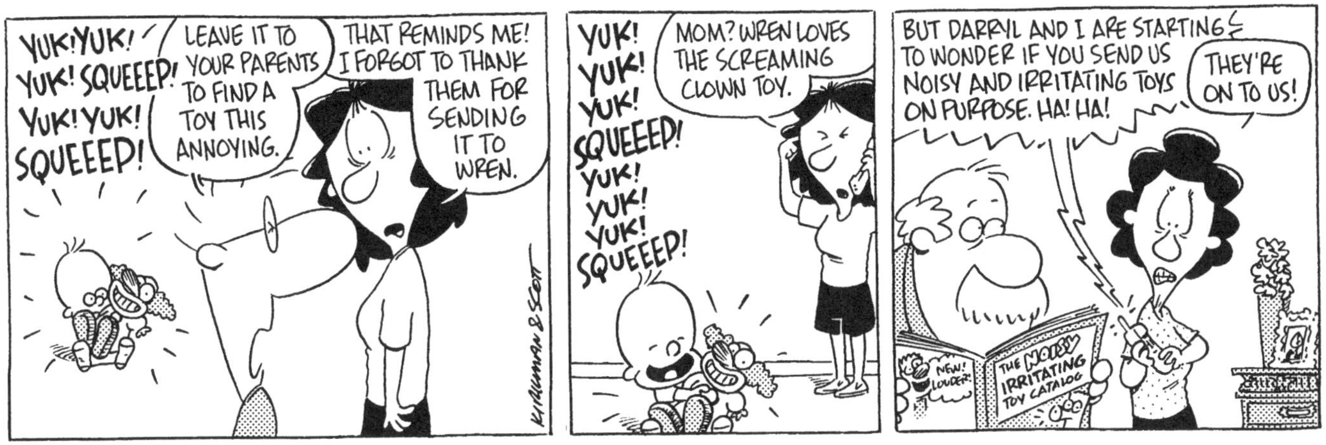
YUK! YUK! YUK! SQUEEEP! YUK! YUK! SQUEEEP!
LEAVE IT TO YOUR PARENTS TO FIND A TOY THIS ANNOYING.
THAT REMINDS ME! I FORGOT TO THANK THEM FOR SENDING IT TO WREN.
YUK! YUK! YUK! SQUEEEP! YUK! YUK! YUK! SQUEEEP!
MOM? WREN LOVES THE SCREAMING CLOWN TOY.
BUT DARRYL AND I ARE STARTING TO WONDER IF YOU SEND US NOISY AND IRRITATING TOYS ON PURPOSE. HA! HA!
THEY'RE ON TO US!
NEW! LOUDER!
THE NOISY IRRITATING TOY CATALOG

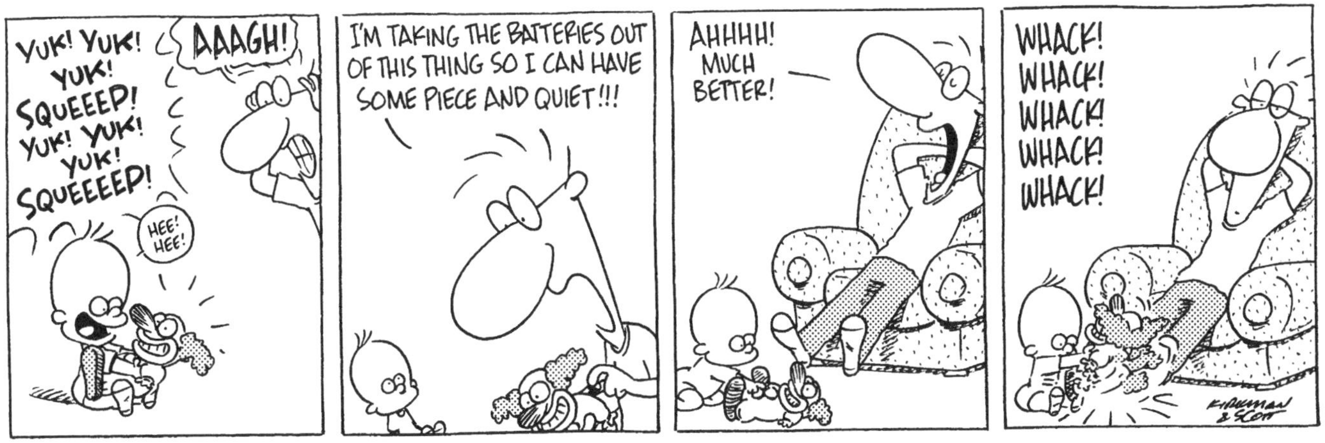
YUK! YUK! YUK! SQUEEEP! YUK! YUK! YUK! SQUEEEEP!
AAAGH!
HEE! HEE!
I'M TAKING THE BATTERIES OUT OF THIS THING SO I CAN HAVE SOME PIECE AND QUIET!!!
AHHHH! MUCH BETTER!
WHACK! WHACK! WHACK! WHACK! WHACK!

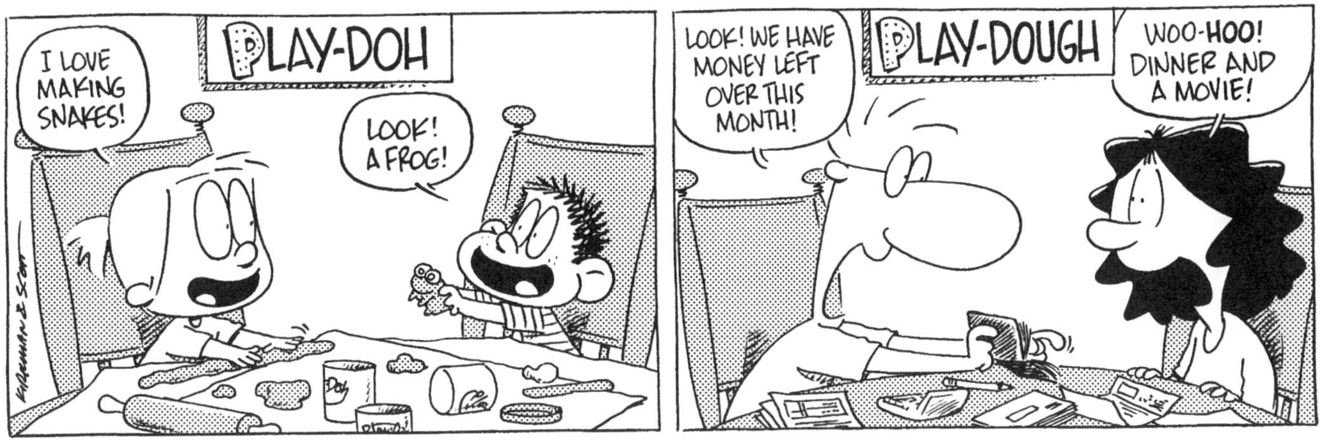
PLAY-DOH
I LOVE MAKING SNAKES!
LOOK! A FROG!
PLAY-DOUGH
LOOK! WE HAVE MONEY LEFT OVER THIS MONTH!
WOO-HOO! DINNER AND A MOVIE!

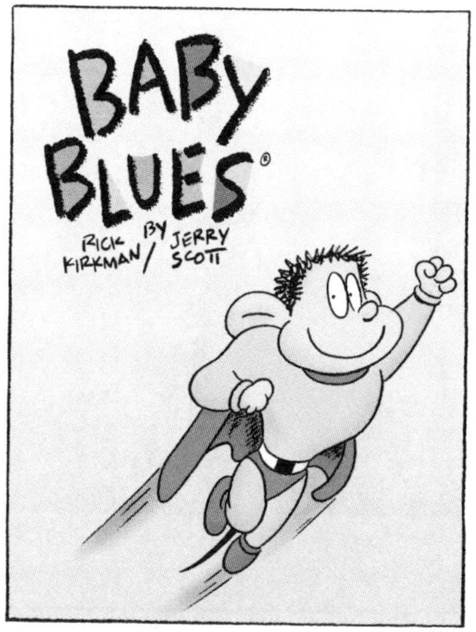
BABY BLUES®
BY RICK KIRKMAN / JERRY SCOTT

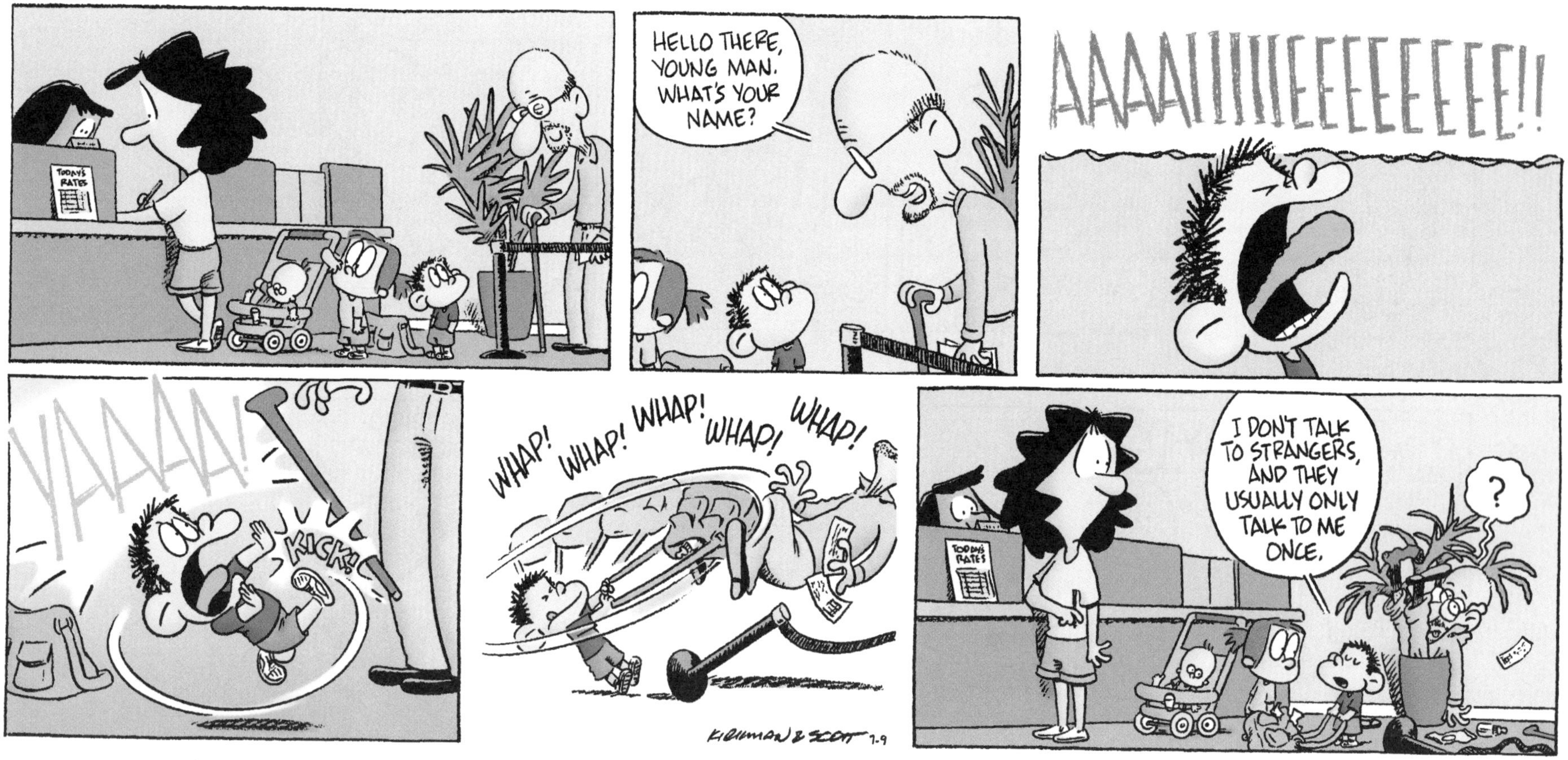
TODAY'S RATES
HELLO THERE, YOUNG MAN. WHAT'S YOUR NAME?
AAAAIIIIIIEEEEEEEE!!
YAAAAA!
KICK!
WHAP! WHAP! WHAP! WHAP! WHAP!
KIRKMAN & SCOTT 7-9
TODAY'S RATES
I DON'T TALK TO STRANGERS, AND THEY USUALLY ONLY TALK TO ME ONCE.
?

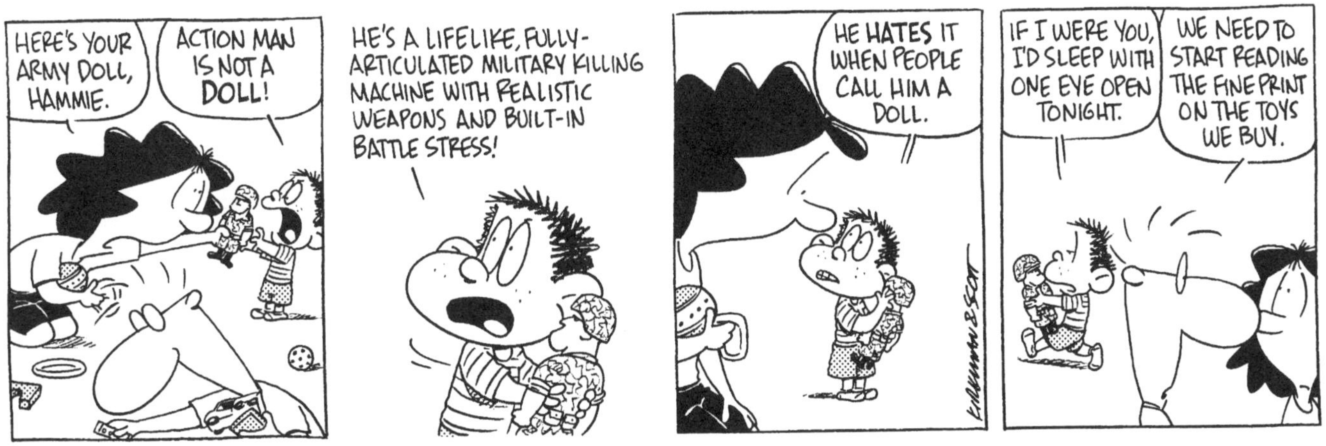
HERE'S YOUR ARMY DOLL, HAMMIE.
ACTION MAN IS NOT A DOLL!
HE'S A LIFELIKE, FULLY-ARTICULATED MILITARY KILLING MACHINE WITH REALISTIC WEAPONS AND BUILT-IN BATTLE STRESS!
HE HATES IT WHEN PEOPLE CALL HIM A DOLL.
IF I WERE YOU, I'D SLEEP WITH ONE EYE OPEN TONIGHT.
WE NEED TO START READING THE FINE PRINT ON THE TOYS WE BUY.
KIRKMAN & SCOTT

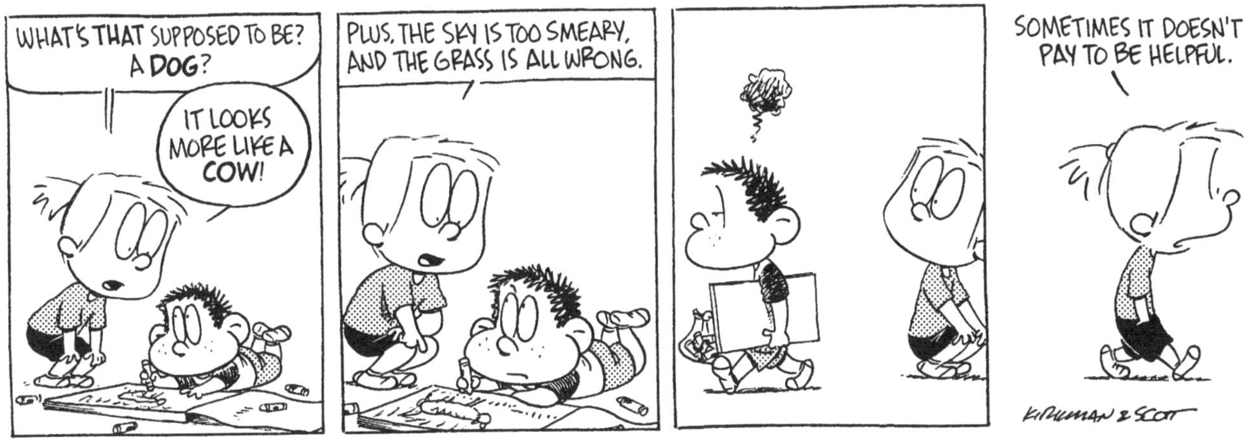
WHAT'S THAT SUPPOSED TO BE? A DOG?
IT LOOKS MORE LIKE A COW!
PLUS, THE SKY IS TOO SMEARY, AND THE GRASS IS ALL WRONG.
SOMETIMES IT DOESN'T PAY TO BE HELPFUL.
KIRKMAN & SCOTT

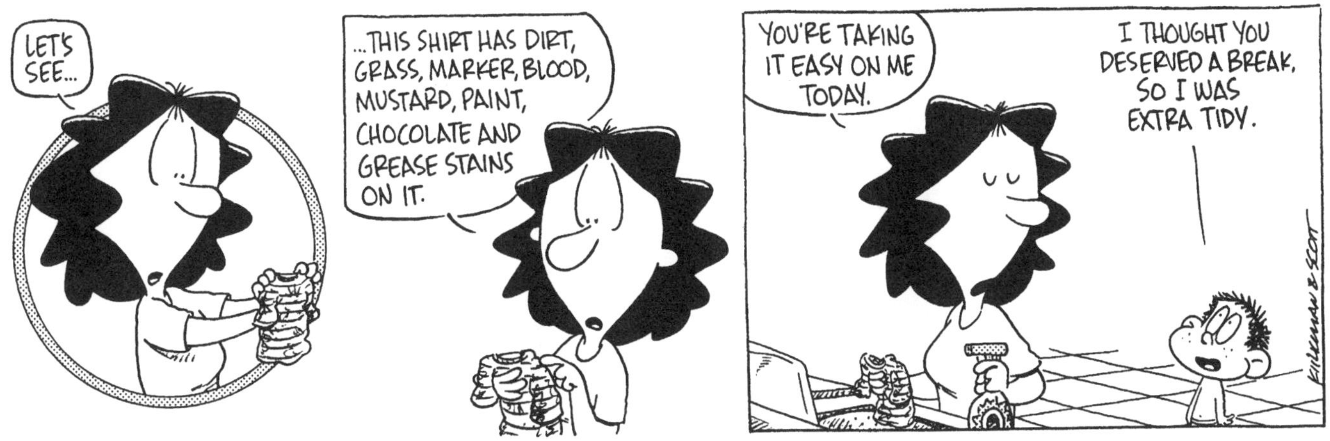
LET'S SEE...
...THIS SHIRT HAS DIRT, GRASS, MARKER, BLOOD, MUSTARD, PAINT, CHOCOLATE AND GREASE STAINS ON IT.
YOU'RE TAKING IT EASY ON ME TODAY.
I THOUGHT YOU DESERVED A BREAK, SO I WAS EXTRA TIDY.
KIRKMAN & SCOTT

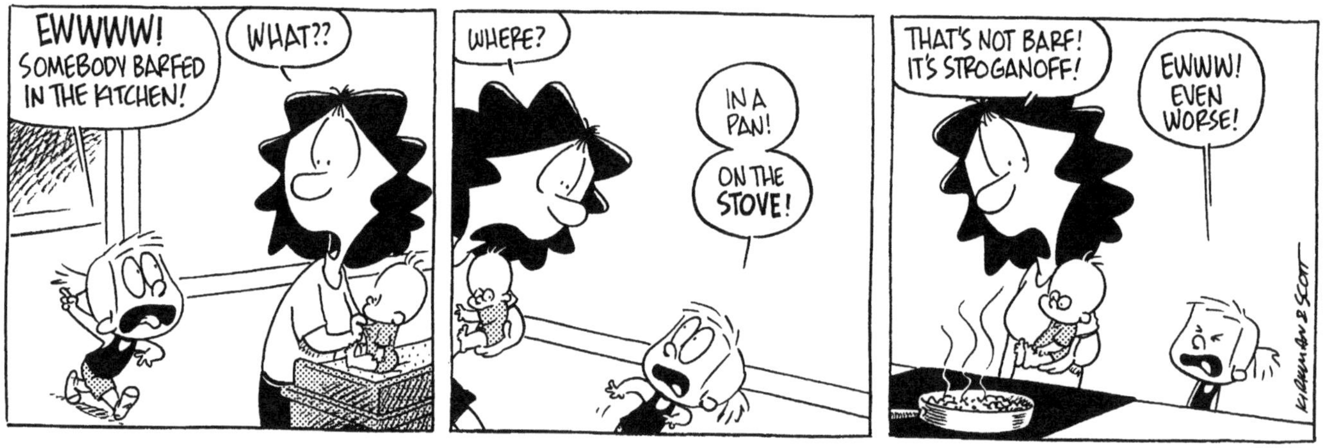
EWWWW!
SOMEBODY BARFED IN THE KITCHEN!
WHAT??
WHERE?
IN A PAN!
ON THE STOVE!
THAT'S NOT BARF! IT'S STROGANOFF!
EWWW! EVEN WORSE!

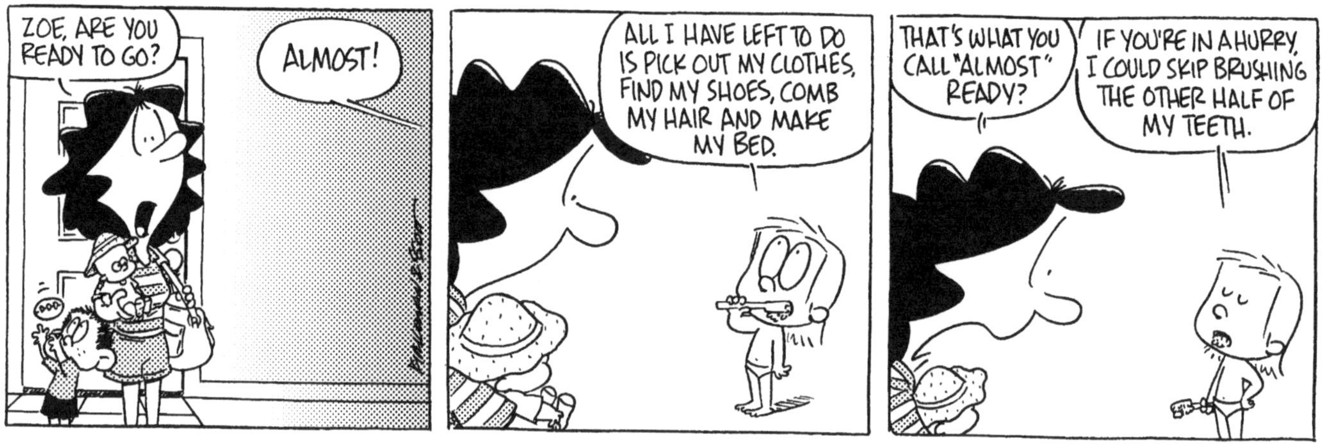
ZOE, ARE YOU READY TO GO?
ALMOST!
ALL I HAVE LEFT TO DO IS PICK OUT MY CLOTHES, FIND MY SHOES, COMB MY HAIR AND MAKE MY BED.
THAT'S WHAT YOU CALL "ALMOST" READY?
IF YOU'RE IN A HURRY, I COULD SKIP BRUSHING THE OTHER HALF OF MY TEETH.

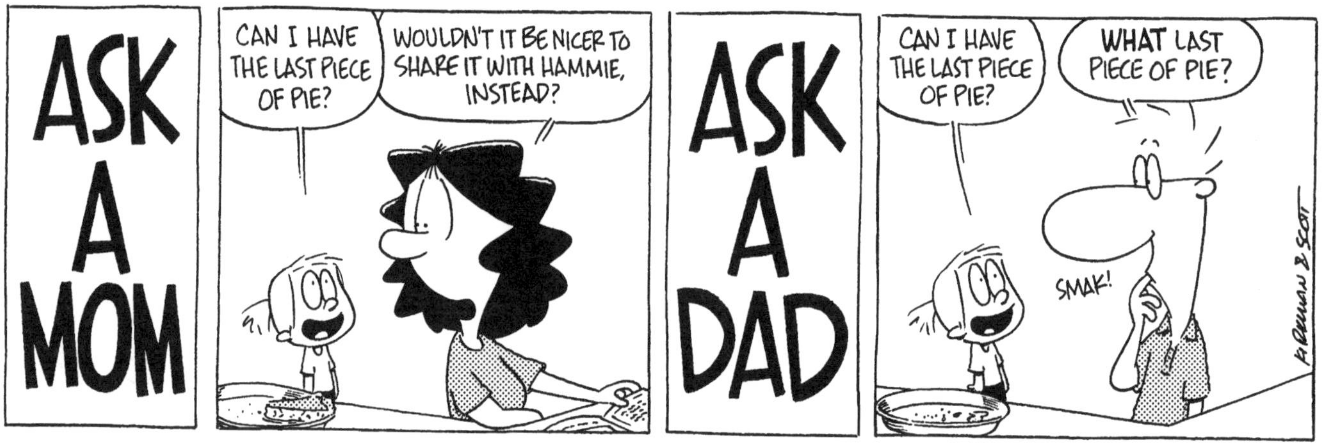
ASK A MOM
CAN I HAVE THE LAST PIECE OF PIE?
WOULDN'T IT BE NICER TO SHARE IT WITH HAMMIE, INSTEAD?
ASK A DAD
CAN I HAVE THE LAST PIECE OF PIE?
WHAT LAST PIECE OF PIE?
SMAK!

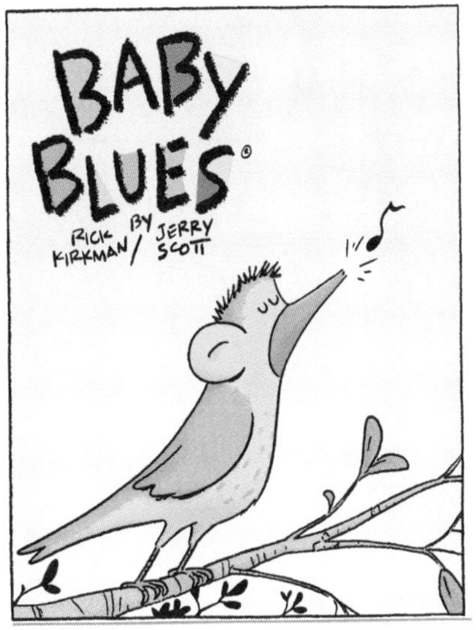
BABY BLUES®
BY RICK KIRKMAN / JERRY SCOTT

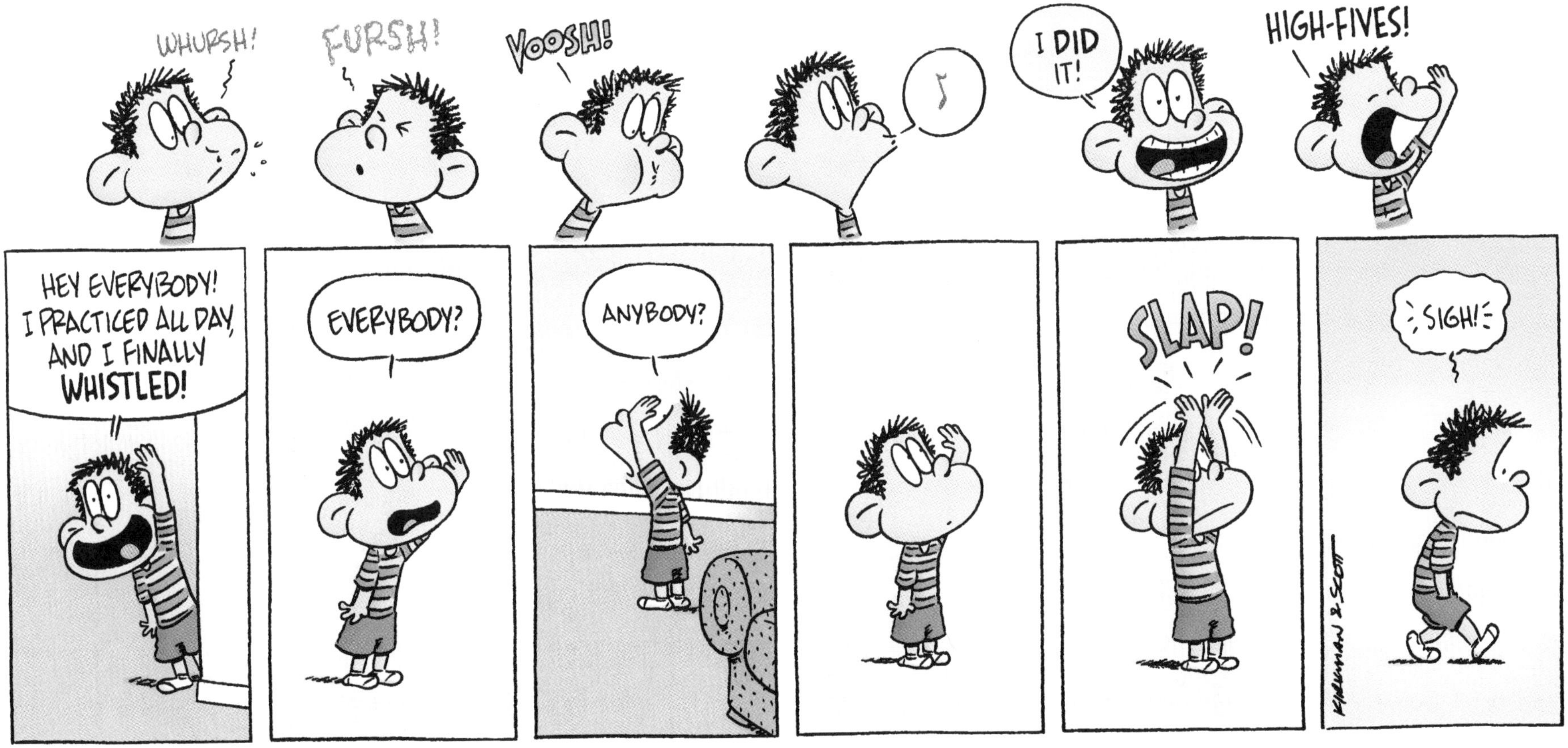
WHURSH!
HEY EVERYBODY! I PRACTICED ALL DAY, AND I FINALLY WHISTLED!
FURSH!
EVERYBODY?
YOOSH!
ANYBODY?
I DID IT!
SLAP!
HIGH-FIVES!
SIGH!
KIRKMAN & SCOTT

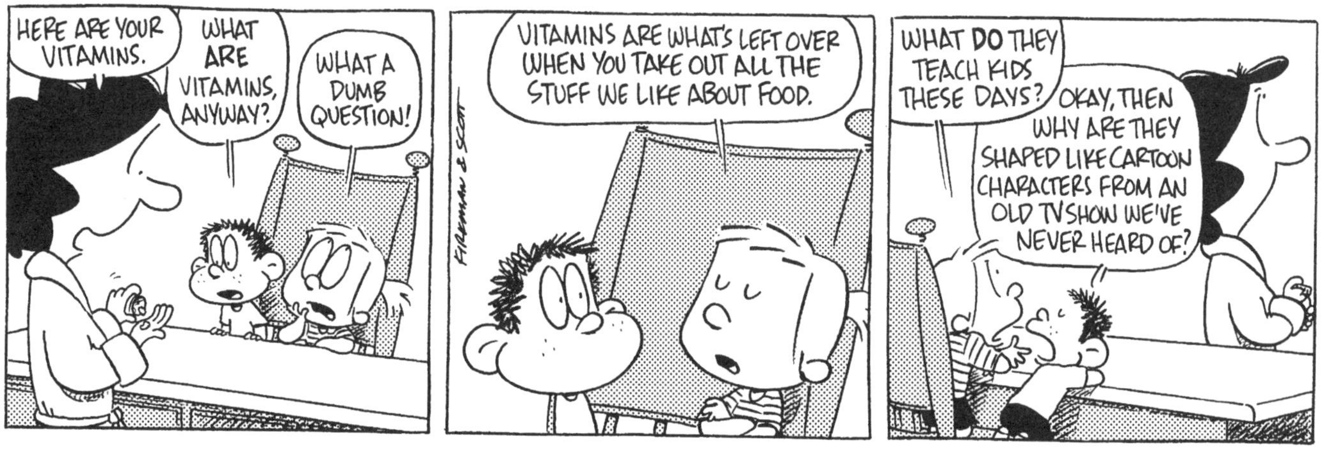
HERE ARE YOUR VITAMINS.
WHAT **ARE** VITAMINS, ANYWAY?
WHAT A DUMB QUESTION!
KIRKMAN & SCOTT
VITAMINS ARE WHAT'S LEFT OVER WHEN YOU TAKE OUT ALL THE STUFF WE LIKE ABOUT FOOD.
WHAT **DO** THEY TEACH KIDS THESE DAYS?
OKAY, THEN WHY ARE THEY SHAPED LIKE CARTOON CHARACTERS FROM AN OLD TV SHOW WE'VE NEVER HEARD OF?

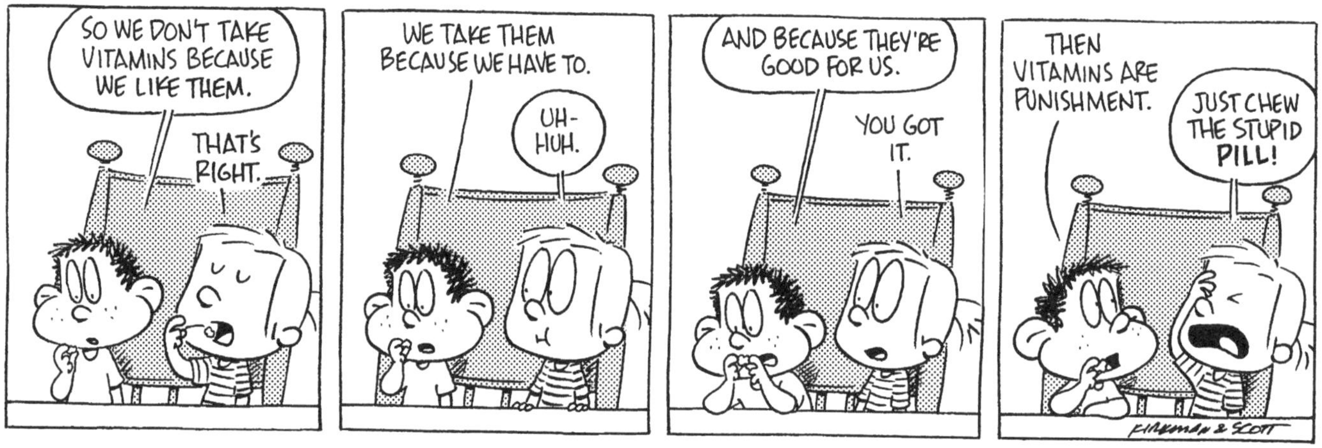
SO WE DON'T TAKE VITAMINS BECAUSE WE LIKE THEM.
THAT'S RIGHT.
WE TAKE THEM BECAUSE WE HAVE TO.
UH-HUH.
AND BECAUSE THEY'RE GOOD FOR US.
YOU GOT IT.
THEN VITAMINS ARE PUNISHMENT.
JUST CHEW THE STUPID **PILL!**
KIRKMAN & SCOTT

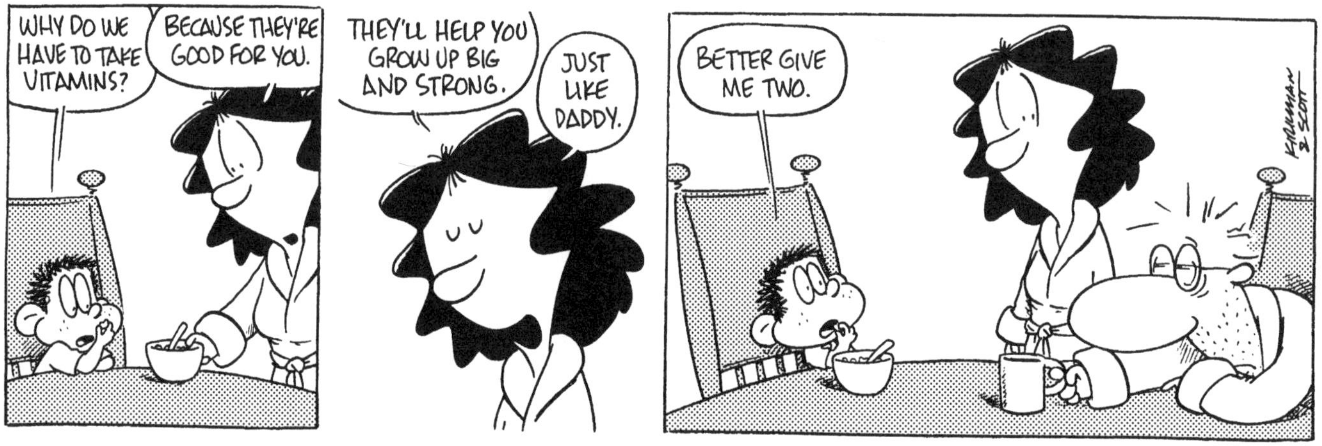
WHY DO WE HAVE TO TAKE VITAMINS?
BECAUSE THEY'RE GOOD FOR YOU.
THEY'LL HELP YOU GROW UP BIG AND STRONG.
JUST LIKE DADDY.
BETTER GIVE ME TWO.
KIRKMAN & SCOTT

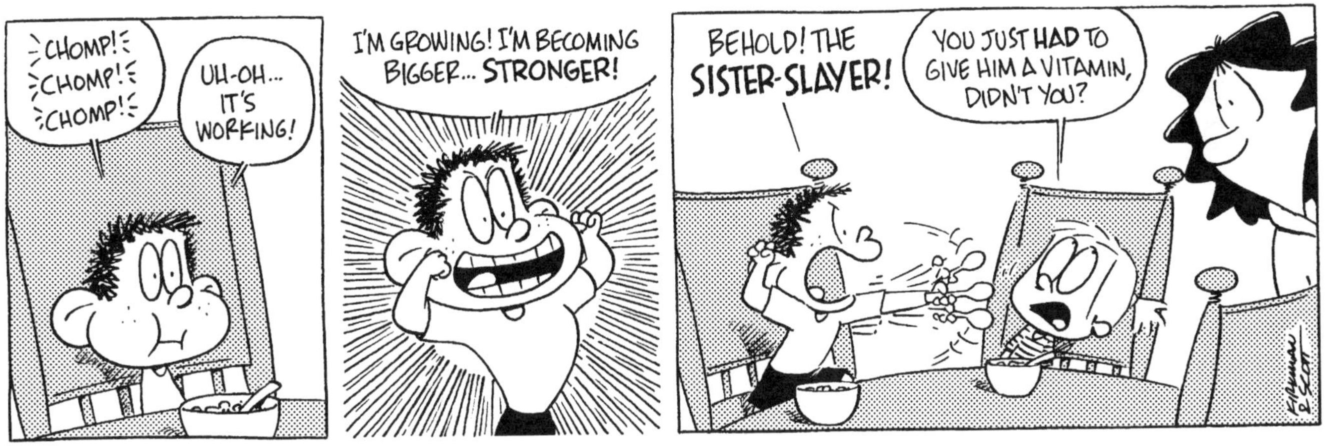
CHOMP! CHOMP! CHOMP!
UH-OH... IT'S WORKING!
I'M GROWING! I'M BECOMING BIGGER... STRONGER!
BEHOLD! THE SISTER-SLAYER!
YOU JUST HAD TO GIVE HIM A VITAMIN, DIDN'T YOU?

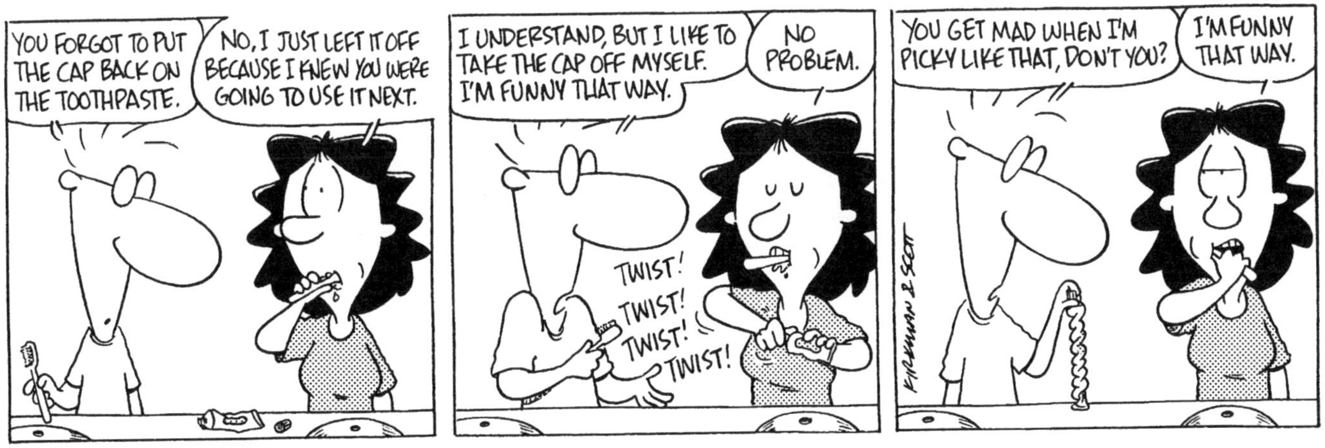
YOU FORGOT TO PUT THE CAP BACK ON THE TOOTHPASTE.
NO, I JUST LEFT IT OFF BECAUSE I KNEW YOU WERE GOING TO USE IT NEXT.
I UNDERSTAND, BUT I LIKE TO TAKE THE CAP OFF MYSELF. I'M FUNNY THAT WAY.
NO PROBLEM.
TWIST! TWIST! TWIST! TWIST!
YOU GET MAD WHEN I'M PICKY LIKE THAT, DON'T YOU?
I'M FUNNY THAT WAY.
KIRKMAN & SCOTT

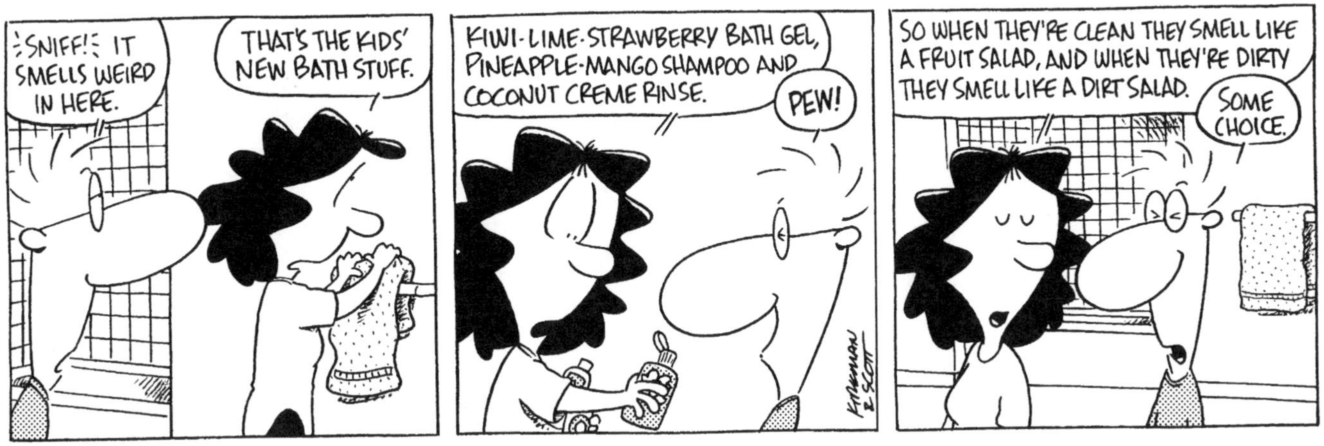
SNIFF! IT SMELLS WEIRD IN HERE.
THAT'S THE KIDS' NEW BATH STUFF.
KIWI-LIME-STRAWBERRY BATH GEL, PINEAPPLE-MANGO SHAMPOO AND COCONUT CREME RINSE.
PEW!
SO WHEN THEY'RE CLEAN THEY SMELL LIKE A FRUIT SALAD, AND WHEN THEY'RE DIRTY THEY SMELL LIKE A DIRT SALAD.
SOME CHOICE.

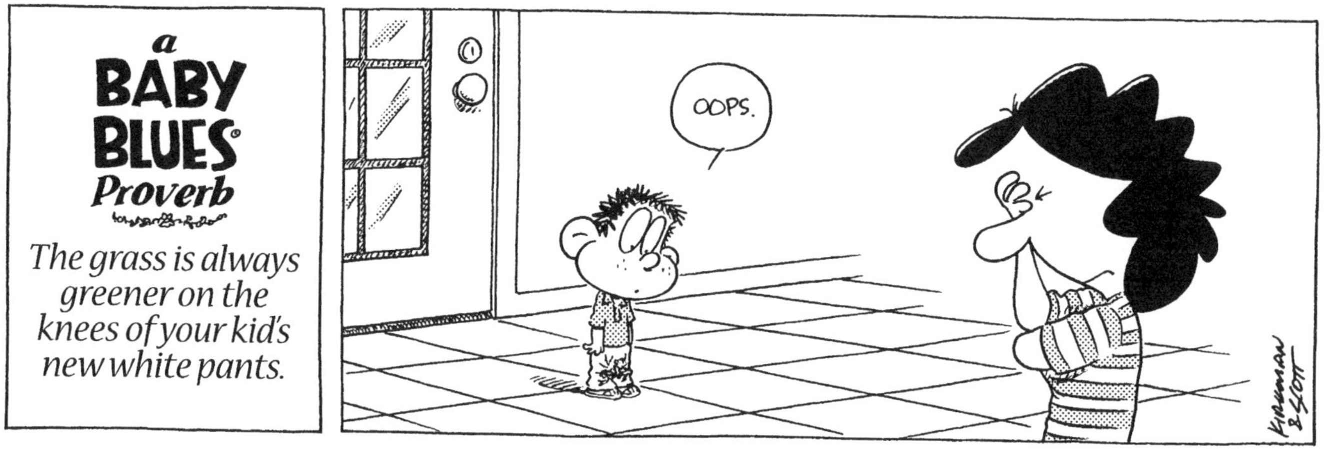
a BABY BLUES Proverb
The grass is always greener on the knees of your kid's new white pants.
OOPS.

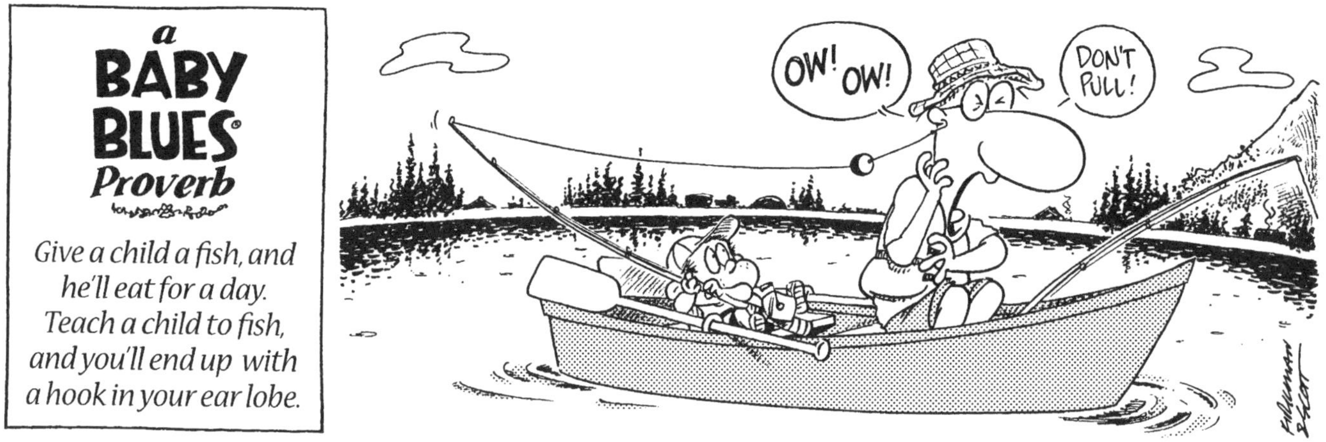
a BABY BLUES Proverb
Give a child a fish, and he'll eat for a day. Teach a child to fish, and you'll end up with a hook in your ear lobe.
OW! OW!
DON'T PULL!

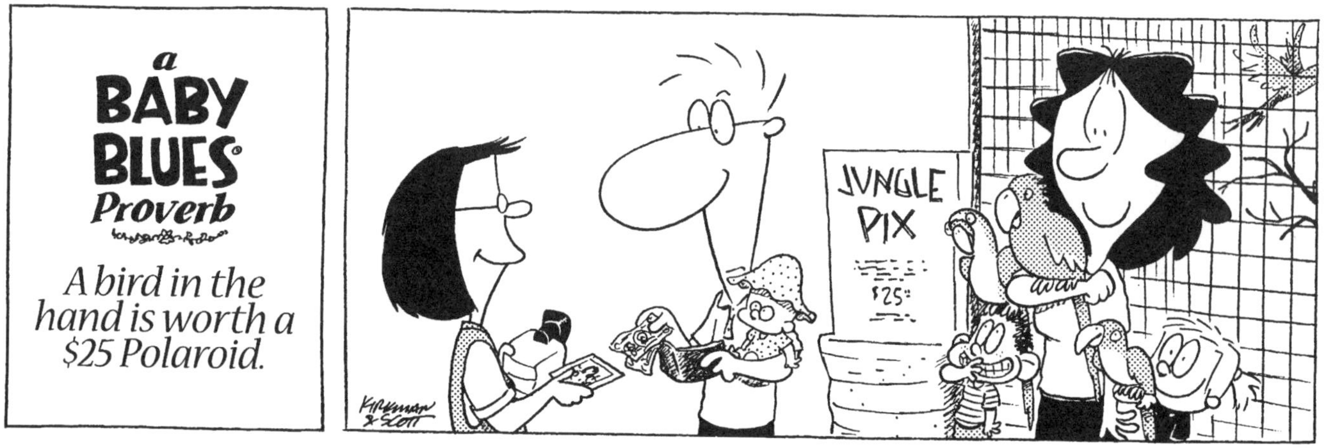
a BABY BLUES Proverb
A bird in the hand is worth a $25 Polaroid.
JUNGLE PIX
$25

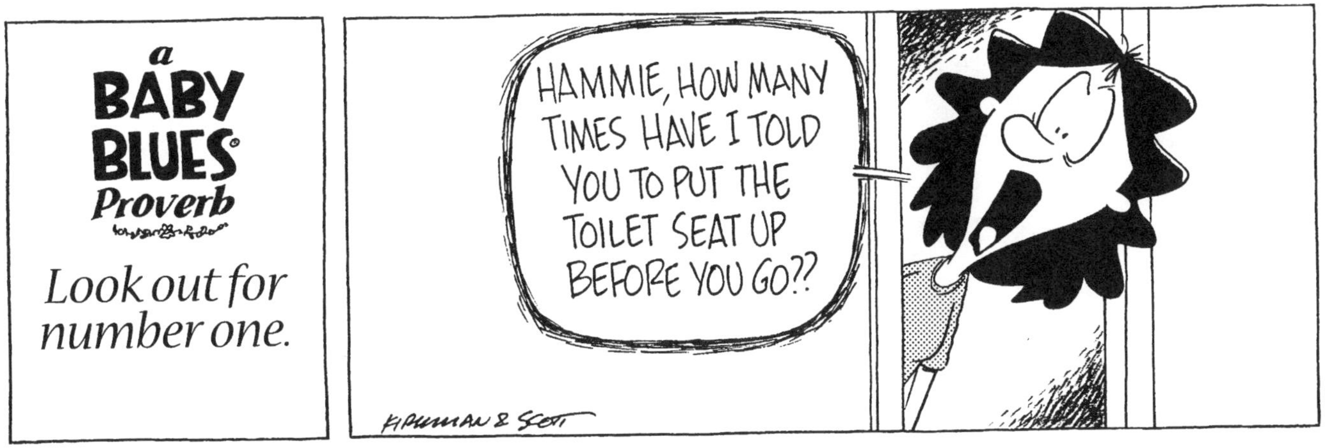
a BABY BLUES Proverb
Look out for number one.
HAMMIE, HOW MANY TIMES HAVE I TOLD YOU TO PUT THE TOILET SEAT UP BEFORE YOU GO??
KIRKMAN & SCOTT

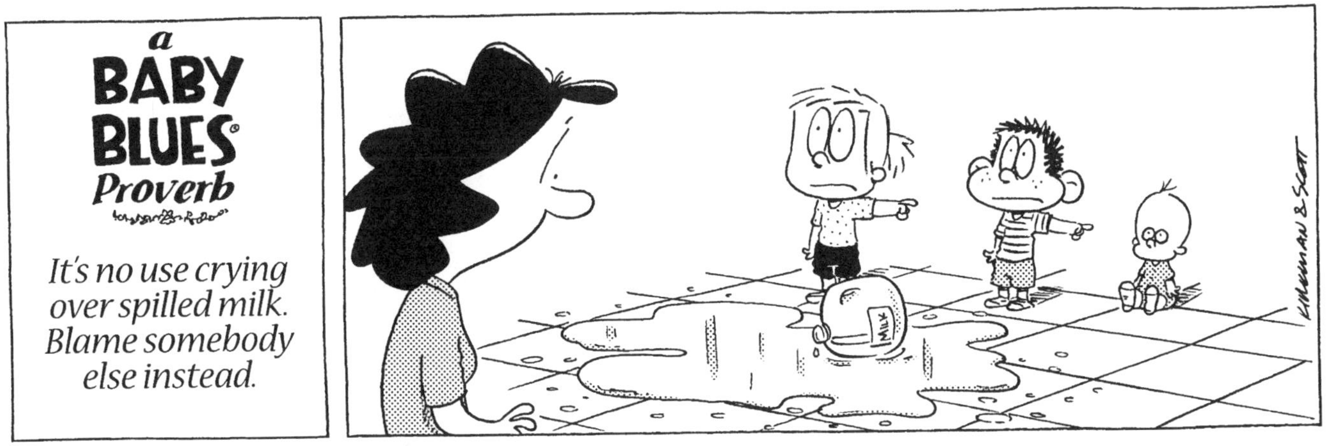
a BABY BLUES Proverb
It's no use crying over spilled milk. Blame somebody else instead.
MILK
KIRKMAN & SCOTT

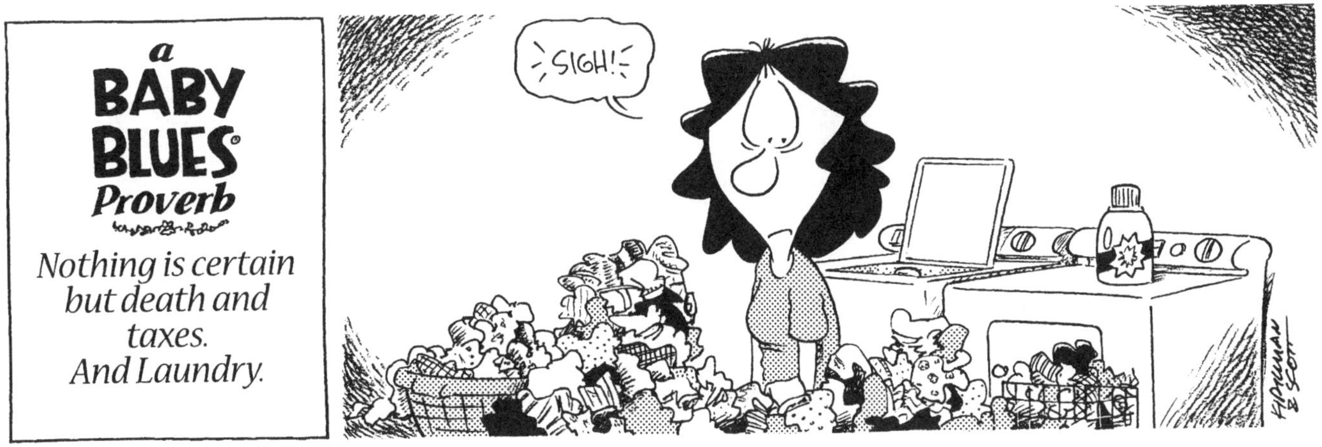
a BABY BLUES Proverb
Nothing is certain but death and taxes. And Laundry.
SIGH!
KIRKMAN & SCOTT

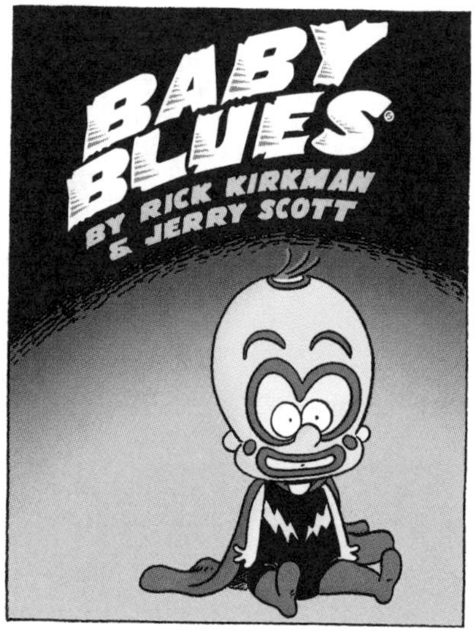
BABY BLUES®
BY RICK KIRKMAN
& JERRY SCOTT

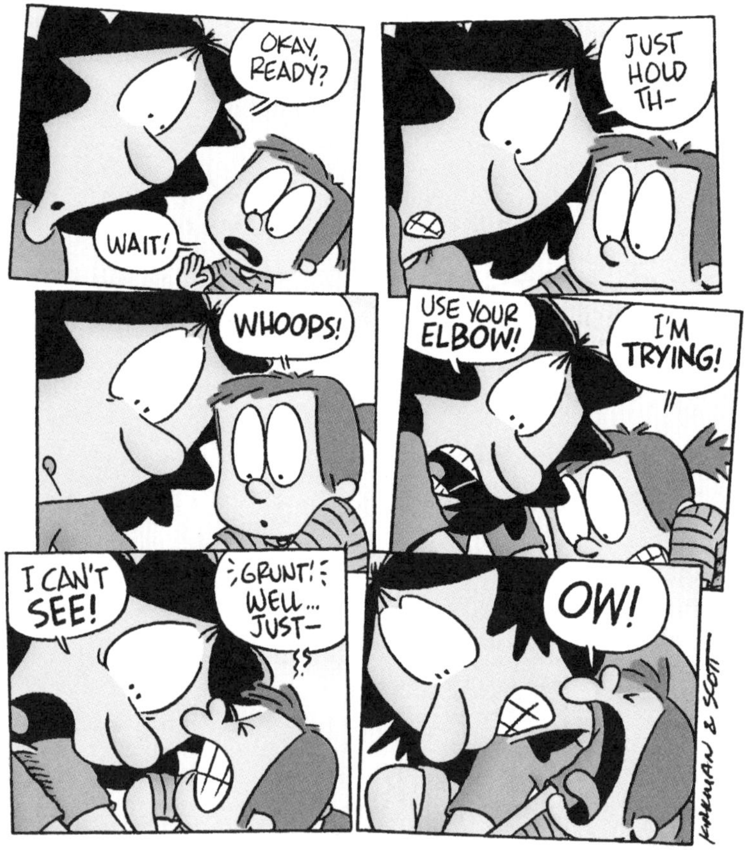
OKAY, READY?
WAIT!
JUST HOLD TH-
WHOOPS!
USE YOUR ELBOW!
I'M TRYING!
I CAN'T SEE!
GRUNT! WELL... JUST-
OW!
KIRKMAN & SCOTT

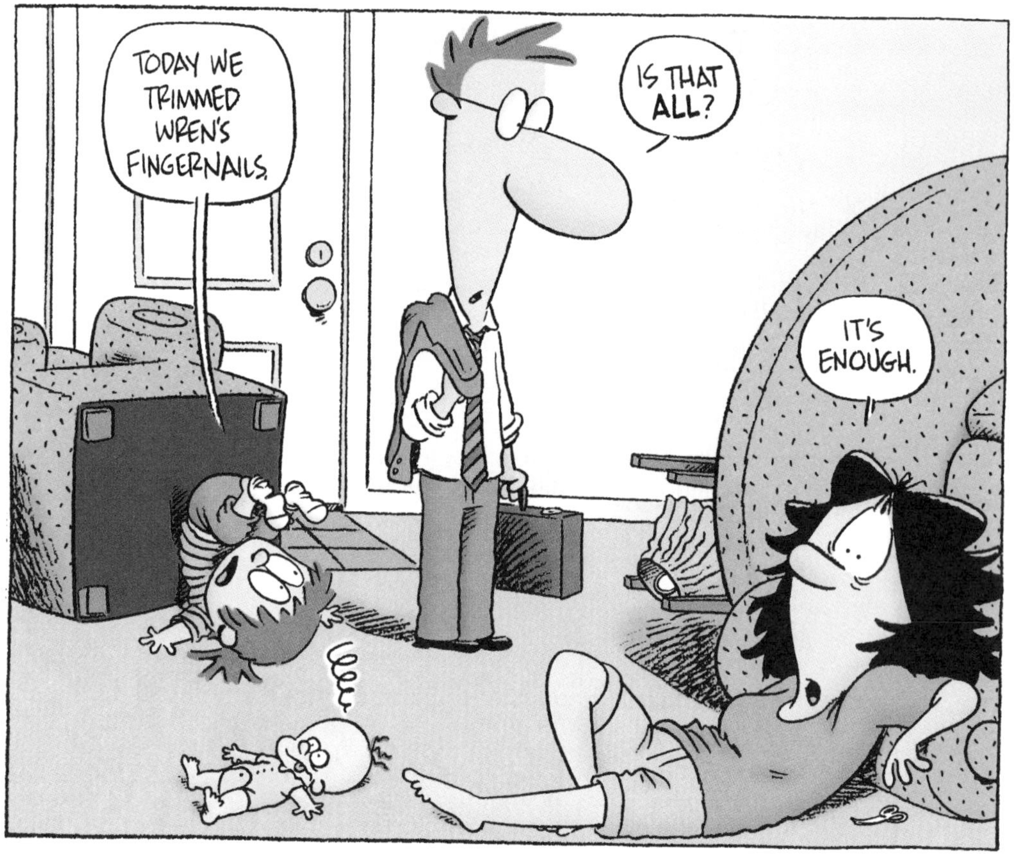
TODAY WE TRIMMED WREN'S FINGERNAILS.
IS THAT ALL?
IT'S ENOUGH.

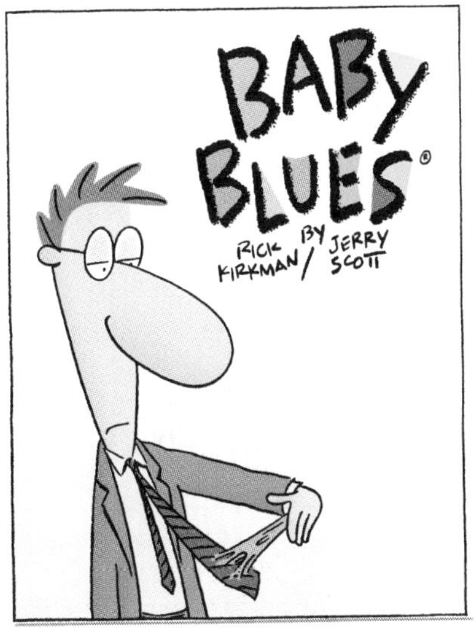
BABY BLUES®
BY RICK KIRKMAN / JERRY SCOTT

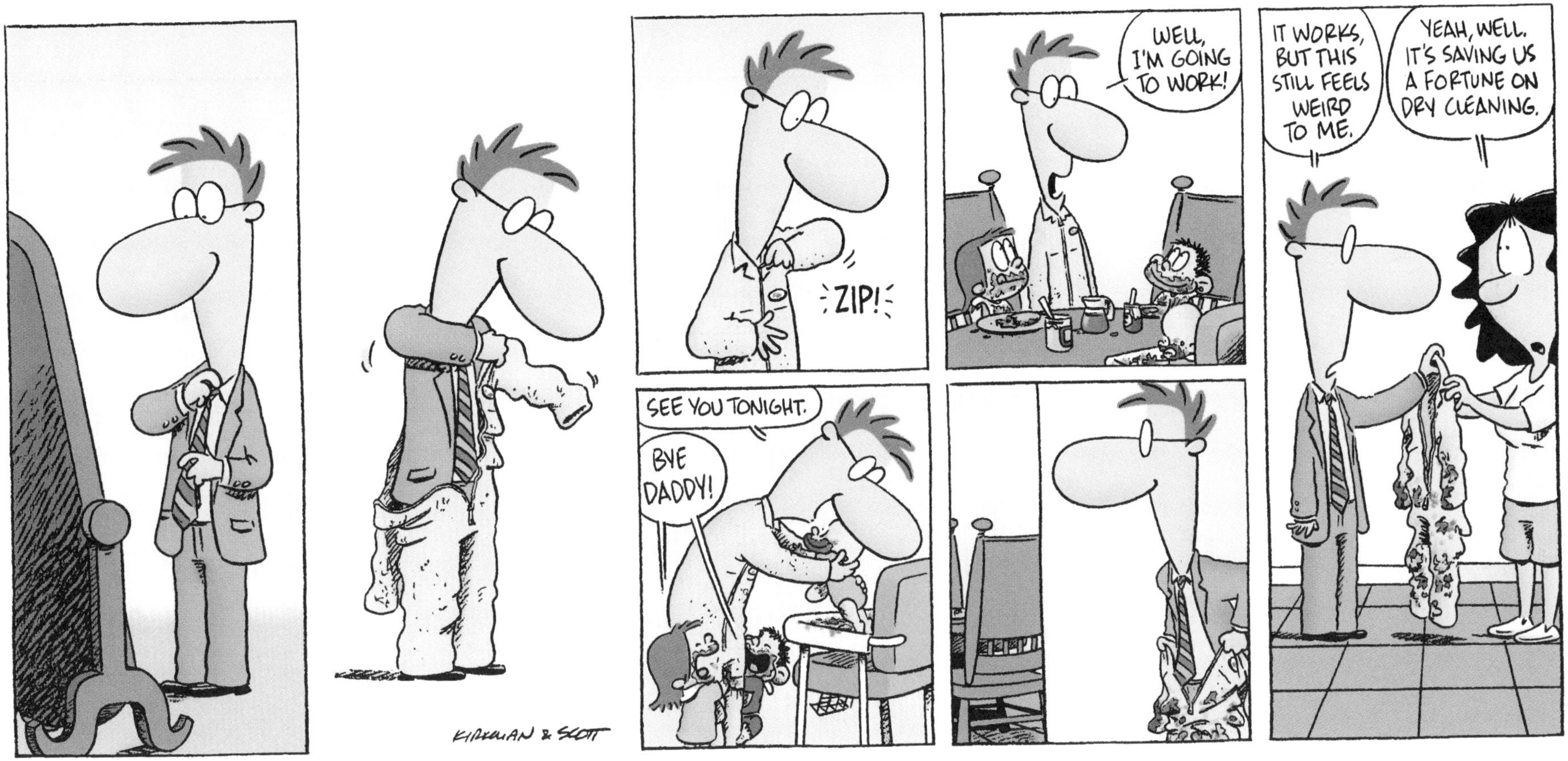
KIRKMAN & SCOTT
ZIP!
WELL, I'M GOING TO WORK!
SEE YOU TONIGHT.
BYE DADDY!
IT WORKS, BUT THIS STILL FEELS WEIRD TO ME.
YEAH, WELL. IT'S SAVING US A FORTUNE ON DRY CLEANING.

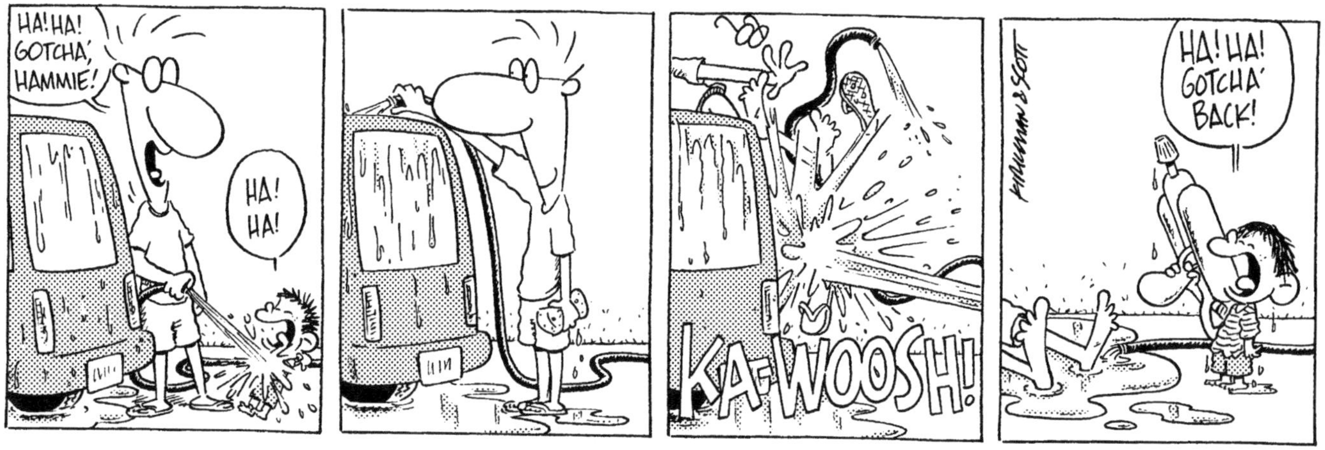
HA! HA! GOTCHA, HAMMIE!
HA! HA!
KA-WOOSH!
HA! HA! GOTCHA BACK!

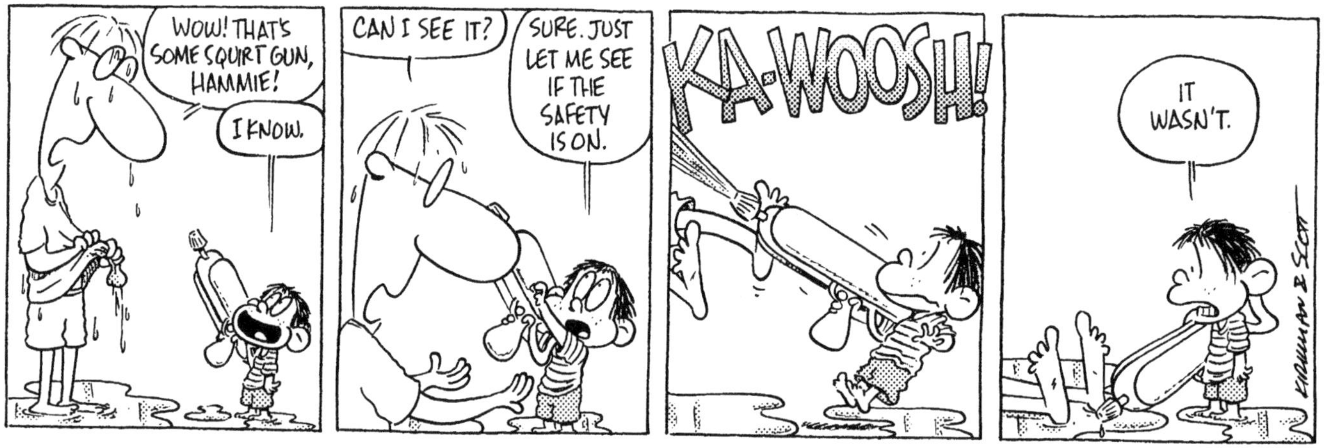
WOW! THAT'S SOME SQUIRT GUN, HAMMIE!
I KNOW.
CAN I SEE IT?
SURE. JUST LET ME SEE IF THE SAFETY IS ON.
KA-WOOSH!
IT WASN'T.

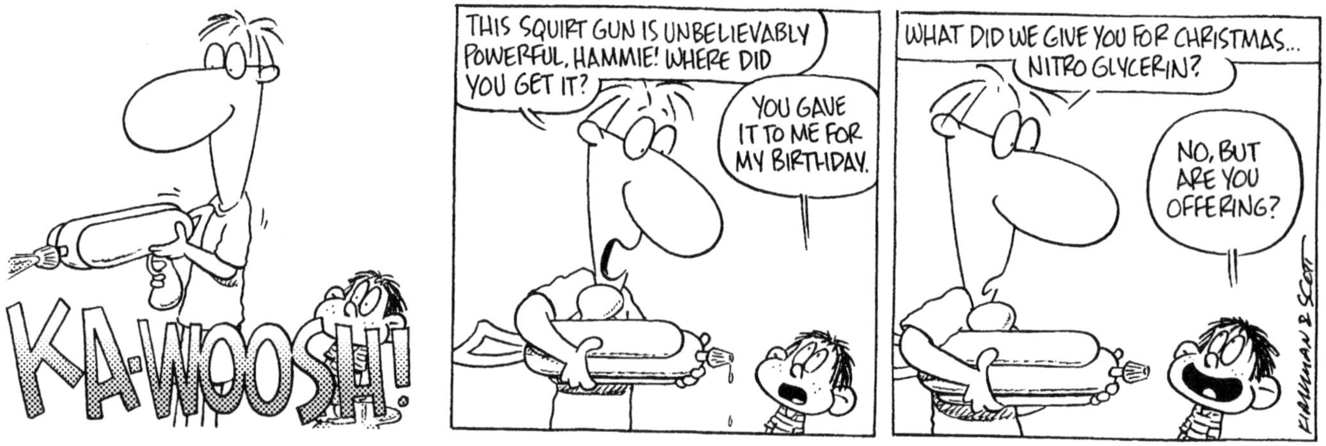
KA-WOOSH!
THIS SQUIRT GUN IS UNBELIEVABLY POWERFUL, HAMMIE! WHERE DID YOU GET IT?
YOU GAVE IT TO ME FOR MY BIRTHDAY.
WHAT DID WE GIVE YOU FOR CHRISTMAS... NITRO GLYCERIN?
NO, BUT ARE YOU OFFERING?

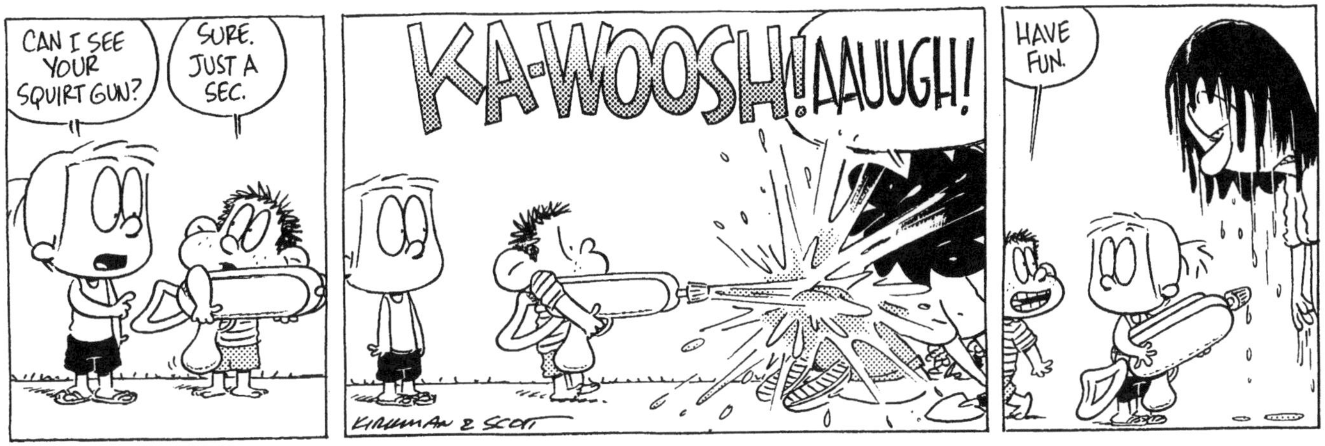
CAN I SEE YOUR SQUIRT GUN?
SURE. JUST A SEC.
KA-WOOSH!
AAUUGH!
HAVE FUN.
KIRKMAN & SCOTT

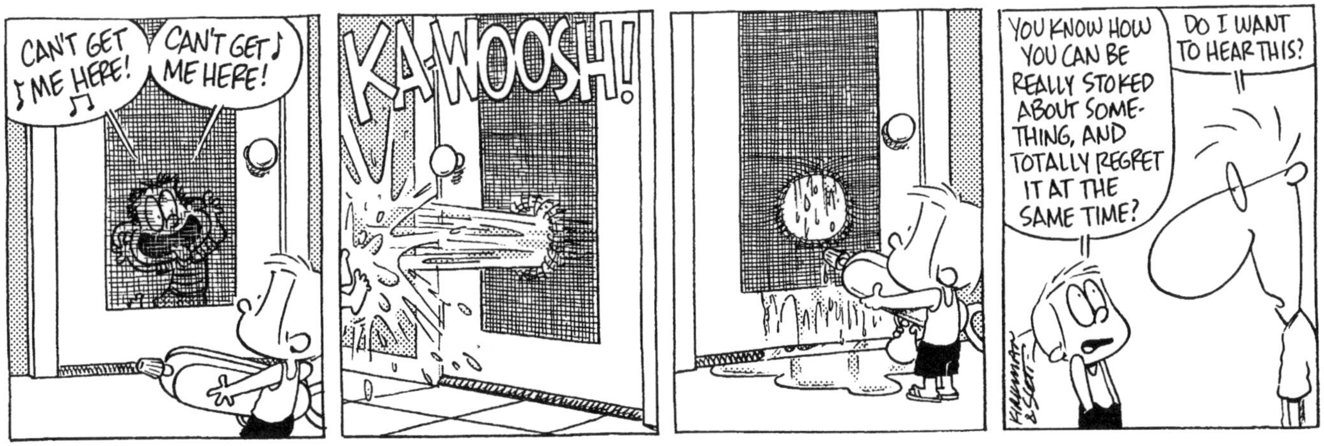
CAN'T GET ME HERE!
CAN'T GET ME HERE!
KA-WOOSH!
YOU KNOW HOW YOU CAN BE REALLY STOKED ABOUT SOME-THING, AND TOTALLY REGRET IT AT THE SAME TIME?
DO I WANT TO HEAR THIS?
KIRKMAN & SCOTT

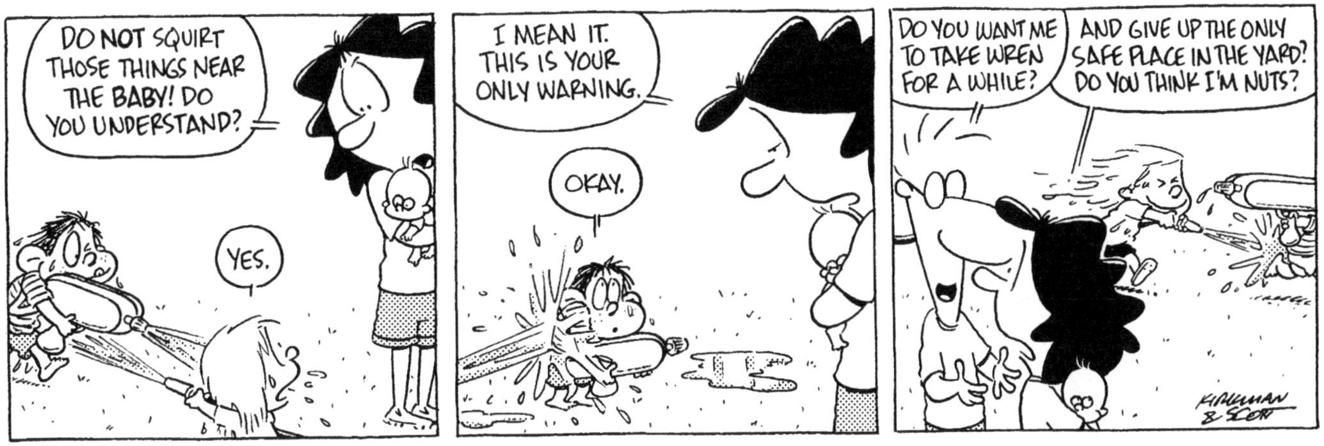
DO NOT SQUIRT THOSE THINGS NEAR THE BABY! DO YOU UNDERSTAND?
YES.
I MEAN IT. THIS IS YOUR ONLY WARNING.
OKAY.
DO YOU WANT ME TO TAKE WREN FOR A WHILE?
AND GIVE UP THE ONLY SAFE PLACE IN THE YARD? DO YOU THINK I'M NUTS?
KIRKMAN & SCOTT

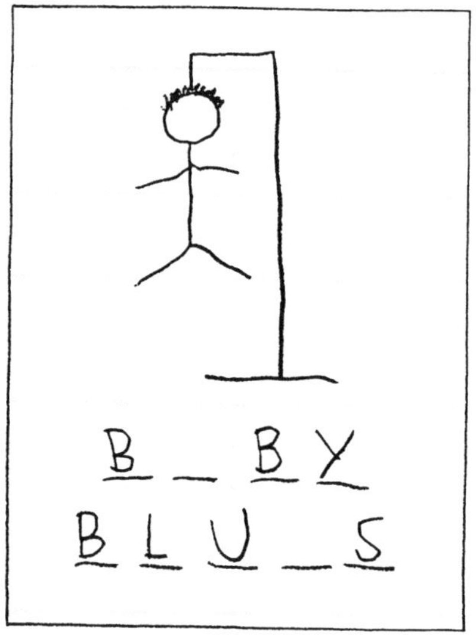
B _ _ B Y
B L U _ _ S

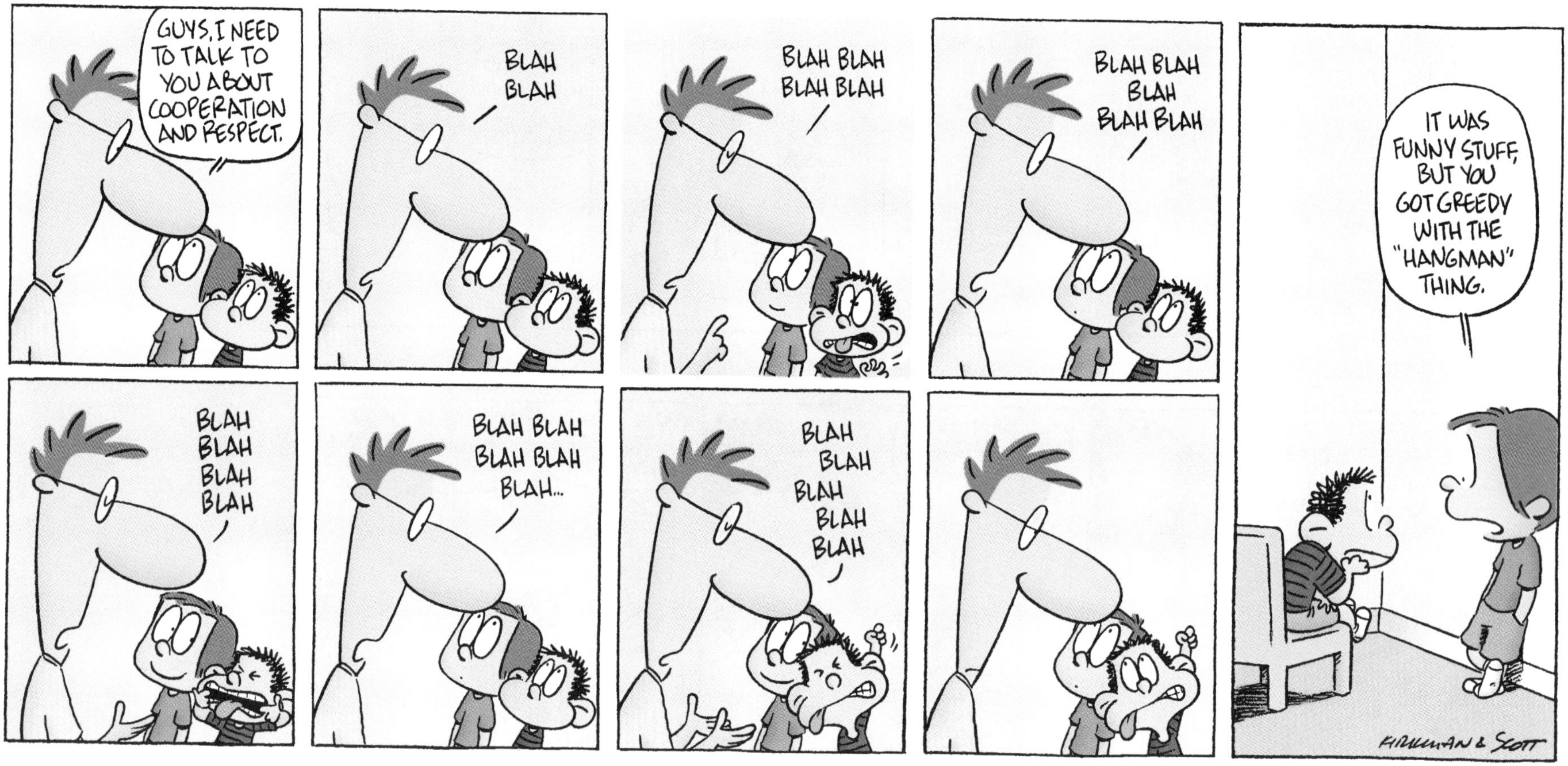
GUYS, I NEED TO TALK TO YOU ABOUT COOPERATION AND RESPECT.
BLAH BLAH
BLAH BLAH BLAH BLAH
BLAH BLAH BLAH BLAH BLAH
BLAH BLAH BLAH BLAH
BLAH BLAH BLAH BLAH BLAH...
BLAH BLAH BLAH BLAH BLAH
IT WAS FUNNY STUFF, BUT YOU GOT GREEDY WITH THE "HANGMAN" THING.
KIRKMAN & SCOTT

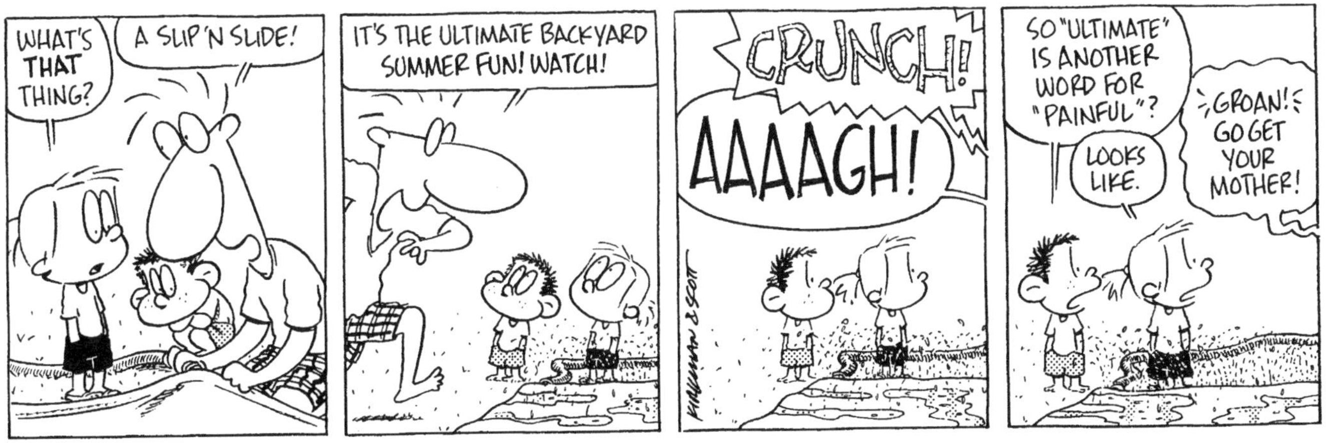
WHAT'S **THAT** THING?
A SLIP 'N SLIDE!
IT'S THE ULTIMATE BACKYARD SUMMER FUN! WATCH!
CRUNCH!
AAAAGH!
SO "ULTIMATE" IS ANOTHER WORD FOR "PAINFUL"?
LOOKS LIKE.
GROAN! GO GET YOUR MOTHER!

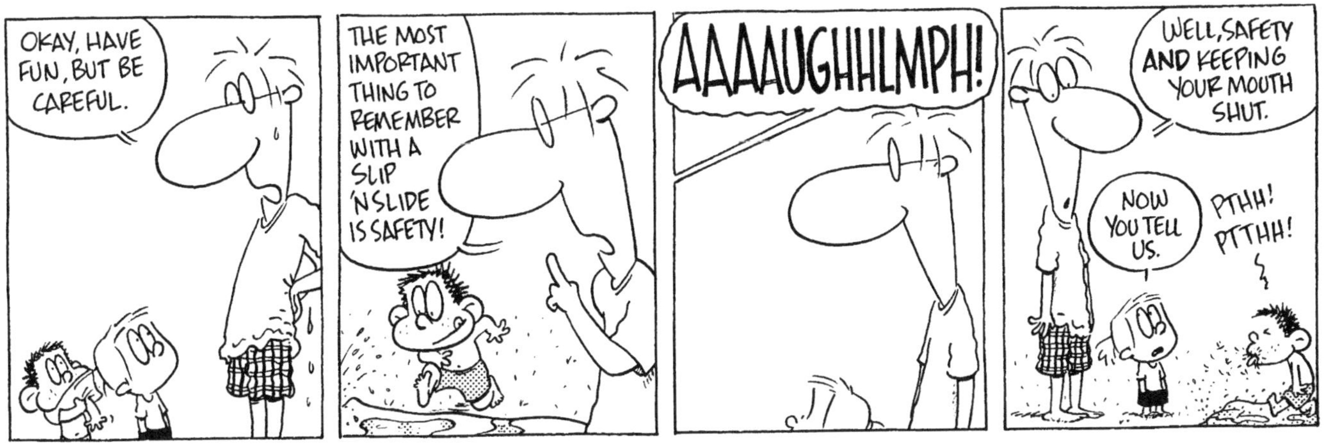
OKAY, HAVE FUN, BUT BE CAREFUL.
THE MOST IMPORTANT THING TO REMEMBER WITH A SLIP 'N SLIDE IS SAFETY!
AAAAUGHHLMPH!
WELL, SAFETY **AND** KEEPING YOUR MOUTH SHUT.
NOW YOU TELL US.
PTHH! PTTHH!

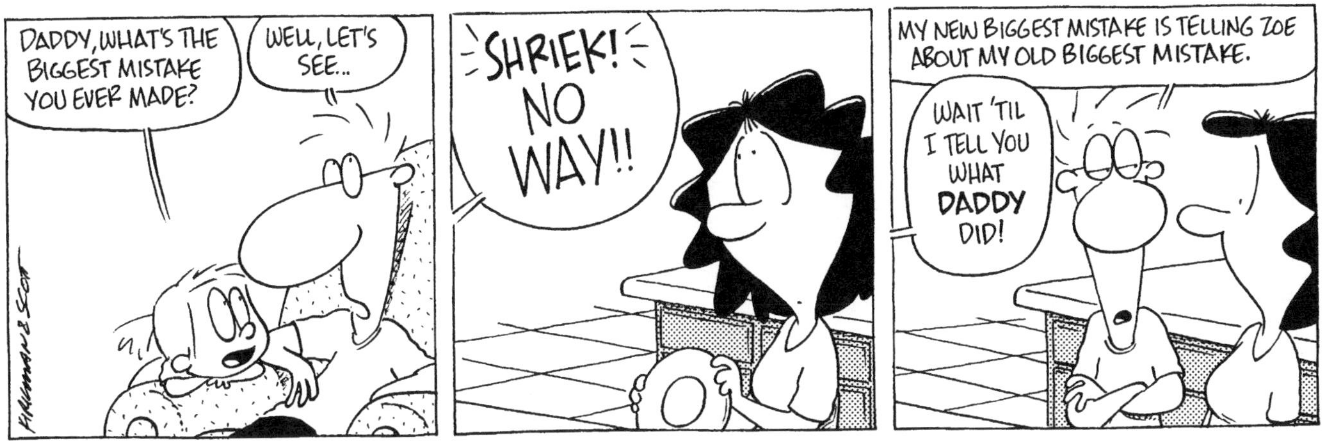
DADDY, WHAT'S THE BIGGEST MISTAKE YOU EVER MADE?
WELL, LET'S SEE...
SHRIEK! NO WAY!!
MY NEW BIGGEST MISTAKE IS TELLING ZOE ABOUT MY OLD BIGGEST MISTAKE.
WAIT 'TIL I TELL YOU WHAT **DADDY** DID!

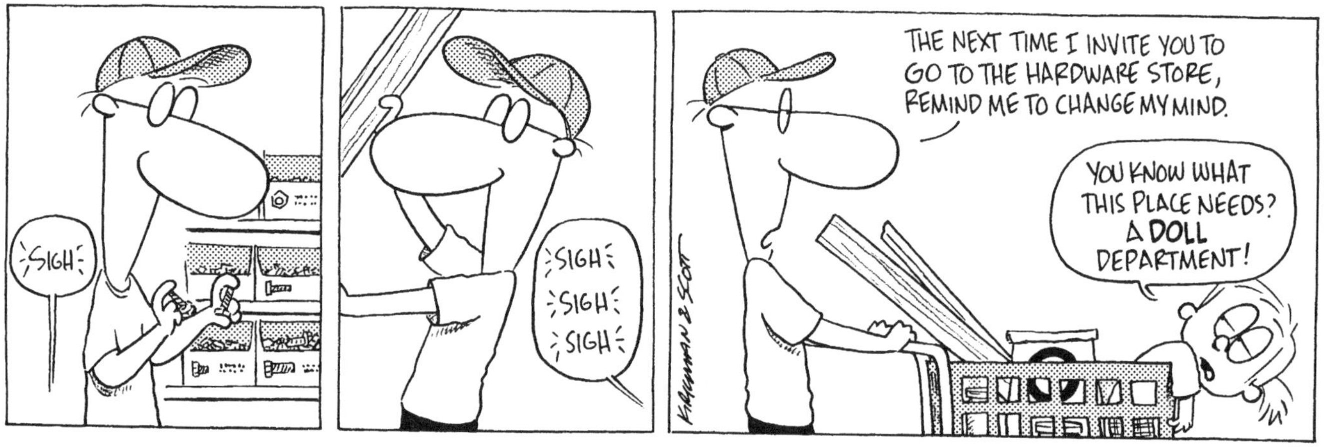
SIGH
SIGH SIGH SIGH
THE NEXT TIME I INVITE YOU TO GO TO THE HARDWARE STORE, REMIND ME TO CHANGE MY MIND.
YOU KNOW WHAT THIS PLACE NEEDS? A **DOLL** DEPARTMENT!
KIRKMAN & SCOTT

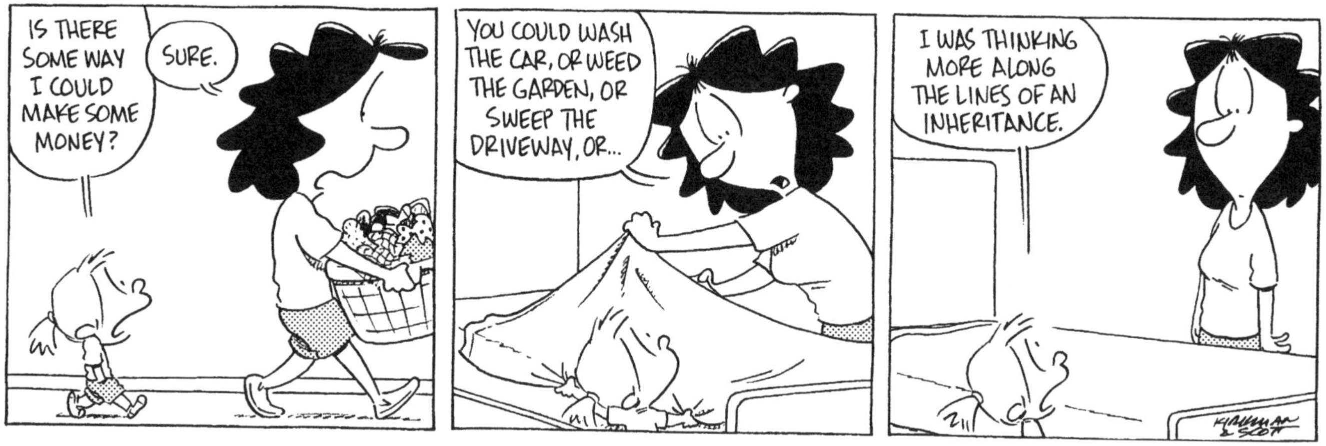
IS THERE SOME WAY I COULD MAKE SOME MONEY?
SURE.
YOU COULD WASH THE CAR, OR WEED THE GARDEN, OR SWEEP THE DRIVEWAY, OR...
I WAS THINKING MORE ALONG THE LINES OF AN INHERITANCE.
KIRKMAN & SCOTT

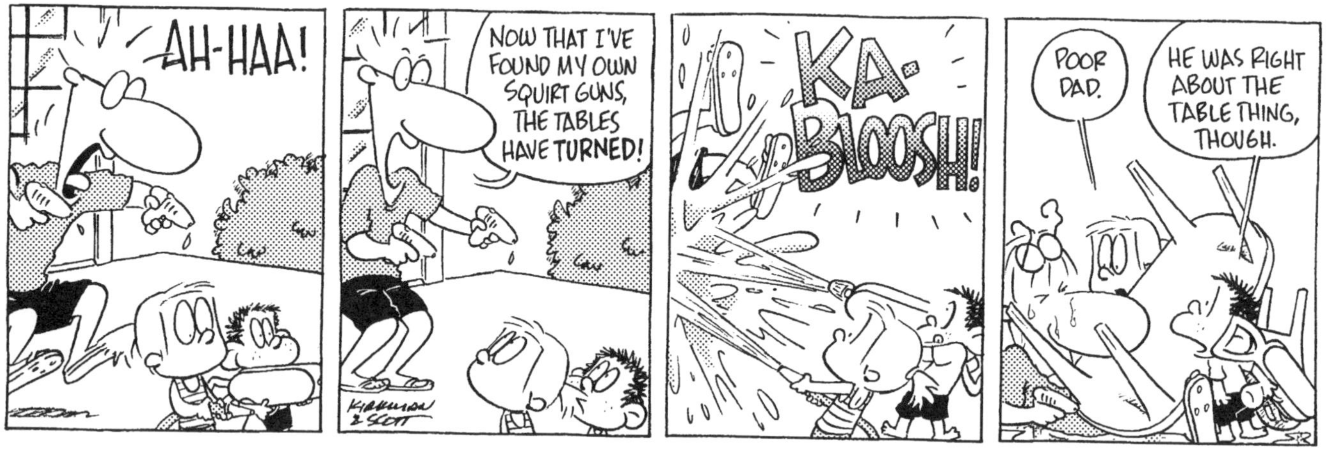
AH-HAA!
NOW THAT I'VE FOUND MY OWN SQUIRT GUNS, THE TABLES HAVE **TURNED**!
KIRKMAN & SCOTT
KA-BLOOSH!
POOR DAD.
HE WAS RIGHT ABOUT THE TABLE THING, THOUGH.

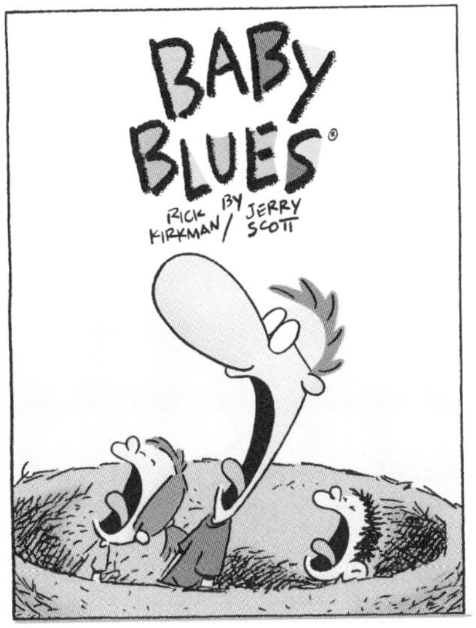
BABY BLUES®
BY RICK KIRKMAN / JERRY SCOTT

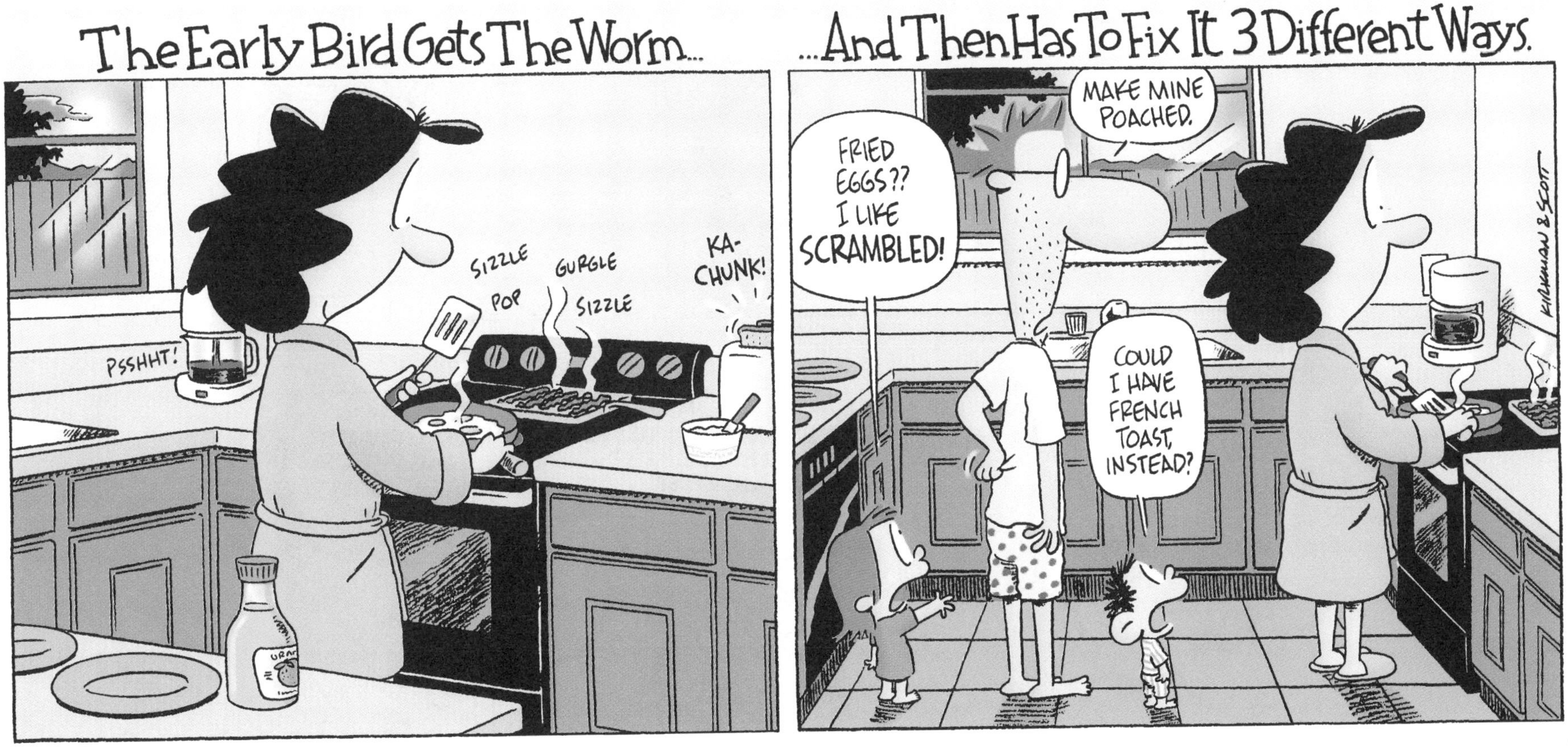
The Early Bird Gets The Worm...
PSSHHT!
SIZZLE
POP
GURGLE
SIZZLE
KA-CHUNK!
...And Then Has To Fix It 3 Different Ways.
FRIED EGGS?? I LIKE SCRAMBLED!
MAKE MINE POACHED.
COULD I HAVE FRENCH TOAST, INSTEAD?
KIRKMAN & SCOTT

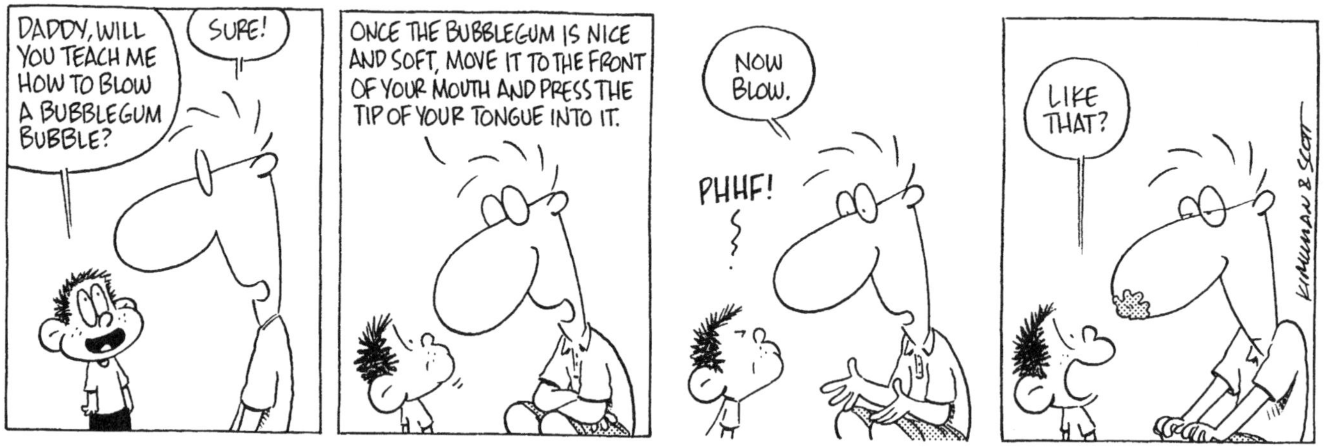
DADDY, WILL YOU TEACH ME HOW TO BLOW A BUBBLEGUM BUBBLE?
SURE!
ONCE THE BUBBLEGUM IS NICE AND SOFT, MOVE IT TO THE FRONT OF YOUR MOUTH AND PRESS THE TIP OF YOUR TONGUE INTO IT.
NOW BLOW.
PHHF!
LIKE THAT?
KIRKMAN & SCOTT

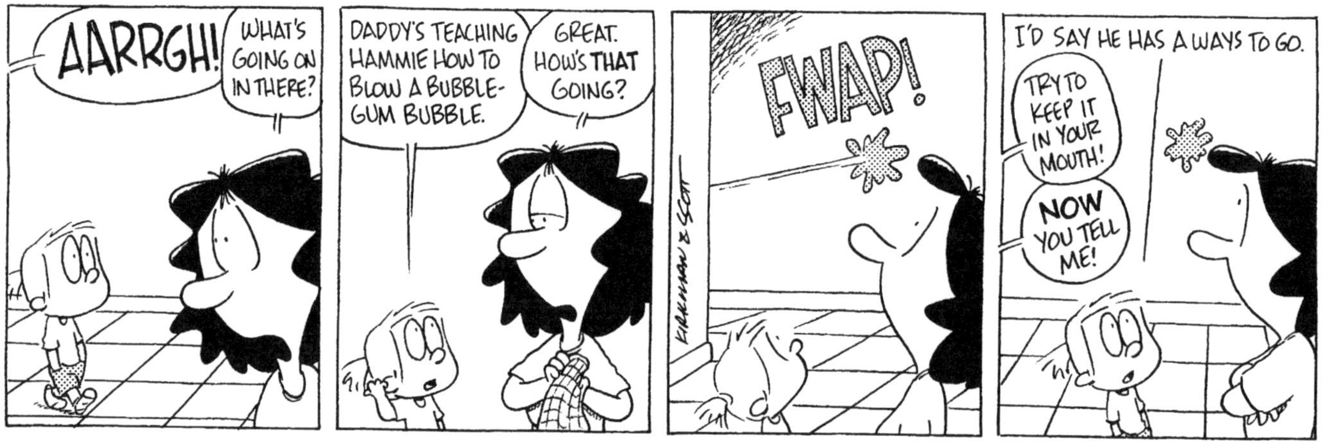
AARRGH!
WHAT'S GOING ON IN THERE?
DADDY'S TEACHING HAMMIE HOW TO BLOW A BUBBLE-GUM BUBBLE.
GREAT. HOW'S THAT GOING?
KIRKMAN & SCOTT
FWAP!
I'D SAY HE HAS A WAYS TO GO.
TRY TO KEEP IT IN YOUR MOUTH!
NOW YOU TELL ME!

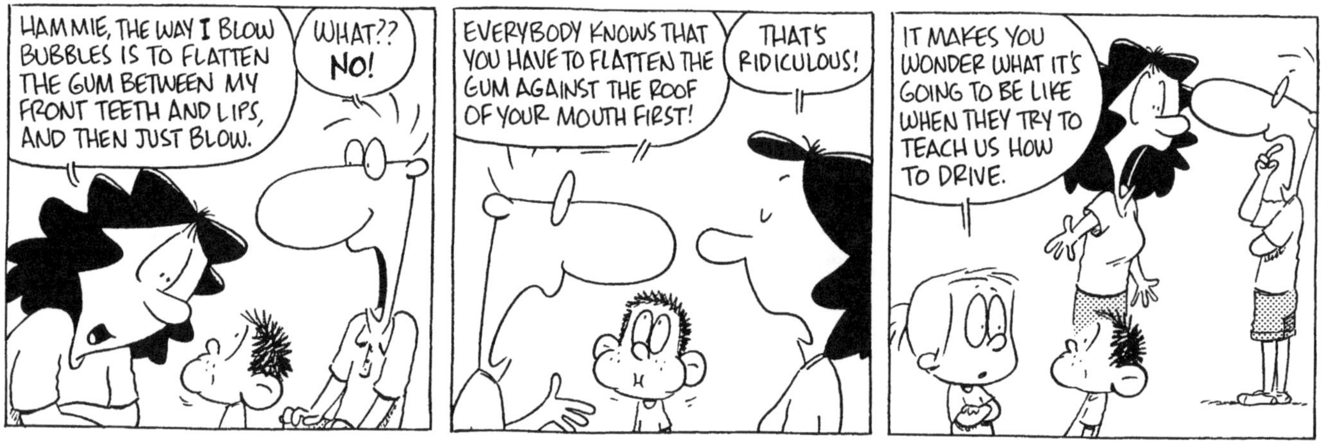
HAMMIE, THE WAY I BLOW BUBBLES IS TO FLATTEN THE GUM BETWEEN MY FRONT TEETH AND LIPS, AND THEN JUST BLOW.
WHAT?? NO!
EVERYBODY KNOWS THAT YOU HAVE TO FLATTEN THE GUM AGAINST THE ROOF OF YOUR MOUTH FIRST!
THAT'S RIDICULOUS!
IT MAKES YOU WONDER WHAT IT'S GOING TO BE LIKE WHEN THEY TRY TO TEACH US HOW TO DRIVE.

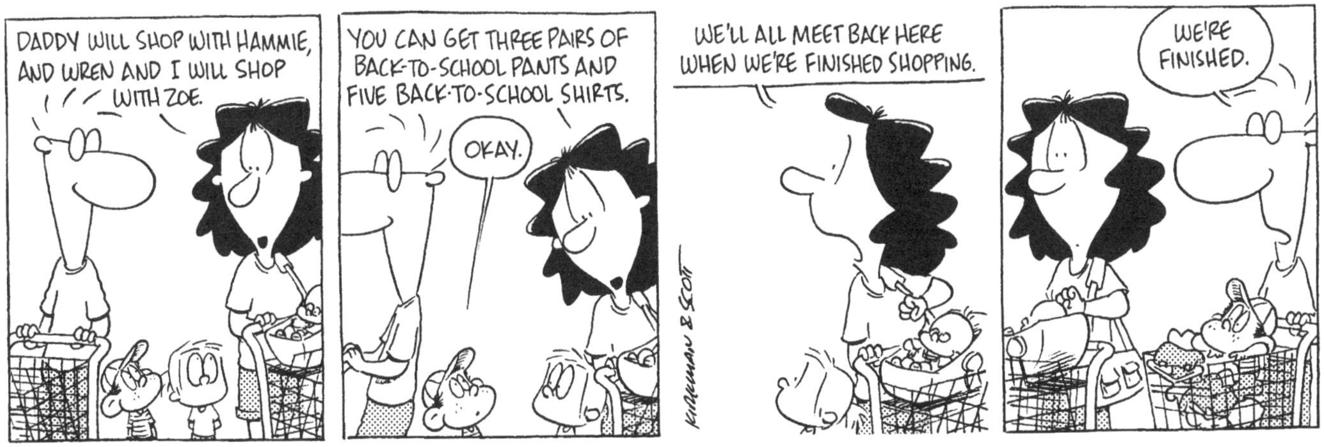
DADDY WILL SHOP WITH HAMMIE, AND WREN AND I WILL SHOP WITH ZOE.
YOU CAN GET THREE PAIRS OF BACK-TO-SCHOOL PANTS AND FIVE BACK-TO-SCHOOL SHIRTS.
OKAY.
KIRKMAN & SCOTT
WE'LL ALL MEET BACK HERE WHEN WE'RE FINISHED SHOPPING.
WE'RE FINISHED.

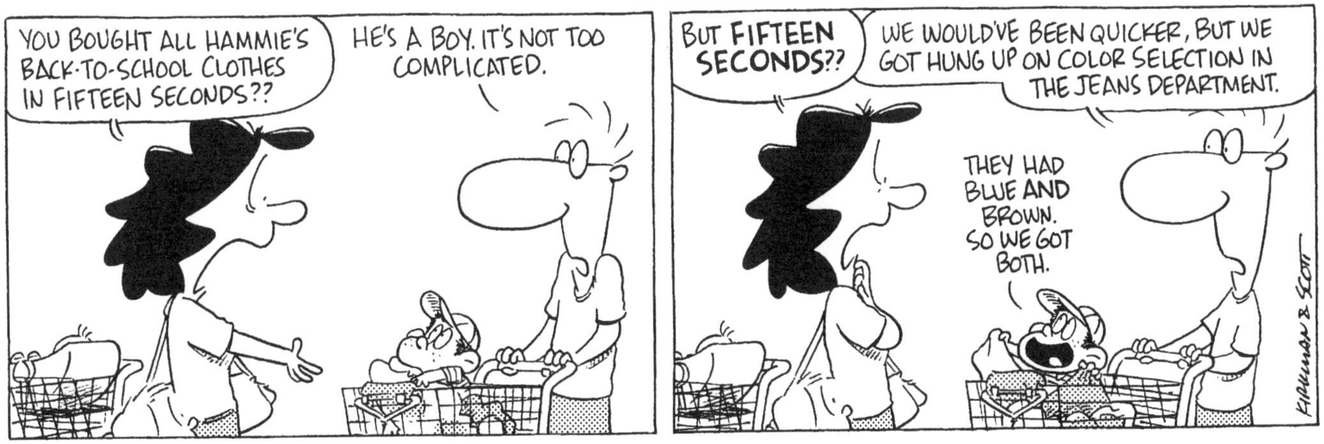
YOU BOUGHT ALL HAMMIE'S BACK-TO-SCHOOL CLOTHES IN FIFTEEN SECONDS??
HE'S A BOY. IT'S NOT TOO COMPLICATED.
BUT **FIFTEEN SECONDS**??
WE WOULD'VE BEEN QUICKER, BUT WE GOT HUNG UP ON COLOR SELECTION IN THE JEANS DEPARTMENT.
THEY HAD BLUE **AND** BROWN. SO WE GOT BOTH.
KIRKMAN & SCOTT

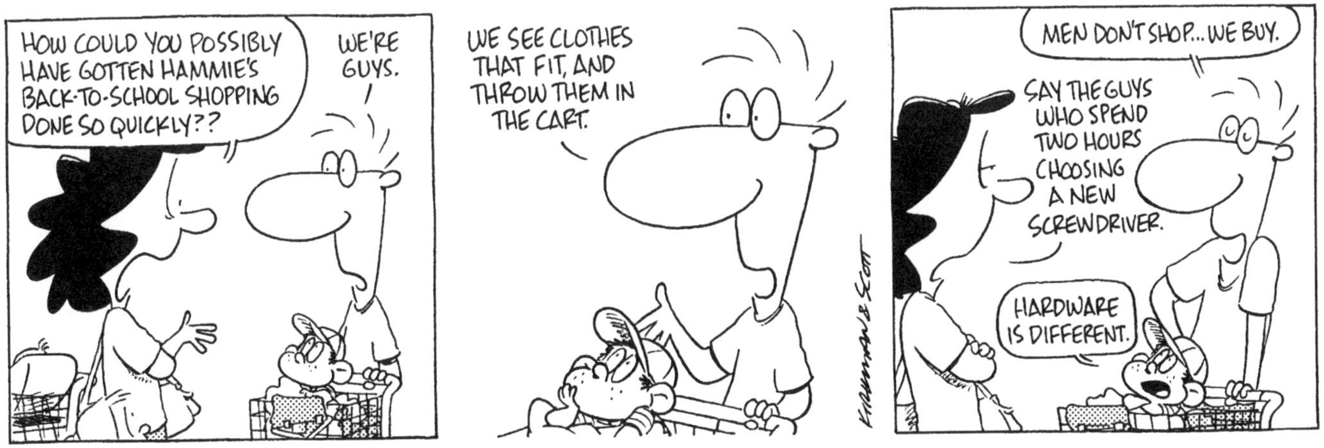
HOW COULD YOU POSSIBLY HAVE GOTTEN HAMMIE'S BACK-TO-SCHOOL SHOPPING DONE SO QUICKLY??
WE'RE GUYS.
WE SEE CLOTHES THAT FIT, AND THROW THEM IN THE CART.
KIRKMAN & SCOTT
MEN DON'T SHOP... WE BUY.
SAY THE GUYS WHO SPEND TWO HOURS CHOOSING A NEW SCREWDRIVER.
HARDWARE IS DIFFERENT.

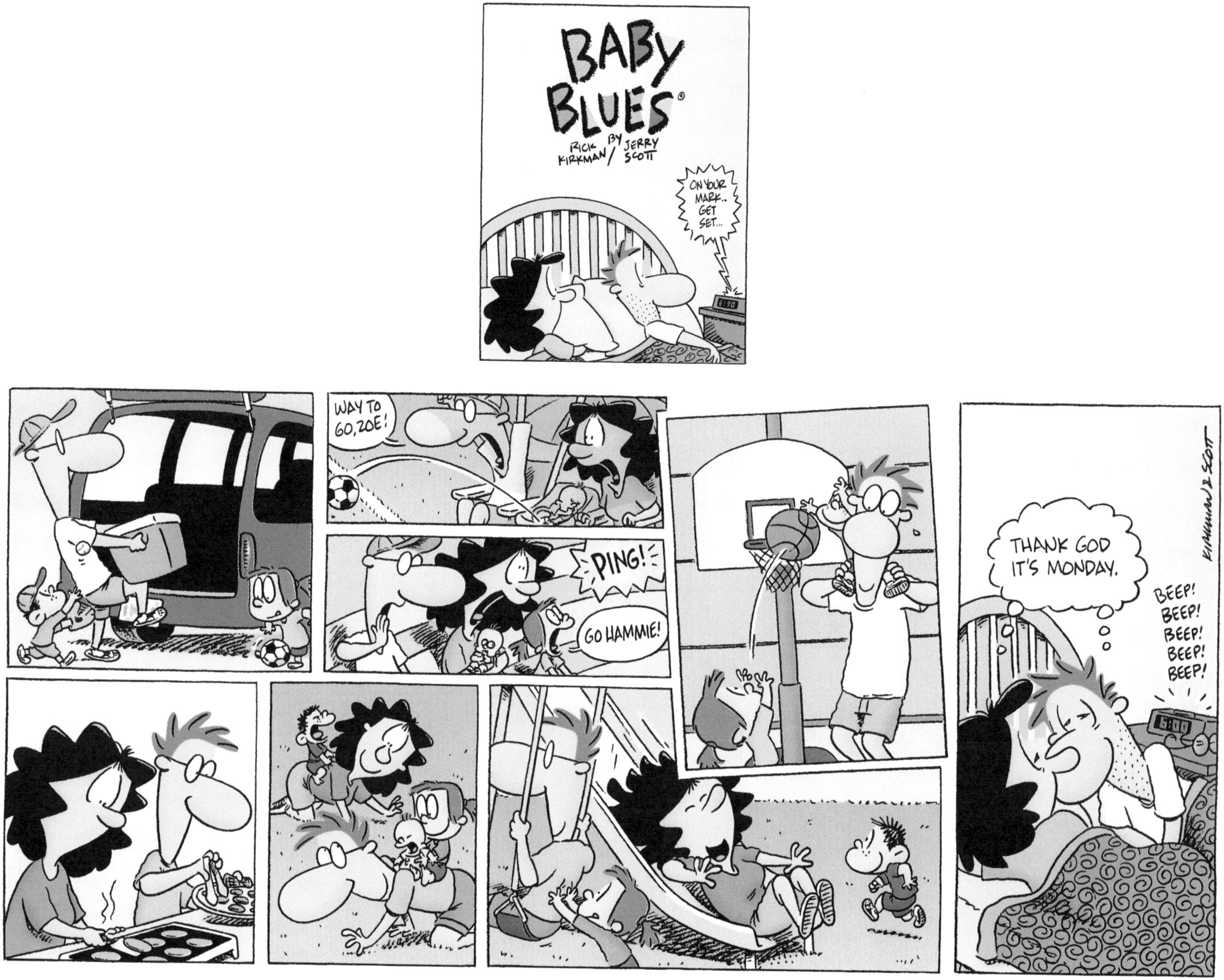
BABY BLUES®
BY RICK KIRKMAN / JERRY SCOTT
ON YOUR MARK.. GET SET...
WAY TO GO, ZOE!
PING!
GO HAMMIE!
THANK GOD IT'S MONDAY.
BEEP! BEEP! BEEP! BEEP! BEEP!
KIRKMAN & SCOTT

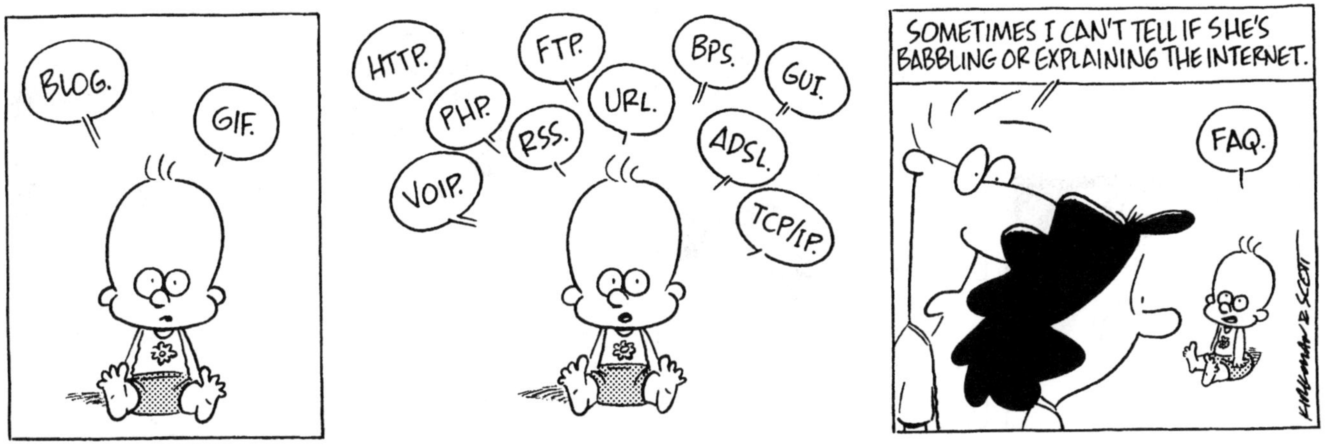
BLOG.
GIF.
HTTP.
PHP.
VOIP.
FTP.
RSS.
URL.
BPS.
GUI.
ADSL.
TCP/IP.
SOMETIMES I CAN'T TELL IF SHE'S BABBLING OR EXPLAINING THE INTERNET.
FAQ.

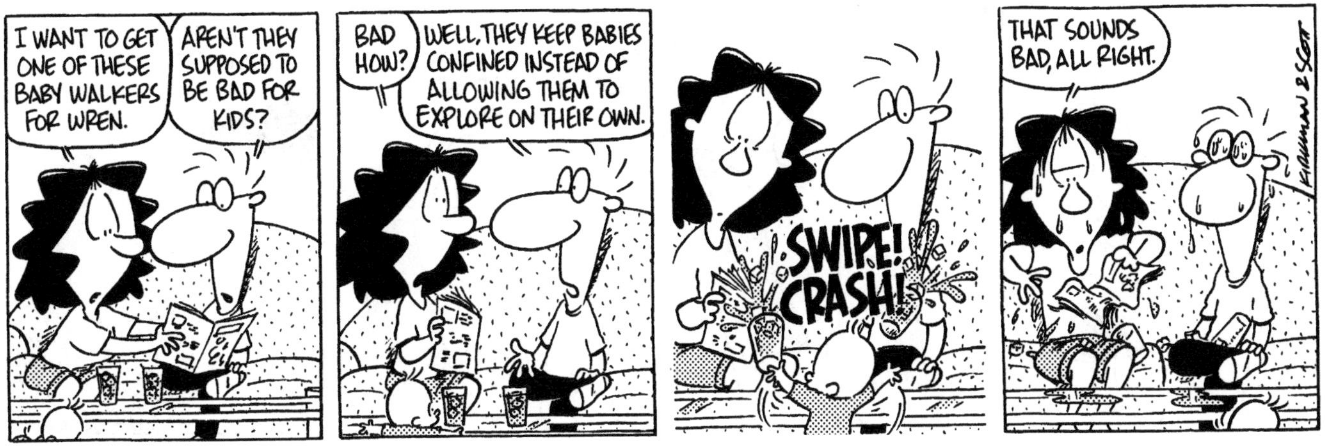
I WANT TO GET ONE OF THESE BABY WALKERS FOR WREN.
AREN'T THEY SUPPOSED TO BE BAD FOR KIDS?
BAD HOW?
WELL, THEY KEEP BABIES CONFINED INSTEAD OF ALLOWING THEM TO EXPLORE ON THEIR OWN.
SWIPE! CRASH!
THAT SOUNDS BAD, ALL RIGHT.

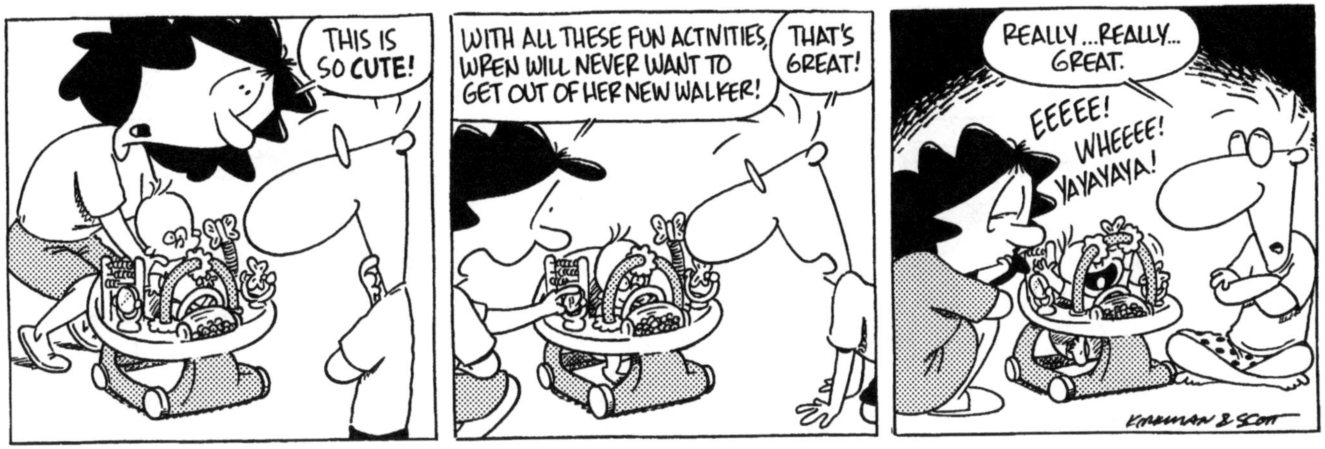
THIS IS SO **CUTE**!
WITH ALL THESE FUN ACTIVITIES, WREN WILL NEVER WANT TO GET OUT OF HER NEW WALKER!
THAT'S GREAT!
REALLY... REALLY... GREAT.
EEEEE! WHEEEE! YAYAYAYA!

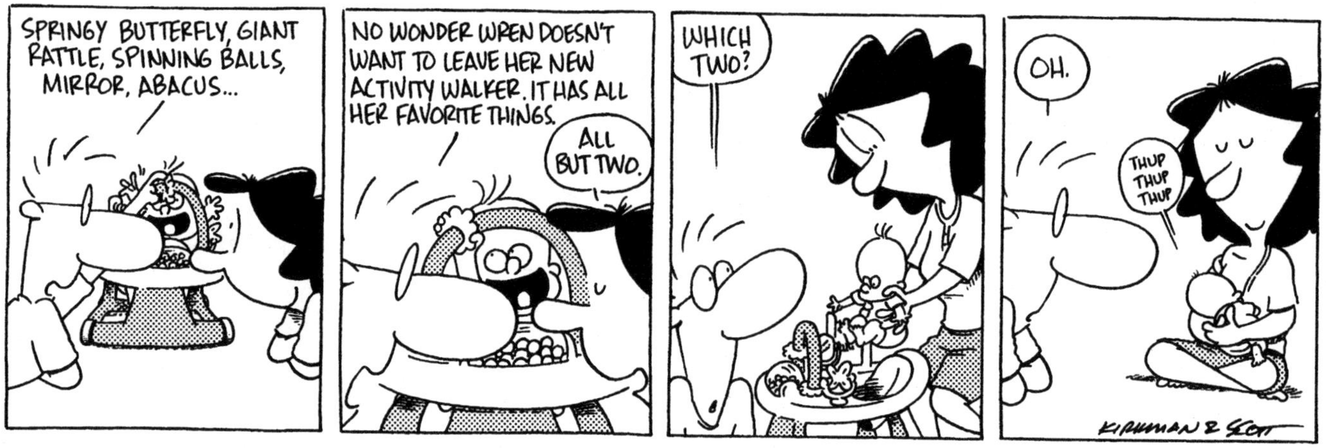
SPRINGY BUTTERFLY, GIANT RATTLE, SPINNING BALLS, MIRROR, ABACUS...
NO WONDER WREN DOESN'T WANT TO LEAVE HER NEW ACTIVITY WALKER. IT HAS ALL HER FAVORITE THINGS.
ALL BUT TWO.
WHICH TWO?
OH.
THUP THUP THUP
KIRKMAN & SCOTT

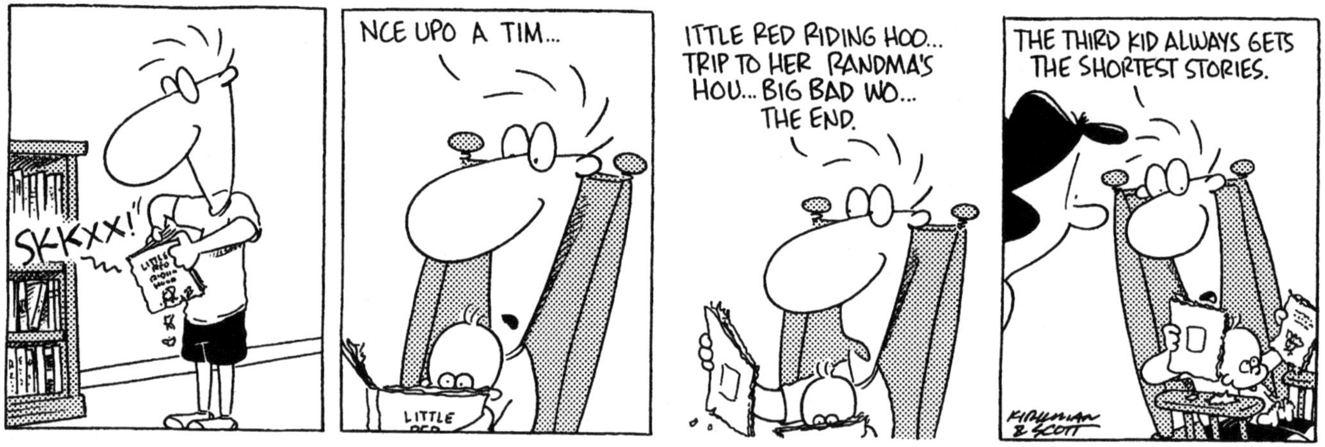
SKKXX!
NCE UPO A TIM...
LITTLE
ITTLE RED RIDING HOO... TRIP TO HER RANDMA'S HOU... BIG BAD WO... THE END.
THE THIRD KID ALWAYS GETS THE SHORTEST STORIES.
KIRKMAN & SCOTT

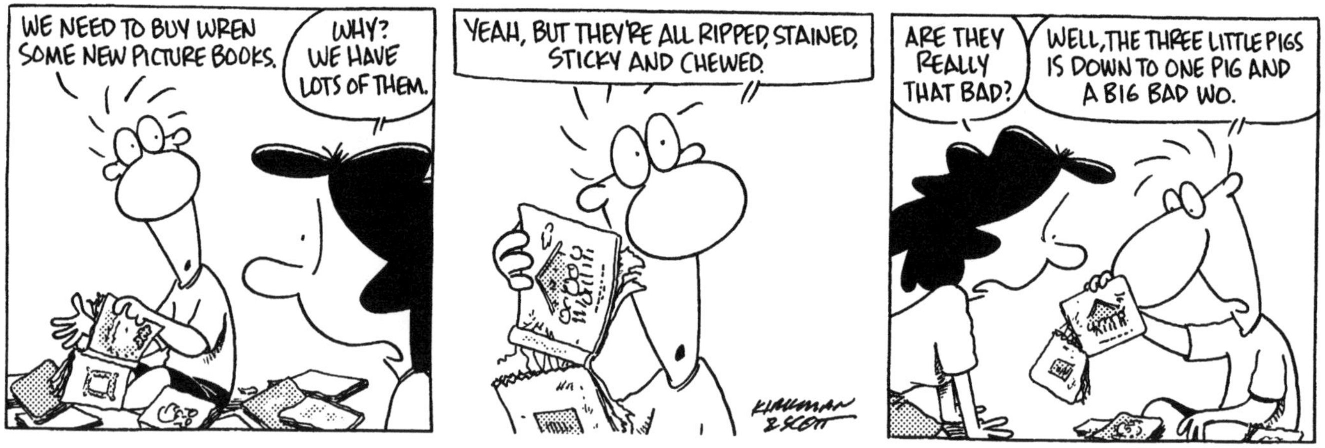
WE NEED TO BUY WREN SOME NEW PICTURE BOOKS.
WHY? WE HAVE LOTS OF THEM.
YEAH, BUT THEY'RE ALL RIPPED, STAINED, STICKY AND CHEWED.
KIRKMAN & SCOTT
ARE THEY REALLY THAT BAD?
WELL, THE THREE LITTLE PIGS IS DOWN TO ONE PIG AND A BIG BAD WO.

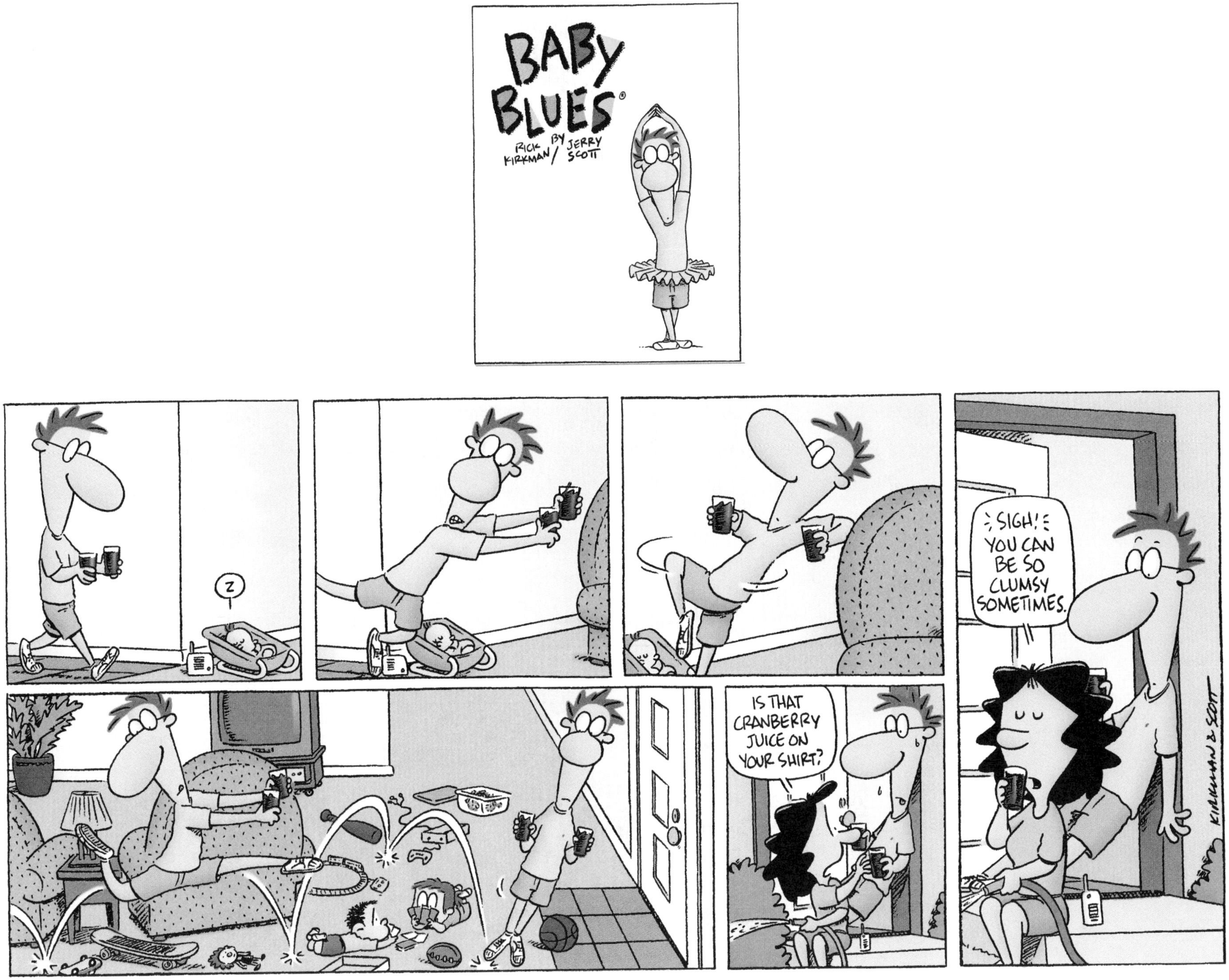
BABY BLUES®
RICK KIRKMAN / JERRY SCOTT
Z
IS THAT CRANBERRY JUICE ON YOUR SHIRT?
SIGH! YOU CAN BE SO CLUMSY SOMETIMES.
KIRKMAN & SCOTT

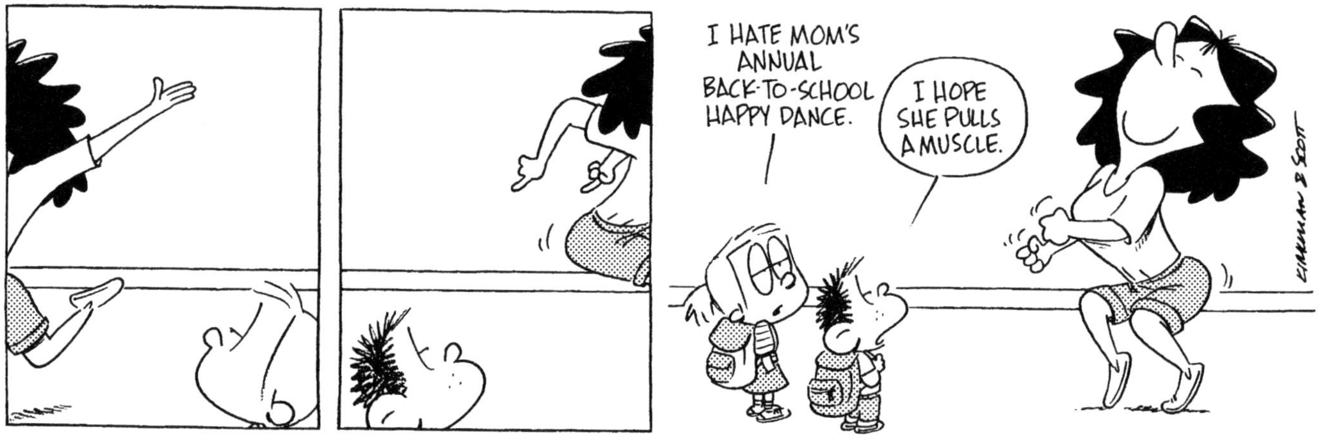
I HATE MOM'S ANNUAL BACK-TO-SCHOOL HAPPY DANCE.
I HOPE SHE PULLS A MUSCLE.

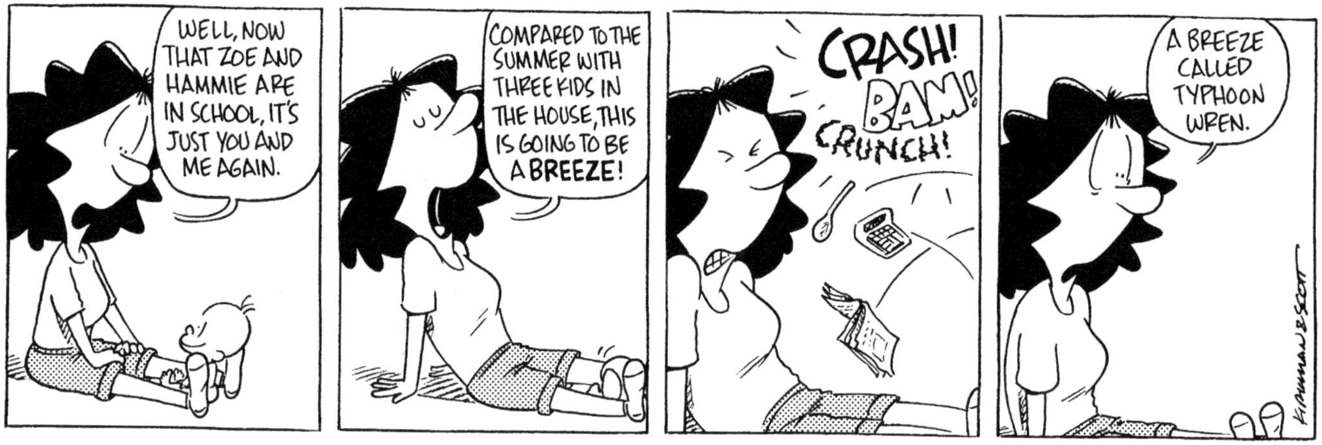
WELL, NOW THAT ZOE AND HAMMIE ARE IN SCHOOL, IT'S JUST YOU AND ME AGAIN.
COMPARED TO THE SUMMER WITH THREE KIDS IN THE HOUSE, THIS IS GOING TO BE A BREEZE!
CRASH!
BAM!
CRUNCH!
A BREEZE CALLED TYPHOON WREN.

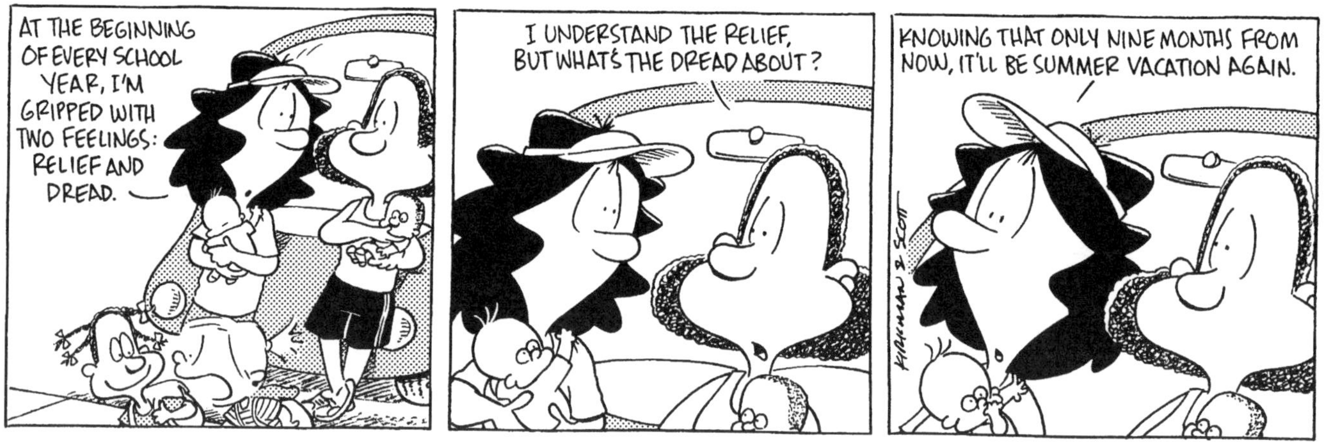
AT THE BEGINNING OF EVERY SCHOOL YEAR, I'M GRIPPED WITH TWO FEELINGS: RELIEF AND DREAD.
I UNDERSTAND THE RELIEF, BUT WHAT'S THE DREAD ABOUT?
KNOWING THAT ONLY NINE MONTHS FROM NOW, IT'LL BE SUMMER VACATION AGAIN.

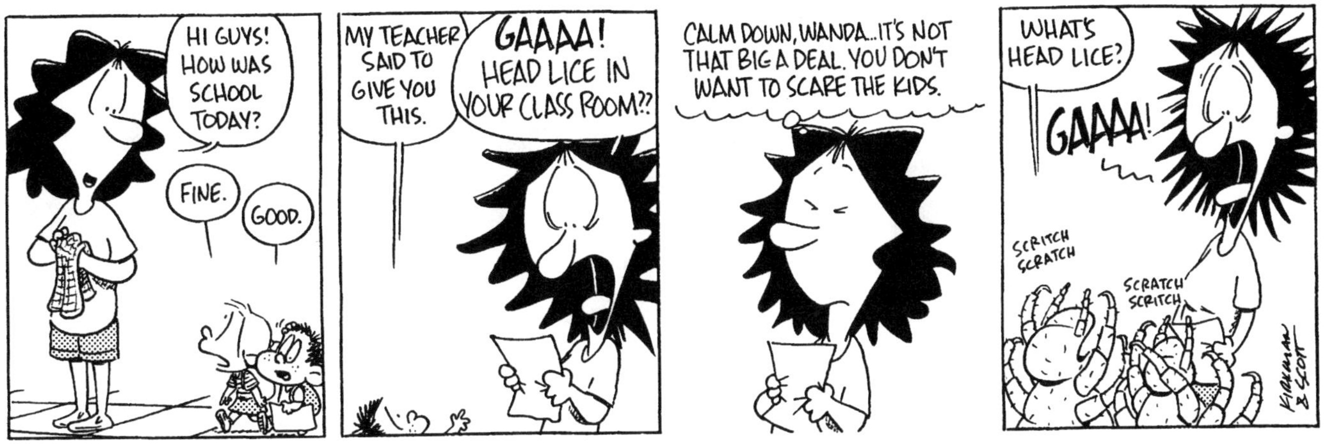
HI GUYS! HOW WAS SCHOOL TODAY?
FINE.
GOOD.
MY TEACHER SAID TO GIVE YOU THIS.
GAAAA! HEAD LICE IN YOUR CLASS ROOM??
CALM DOWN, WANDA...IT'S NOT THAT BIG A DEAL. YOU DON'T WANT TO SCARE THE KIDS.
WHAT'S HEAD LICE?
GAAAA!
SCRITCH SCRATCH
SCRATCH SCRITCH
KIRKMAN & SCOTT

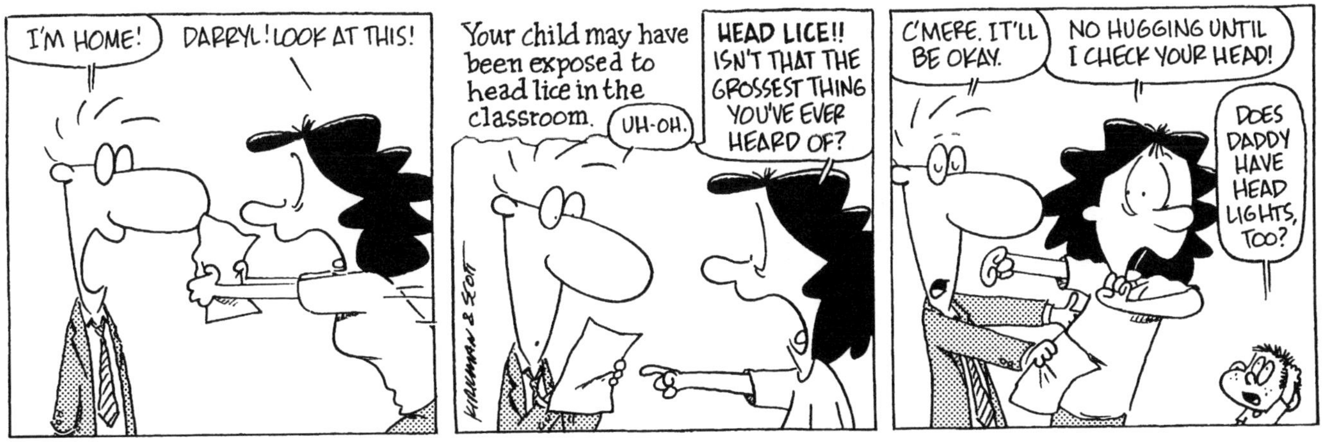
I'M HOME!
DARRYL! LOOK AT THIS!
Your child may have been exposed to head lice in the classroom.
UH-OH.
HEAD LICE!! ISN'T THAT THE GROSSEST THING YOU'VE EVER HEARD OF?
KIRKMAN & SCOTT
C'MERE. IT'LL BE OKAY.
NO HUGGING UNTIL I CHECK YOUR HEAD!
DOES DADDY HAVE HEAD LIGHTS, TOO?

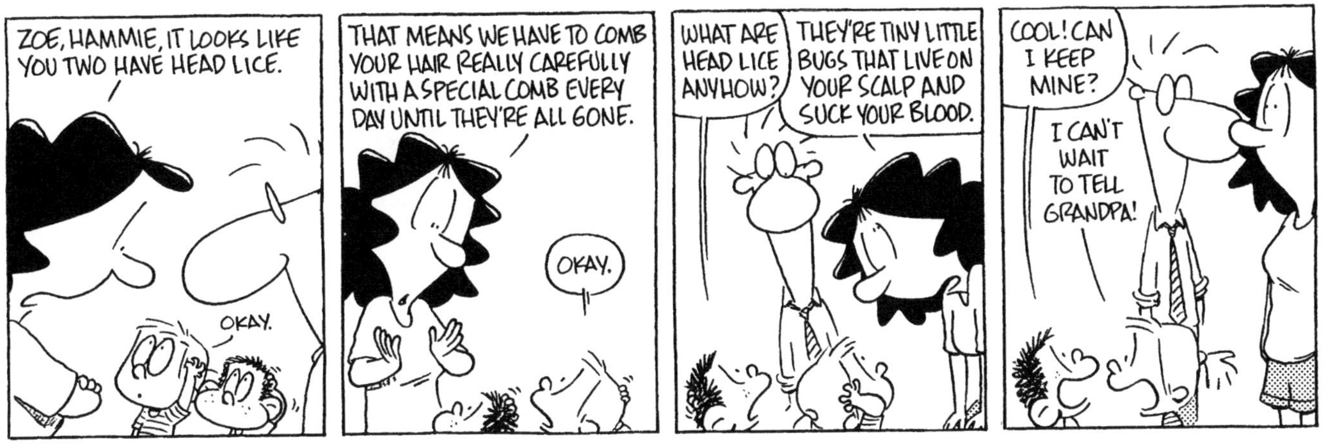
ZOE, HAMMIE, IT LOOKS LIKE YOU TWO HAVE HEAD LICE.
OKAY.
THAT MEANS WE HAVE TO COMB YOUR HAIR REALLY CAREFULLY WITH A SPECIAL COMB EVERY DAY UNTIL THEY'RE ALL GONE.
OKAY.
WHAT ARE HEAD LICE ANYHOW?
THEY'RE TINY LITTLE BUGS THAT LIVE ON YOUR SCALP AND SUCK YOUR BLOOD.
COOL! CAN I KEEP MINE?
I CAN'T WAIT TO TELL GRANDPA!

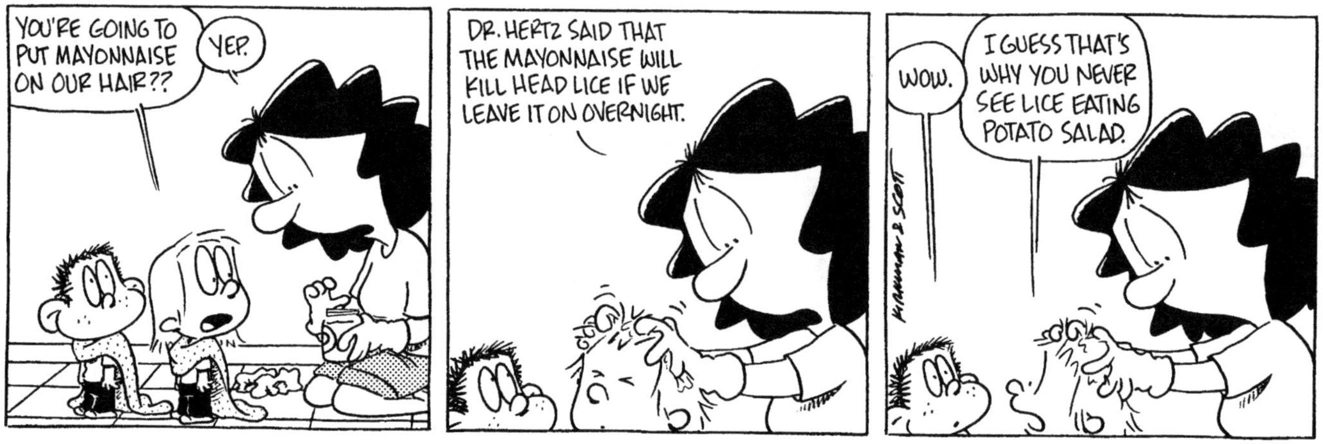
YOU'RE GOING TO PUT MAYONNAISE ON OUR HAIR??
YEP.
DR. HERTZ SAID THAT THE MAYONNAISE WILL KILL HEAD LICE IF WE LEAVE IT ON OVERNIGHT.
WOW.
I GUESS THAT'S WHY YOU NEVER SEE LICE EATING POTATO SALAD.

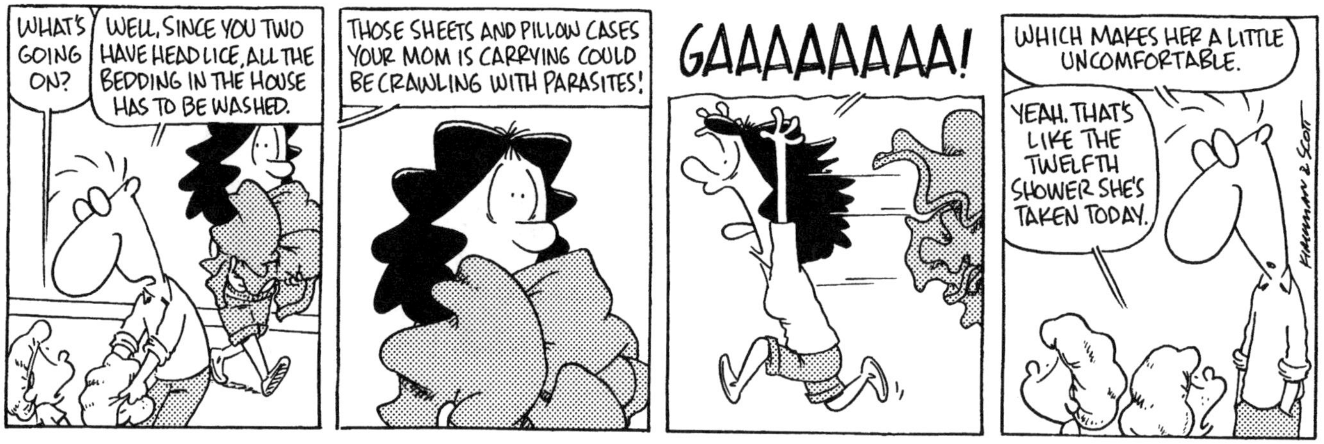
WHAT'S GOING ON?
WELL, SINCE YOU TWO HAVE HEAD LICE, ALL THE BEDDING IN THE HOUSE HAS TO BE WASHED.
THOSE SHEETS AND PILLOW CASES YOUR MOM IS CARRYING COULD BE CRAWLING WITH PARASITES!
GAAAAAAAA!
WHICH MAKES HER A LITTLE UNCOMFORTABLE.
YEAH. THAT'S LIKE THE TWELFTH SHOWER SHE'S TAKEN TODAY.

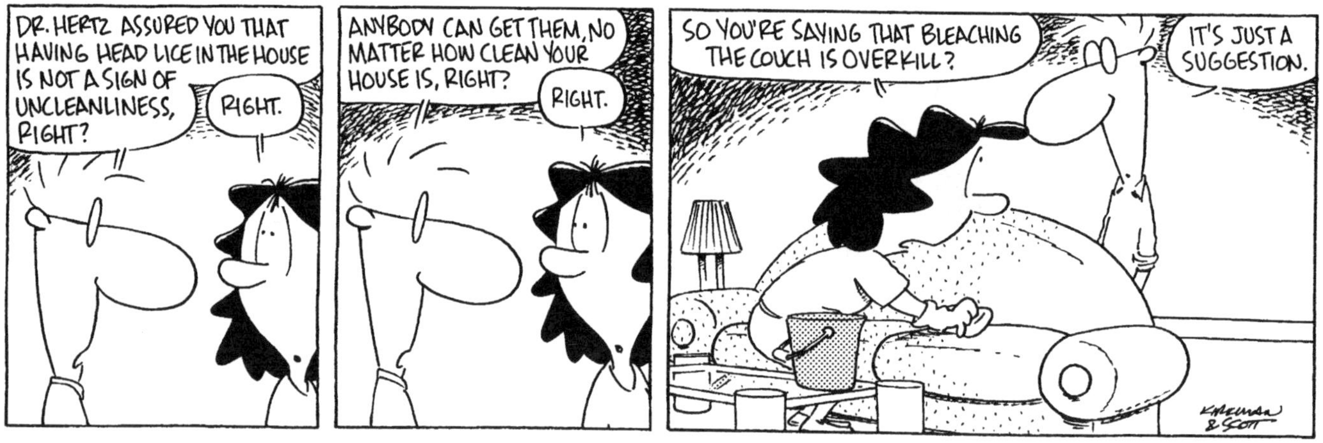
DR. HERTZ ASSURED YOU THAT HAVING HEAD LICE IN THE HOUSE IS NOT A SIGN OF UNCLEANLINESS, RIGHT?
RIGHT.
ANYBODY CAN GET THEM, NO MATTER HOW CLEAN YOUR HOUSE IS, RIGHT?
RIGHT.
SO YOU'RE SAYING THAT BLEACHING THE COUCH IS OVERKILL?
IT'S JUST A SUGGESTION.

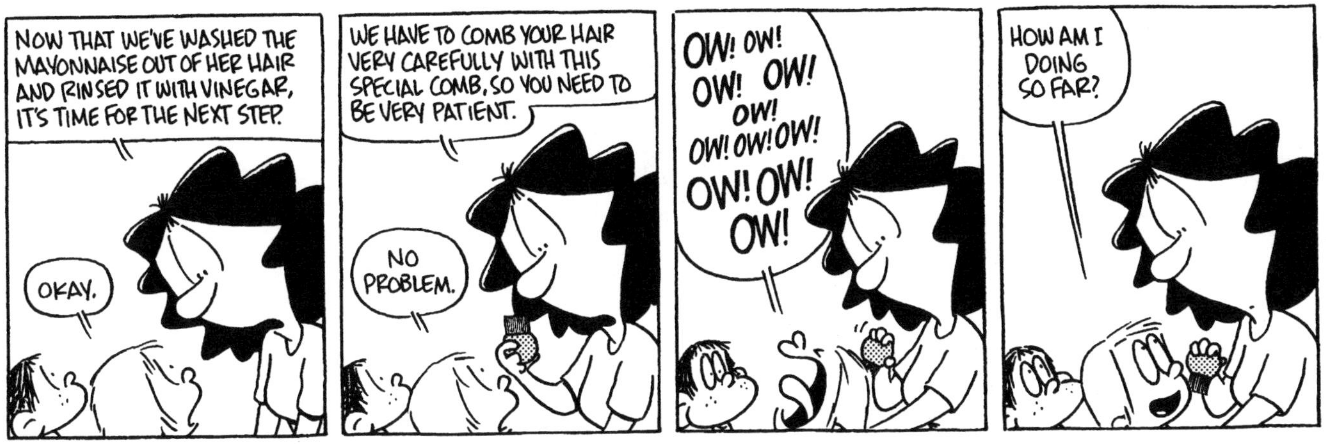
NOW THAT WE'VE WASHED THE MAYONNAISE OUT OF HER HAIR AND RINSED IT WITH VINEGAR, IT'S TIME FOR THE NEXT STEP.
OKAY.
WE HAVE TO COMB YOUR HAIR VERY CAREFULLY WITH THIS SPECIAL COMB, SO YOU NEED TO BE VERY PATIENT.
NO PROBLEM.
OW! OW! OW! OW! OW! OW! OW! OW! OW! OW! OW!
HOW AM I DOING SO FAR?

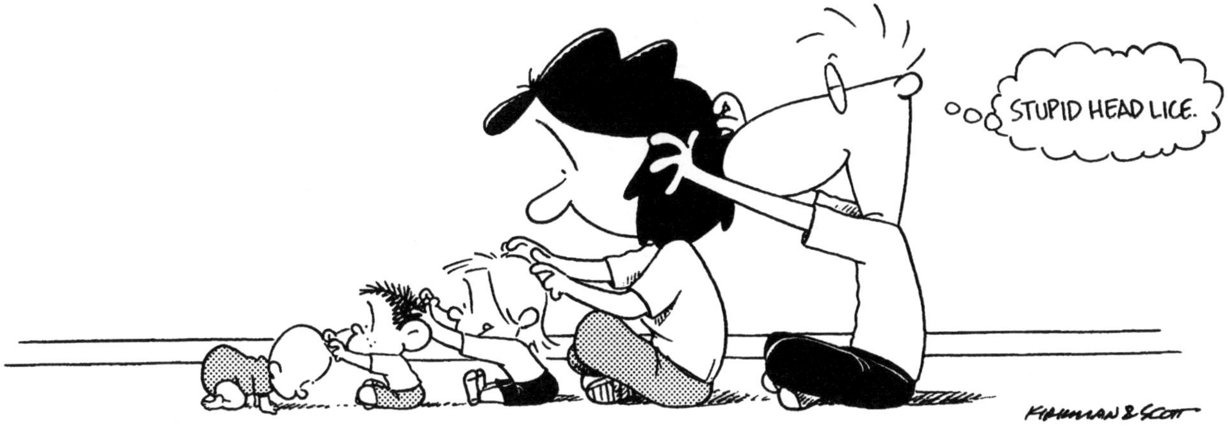
STUPID HEAD LICE.
KIRKMAN & SCOTT

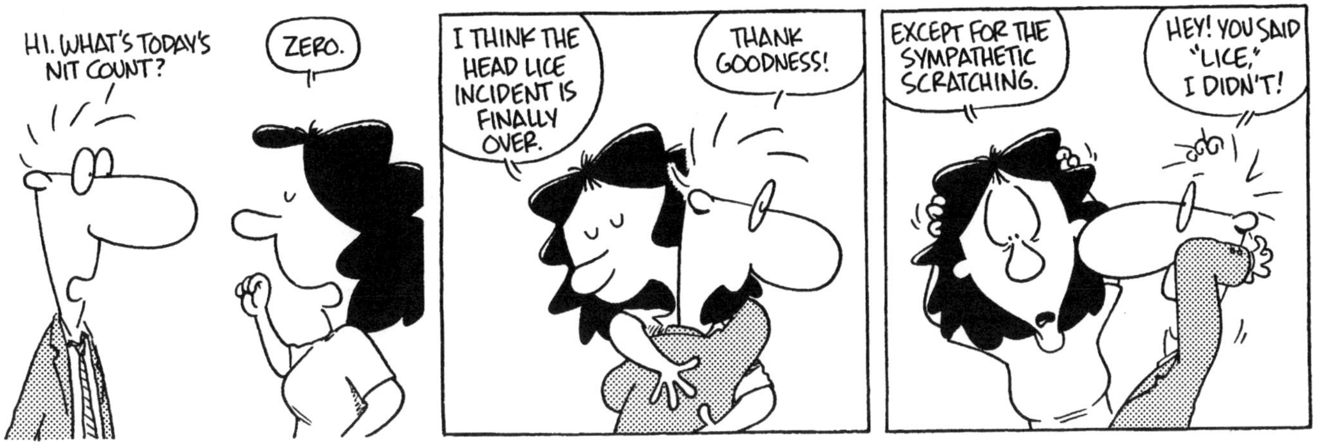
HI. WHAT'S TODAY'S NIT COUNT?
ZERO.
I THINK THE HEAD LICE INCIDENT IS FINALLY OVER.
THANK GOODNESS!
EXCEPT FOR THE SYMPATHETIC SCRATCHING.
HEY! YOU SAID "LICE," I DIDN'T!

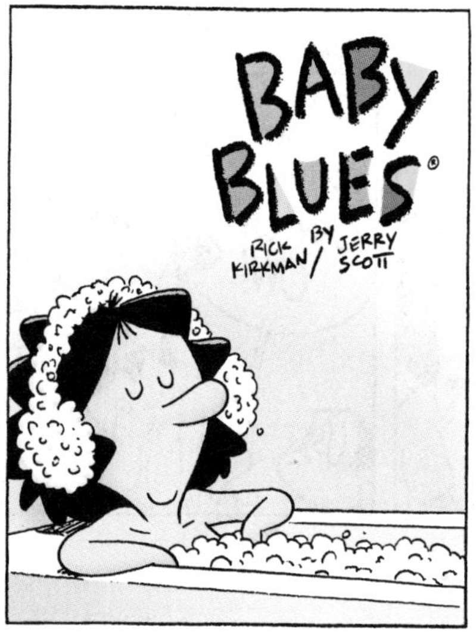

BABY BLUES®
BY RICK KIRKMAN / JERRY SCOTT

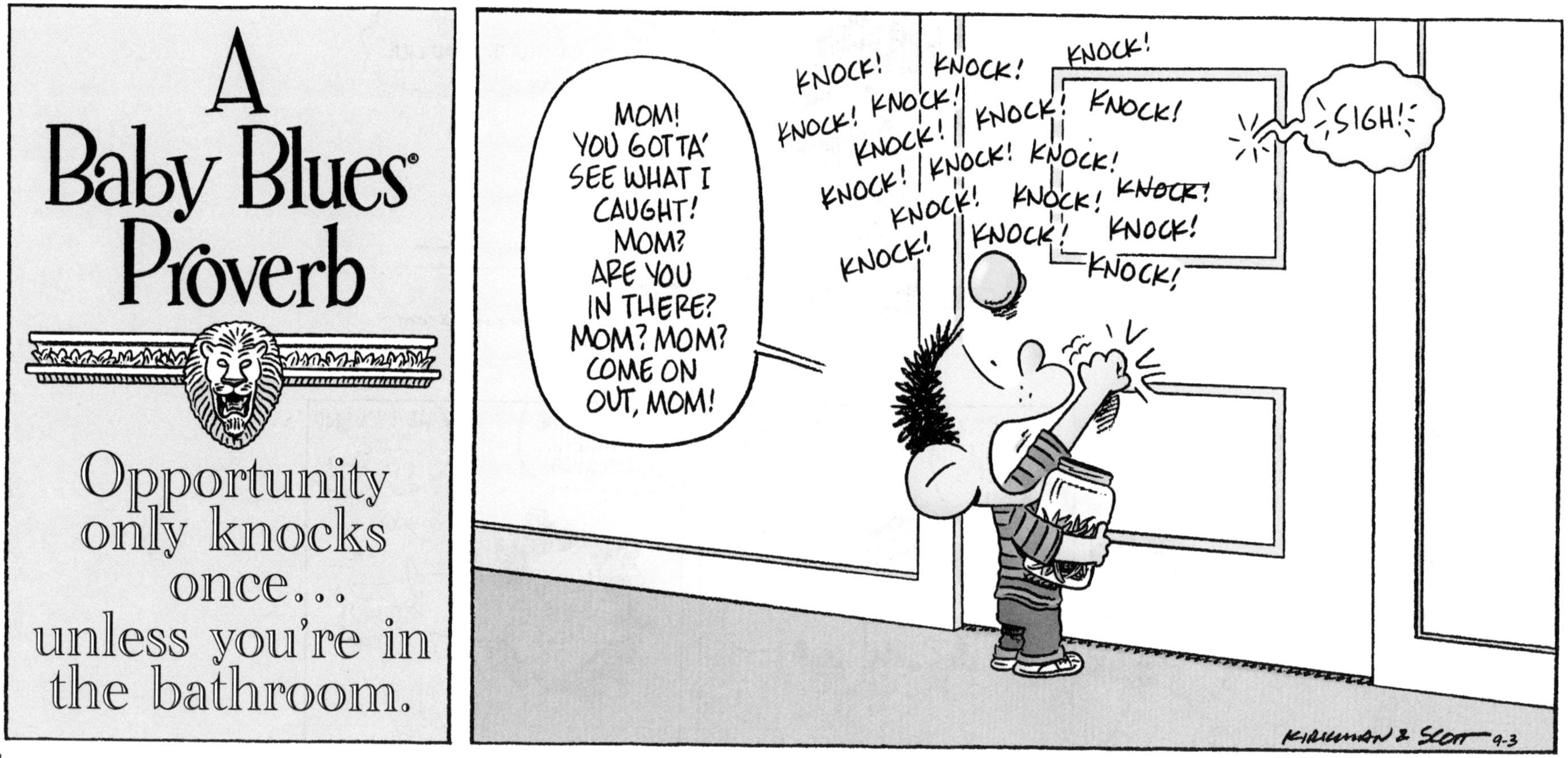

A Baby Blues® Proverb
Opportunity only knocks once... unless you're in the bathroom.
MOM! YOU GOTTA' SEE WHAT I CAUGHT! MOM? ARE YOU IN THERE? MOM? MOM? COME ON OUT, MOM!
KNOCK! KNOCK! KNOCK!
KNOCK! KNOCK! KNOCK! KNOCK!
KNOCK!
KNOCK! KNOCK! KNOCK!
KNOCK! KNOCK! KNOCK!
KNOCK! KNOCK! KNOCK!
KNOCK!
SIGH!
KIRKMAN & SCOTT 9-3

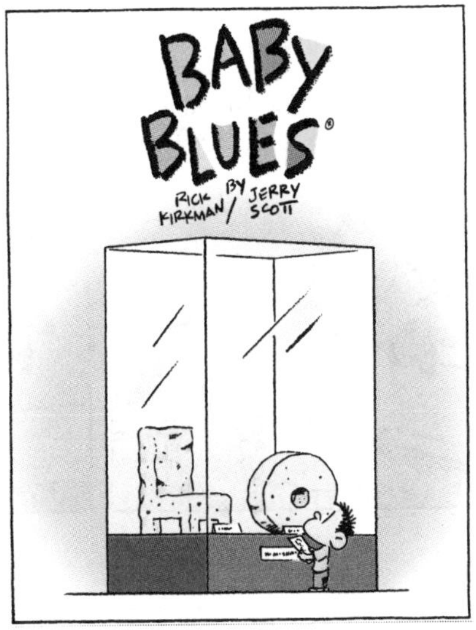
BABY BLUES®
BY RICK KIRKMAN / JERRY SCOTT

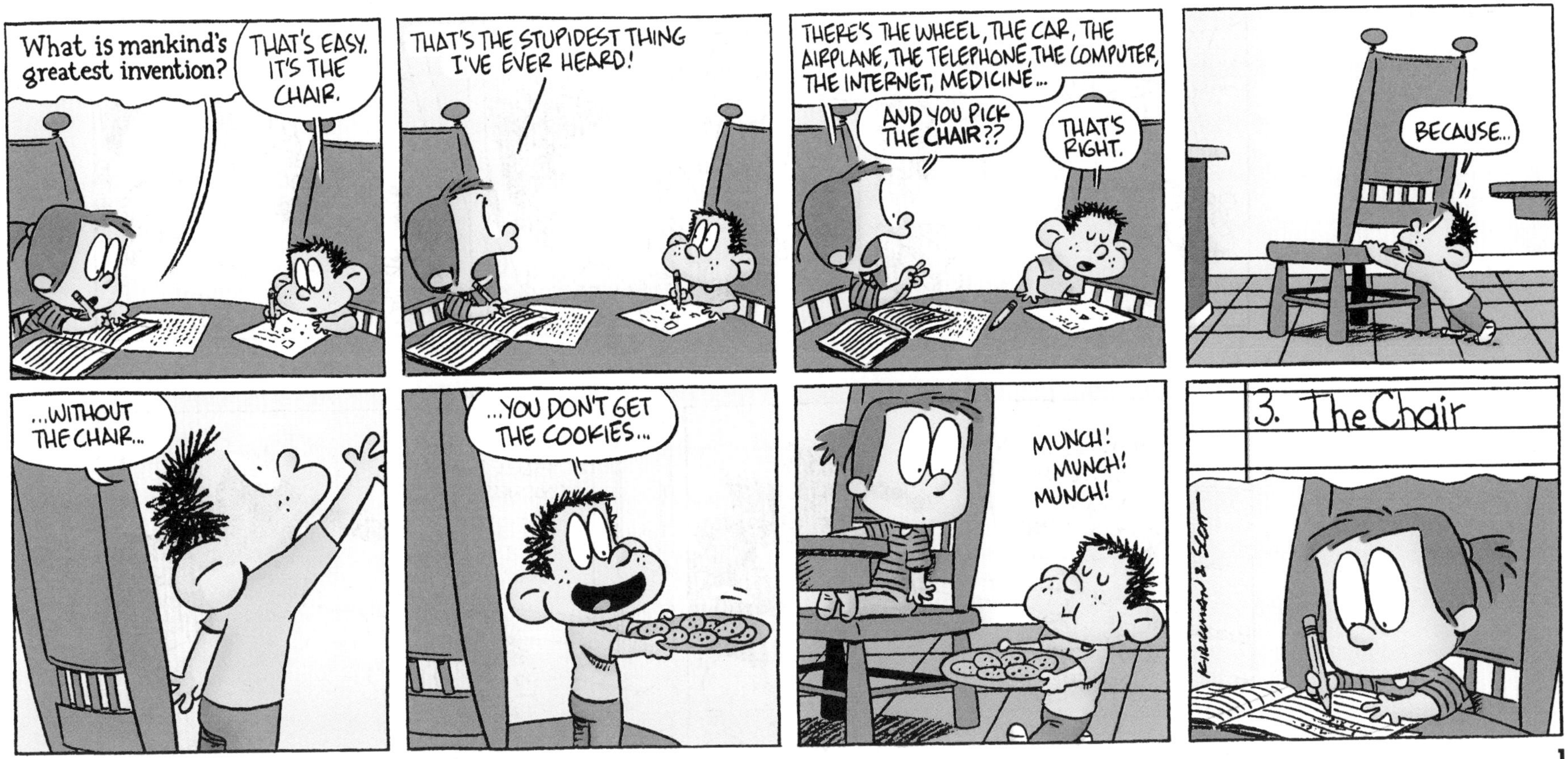
What is mankind's greatest invention?
THAT'S EASY. IT'S THE CHAIR.
THAT'S THE STUPIDEST THING I'VE EVER HEARD!
THERE'S THE WHEEL, THE CAR, THE AIRPLANE, THE TELEPHONE, THE COMPUTER, THE INTERNET, MEDICINE...
AND YOU PICK THE CHAIR??
THAT'S RIGHT.
BECAUSE...
...WITHOUT THE CHAIR...
...YOU DON'T GET THE COOKIES...
MUNCH! MUNCH! MUNCH!
3. The Chair
KIRKMAN & SCOTT

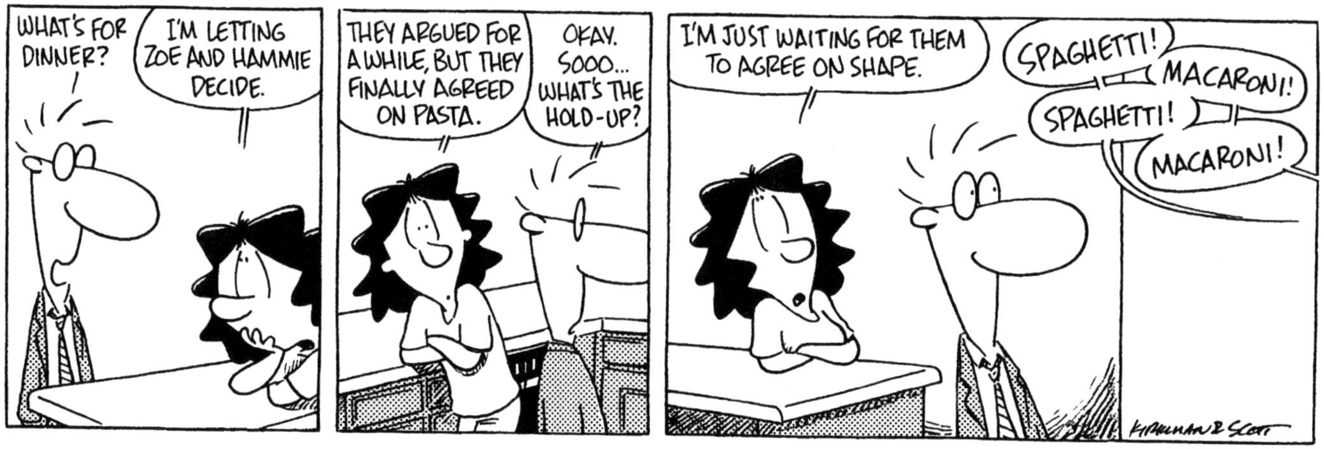
WHAT'S FOR DINNER?
I'M LETTING ZOE AND HAMMIE DECIDE.
THEY ARGUED FOR A WHILE, BUT THEY FINALLY AGREED ON PASTA.
OKAY. SOOO... WHAT'S THE HOLD-UP?
I'M JUST WAITING FOR THEM TO AGREE ON SHAPE.
SPAGHETTI!
MACARONI!
SPAGHETTI!
MACARONI!
KIRKMAN & SCOTT

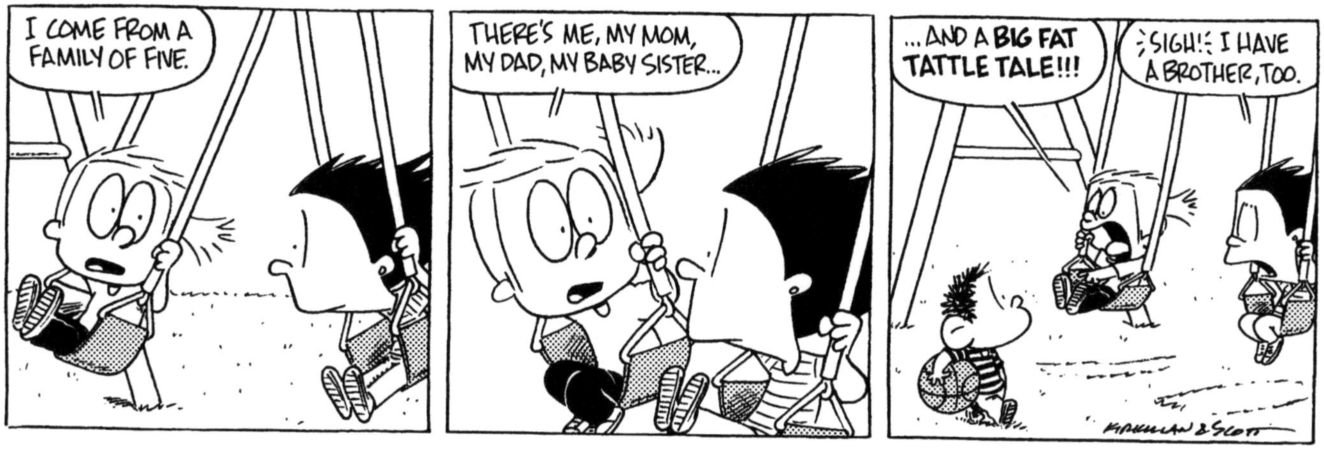
I COME FROM A FAMILY OF FIVE.
THERE'S ME, MY MOM, MY DAD, MY BABY SISTER...
...AND A **BIG FAT TATTLE TALE!!!**
SIGH! I HAVE A BROTHER, TOO.
KIRKMAN & SCOTT

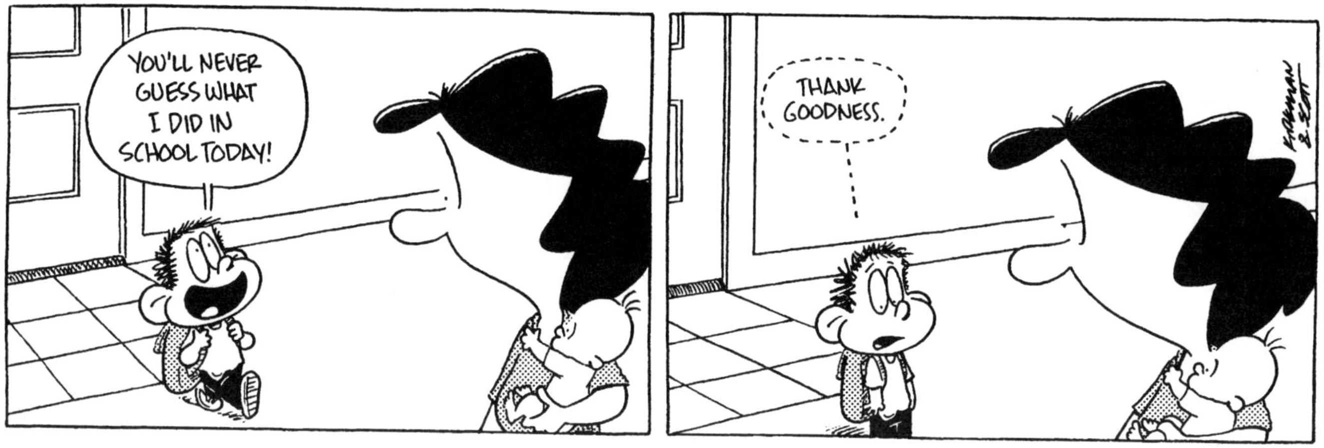
YOU'LL NEVER GUESS WHAT I DID IN SCHOOL TODAY!
THANK GOODNESS.
KIRKMAN & SCOTT

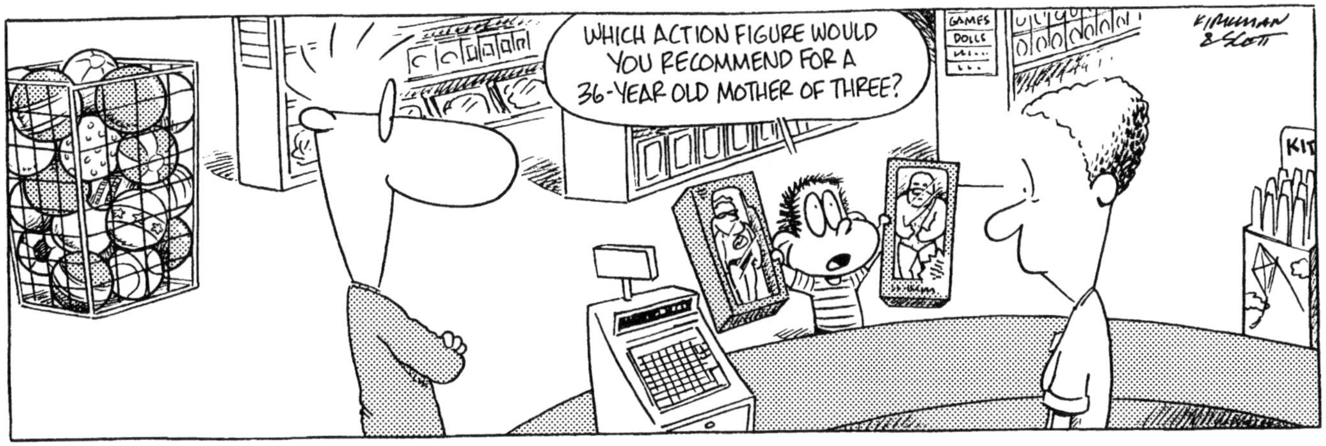
KIRKMAN & SCOTT
WHICH ACTION FIGURE WOULD YOU RECOMMEND FOR A 36-YEAR OLD MOTHER OF THREE?
GAMES
DOLLS

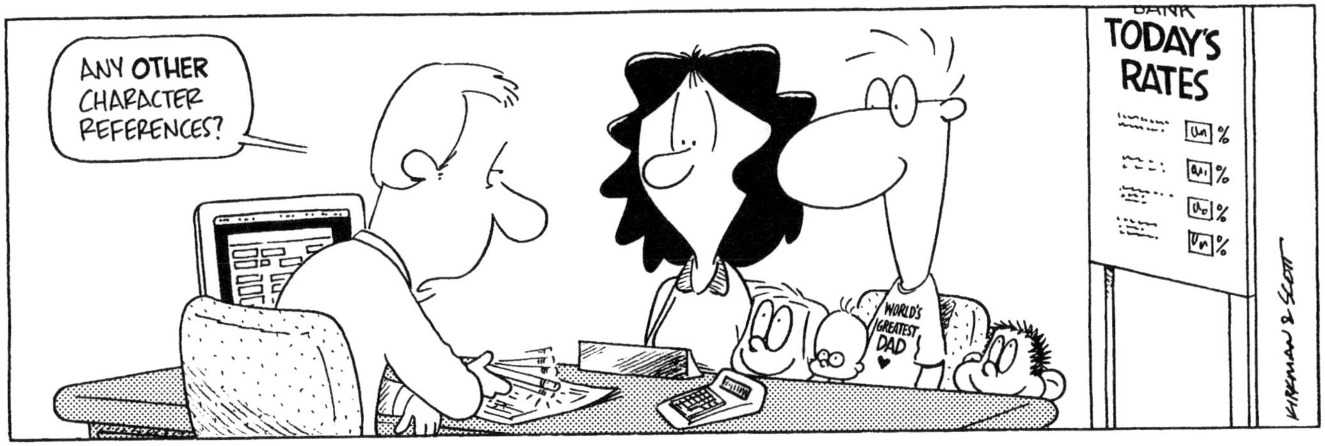
ANY **OTHER** CHARACTER REFERENCES?
TODAY'S RATES
WORLD'S GREATEST DAD
KIRKMAN & SCOTT

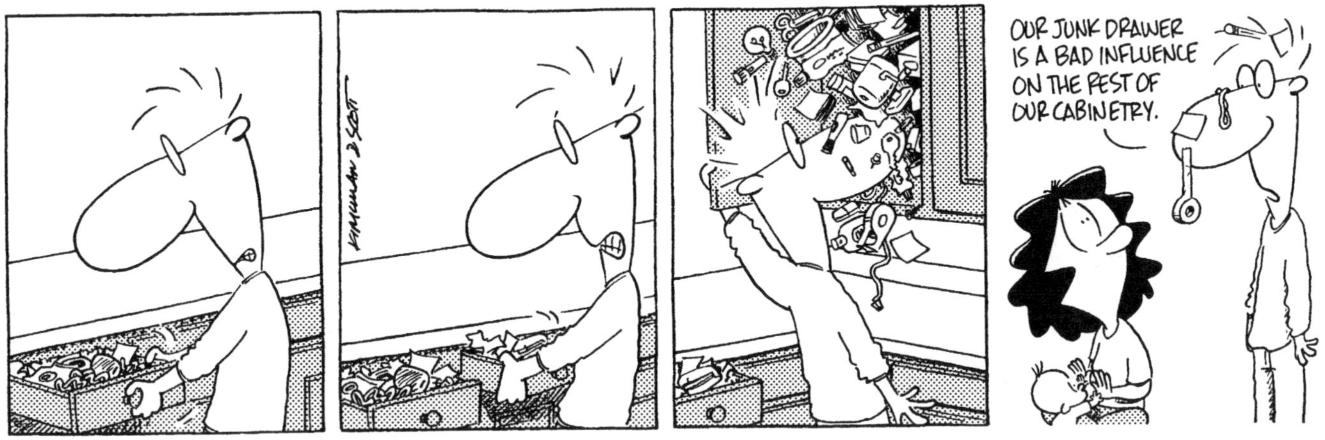
KIRKMAN & SCOTT
OUR JUNK DRAWER IS A BAD INFLUENCE ON THE REST OF OUR CABINETRY.

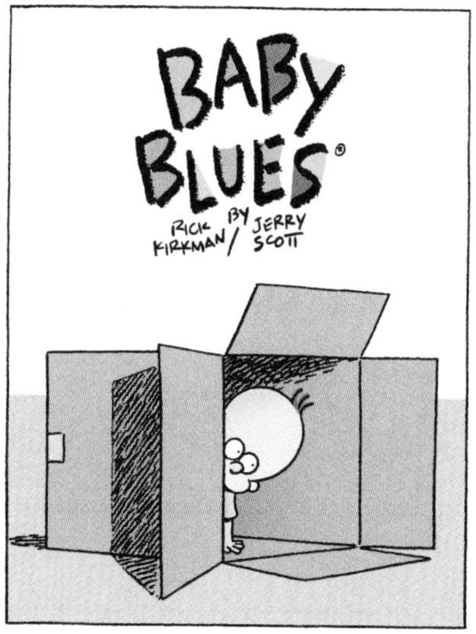
BABY BLUES®
BY RICK KIRKMAN / JERRY SCOTT

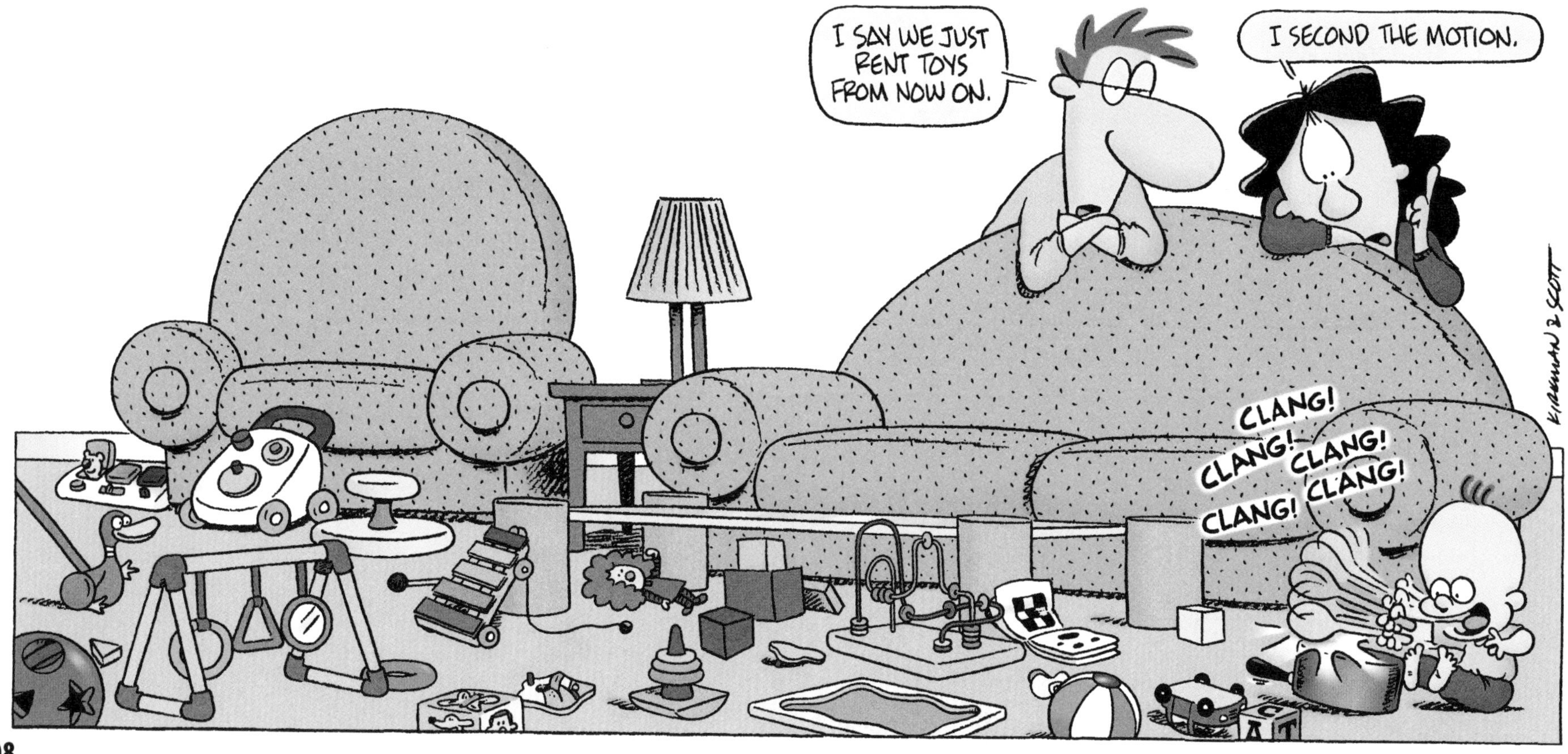
I SAY WE JUST RENT TOYS FROM NOW ON.
I SECOND THE MOTION.
CLANG! CLANG! CLANG! CLANG! CLANG!
KIRKMAN & SCOTT

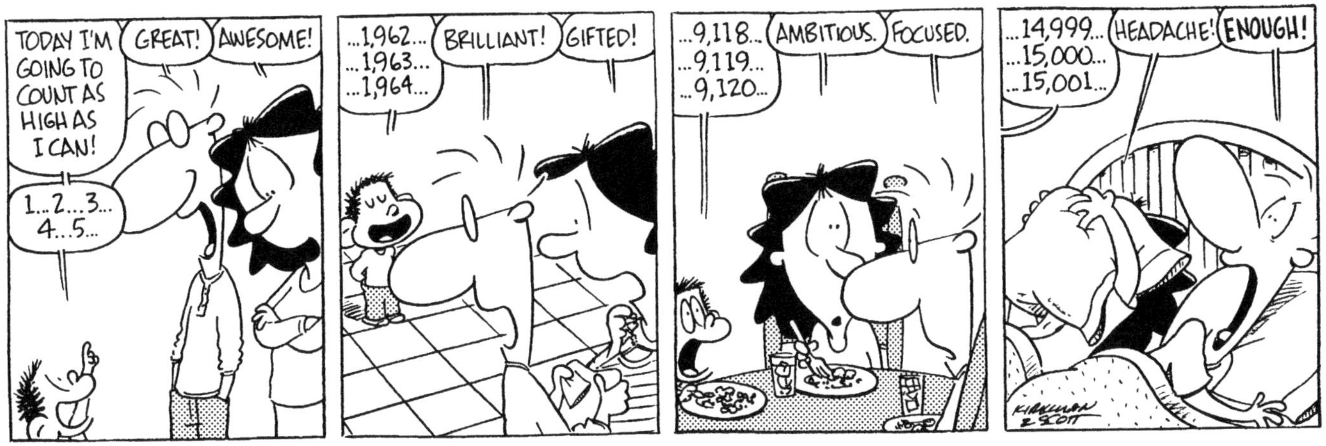
TODAY I'M GOING TO COUNT AS HIGH AS I CAN!
GREAT!
AWESOME!
1...2...3... 4...5...
...1,962... ...1,963... ...1,964...
BRILLIANT!
GIFTED!
...9,118... ...9,119... ...9,120...
AMBITIOUS.
FOCUSED.
...14,999... ...15,000... ...15,001...
HEADACHE!
ENOUGH!

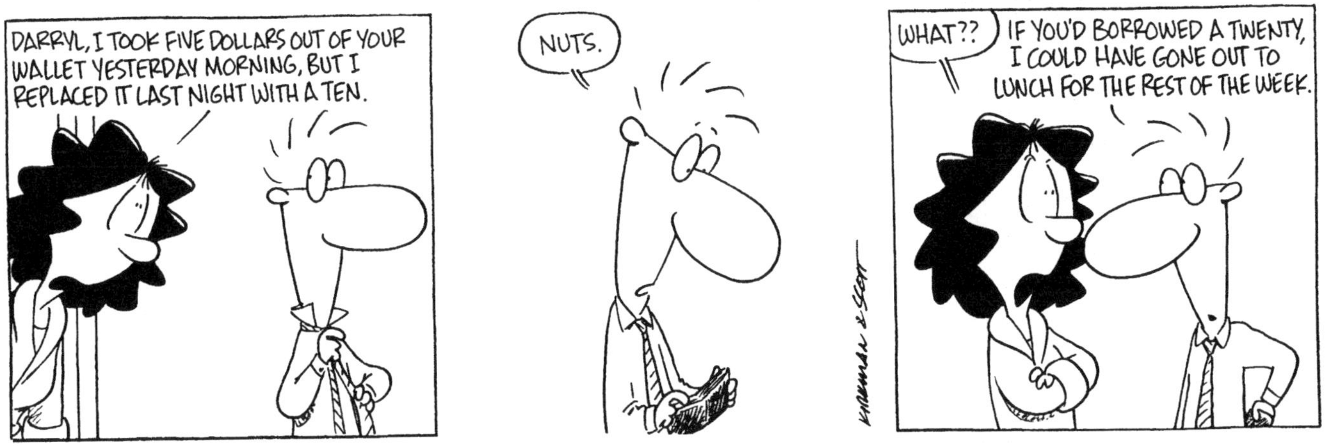
DARRYL, I TOOK FIVE DOLLARS OUT OF YOUR WALLET YESTERDAY MORNING, BUT I REPLACED IT LAST NIGHT WITH A TEN.
NUTS.
WHAT??
IF YOU'D BORROWED A TWENTY, I COULD HAVE GONE OUT TO LUNCH FOR THE REST OF THE WEEK.

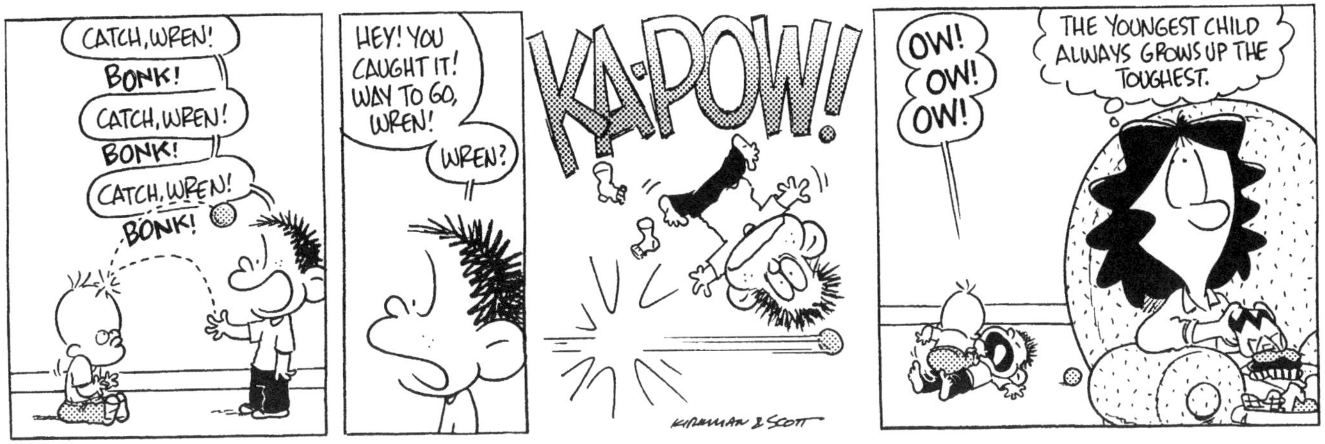
CATCH, WREN!
BONK!
CATCH, WREN!
BONK!
CATCH, WREN!
BONK!
HEY! YOU CAUGHT IT! WAY TO GO, WREN!
WREN?
KA-POW!
OW! OW! OW!
THE YOUNGEST CHILD ALWAYS GROWS UP THE TOUGHEST.

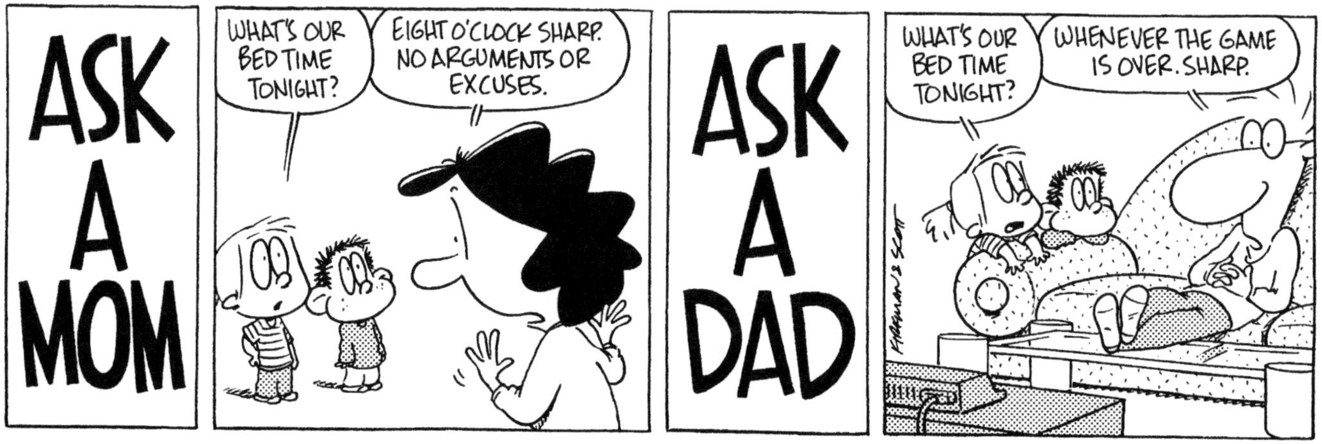
ASK A MOM
WHAT'S OUR BED TIME TONIGHT?
EIGHT O'CLOCK SHARP. NO ARGUMENTS OR EXCUSES.
ASK A DAD
WHAT'S OUR BED TIME TONIGHT?
WHENEVER THE GAME IS OVER. SHARP.

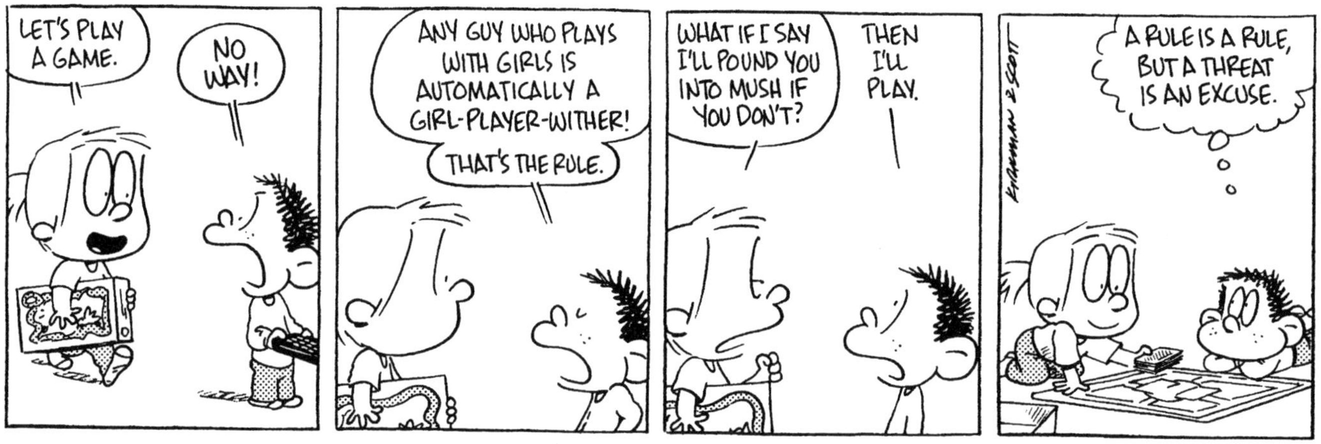
LET'S PLAY A GAME.
NO WAY!
ANY GUY WHO PLAYS WITH GIRLS IS AUTOMATICALLY A GIRL-PLAYER-WITHER!
THAT'S THE RULE.
WHAT IF I SAY I'LL POUND YOU INTO MUSH IF YOU DON'T?
THEN I'LL PLAY.
A RULE IS A RULE, BUT A THREAT IS AN EXCUSE.

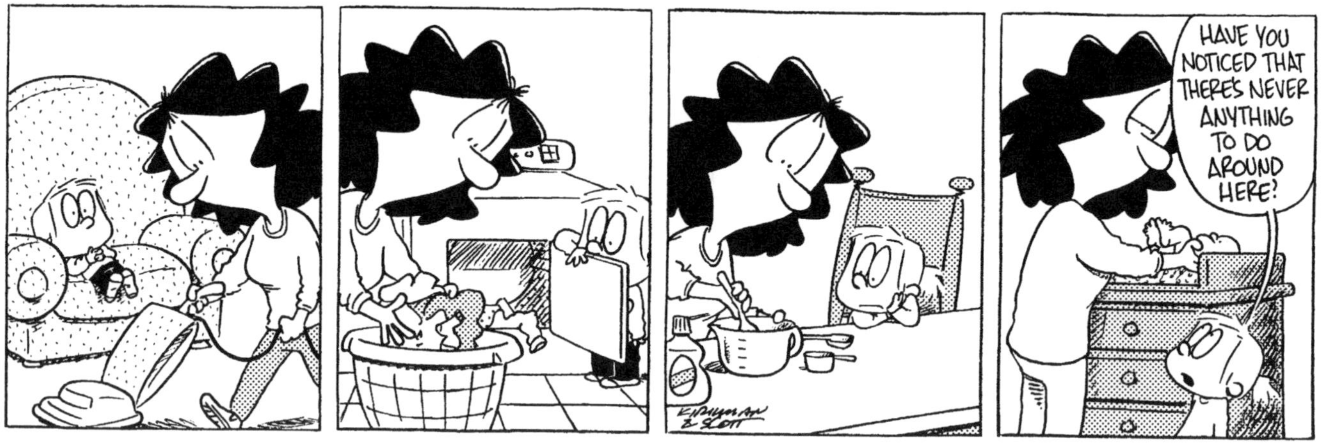
HAVE YOU NOTICED THAT THERE'S NEVER ANYTHING TO DO AROUND HERE?

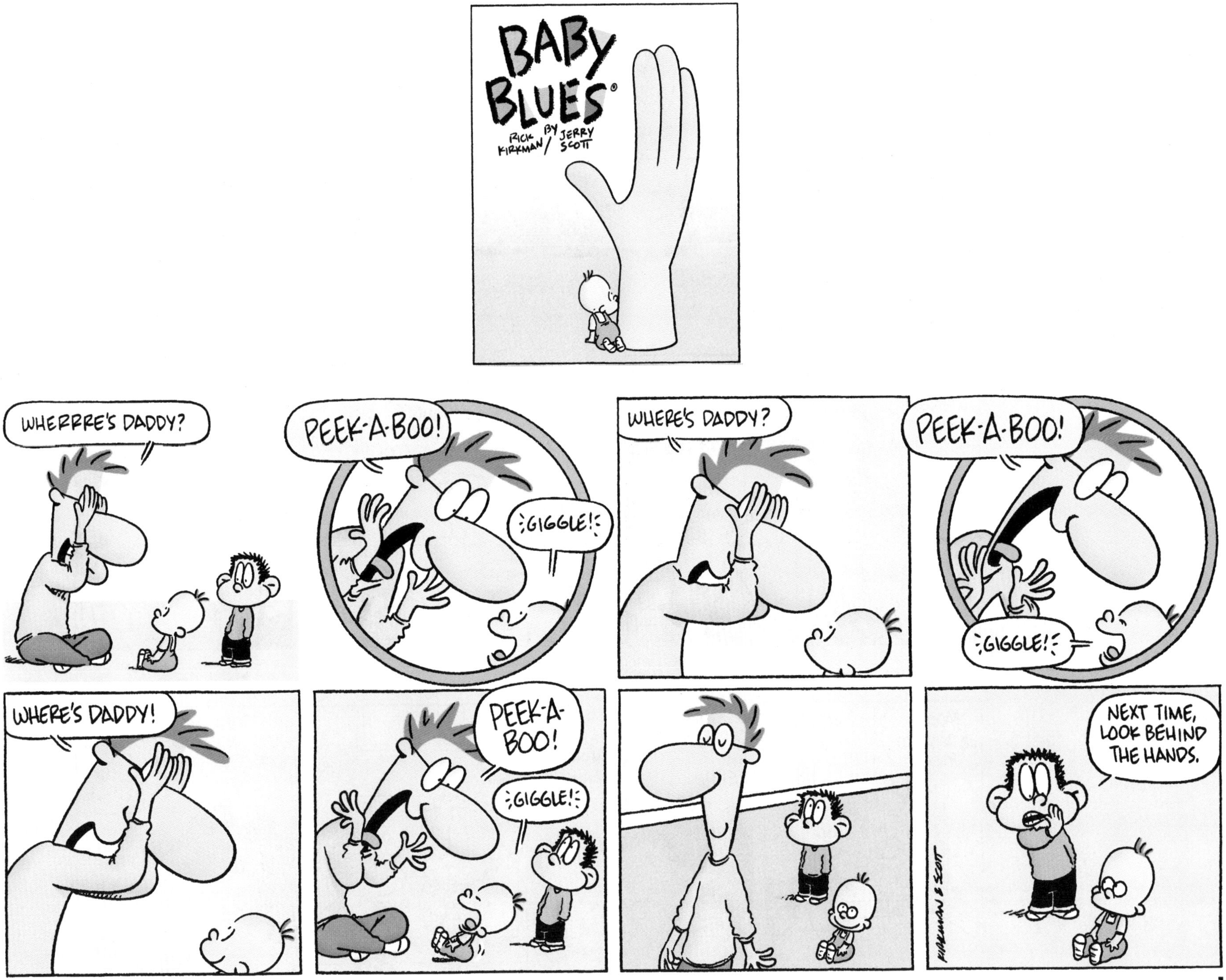
BABY BLUES®
BY RICK KIRKMAN / JERRY SCOTT
WHERRRE'S DADDY?
PEEK-A-BOO!
GIGGLE!
WHERE'S DADDY?
PEEK-A-BOO!
GIGGLE!
WHERE'S DADDY!
PEEK-A-BOO!
GIGGLE!
NEXT TIME, LOOK BEHIND THE HANDS.
KIRKMAN & SCOTT

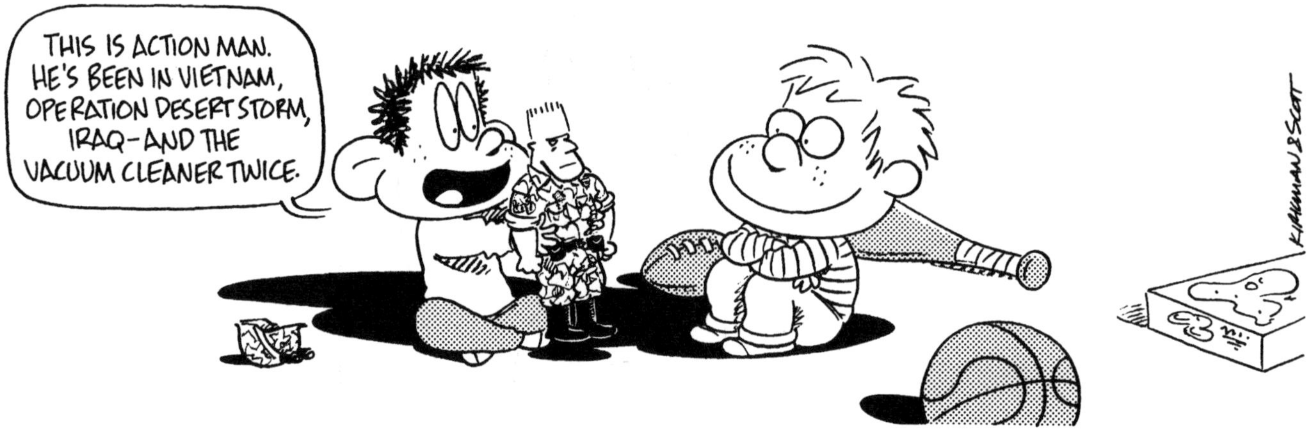
THIS IS ACTION MAN. HE'S BEEN IN VIETNAM, OPERATION DESERT STORM, IRAQ—AND THE VACUUM CLEANER TWICE.

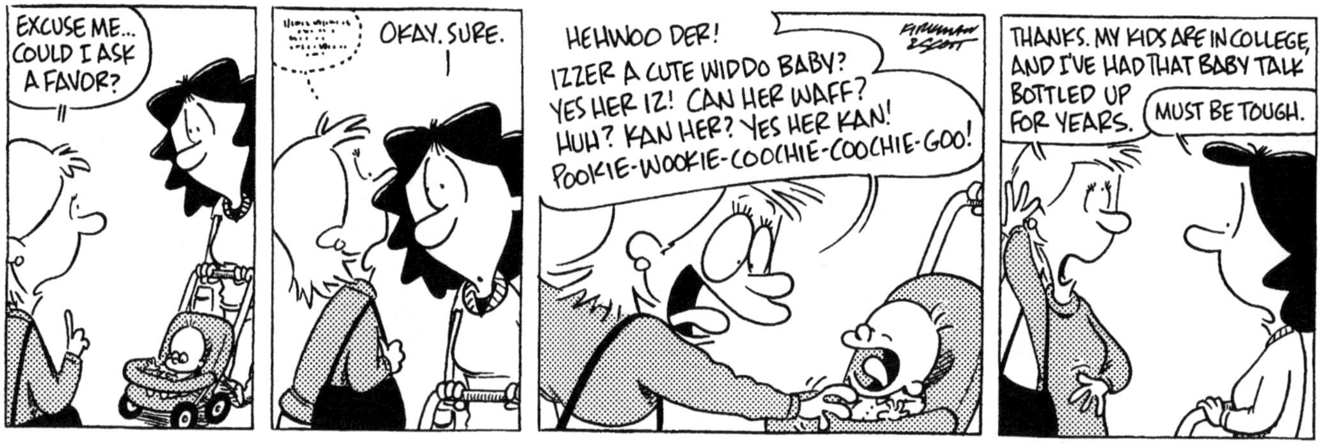
EXCUSE ME... COULD I ASK A FAVOR?
OKAY. SURE.
HEHWOO DER! IZZER A CUTE WIDDO BABY? YES HER IZ! CAN HER WAFF? HUH? KAN HER? YES HER KAN! POOKIE-WOOKIE-COOCHIE-COOCHIE-GOO!
THANKS. MY KIDS ARE IN COLLEGE, AND I'VE HAD THAT BABY TALK BOTTLED UP FOR YEARS.
MUST BE TOUGH.

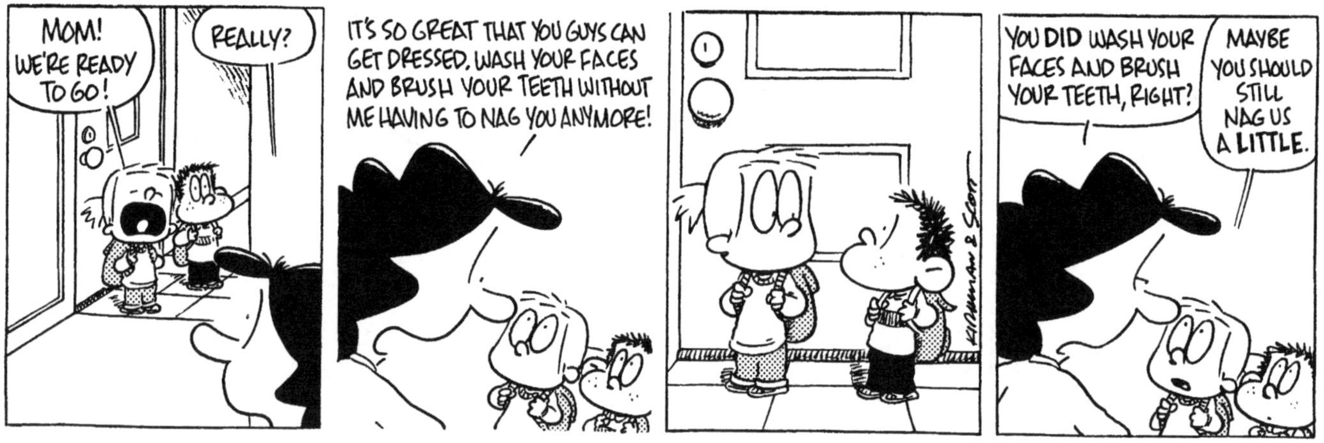
MOM! WE'RE READY TO GO!
REALLY?
IT'S SO GREAT THAT YOU GUYS CAN GET DRESSED, WASH YOUR FACES AND BRUSH YOUR TEETH WITHOUT ME HAVING TO NAG YOU ANYMORE!
YOU **DID** WASH YOUR FACES AND BRUSH YOUR TEETH, RIGHT?
MAYBE YOU SHOULD STILL NAG US A **LITTLE**.

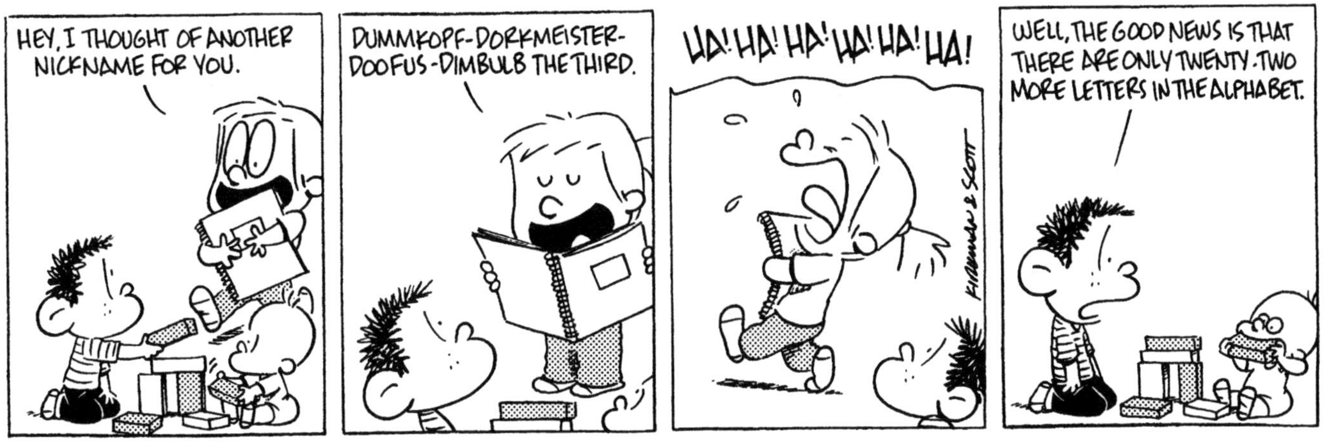
HEY, I THOUGHT OF ANOTHER NICKNAME FOR YOU.
DUMMKOPF-DORKMEISTER-DOOFUS-DIMBULB THE THIRD.
HA! HA! HA! HA! HA! HA!
KIRKMAN & SCOTT
WELL, THE GOOD NEWS IS THAT THERE ARE ONLY TWENTY-TWO MORE LETTERS IN THE ALPHABET.

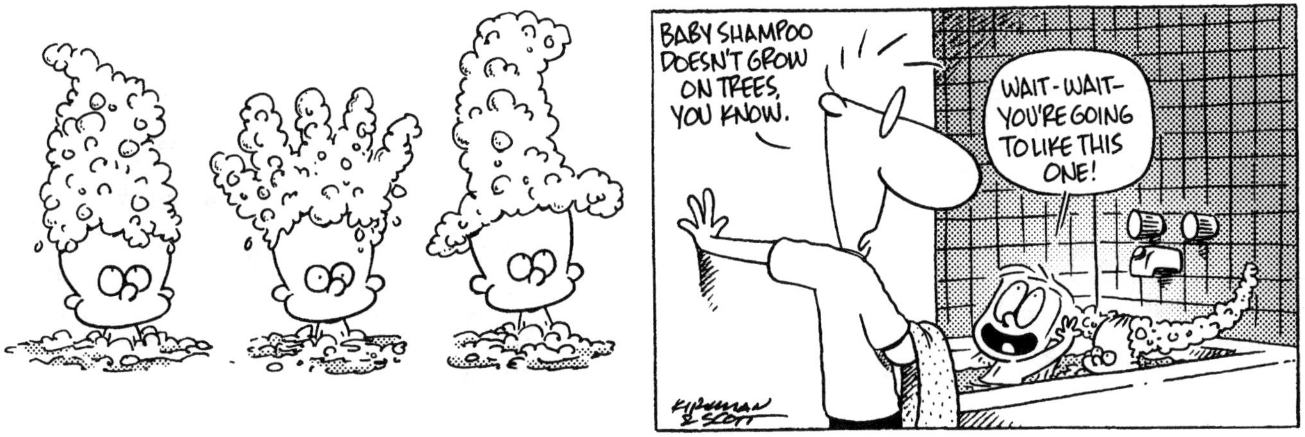
BABY SHAMPOO DOESN'T GROW ON TREES, YOU KNOW.
WAIT-WAIT-YOU'RE GOING TO LIKE THIS ONE!
KIRKMAN & SCOTT

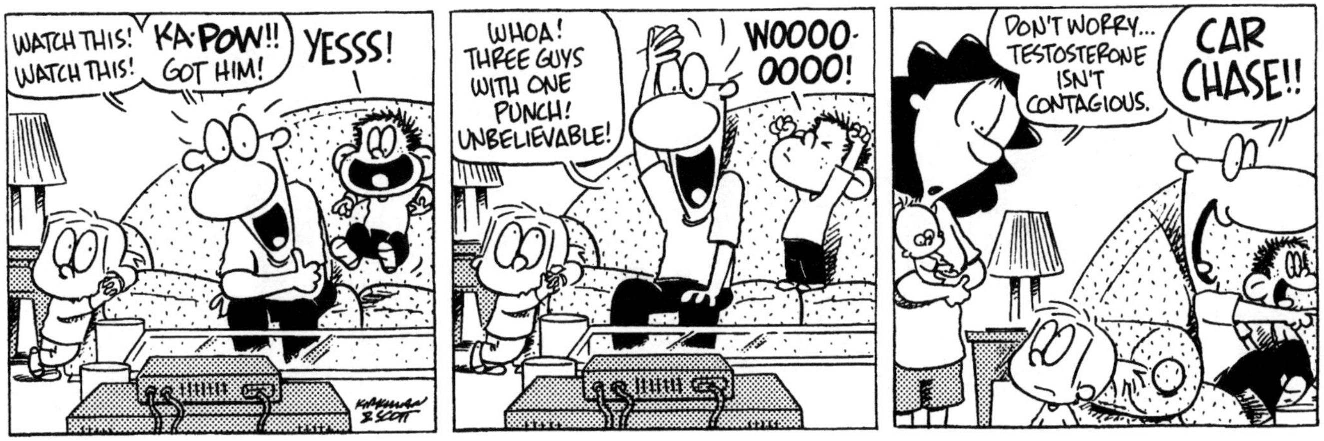
WATCH THIS! WATCH THIS!
KA-POW!! GOT HIM!
YESSS!
KIRKMAN & SCOTT
WHOA! THREE GUYS WITH ONE PUNCH! UNBELIEVABLE!
WOOOO-OOOO!
DON'T WORRY... TESTOSTERONE ISN'T CONTAGIOUS.
CAR CHASE!!

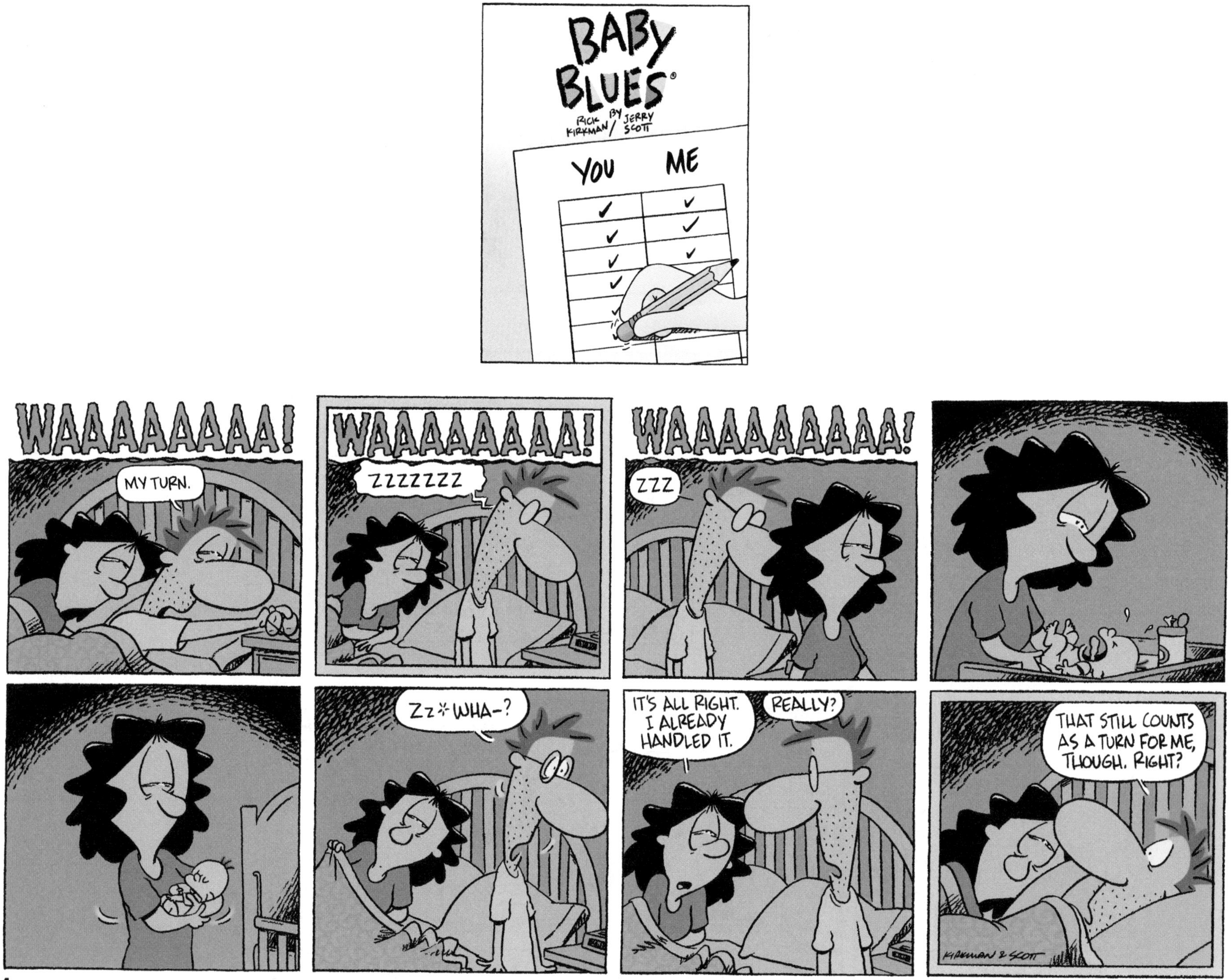

BABY BLUES®
RICK KIRKMAN / BY JERRY SCOTT
YOU
ME
WAAAAAAAA!
MY TURN.
WAAAAAAAAA!
ZZZZZZZ
WAAAAAAAAAA!
ZZZ
Zz✳WHA-?
IT'S ALL RIGHT. I ALREADY HANDLED IT.
REALLY?
THAT STILL COUNTS AS A TURN FOR ME, THOUGH. RIGHT?
KIRKMAN & SCOTT

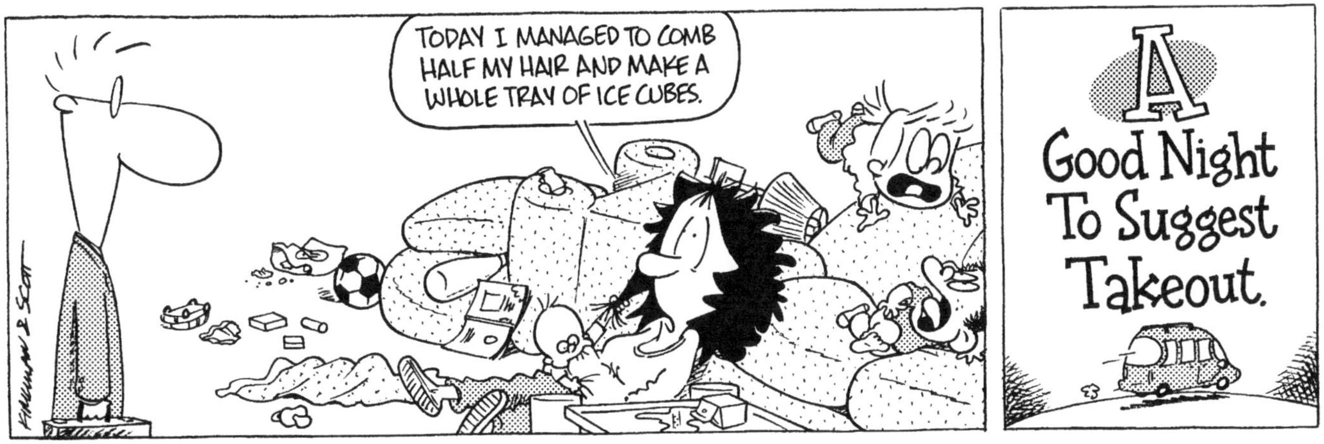
TODAY I MANAGED TO COMB HALF MY HAIR AND MAKE A WHOLE TRAY OF ICE CUBES.
A Good Night To Suggest Takeout.

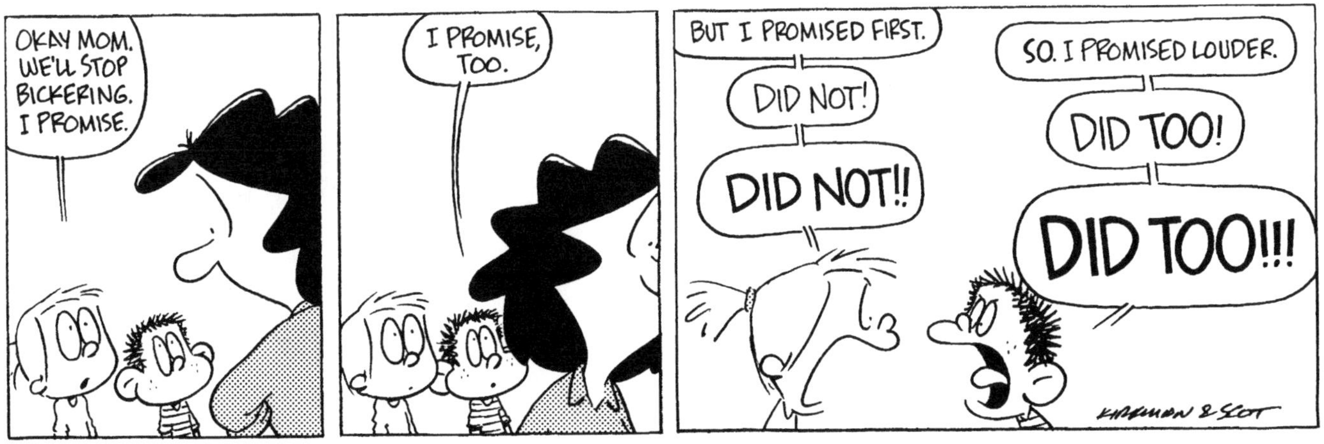
OKAY MOM. WE'LL STOP BICKERING. I PROMISE.
I PROMISE, TOO.
BUT I PROMISED FIRST.
SO. I PROMISED LOUDER.
DID NOT!
DID TOO!
DID NOT!!
DID TOO!!!

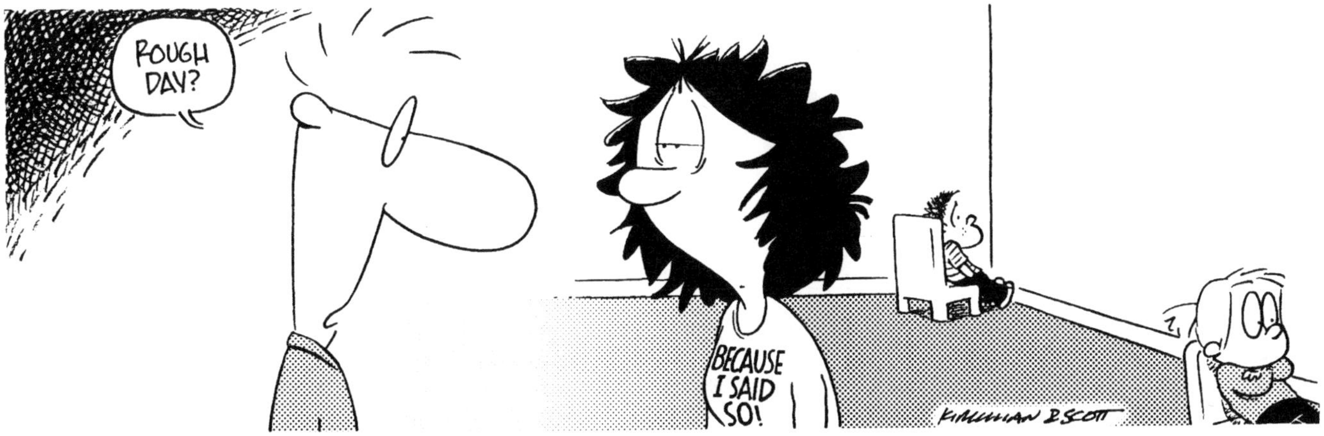
ROUGH DAY?
BECAUSE I SAID SO!

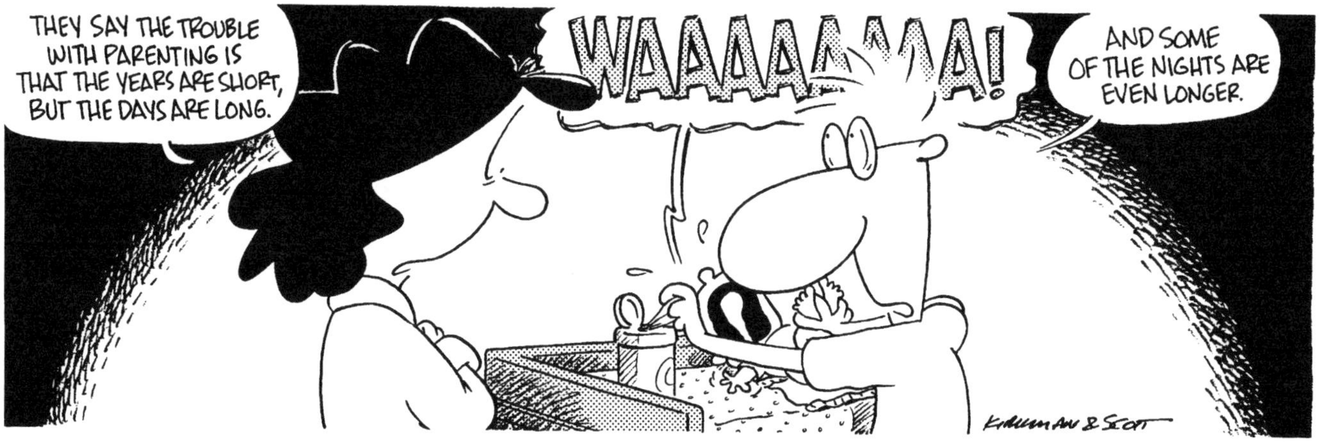
THEY SAY THE TROUBLE WITH PARENTING IS THAT THE YEARS ARE SHORT, BUT THE DAYS ARE LONG.
WAAAAAAAA!
AND SOME OF THE NIGHTS ARE EVEN LONGER.
KIRKMAN & SCOTT

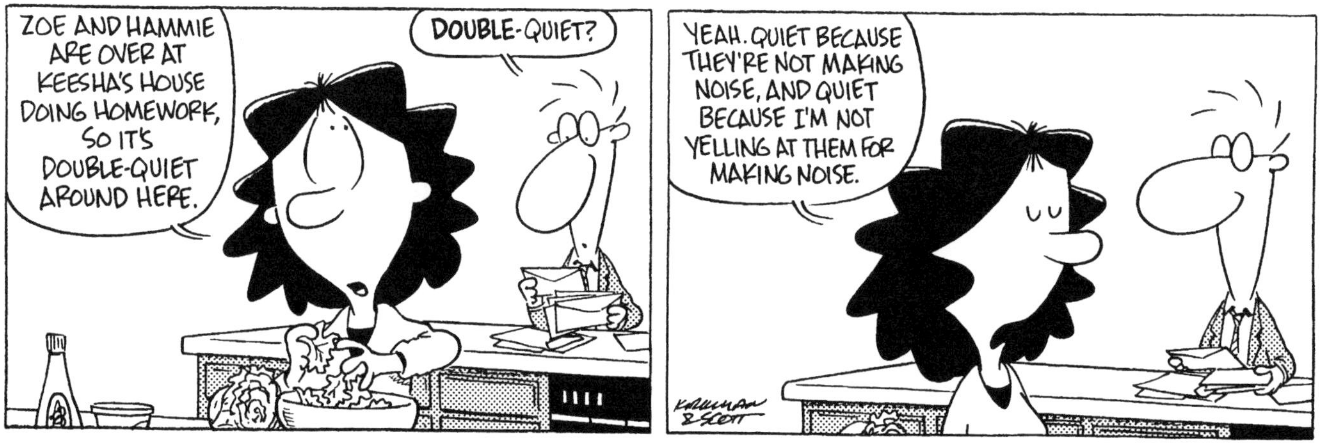
ZOE AND HAMMIE ARE OVER AT KEESHA'S HOUSE DOING HOMEWORK, SO IT'S DOUBLE-QUIET AROUND HERE.
DOUBLE-QUIET?
YEAH. QUIET BECAUSE THEY'RE NOT MAKING NOISE, AND QUIET BECAUSE I'M NOT YELLING AT THEM FOR MAKING NOISE.
KIRKMAN & SCOTT

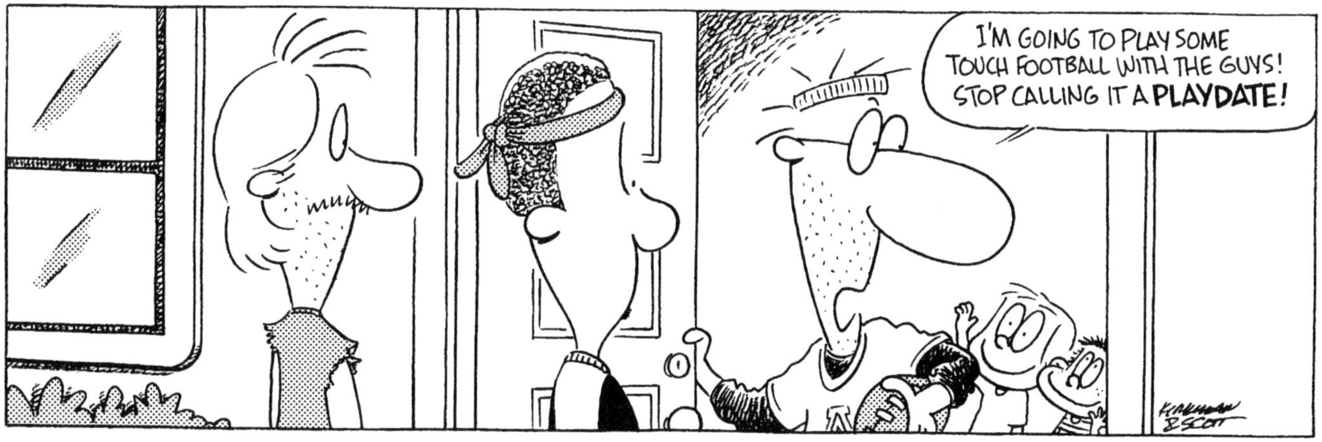
I'M GOING TO PLAY SOME TOUCH FOOTBALL WITH THE GUYS! STOP CALLING IT A PLAYDATE!
KIRKMAN & SCOTT

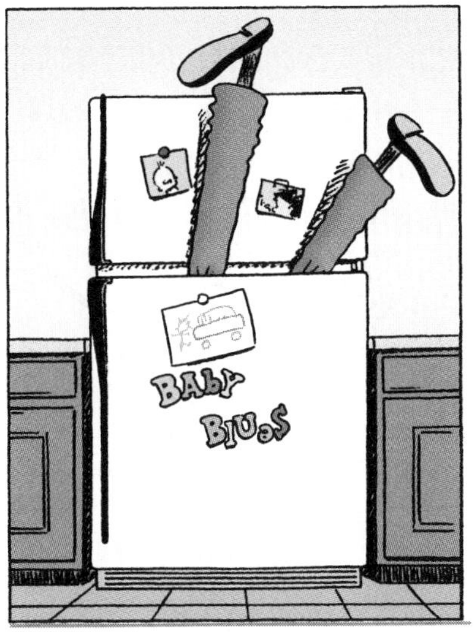
BABY BLUES

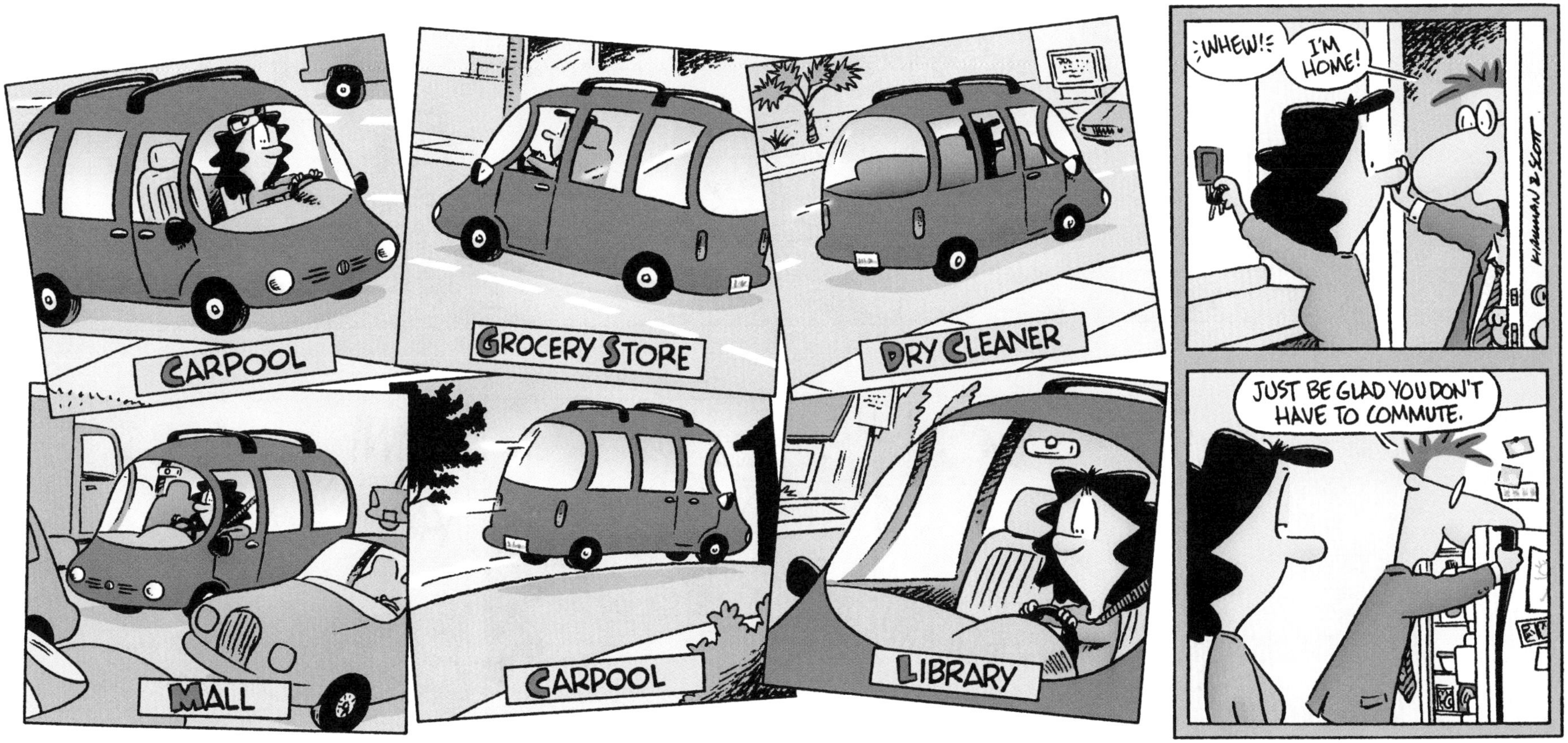
CARPOOL
GROCERY STORE
DRY CLEANER
MALL
CARPOOL
LIBRARY
WHEW!
I'M HOME!
JUST BE GLAD YOU DON'T HAVE TO COMMUTE.

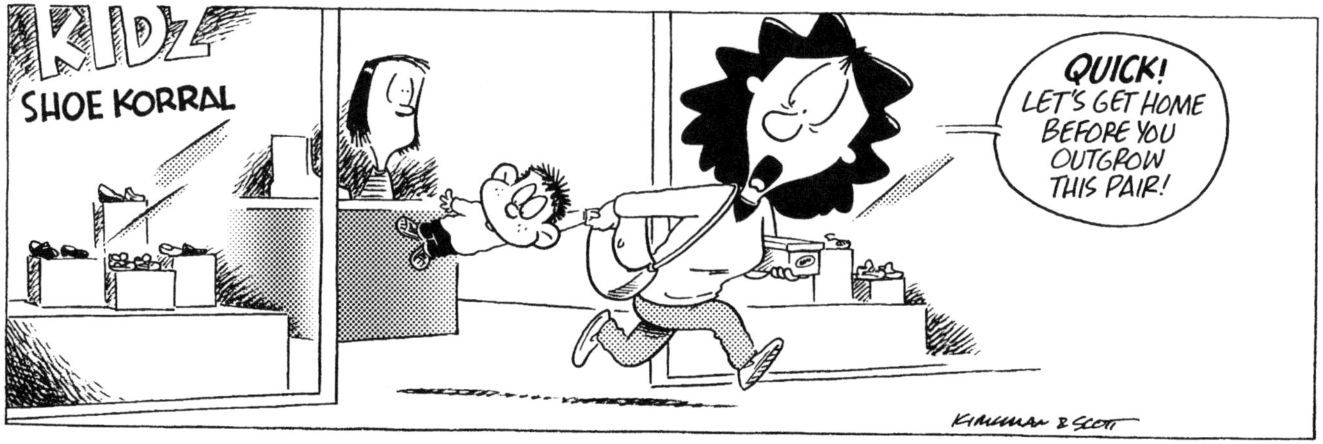
KIDZ
SHOE KORRAL
QUICK! LET'S GET HOME BEFORE YOU OUTGROW THIS PAIR!
KIRKMAN & SCOTT

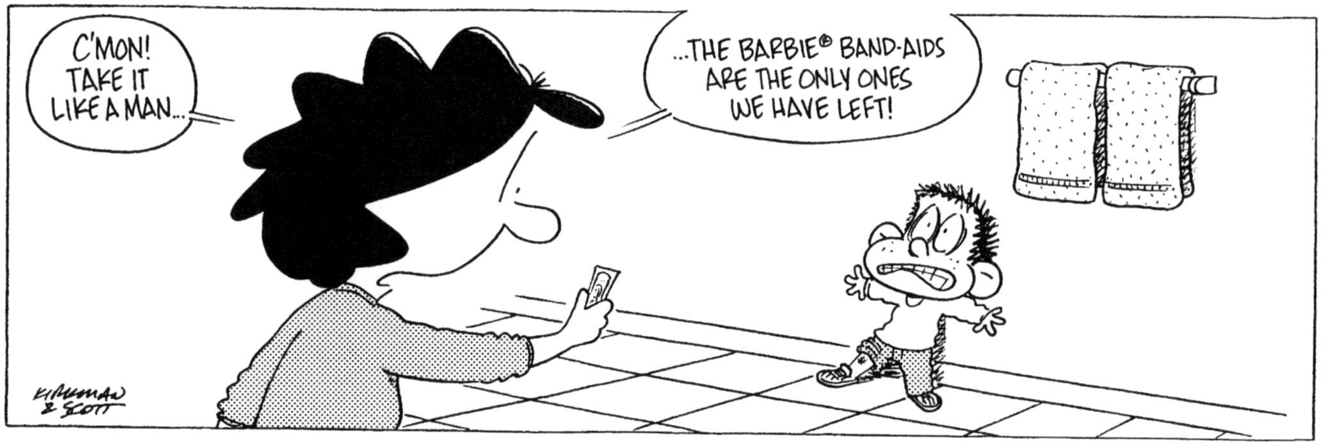
C'MON! TAKE IT LIKE A MAN...
...THE BARBIE® BAND-AIDS ARE THE ONLY ONES WE HAVE LEFT!
KIRKMAN & SCOTT

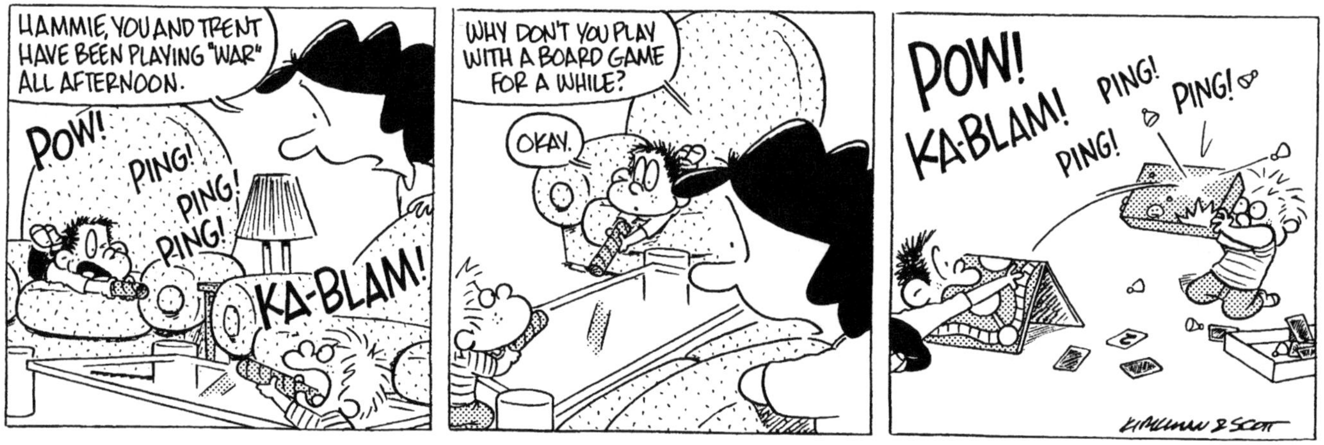
HAMMIE, YOU AND TRENT HAVE BEEN PLAYING "WAR" ALL AFTERNOON.
POW!
PING!
PING!
PING!
KA-BLAM!
WHY DON'T YOU PLAY WITH A BOARD GAME FOR A WHILE?
OKAY.
POW!
KA-BLAM!
PING!
PING!
PING!
KIRKMAN & SCOTT

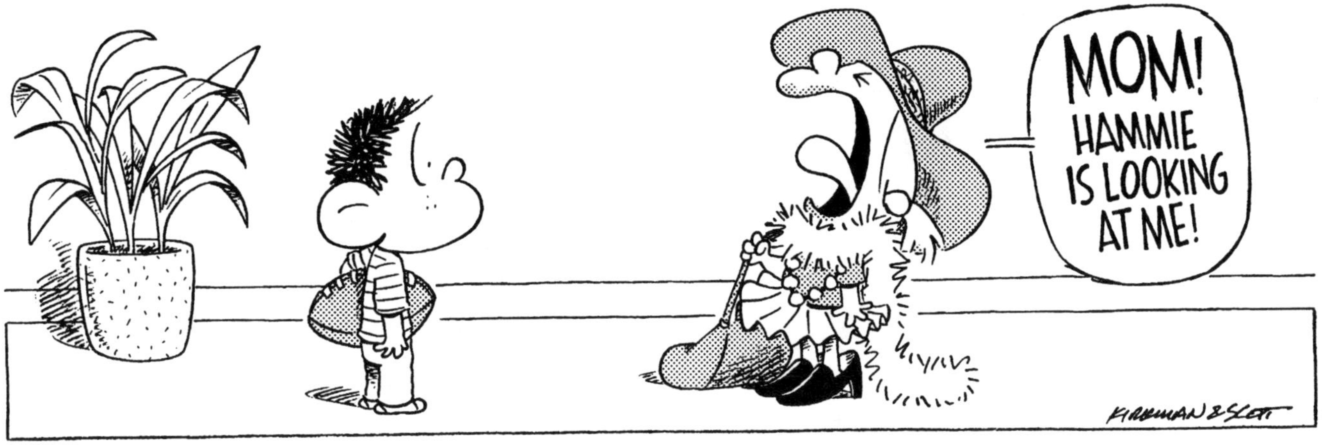
MOM! HAMMIE IS LOOKING AT ME!
KIRKMAN & SCOTT

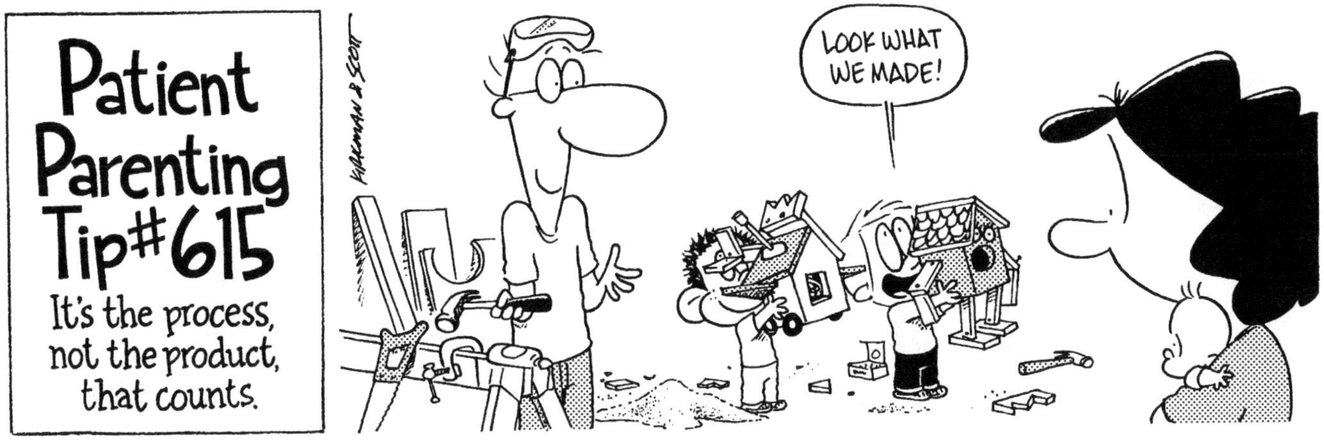
Patient Parenting Tip#615
It's the process, not the product, that counts.
KIRKMAN & SCOTT
LOOK WHAT WE MADE!

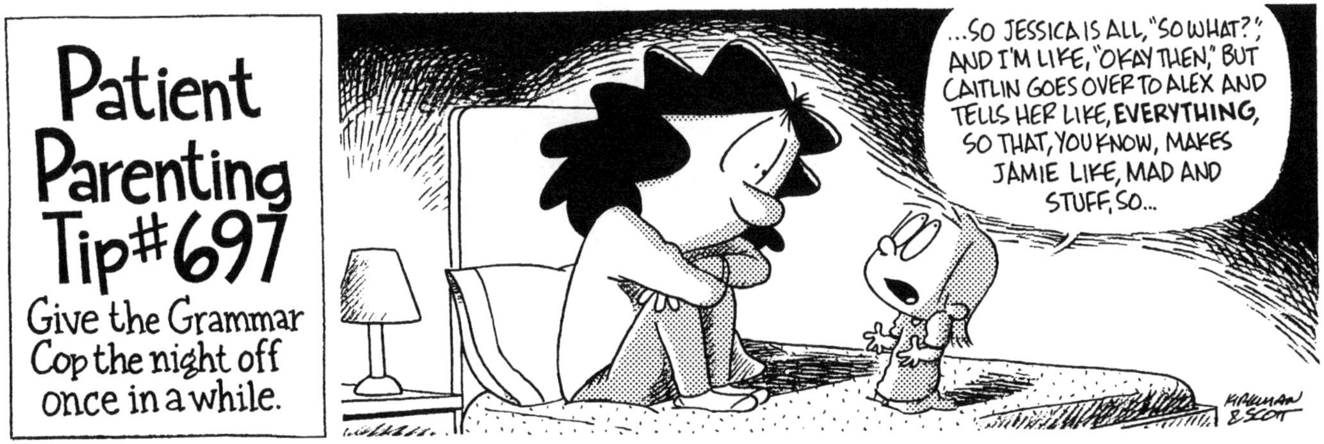
Patient Parenting Tip#697
Give the Grammar Cop the night off once in a while.
...SO JESSICA IS ALL, "SO WHAT?", AND I'M LIKE, "OKAY THEN," BUT CAITLIN GOES OVER TO ALEX AND TELLS HER LIKE, EVERYTHING, SO THAT, YOU KNOW, MAKES JAMIE LIKE, MAD AND STUFF, SO...
KIRKMAN & SCOTT

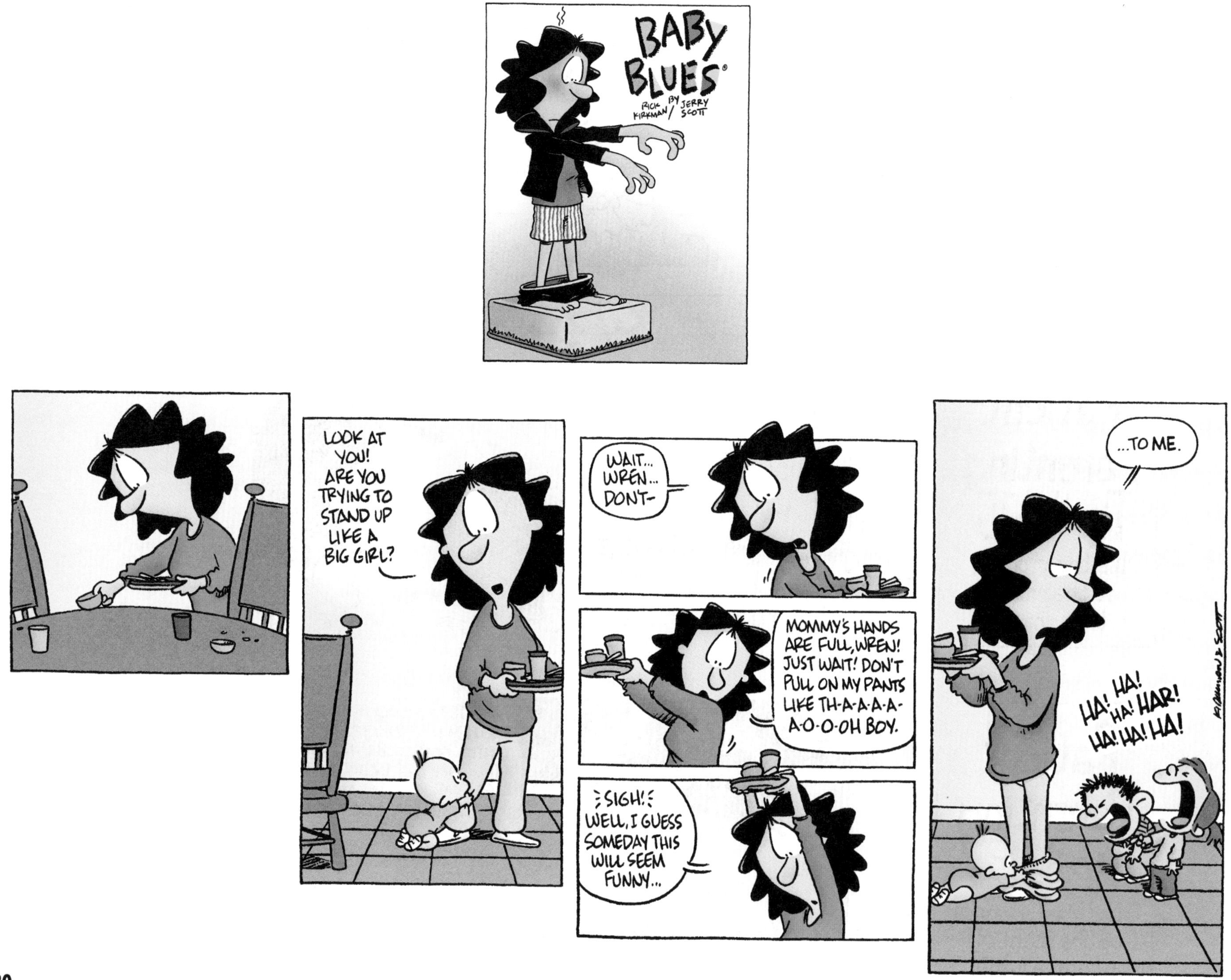
BABY BLUES®
BY RICK KIRKMAN / JERRY SCOTT
LOOK AT YOU! ARE YOU TRYING TO STAND UP LIKE A BIG GIRL?
WAIT... WREN... DON'T-
MOMMY'S HANDS ARE FULL, WREN! JUST WAIT! DON'T PULL ON MY PANTS LIKE TH-A-A-A-A-A-O-O-OH BOY.
SIGH! WELL, I GUESS SOMEDAY THIS WILL SEEM FUNNY...
...TO ME.
HA! HA! HA! HAR! HA! HA! HA!

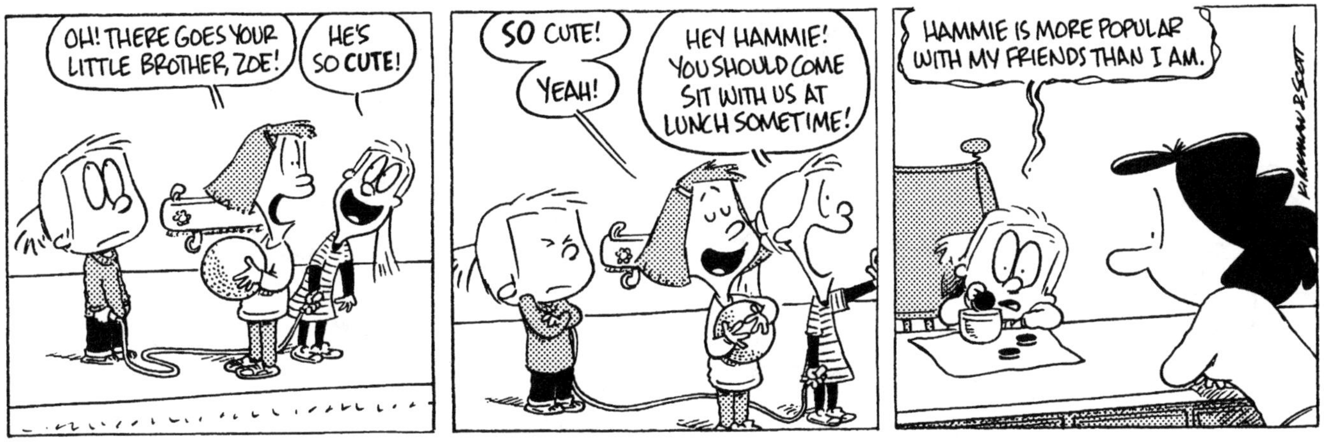
OH! THERE GOES YOUR LITTLE BROTHER, ZOE!
HE'S SO CUTE!
SO CUTE!
YEAH!
HEY HAMMIE! YOU SHOULD COME SIT WITH US AT LUNCH SOMETIME!
HAMMIE IS MORE POPULAR WITH MY FRIENDS THAN I AM.

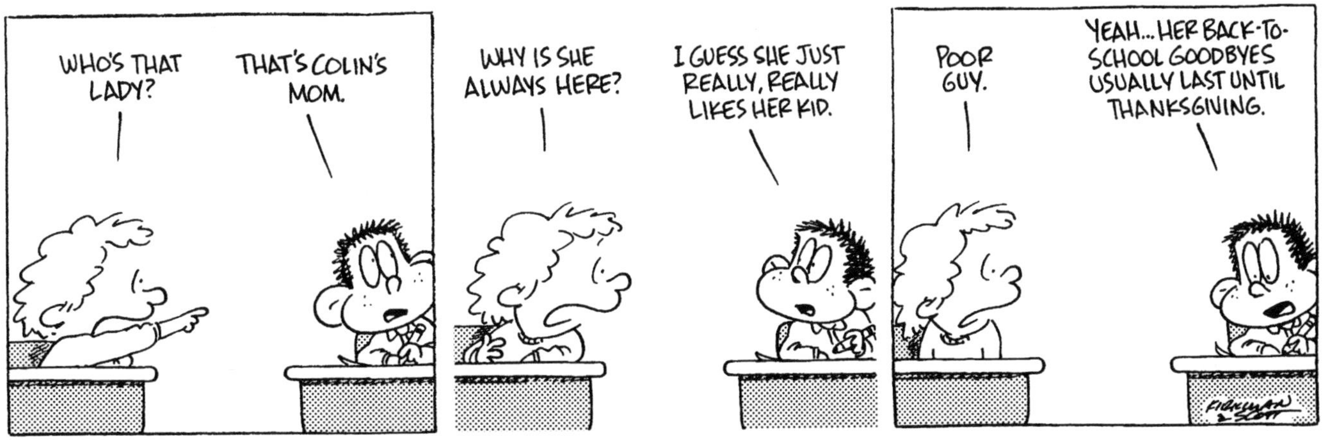
WHO'S THAT LADY?
THAT'S COLIN'S MOM.
WHY IS SHE ALWAYS HERE?
I GUESS SHE JUST REALLY, REALLY LIKES HER KID.
POOR GUY.
YEAH... HER BACK-TO-SCHOOL GOODBYES USUALLY LAST UNTIL THANKSGIVING.

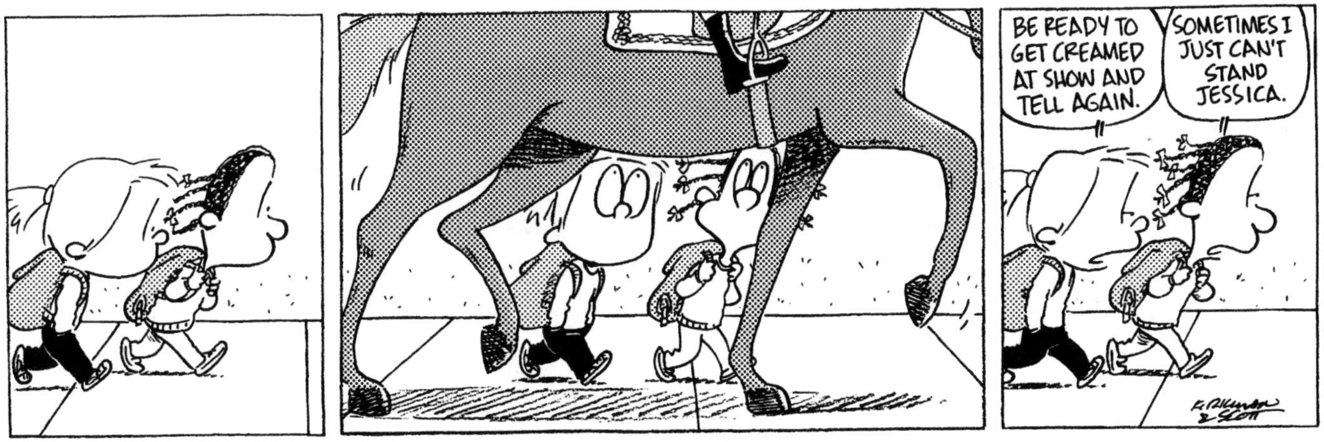
BE READY TO GET CREAMED AT SHOW AND TELL AGAIN.
SOMETIMES I JUST CAN'T STAND JESSICA.

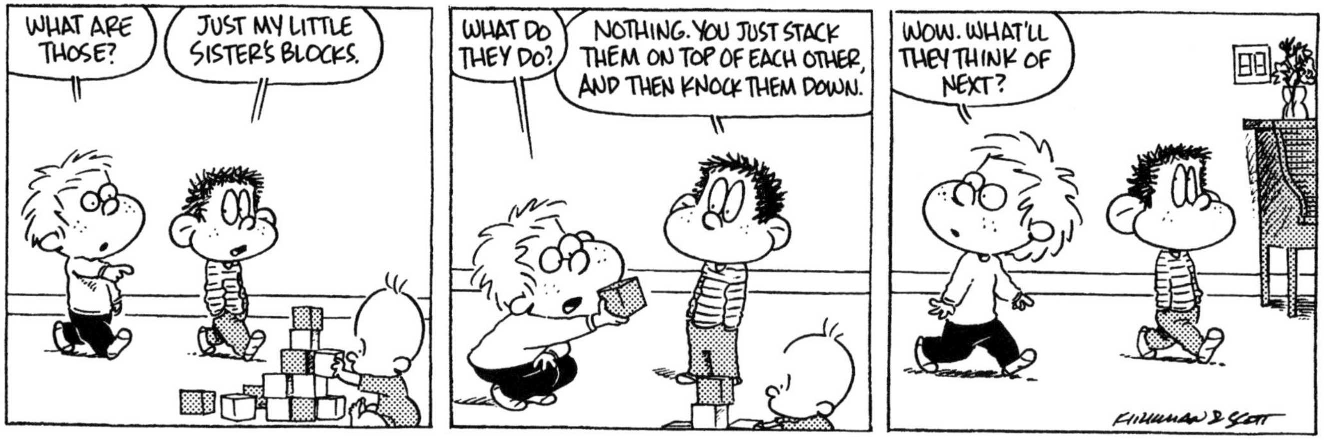
WHAT ARE THOSE?
JUST MY LITTLE SISTER'S BLOCKS.
WHAT DO THEY DO?
NOTHING. YOU JUST STACK THEM ON TOP OF EACH OTHER, AND THEN KNOCK THEM DOWN.
WOW. WHAT'LL THEY THINK OF NEXT?

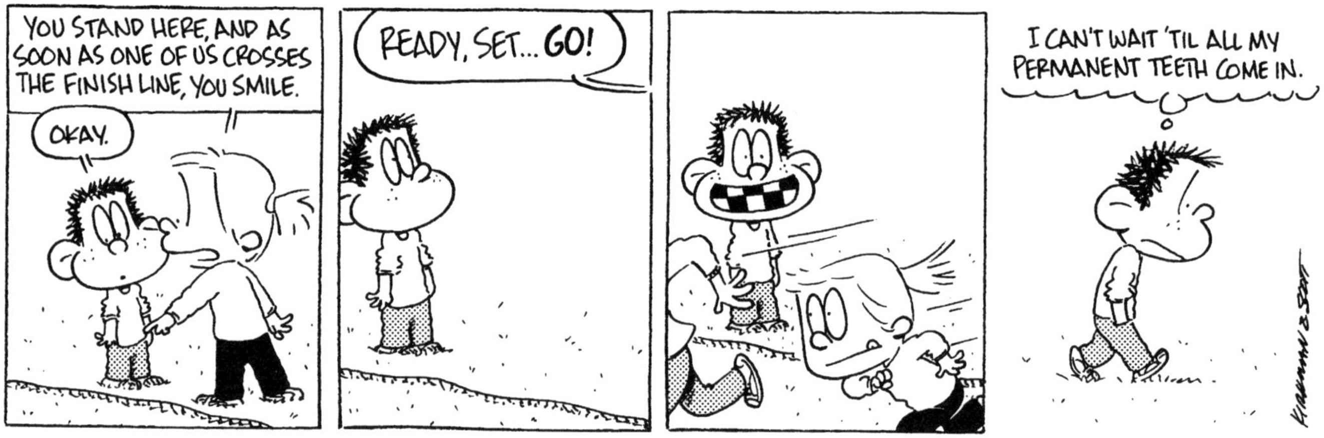
YOU STAND HERE, AND AS SOON AS ONE OF US CROSSES THE FINISH LINE, YOU SMILE.
OKAY.
READY, SET... GO!
I CAN'T WAIT 'TIL ALL MY PERMANENT TEETH COME IN.

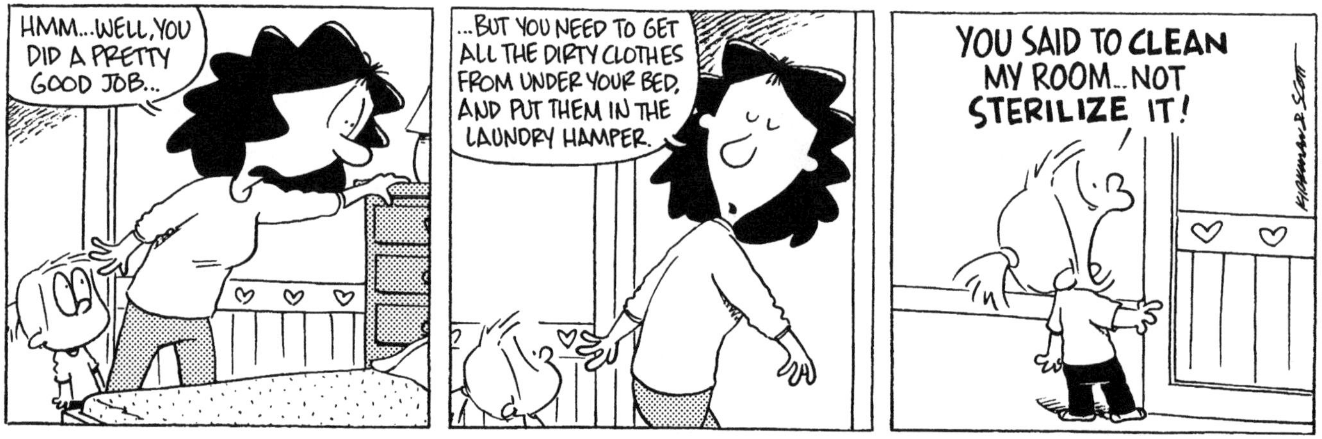
HMM...WELL, YOU DID A PRETTY GOOD JOB...
...BUT YOU NEED TO GET ALL THE DIRTY CLOTHES FROM UNDER YOUR BED, AND PUT THEM IN THE LAUNDRY HAMPER.
YOU SAID TO CLEAN MY ROOM...NOT STERILIZE IT!

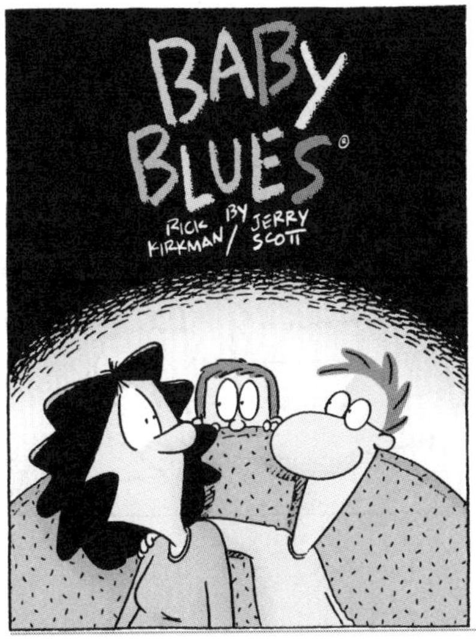
BABY BLUES®
RICK KIRKMAN / BY JERRY SCOTT

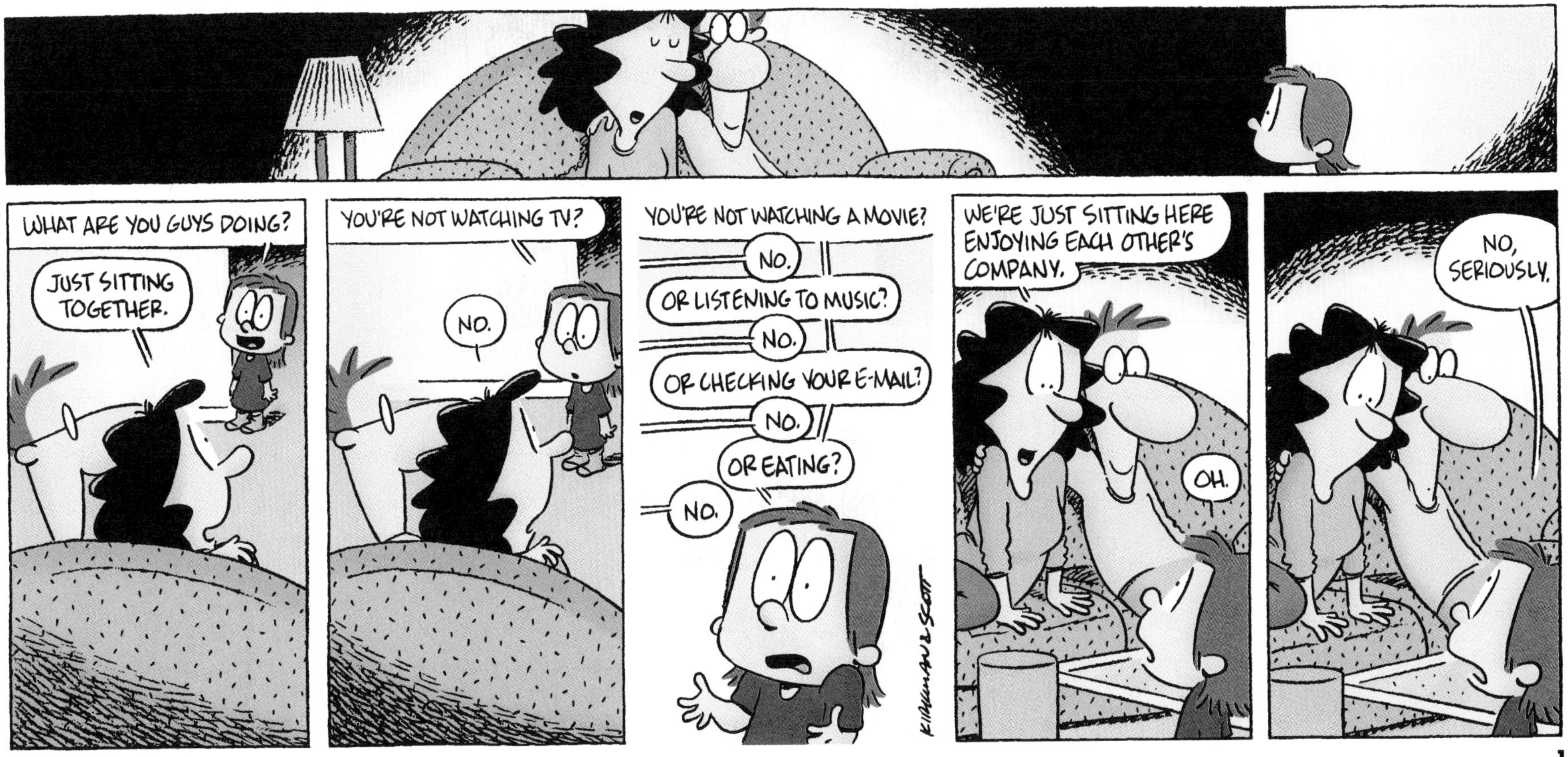
WHAT ARE YOU GUYS DOING?
JUST SITTING TOGETHER.
YOU'RE NOT WATCHING TV?
NO.
YOU'RE NOT WATCHING A MOVIE?
NO.
OR LISTENING TO MUSIC?
NO.
OR CHECKING YOUR E-MAIL?
NO.
OR EATING?
NO.
KIRKMAN & SCOTT
WE'RE JUST SITTING HERE ENJOYING EACH OTHER'S COMPANY.
OH.
NO, SERIOUSLY.

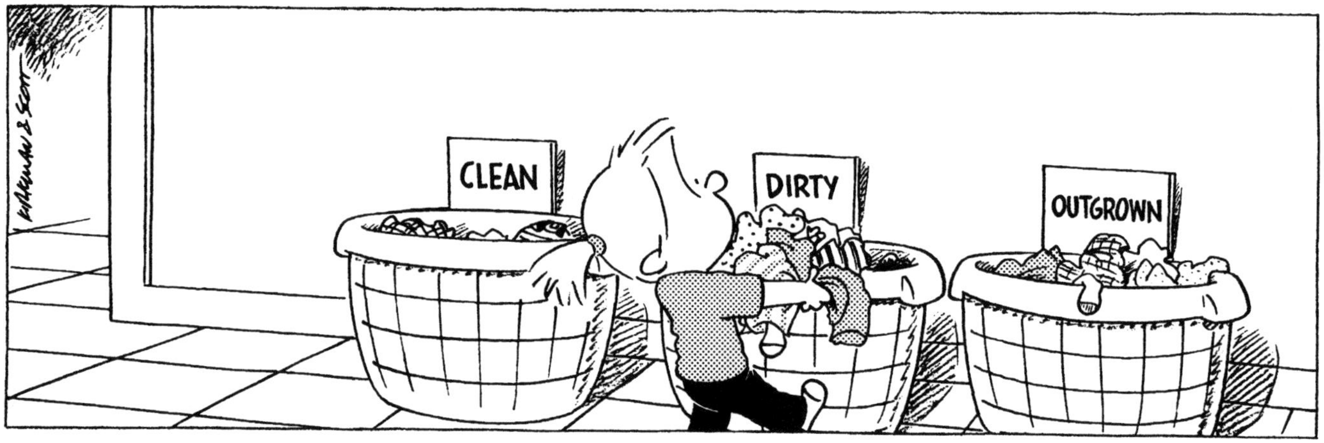
CLEAN
DIRTY
OUTGROWN

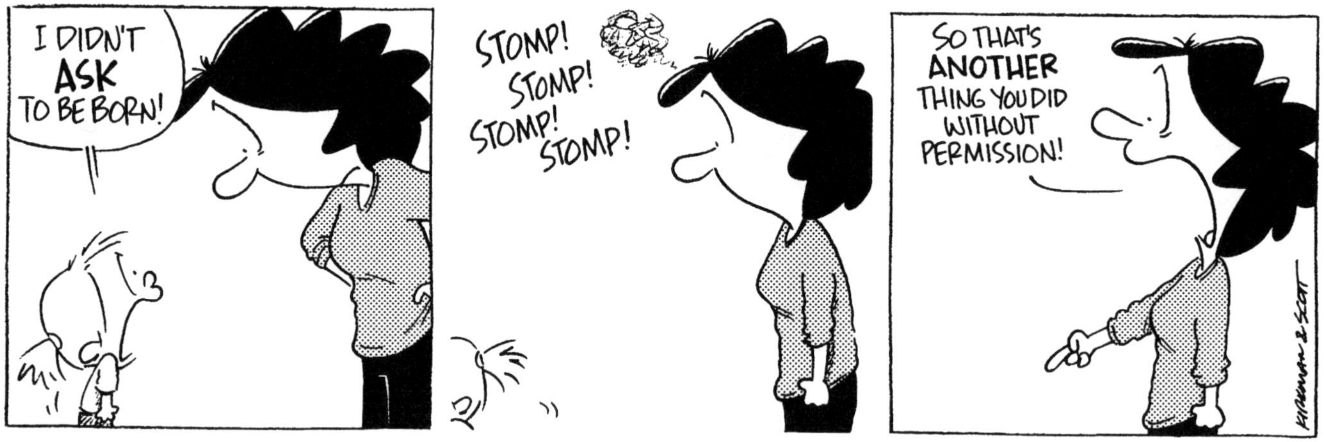
I DIDN'T **ASK** TO BE BORN!
STOMP! STOMP! STOMP! STOMP!
SO THAT'S **ANOTHER** THING YOU DID WITHOUT PERMISSION!

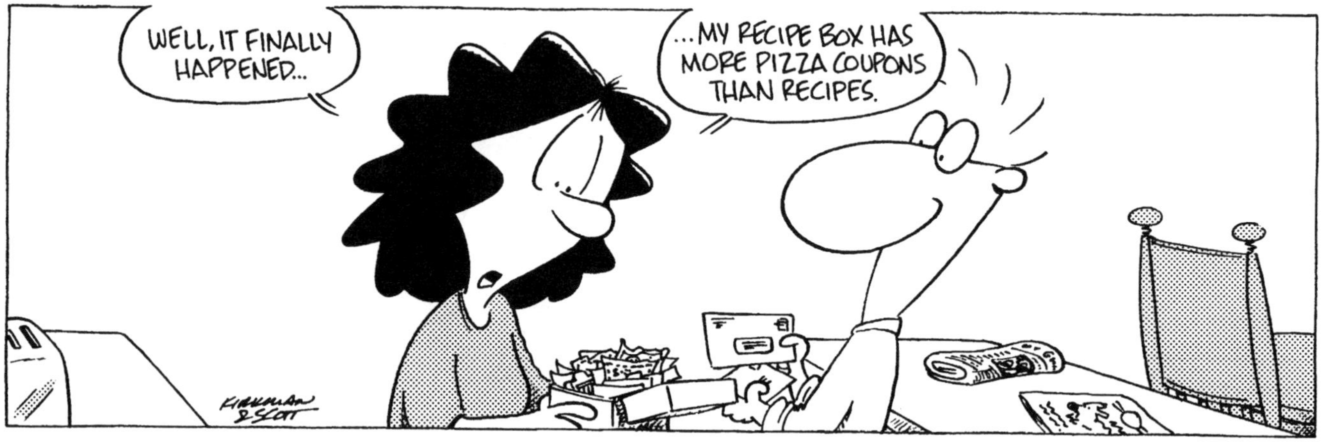
WELL, IT FINALLY HAPPENED...
...MY RECIPE BOX HAS MORE PIZZA COUPONS THAN RECIPES.

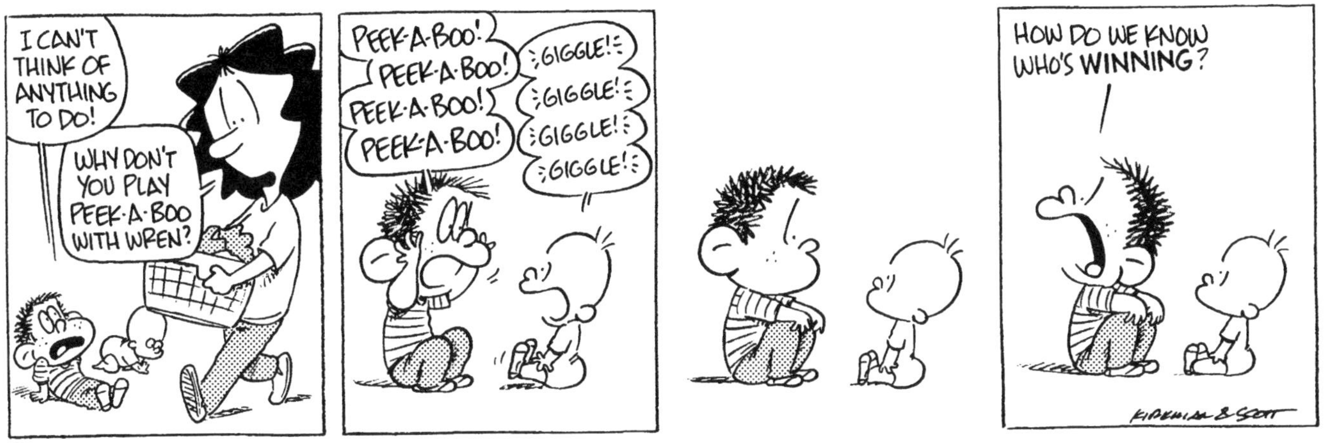
I CAN'T THINK OF ANYTHING TO DO!
WHY DON'T YOU PLAY PEEK-A-BOO WITH WREN?
PEEK-A-BOO!
PEEK-A-BOO!
PEEK-A-BOO!
PEEK-A-BOO!
GIGGLE!
GIGGLE!
GIGGLE!
GIGGLE!
HOW DO WE KNOW WHO'S WINNING?

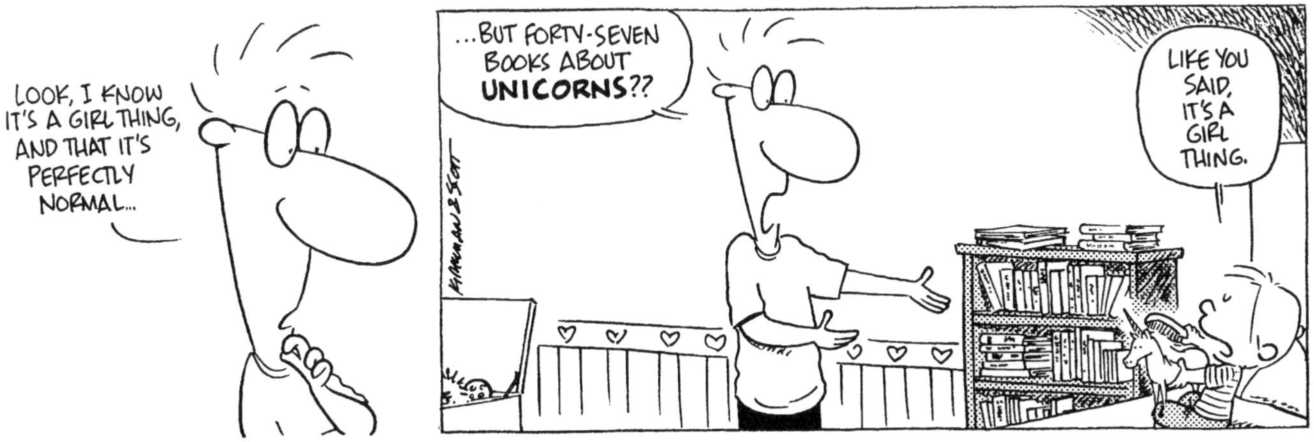
LOOK, I KNOW IT'S A GIRL THING, AND THAT IT'S PERFECTLY NORMAL...
...BUT FORTY-SEVEN BOOKS ABOUT UNICORNS??
LIKE YOU SAID, IT'S A GIRL THING.

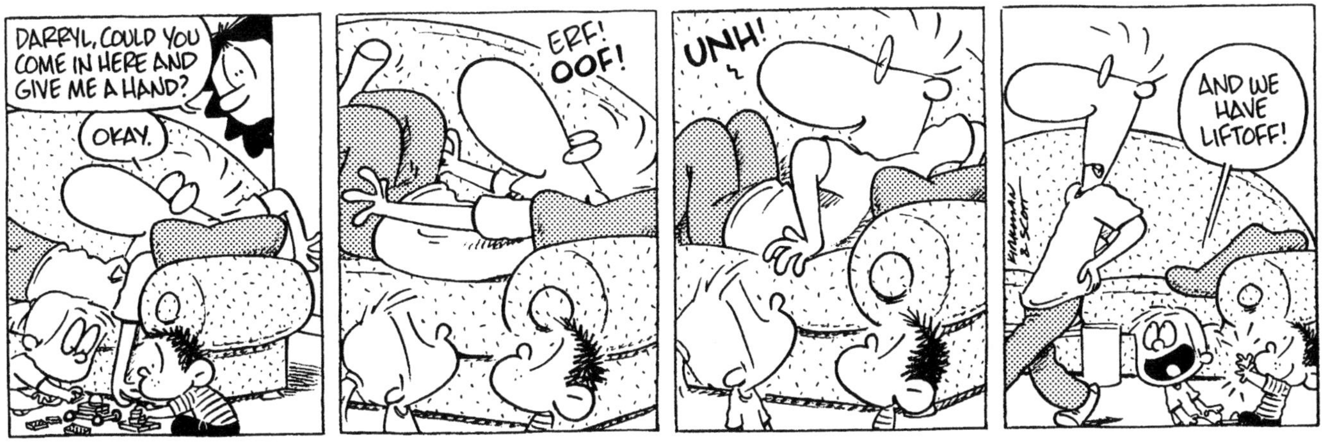
DARRYL, COULD YOU COME IN HERE AND GIVE ME A HAND?
OKAY.
ERF! OOF!
UNH!
AND WE HAVE LIFTOFF!

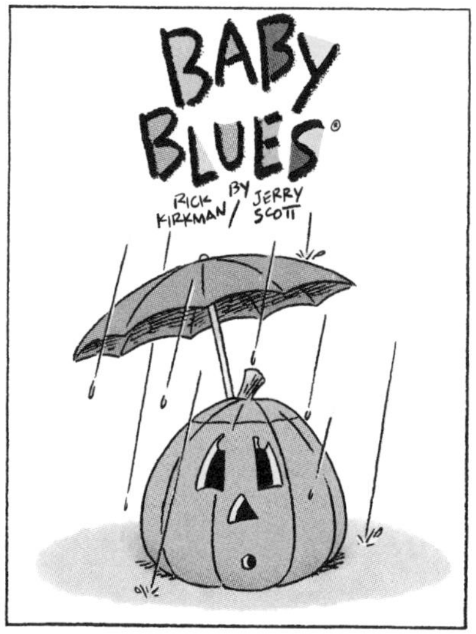
BABY BLUES®
BY RICK KIRKMAN / JERRY SCOTT

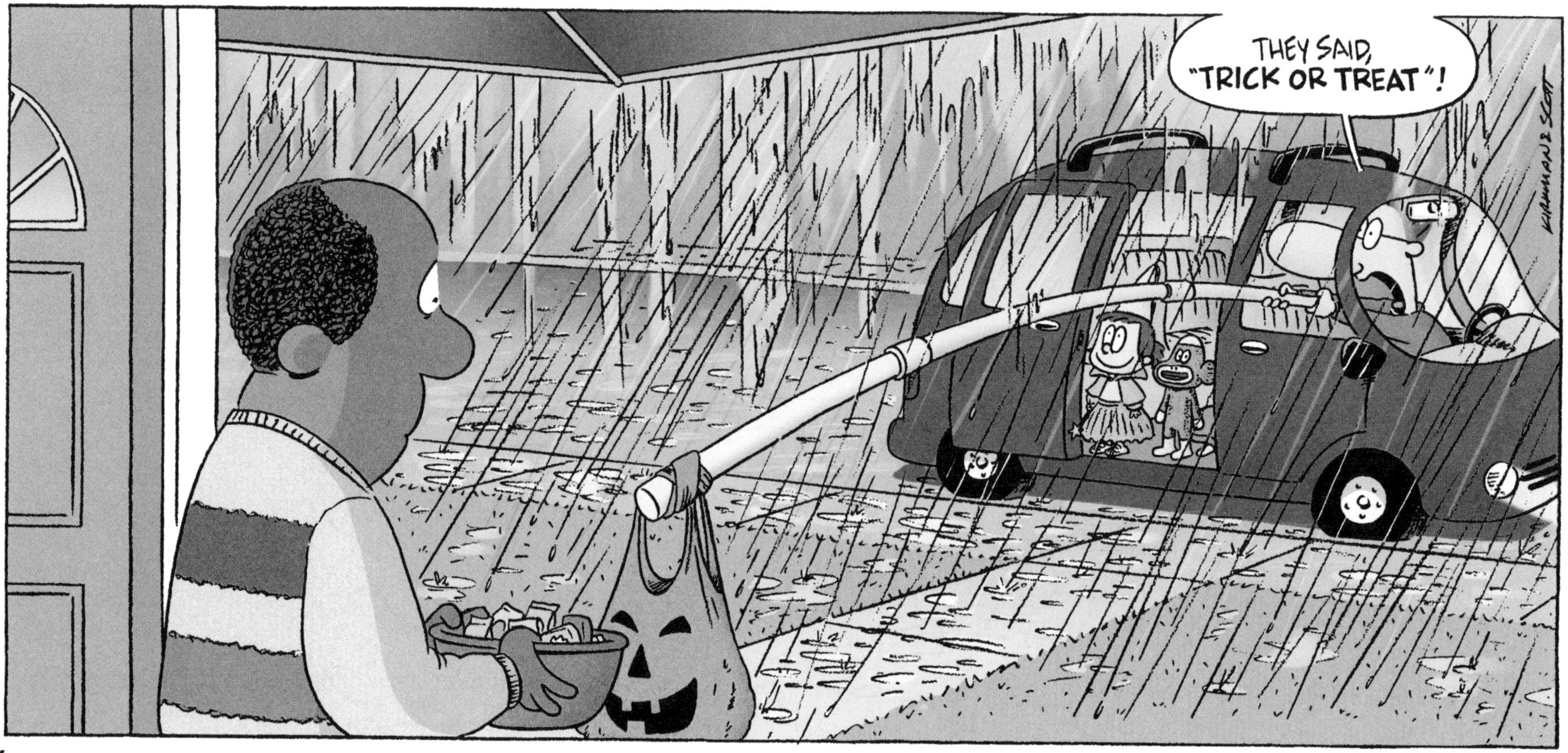
THEY SAID, "TRICK OR TREAT"!

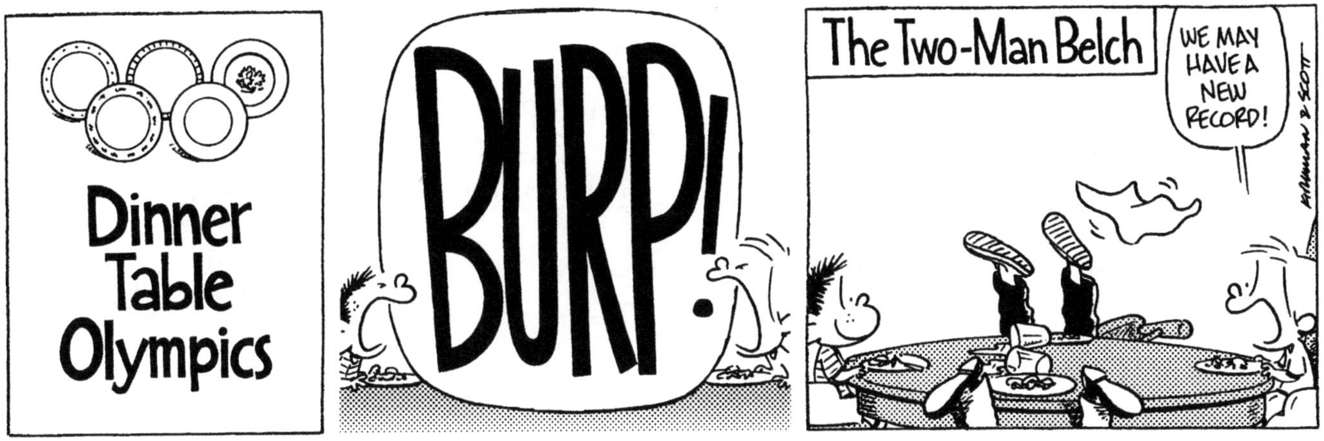
Dinner Table Olympics
BURP!
The Two-Man Belch
WE MAY HAVE A NEW RECORD!
KIRKMAN & SCOTT

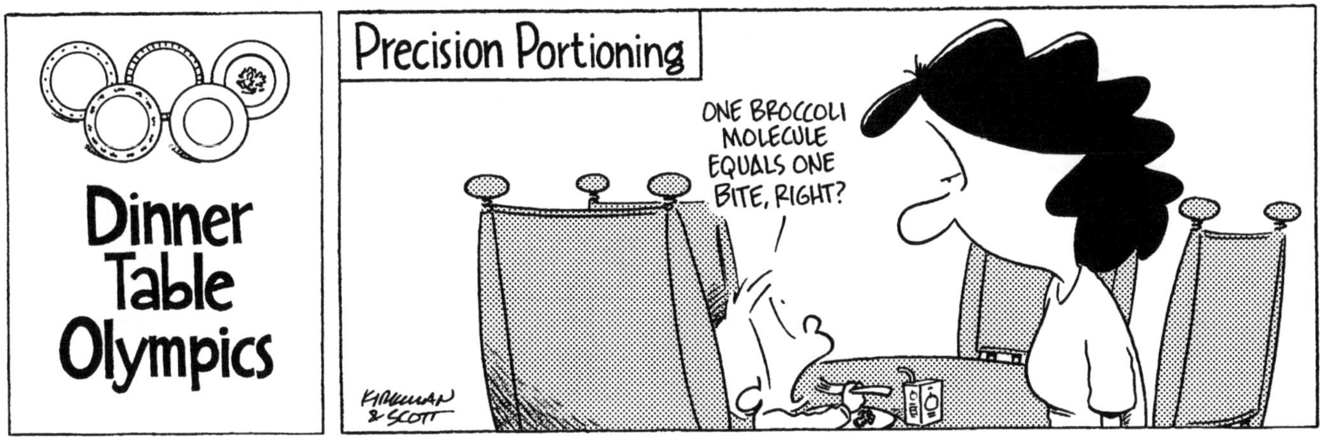
Dinner Table Olympics
Precision Portioning
ONE BROCCOLI MOLECULE EQUALS ONE BITE, RIGHT?
KIRKMAN & SCOTT

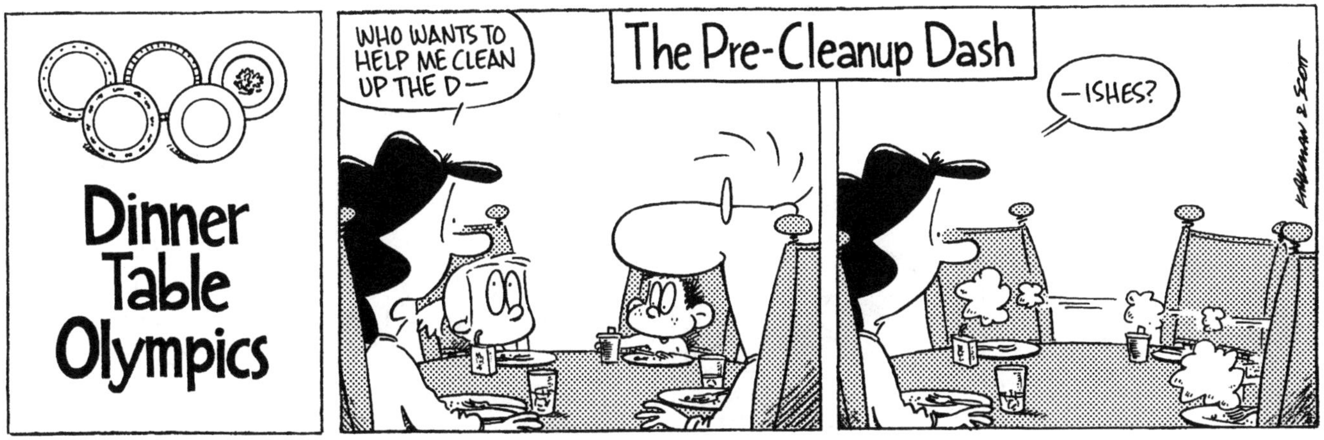
Dinner Table Olympics
The Pre-Cleanup Dash
WHO WANTS TO HELP ME CLEAN UP THE D—
—ISHES?
KIRKMAN & SCOTT

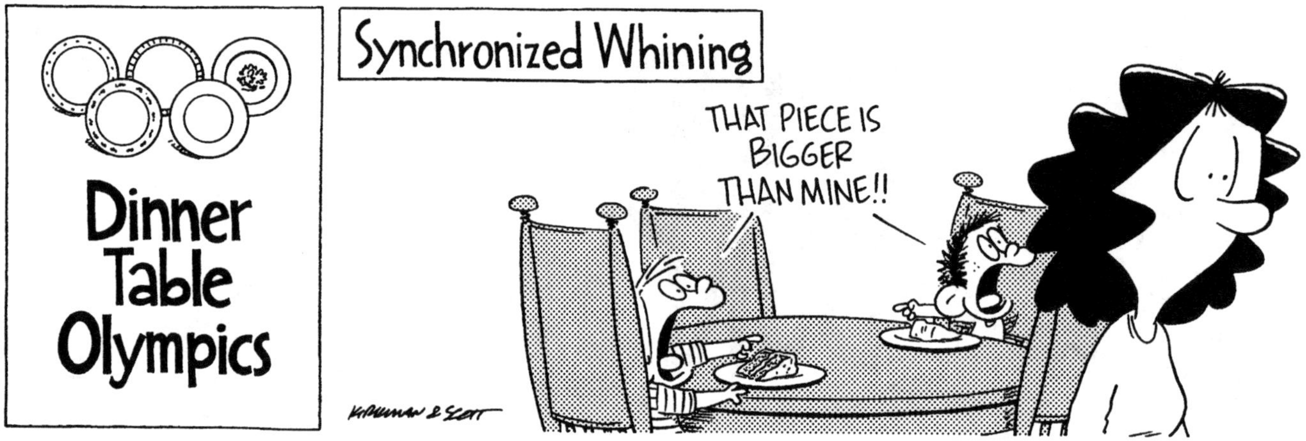
Dinner Table Olympics
Synchronized Whining
THAT PIECE IS BIGGER THAN MINE!!

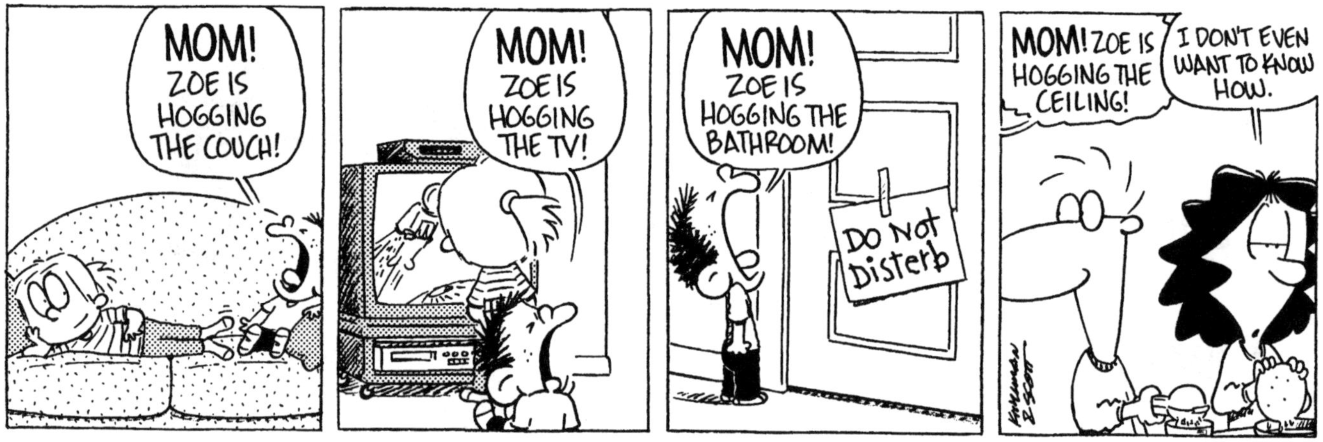
MOM! ZOE IS HOGGING THE COUCH!
MOM! ZOE IS HOGGING THE TV!
MOM! ZOE IS HOGGING THE BATHROOM!
DO NOT DISTERB
MOM! ZOE IS HOGGING THE CEILING!
I DON'T EVEN WANT TO KNOW HOW.

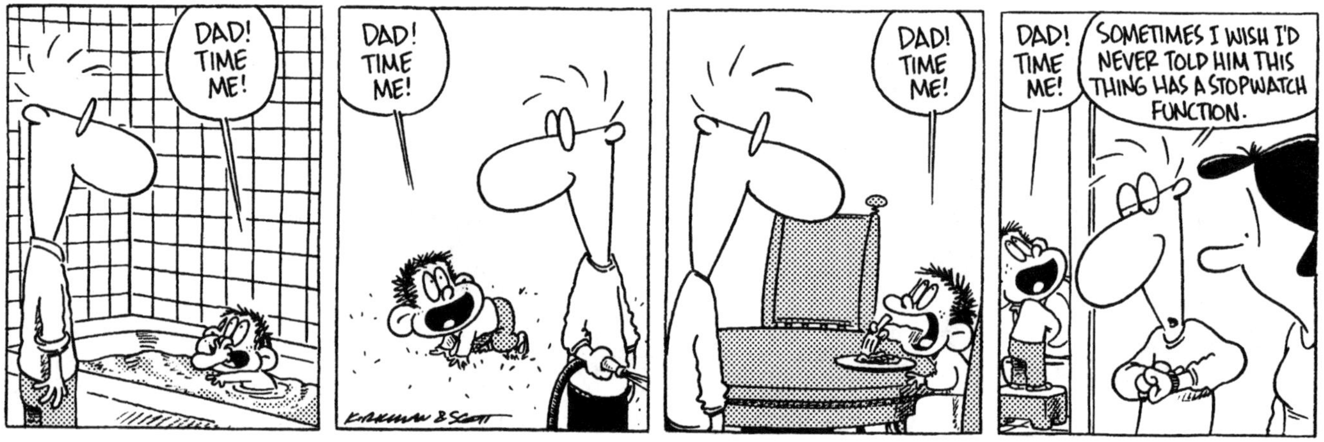
DAD! TIME ME!
DAD! TIME ME!
DAD! TIME ME!
DAD! TIME ME!
SOMETIMES I WISH I'D NEVER TOLD HIM THIS THING HAS A STOPWATCH FUNCTION.

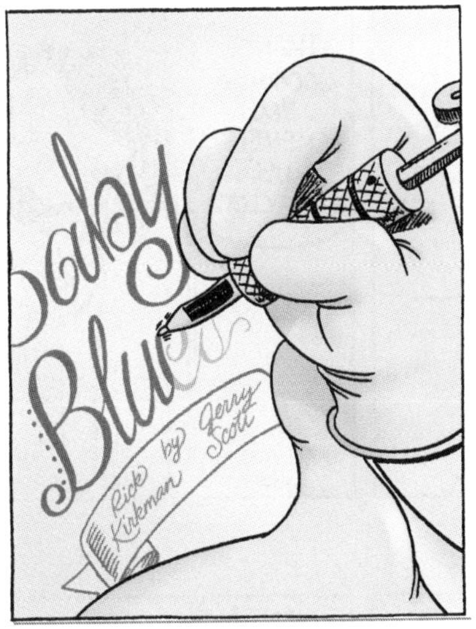
Baby Blues
Rick Kirkman by Jerry Scott

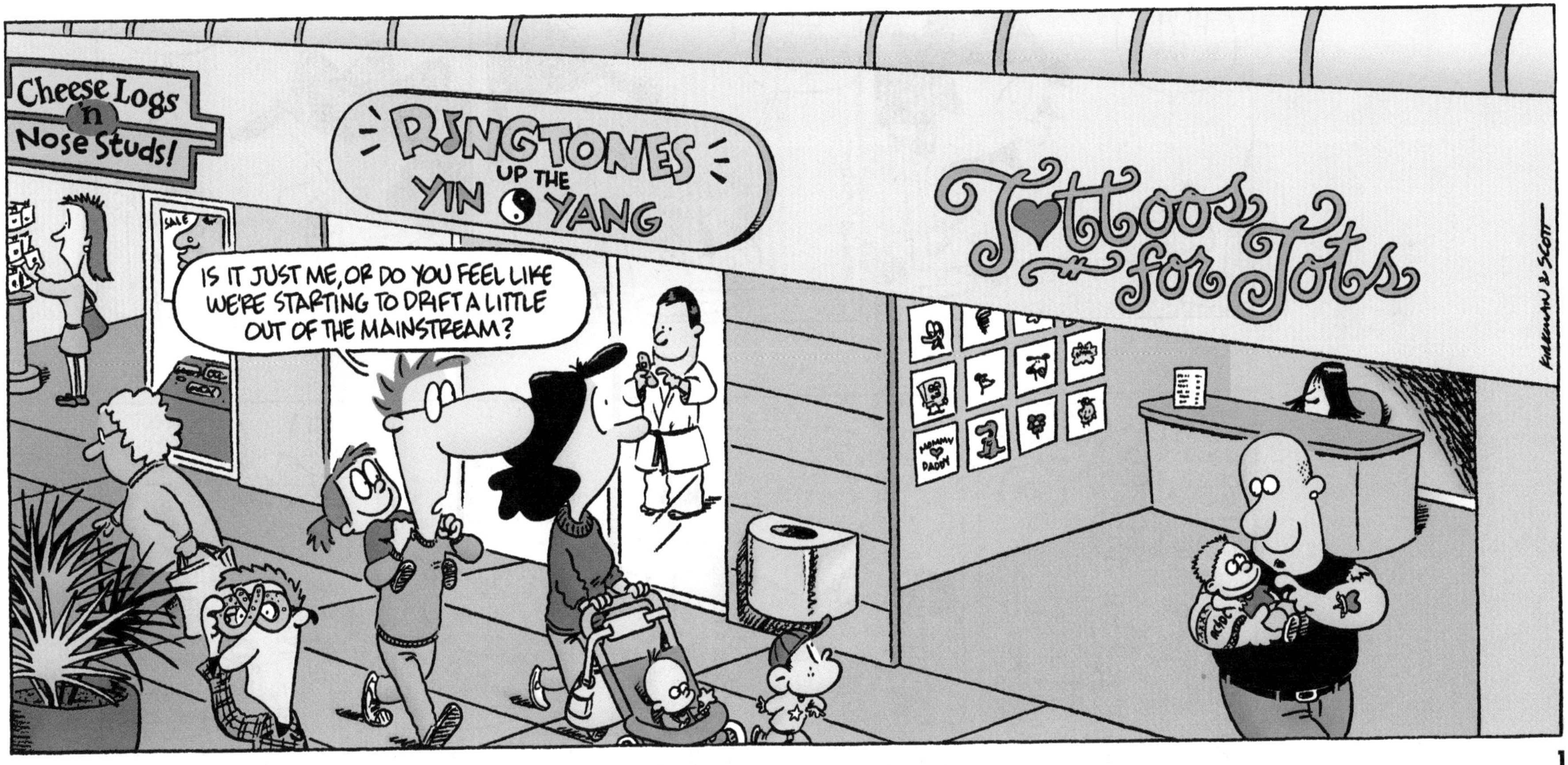
Cheese Logs 'n Nose Studs!
RINGTONES UP THE YIN YANG
Tattoos for Tots
IS IT JUST ME, OR DO YOU FEEL LIKE WE'RE STARTING TO DRIFT A LITTLE OUT OF THE MAINSTREAM?
KIRKMAN & SCOTT

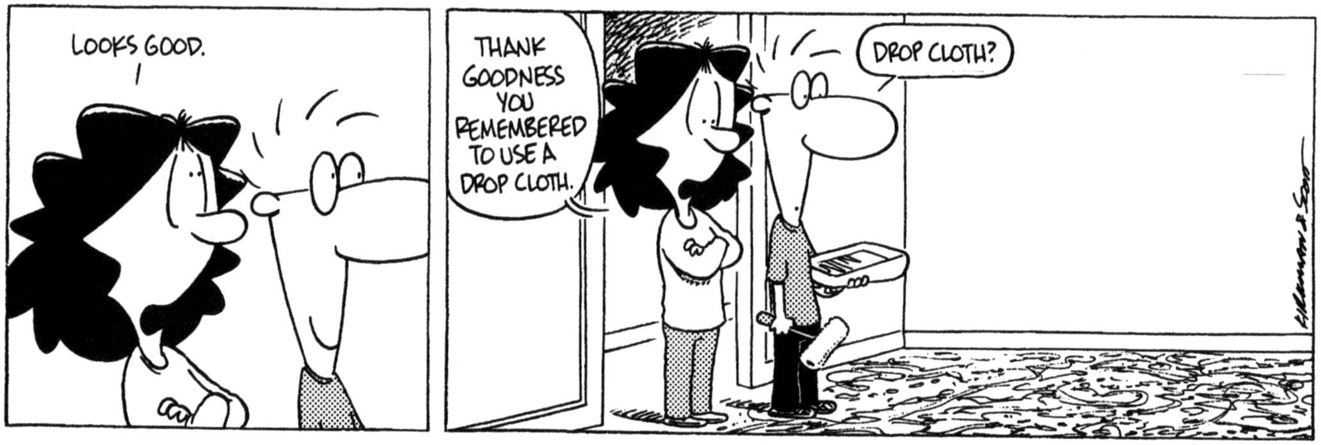
LOOKS GOOD.
THANK GOODNESS YOU REMEMBERED TO USE A DROP CLOTH.
DROP CLOTH?

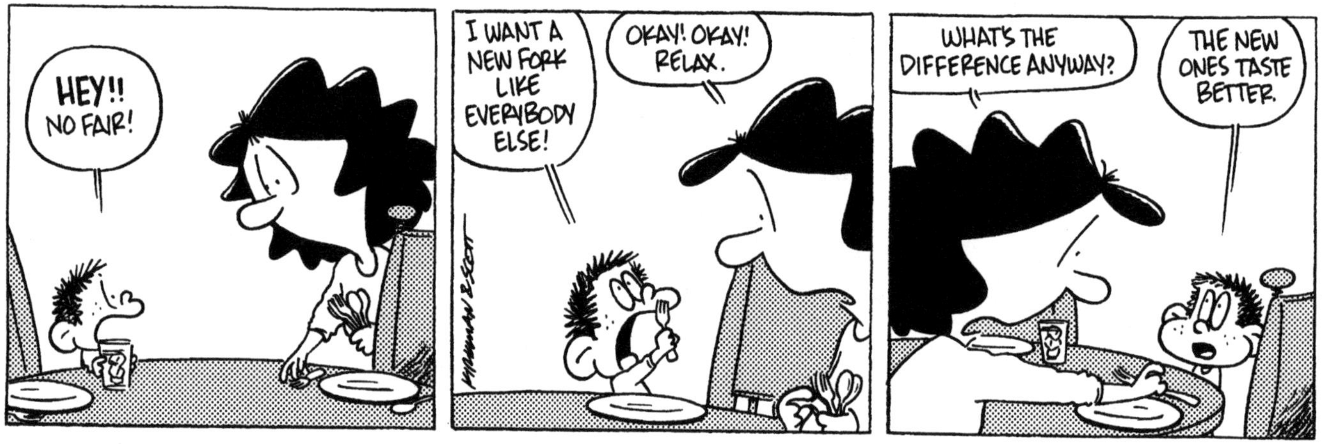
HEY!! NO FAIR!
I WANT A NEW FORK LIKE EVERYBODY ELSE!
OKAY! OKAY! RELAX.
WHAT'S THE DIFFERENCE ANYWAY?
THE NEW ONES TASTE BETTER.

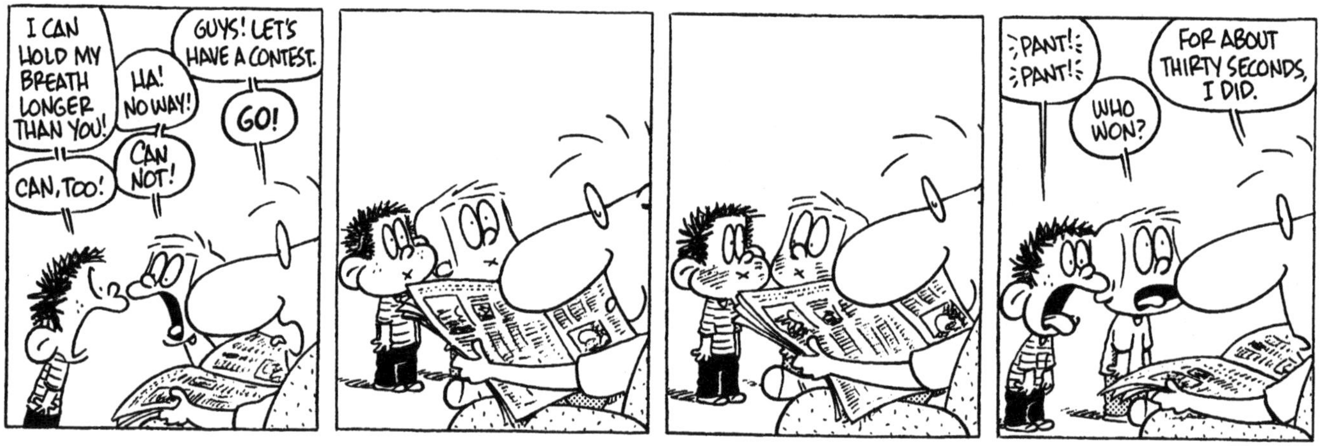
I CAN HOLD MY BREATH LONGER THAN YOU!
HA! NO WAY!
CAN, TOO!
CAN NOT!
GUYS! LET'S HAVE A CONTEST.
GO!
PANT! PANT!
WHO WON?
FOR ABOUT THIRTY SECONDS, I DID.

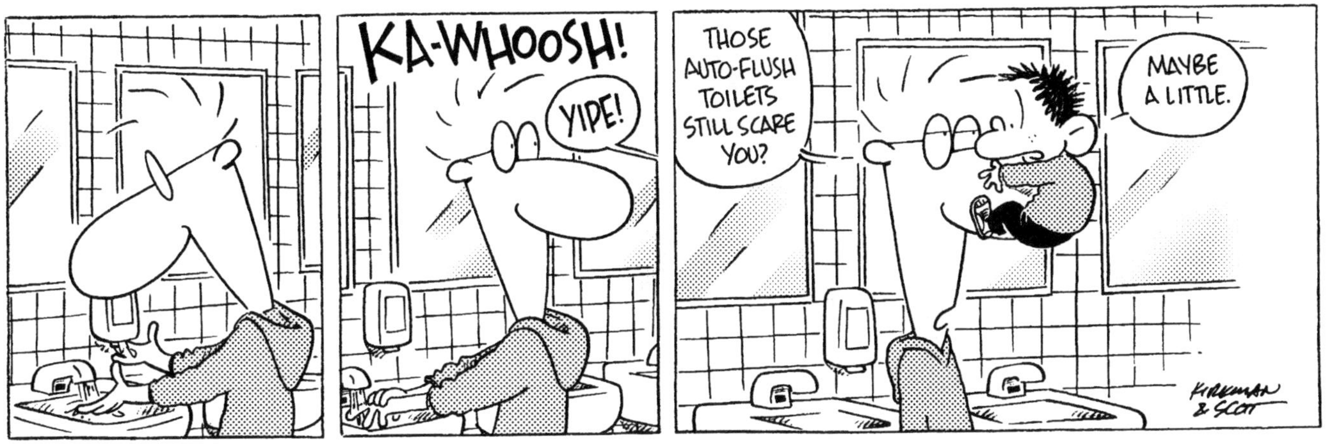
KA-WHOOSH!
YIPE!
THOSE AUTO-FLUSH TOILETS STILL SCARE YOU?
MAYBE A LITTLE.

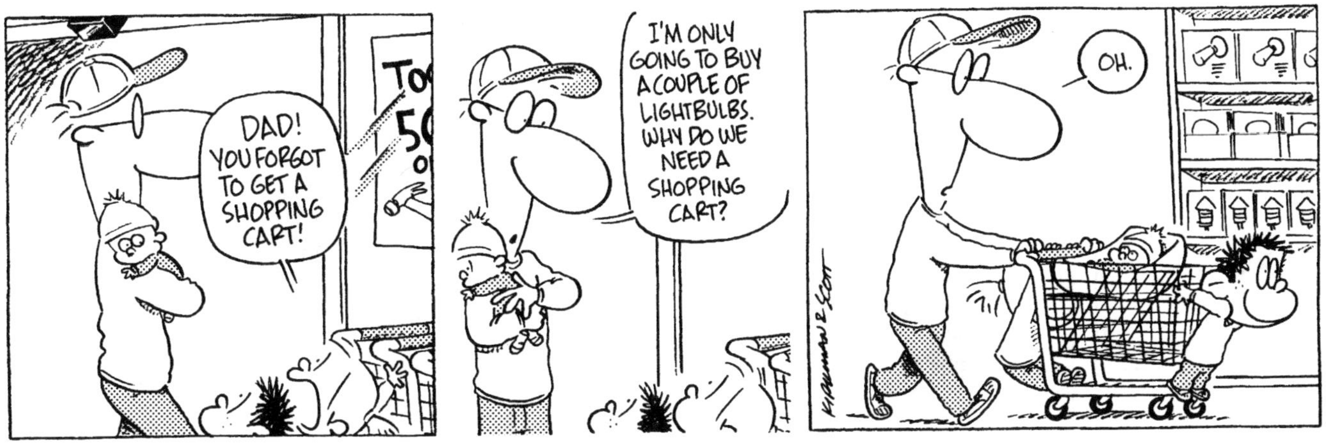
DAD! YOU FORGOT TO GET A SHOPPING CART!
I'M ONLY GOING TO BUY A COUPLE OF LIGHTBULBS. WHY DO WE NEED A SHOPPING CART?
OH.

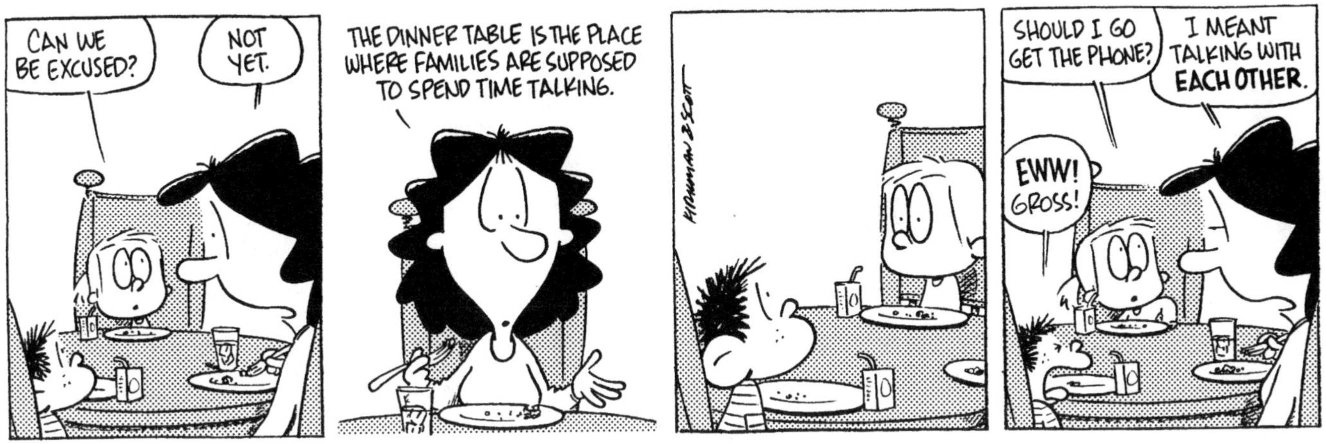
CAN WE BE EXCUSED?
NOT YET.
THE DINNER TABLE IS THE PLACE WHERE FAMILIES ARE SUPPOSED TO SPEND TIME TALKING.
SHOULD I GO GET THE PHONE?
I MEANT TALKING WITH **EACH OTHER**.
EWW! GROSS!

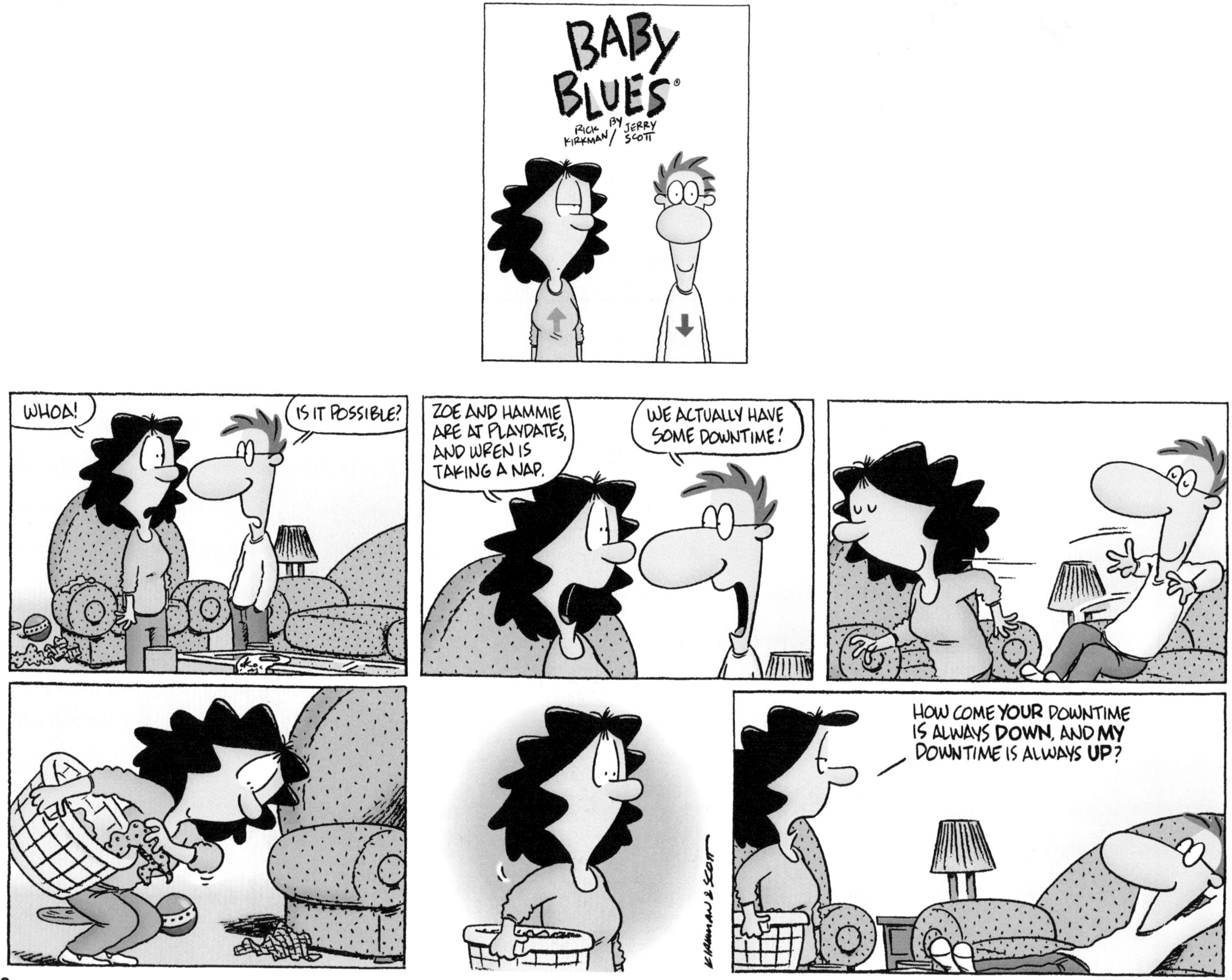
BABY BLUES®
BY RICK KIRKMAN / JERRY SCOTT
WHOA!
IS IT POSSIBLE?
ZOE AND HAMMIE ARE AT PLAYDATES, AND WREN IS TAKING A NAP.
WE ACTUALLY HAVE SOME DOWNTIME!
KIRKMAN & SCOTT
HOW COME YOUR DOWNTIME IS ALWAYS DOWN, AND MY DOWNTIME IS ALWAYS UP?

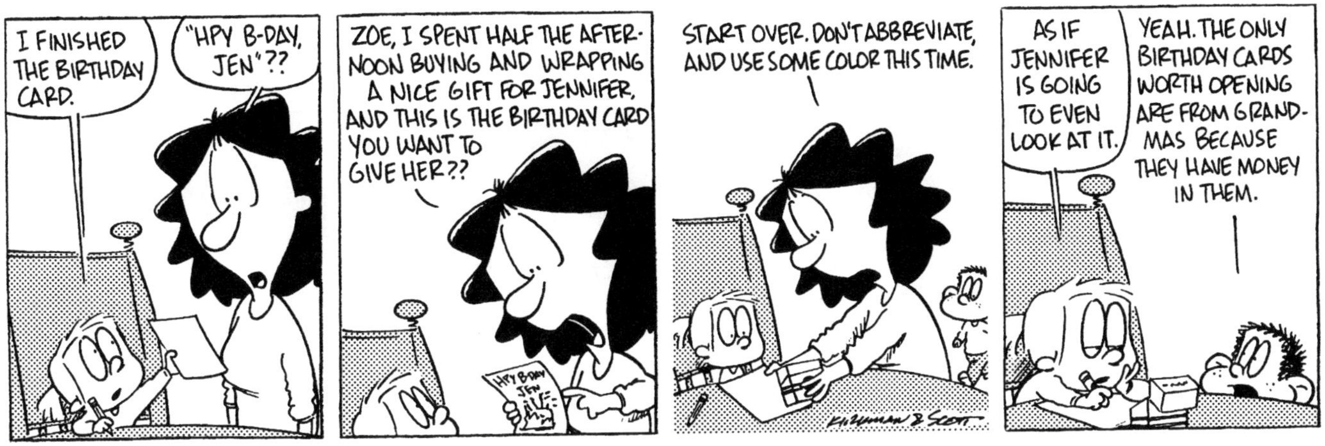
I FINISHED THE BIRTHDAY CARD.
"HPY B-DAY, JEN"??
ZOE, I SPENT HALF THE AFTERNOON BUYING AND WRAPPING A NICE GIFT FOR JENNIFER, AND THIS IS THE BIRTHDAY CARD YOU WANT TO GIVE HER??
START OVER. DON'T ABBREVIATE, AND USE SOME COLOR THIS TIME.
AS IF JENNIFER IS GOING TO EVEN LOOK AT IT.
YEAH. THE ONLY BIRTHDAY CARDS WORTH OPENING ARE FROM GRANDMAS BECAUSE THEY HAVE MONEY IN THEM.

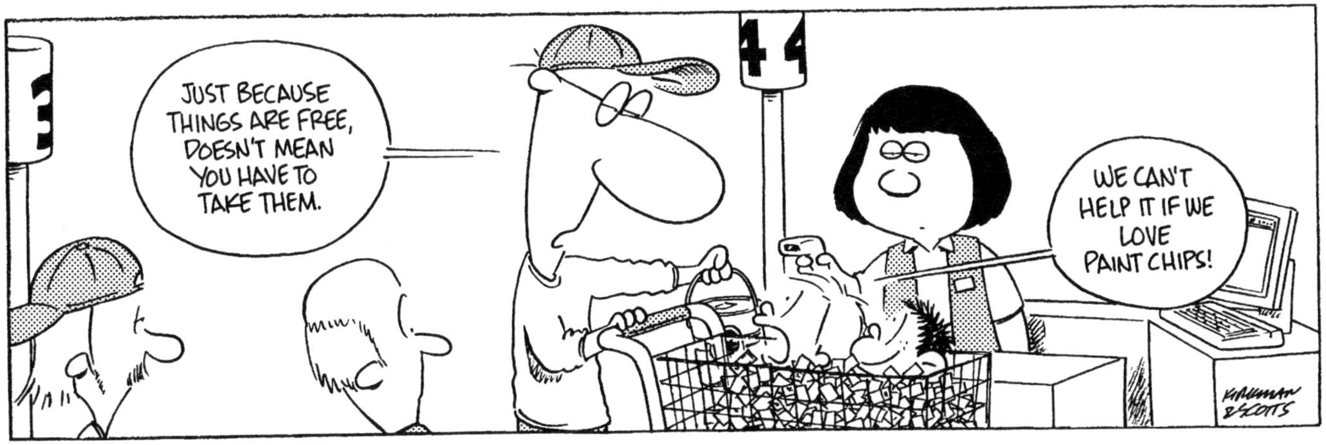
JUST BECAUSE THINGS ARE FREE, DOESN'T MEAN YOU HAVE TO TAKE THEM.
WE CAN'T HELP IT IF WE LOVE PAINT CHIPS!

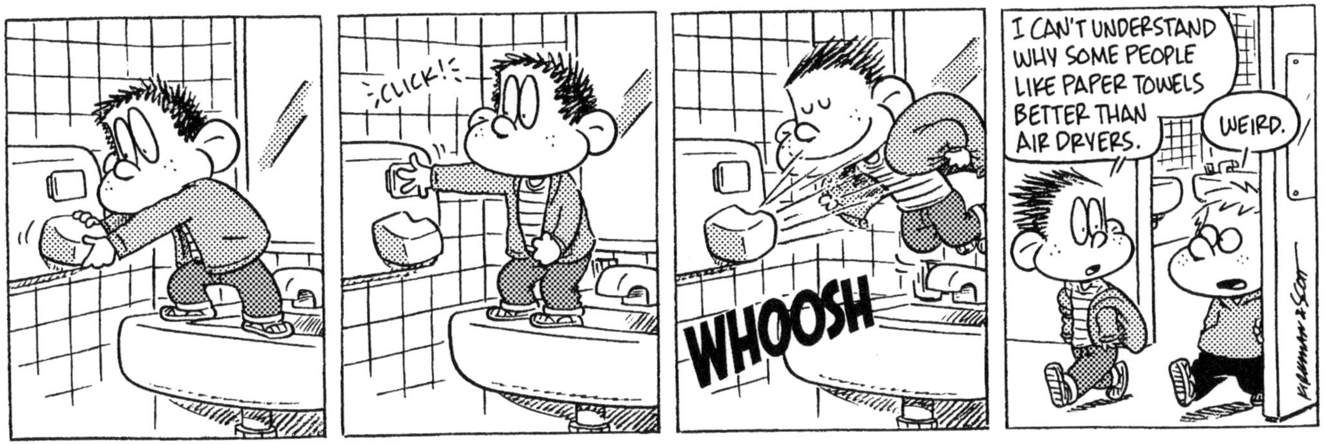
CLICK!
WHOOSH
I CAN'T UNDERSTAND WHY SOME PEOPLE LIKE PAPER TOWELS BETTER THAN AIR DRYERS.
WEIRD.

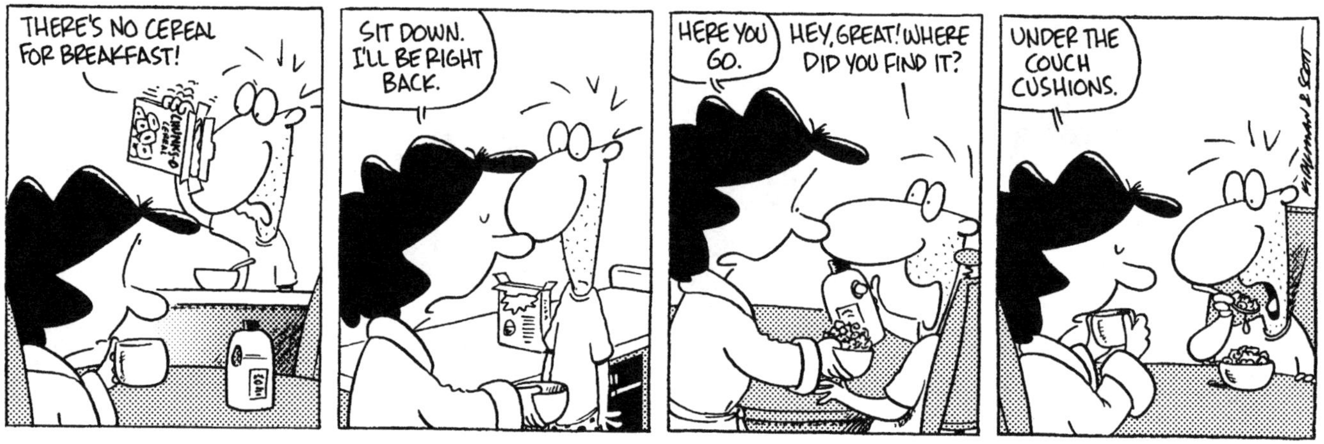
THERE'S NO CEREAL FOR BREAKFAST!
SIT DOWN. I'LL BE RIGHT BACK.
HERE YOU GO.
HEY, GREAT! WHERE DID YOU FIND IT?
UNDER THE COUCH CUSHIONS.

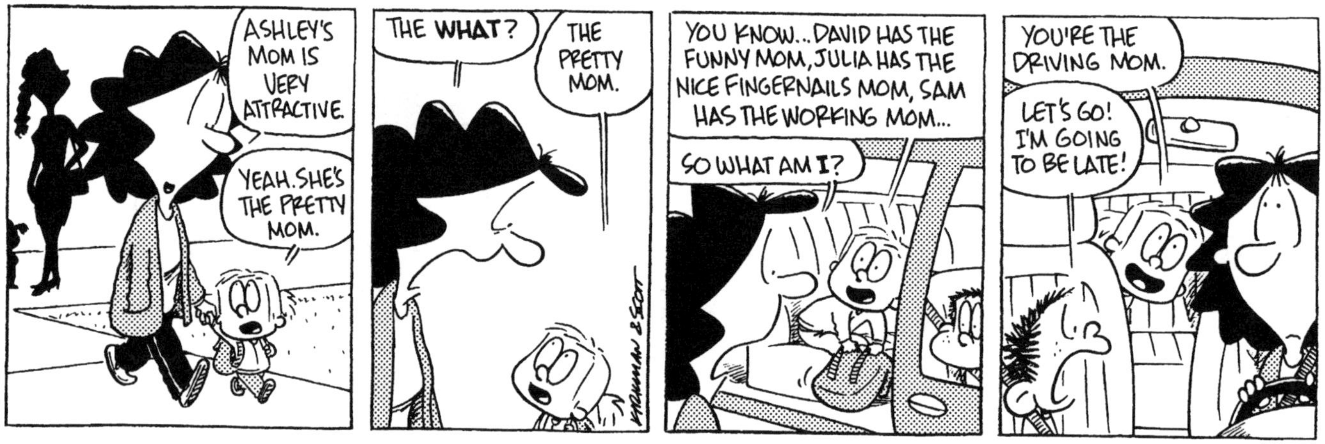
ASHLEY'S MOM IS VERY ATTRACTIVE.
YEAH. SHE'S THE PRETTY MOM.
THE **WHAT**?
THE PRETTY MOM.
YOU KNOW... DAVID HAS THE FUNNY MOM, JULIA HAS THE NICE FINGERNAILS MOM, SAM HAS THE WORKING MOM...
SO WHAT AM **I**?
YOU'RE THE DRIVING MOM.
LET'S GO! I'M GOING TO BE LATE!

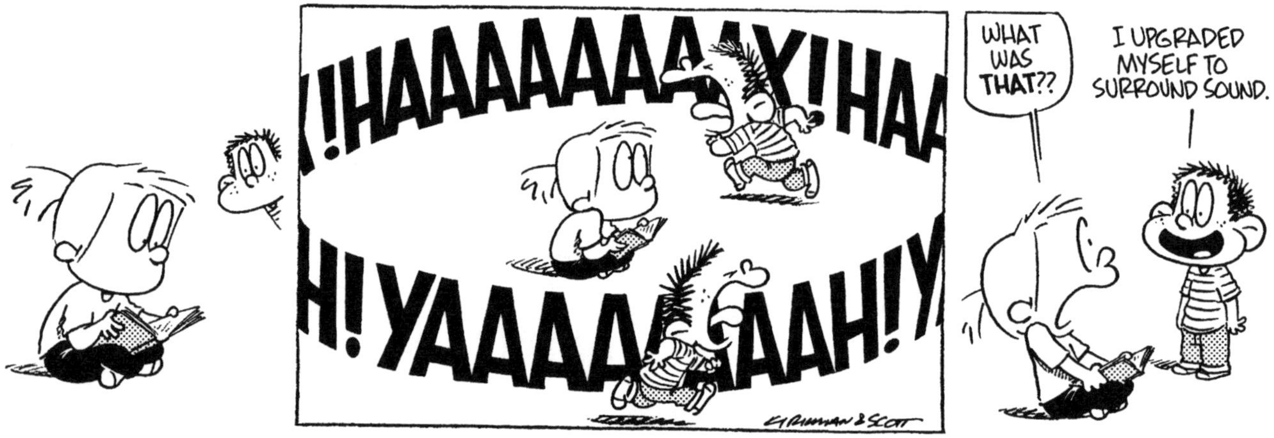
!HAAAAAAAAY!HAA
H!YAAAAAAAAH!Y
WHAT WAS **THAT**??
I UPGRADED MYSELF TO SURROUND SOUND.

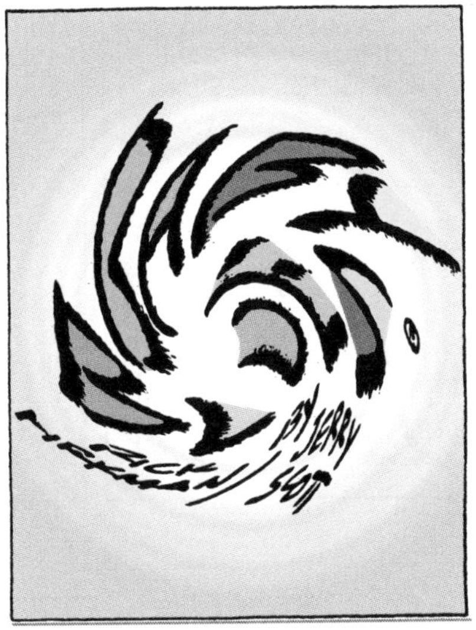

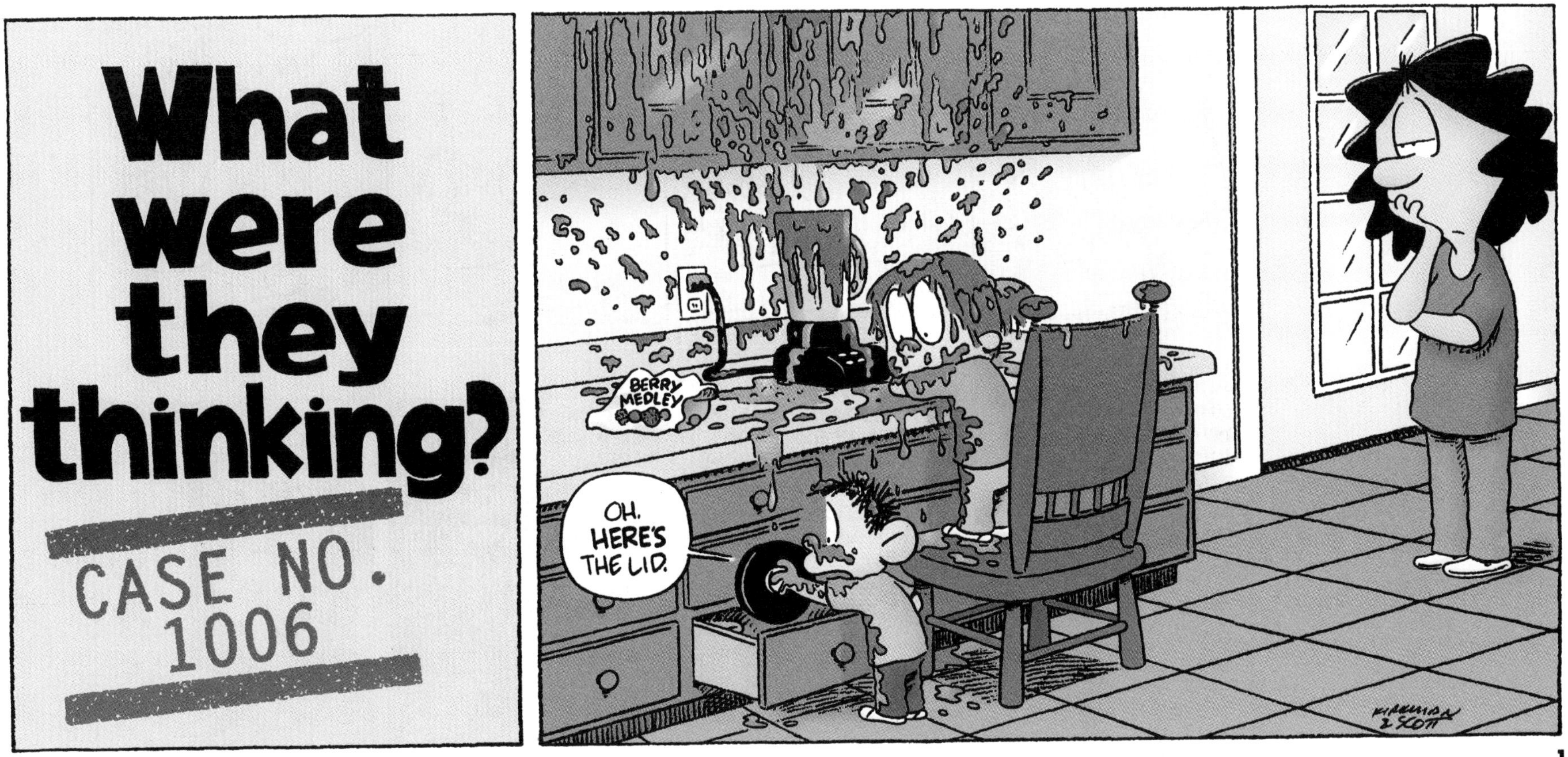
What were they thinking?
CASE NO. 1006
BERRY MEDLEY
OH. HERE'S THE LID.

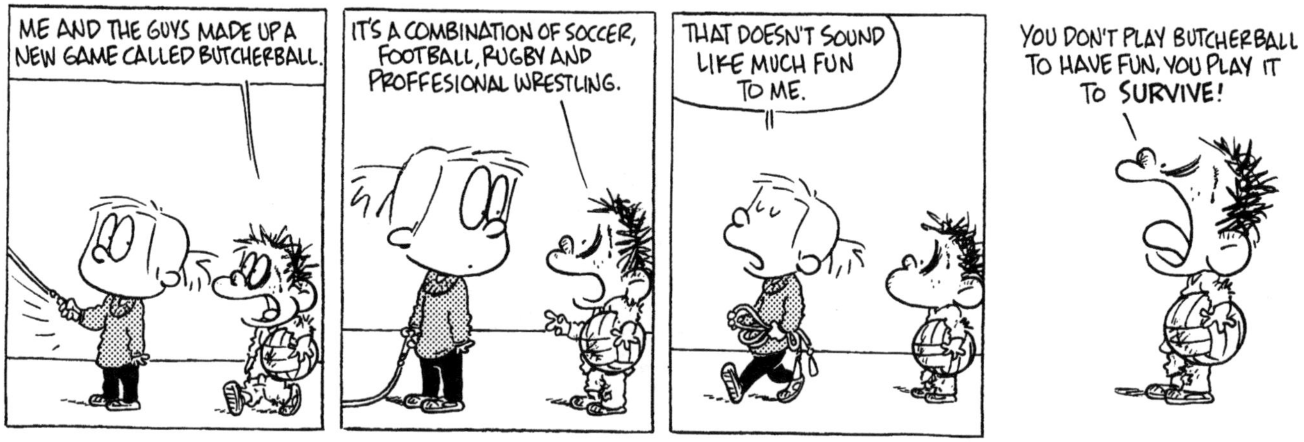
ME AND THE GUYS MADE UP A NEW GAME CALLED BUTCHERBALL.
IT'S A COMBINATION OF SOCCER, FOOTBALL, RUGBY AND PROFFESIONAL WRESTLING.
THAT DOESN'T SOUND LIKE MUCH FUN TO ME.
YOU DON'T PLAY BUTCHERBALL TO HAVE FUN, YOU PLAY IT TO **SURVIVE**!

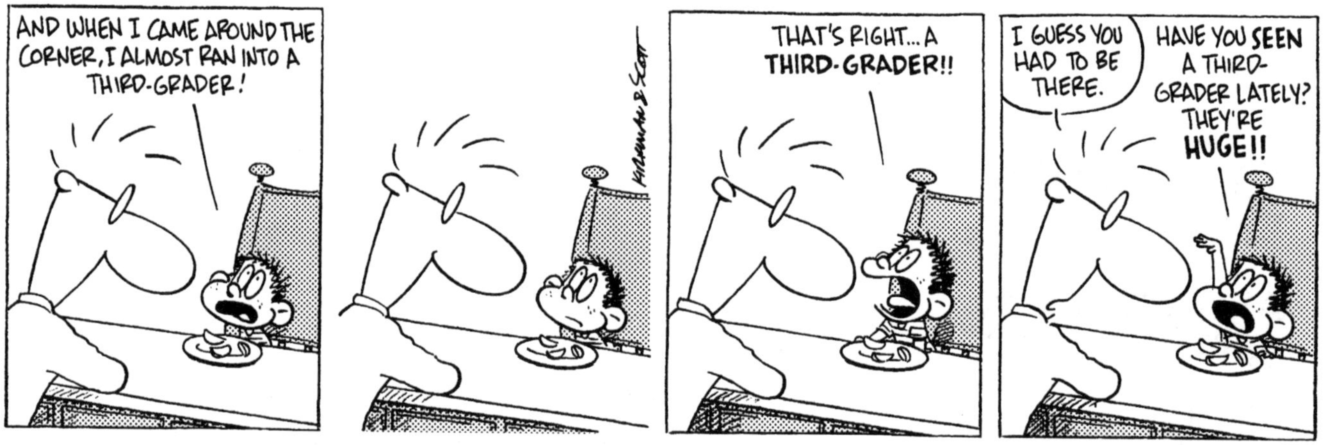
AND WHEN I CAME AROUND THE CORNER, I ALMOST RAN INTO A THIRD-GRADER!
THAT'S RIGHT... A **THIRD-GRADER**!!
I GUESS YOU HAD TO BE THERE.
HAVE YOU **SEEN** A THIRD-GRADER LATELY? THEY'RE **HUGE**!!

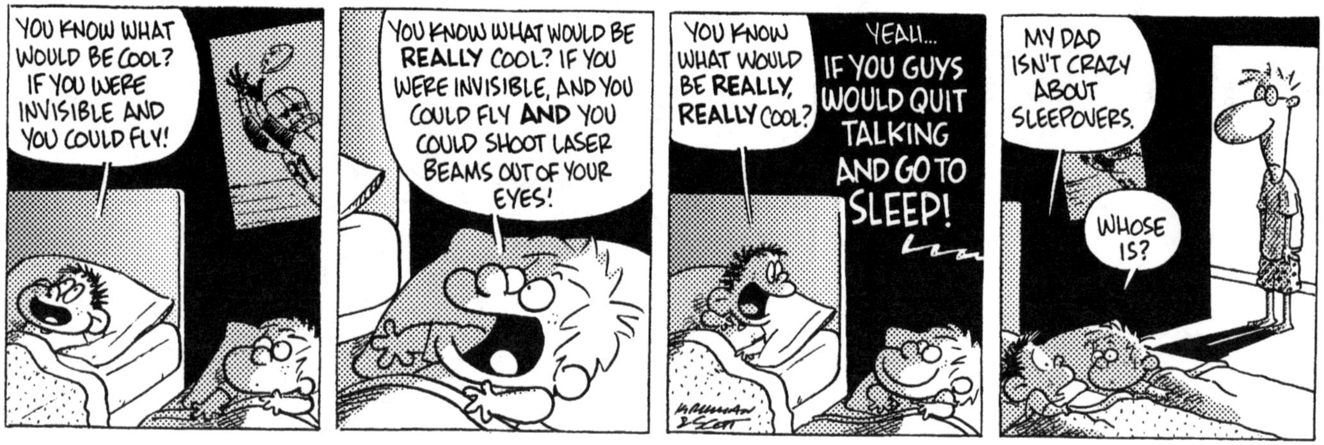
YOU KNOW WHAT WOULD BE COOL? IF YOU WERE INVISIBLE AND YOU COULD FLY!
YOU KNOW WHAT WOULD BE **REALLY** COOL? IF YOU WERE INVISIBLE, AND YOU COULD FLY **AND** YOU COULD SHOOT LASER BEAMS OUT OF YOUR EYES!
YOU KNOW WHAT WOULD BE **REALLY, REALLY** COOL?
YEAH... IF YOU GUYS WOULD QUIT TALKING AND GO TO SLEEP!
MY DAD ISN'T CRAZY ABOUT SLEEPOVERS.
WHOSE IS?

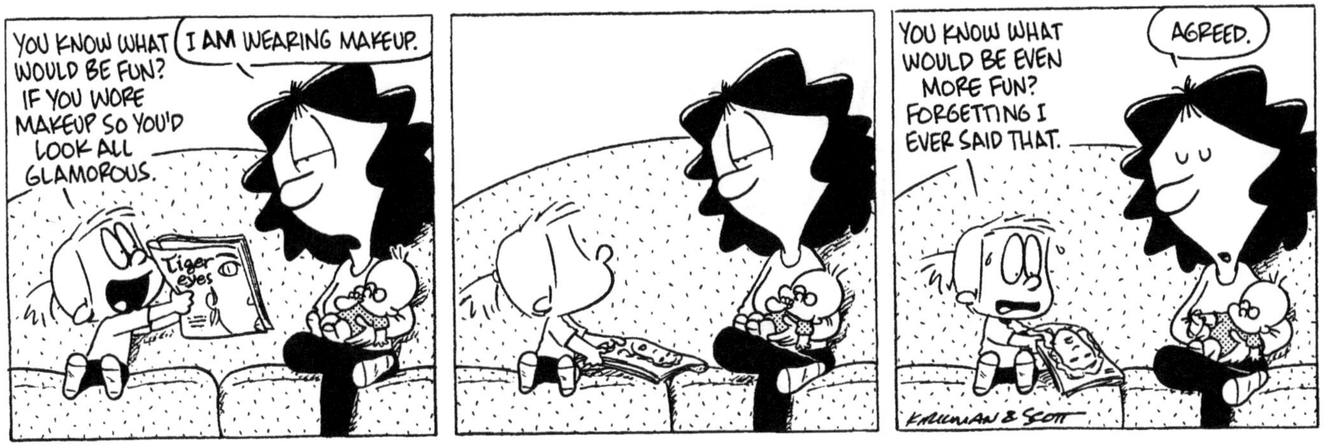
YOU KNOW WHAT WOULD BE FUN? IF YOU WORE MAKEUP SO YOU'D LOOK ALL GLAMOROUS.
I AM WEARING MAKEUP.
Tiger eyes
YOU KNOW WHAT WOULD BE EVEN MORE FUN? FORGETTING I EVER SAID THAT.
AGREED.
KIRKMAN & SCOTT

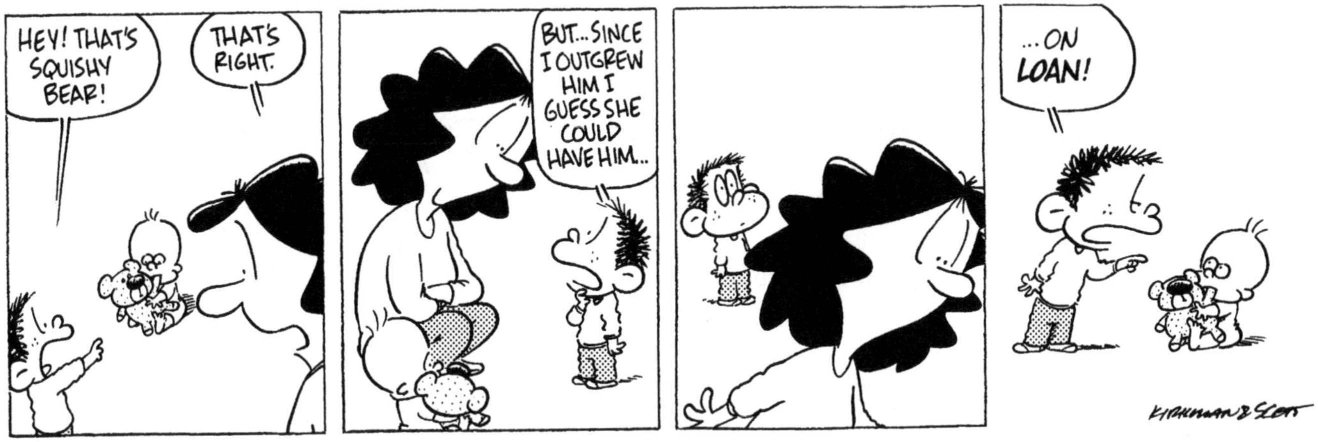
HEY! THAT'S SQUISHY BEAR!
THAT'S RIGHT.
BUT... SINCE I OUTGREW HIM I GUESS SHE COULD HAVE HIM...
...ON LOAN!
KIRKMAN & SCOTT

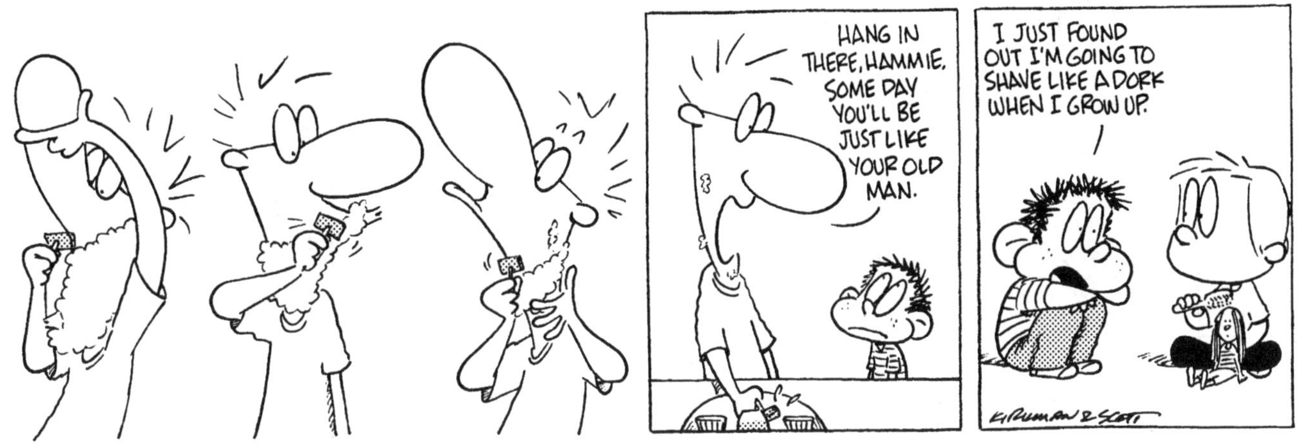
HANG IN THERE, HAMMIE. SOME DAY YOU'LL BE JUST LIKE YOUR OLD MAN.
I JUST FOUND OUT I'M GOING TO SHAVE LIKE A DORK WHEN I GROW UP.
KIRKMAN & SCOTT

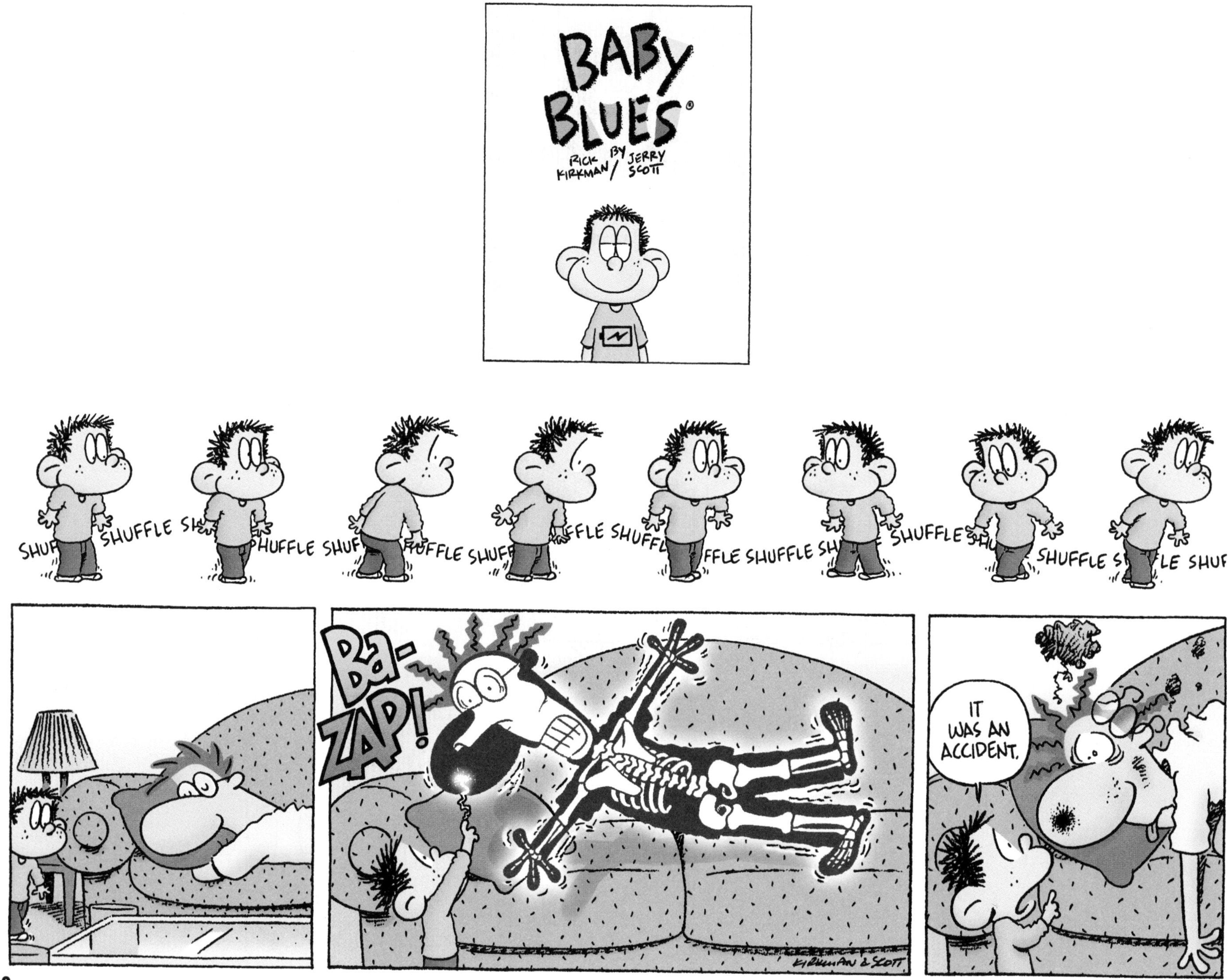
BABY BLUES®
BY RICK KIRKMAN / JERRY SCOTT
SHUF SHUFFLE SH HUFFLE SHUF UFFLE SHUF FFLE SHUFFL FFLE SHUFFLE SH SHUFFLE SH SHUFFLE S LE SHUF
Ba-ZAP!
KIRKMAN & SCOTT
IT WAS AN ACCIDENT.

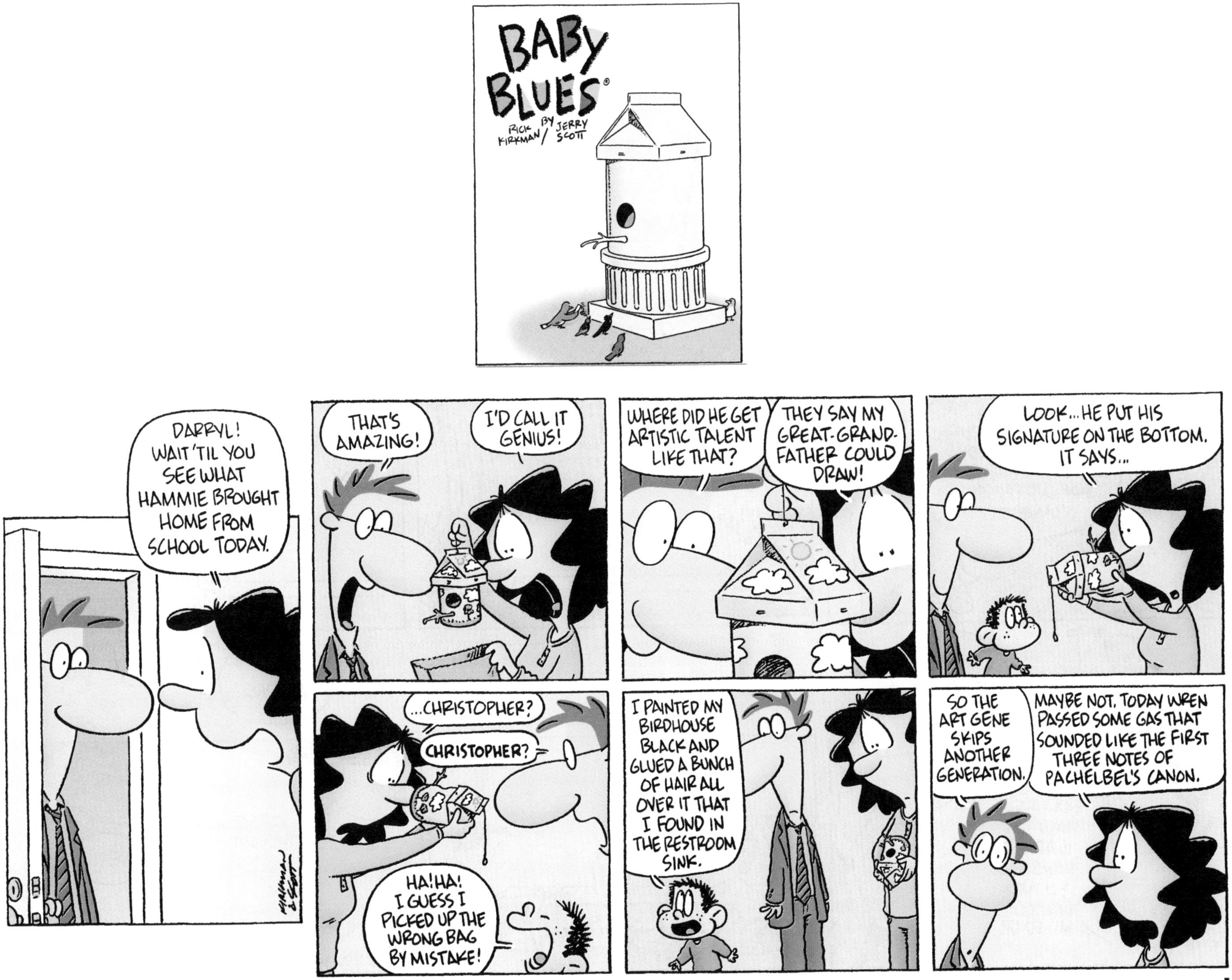
BABY BLUES®
BY RICK KIRKMAN / JERRY SCOTT
DARRYL! WAIT 'TIL YOU SEE WHAT HAMMIE BROUGHT HOME FROM SCHOOL TODAY.
THAT'S AMAZING!
I'D CALL IT GENIUS!
WHERE DID HE GET ARTISTIC TALENT LIKE THAT?
THEY SAY MY GREAT-GRAND-FATHER COULD DRAW!
LOOK... HE PUT HIS SIGNATURE ON THE BOTTOM. IT SAYS...
...CHRISTOPHER?
CHRISTOPHER?
HA! HA! I GUESS I PICKED UP THE WRONG BAG BY MISTAKE!
I PAINTED MY BIRDHOUSE BLACK AND GLUED A BUNCH OF HAIR ALL OVER IT THAT I FOUND IN THE RESTROOM SINK.
SO THE ART GENE SKIPS ANOTHER GENERATION.
MAYBE NOT. TODAY WREN PASSED SOME GAS THAT SOUNDED LIKE THE FIRST THREE NOTES OF PACHELBEL'S CANON.

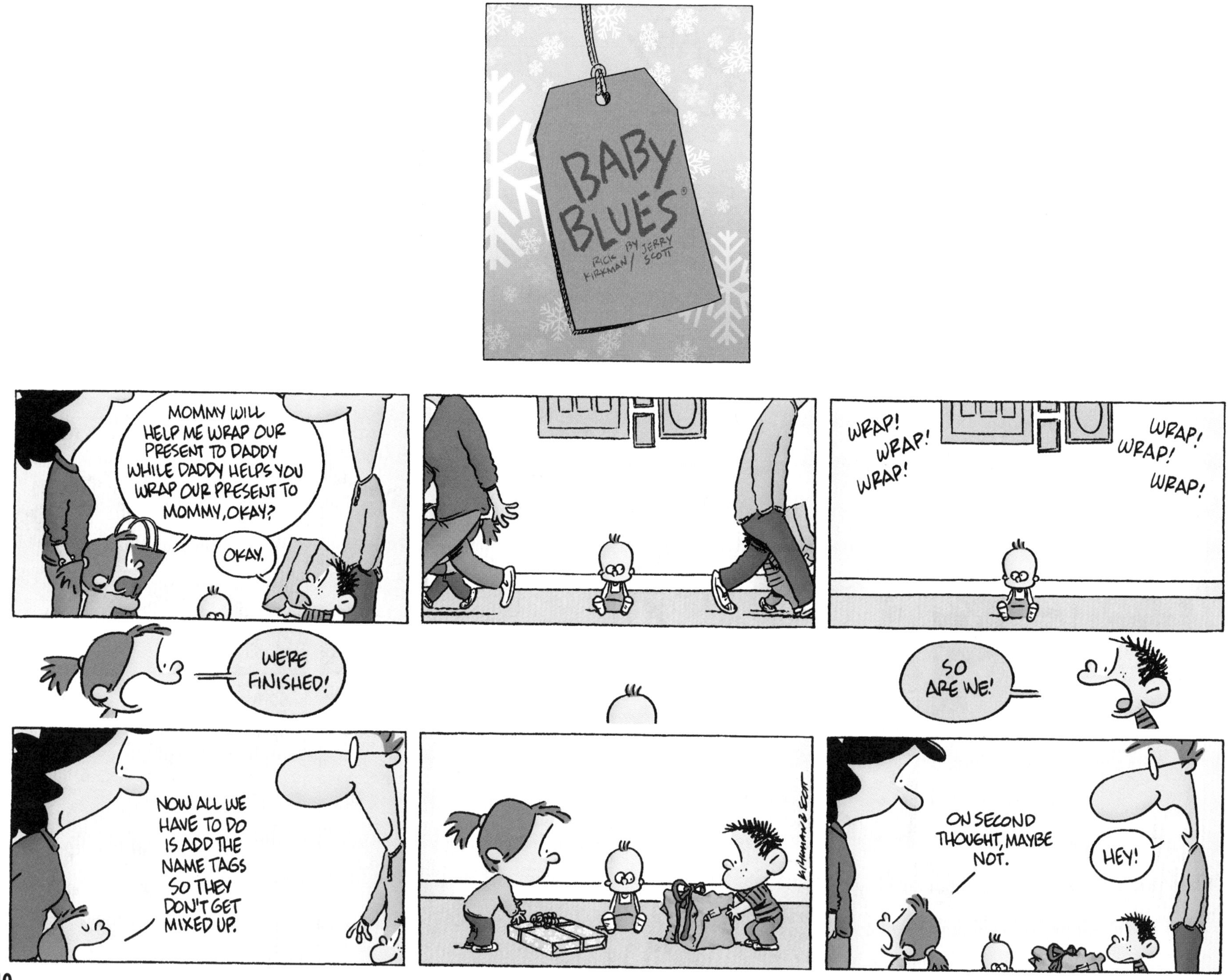
BABY BLUES®
RICK KIRKMAN / BY JERRY SCOTT
MOMMY WILL HELP ME WRAP OUR PRESENT TO DADDY WHILE DADDY HELPS YOU WRAP OUR PRESENT TO MOMMY, OKAY?
OKAY.
WRAP! WRAP! WRAP!
WRAP! WRAP! WRAP!
WE'RE FINISHED!
SO ARE WE!
NOW ALL WE HAVE TO DO IS ADD THE NAME TAGS SO THEY DON'T GET MIXED UP.
ON SECOND THOUGHT, MAYBE NOT.
HEY!

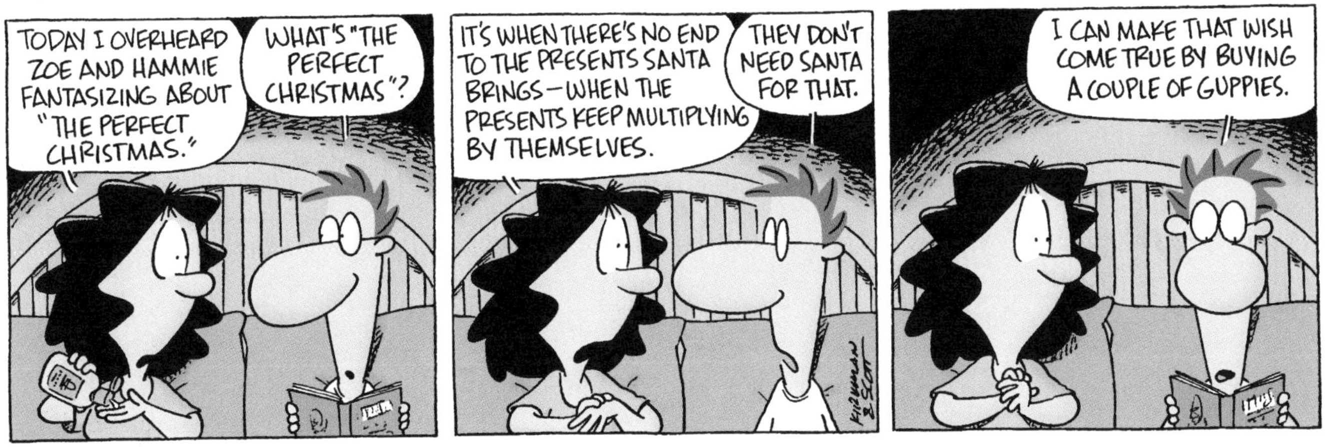
TODAY I OVERHEARD ZOE AND HAMMIE FANTASIZING ABOUT "THE PERFECT CHRISTMAS."
WHAT'S "THE PERFECT CHRISTMAS"?
IT'S WHEN THERE'S NO END TO THE PRESENTS SANTA BRINGS—WHEN THE PRESENTS KEEP MULTIPLYING BY THEMSELVES.
THEY DON'T NEED SANTA FOR THAT.
I CAN MAKE THAT WISH COME TRUE BY BUYING A COUPLE OF GUPPIES.

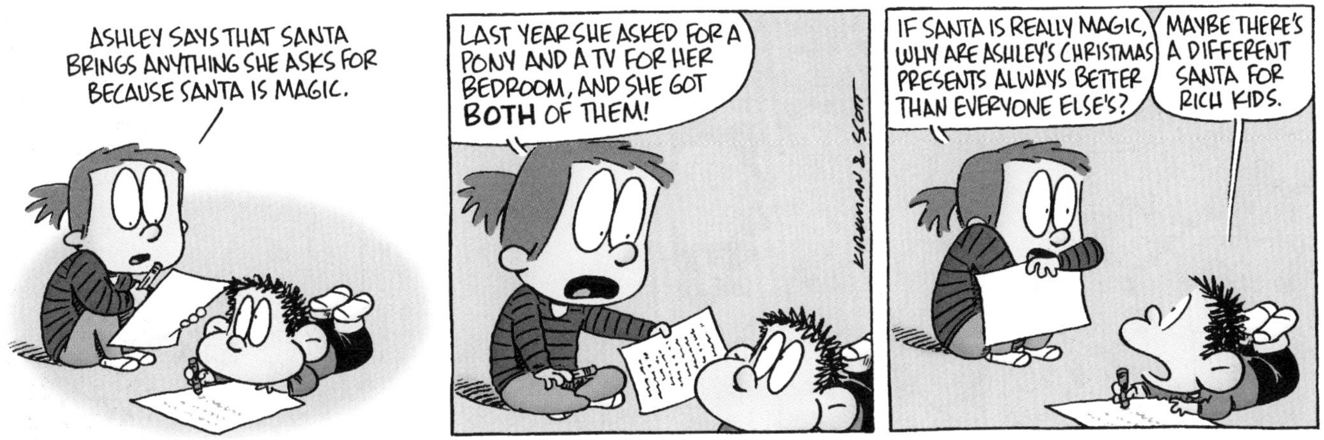
ASHLEY SAYS THAT SANTA BRINGS ANYTHING SHE ASKS FOR BECAUSE SANTA IS MAGIC.
LAST YEAR SHE ASKED FOR A PONY AND A TV FOR HER BEDROOM, AND SHE GOT **BOTH** OF THEM!
IF SANTA IS REALLY MAGIC, WHY ARE ASHLEY'S CHRISTMAS PRESENTS ALWAYS BETTER THAN EVERYONE ELSE'S?
MAYBE THERE'S A DIFFERENT SANTA FOR RICH KIDS.

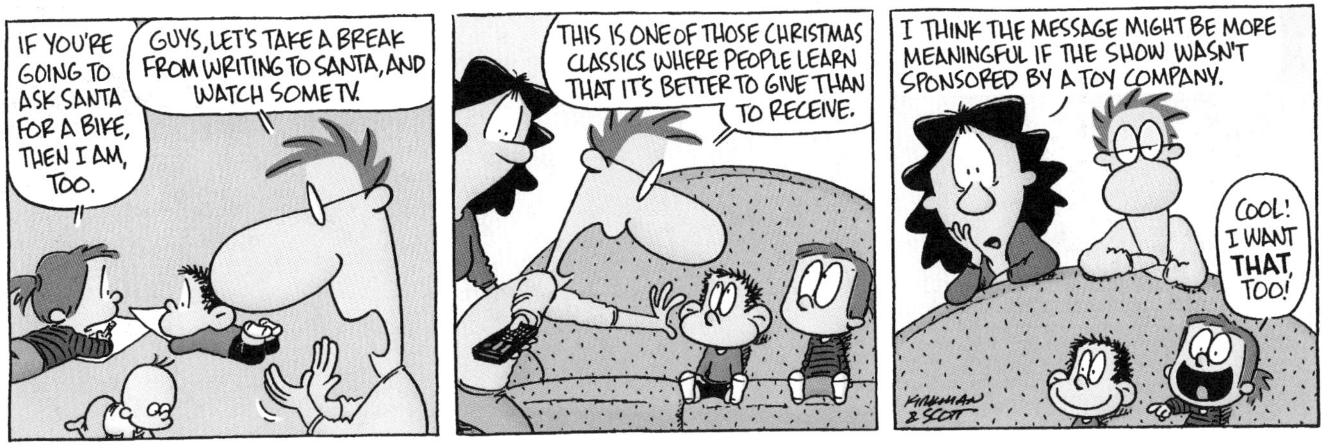
IF YOU'RE GOING TO ASK SANTA FOR A BIKE, THEN I AM, TOO.
GUYS, LET'S TAKE A BREAK FROM WRITING TO SANTA, AND WATCH SOME TV.
THIS IS ONE OF THOSE CHRISTMAS CLASSICS WHERE PEOPLE LEARN THAT IT'S BETTER TO GIVE THAN TO RECEIVE.
I THINK THE MESSAGE MIGHT BE MORE MEANINGFUL IF THE SHOW WASN'T SPONSORED BY A TOY COMPANY.
COOL! I WANT **THAT**, TOO!

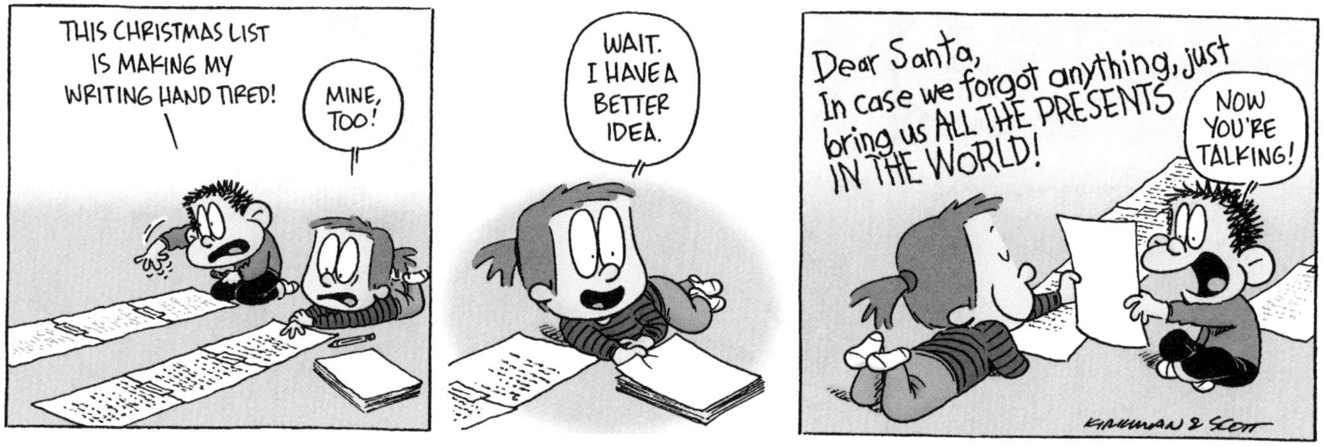
THIS CHRISTMAS LIST IS MAKING MY WRITING HAND TIRED!
MINE, TOO!
WAIT. I HAVE A BETTER IDEA.
Dear Santa,
In case we forgot anything, just bring us ALL THE PRESENTS IN THE WORLD!
NOW YOU'RE TALKING!
KIRKMAN & SCOTT

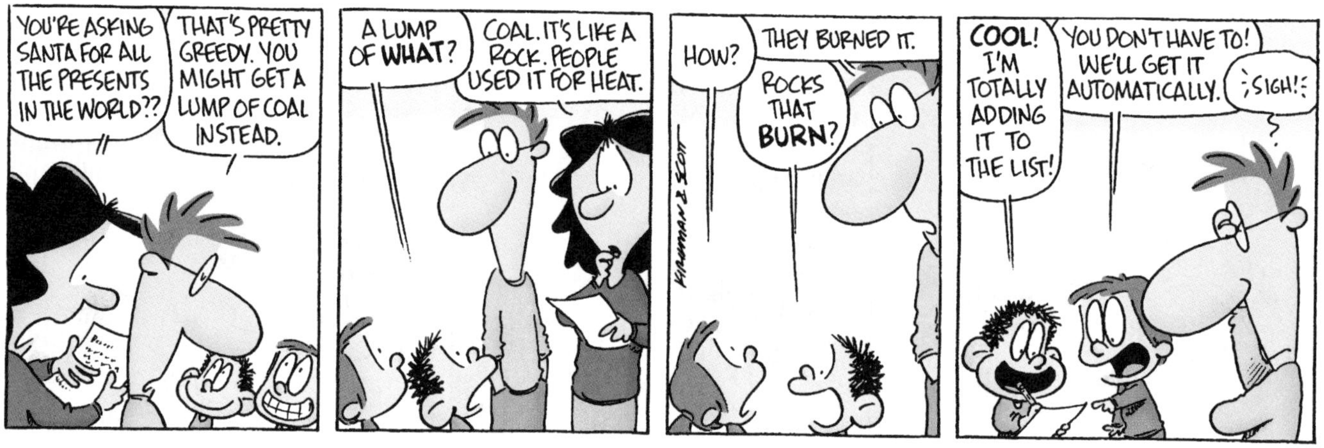
YOU'RE ASKING SANTA FOR ALL THE PRESENTS IN THE WORLD??
THAT'S PRETTY GREEDY. YOU MIGHT GET A LUMP OF COAL INSTEAD.
A LUMP OF **WHAT**?
COAL. IT'S LIKE A ROCK. PEOPLE USED IT FOR HEAT.
KIRKMAN & SCOTT
HOW?
THEY BURNED IT.
ROCKS THAT **BURN**?
COOL! I'M TOTALLY ADDING IT TO THE LIST!
YOU DON'T HAVE TO! WE'LL GET IT AUTOMATICALLY.
SIGH!

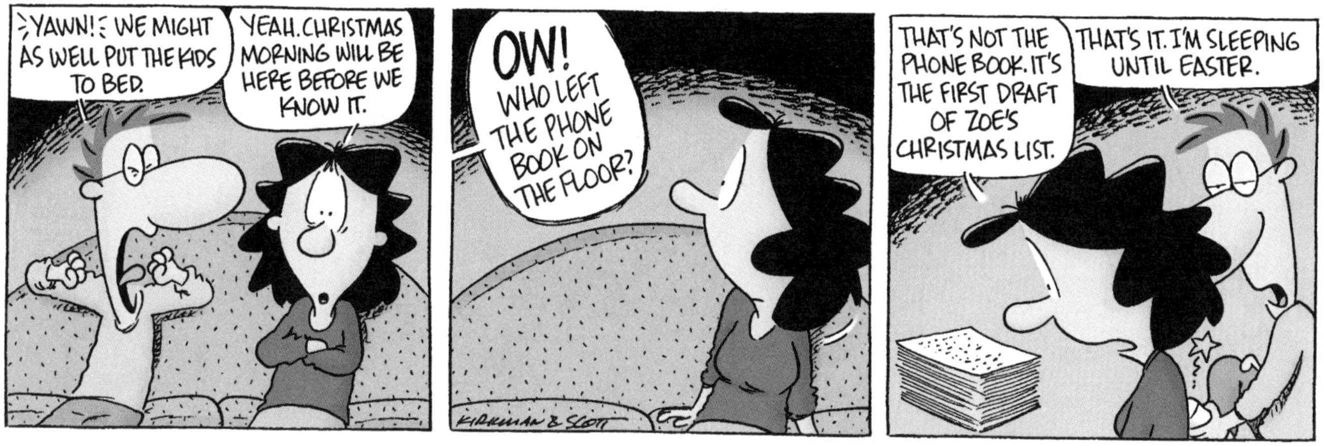
YAWN! WE MIGHT AS WELL PUT THE KIDS TO BED.
YEAH. CHRISTMAS MORNING WILL BE HERE BEFORE WE KNOW IT.
OW!
WHO LEFT THE PHONE BOOK ON THE FLOOR?
KIRKMAN & SCOTT
THAT'S NOT THE PHONE BOOK. IT'S THE FIRST DRAFT OF ZOE'S CHRISTMAS LIST.
THAT'S IT. I'M SLEEPING UNTIL EASTER.

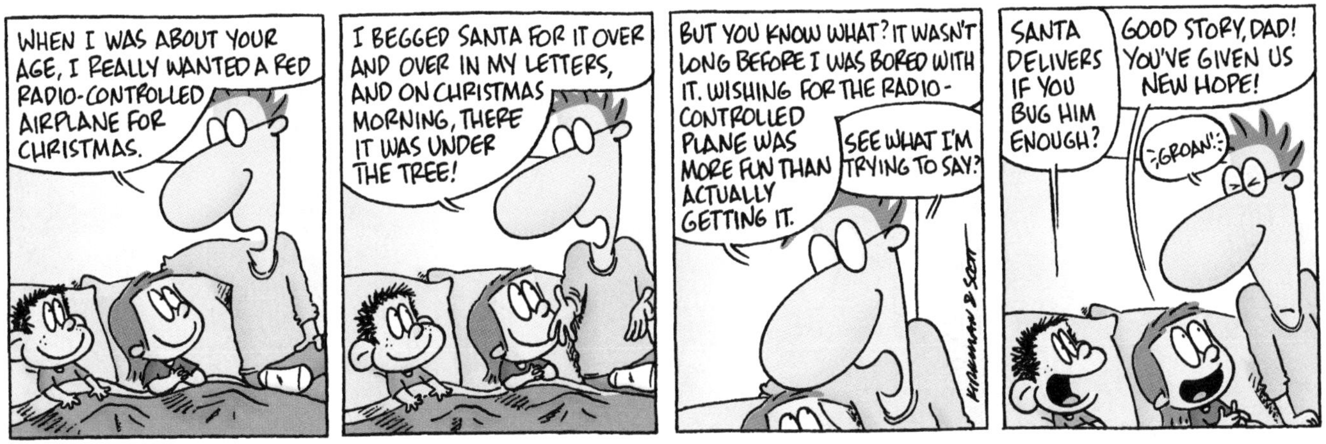
WHEN I WAS ABOUT YOUR AGE, I REALLY WANTED A RED RADIO-CONTROLLED AIRPLANE FOR CHRISTMAS.
I BEGGED SANTA FOR IT OVER AND OVER IN MY LETTERS, AND ON CHRISTMAS MORNING, THERE IT WAS UNDER THE TREE!
BUT YOU KNOW WHAT? IT WASN'T LONG BEFORE I WAS BORED WITH IT. WISHING FOR THE RADIO-CONTROLLED PLANE WAS MORE FUN THAN ACTUALLY GETTING IT.
SEE WHAT I'M TRYING TO SAY?
SANTA DELIVERS IF YOU BUG HIM ENOUGH?
GOOD STORY, DAD! YOU'VE GIVEN US NEW HOPE!
GROAN!

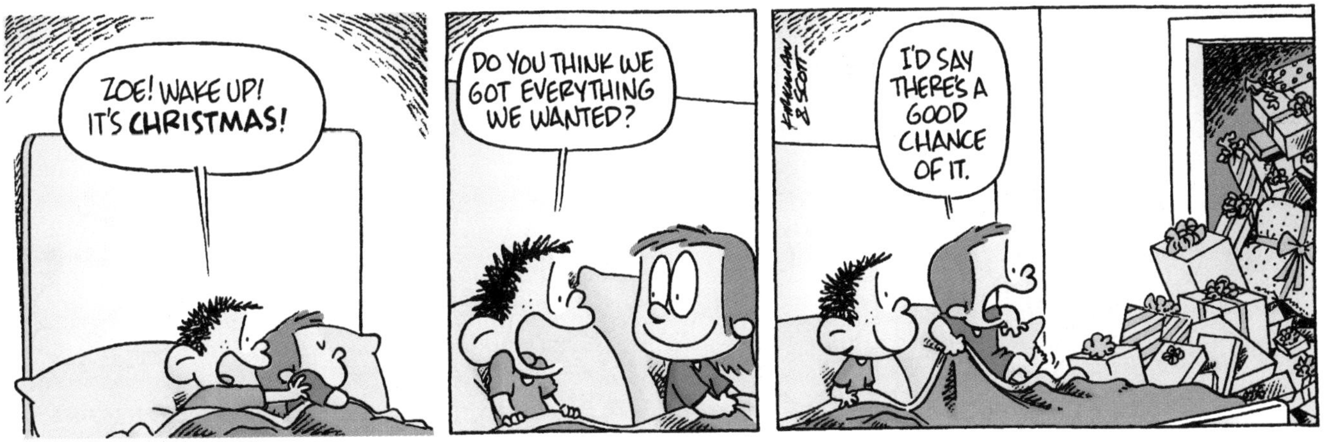
ZOE! WAKE UP! IT'S **CHRISTMAS!**
DO YOU THINK WE GOT EVERYTHING WE WANTED?
I'D SAY THERE'S A GOOD CHANCE OF IT.

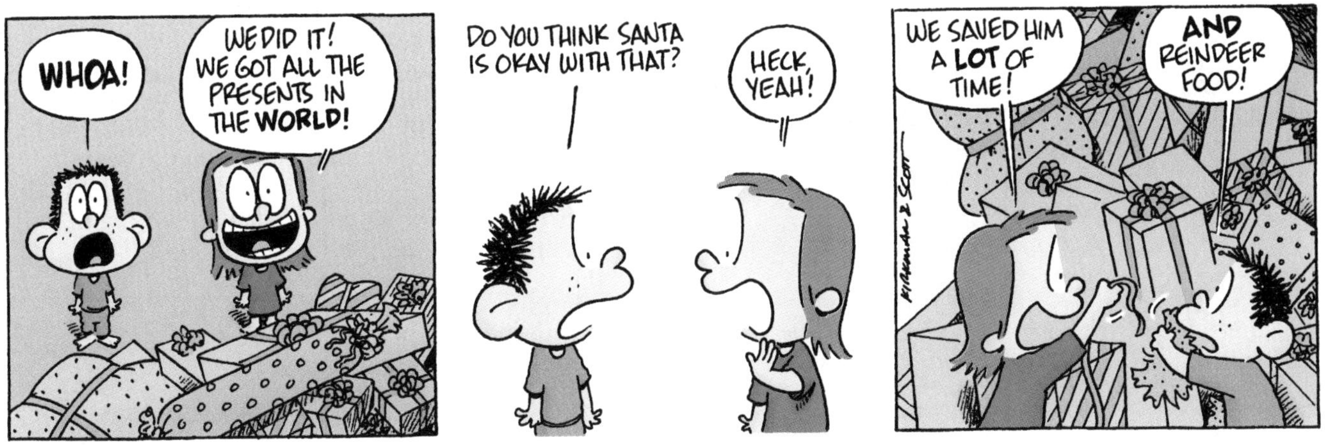
WHOA!
WE DID IT! WE GOT ALL THE PRESENTS IN THE **WORLD!**
DO YOU THINK SANTA IS OKAY WITH THAT?
HECK, YEAH!
WE SAVED HIM A **LOT** OF TIME!
AND REINDEER FOOD!

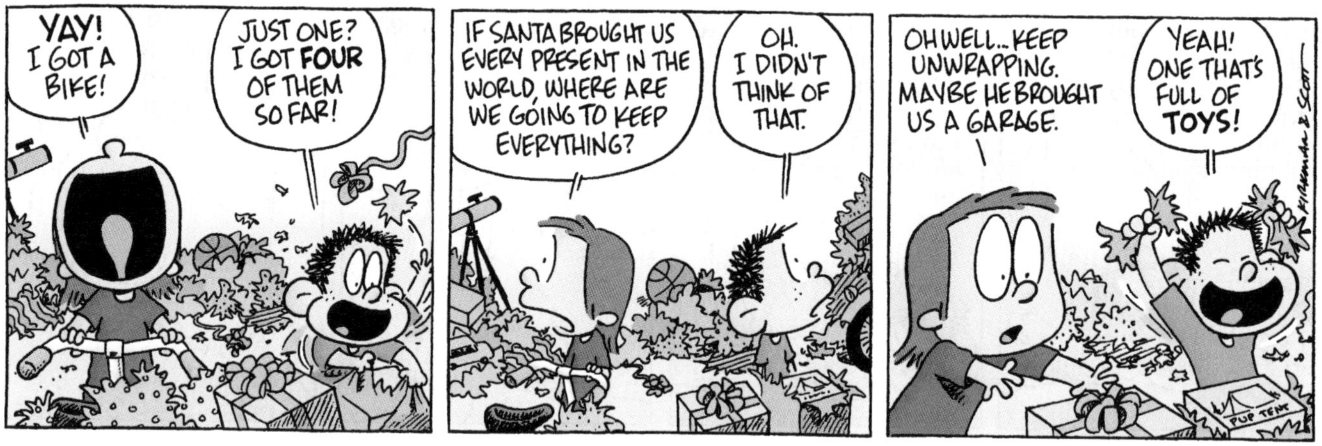
YAY! I GOT A BIKE!
JUST ONE? I GOT **FOUR** OF THEM SO FAR!
IF SANTA BROUGHT US EVERY PRESENT IN THE WORLD, WHERE ARE WE GOING TO KEEP EVERYTHING?
OH. I DIDN'T THINK OF THAT.
OH WELL... KEEP UNWRAPPING. MAYBE HE BROUGHT US A GARAGE.
YEAH! ONE THAT'S FULL OF **TOYS**!
PUP TENT

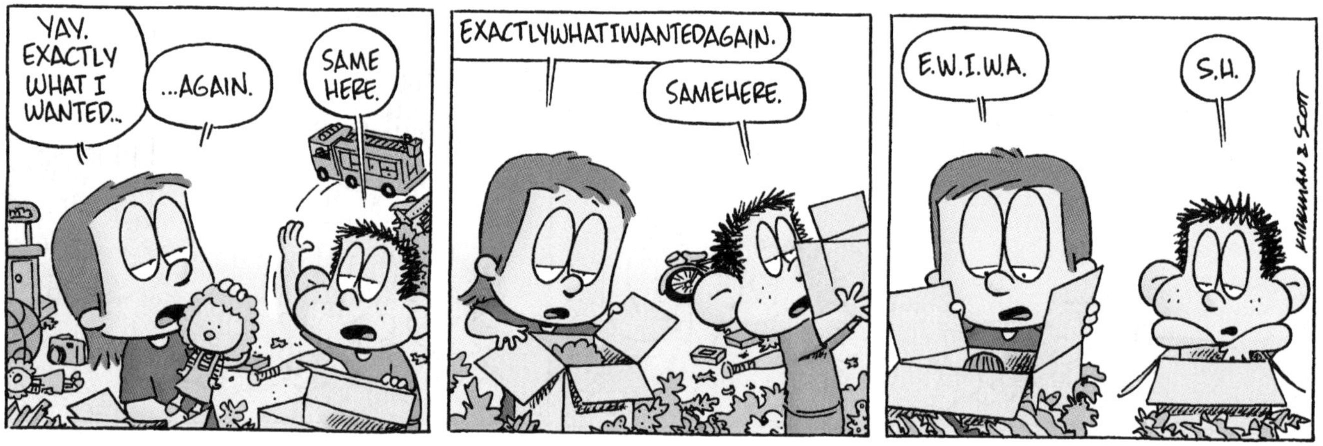
YAY. EXACTLY WHAT I WANTED...
...AGAIN.
SAME HERE.
EXACTLYWHATIWANTEDAGAIN.
SAMEHERE.
E.W.I.W.A.
S.H.

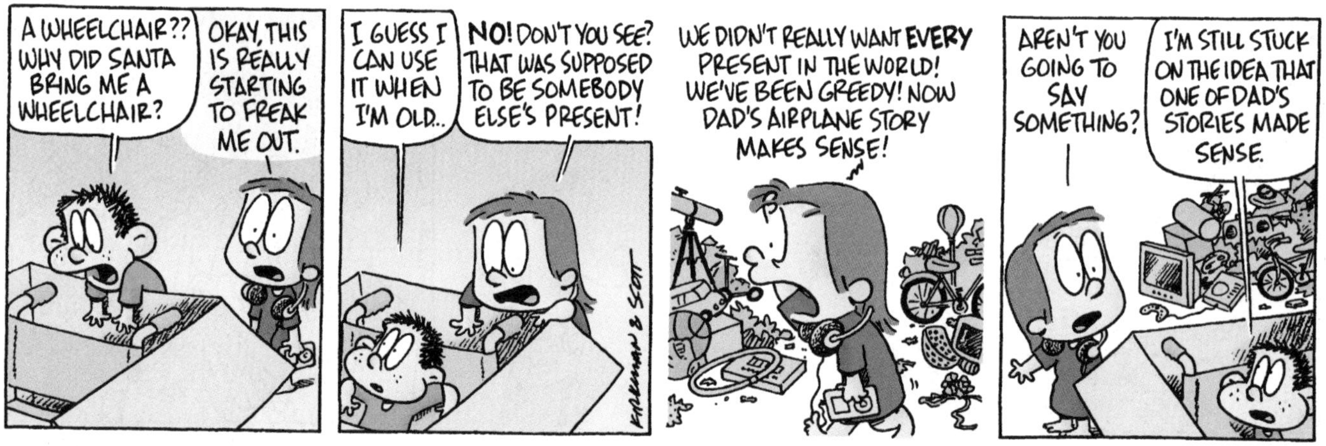
A WHEELCHAIR?? WHY DID SANTA BRING ME A WHEELCHAIR?
OKAY, THIS IS REALLY STARTING TO FREAK ME OUT.
I GUESS I CAN USE IT WHEN I'M OLD...
NO! DON'T YOU SEE? THAT WAS SUPPOSED TO BE SOMEBODY ELSE'S PRESENT!
WE DIDN'T REALLY WANT **EVERY** PRESENT IN THE WORLD! WE'VE BEEN GREEDY! NOW DAD'S AIRPLANE STORY MAKES SENSE!
AREN'T YOU GOING TO SAY SOMETHING?
I'M STILL STUCK ON THE IDEA THAT ONE OF DAD'S STORIES MADE SENSE.

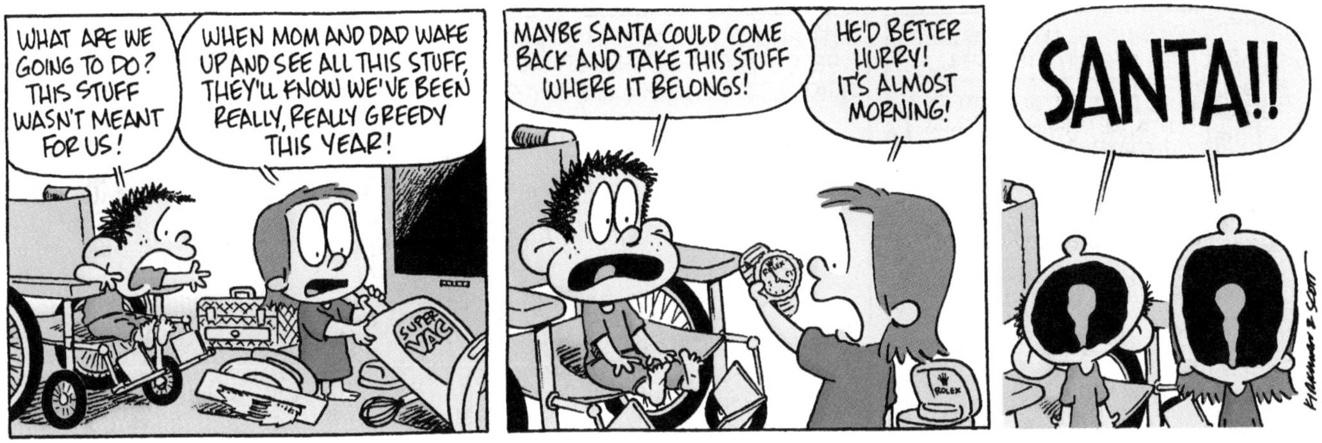
WHAT ARE WE GOING TO DO? THIS STUFF WASN'T MEANT FOR US!
WHEN MOM AND DAD WAKE UP AND SEE ALL THIS STUFF, THEY'LL KNOW WE'VE BEEN REALLY, REALLY GREEDY THIS YEAR!
SUPER VAC
MAYBE SANTA COULD COME BACK AND TAKE THIS STUFF WHERE IT BELONGS!
HE'D BETTER HURRY! IT'S ALMOST MORNING!
SANTA!!

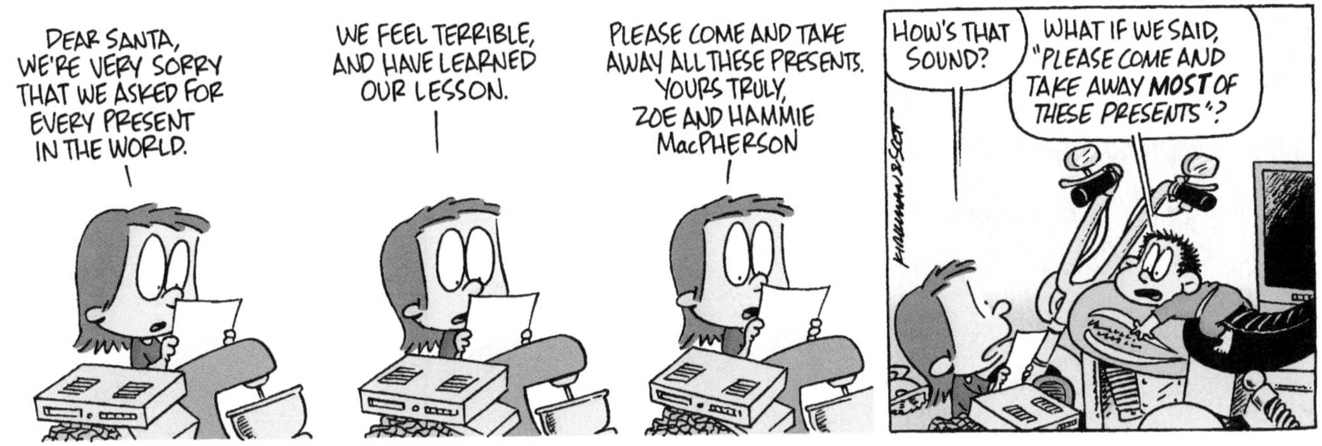
DEAR SANTA, WE'RE VERY SORRY THAT WE ASKED FOR EVERY PRESENT IN THE WORLD.
WE FEEL TERRIBLE, AND HAVE LEARNED OUR LESSON.
PLEASE COME AND TAKE AWAY ALL THESE PRESENTS. YOURS TRULY, ZOE AND HAMMIE MacPHERSON
HOW'S THAT SOUND?
WHAT IF WE SAID, "PLEASE COME AND TAKE AWAY MOST OF THESE PRESENTS"?

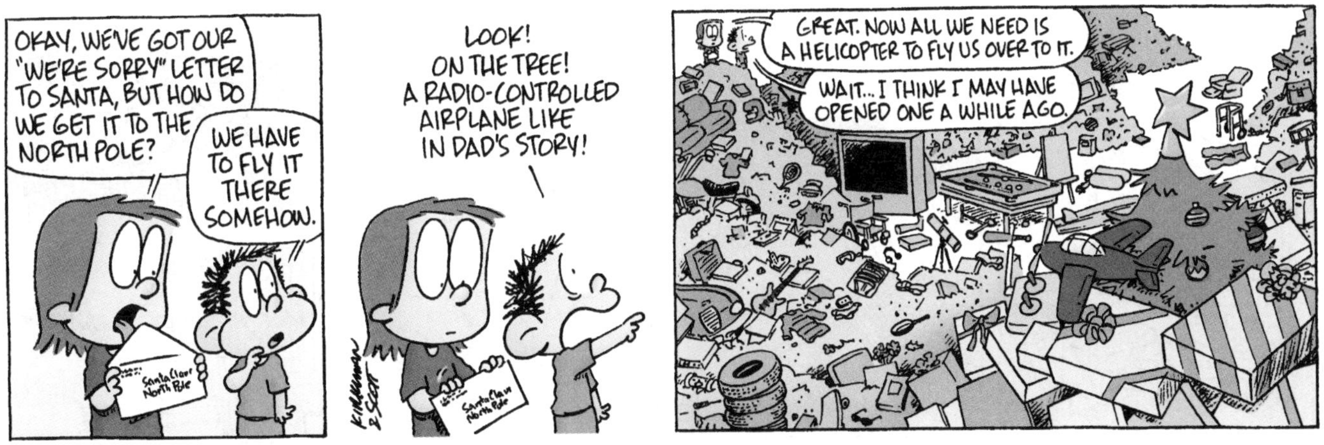
OKAY, WE'VE GOT OUR "WE'RE SORRY" LETTER TO SANTA, BUT HOW DO WE GET IT TO THE NORTH POLE?
WE HAVE TO FLY IT THERE SOMEHOW.
LOOK! ON THE TREE! A RADIO-CONTROLLED AIRPLANE LIKE IN DAD'S STORY!
GREAT. NOW ALL WE NEED IS A HELICOPTER TO FLY US OVER TO IT.
WAIT... I THINK I MAY HAVE OPENED ONE A WHILE AGO.

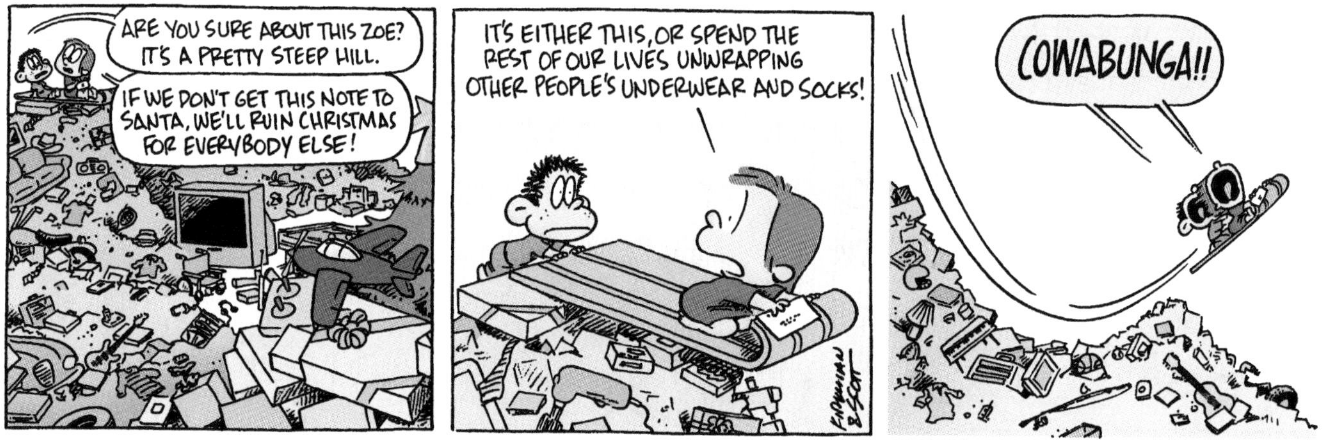
ARE YOU SURE ABOUT THIS ZOE? IT'S A PRETTY STEEP HILL.
IF WE DON'T GET THIS NOTE TO SANTA, WE'LL RUIN CHRISTMAS FOR EVERYBODY ELSE!
IT'S EITHER THIS, OR SPEND THE REST OF OUR LIVES UNWRAPPING OTHER PEOPLE'S UNDERWEAR AND SOCKS!
COWABUNGA!!

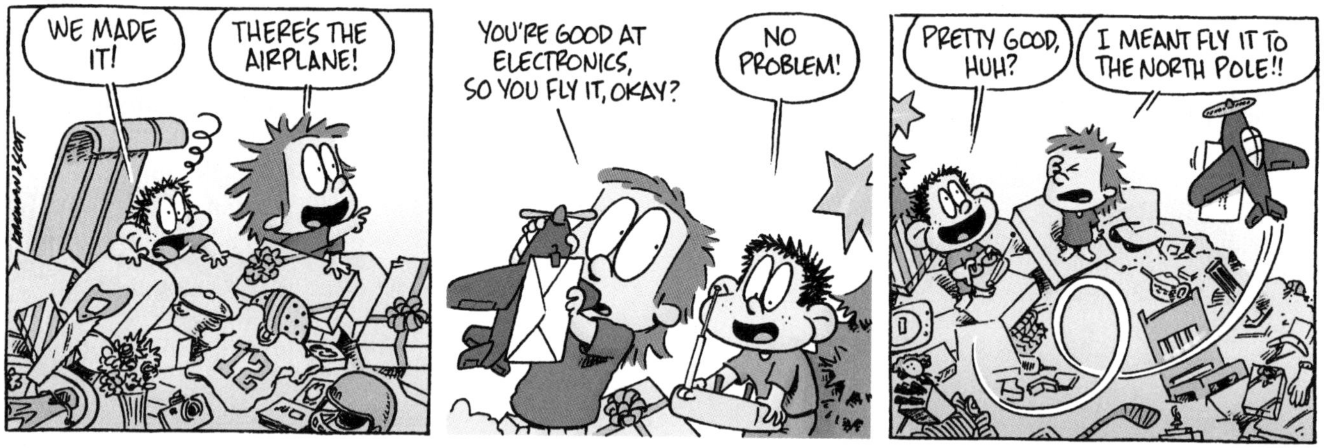
WE MADE IT!
THERE'S THE AIRPLANE!
YOU'RE GOOD AT ELECTRONICS, SO YOU FLY IT, OKAY?
NO PROBLEM!
PRETTY GOOD, HUH?
I MEANT FLY IT TO THE NORTH POLE!!

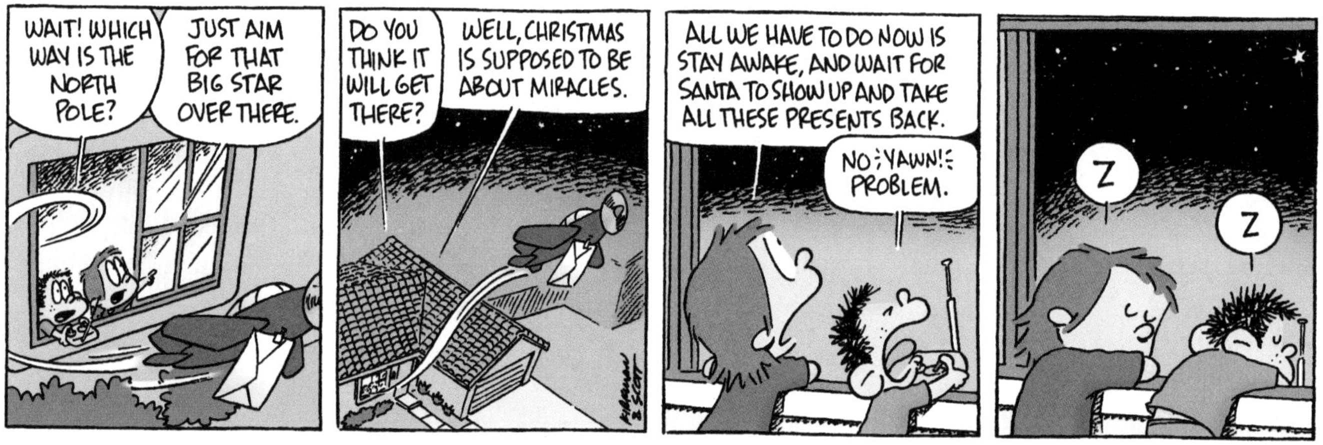
WAIT! WHICH WAY IS THE NORTH POLE?
JUST AIM FOR THAT BIG STAR OVER THERE.
DO YOU THINK IT WILL GET THERE?
WELL, CHRISTMAS IS SUPPOSED TO BE ABOUT MIRACLES.
ALL WE HAVE TO DO NOW IS STAY AWAKE, AND WAIT FOR SANTA TO SHOW UP AND TAKE ALL THESE PRESENTS BACK.
NO *YAWN!* PROBLEM.
Z
Z

ZOE! WAKE UP! IT'S CHRISTMAS!

DO YOU SEE WHAT I SEE?

I THINK SO.

YAY! SANTA DIDN'T BRING US EVERYTHING WE ASKED FOR!!

KIRKMAN & SCOTT

SEE? LOOK! IT'S THE PERFECT CHRISTMAS!

NO WHEELCHAIRS, NO VACUUM CLEANERS, NO BULLDOZERS...

SANTA CAME BACK AND MADE EVERYTHING RIGHT AGAIN.

WHAT WAS IN THAT EGGNOG YOU GAVE ME LAST NIGHT?

PHOOEY! I GUESS HE TOOK THE HARLEY, TOO.

SO THIS IS THE PERFECT CHRISTMAS, EVEN THOUGH YOU DIDN'T GET EVERY PRESENT IN THE WORLD?

THE PERFECT CHRISTMAS ISN'T JUST ABOUT THE PRESENTS YOU GET, MOM.

IT'S ABOUT NOT BEING GREEDY. IT'S ABOUT ONE OF DAD'S STORIES HAVING A POINT, AND NOT HAVING TO RIDE A TOBOGGAN TO THE CHRISTMAS TREE!

DID YOU UNDERSTAND ANY OF THAT?

DOES IT MATTER? THEY'RE HAPPY.

KIRKMAN & SCOTT

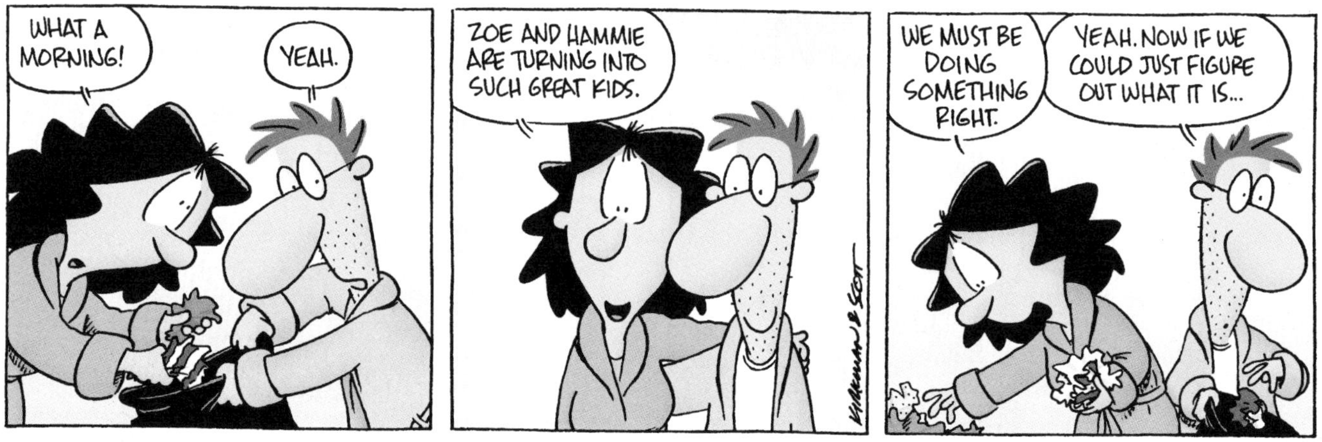
WHAT A MORNING!
YEAH.
ZOE AND HAMMIE ARE TURNING INTO SUCH GREAT KIDS.
WE MUST BE DOING SOMETHING RIGHT.
YEAH. NOW IF WE COULD JUST FIGURE OUT WHAT IT IS...

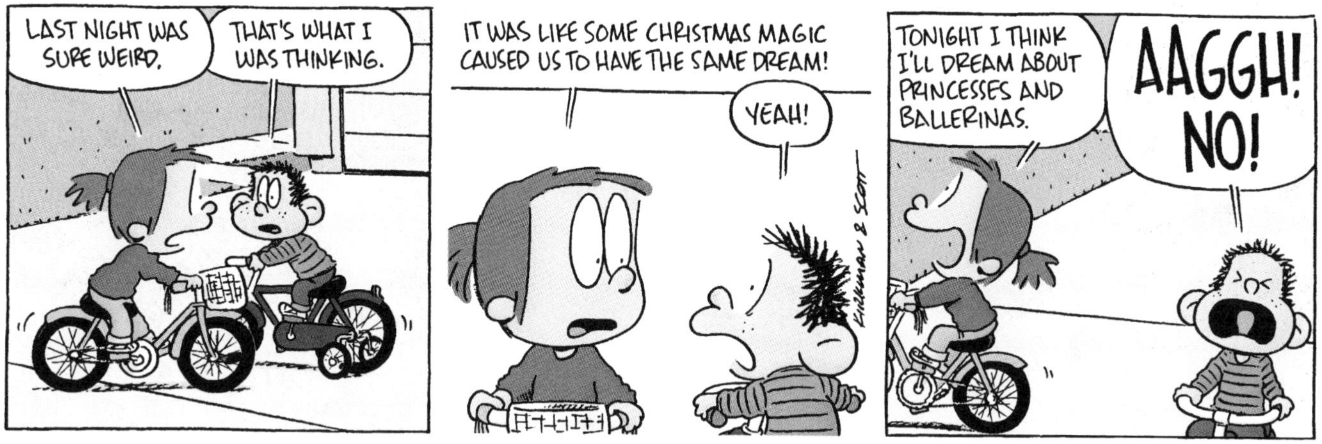
LAST NIGHT WAS SURE WEIRD.
THAT'S WHAT I WAS THINKING.
IT WAS LIKE SOME CHRISTMAS MAGIC CAUSED US TO HAVE THE SAME DREAM!
YEAH!
TONIGHT I THINK I'LL DREAM ABOUT PRINCESSES AND BALLERINAS.
AAGGH! NO!

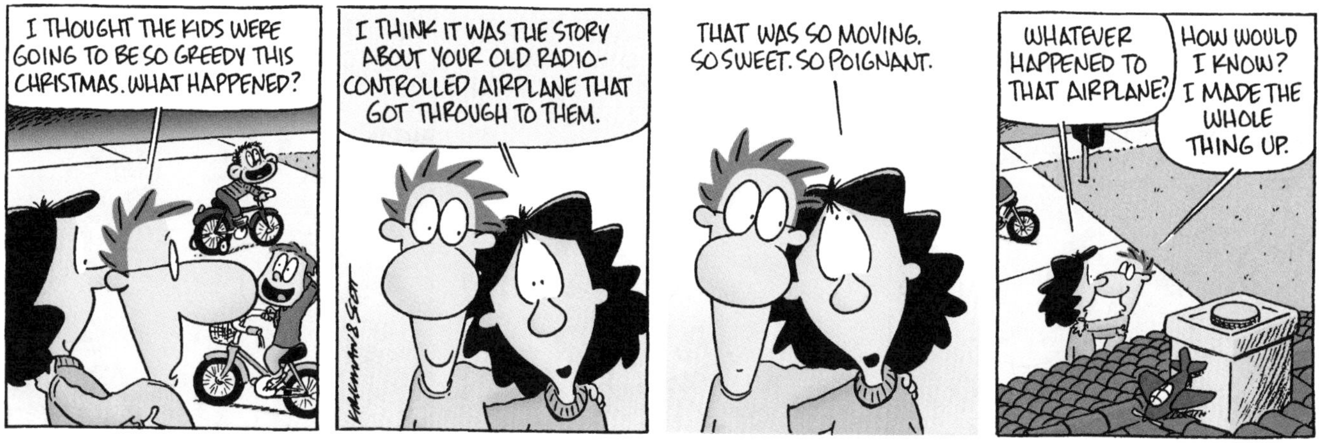
I THOUGHT THE KIDS WERE GOING TO BE SO GREEDY THIS CHRISTMAS. WHAT HAPPENED?
I THINK IT WAS THE STORY ABOUT YOUR OLD RADIO-CONTROLLED AIRPLANE THAT GOT THROUGH TO THEM.
THAT WAS SO MOVING. SO SWEET. SO POIGNANT.
WHATEVER HAPPENED TO THAT AIRPLANE?
HOW WOULD I KNOW? I MADE THE WHOLE THING UP.

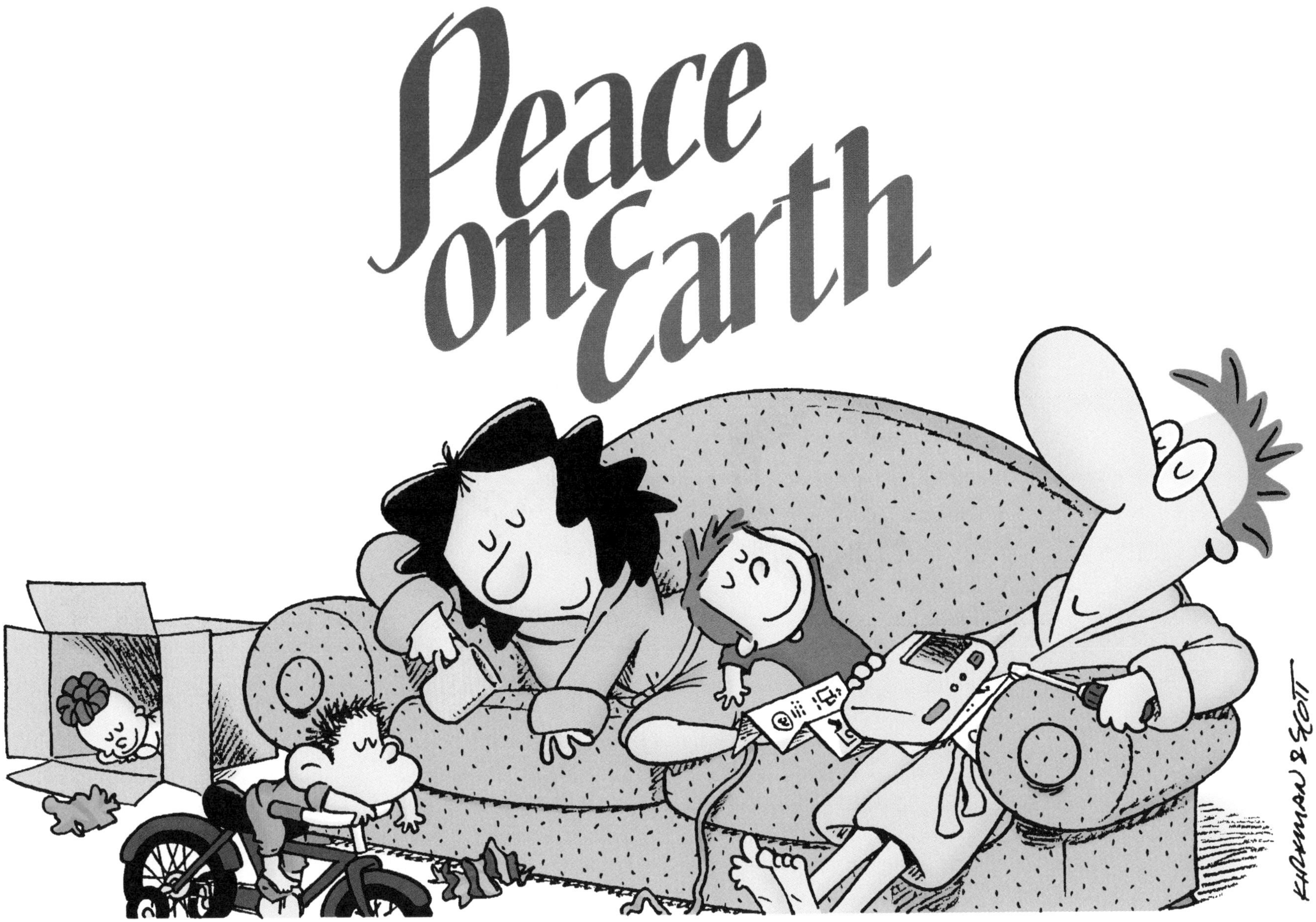
Peace on Earth
KIRKMAN & SCOTT

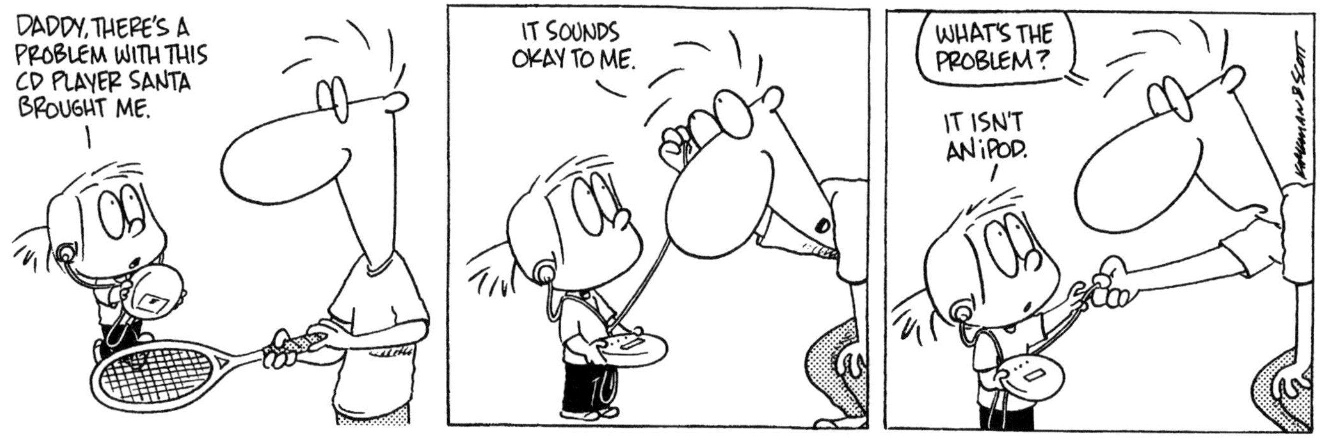
DADDY, THERE'S A PROBLEM WITH THIS CD PLAYER SANTA BROUGHT ME.
IT SOUNDS OKAY TO ME.
WHAT'S THE PROBLEM?
IT ISN'T AN iPOD.

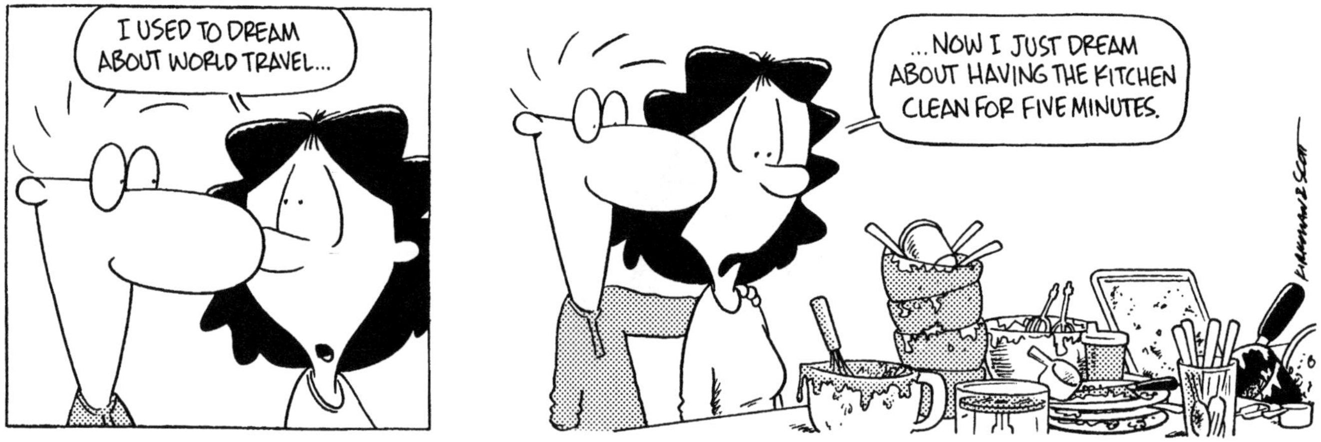
I USED TO DREAM ABOUT WORLD TRAVEL...
... NOW I JUST DREAM ABOUT HAVING THE KITCHEN CLEAN FOR FIVE MINUTES.

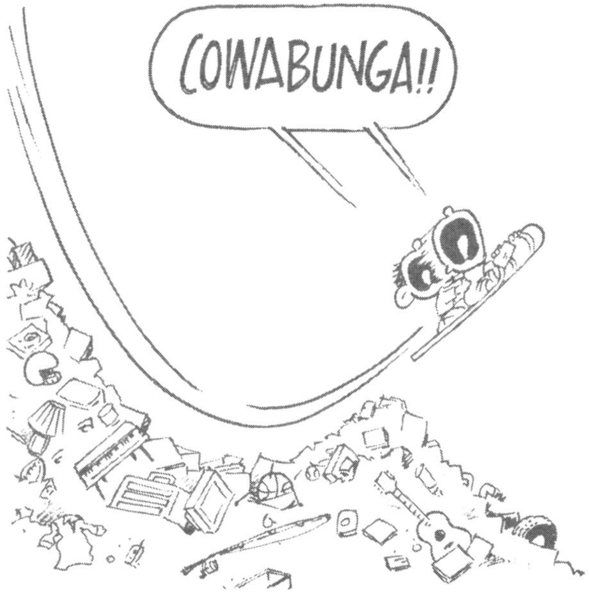
COWABUNGA!!

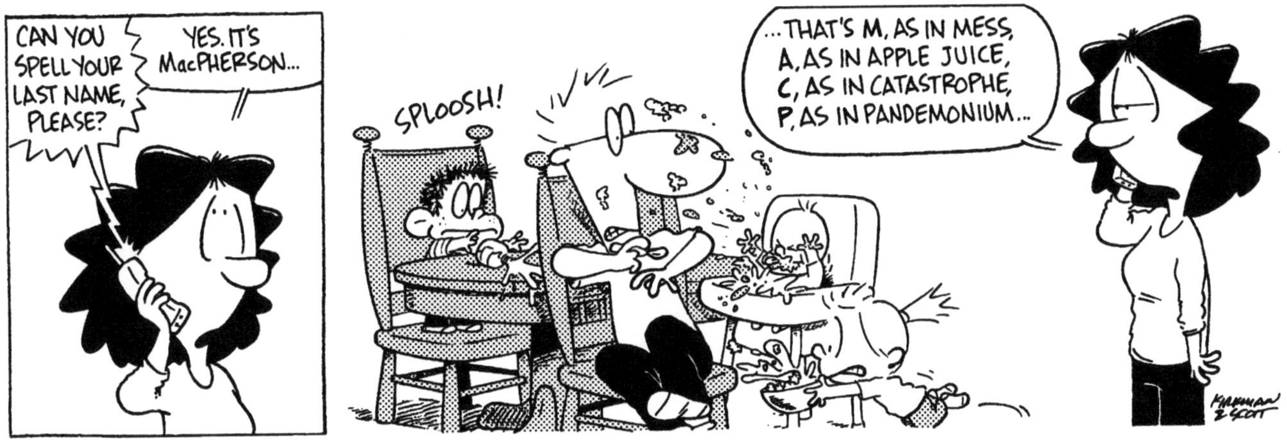
CAN YOU SPELL YOUR LAST NAME, PLEASE?
YES. IT'S MacPHERSON...
SPLOOSH!
...THAT'S M, AS IN MESS, A, AS IN APPLE JUICE, C, AS IN CATASTROPHE, P, AS IN PANDEMONIUM...

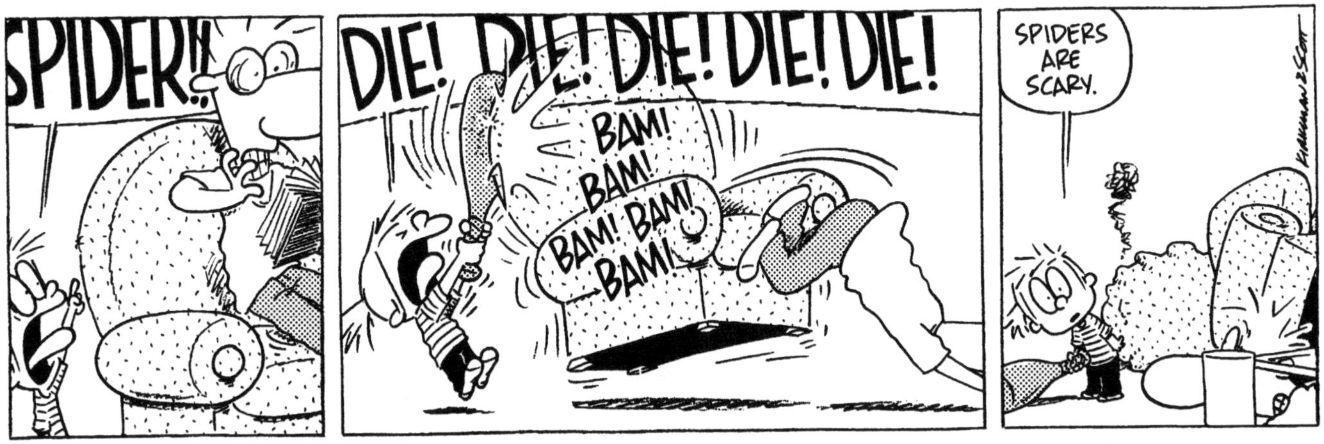
SPIDER!!
DIE! DIE! DIE! DIE! DIE!
BAM! BAM! BAM! BAM! BAM! BAM!
SPIDERS ARE SCARY.

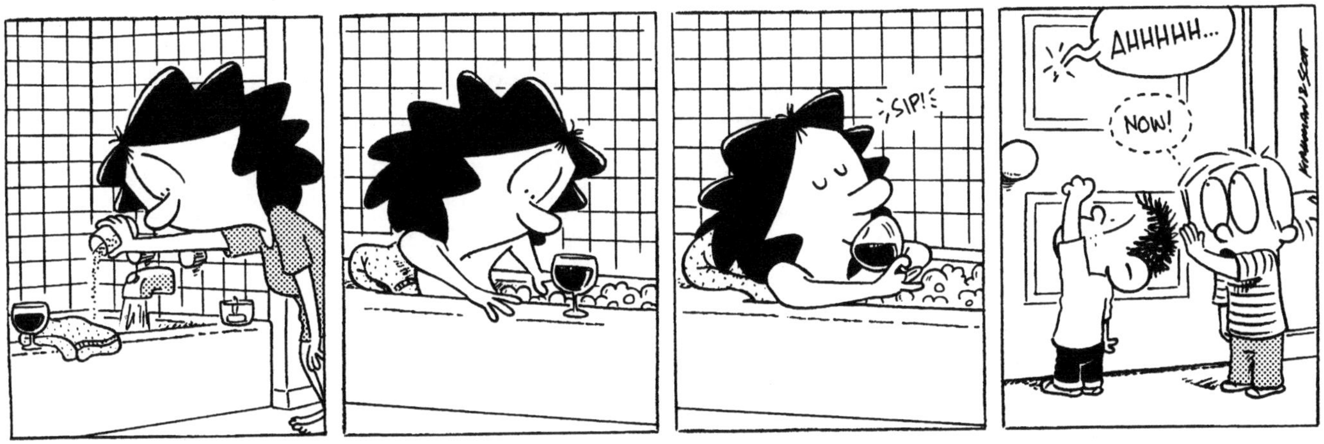
SIP!
AHHHHH...
NOW!

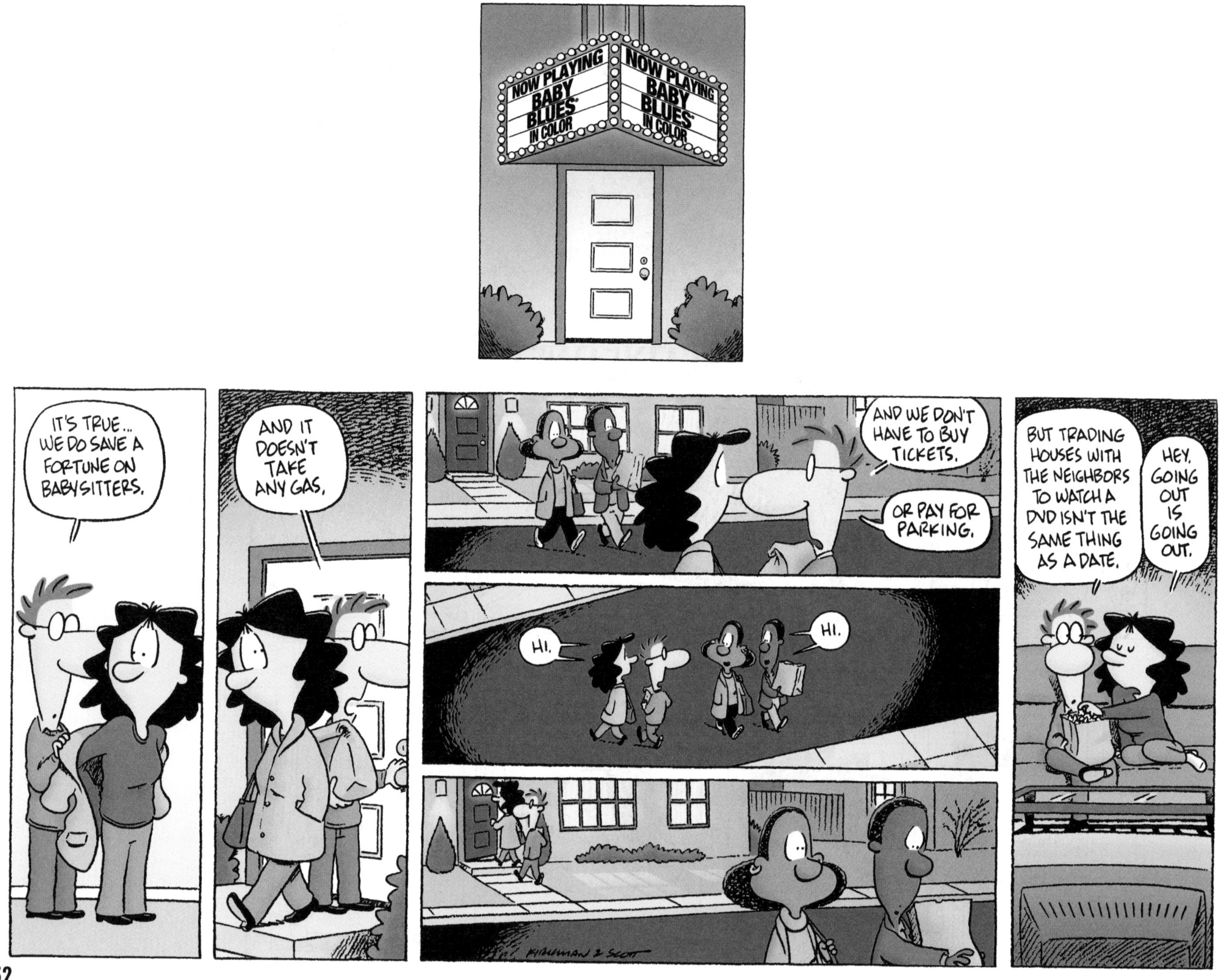
NOW PLAYING
BABY BLUES®
IN COLOR
NOW PLAYING
BABY BLUES®
IN COLOR
IT'S TRUE... WE DO SAVE A FORTUNE ON BABYSITTERS.
AND IT DOESN'T TAKE ANY GAS.
AND WE DON'T HAVE TO BUY TICKETS.
OR PAY FOR PARKING.
HI.
HI.
KIRKMAN & SCOTT
BUT TRADING HOUSES WITH THE NEIGHBORS TO WATCH A DVD ISN'T THE SAME THING AS A DATE.
HEY. GOING OUT IS GOING OUT.

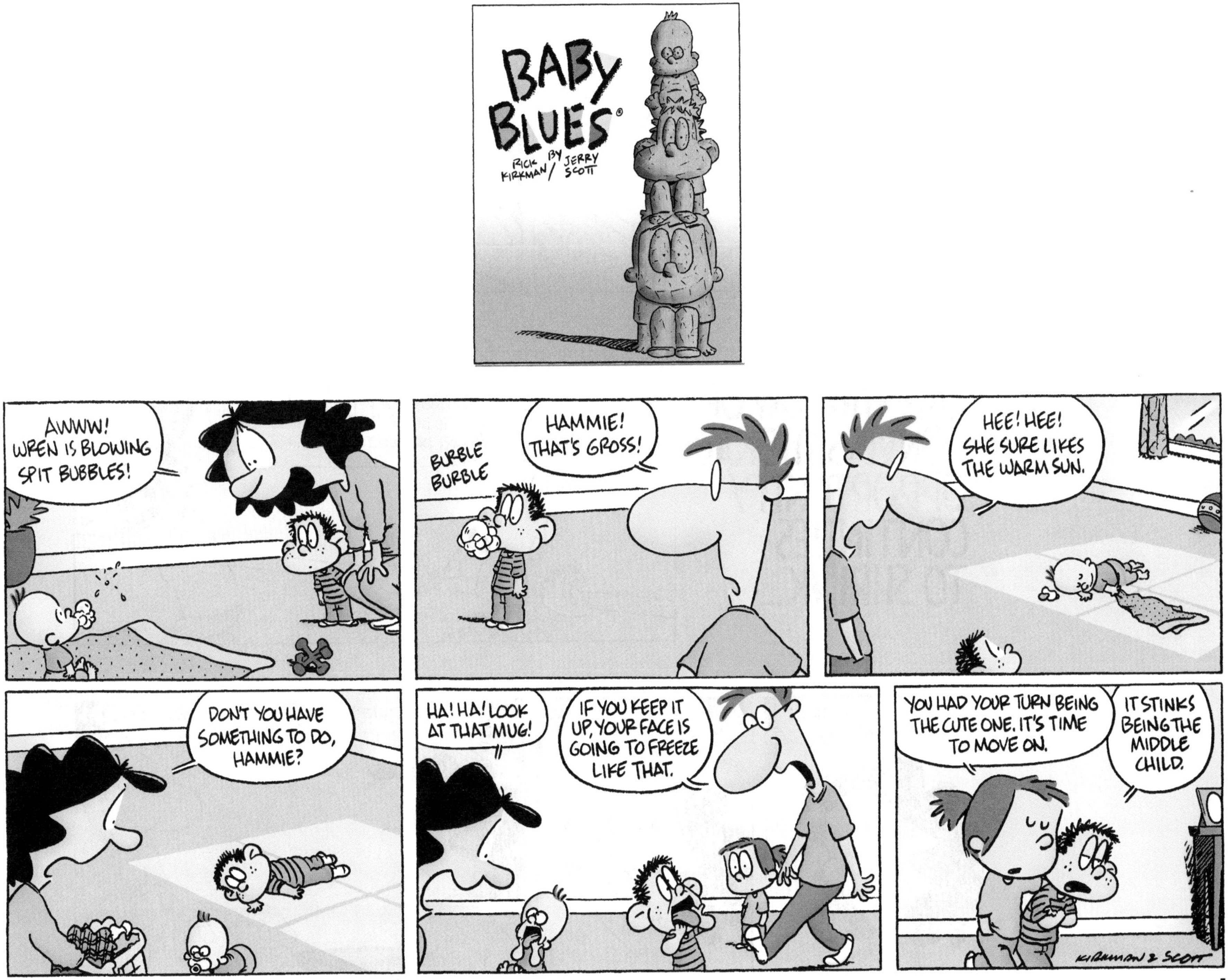
BABY BLUES®
BY RICK KIRKMAN / JERRY SCOTT
AWWW! WREN IS BLOWING SPIT BUBBLES!
BURBLE BURBLE
HAMMIE! THAT'S GROSS!
HEE! HEE! SHE SURE LIKES THE WARM SUN.
DON'T YOU HAVE SOMETHING TO DO, HAMMIE?
HA! HA! LOOK AT THAT MUG!
IF YOU KEEP IT UP, YOUR FACE IS GOING TO FREEZE LIKE THAT.
YOU HAD YOUR TURN BEING THE CUTE ONE. IT'S TIME TO MOVE ON.
IT STINKS BEING THE MIDDLE CHILD.
KIRKMAN & SCOTT

RIINN-NNGGG-
TAP!
YAWN!
ON YOUR MARK... GET SET...
SHE STARTED IT!!
...GO.

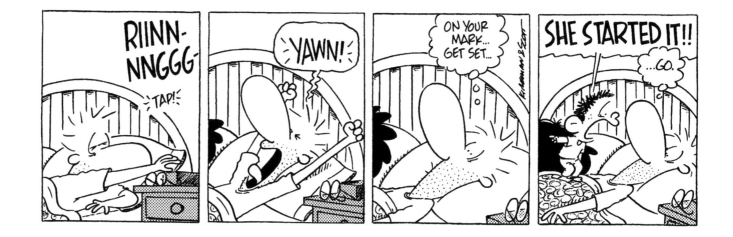

THE WINDOW OF CONVERSATIONAL OPPORTUNITY CONTINUES TO SHRINK...

REMIND ME TO FINISH THE STORY I STARTED TO TELL YOU THIS MORNING AFTER THE KIDS GO TO BED, BUT BEFORE I FALL ASLEEP OR FORGET IT ALTOGETHER.

WE DEPEND ON TECHNOLOGY TOO MUCH AROUND HERE...
...SO TONIGHT WE'RE GOING BACK TO BASICS BY COOKING OVER AN OPEN FIRE UNDER THE STARS!
HOW DOES THAT SOUND?
MICROWAVE'S BUSTED, HUH?

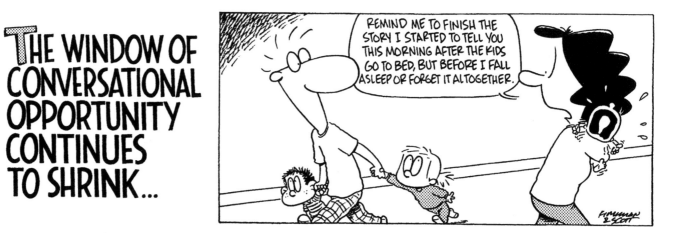

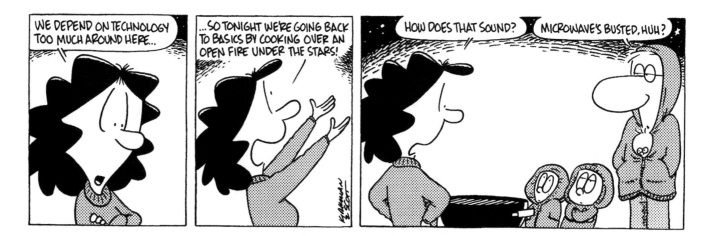

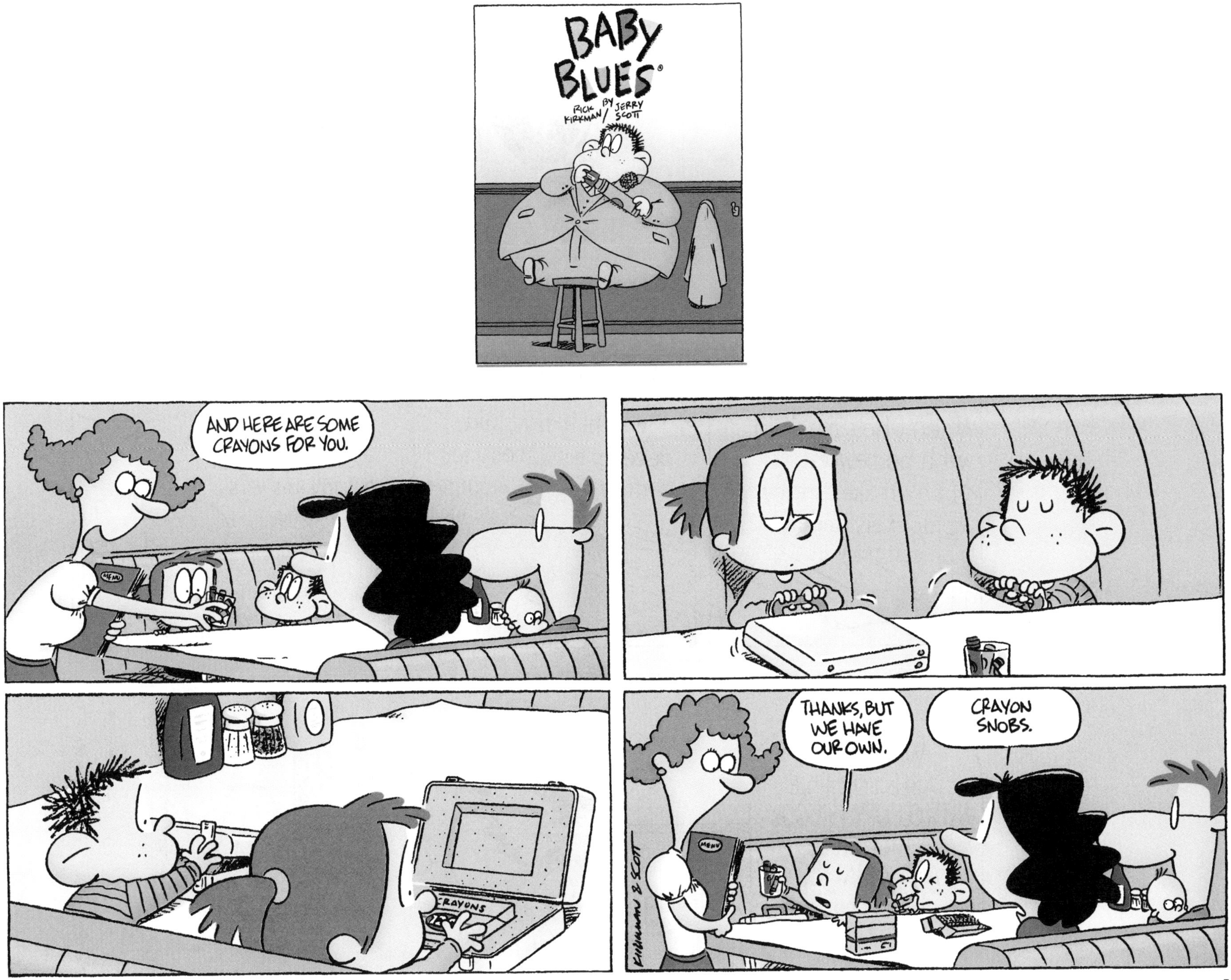
BABY BLUES®
BY RICK KIRKMAN / JERRY SCOTT
AND HERE ARE SOME CRAYONS FOR YOU.
MENU
CRAYONS
THANKS, BUT WE HAVE OUR OWN.
CRAYON SNOBS.
MENU
KIRKMAN & SCOTT

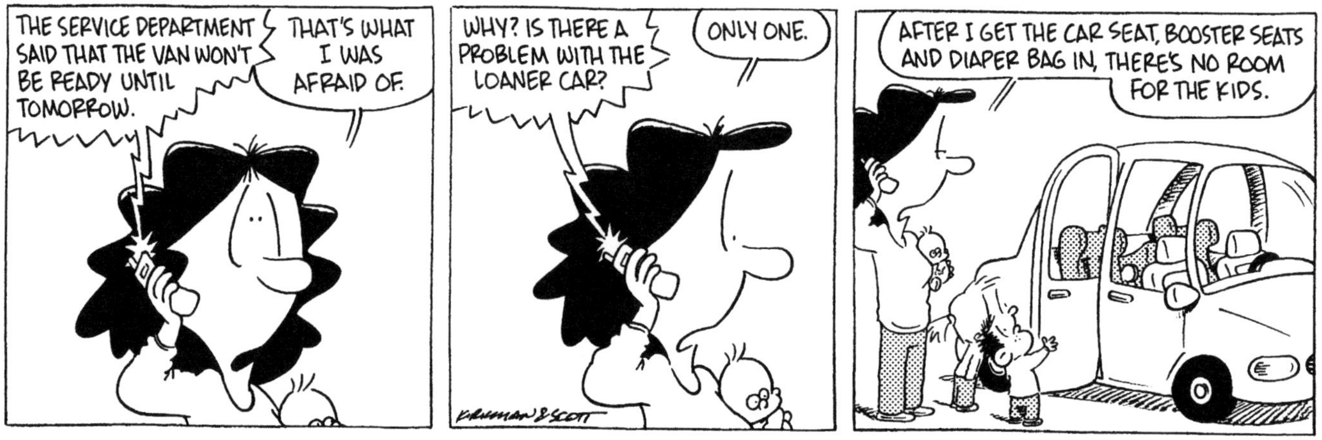
THE SERVICE DEPARTMENT SAID THAT THE VAN WON'T BE READY UNTIL TOMORROW.
THAT'S WHAT I WAS AFRAID OF.
WHY? IS THERE A PROBLEM WITH THE LOANER CAR?
ONLY ONE.
AFTER I GET THE CAR SEAT, BOOSTER SEATS AND DIAPER BAG IN, THERE'S NO ROOM FOR THE KIDS.

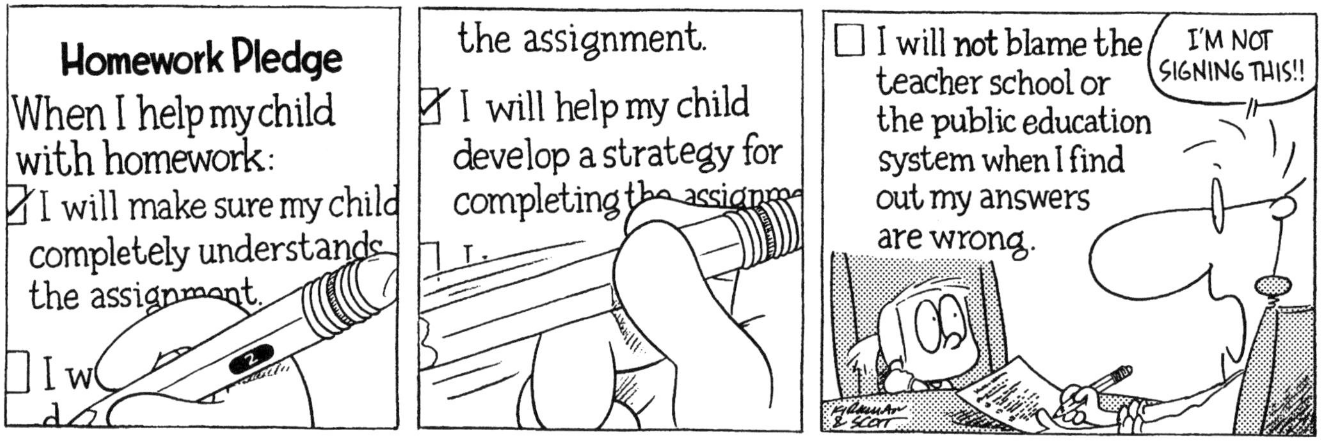
Homework Pledge
When I help my child with homework:
I will make sure my child completely understands the assignment.
the assignment.
I will help my child develop a strategy for completing the
I will not blame the teacher school or the public education system when I find out my answers are wrong.
I'M NOT SIGNING THIS!!

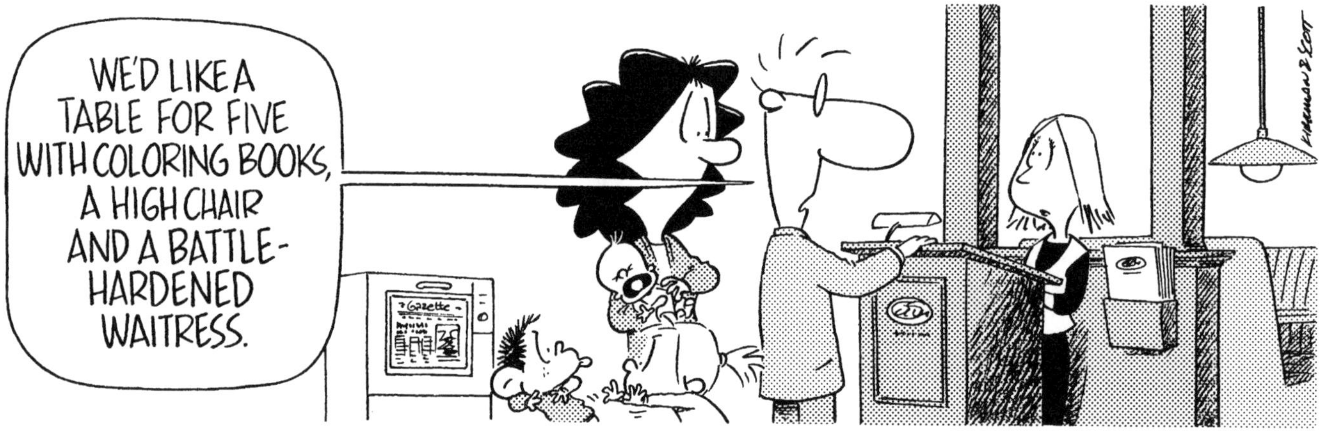
WE'D LIKE A TABLE FOR FIVE WITH COLORING BOOKS, A HIGH CHAIR AND A BATTLE-HARDENED WAITRESS.

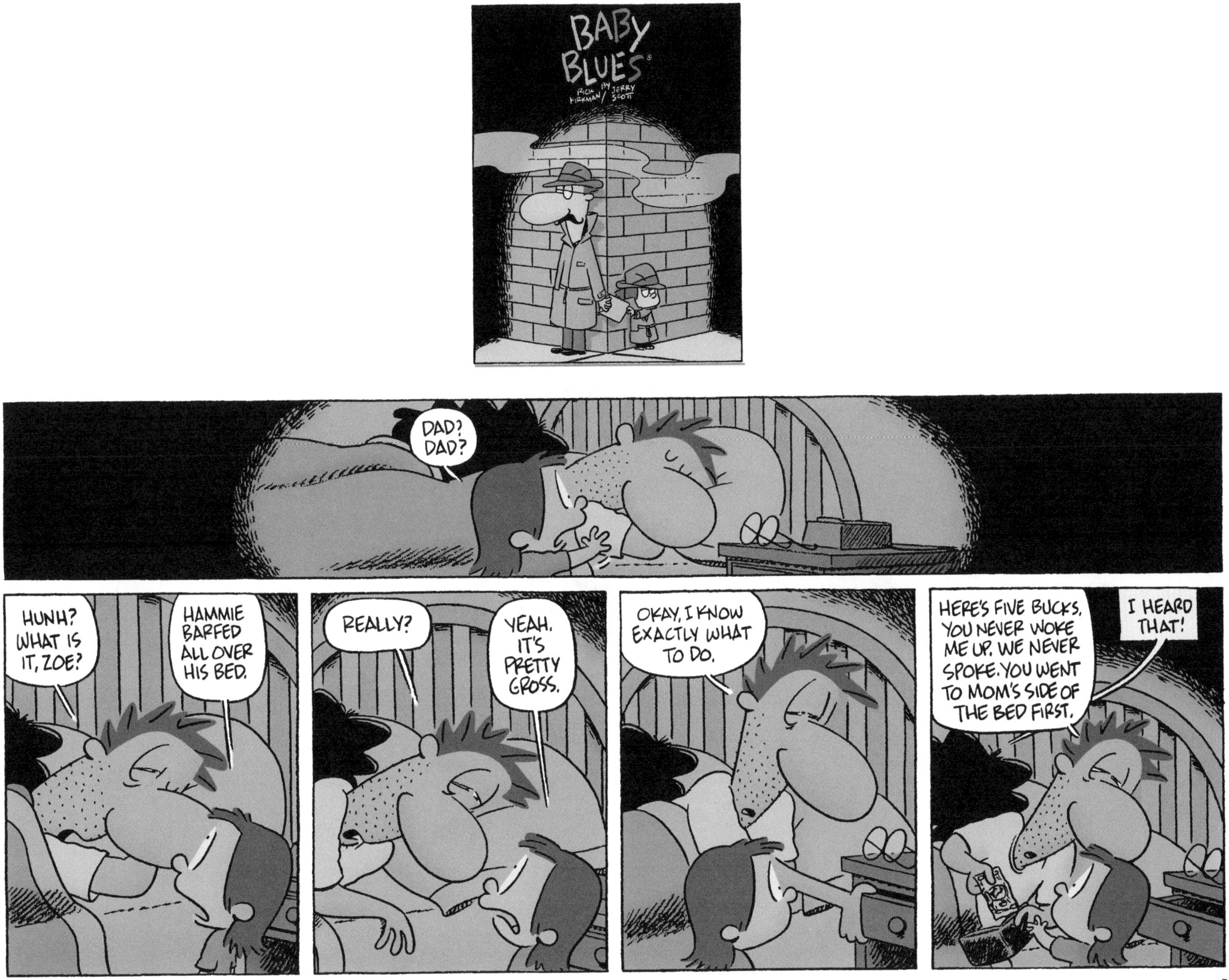
BABY BLUES®
BY RICK KIRKMAN / JERRY SCOTT
DAD? DAD?
HUNH? WHAT IS IT, ZOE?
HAMMIE BARFED ALL OVER HIS BED.
REALLY?
YEAH. IT'S PRETTY GROSS.
OKAY, I KNOW EXACTLY WHAT TO DO.
HERE'S FIVE BUCKS. YOU NEVER WOKE ME UP. WE NEVER SPOKE. YOU WENT TO MOM'S SIDE OF THE BED FIRST.
I HEARD THAT!

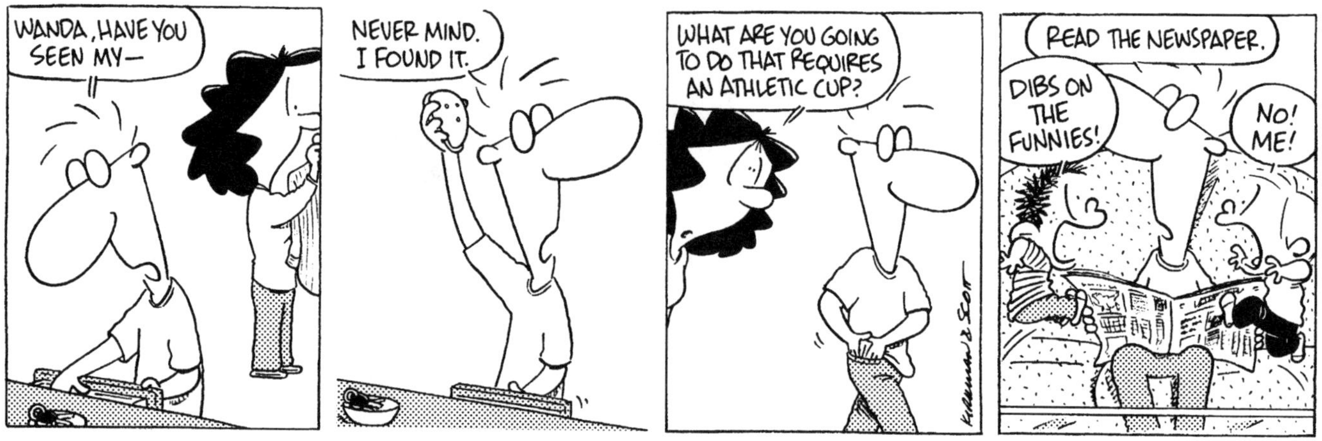
WANDA, HAVE YOU SEEN MY—
NEVER MIND. I FOUND IT.
WHAT ARE YOU GOING TO DO THAT REQUIRES AN ATHLETIC CUP?
READ THE NEWSPAPER.
DIBS ON THE FUNNIES!
NO! ME!

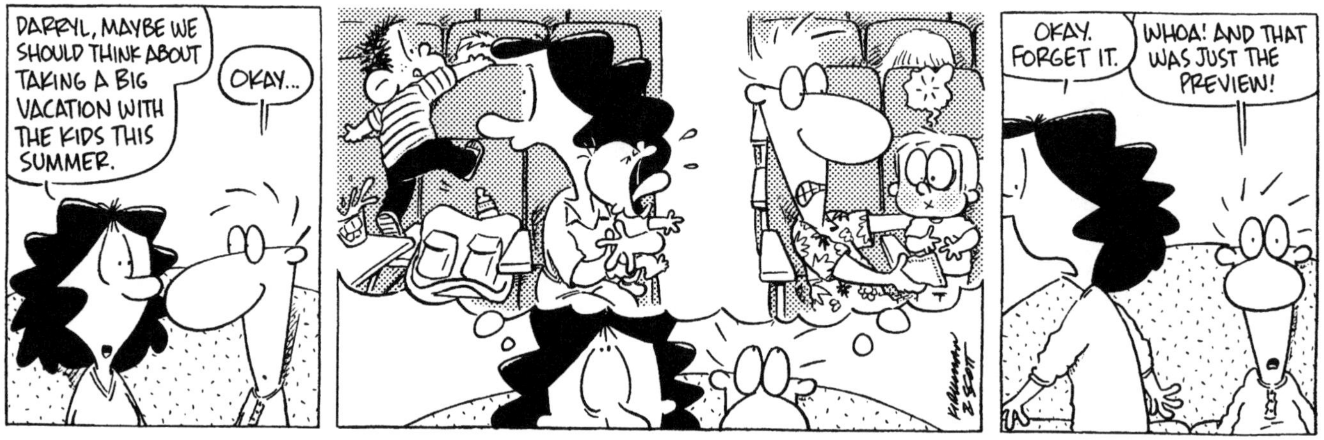
DARRYL, MAYBE WE SHOULD THINK ABOUT TAKING A BIG VACATION WITH THE KIDS THIS SUMMER.
OKAY...
OKAY. FORGET IT.
WHOA! AND THAT WAS JUST THE PREVIEW!

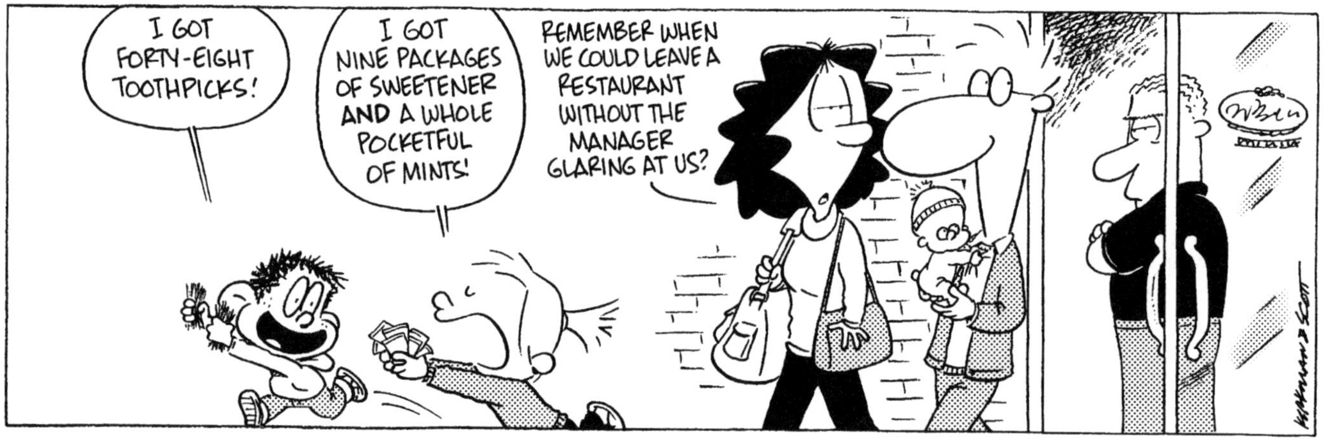
I GOT FORTY-EIGHT TOOTHPICKS!
I GOT NINE PACKAGES OF SWEETENER AND A WHOLE POCKETFUL OF MINTS!
REMEMBER WHEN WE COULD LEAVE A RESTAURANT WITHOUT THE MANAGER GLARING AT US?

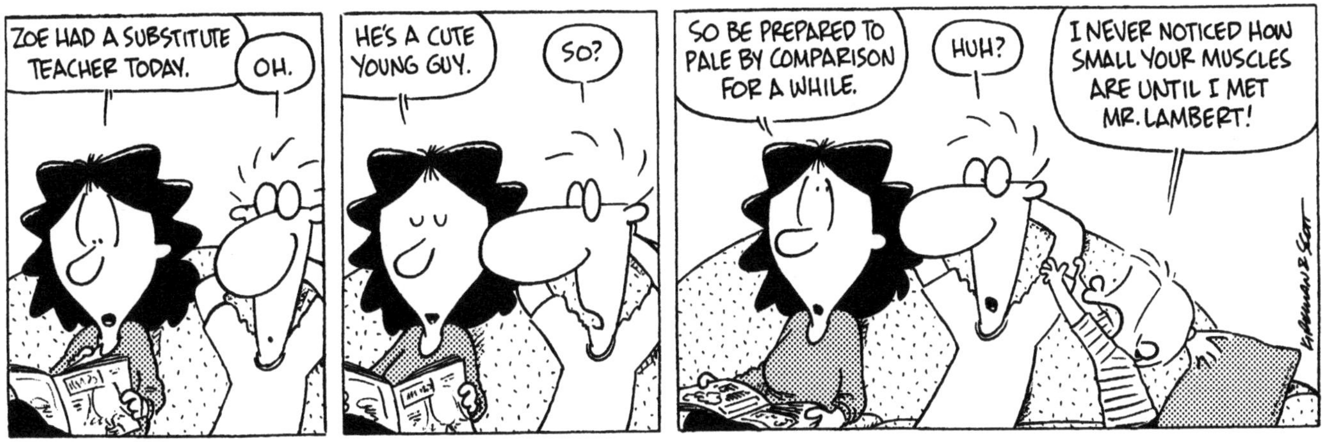
ZOE HAD A SUBSTITUTE TEACHER TODAY.
OH.
HE'S A CUTE YOUNG GUY.
SO?
SO BE PREPARED TO PALE BY COMPARISON FOR A WHILE.
HUH?
I NEVER NOTICED HOW SMALL YOUR MUSCLES ARE UNTIL I MET MR. LAMBERT!

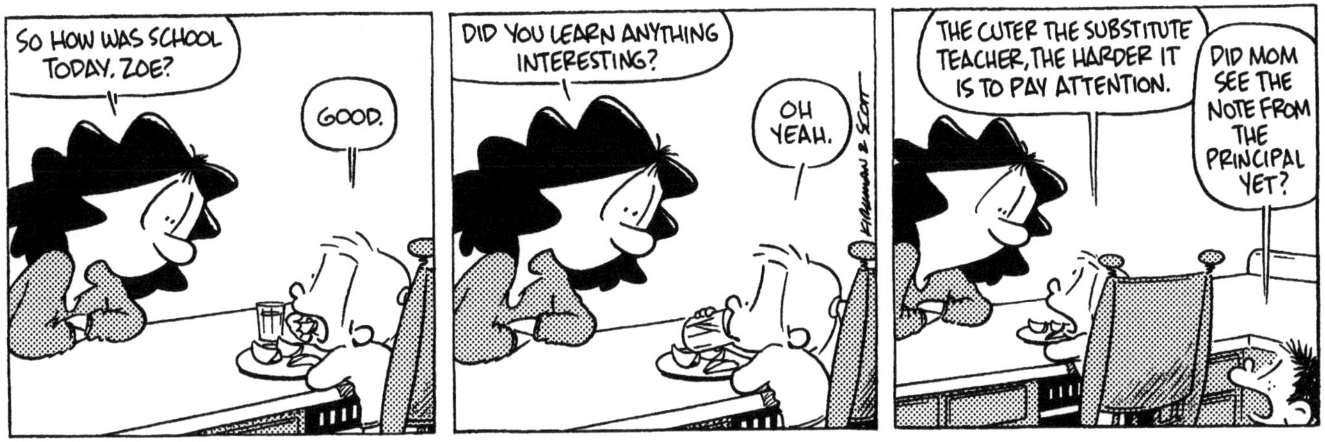
SO HOW WAS SCHOOL TODAY, ZOE?
GOOD.
DID YOU LEARN ANYTHING INTERESTING?
OH YEAH.
THE CUTER THE SUBSTITUTE TEACHER, THE HARDER IT IS TO PAY ATTENTION.
DID MOM SEE THE NOTE FROM THE PRINCIPAL YET?

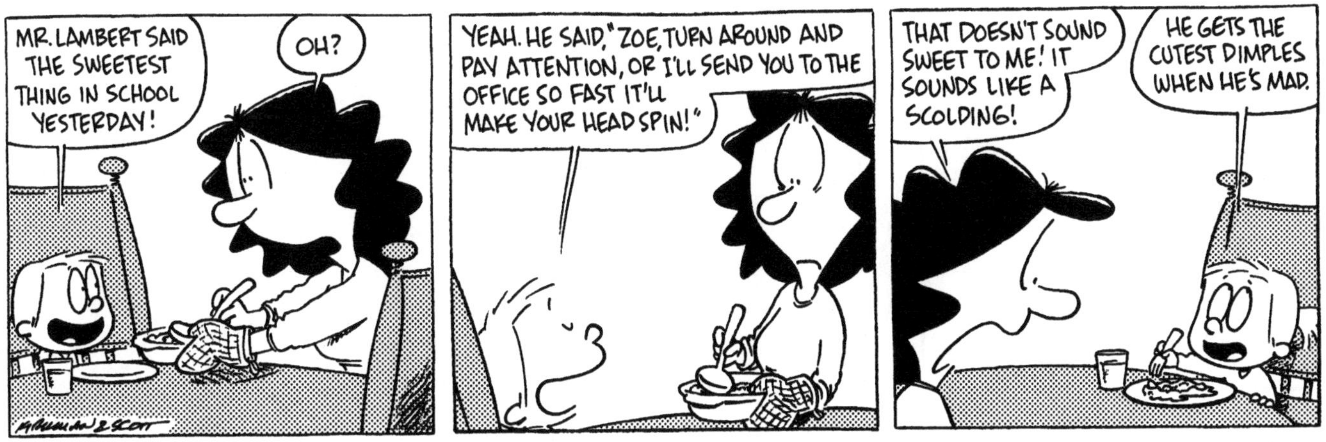
MR. LAMBERT SAID THE SWEETEST THING IN SCHOOL YESTERDAY!
OH?
YEAH. HE SAID, "ZOE, TURN AROUND AND PAY ATTENTION, OR I'LL SEND YOU TO THE OFFICE SO FAST IT'LL MAKE YOUR HEAD SPIN!"
THAT DOESN'T SOUND SWEET TO ME! IT SOUNDS LIKE A SCOLDING!
HE GETS THE CUTEST DIMPLES WHEN HE'S MAD.

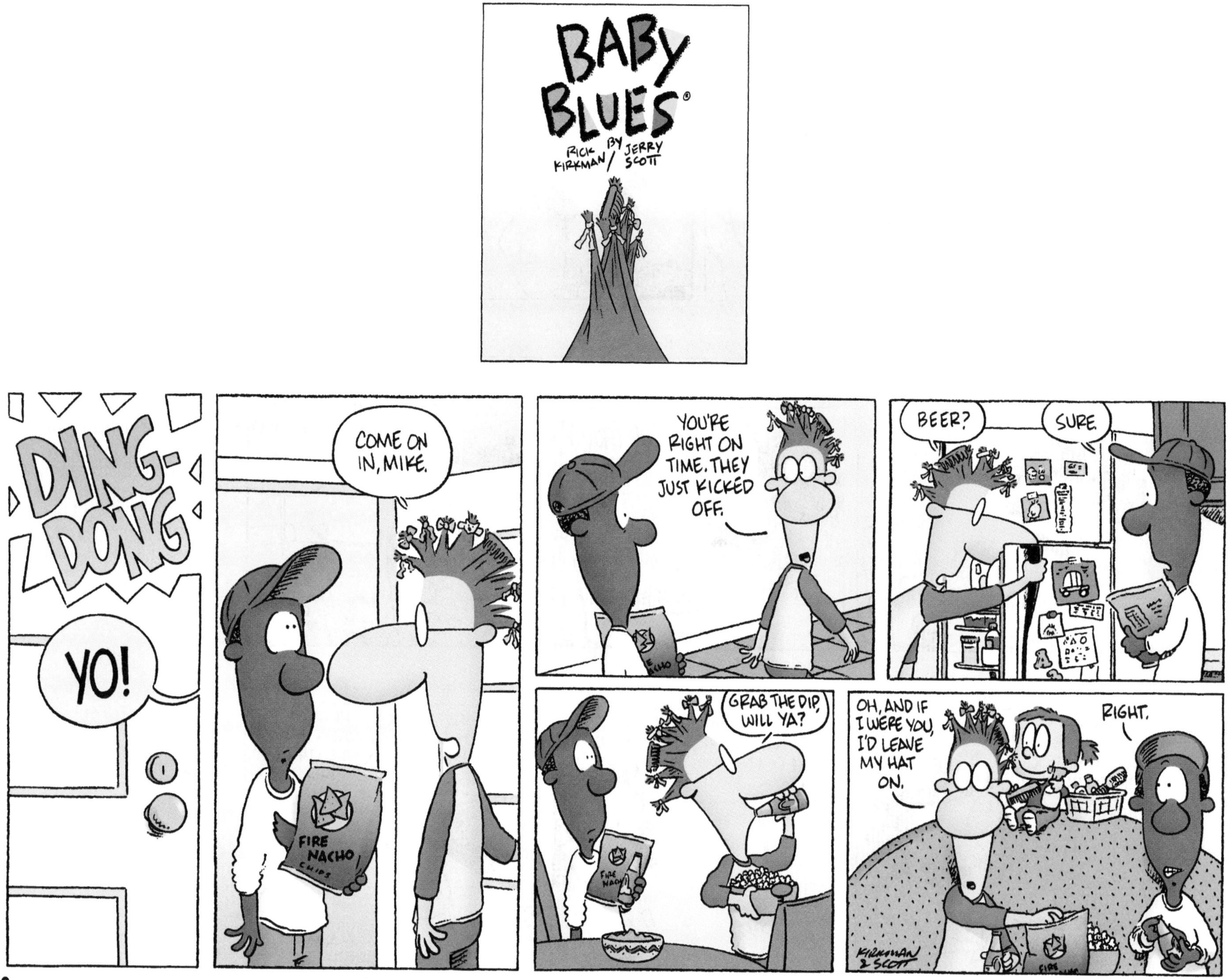
BABY BLUES®
BY RICK KIRKMAN / JERRY SCOTT
DING-DONG
YO!
COME ON IN, MIKE.
FIRE NACHO CHIPS
YOU'RE RIGHT ON TIME. THEY JUST KICKED OFF.
BEER?
SURE.
GRAB THE DIP, WILL YA?
OH, AND IF I WERE YOU, I'D LEAVE MY HAT ON.
RIGHT.
KIRKMAN & SCOTT

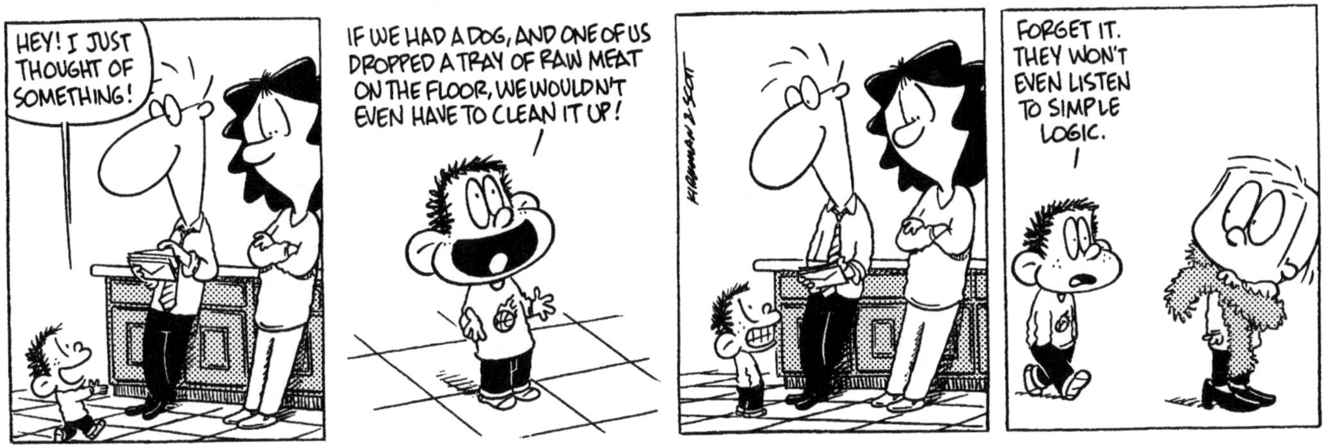
HEY! I JUST THOUGHT OF SOMETHING!
IF WE HAD A DOG, AND ONE OF US DROPPED A TRAY OF RAW MEAT ON THE FLOOR, WE WOULDN'T EVEN HAVE TO CLEAN IT UP!
FORGET IT. THEY WON'T EVEN LISTEN TO SIMPLE LOGIC.

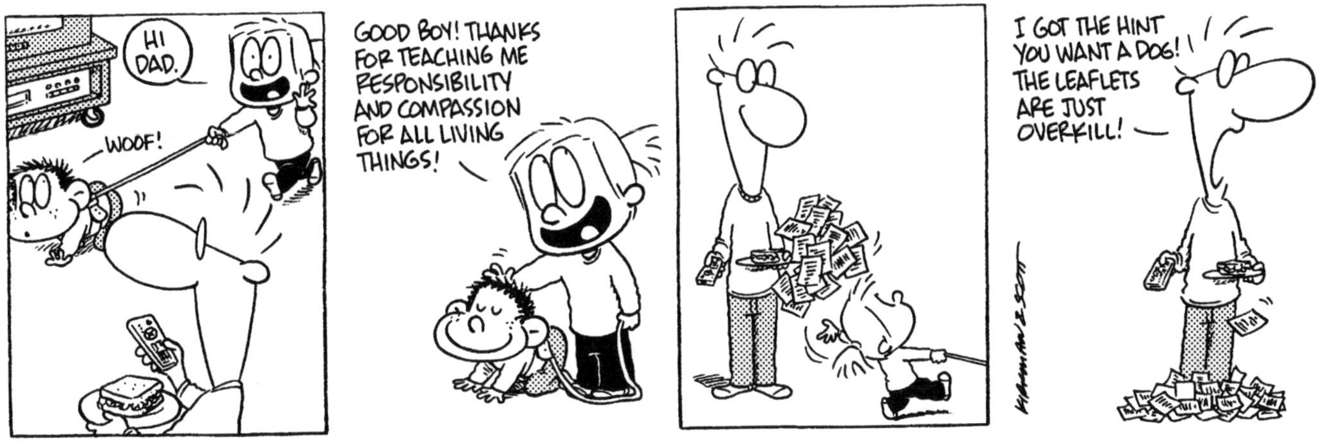
HI DAD.
WOOF!
GOOD BOY! THANKS FOR TEACHING ME RESPONSIBILITY AND COMPASSION FOR ALL LIVING THINGS!
I GOT THE HINT YOU WANT A DOG! THE LEAFLETS ARE JUST OVERKILL!

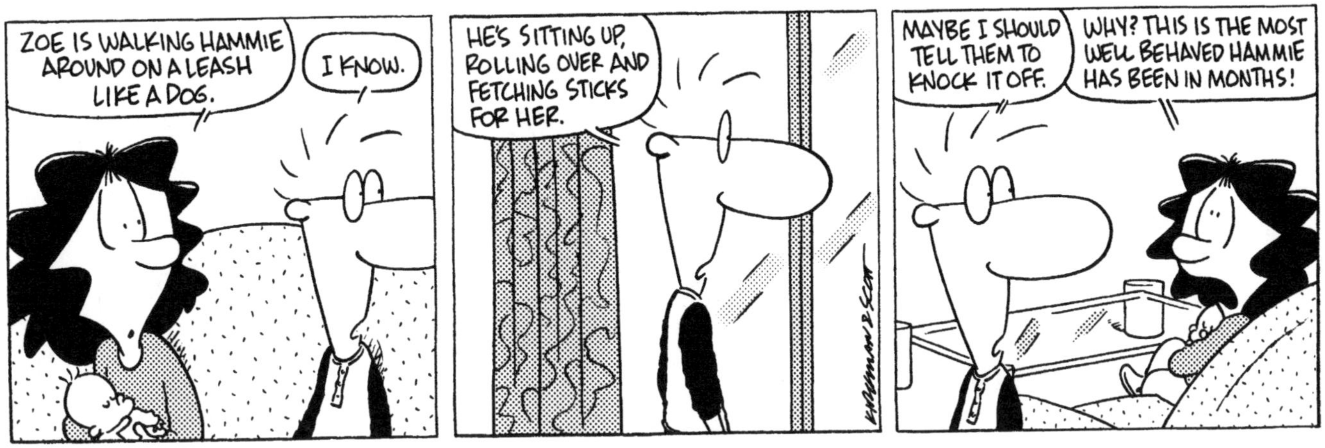
ZOE IS WALKING HAMMIE AROUND ON A LEASH LIKE A DOG.
I KNOW.
HE'S SITTING UP, ROLLING OVER AND FETCHING STICKS FOR HER.
MAYBE I SHOULD TELL THEM TO KNOCK IT OFF.
WHY? THIS IS THE MOST WELL BEHAVED HAMMIE HAS BEEN IN MONTHS!

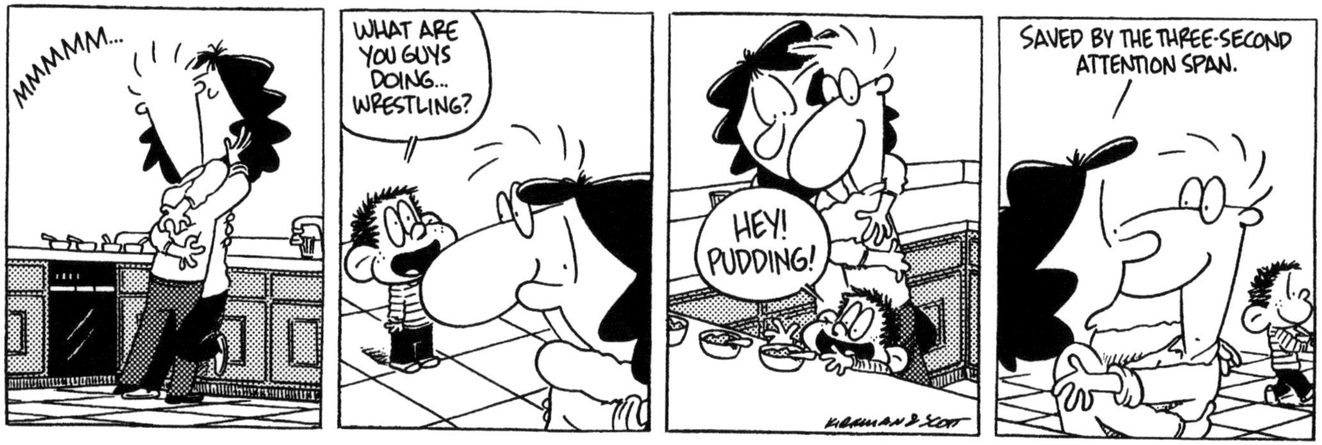
MMMMM...
WHAT ARE YOU GUYS DOING... WRESTLING?
HEY! PUDDING!
SAVED BY THE THREE-SECOND ATTENTION SPAN.

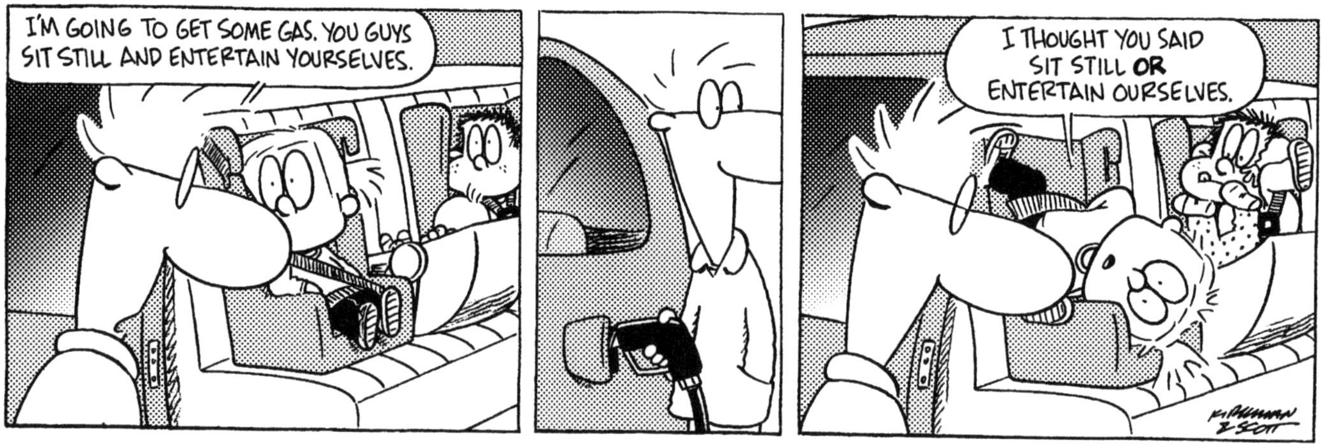
I'M GOING TO GET SOME GAS. YOU GUYS SIT STILL AND ENTERTAIN YOURSELVES.
I THOUGHT YOU SAID SIT STILL **OR** ENTERTAIN OURSELVES.

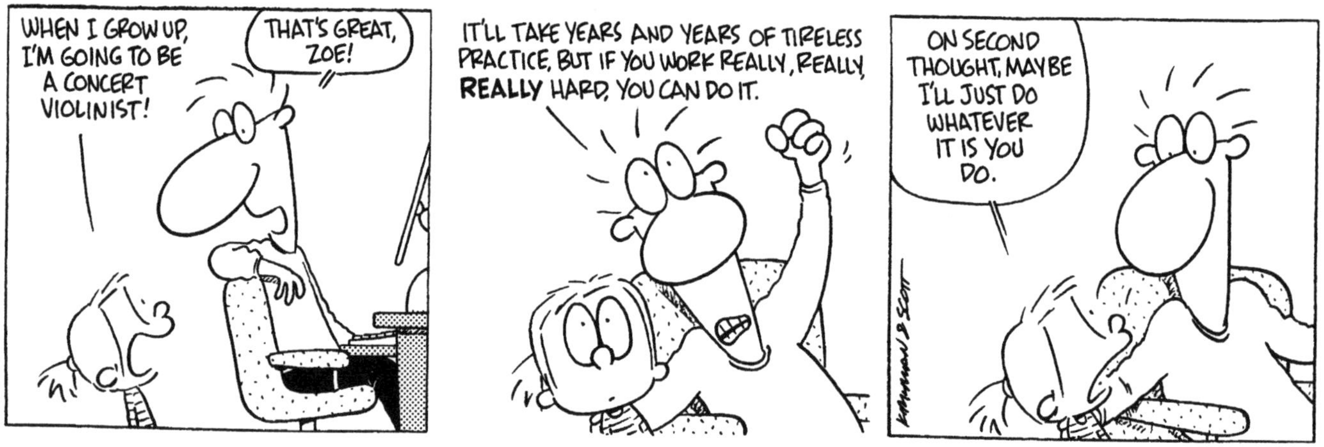
WHEN I GROW UP, I'M GOING TO BE A CONCERT VIOLINIST!
THAT'S GREAT, ZOE!
IT'LL TAKE YEARS AND YEARS OF TIRELESS PRACTICE, BUT IF YOU WORK REALLY, REALLY, **REALLY** HARD, YOU CAN DO IT.
ON SECOND THOUGHT, MAYBE I'LL JUST DO WHATEVER IT IS YOU DO.

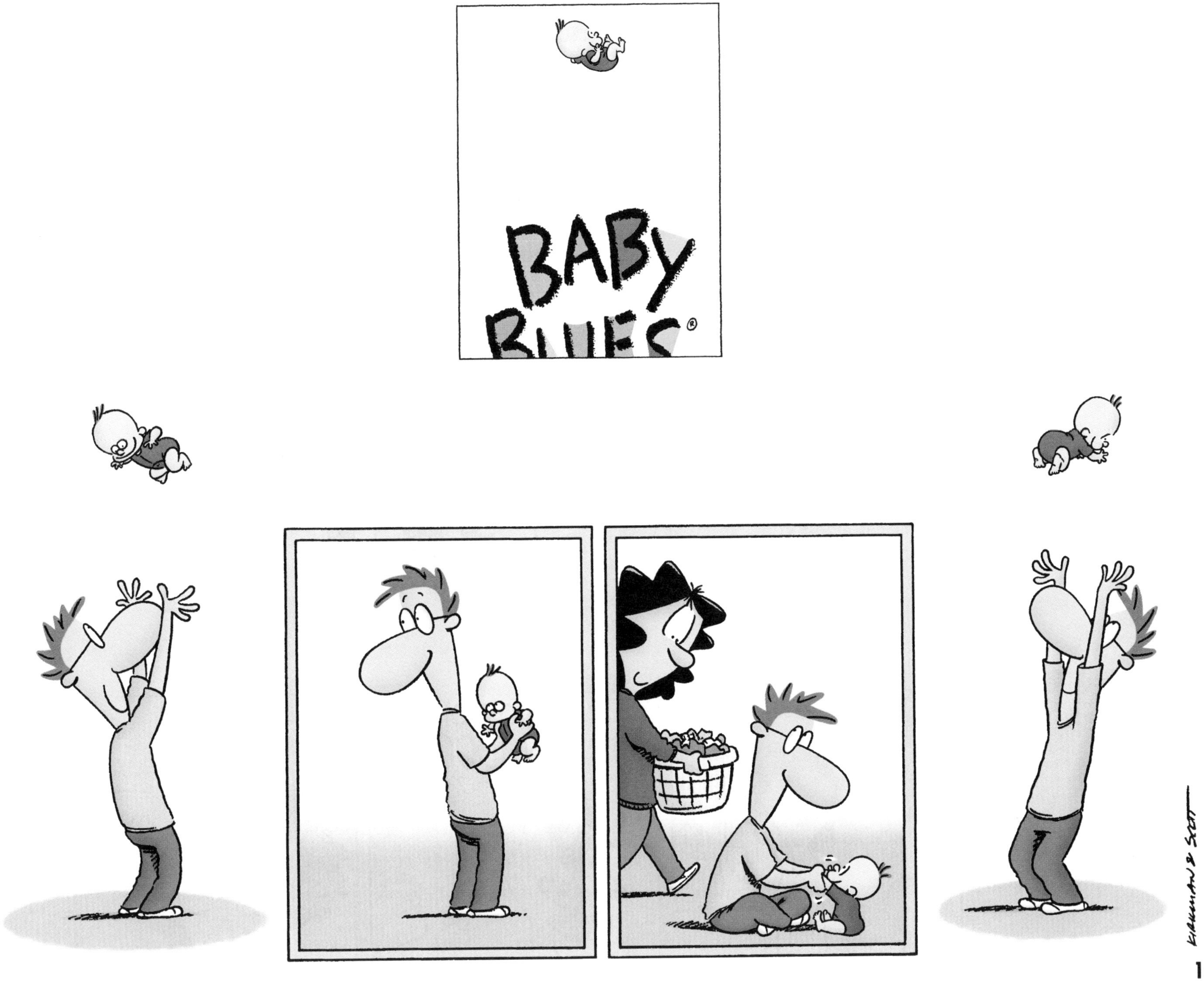
BABY
KIRKMAN & SCOTT

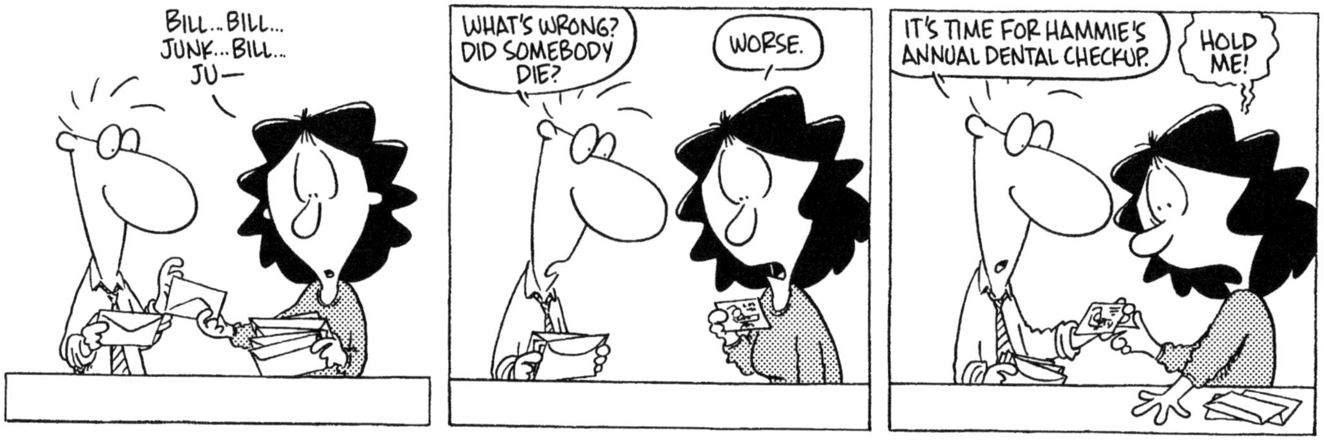
BILL... BILL... JUNK... BILL... JU—
WHAT'S WRONG? DID SOMEBODY DIE?
WORSE.
IT'S TIME FOR HAMMIE'S ANNUAL DENTAL CHECKUP.
HOLD ME!

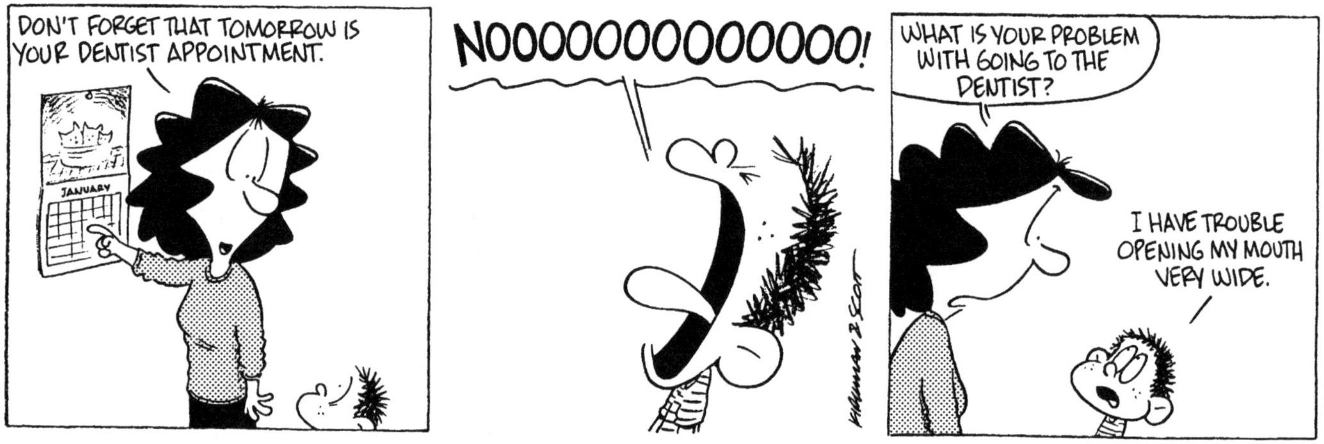
DON'T FORGET THAT TOMORROW IS YOUR DENTIST APPOINTMENT.
JANUARY
NOOOOOOOOOOOOO!
WHAT IS YOUR PROBLEM WITH GOING TO THE DENTIST?
I HAVE TROUBLE OPENING MY MOUTH VERY WIDE.

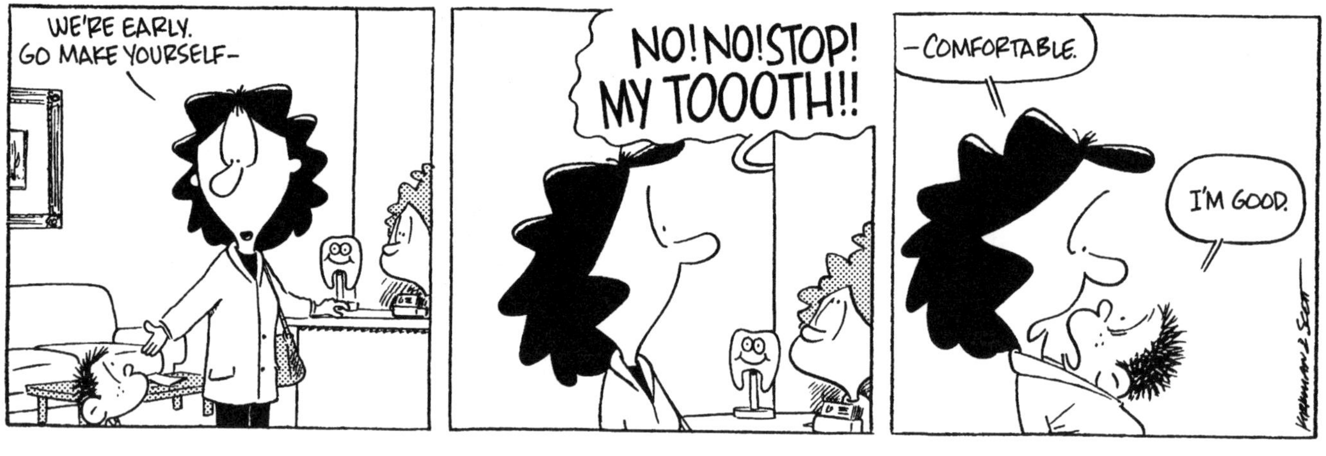
WE'RE EARLY. GO MAKE YOURSELF—
NO! NO! STOP! MY TOOOTH!!
—COMFORTABLE.
I'M GOOD.

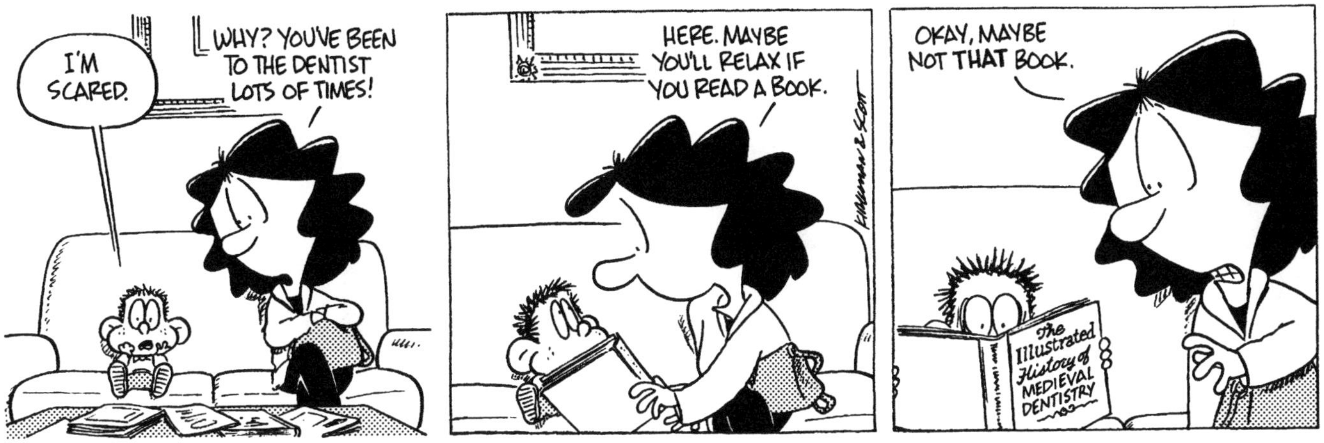
I'M SCARED.
WHY? YOU'VE BEEN TO THE DENTIST LOTS OF TIMES!
HERE. MAYBE YOU'LL RELAX IF YOU READ A BOOK.
OKAY, MAYBE NOT **THAT** BOOK.
The Illustrated History of MEDIEVAL DENTISTRY

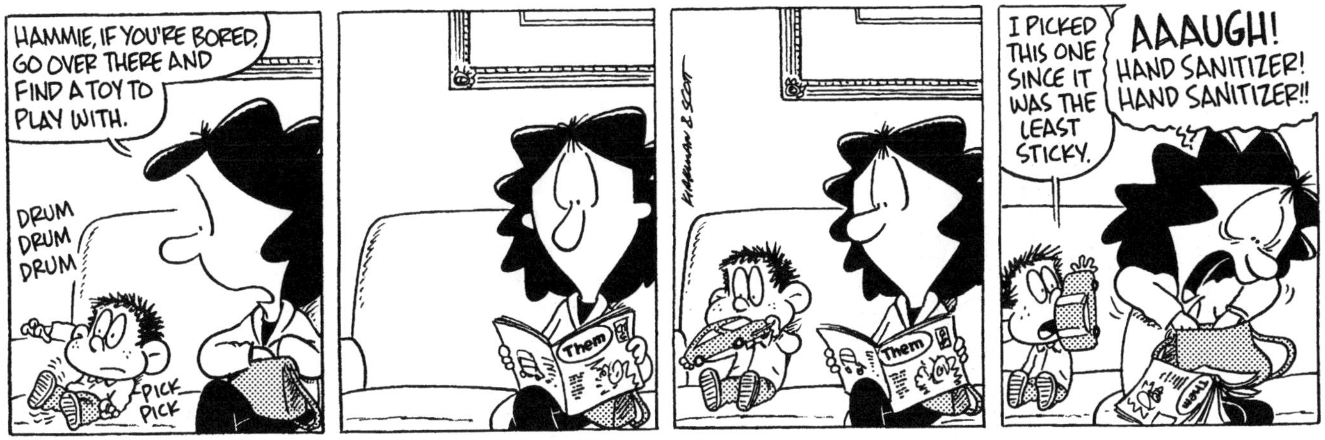
HAMMIE, IF YOU'RE BORED, GO OVER THERE AND FIND A TOY TO PLAY WITH.
DRUM DRUM DRUM
PICK PICK
Them
Them
I PICKED THIS ONE SINCE IT WAS THE LEAST STICKY.
AAAUGH! HAND SANITIZER! HAND SANITIZER!!

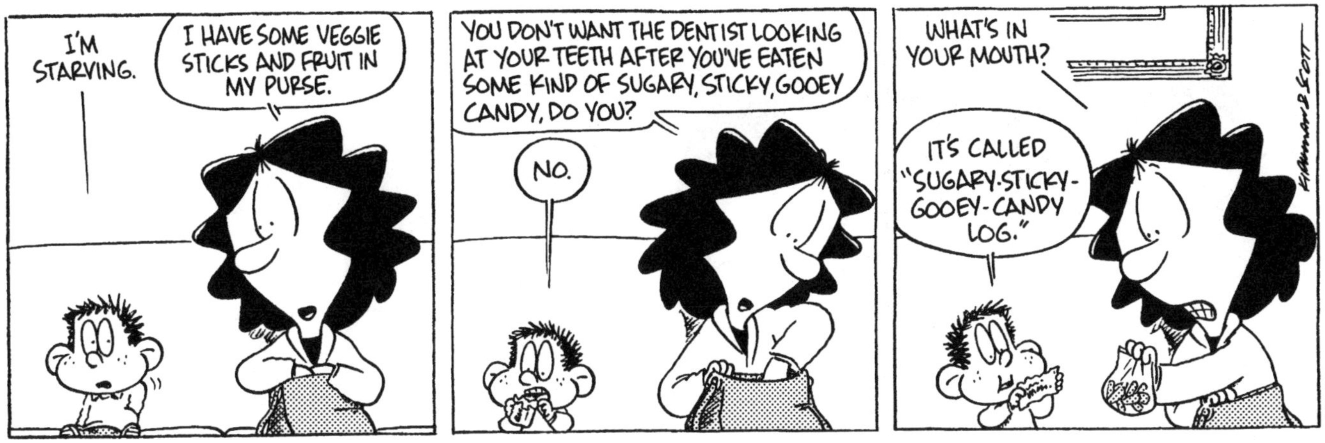
I'M STARVING.
I HAVE SOME VEGGIE STICKS AND FRUIT IN MY PURSE.
YOU DON'T WANT THE DENTIST LOOKING AT YOUR TEETH AFTER YOU'VE EATEN SOME KIND OF SUGARY, STICKY, GOOEY CANDY, DO YOU?
NO.
WHAT'S IN YOUR MOUTH?
IT'S CALLED "SUGARY-STICKY-GOOEY-CANDY LOG."

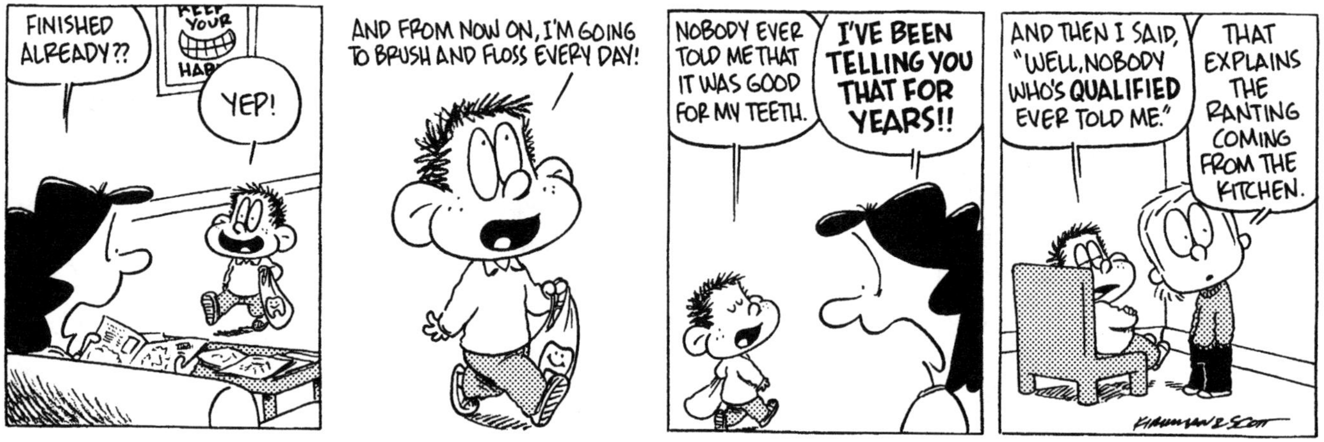
FINISHED ALREADY??
YEP!
AND FROM NOW ON, I'M GOING TO BRUSH AND FLOSS EVERY DAY!
NOBODY EVER TOLD ME THAT IT WAS GOOD FOR MY TEETH.
I'VE BEEN TELLING YOU THAT FOR YEARS!!
AND THEN I SAID, "WELL, NOBODY WHO'S QUALIFIED EVER TOLD ME."
THAT EXPLAINS THE RANTING COMING FROM THE KITCHEN.

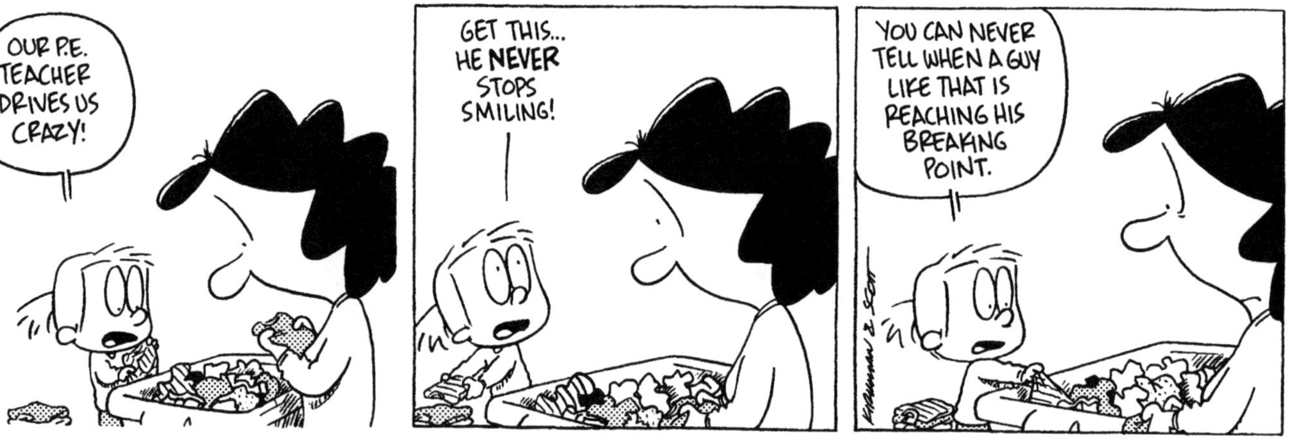
OUR P.E. TEACHER DRIVES US CRAZY!
GET THIS... HE NEVER STOPS SMILING!
YOU CAN NEVER TELL WHEN A GUY LIKE THAT IS REACHING HIS BREAKING POINT.

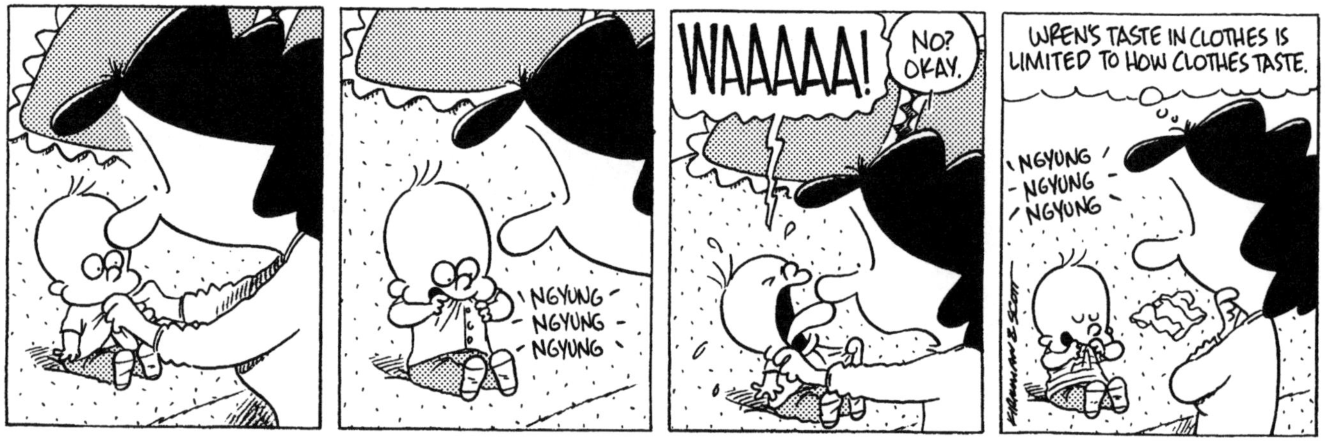
NGYUNG
NGYUNG
NGYUNG
WAAAAA!
NO? OKAY.
WREN'S TASTE IN CLOTHES IS LIMITED TO HOW CLOTHES TASTE.
NGYUNG
NGYUNG
NGYUNG

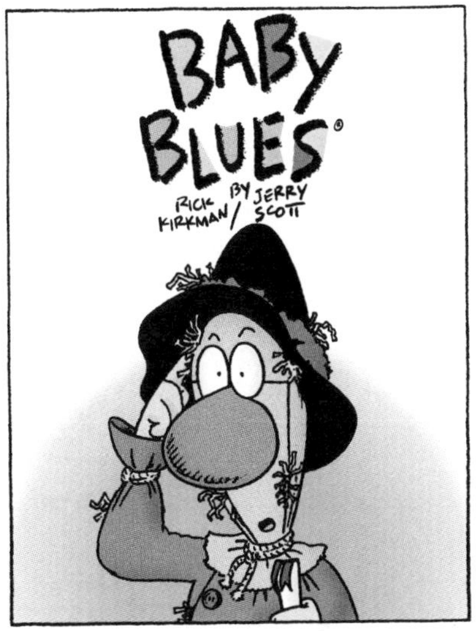
BABY BLUES®
BY RICK KIRKMAN / JERRY SCOTT

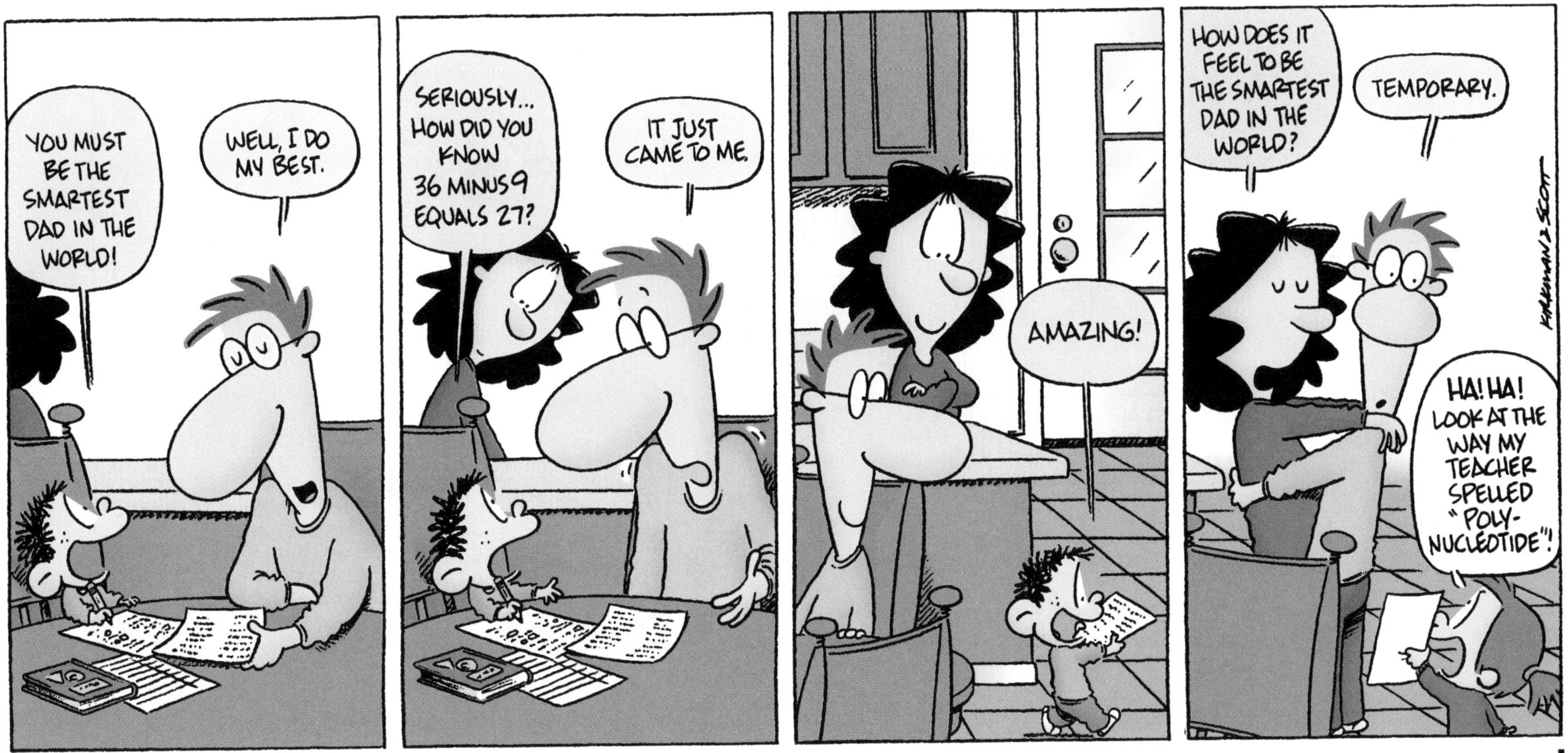
YOU MUST BE THE SMARTEST DAD IN THE WORLD!
WELL, I DO MY BEST.
SERIOUSLY... HOW DID YOU KNOW 36 MINUS 9 EQUALS 27?
IT JUST CAME TO ME.
AMAZING!
HOW DOES IT FEEL TO BE THE SMARTEST DAD IN THE WORLD?
TEMPORARY.
HA! HA! LOOK AT THE WAY MY TEACHER SPELLED "POLY-NUCLEOTIDE"!
KIRKMAN & SCOTT

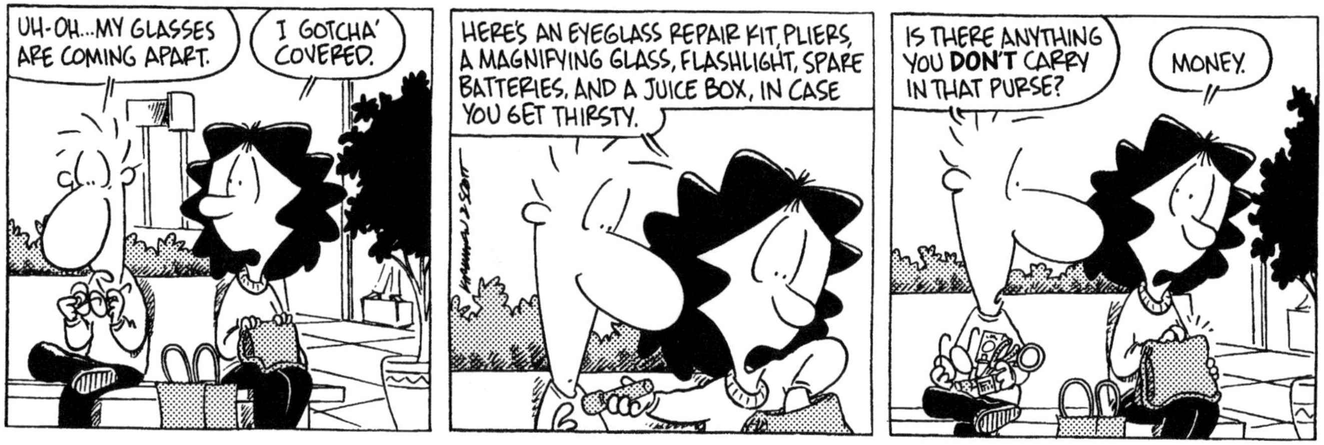
UH-OH...MY GLASSES ARE COMING APART.
I GOTCHA' COVERED.
HERE'S AN EYEGLASS REPAIR KIT, PLIERS, A MAGNIFYING GLASS, FLASHLIGHT, SPARE BATTERIES, AND A JUICE BOX, IN CASE YOU GET THIRSTY.
IS THERE ANYTHING YOU **DON'T** CARRY IN THAT PURSE?
MONEY.

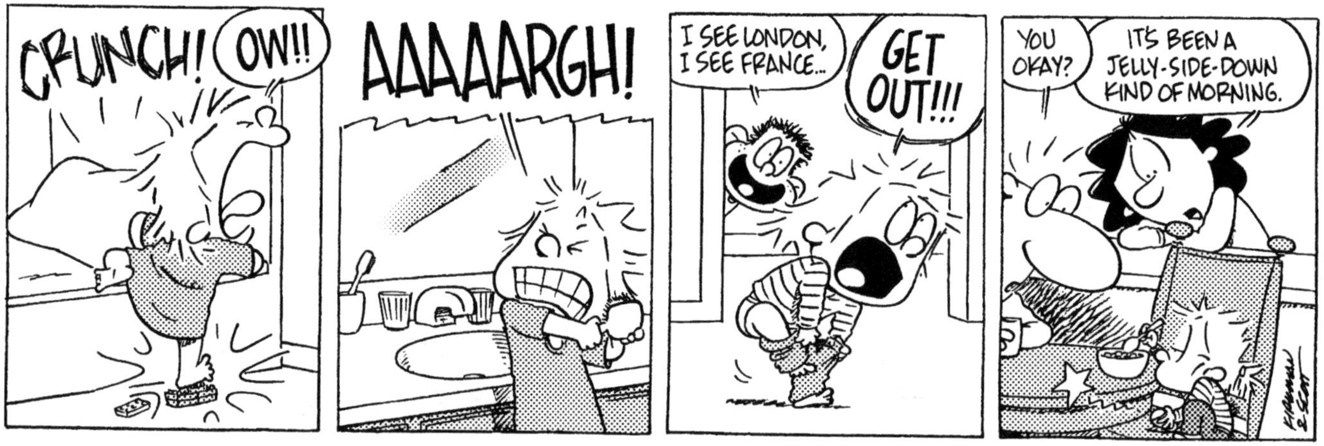
CRUNCH!
OW!!
AAAAARGH!
I SEE LONDON, I SEE FRANCE...
GET OUT!!!
YOU OKAY?
IT'S BEEN A JELLY-SIDE-DOWN KIND OF MORNING.

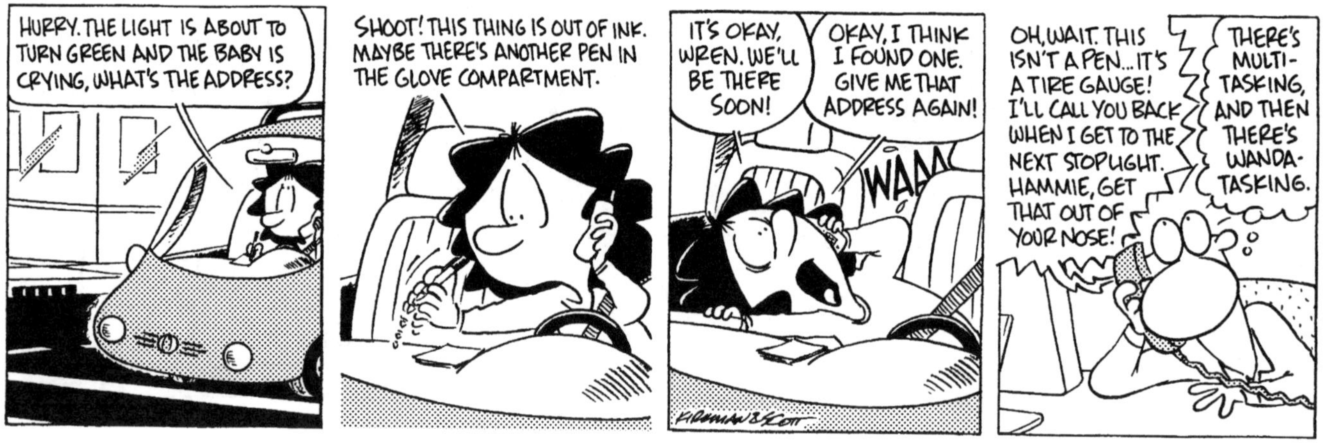
HURRY. THE LIGHT IS ABOUT TO TURN GREEN AND THE BABY IS CRYING. WHAT'S THE ADDRESS?
SHOOT! THIS THING IS OUT OF INK. MAYBE THERE'S ANOTHER PEN IN THE GLOVE COMPARTMENT.
IT'S OKAY, WREN. WE'LL BE THERE SOON!
OKAY, I THINK I FOUND ONE. GIVE ME THAT ADDRESS AGAIN!
OH, WAIT. THIS ISN'T A PEN... IT'S A TIRE GAUGE! I'LL CALL YOU BACK WHEN I GET TO THE NEXT STOPLIGHT. HAMMIE, GET THAT OUT OF YOUR NOSE!
THERE'S MULTI-TASKING, AND THEN THERE'S WANDA-TASKING.

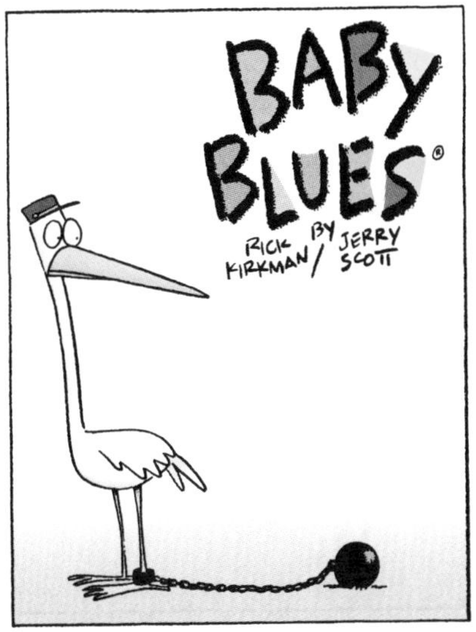
BABY BLUES®
BY RICK KIRKMAN / JERRY SCOTT

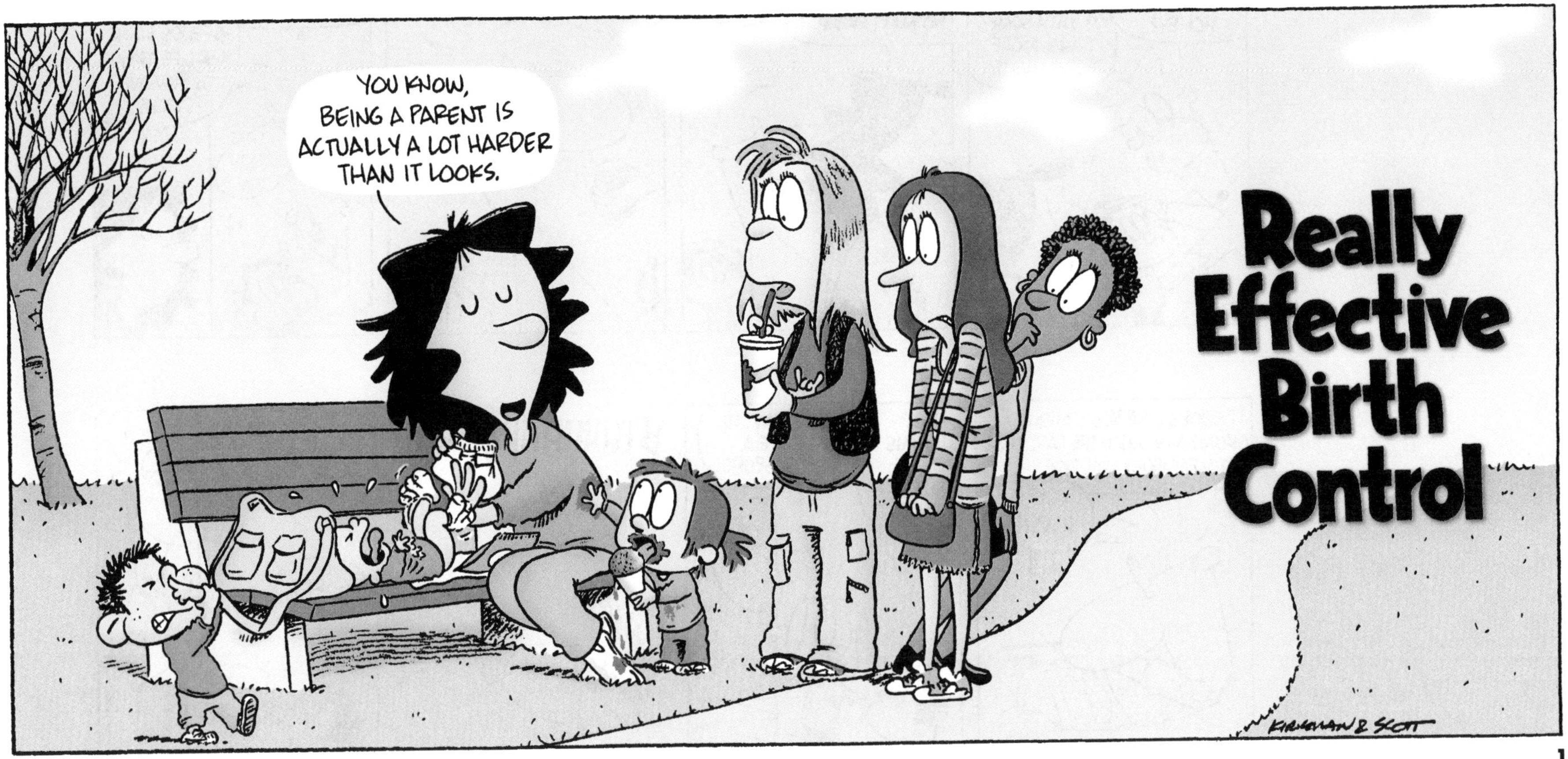
YOU KNOW, BEING A PARENT IS ACTUALLY A LOT HARDER THAN IT LOOKS.
Really Effective Birth Control
KIRKMAN & SCOTT

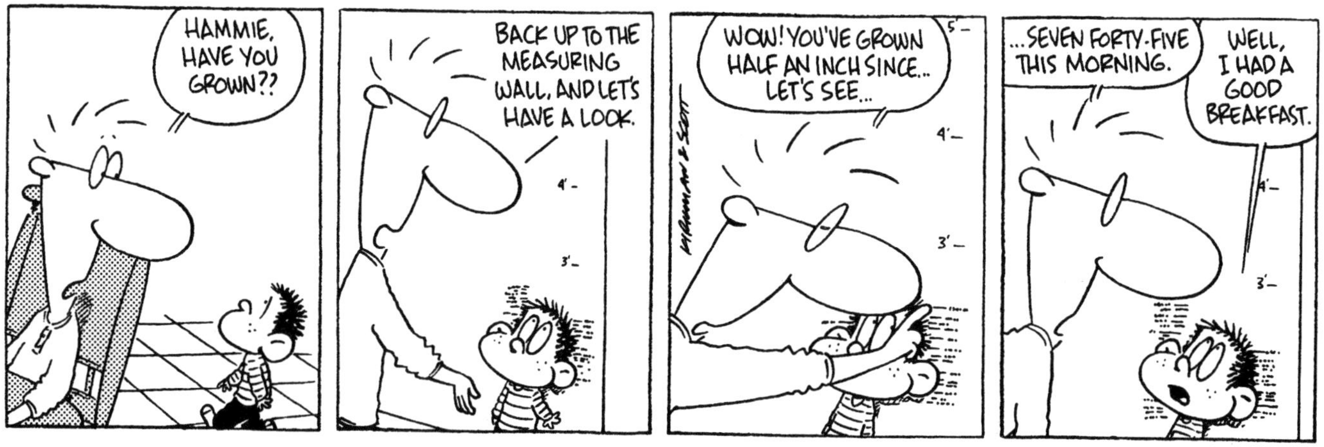
HAMMIE, HAVE YOU GROWN??
BACK UP TO THE MEASURING WALL, AND LET'S HAVE A LOOK.
WOW! YOU'VE GROWN HALF AN INCH SINCE... LET'S SEE...
...SEVEN FORTY-FIVE THIS MORNING.
WELL, I HAD A GOOD BREAKFAST.

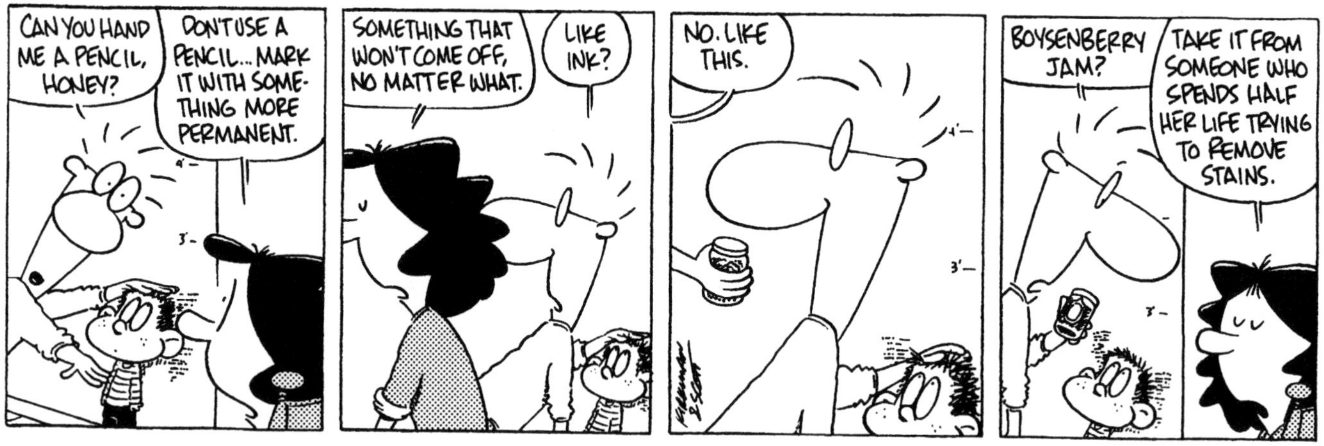
CAN YOU HAND ME A PENCIL, HONEY?
DON'T USE A PENCIL... MARK IT WITH SOMETHING MORE PERMANENT.
SOMETHING THAT WON'T COME OFF, NO MATTER WHAT.
LIKE INK?
NO. LIKE THIS.
BOYSENBERRY JAM?
TAKE IT FROM SOMEONE WHO SPENDS HALF HER LIFE TRYING TO REMOVE STAINS.

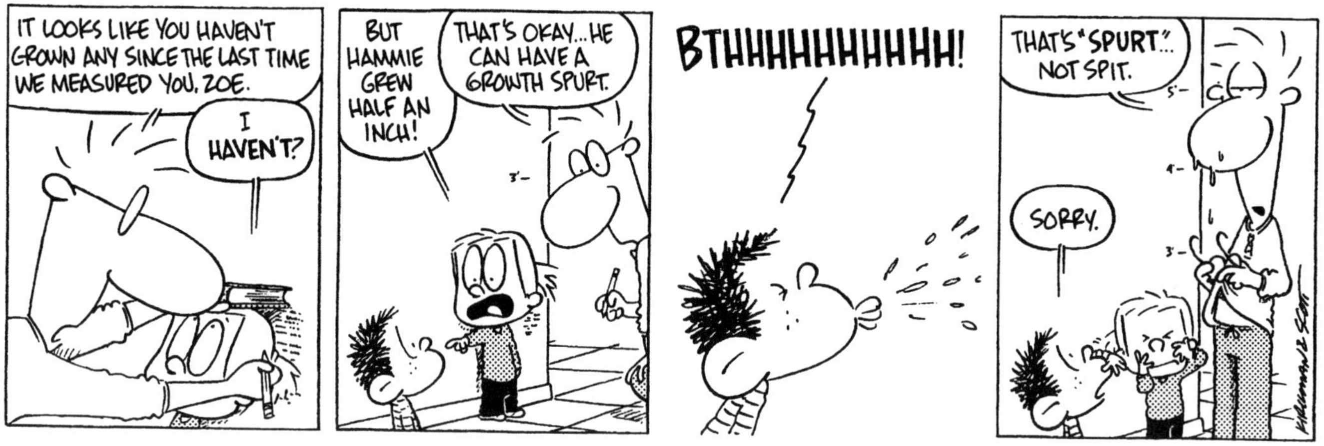
IT LOOKS LIKE YOU HAVEN'T GROWN ANY SINCE THE LAST TIME WE MEASURED YOU, ZOE.
I HAVEN'T?
BUT HAMMIE GREW HALF AN INCH!
THAT'S OKAY... HE CAN HAVE A GROWTH SPURT.
BTHHHHHHHHHH!
THAT'S "SPURT"... NOT SPIT.
SORRY.

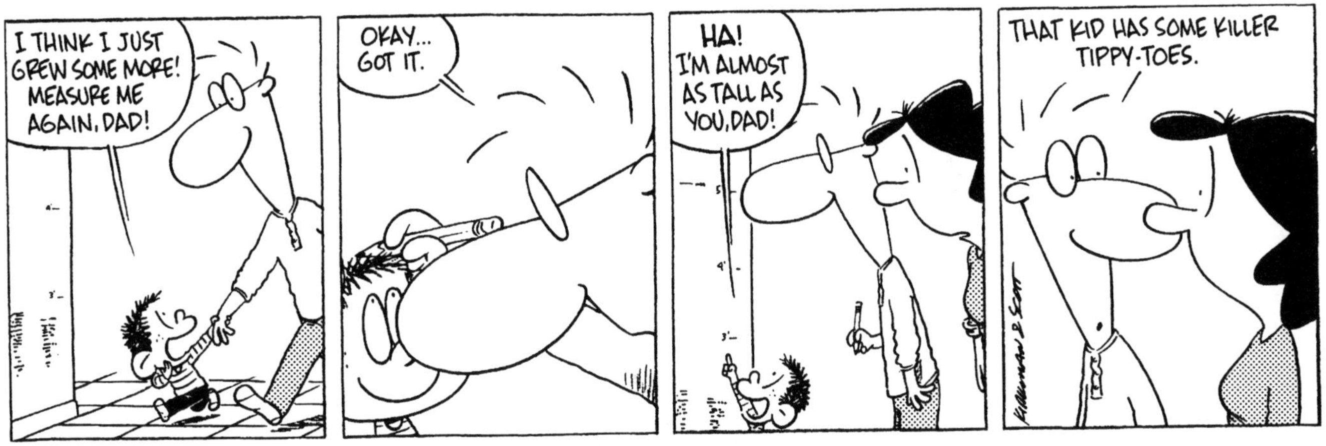
I THINK I JUST GREW SOME MORE! MEASURE ME AGAIN, DAD!
OKAY... GOT IT.
HA! I'M ALMOST AS TALL AS YOU, DAD!
THAT KID HAS SOME KILLER TIPPY-TOES.

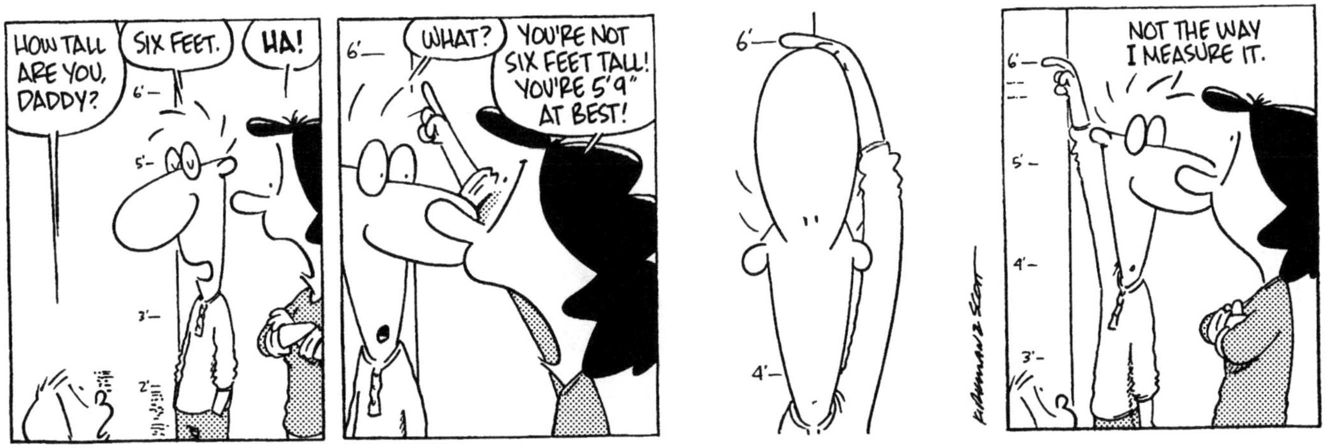
HOW TALL ARE YOU, DADDY?
SIX FEET.
HA!
WHAT?
YOU'RE NOT SIX FEET TALL! YOU'RE 5'9" AT BEST!
NOT THE WAY I MEASURE IT.

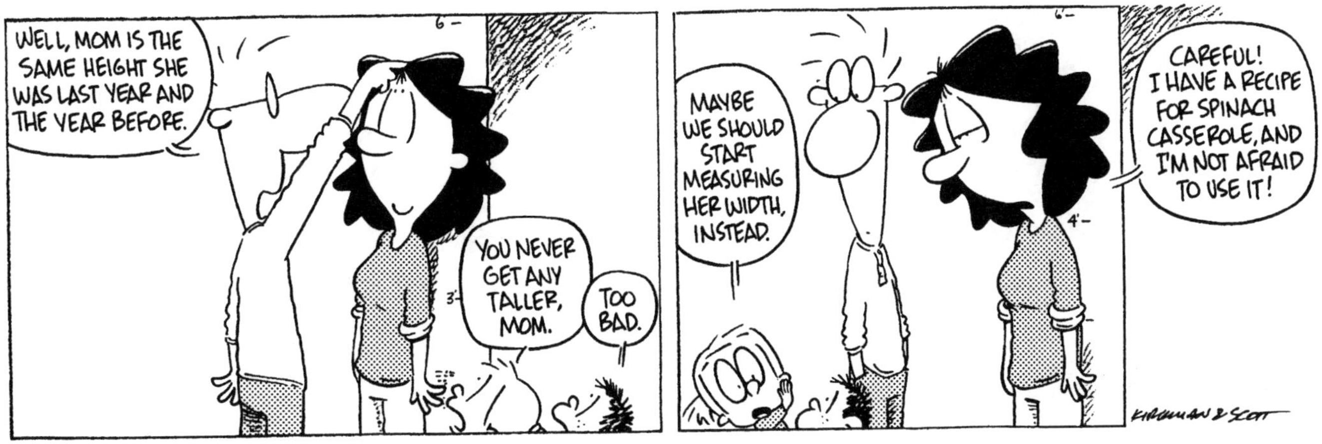
WELL, MOM IS THE SAME HEIGHT SHE WAS LAST YEAR AND THE YEAR BEFORE.
YOU NEVER GET ANY TALLER, MOM.
TOO BAD.
MAYBE WE SHOULD START MEASURING HER WIDTH, INSTEAD.
CAREFUL! I HAVE A RECIPE FOR SPINACH CASSEROLE, AND I'M NOT AFRAID TO USE IT!

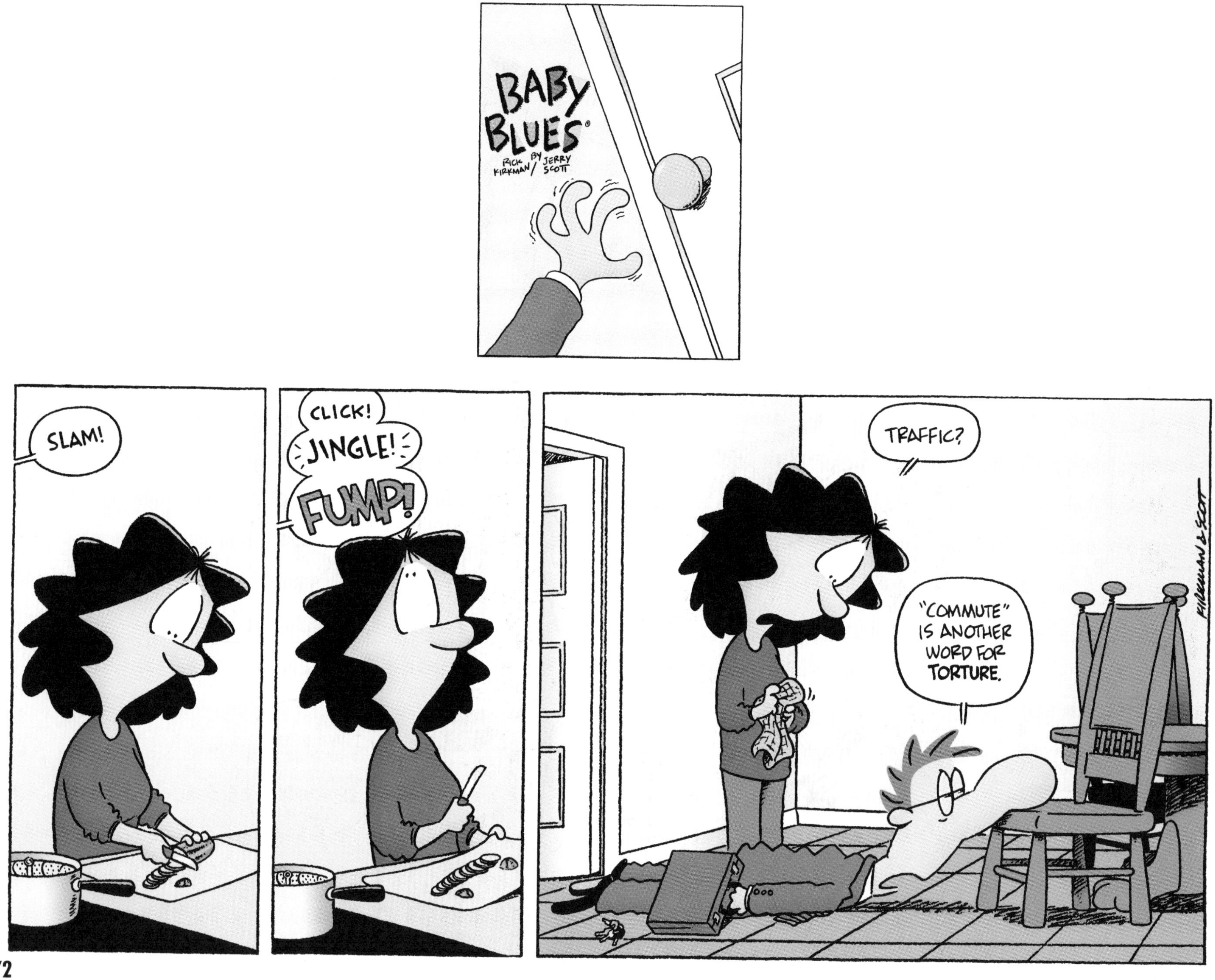
BABY BLUES®
RICK KIRKMAN / BY JERRY SCOTT
SLAM!
CLICK!
JINGLE!
FUMP!
TRAFFIC?
"COMMUTE" IS ANOTHER WORD FOR TORTURE.
KIRKMAN & SCOTT

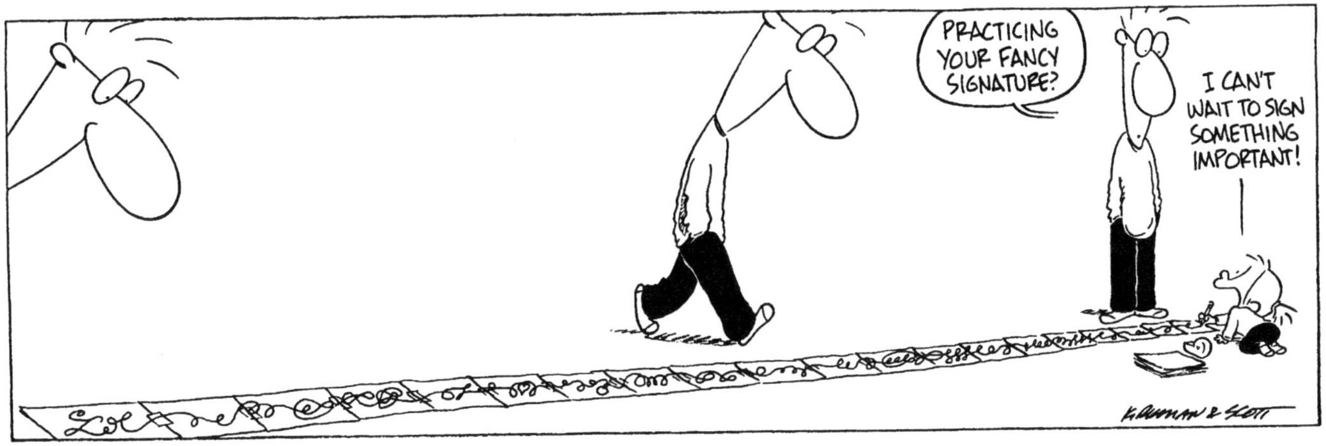
PRACTICING YOUR FANCY SIGNATURE?
I CAN'T WAIT TO SIGN SOMETHING IMPORTANT!
KIRKMAN & SCOTT

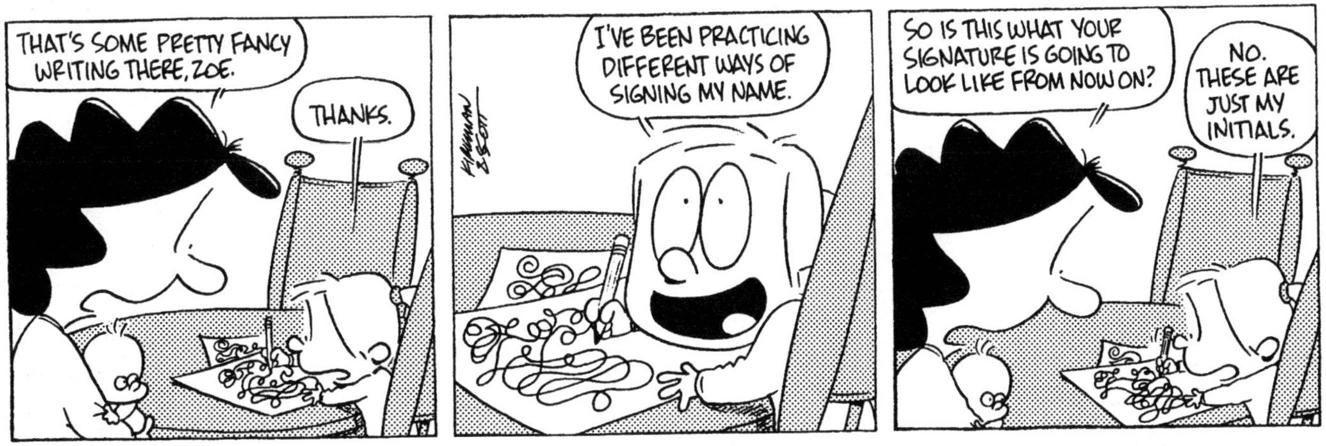
THAT'S SOME PRETTY FANCY WRITING THERE, ZOE.
THANKS.
KIRKMAN & SCOTT
I'VE BEEN PRACTICING DIFFERENT WAYS OF SIGNING MY NAME.
SO IS THIS WHAT YOUR SIGNATURE IS GOING TO LOOK LIKE FROM NOW ON?
NO. THESE ARE JUST MY INITIALS.

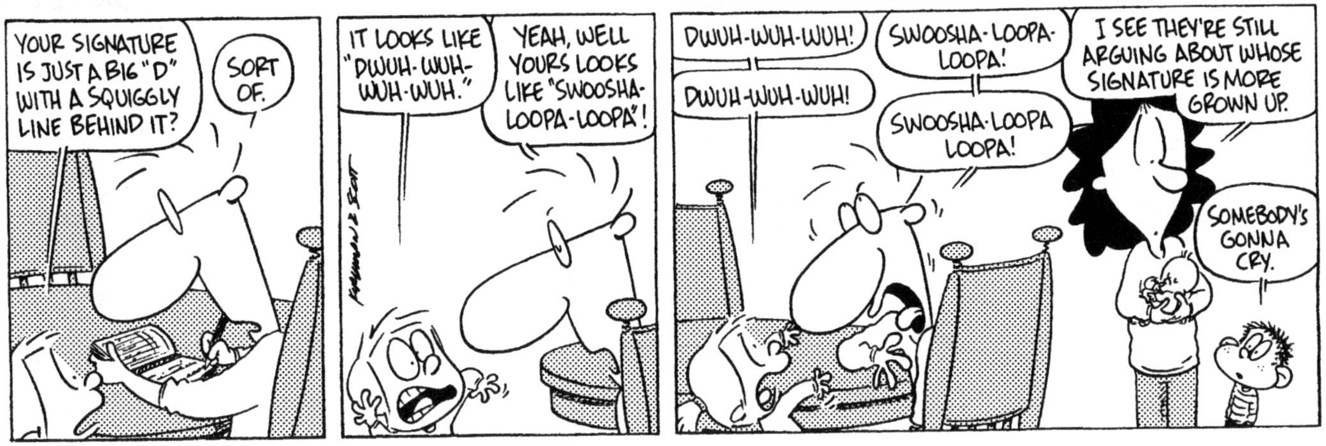
YOUR SIGNATURE IS JUST A BIG "D" WITH A SQUIGGLY LINE BEHIND IT?
SORT OF.
IT LOOKS LIKE "DWUH-WUH-WUH-WUH."
YEAH, WELL YOURS LOOKS LIKE "SWOOSHA-LOOPA-LOOPA"!
KIRKMAN & SCOTT
DWUH-WUH-WUH!
SWOOSHA-LOOPA-LOOPA!
DWUH-WUH-WUH!
SWOOSHA-LOOPA LOOPA!
I SEE THEY'RE STILL ARGUING ABOUT WHOSE SIGNATURE IS MORE GROWN UP.
SOMEBODY'S GONNA CRY.

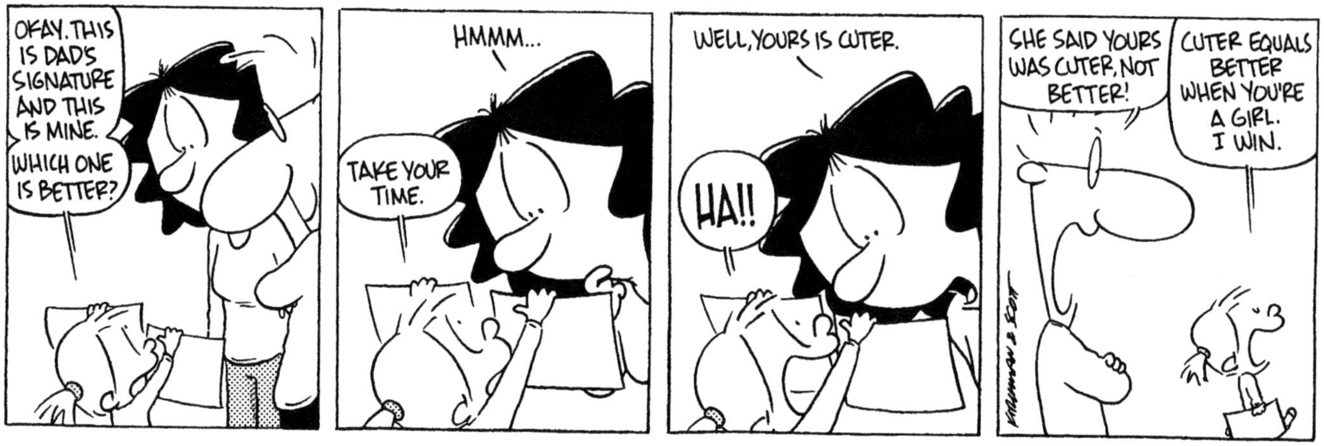
OKAY. THIS IS DAD'S SIGNATURE AND THIS IS MINE.
WHICH ONE IS BETTER?
HMMM...
TAKE YOUR TIME.
WELL, YOURS IS CUTER.
HA!!
SHE SAID YOURS WAS CUTER, NOT BETTER!
CUTER EQUALS BETTER WHEN YOU'RE A GIRL. I WIN.

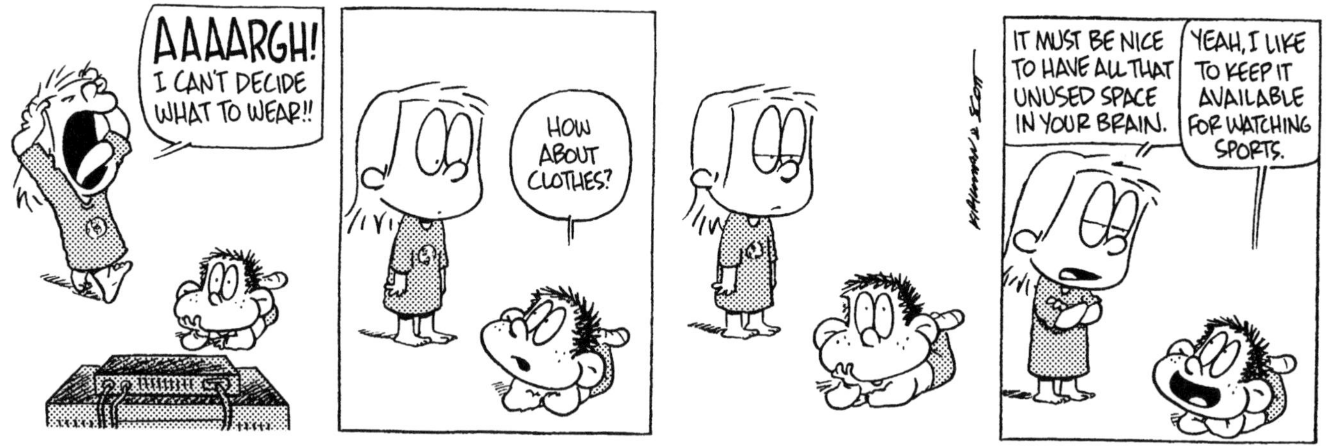
AAAARGH! I CAN'T DECIDE WHAT TO WEAR!!
HOW ABOUT CLOTHES?
IT MUST BE NICE TO HAVE ALL THAT UNUSED SPACE IN YOUR BRAIN.
YEAH, I LIKE TO KEEP IT AVAILABLE FOR WATCHING SPORTS.

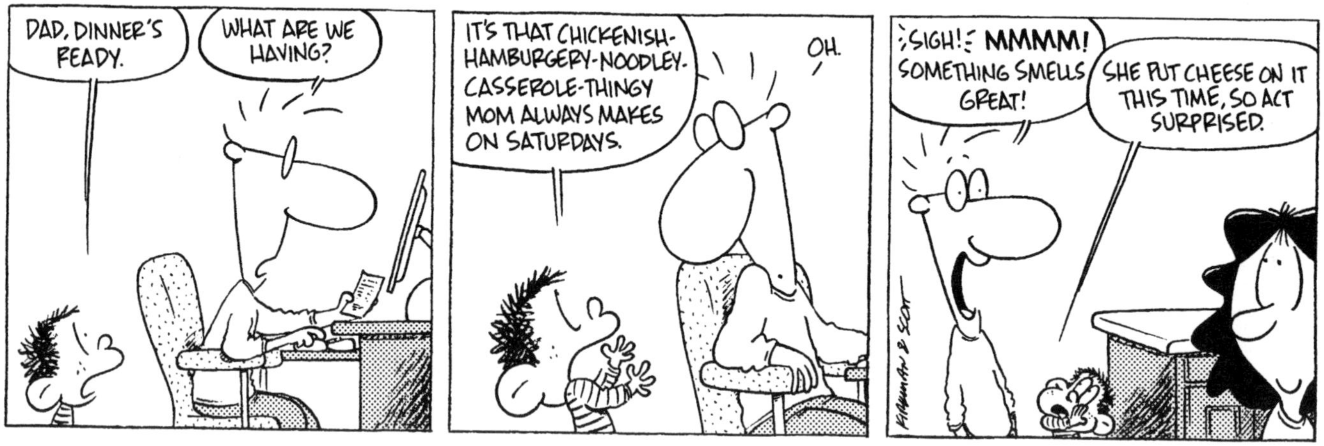
DAD, DINNER'S READY.
WHAT ARE WE HAVING?
IT'S THAT CHICKENISH-HAMBURGERY-NOODLEY-CASSEROLE-THINGY MOM ALWAYS MAKES ON SATURDAYS.
OH.
SIGH! MMMM! SOMETHING SMELLS GREAT!
SHE PUT CHEESE ON IT THIS TIME, SO ACT SURPRISED.

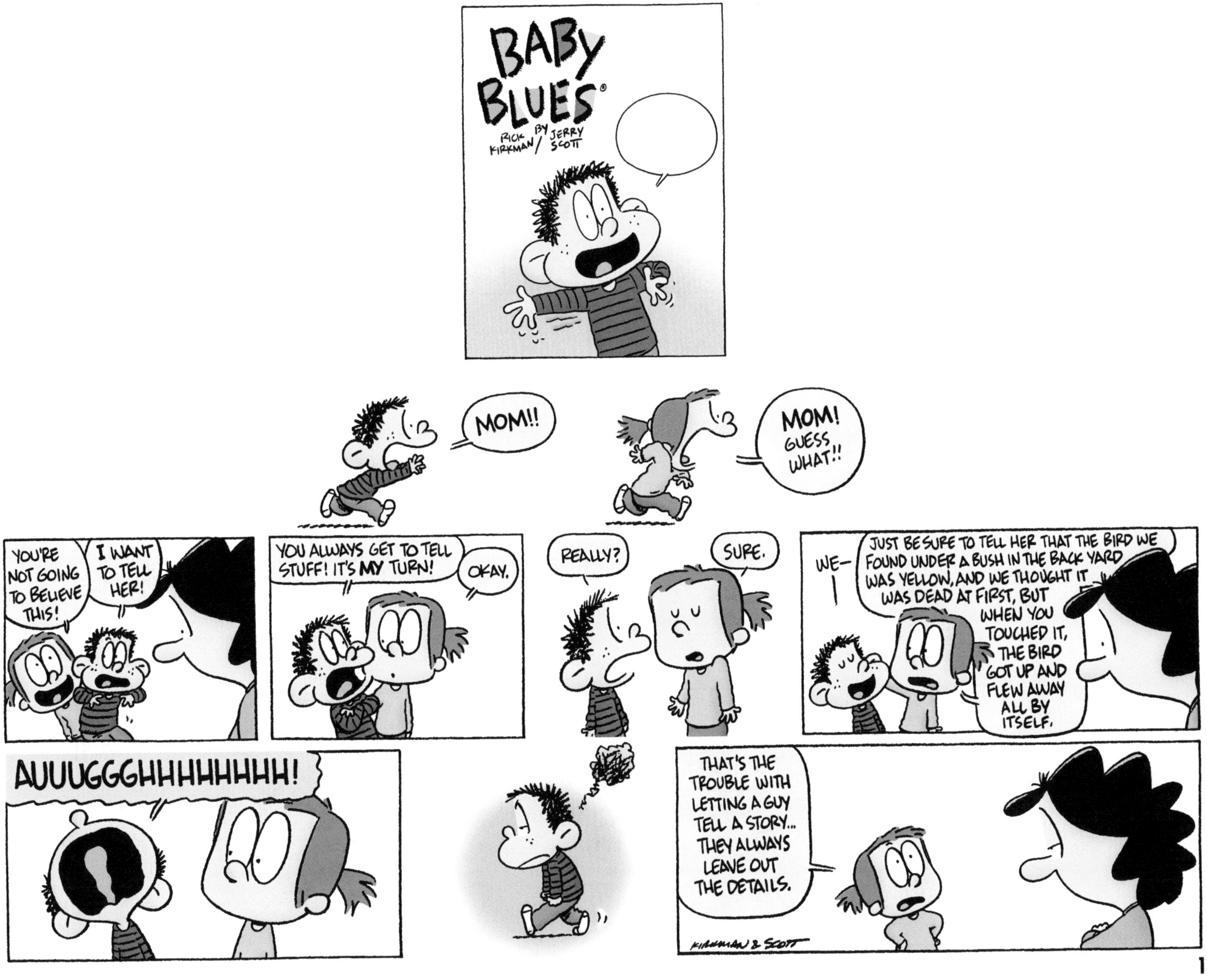
BABY BLUES®
BY RICK KIRKMAN / JERRY SCOTT
MOM!!
MOM! GUESS WHAT!!
YOU'RE NOT GOING TO BELIEVE THIS!
I WANT TO TELL HER!
YOU ALWAYS GET TO TELL STUFF! IT'S MY TURN!
OKAY.
REALLY?
SURE.
WE–
JUST BE SURE TO TELL HER THAT THE BIRD WE FOUND UNDER A BUSH IN THE BACK YARD WAS YELLOW, AND WE THOUGHT IT WAS DEAD AT FIRST, BUT WHEN YOU TOUCHED IT, THE BIRD GOT UP AND FLEW AWAY ALL BY ITSELF.
AUUUGGGHHHHHHHH!
THAT'S THE TROUBLE WITH LETTING A GUY TELL A STORY... THEY ALWAYS LEAVE OUT THE DETAILS.
KIRKMAN & SCOTT

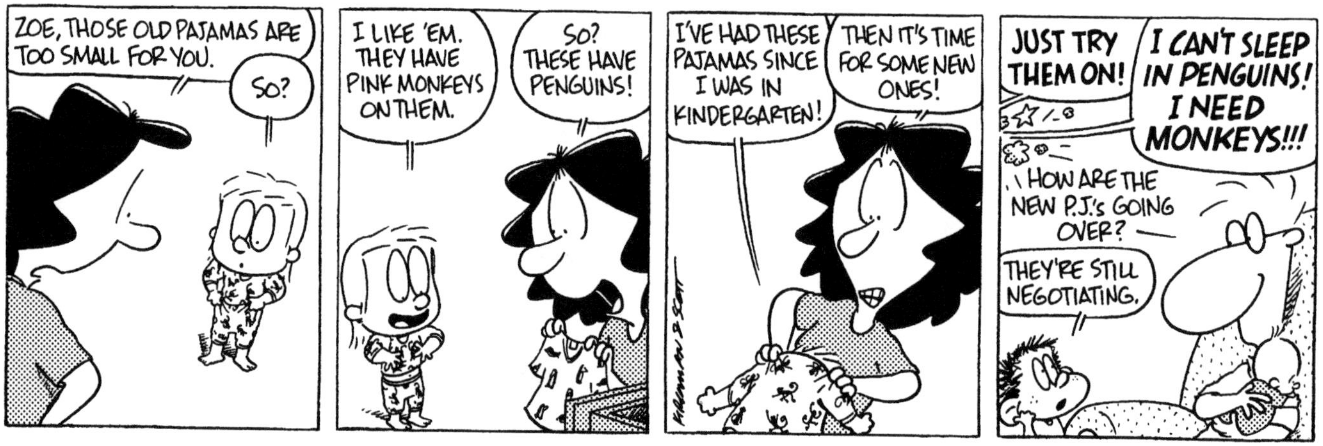
ZOE, THOSE OLD PAJAMAS ARE TOO SMALL FOR YOU.
SO?
I LIKE 'EM. THEY HAVE PINK MONKEYS ON THEM.
SO? THESE HAVE PENGUINS!
I'VE HAD THESE PAJAMAS SINCE I WAS IN KINDERGARTEN!
THEN IT'S TIME FOR SOME NEW ONES!
JUST TRY THEM ON!
I CAN'T SLEEP IN PENGUINS! I NEED MONKEYS!!!
HOW ARE THE NEW P.J.'s GOING OVER?
THEY'RE STILL NEGOTIATING.

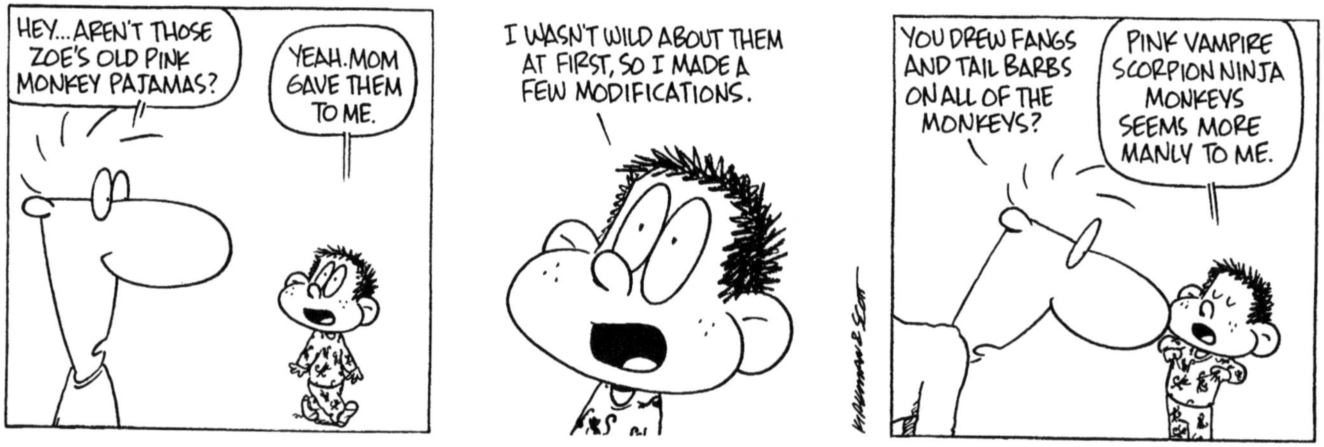
HEY... AREN'T THOSE ZOE'S OLD PINK MONKEY PAJAMAS?
YEAH. MOM GAVE THEM TO ME.
I WASN'T WILD ABOUT THEM AT FIRST, SO I MADE A FEW MODIFICATIONS.
YOU DREW FANGS AND TAIL BARBS ON ALL OF THE MONKEYS?
PINK VAMPIRE SCORPION NINJA MONKEYS SEEMS MORE MANLY TO ME.

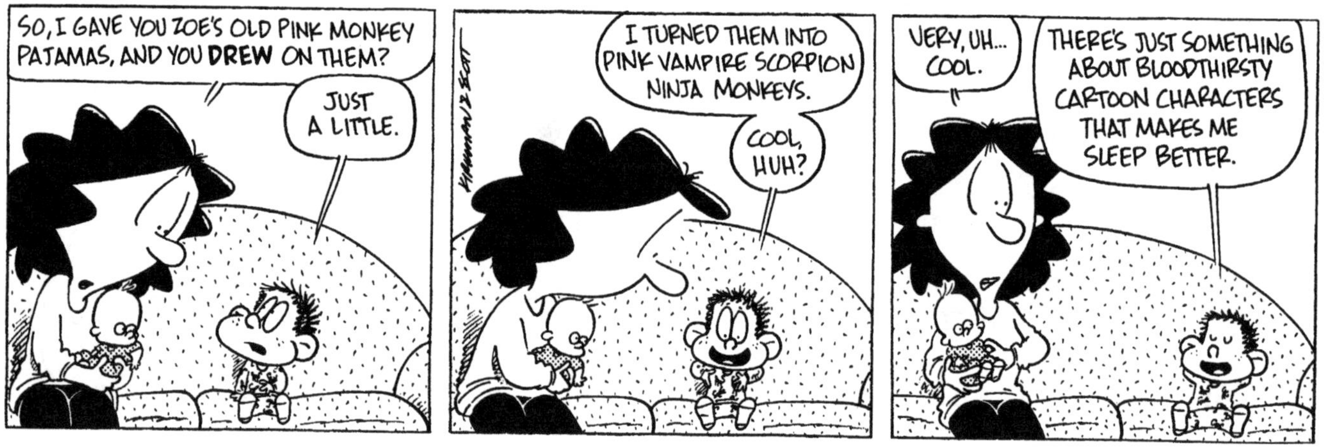
SO, I GAVE YOU ZOE'S OLD PINK MONKEY PAJAMAS, AND YOU DREW ON THEM?
JUST A LITTLE.
I TURNED THEM INTO PINK VAMPIRE SCORPION NINJA MONKEYS.
COOL, HUH?
VERY, UH... COOL.
THERE'S JUST SOMETHING ABOUT BLOODTHIRSTY CARTOON CHARACTERS THAT MAKES ME SLEEP BETTER.

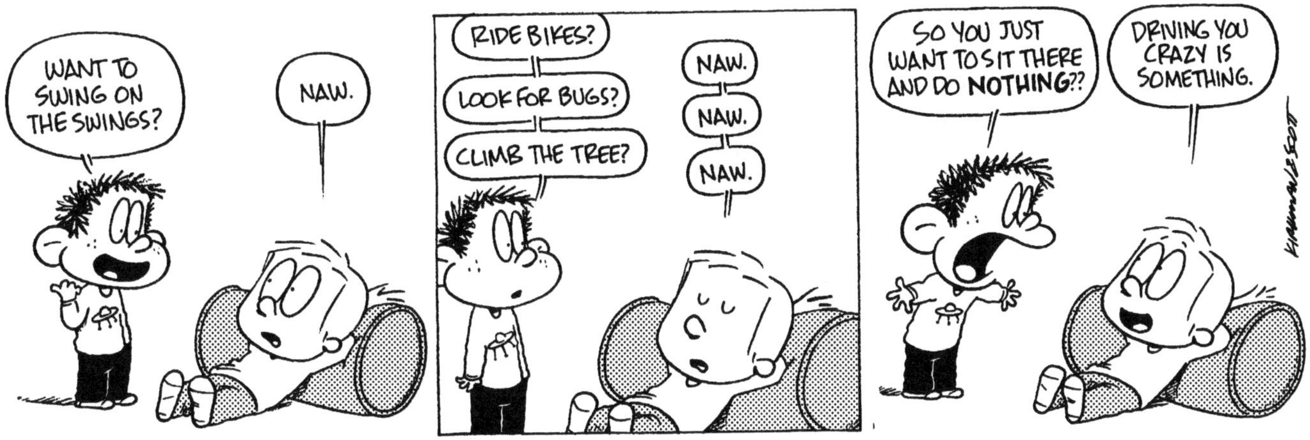
WANT TO SWING ON THE SWINGS?
NAW.
RIDE BIKES?
NAW.
LOOK FOR BUGS?
NAW.
CLIMB THE TREE?
NAW.
SO YOU JUST WANT TO SIT THERE AND DO **NOTHING**??
DRIVING YOU CRAZY IS SOMETHING.

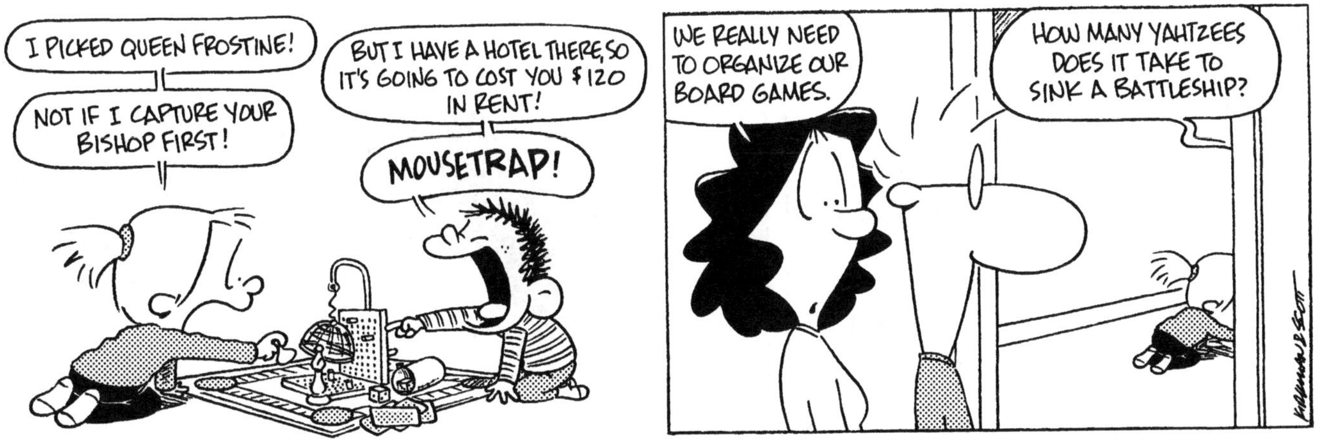
I PICKED QUEEN FROSTINE!
NOT IF I CAPTURE YOUR BISHOP FIRST!
BUT I HAVE A HOTEL THERE, SO IT'S GOING TO COST YOU $120 IN RENT!
MOUSETRAP!
WE REALLY NEED TO ORGANIZE OUR BOARD GAMES.
HOW MANY YAHTZEES DOES IT TAKE TO SINK A BATTLESHIP?

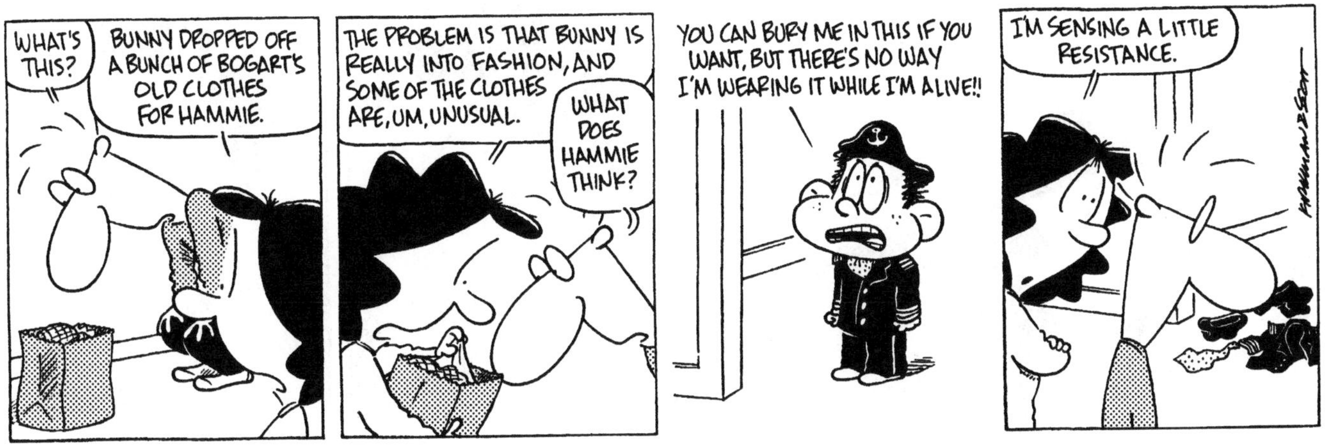
WHAT'S THIS?
BUNNY DROPPED OFF A BUNCH OF BOGART'S OLD CLOTHES FOR HAMMIE.
THE PROBLEM IS THAT BUNNY IS REALLY INTO FASHION, AND SOME OF THE CLOTHES ARE, UM, UNUSUAL.
WHAT DOES HAMMIE THINK?
YOU CAN BURY ME IN THIS IF YOU WANT, BUT THERE'S NO WAY I'M WEARING IT WHILE I'M ALIVE!!
I'M SENSING A LITTLE RESISTANCE.

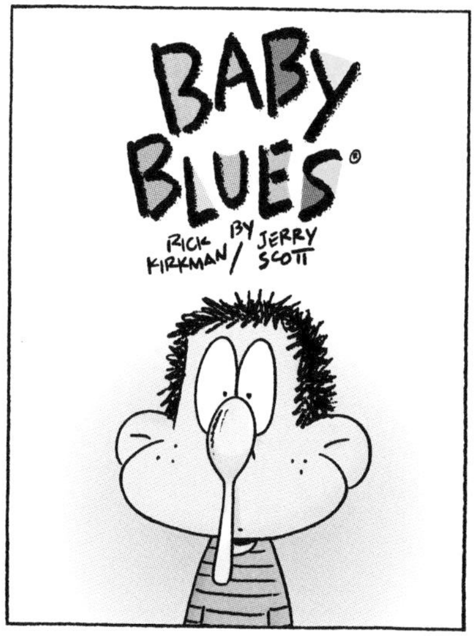
BABY BLUES®
RICK KIRKMAN / BY / JERRY SCOTT

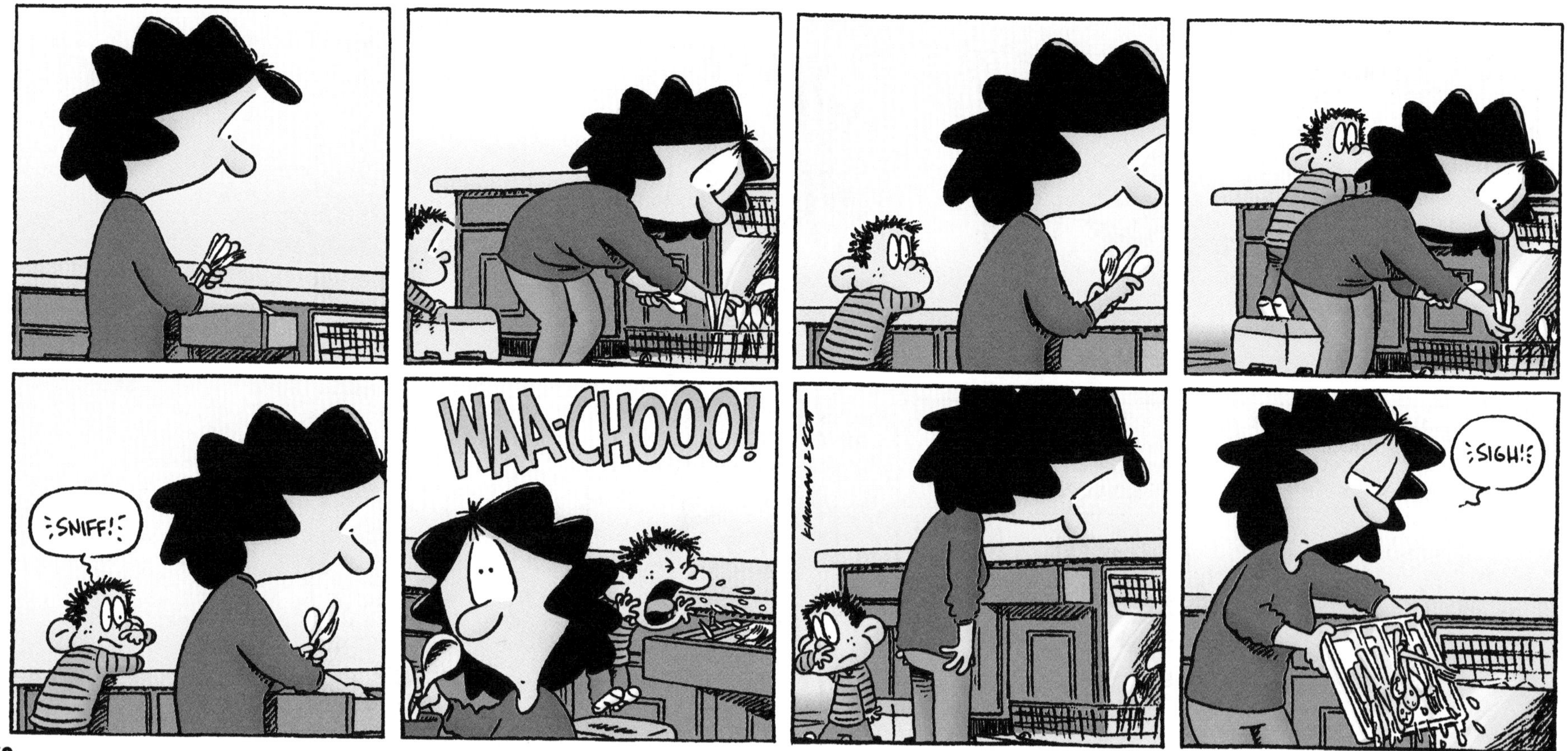
SNIFF!
WAA-CHOOO!
KIRKMAN & SCOTT
SIGH!

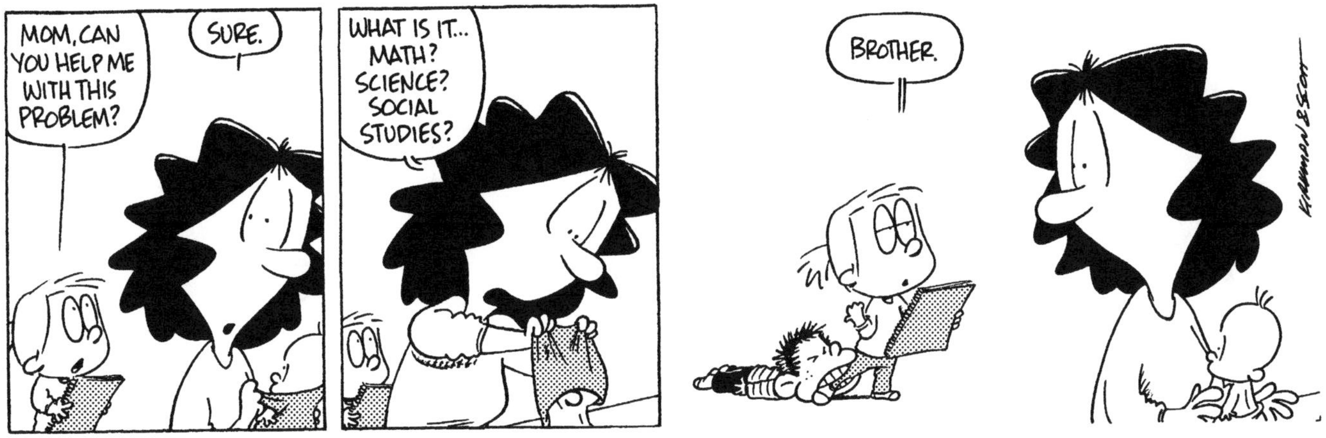
MOM, CAN YOU HELP ME WITH THIS PROBLEM?
SURE.
WHAT IS IT... MATH? SCIENCE? SOCIAL STUDIES?
BROTHER.

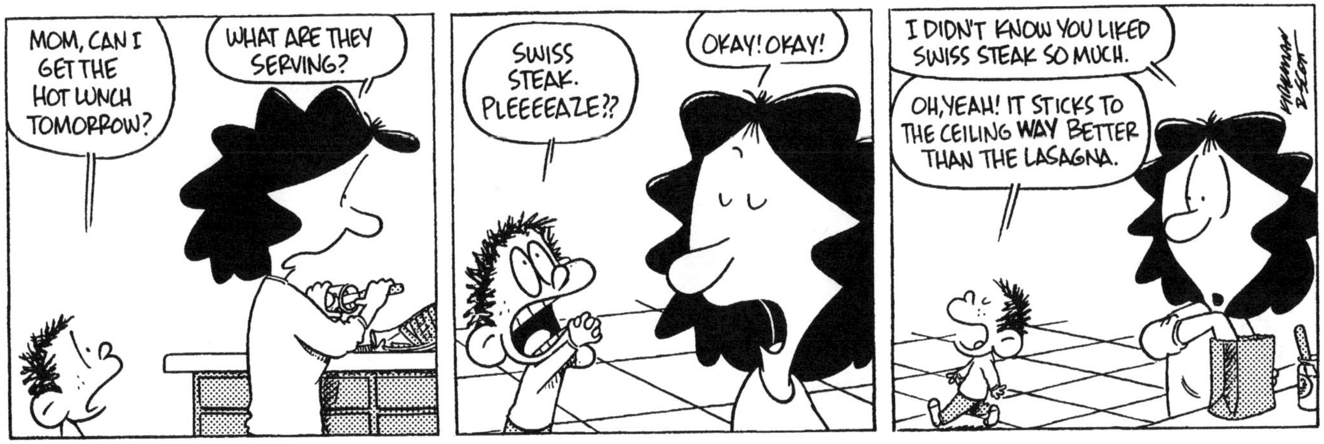
MOM, CAN I GET THE HOT LUNCH TOMORROW?
WHAT ARE THEY SERVING?
SWISS STEAK. PLEEEEAZE??
OKAY! OKAY!
I DIDN'T KNOW YOU LIKED SWISS STEAK SO MUCH.
OH, YEAH! IT STICKS TO THE CEILING WAY BETTER THAN THE LASAGNA.

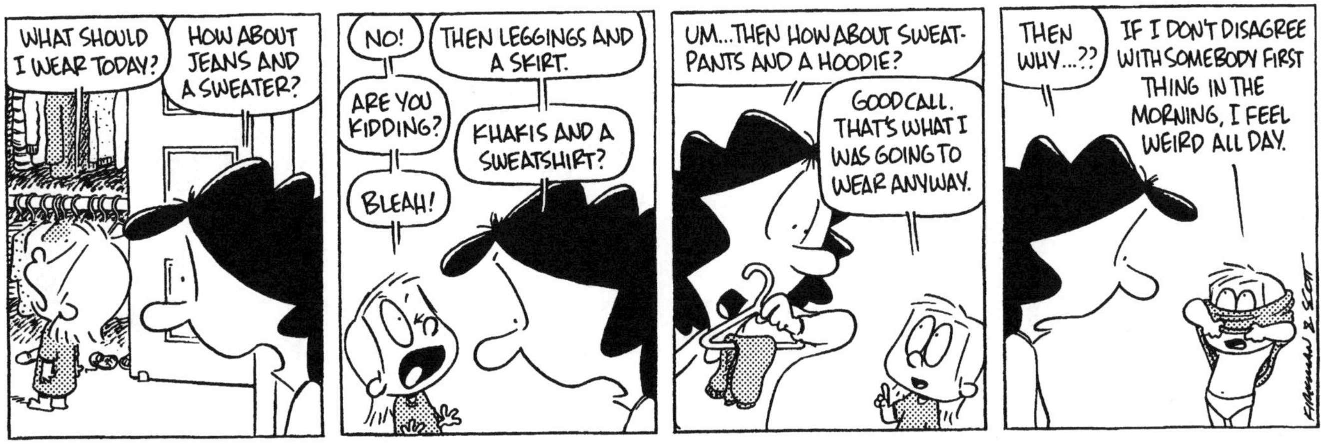
WHAT SHOULD I WEAR TODAY?
HOW ABOUT JEANS AND A SWEATER?
NO!
THEN LEGGINGS AND A SKIRT.
ARE YOU KIDDING?
KHAKIS AND A SWEATSHIRT?
BLEAH!
UM...THEN HOW ABOUT SWEAT-PANTS AND A HOODIE?
GOOD CALL. THAT'S WHAT I WAS GOING TO WEAR ANYWAY.
THEN WHY...??
IF I DON'T DISAGREE WITH SOMEBODY FIRST THING IN THE MORNING, I FEEL WEIRD ALL DAY.

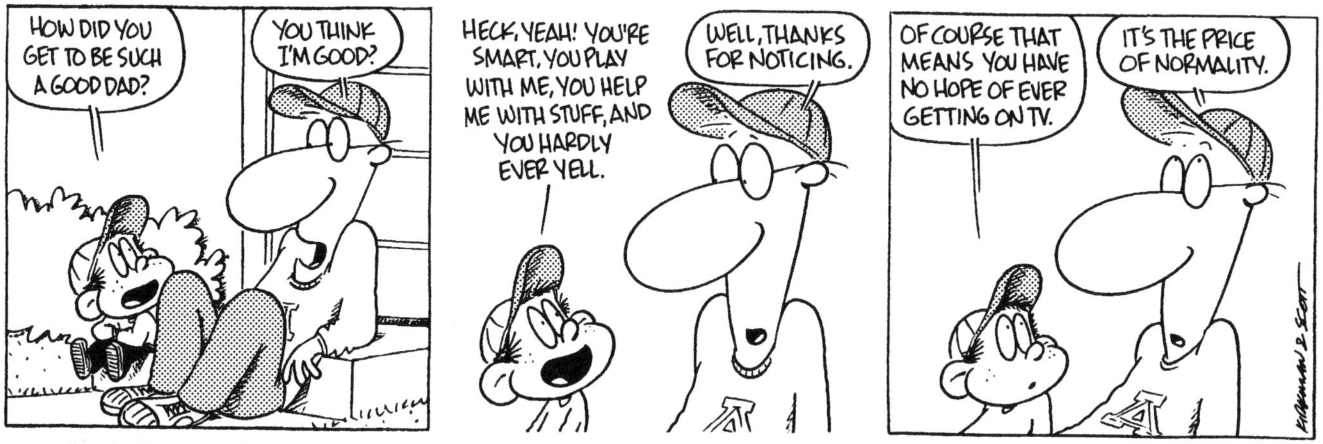
HOW DID YOU GET TO BE SUCH A GOOD DAD?
YOU THINK I'M GOOD?
HECK, YEAH! YOU'RE SMART, YOU PLAY WITH ME, YOU HELP ME WITH STUFF, AND YOU HARDLY EVER YELL.
WELL, THANKS FOR NOTICING.
OF COURSE THAT MEANS YOU HAVE NO HOPE OF EVER GETTING ON TV.
IT'S THE PRICE OF NORMALITY.
KIRKMAN & SCOTT

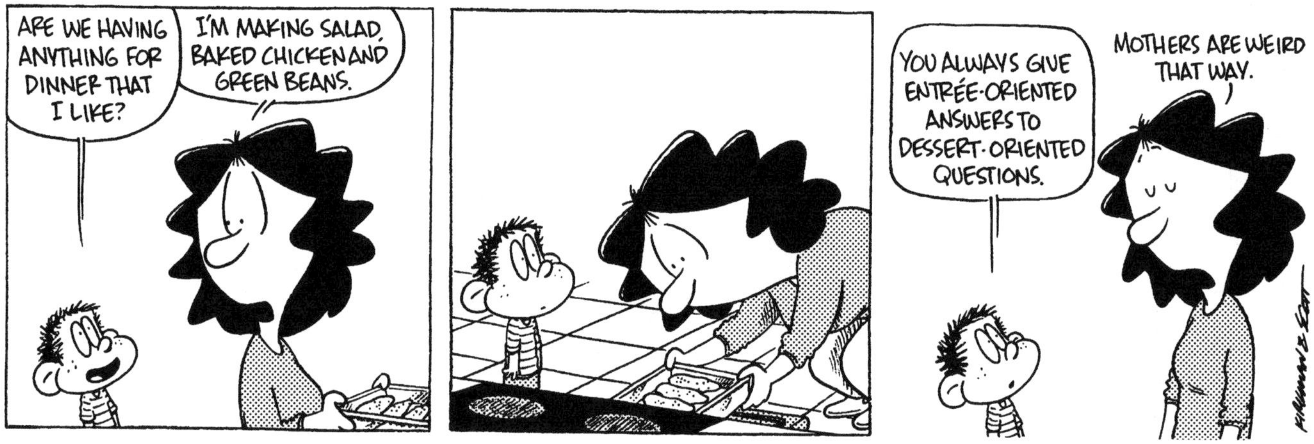
ARE WE HAVING ANYTHING FOR DINNER THAT I LIKE?
I'M MAKING SALAD, BAKED CHICKEN AND GREEN BEANS.
YOU ALWAYS GIVE ENTRÉE-ORIENTED ANSWERS TO DESSERT-ORIENTED QUESTIONS.
MOTHERS ARE WEIRD THAT WAY.
KIRKMAN & SCOTT

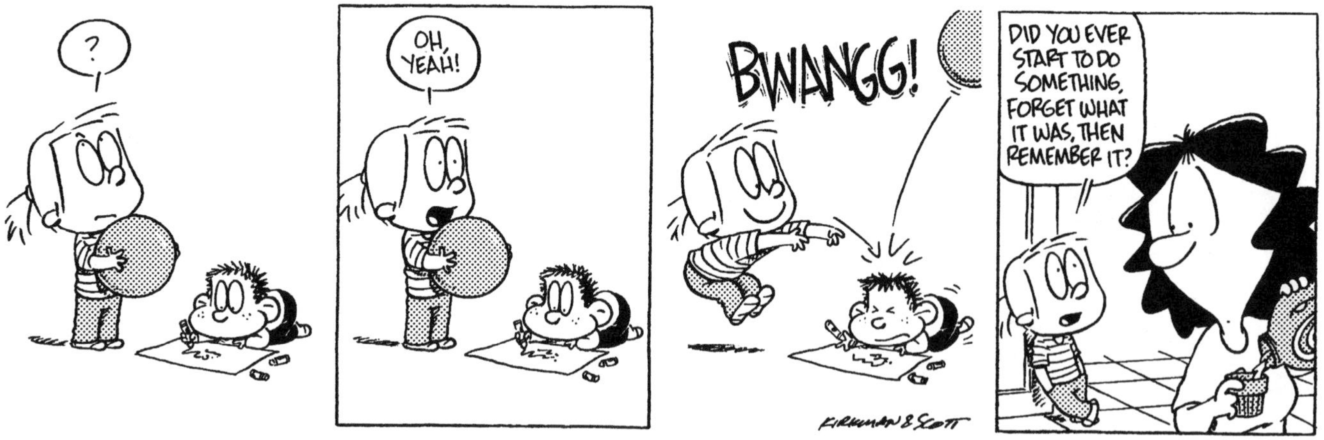
?
OH, YEAH!
BWANGG!
DID YOU EVER START TO DO SOMETHING, FORGET WHAT IT WAS, THEN REMEMBER IT?
KIRKMAN & SCOTT

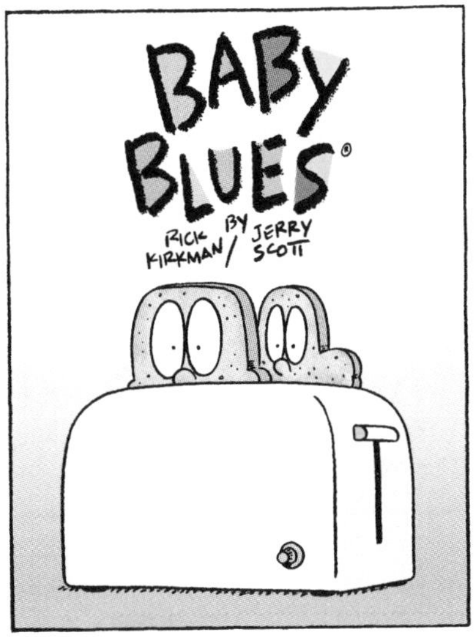
BABY BLUES®
RICK KIRKMAN / BY JERRY SCOTT

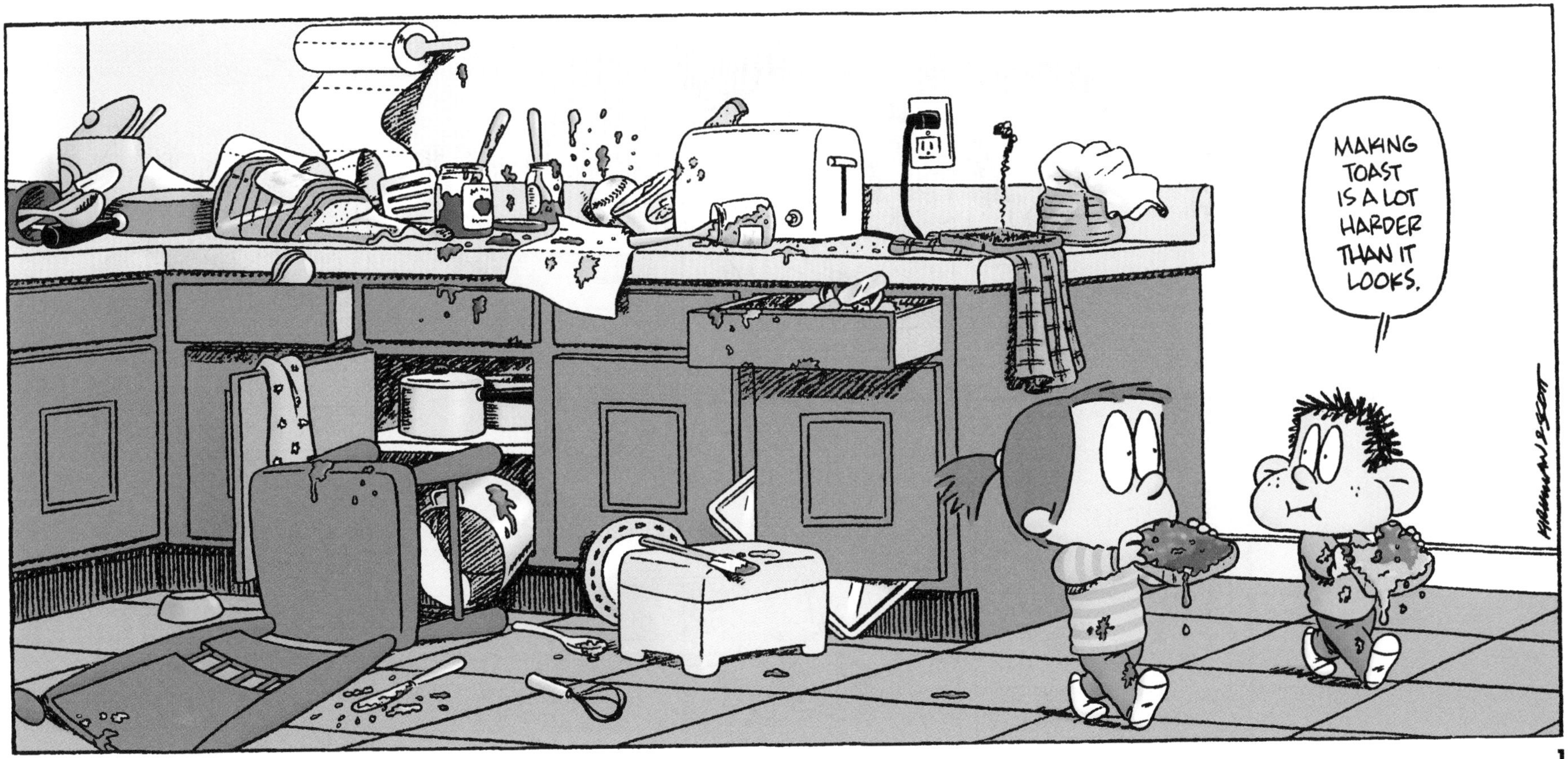
MAKING TOAST IS A LOT HARDER THAN IT LOOKS.

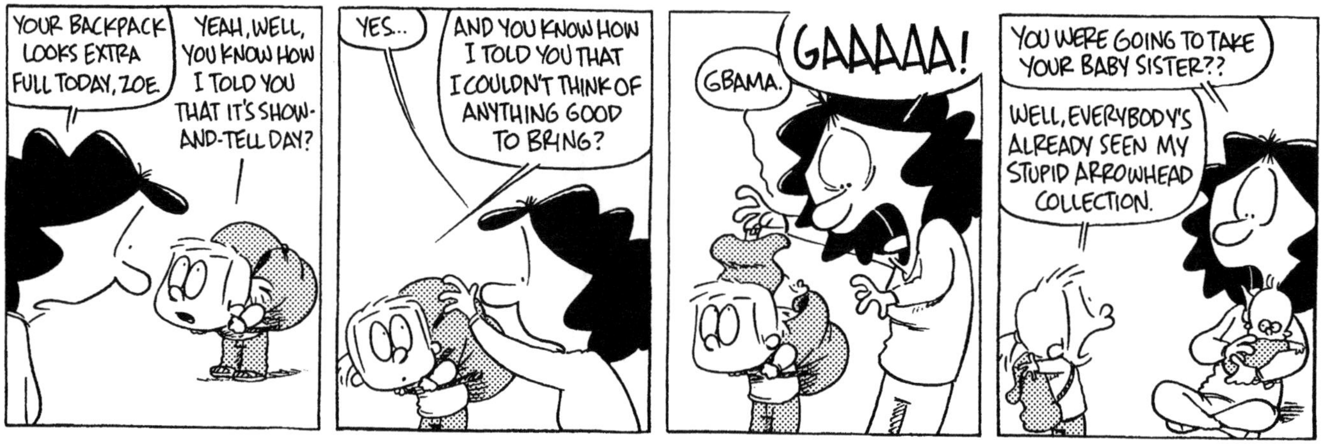
YOUR BACKPACK LOOKS EXTRA FULL TODAY, ZOE.
YEAH, WELL, YOU KNOW HOW I TOLD YOU THAT IT'S SHOW-AND-TELL DAY?
YES...
AND YOU KNOW HOW I TOLD YOU THAT I COULDN'T THINK OF ANYTHING GOOD TO BRING?
GBAMA.
GAAAAA!
YOU WERE GOING TO TAKE YOUR BABY SISTER??
WELL, EVERYBODY'S ALREADY SEEN MY STUPID ARROWHEAD COLLECTION.

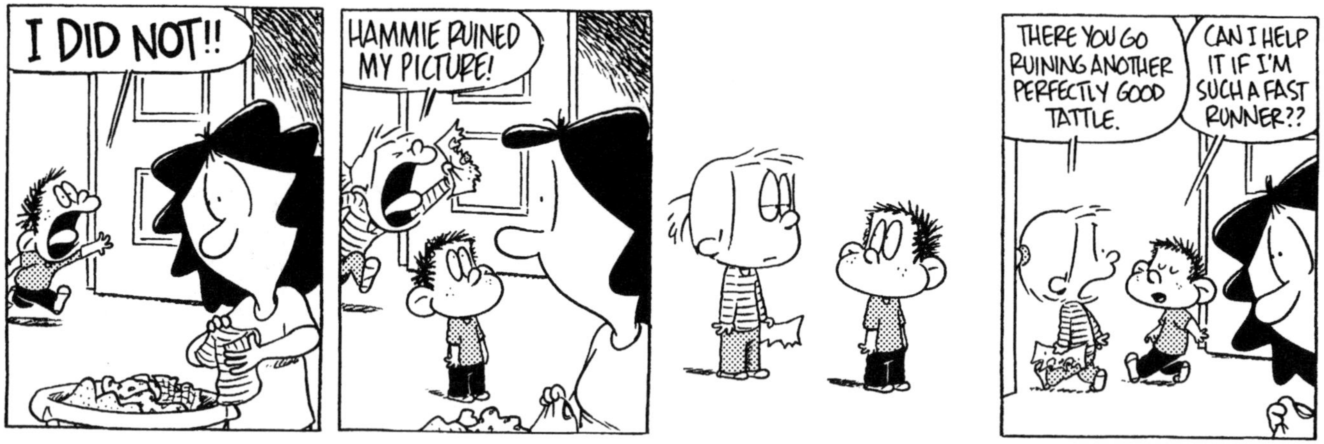
I DID NOT!!
HAMMIE RUINED MY PICTURE!
THERE YOU GO RUINING ANOTHER PERFECTLY GOOD TATTLE.
CAN I HELP IT IF I'M SUCH A FAST RUNNER??

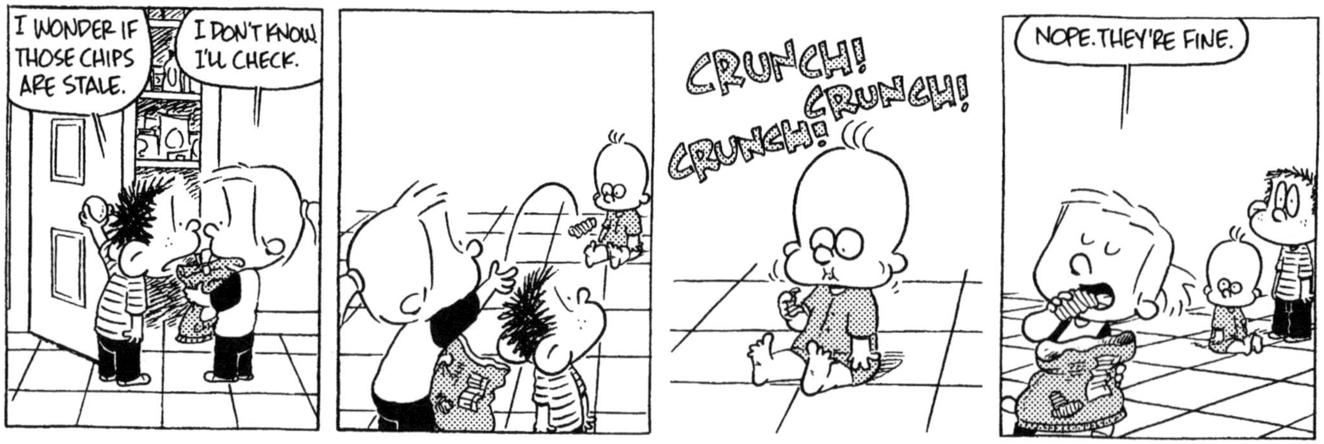
I WONDER IF THOSE CHIPS ARE STALE.
I DON'T KNOW. I'LL CHECK.
CRUNCH!
CRUNCH! CRUNCH!
NOPE. THEY'RE FINE.

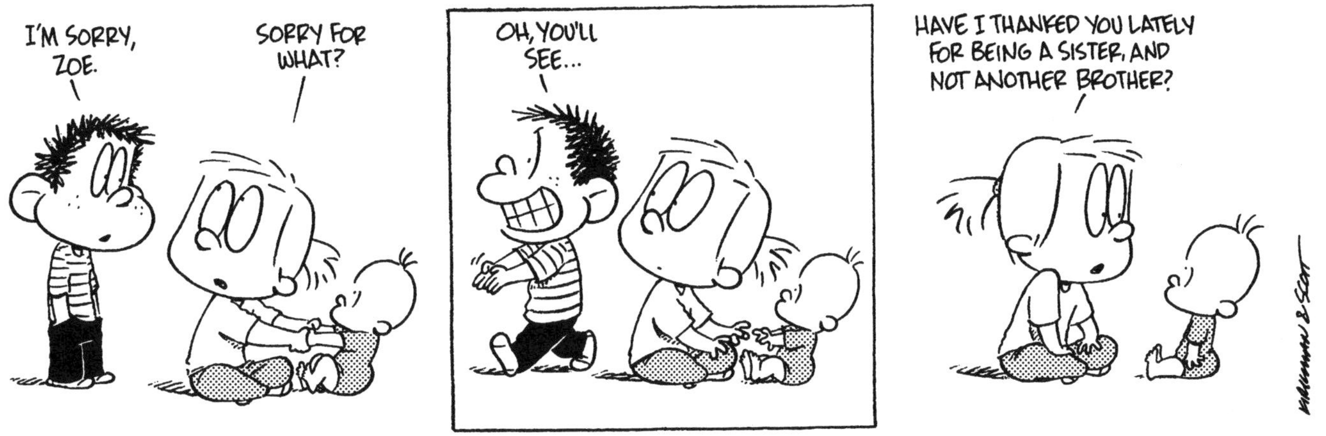
I'M SORRY, ZOE.
SORRY FOR WHAT?
OH, YOU'LL SEE...
HAVE I THANKED YOU LATELY FOR BEING A SISTER, AND NOT ANOTHER BROTHER?

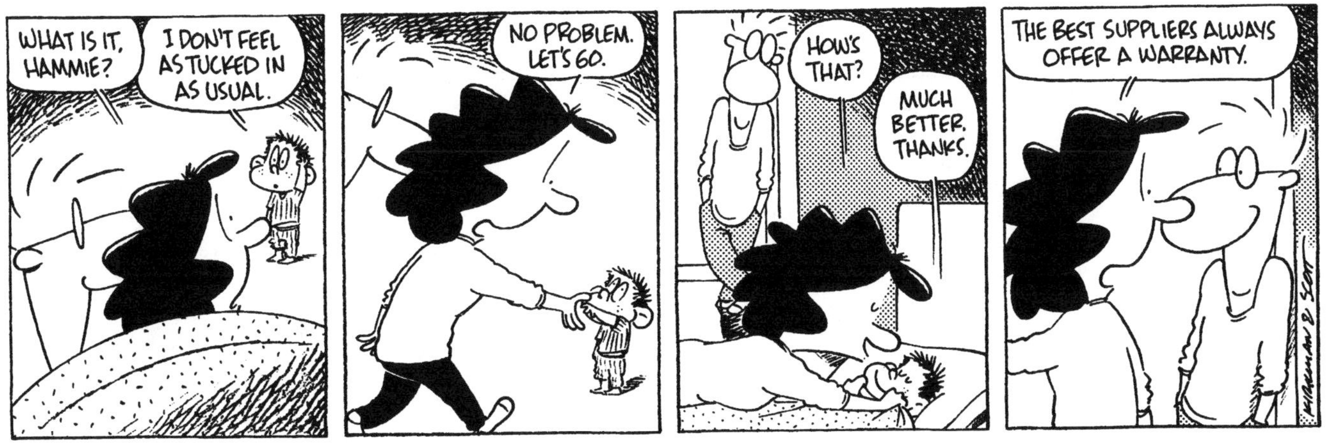
WHAT IS IT, HAMMIE?
I DON'T FEEL AS TUCKED IN AS USUAL.
NO PROBLEM. LET'S GO.
HOW'S THAT?
MUCH BETTER. THANKS.
THE BEST SUPPLIERS ALWAYS OFFER A WARRANTY.

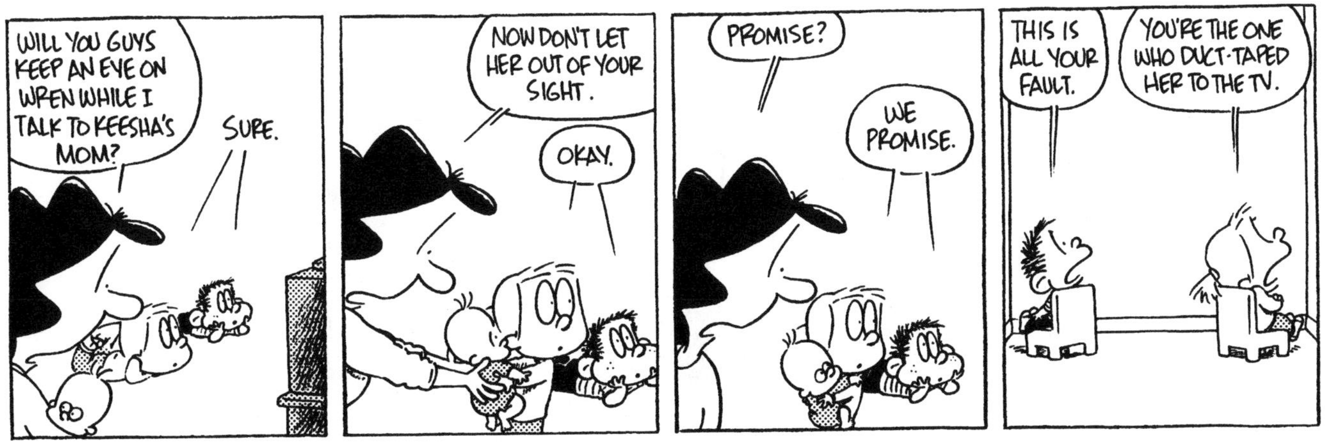
WILL YOU GUYS KEEP AN EYE ON WREN WHILE I TALK TO KEESHA'S MOM?
SURE.
NOW DON'T LET HER OUT OF YOUR SIGHT.
OKAY.
PROMISE?
WE PROMISE.
THIS IS ALL YOUR FAULT.
YOU'RE THE ONE WHO DUCT-TAPED HER TO THE TV.

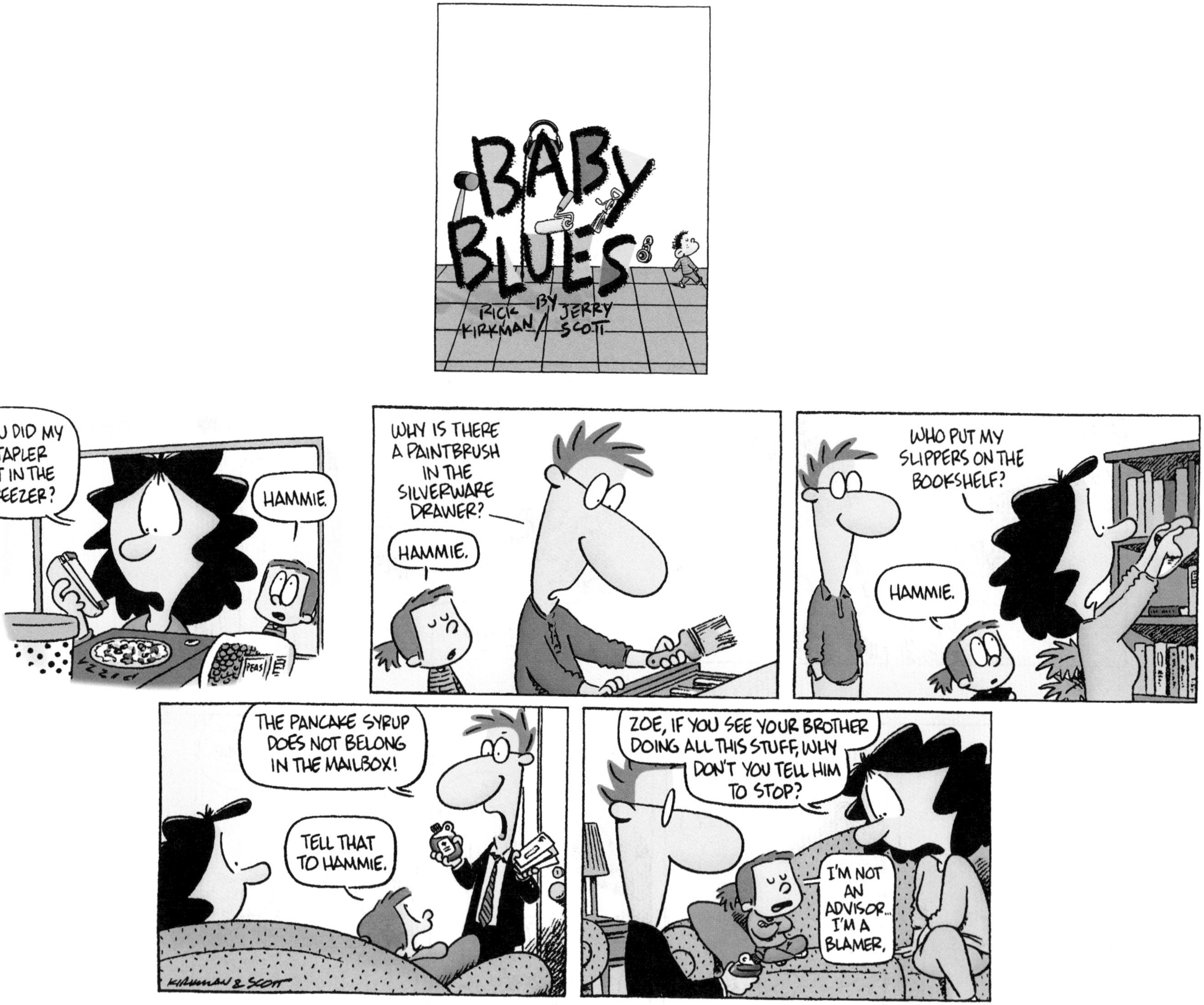
BABY BLUES
BY RICK KIRKMAN / JERRY SCOTT
HOW DID MY STAPLER GET IN THE FREEZER?
HAMMIE.
WHY IS THERE A PAINTBRUSH IN THE SILVERWARE DRAWER?
HAMMIE.
WHO PUT MY SLIPPERS ON THE BOOKSHELF?
HAMMIE.
THE PANCAKE SYRUP DOES NOT BELONG IN THE MAILBOX!
TELL THAT TO HAMMIE.
ZOE, IF YOU SEE YOUR BROTHER DOING ALL THIS STUFF, WHY DON'T YOU TELL HIM TO STOP?
I'M NOT AN ADVISOR... I'M A BLAMER.
KIRKMAN & SCOTT

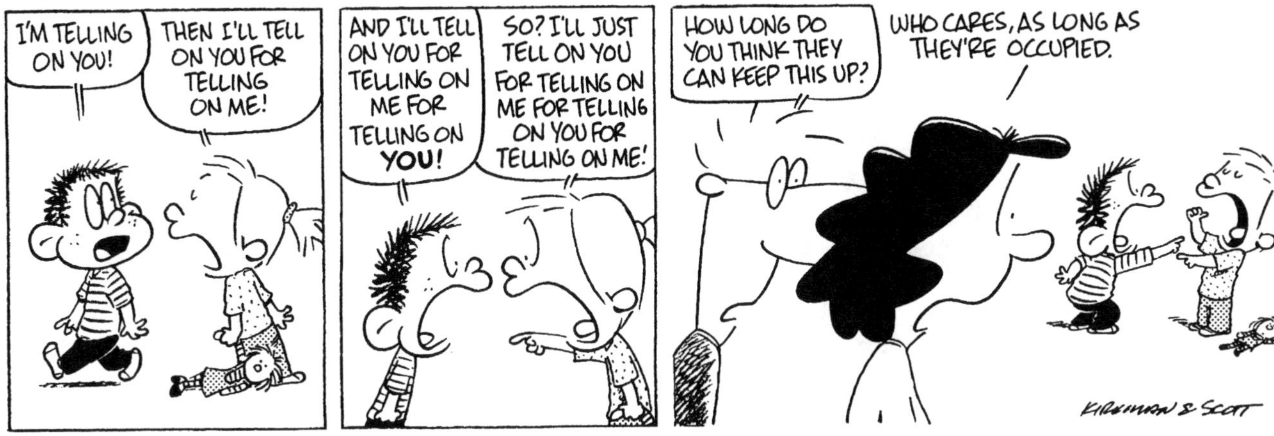
I'M TELLING ON YOU!
THEN I'LL TELL ON YOU FOR TELLING ON ME!
AND I'LL TELL ON YOU FOR TELLING ON ME FOR TELLING ON **YOU**!
SO? I'LL JUST TELL ON YOU FOR TELLING ON ME FOR TELLING ON YOU FOR TELLING ON ME!
HOW LONG DO YOU THINK THEY CAN KEEP THIS UP?
WHO CARES, AS LONG AS THEY'RE OCCUPIED.
KIRKMAN & SCOTT

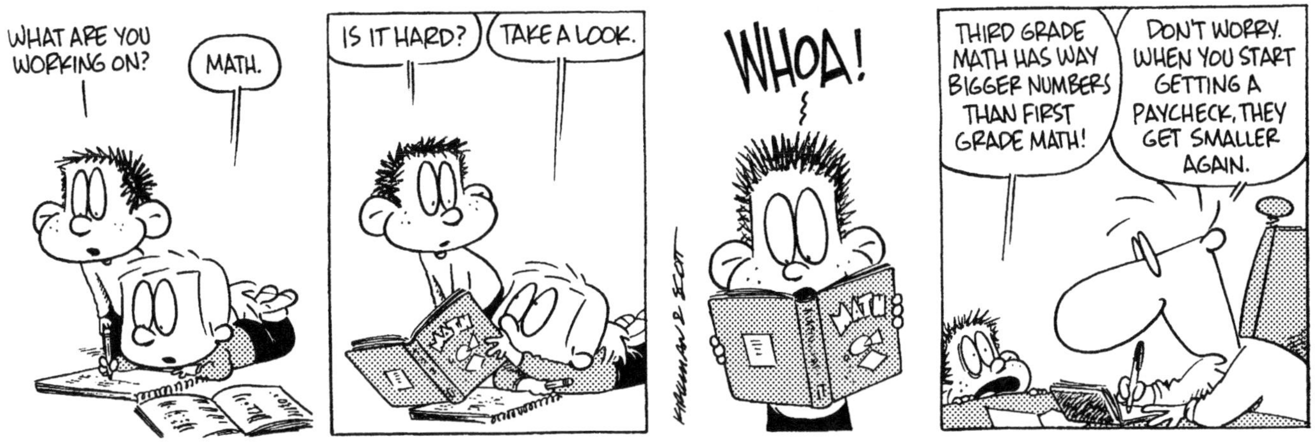
WHAT ARE YOU WORKING ON?
MATH.
IS IT HARD?
TAKE A LOOK.
WHOA!
KIRKMAN & SCOTT
THIRD GRADE MATH HAS WAY BIGGER NUMBERS THAN FIRST GRADE MATH!
DON'T WORRY. WHEN YOU START GETTING A PAYCHECK, THEY GET SMALLER AGAIN.

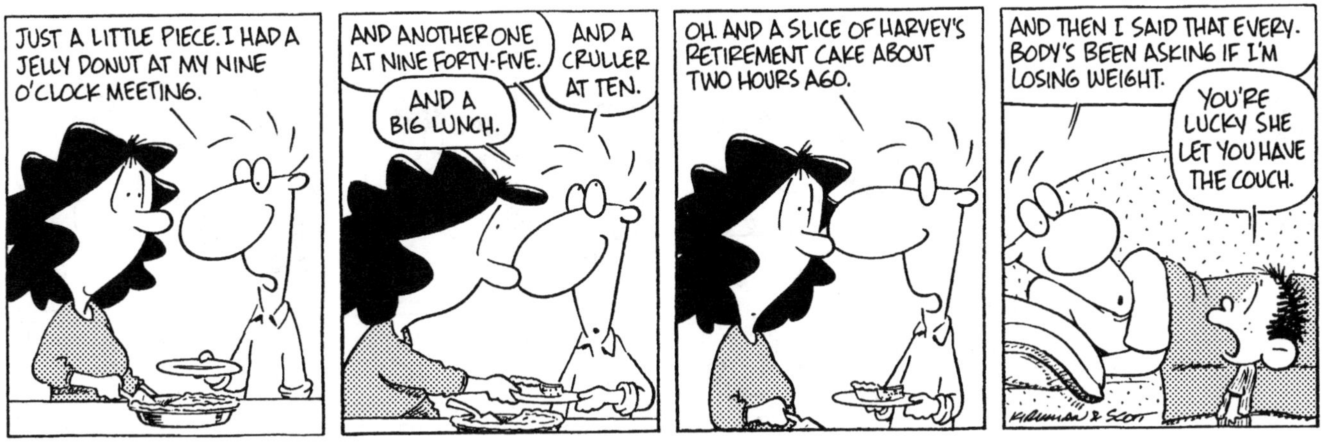
JUST A LITTLE PIECE. I HAD A JELLY DONUT AT MY NINE O'CLOCK MEETING.
AND ANOTHER ONE AT NINE FORTY-FIVE.
AND A CRULLER AT TEN.
AND A BIG LUNCH.
OH. AND A SLICE OF HARVEY'S RETIREMENT CAKE ABOUT TWO HOURS AGO.
AND THEN I SAID THAT EVERY-BODY'S BEEN ASKING IF I'M LOSING WEIGHT.
YOU'RE LUCKY SHE LET YOU HAVE THE COUCH.
KIRKMAN & SCOTT

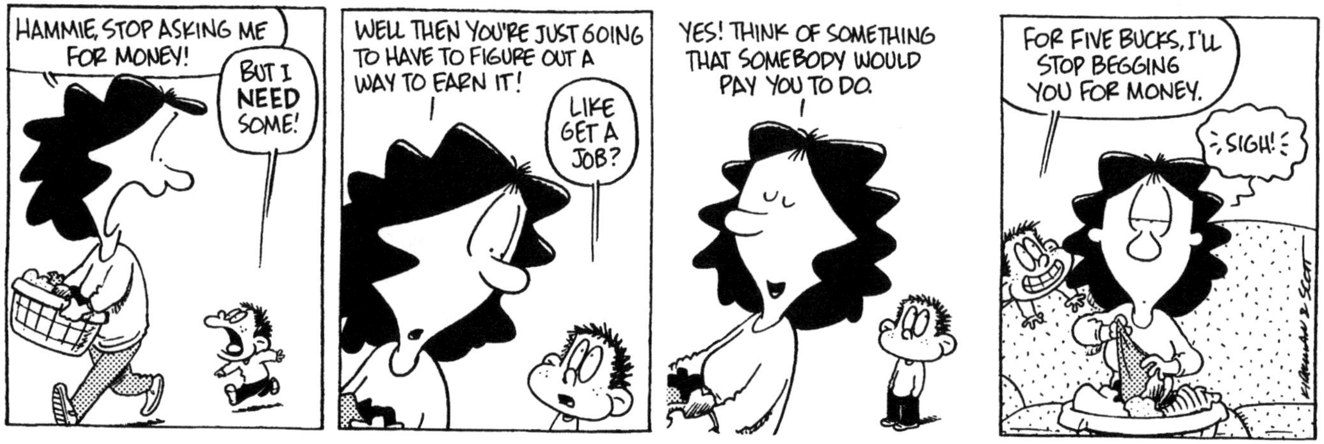
HAMMIE, STOP ASKING ME FOR MONEY!
BUT I NEED SOME!
WELL THEN YOU'RE JUST GOING TO HAVE TO FIGURE OUT A WAY TO EARN IT!
LIKE GET A JOB?
YES! THINK OF SOMETHING THAT SOMEBODY WOULD PAY YOU TO DO.
FOR FIVE BUCKS, I'LL STOP BEGGING YOU FOR MONEY.
SIGH!

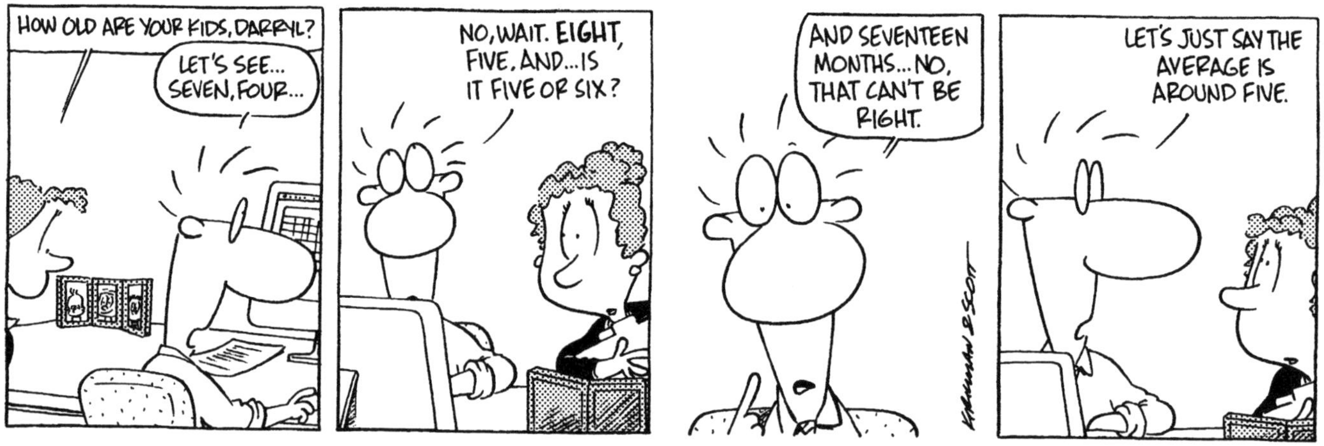
HOW OLD ARE YOUR KIDS, DARRYL?
LET'S SEE... SEVEN, FOUR...
NO, WAIT. EIGHT, FIVE, AND...IS IT FIVE OR SIX?
AND SEVENTEEN MONTHS...NO, THAT CAN'T BE RIGHT.
LET'S JUST SAY THE AVERAGE IS AROUND FIVE.

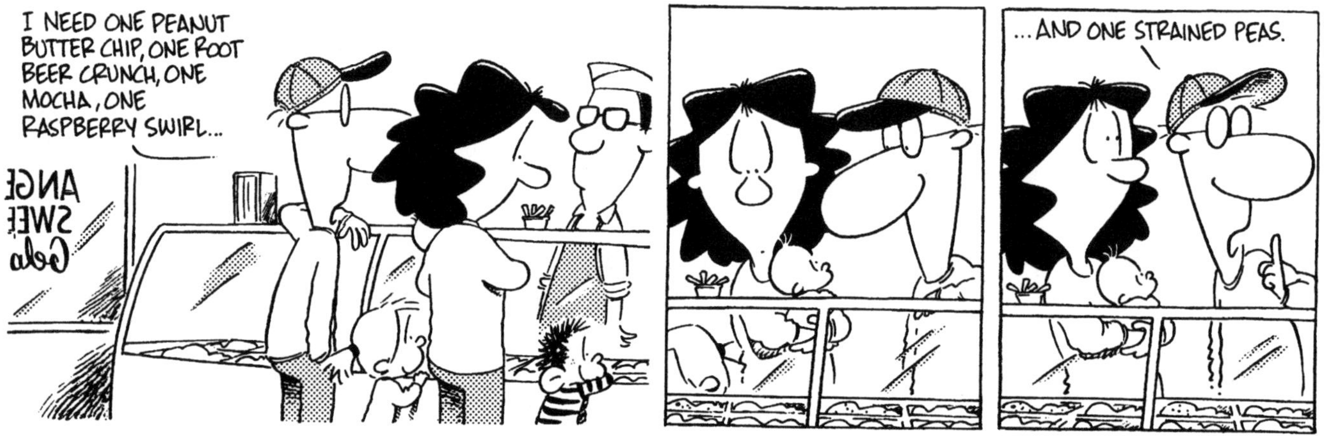
I NEED ONE PEANUT BUTTER CHIP, ONE ROOT BEER CRUNCH, ONE MOCHA, ONE RASPBERRY SWIRL...
...AND ONE STRAINED PEAS.

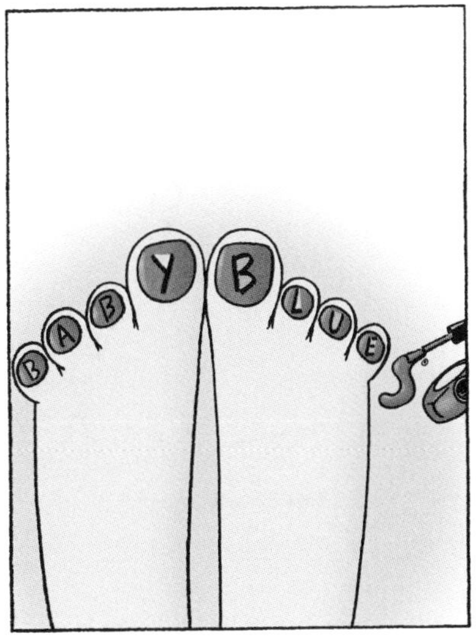
BABY BLUES

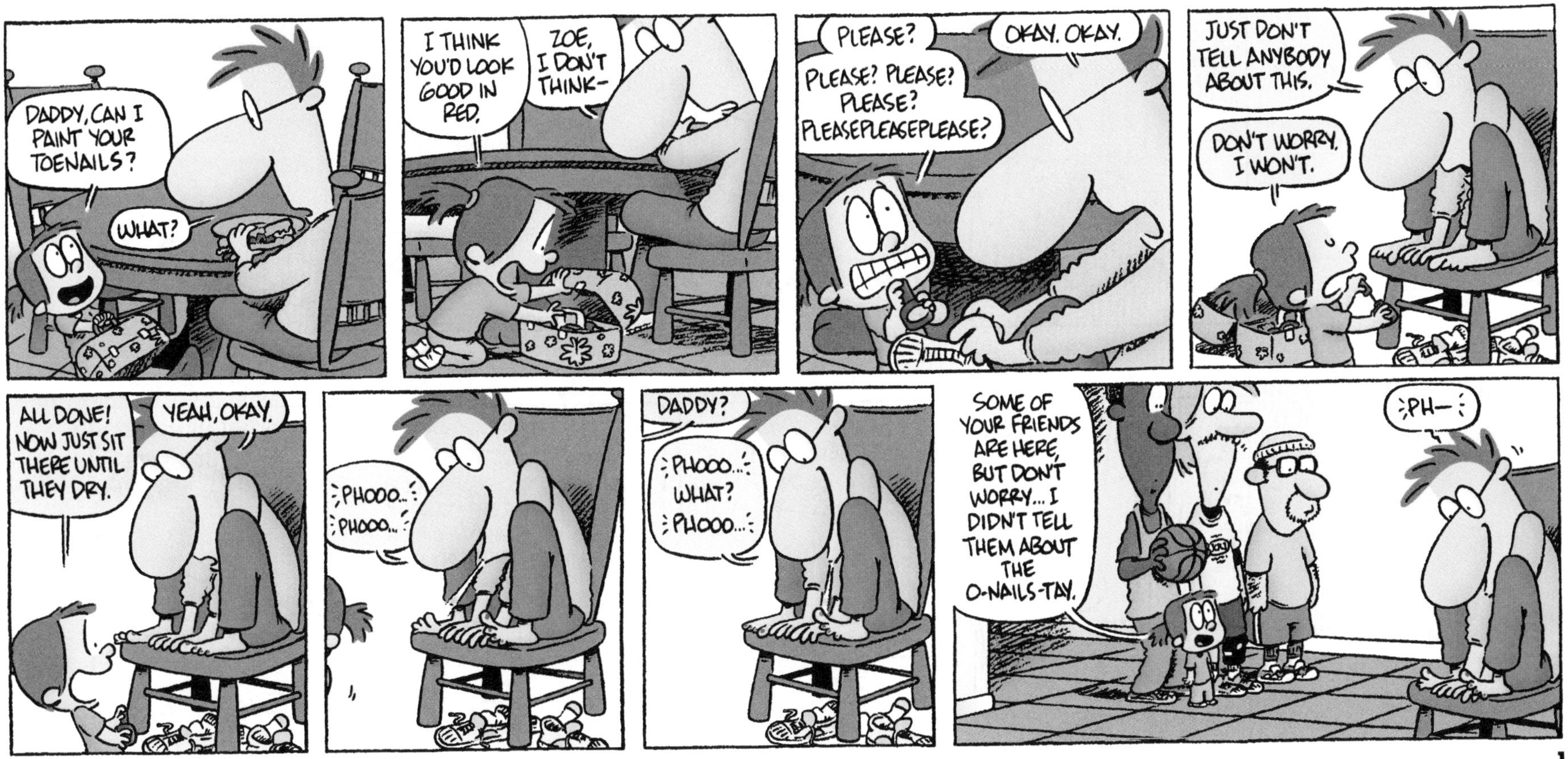
DADDY, CAN I PAINT YOUR TOENAILS?
WHAT?
I THINK YOU'D LOOK GOOD IN RED.
ZOE, I DON'T THINK-
PLEASE?
PLEASE? PLEASE? PLEASE? PLEASEPLEASEPLEASE?
OKAY. OKAY.
JUST DON'T TELL ANYBODY ABOUT THIS.
DON'T WORRY, I WON'T.
ALL DONE! NOW JUST SIT THERE UNTIL THEY DRY.
YEAH, OKAY.
PHOOO...
PHOOO...
DADDY?
PHOOO... WHAT? PHOOO...
SOME OF YOUR FRIENDS ARE HERE, BUT DON'T WORRY... I DIDN'T TELL THEM ABOUT THE O-NAILS-TAY.
PH-

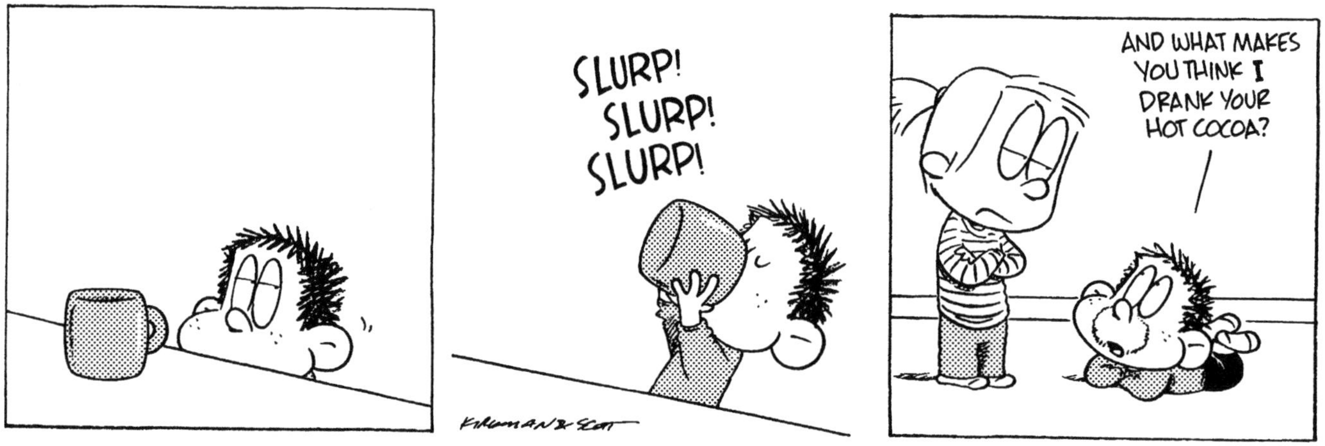
SLURP!
SLURP!
SLURP!
AND WHAT MAKES YOU THINK I DRANK YOUR HOT COCOA?

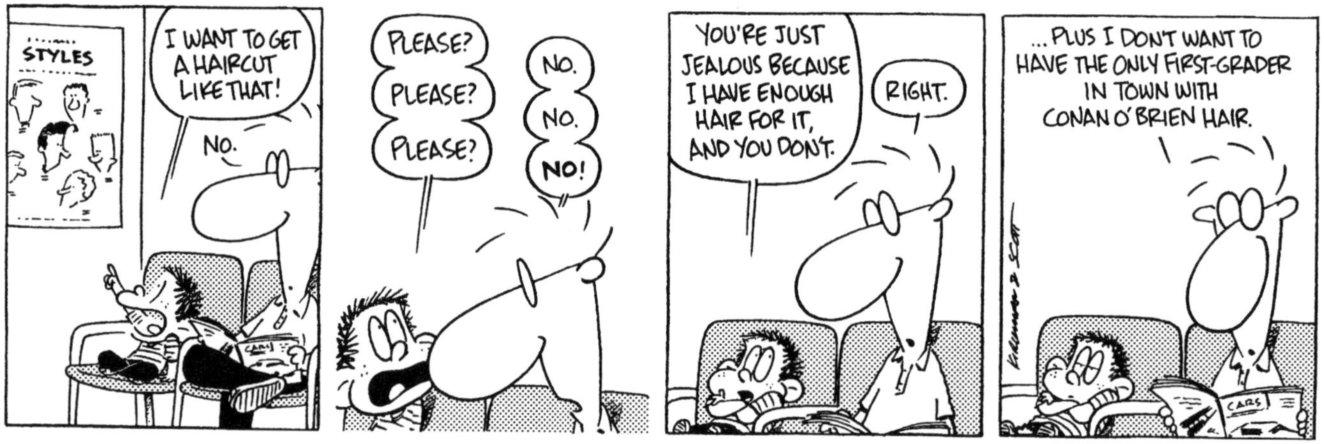
STYLES
I WANT TO GET A HAIRCUT LIKE THAT!
NO.
PLEASE?
PLEASE?
PLEASE?
NO.
NO.
NO!
YOU'RE JUST JEALOUS BECAUSE I HAVE ENOUGH HAIR FOR IT, AND YOU DON'T.
RIGHT.
...PLUS I DON'T WANT TO HAVE THE ONLY FIRST-GRADER IN TOWN WITH CONAN O'BRIEN HAIR.
CARS

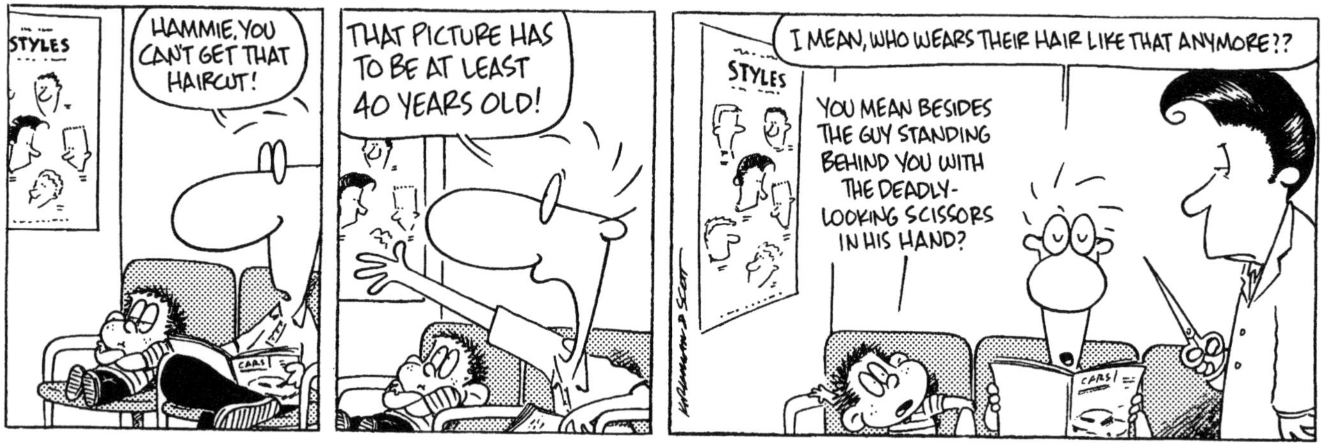
STYLES
HAMMIE, YOU CAN'T GET THAT HAIRCUT!
THAT PICTURE HAS TO BE AT LEAST 40 YEARS OLD!
I MEAN, WHO WEARS THEIR HAIR LIKE THAT ANYMORE??
YOU MEAN BESIDES THE GUY STANDING BEHIND YOU WITH THE DEADLY-LOOKING SCISSORS IN HIS HAND?
CARS

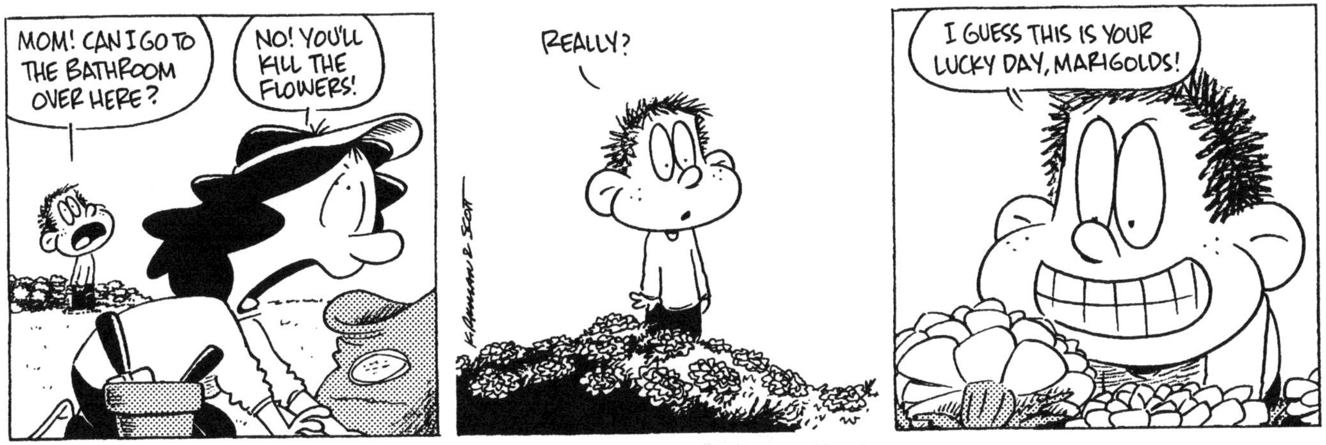
MOM! CAN I GO TO THE BATHROOM OVER HERE?
NO! YOU'LL KILL THE FLOWERS!
REALLY?
I GUESS THIS IS YOUR LUCKY DAY, MARIGOLDS!

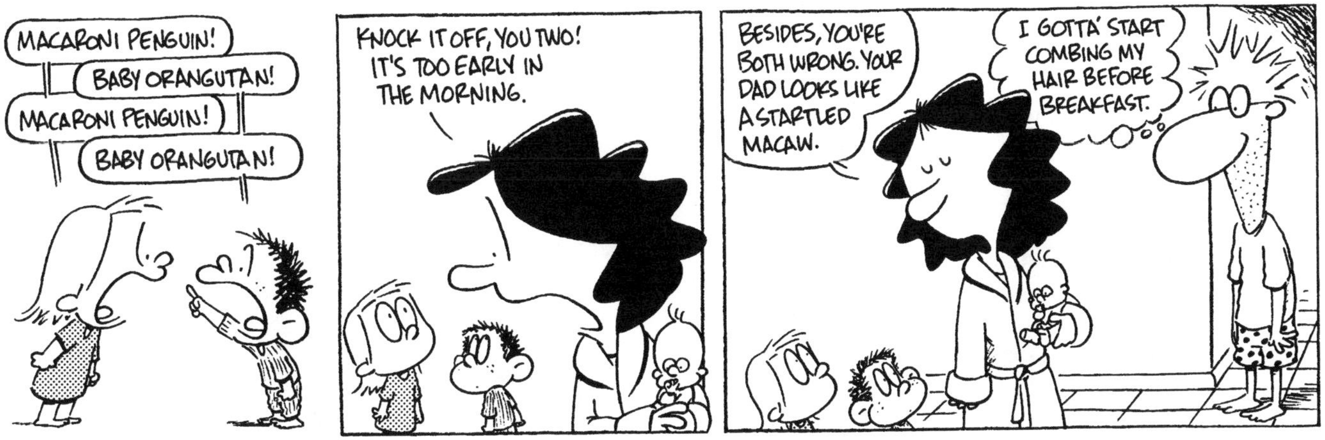
MACARONI PENGUIN!
BABY ORANGUTAN!
MACARONI PENGUIN!
BABY ORANGUTAN!
KNOCK IT OFF, YOU TWO! IT'S TOO EARLY IN THE MORNING.
BESIDES, YOU'RE BOTH WRONG. YOUR DAD LOOKS LIKE A STARTLED MACAW.
I GOTTA' START COMBING MY HAIR BEFORE BREAKFAST.

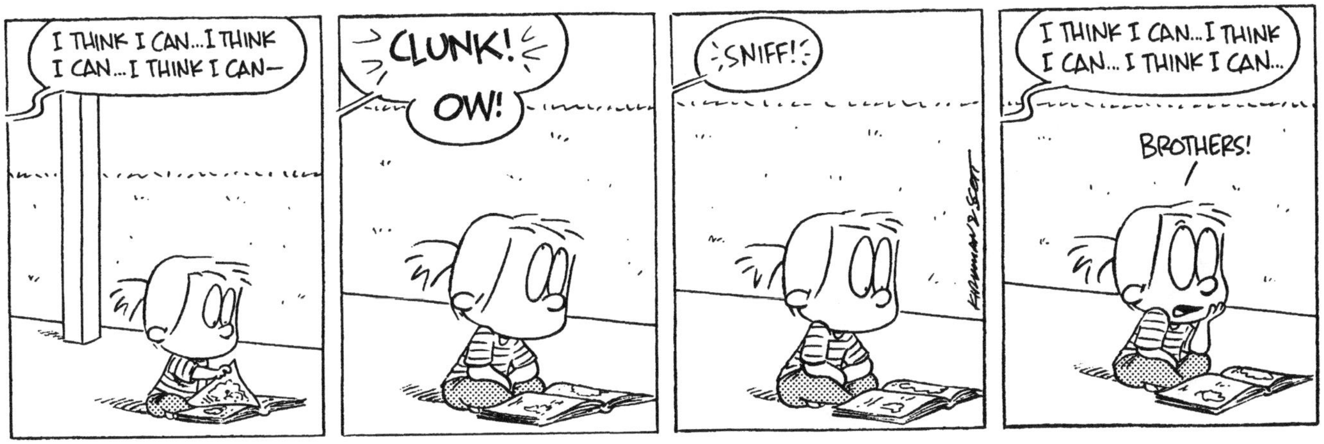
I THINK I CAN... I THINK I CAN... I THINK I CAN—
CLUNK!
OW!
SNIFF!
I THINK I CAN... I THINK I CAN... I THINK I CAN...
BROTHERS!

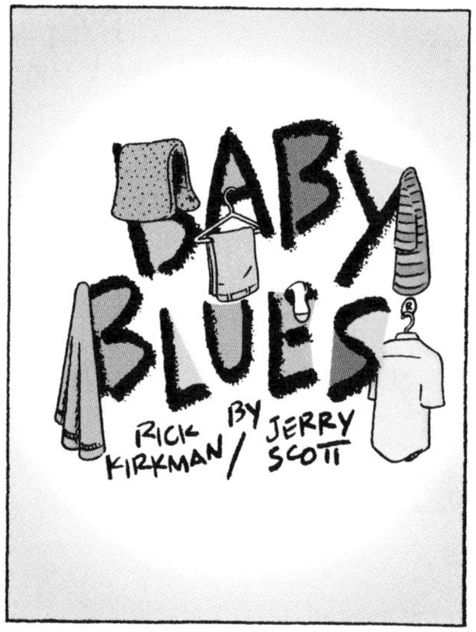
BABY BLUES
BY RICK KIRKMAN / JERRY SCOTT

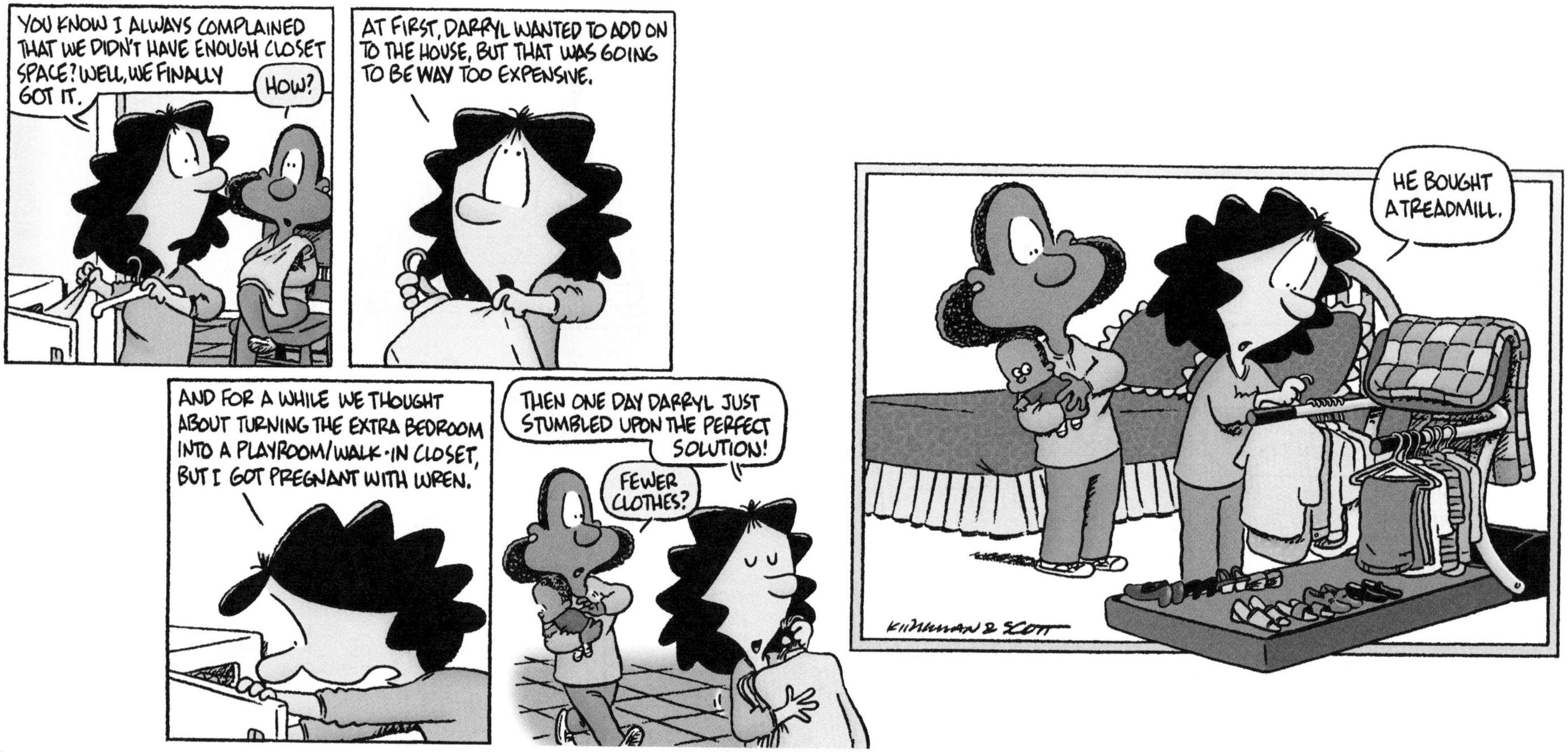
YOU KNOW I ALWAYS COMPLAINED THAT WE DIDN'T HAVE ENOUGH CLOSET SPACE? WELL, WE FINALLY GOT IT.
HOW?
AT FIRST, DARRYL WANTED TO ADD ON TO THE HOUSE, BUT THAT WAS GOING TO BE WAY TOO EXPENSIVE.
AND FOR A WHILE WE THOUGHT ABOUT TURNING THE EXTRA BEDROOM INTO A PLAYROOM/WALK-IN CLOSET, BUT I GOT PREGNANT WITH WREN.
THEN ONE DAY DARRYL JUST STUMBLED UPON THE PERFECT SOLUTION!
FEWER CLOTHES?
HE BOUGHT A TREADMILL.
KIRKMAN & SCOTT

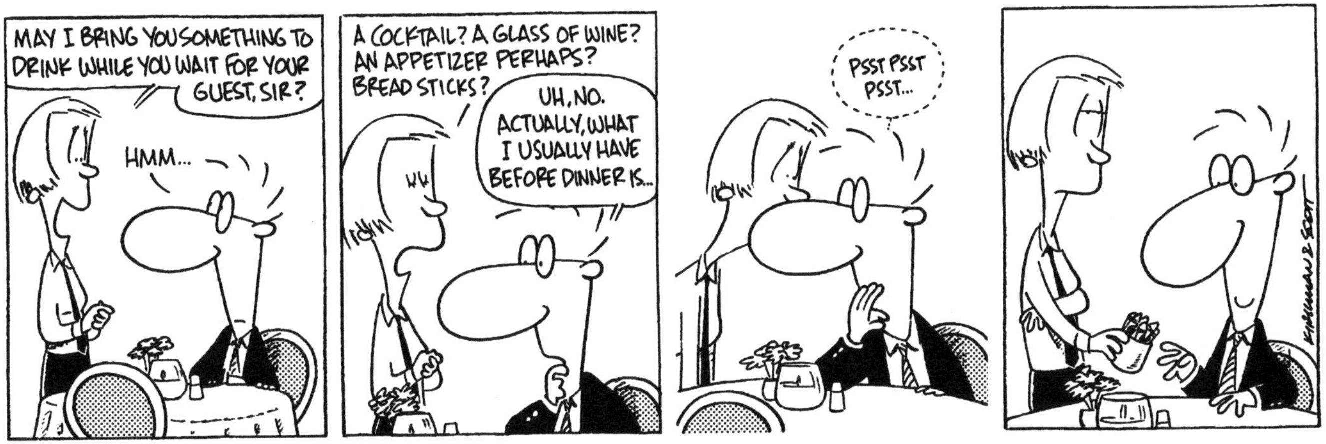
MAY I BRING YOU SOMETHING TO DRINK WHILE YOU WAIT FOR YOUR GUEST, SIR?
HMM...
A COCKTAIL? A GLASS OF WINE? AN APPETIZER PERHAPS? BREAD STICKS?
UH, NO. ACTUALLY, WHAT I USUALLY HAVE BEFORE DINNER IS...
PSST PSST PSST...
KIRKMAN & SCOTT

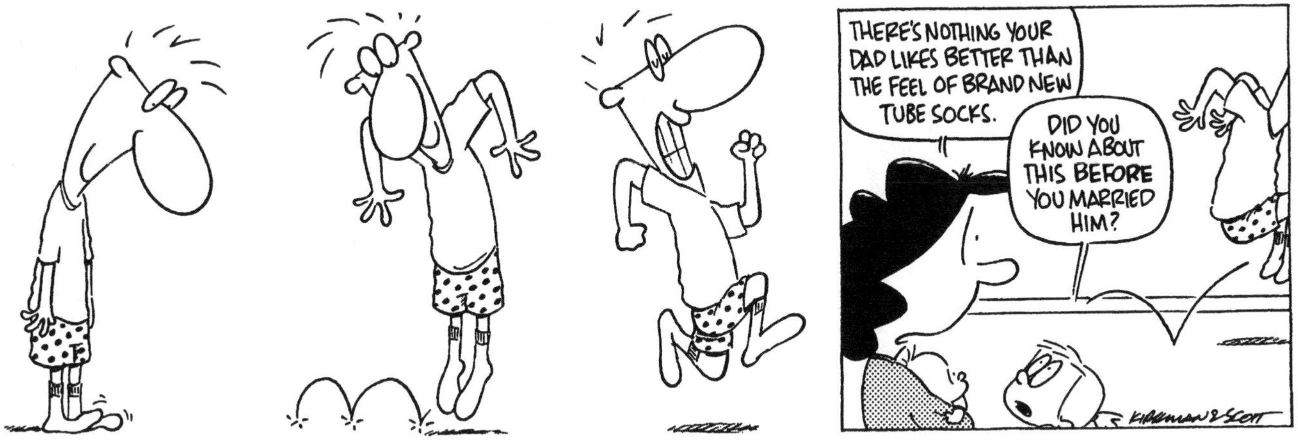
THERE'S NOTHING YOUR DAD LIKES BETTER THAN THE FEEL OF BRAND NEW TUBE SOCKS.
DID YOU KNOW ABOUT THIS BEFORE YOU MARRIED HIM?
KIRKMAN & SCOTT

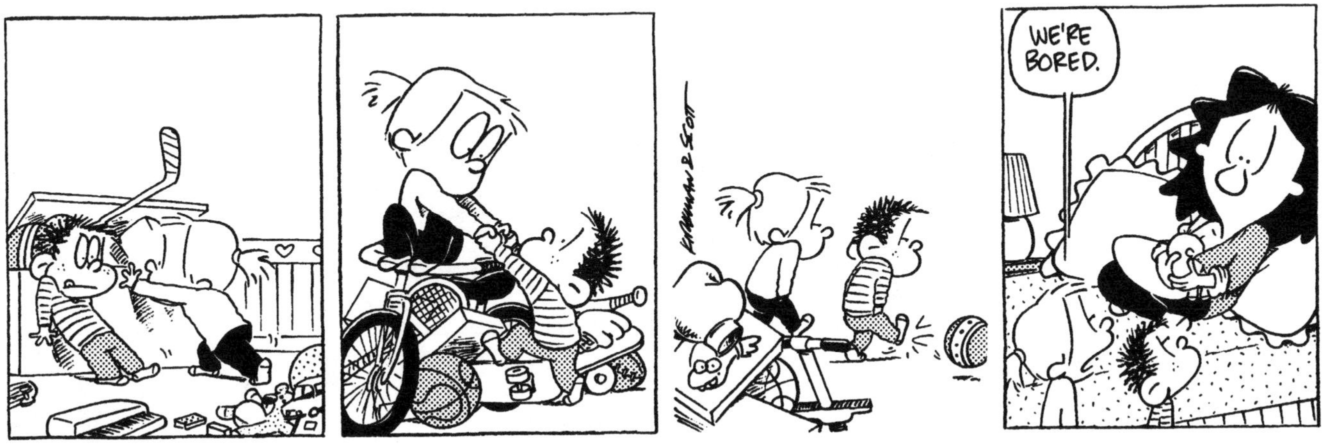
KIRKMAN & SCOTT
WE'RE BORED.

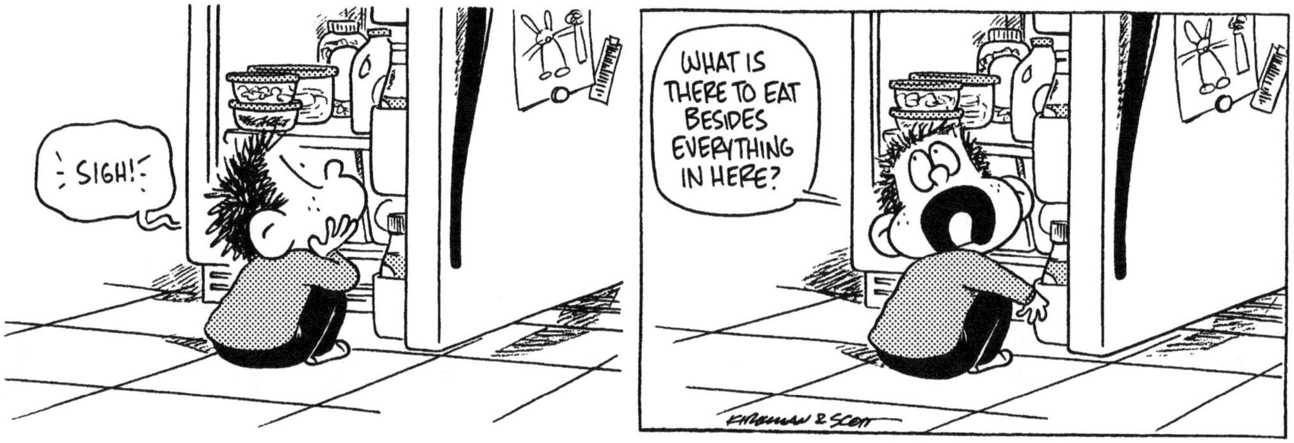
SIGH!
WHAT IS THERE TO EAT BESIDES EVERYTHING IN HERE?
KIRKMAN & SCOTT

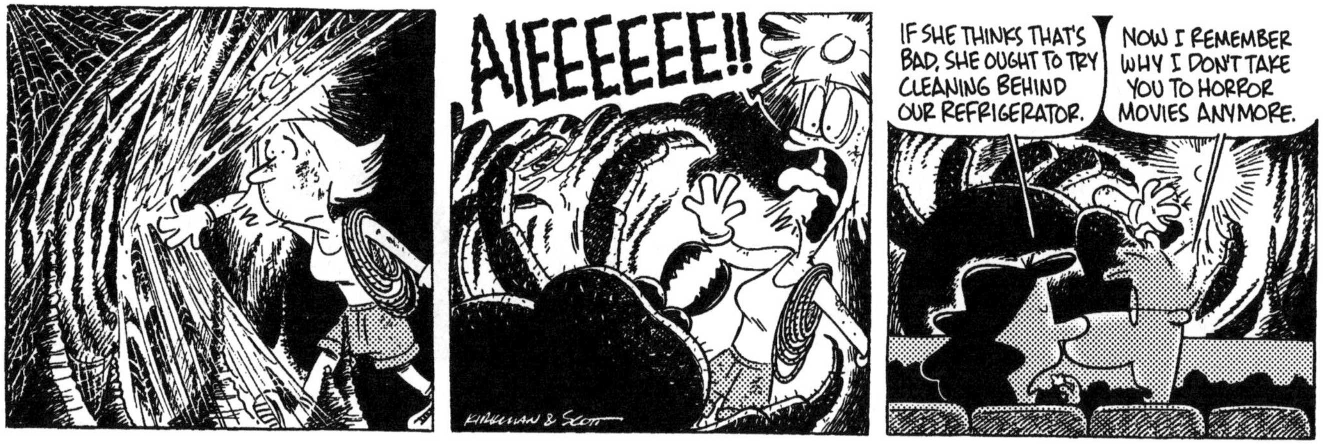
AIEEEEEE!!
KIRKMAN & SCOTT
IF SHE THINKS THAT'S BAD, SHE OUGHT TO TRY CLEANING BEHIND OUR REFRIGERATOR.
NOW I REMEMBER WHY I DON'T TAKE YOU TO HORROR MOVIES ANYMORE.

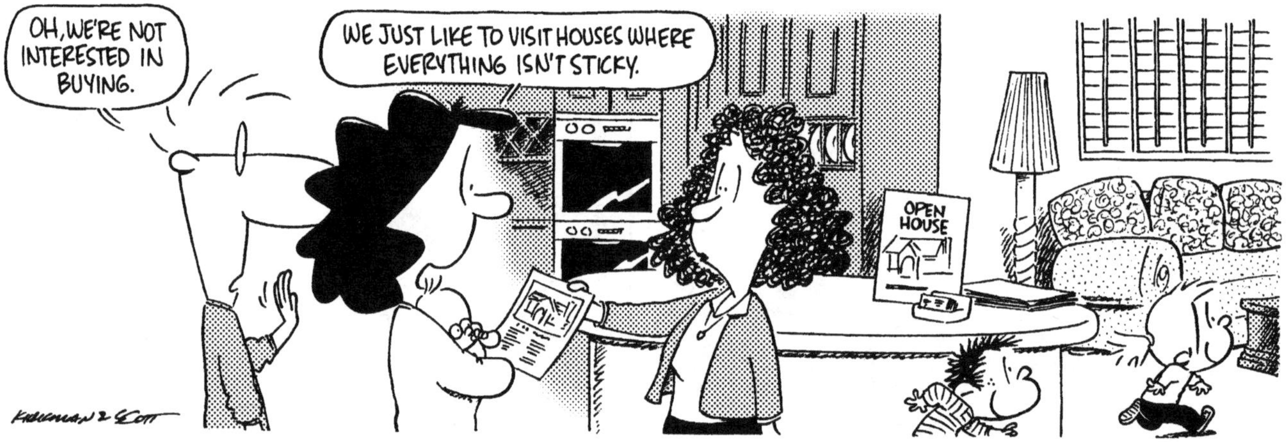
OH, WE'RE NOT INTERESTED IN BUYING.
WE JUST LIKE TO VISIT HOUSES WHERE EVERYTHING ISN'T STICKY.
OPEN HOUSE
KIRKMAN & SCOTT

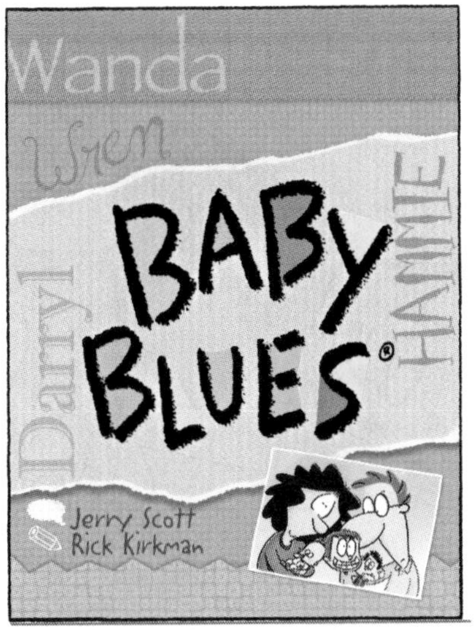
Wanda
Wren
Darryl
BABY BLUES®
HAMMIE
Jerry Scott
Rick Kirkman

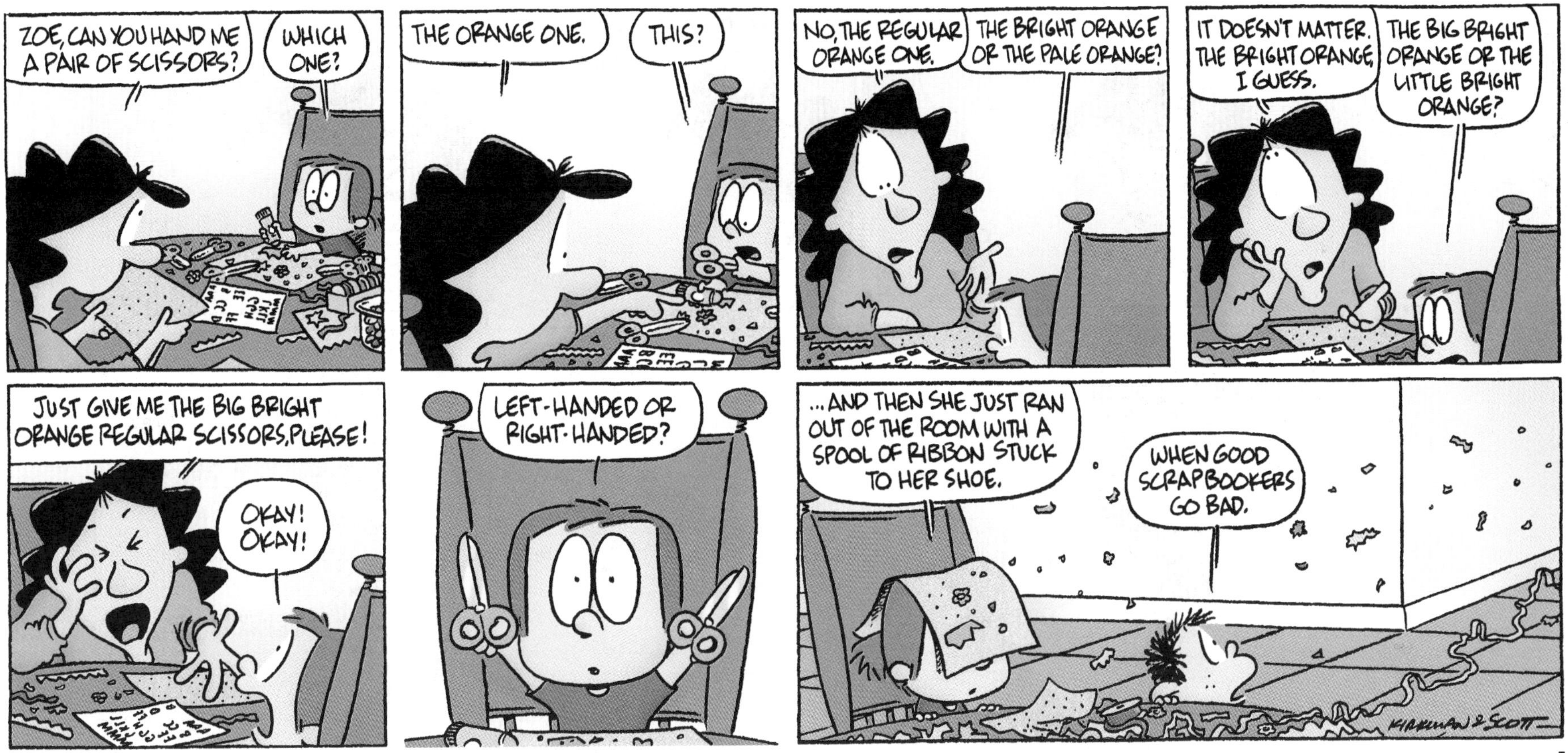
ZOE, CAN YOU HAND ME A PAIR OF SCISSORS?
WHICH ONE?
THE ORANGE ONE.
THIS?
NO, THE REGULAR ORANGE ONE.
THE BRIGHT ORANGE OR THE PALE ORANGE?
IT DOESN'T MATTER. THE BRIGHT ORANGE, I GUESS.
THE BIG BRIGHT ORANGE OR THE LITTLE BRIGHT ORANGE?
JUST GIVE ME THE BIG BRIGHT ORANGE REGULAR SCISSORS, PLEASE!
OKAY! OKAY!
LEFT-HANDED OR RIGHT-HANDED?
...AND THEN SHE JUST RAN OUT OF THE ROOM WITH A SPOOL OF RIBBON STUCK TO HER SHOE.
WHEN GOOD SCRAPBOOKERS GO BAD.
KIRKMAN & SCOTT

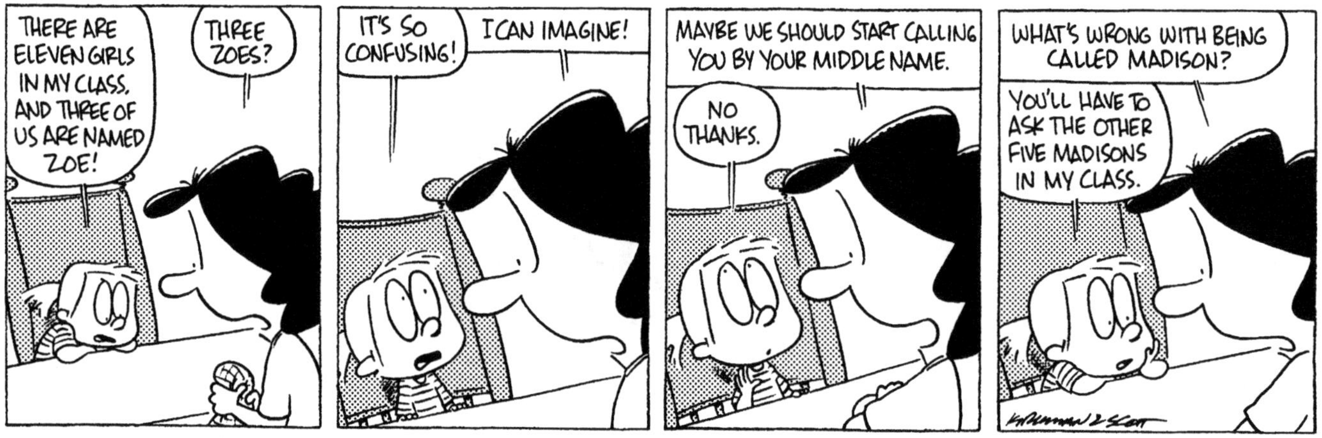
THERE ARE ELEVEN GIRLS IN MY CLASS, AND THREE OF US ARE NAMED ZOE!
THREE ZOES?
IT'S SO CONFUSING!
I CAN IMAGINE!
MAYBE WE SHOULD START CALLING YOU BY YOUR MIDDLE NAME.
NO THANKS.
WHAT'S WRONG WITH BEING CALLED MADISON?
YOU'LL HAVE TO ASK THE OTHER FIVE MADISONS IN MY CLASS.

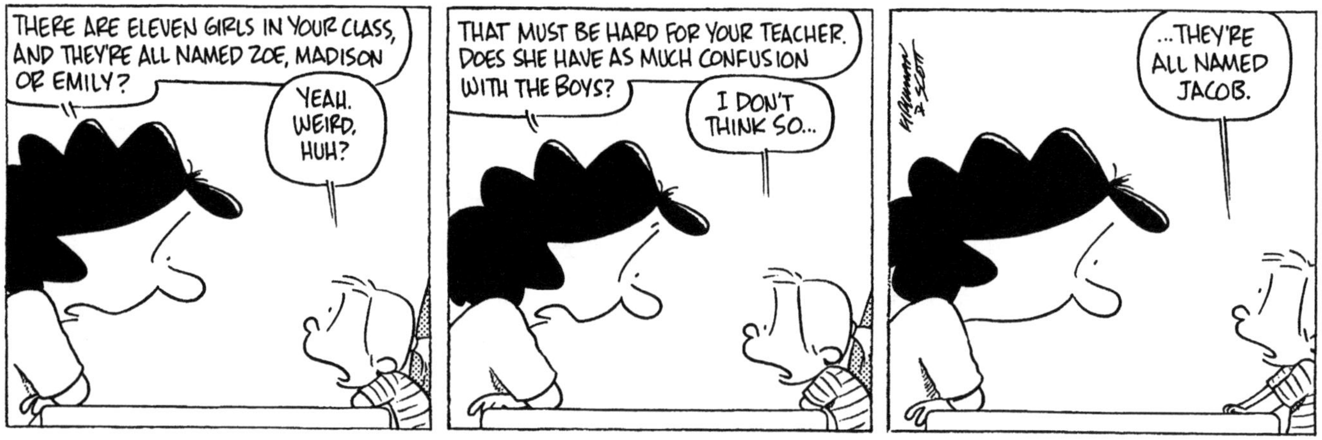
THERE ARE ELEVEN GIRLS IN YOUR CLASS, AND THEY'RE ALL NAMED ZOE, MADISON OR EMILY?
YEAH. WEIRD, HUH?
THAT MUST BE HARD FOR YOUR TEACHER. DOES SHE HAVE AS MUCH CONFUSION WITH THE BOYS?
I DON'T THINK SO...
...THEY'RE ALL NAMED JACOB.

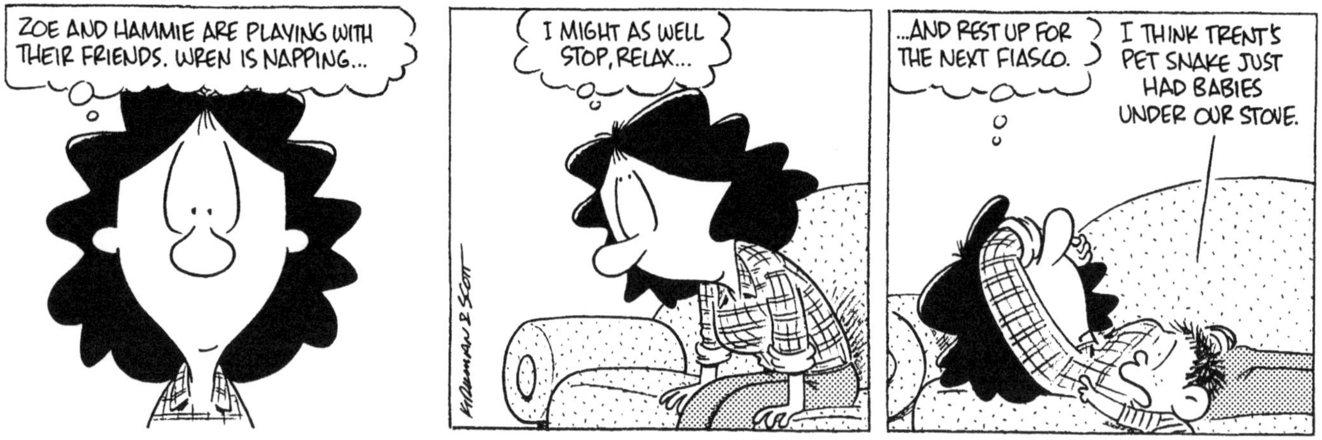
ZOE AND HAMMIE ARE PLAYING WITH THEIR FRIENDS. WREN IS NAPPING...
I MIGHT AS WELL STOP, RELAX...
...AND REST UP FOR THE NEXT FIASCO.
I THINK TRENT'S PET SNAKE JUST HAD BABIES UNDER OUR STOVE.

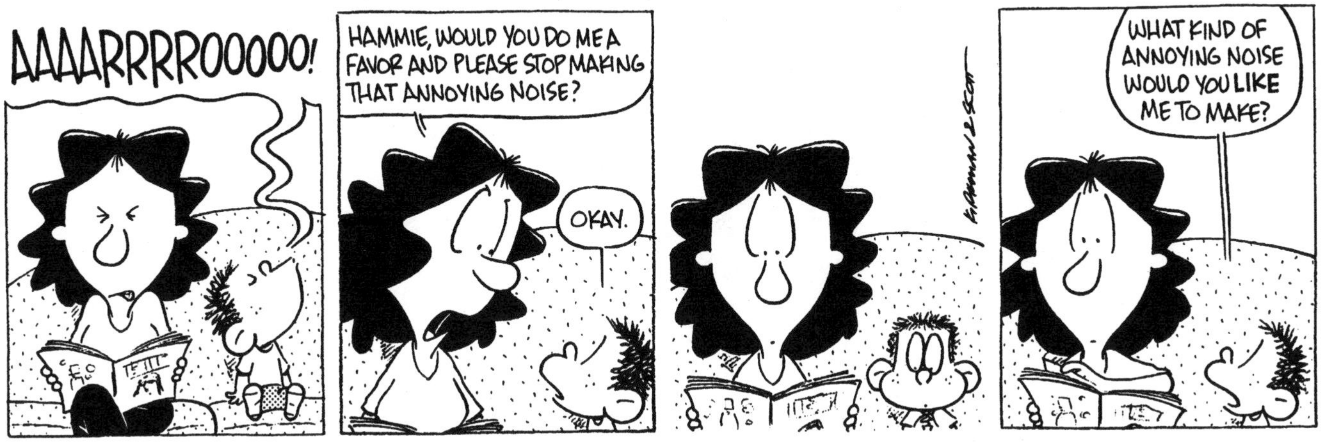
AAAARRRROOOOO!
HAMMIE, WOULD YOU DO ME A FAVOR AND PLEASE STOP MAKING THAT ANNOYING NOISE?
OKAY.
WHAT KIND OF ANNOYING NOISE WOULD YOU **LIKE** ME TO MAKE?

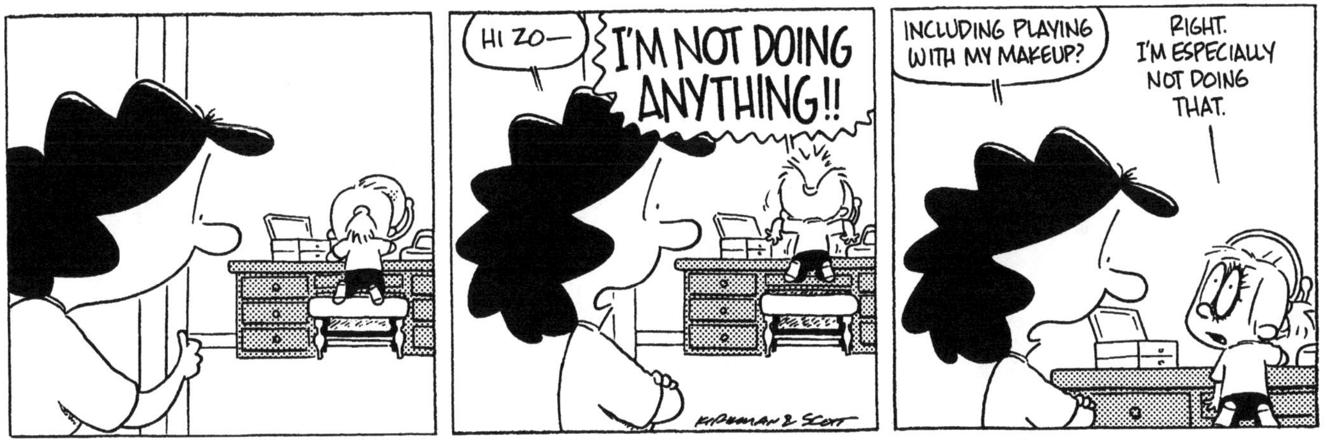
HI ZO—
I'M NOT DOING ANYTHING!!
INCLUDING PLAYING WITH MY MAKEUP?
RIGHT. I'M ESPECIALLY NOT DOING THAT.

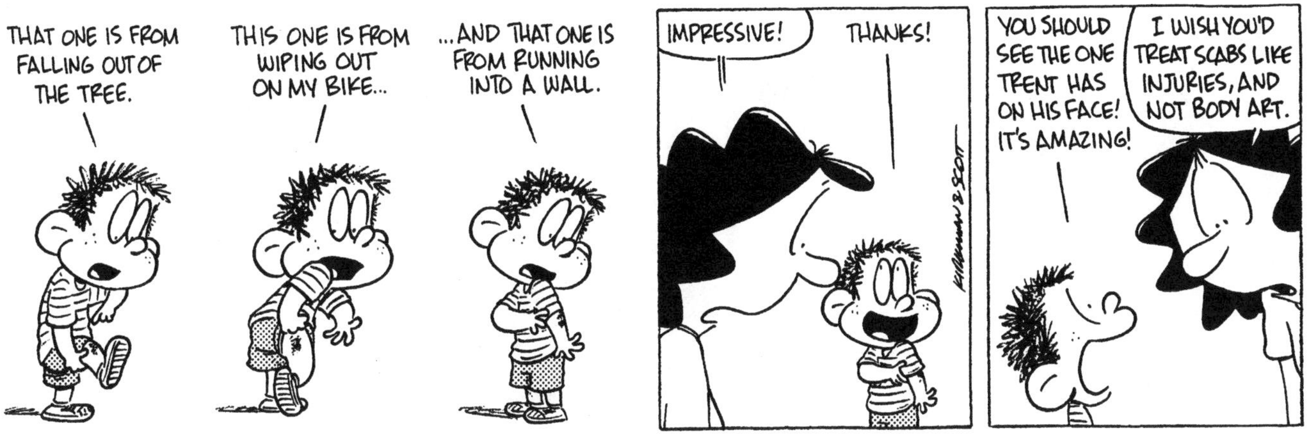
THAT ONE IS FROM FALLING OUT OF THE TREE.
THIS ONE IS FROM WIPING OUT ON MY BIKE...
...AND THAT ONE IS FROM RUNNING INTO A WALL.
IMPRESSIVE!
THANKS!
YOU SHOULD SEE THE ONE TRENT HAS ON HIS FACE! IT'S AMAZING!
I WISH YOU'D TREAT SCABS LIKE INJURIES, AND NOT BODY ART.

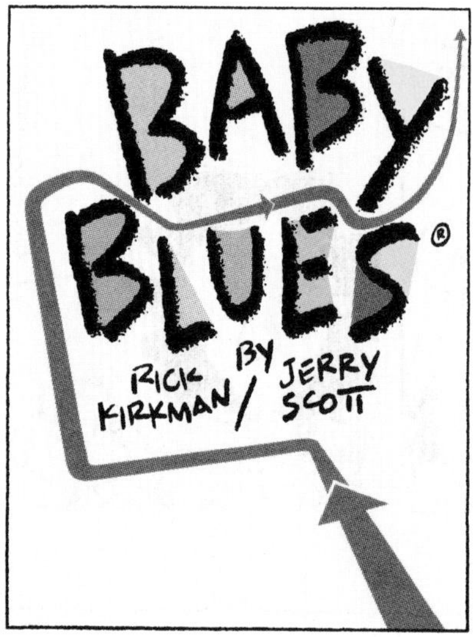
BABY BLUES®
BY
RICK KIRKMAN / JERRY SCOTT

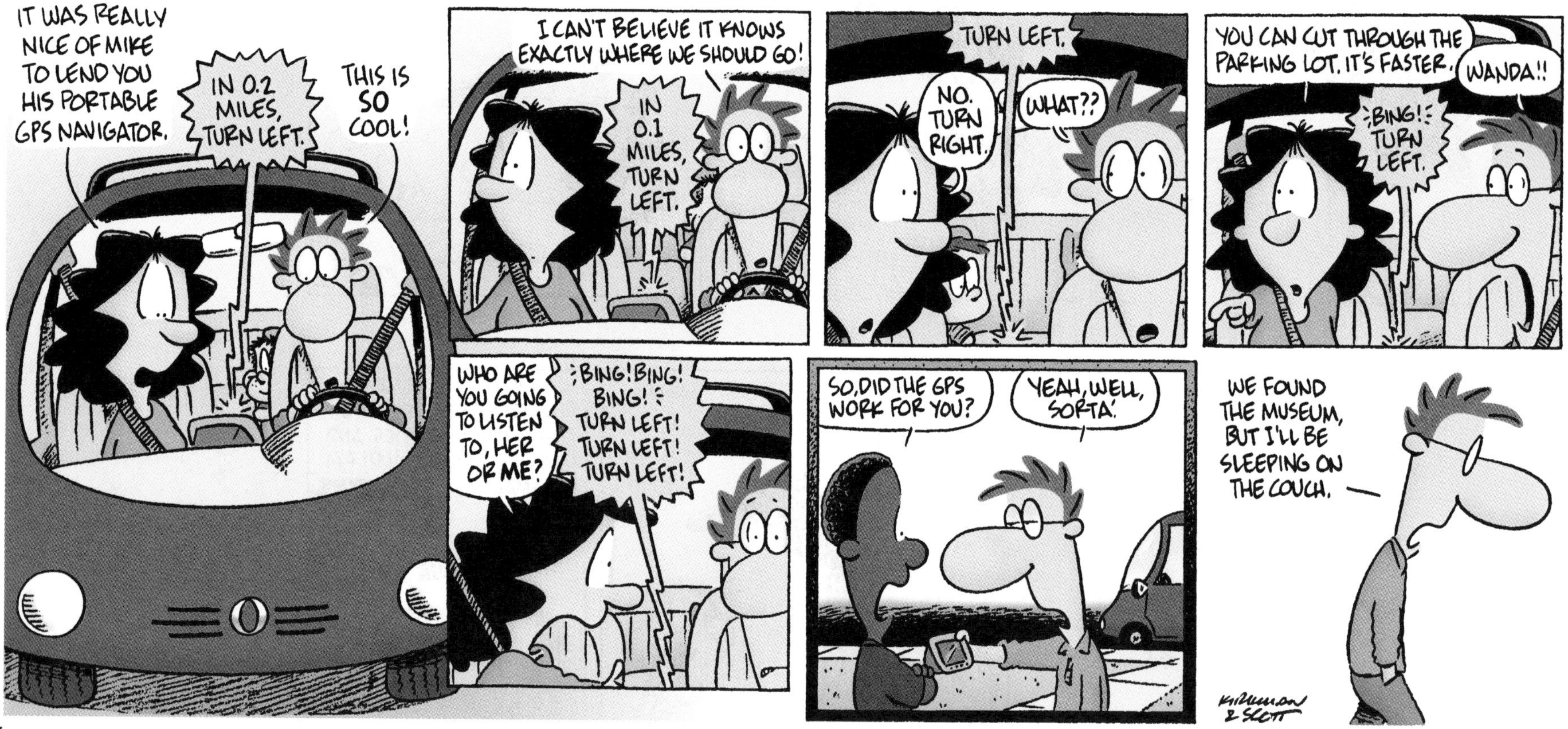
IT WAS REALLY NICE OF MIKE TO LEND YOU HIS PORTABLE GPS NAVIGATOR.
IN 0.2 MILES, TURN LEFT.
THIS IS SO COOL!
I CAN'T BELIEVE IT KNOWS EXACTLY WHERE WE SHOULD GO!
IN 0.1 MILES, TURN LEFT.
TURN LEFT.
NO. TURN RIGHT.
WHAT??
YOU CAN CUT THROUGH THE PARKING LOT. IT'S FASTER.
BING! TURN LEFT.
WANDA!!
WHO ARE YOU GOING TO LISTEN TO, HER OR ME?
BING! BING! BING! TURN LEFT! TURN LEFT! TURN LEFT!
SO, DID THE GPS WORK FOR YOU?
YEAH, WELL, SORTA.
WE FOUND THE MUSEUM, BUT I'LL BE SLEEPING ON THE COUCH.
KIRKMAN & SCOTT

BEFORE & AFTER

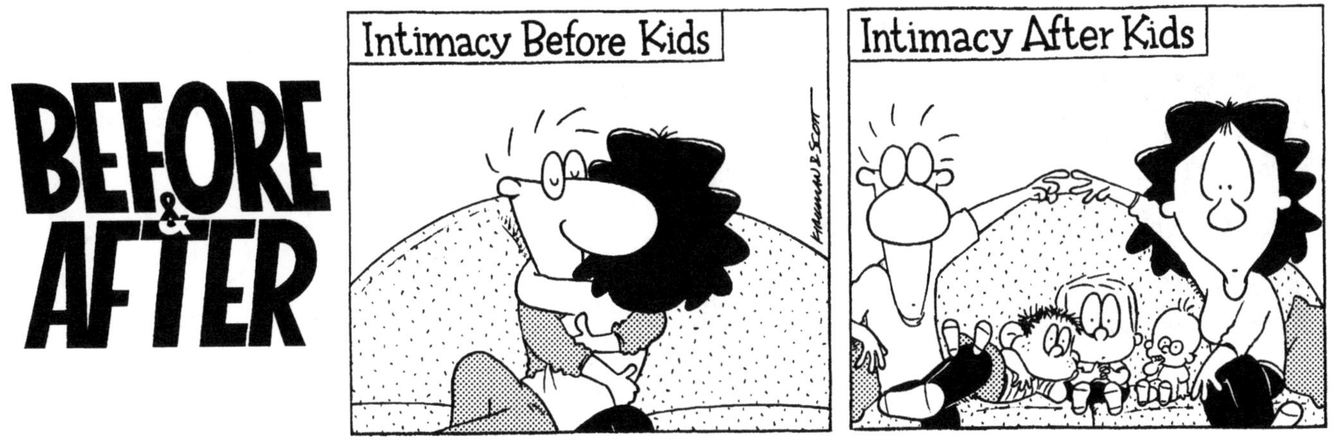
Intimacy Before Kids
Intimacy After Kids

BEFORE & AFTER

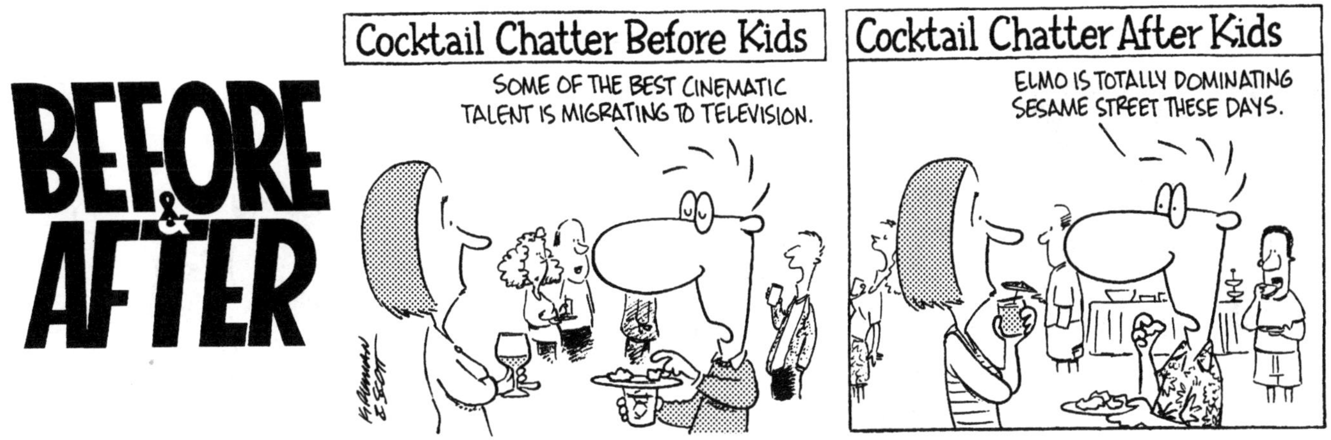
Cocktail Chatter Before Kids
SOME OF THE BEST CINEMATIC TALENT IS MIGRATING TO TELEVISION.
Cocktail Chatter After Kids
ELMO IS TOTALLY DOMINATING SESAME STREET THESE DAYS.

BEFORE & AFTER

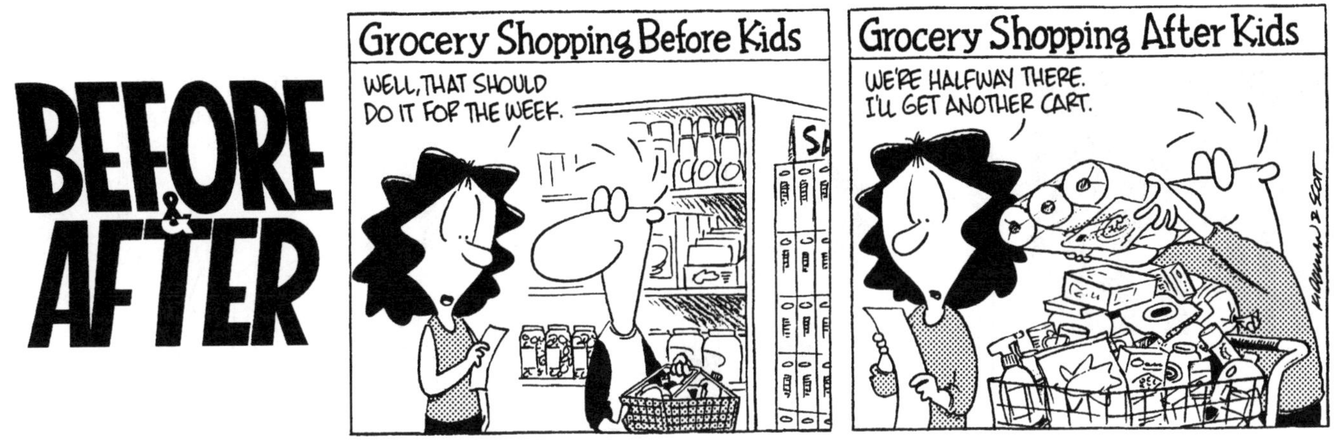
Grocery Shopping Before Kids
WELL, THAT SHOULD DO IT FOR THE WEEK.
Grocery Shopping After Kids
WE'RE HALFWAY THERE. I'LL GET ANOTHER CART.

BEFORE & AFTER

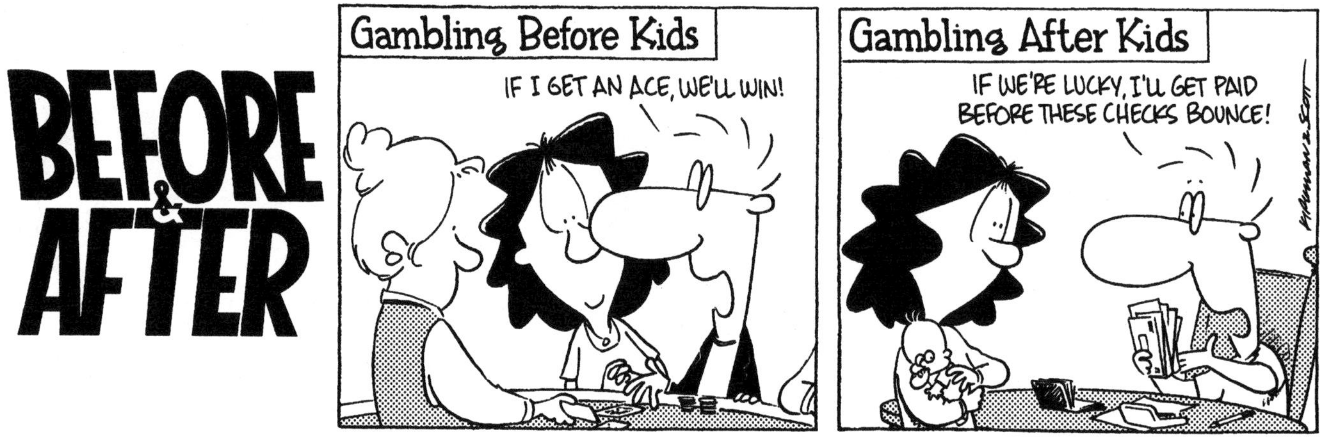
Gambling Before Kids
IF I GET AN ACE, WE'LL WIN!
Gambling After Kids
IF WE'RE LUCKY, I'LL GET PAID BEFORE THESE CHECKS BOUNCE!

BEFORE & AFTER

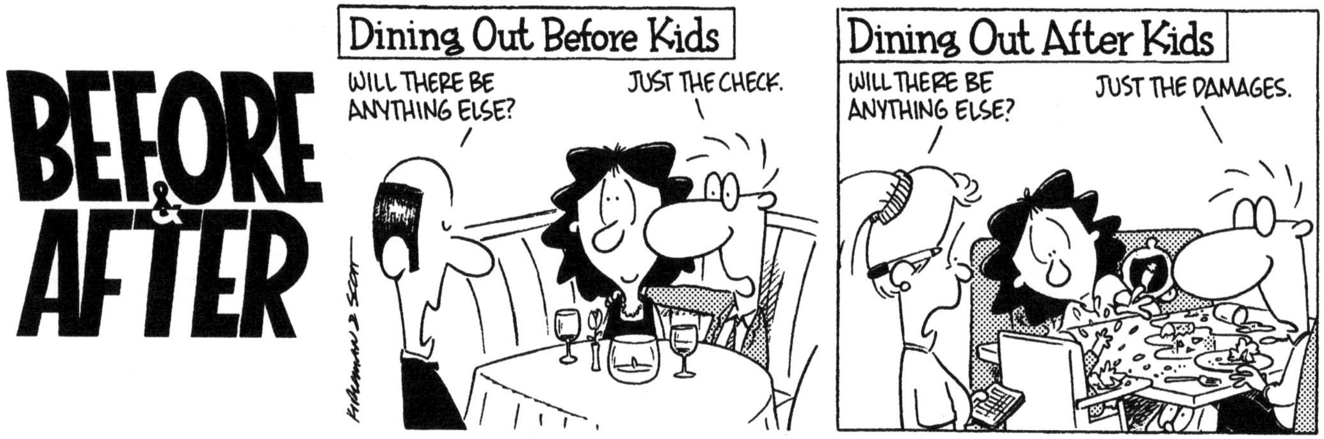
Dining Out Before Kids
WILL THERE BE ANYTHING ELSE?
JUST THE CHECK.
Dining Out After Kids
WILL THERE BE ANYTHING ELSE?
JUST THE DAMAGES.

BEFORE & AFTER

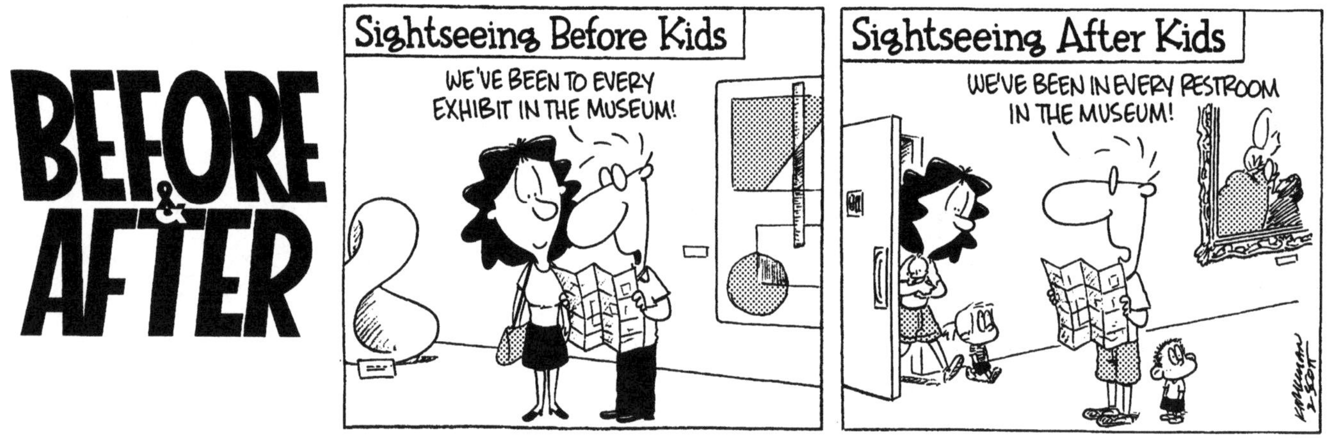
Sightseeing Before Kids
WE'VE BEEN TO EVERY EXHIBIT IN THE MUSEUM!
Sightseeing After Kids
WE'VE BEEN IN EVERY RESTROOM IN THE MUSEUM!

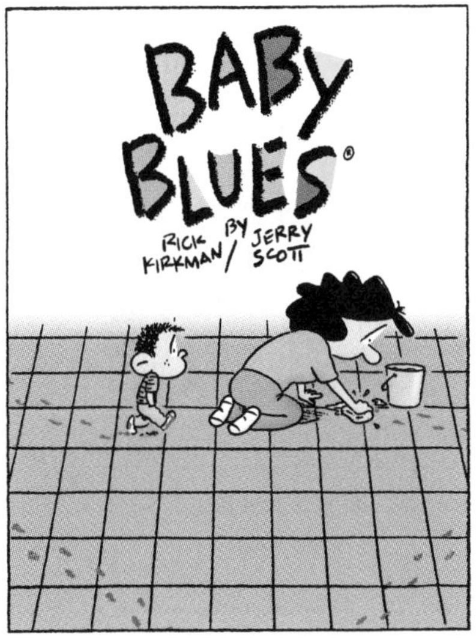
BABY BLUES®
BY RICK KIRKMAN / JERRY SCOTT

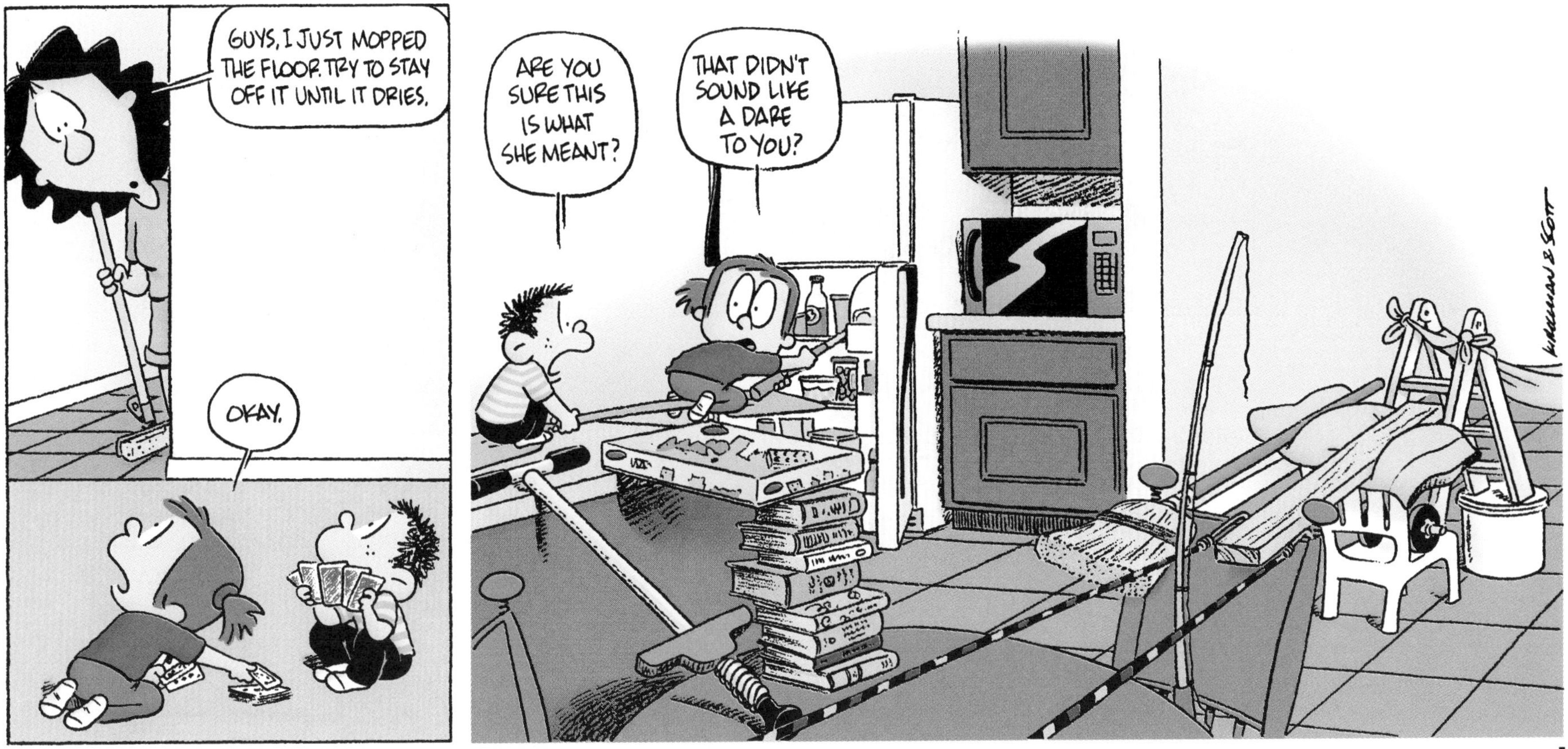
GUYS, I JUST MOPPED THE FLOOR. TRY TO STAY OFF IT UNTIL IT DRIES.
OKAY.
ARE YOU SURE THIS IS WHAT SHE MEANT?
THAT DIDN'T SOUND LIKE A DARE TO YOU?
KIRKMAN & SCOTT

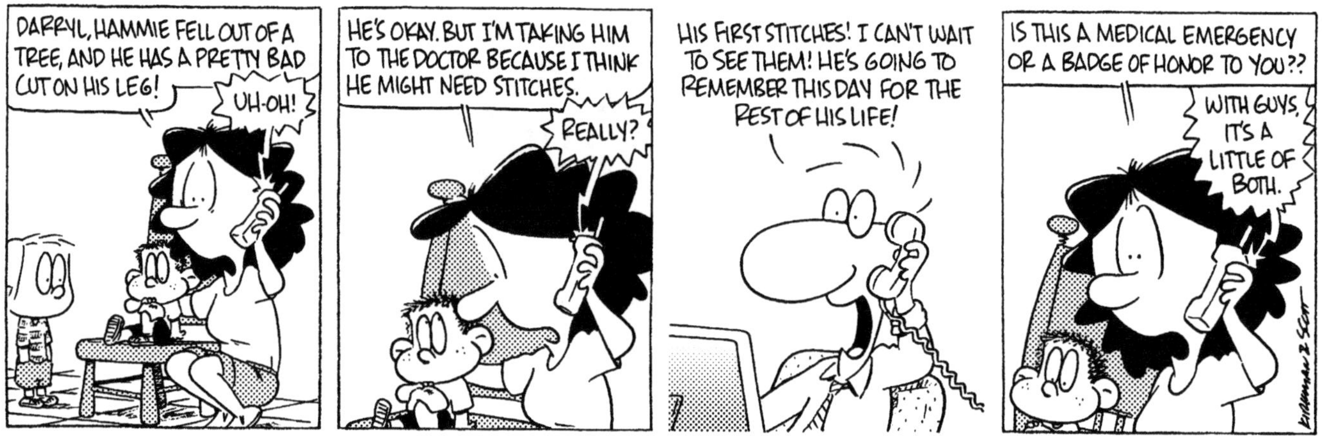
DARRYL, HAMMIE FELL OUT OF A TREE, AND HE HAS A PRETTY BAD CUT ON HIS LEG!
UH-OH!
HE'S OKAY. BUT I'M TAKING HIM TO THE DOCTOR BECAUSE I THINK HE MIGHT NEED STITCHES.
REALLY?
HIS FIRST STITCHES! I CAN'T WAIT TO SEE THEM! HE'S GOING TO REMEMBER THIS DAY FOR THE REST OF HIS LIFE!
IS THIS A MEDICAL EMERGENCY OR A BADGE OF HONOR TO YOU??
WITH GUYS, IT'S A LITTLE OF BOTH.

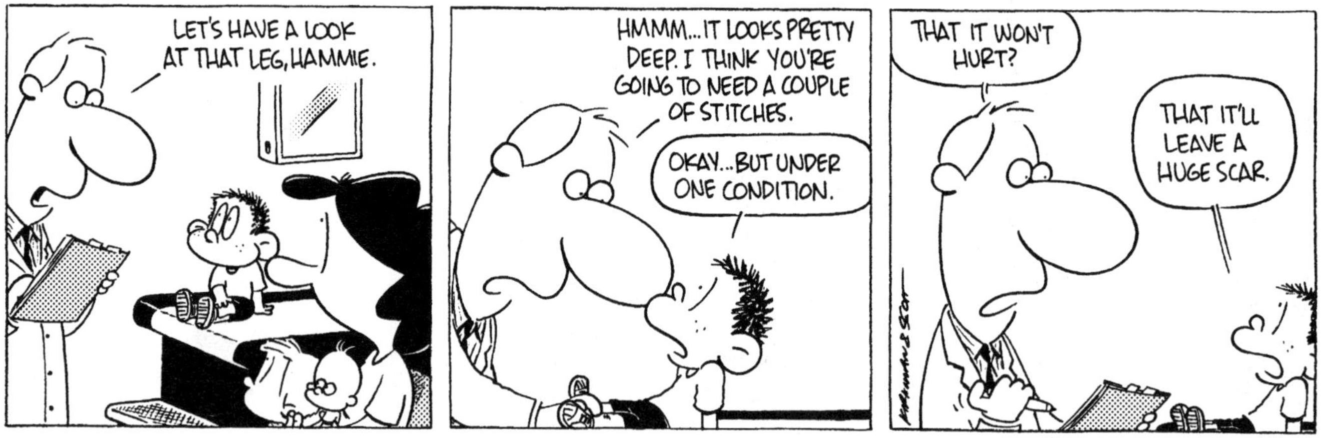
LET'S HAVE A LOOK AT THAT LEG, HAMMIE.
HMMM... IT LOOKS PRETTY DEEP. I THINK YOU'RE GOING TO NEED A COUPLE OF STITCHES.
OKAY... BUT UNDER ONE CONDITION.
THAT IT WON'T HURT?
THAT IT'LL LEAVE A HUGE SCAR.

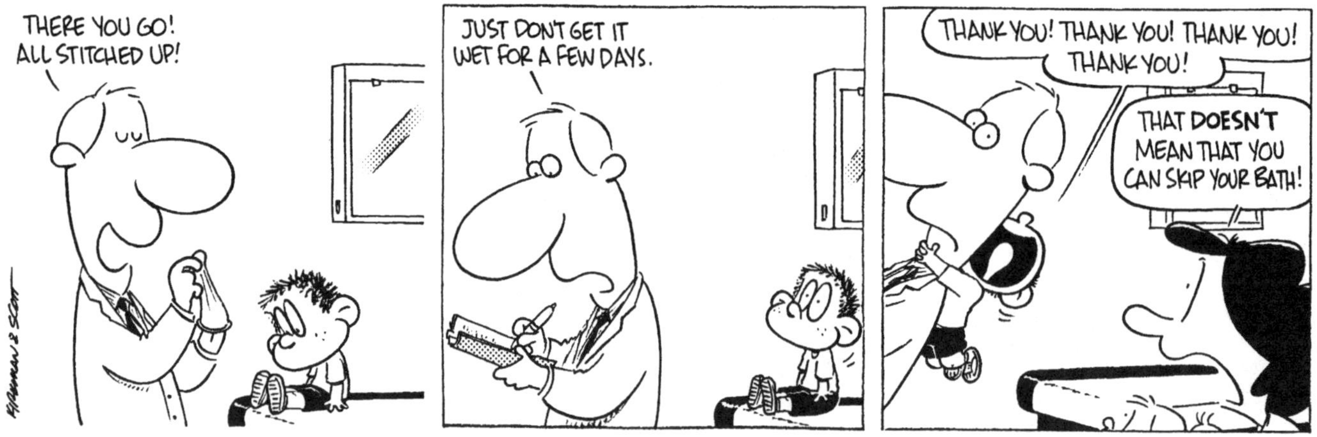
THERE YOU GO! ALL STITCHED UP!
JUST DON'T GET IT WET FOR A FEW DAYS.
THANK YOU! THANK YOU! THANK YOU! THANK YOU!
THAT **DOESN'T** MEAN THAT YOU CAN SKIP YOUR BATH!

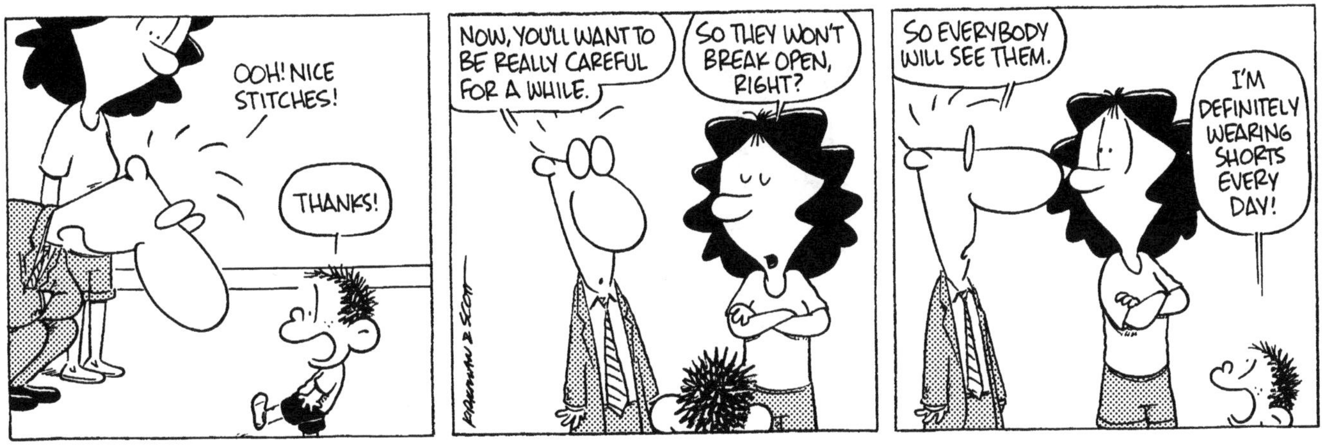
OOH! NICE STITCHES!
THANKS!
NOW, YOU'LL WANT TO BE REALLY CAREFUL FOR A WHILE.
SO THEY WON'T BREAK OPEN, RIGHT?
SO EVERYBODY WILL SEE THEM.
I'M DEFINITELY WEARING SHORTS EVERY DAY!

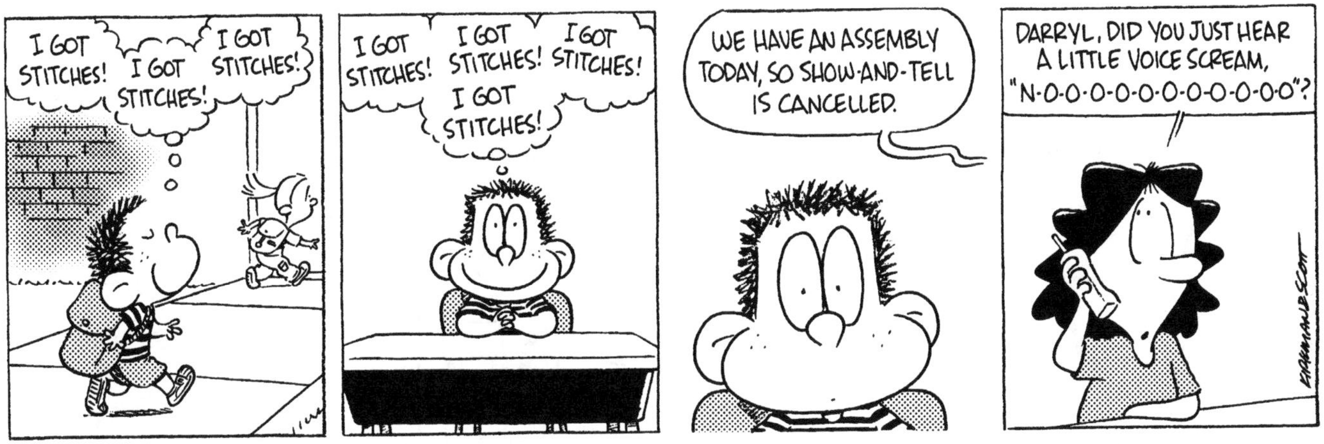
I GOT STITCHES!
I GOT STITCHES!
I GOT STITCHES!
I GOT STITCHES!
I GOT STITCHES!
I GOT STITCHES!
I GOT STITCHES!
WE HAVE AN ASSEMBLY TODAY, SO SHOW-AND-TELL IS CANCELLED.
DARRYL, DID YOU JUST HEAR A LITTLE VOICE SCREAM, "N-O-O-O-O-O-O-O-O-O-O-O"?

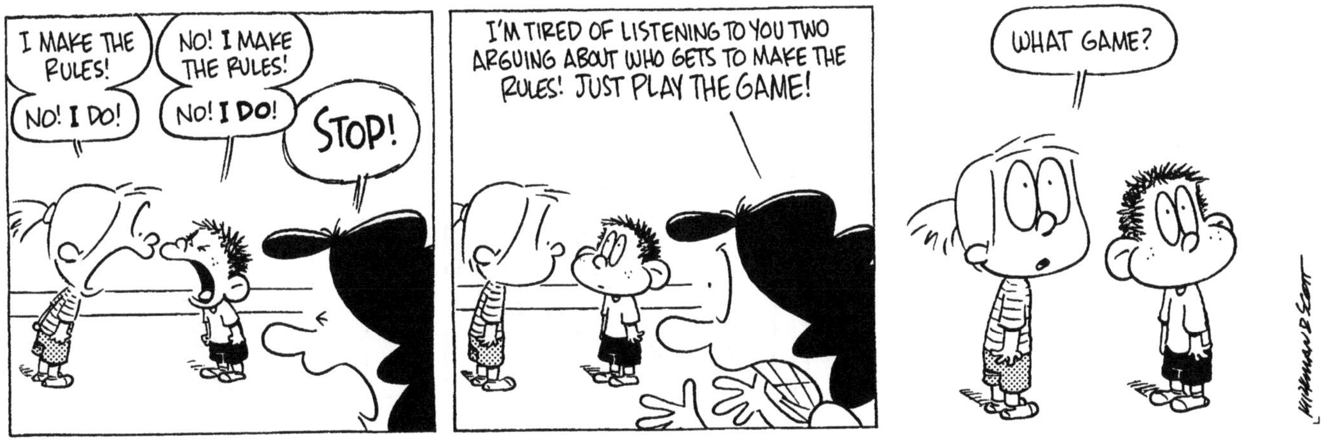
I MAKE THE RULES!
NO! I MAKE THE RULES!
NO! **I DO!**
NO! **I DO!**
STOP!
I'M TIRED OF LISTENING TO YOU TWO ARGUING ABOUT WHO GETS TO MAKE THE RULES! JUST PLAY THE GAME!
WHAT GAME?

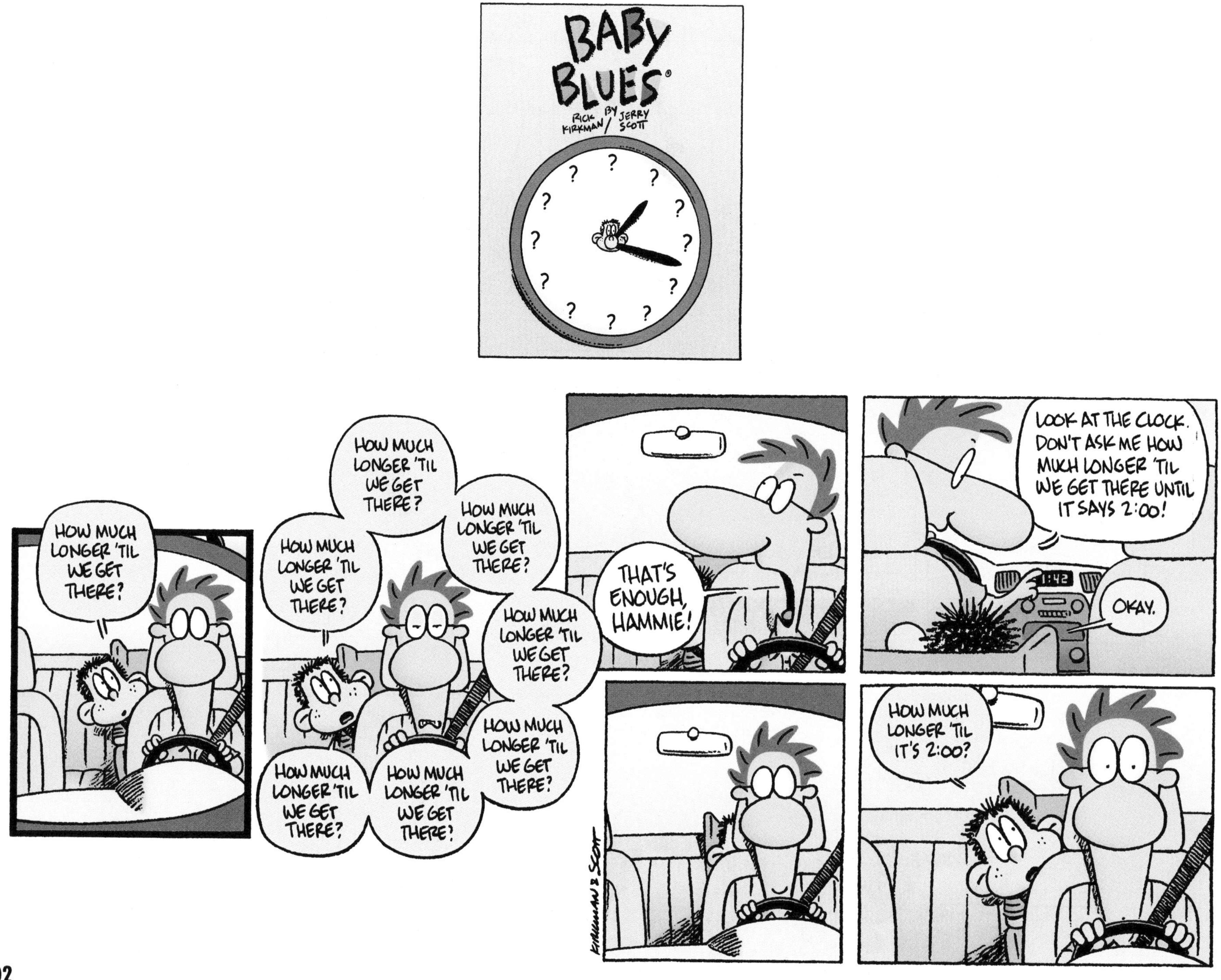
BABY BLUES®
BY RICK KIRKMAN / JERRY SCOTT
HOW MUCH LONGER 'TIL WE GET THERE?
HOW MUCH LONGER 'TIL WE GET THERE?
HOW MUCH LONGER 'TIL WE GET THERE?
HOW MUCH LONGER 'TIL WE GET THERE?
HOW MUCH LONGER 'TIL WE GET THERE?
HOW MUCH LONGER 'TIL WE GET THERE?
HOW MUCH LONGER 'TIL WE GET THERE?
HOW MUCH LONGER 'TIL WE GET THERE?
THAT'S ENOUGH, HAMMIE!
LOOK AT THE CLOCK. DON'T ASK ME HOW MUCH LONGER 'TIL WE GET THERE UNTIL IT SAYS 2:00!
1:42
OKAY.
HOW MUCH LONGER 'TIL IT'S 2:00?
KIRKMAN & SCOTT

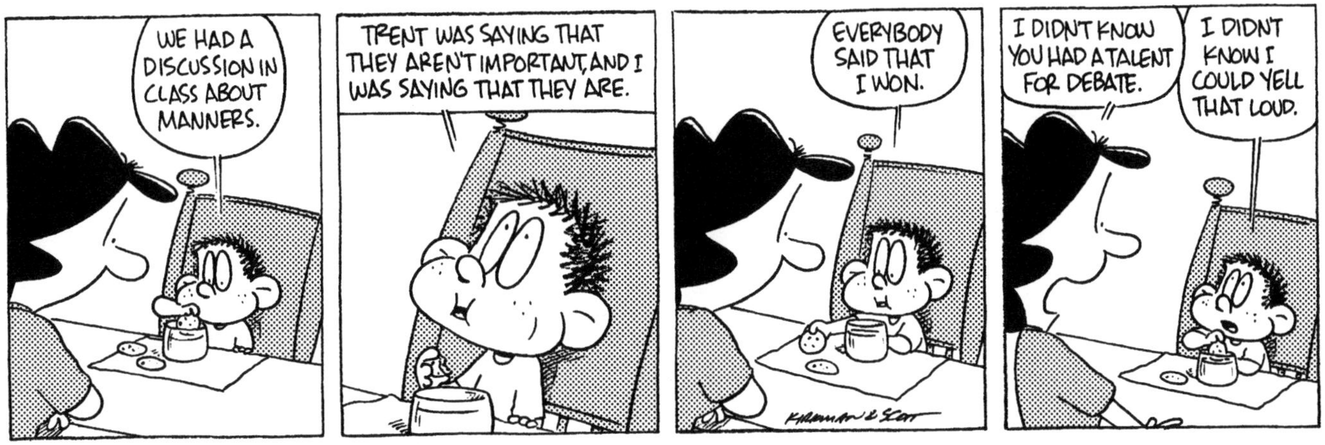
WE HAD A DISCUSSION IN CLASS ABOUT MANNERS.
TRENT WAS SAYING THAT THEY AREN'T IMPORTANT, AND I WAS SAYING THAT THEY ARE.
EVERYBODY SAID THAT I WON.
I DIDN'T KNOW YOU HAD A TALENT FOR DEBATE.
I DIDN'T KNOW I COULD YELL THAT LOUD.

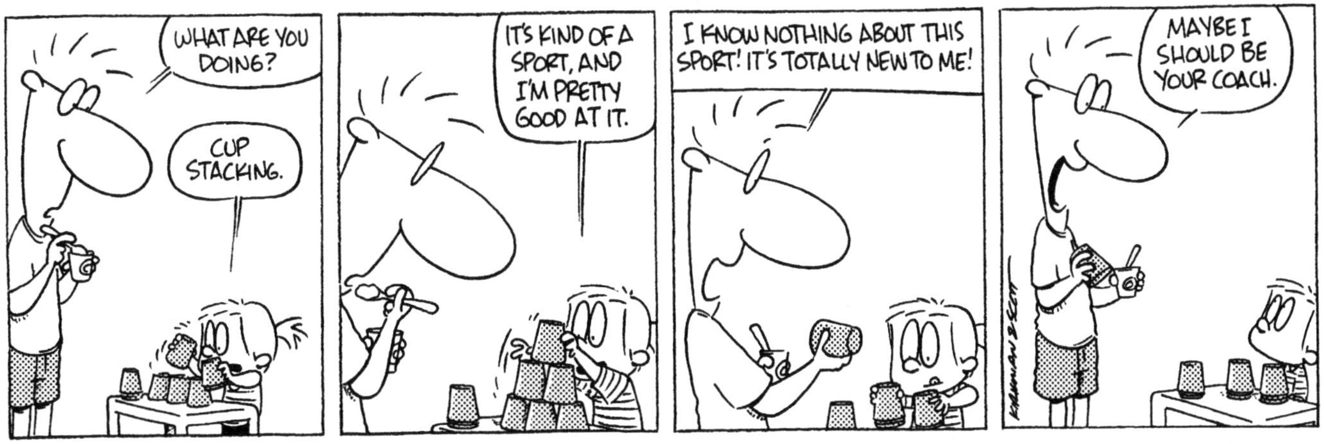
WHAT ARE YOU DOING?
CUP STACKING.
IT'S KIND OF A SPORT, AND I'M PRETTY GOOD AT IT.
I KNOW NOTHING ABOUT THIS SPORT! IT'S TOTALLY NEW TO ME!
MAYBE I SHOULD BE YOUR COACH.

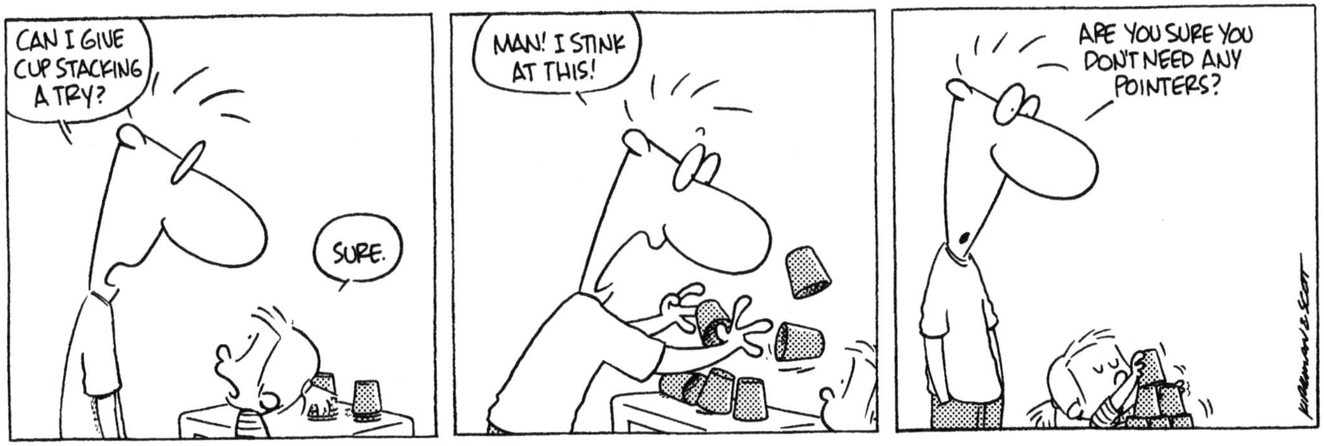
CAN I GIVE CUP STACKING A TRY?
SURE.
MAN! I STINK AT THIS!
ARE YOU SURE YOU DON'T NEED ANY POINTERS?

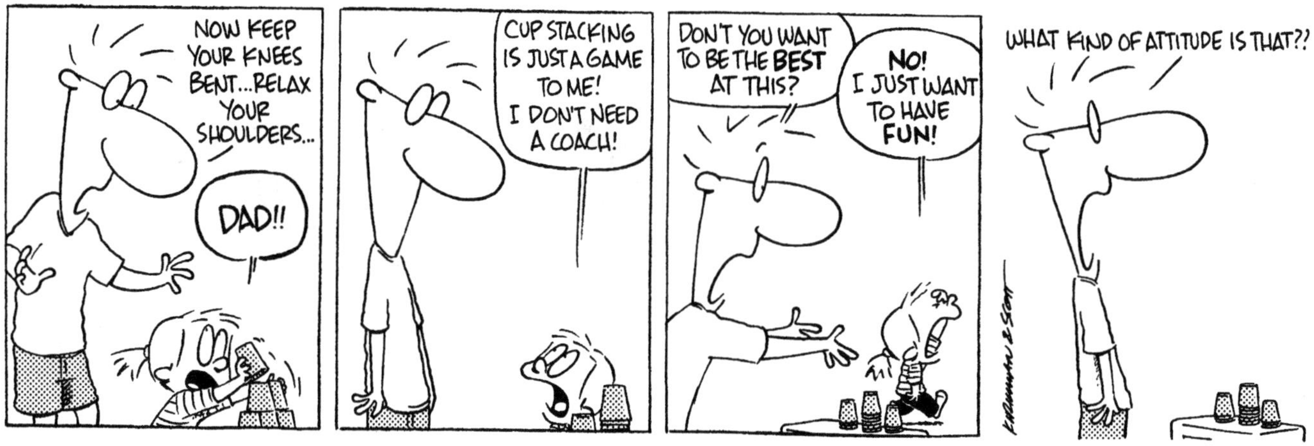
NOW KEEP YOUR KNEES BENT...RELAX YOUR SHOULDERS...
DAD!!
CUP STACKING IS JUST A GAME TO ME! I DON'T NEED A COACH!
DON'T YOU WANT TO BE THE **BEST** AT THIS?
NO! I JUST WANT TO HAVE **FUN!**
WHAT KIND OF ATTITUDE IS THAT??

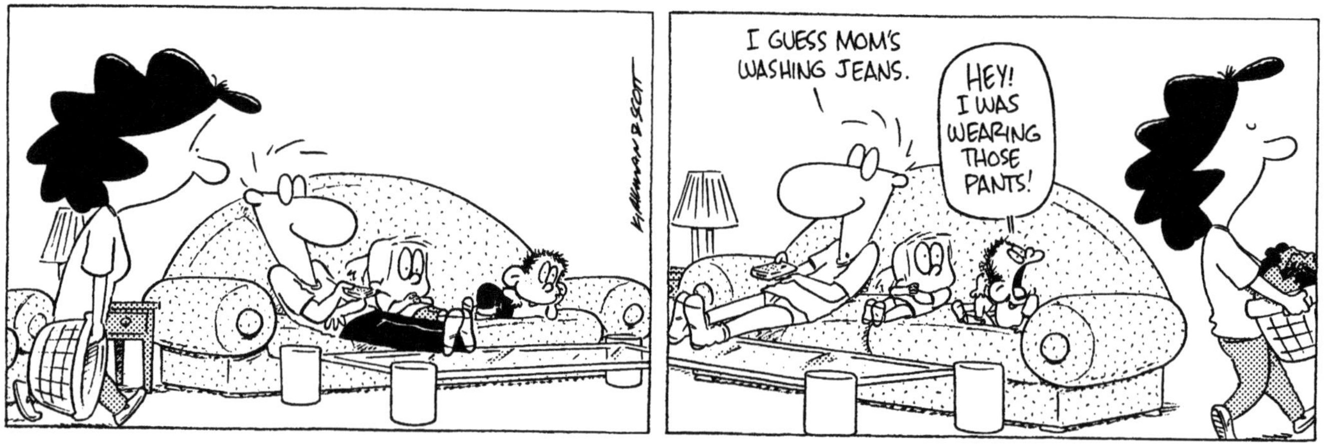
I GUESS MOM'S WASHING JEANS.
HEY! I WAS WEARING THOSE PANTS!

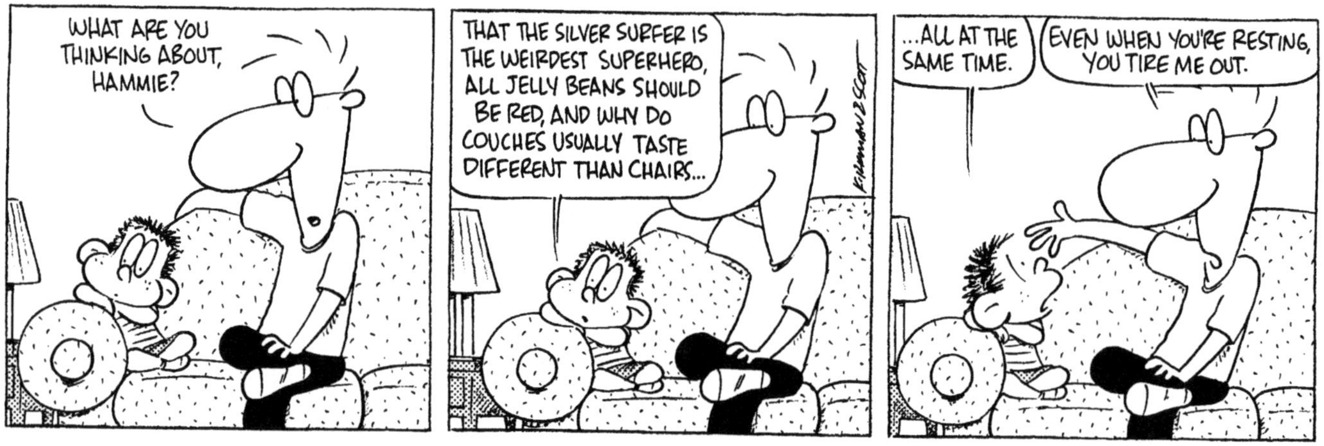
WHAT ARE YOU THINKING ABOUT, HAMMIE?
THAT THE SILVER SURFER IS THE WEIRDEST SUPERHERO, ALL JELLY BEANS SHOULD BE RED, AND WHY DO COUCHES USUALLY TASTE DIFFERENT THAN CHAIRS...
...ALL AT THE SAME TIME.
EVEN WHEN YOU'RE RESTING, YOU TIRE ME OUT.

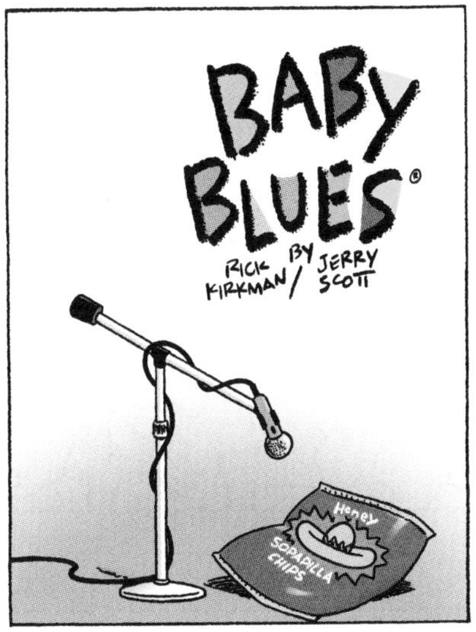
BABY BLUES®
BY RICK KIRKMAN / JERRY SCOTT
Honey
SOPAPILLA CHIPS

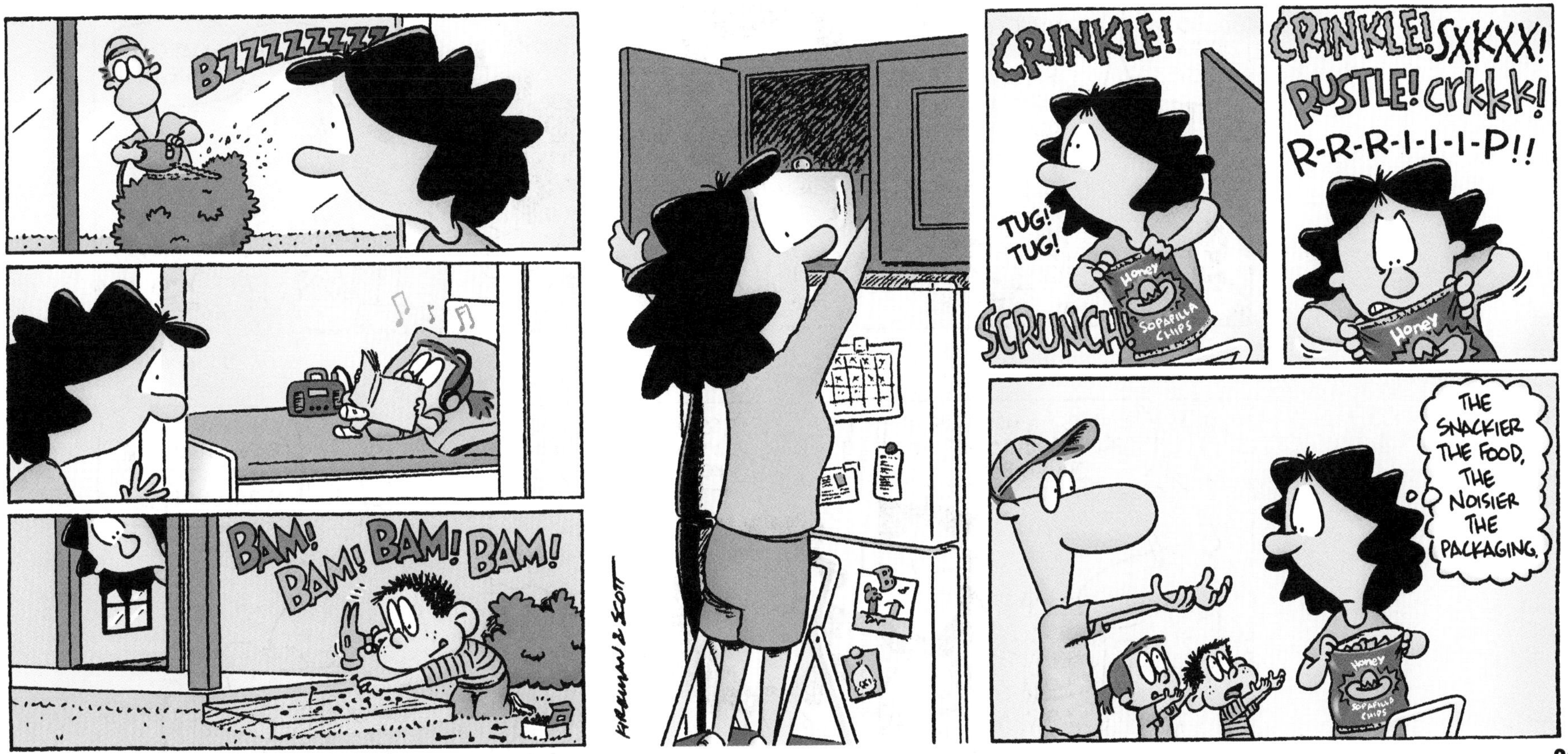
BZZZZZZZZZ
BAM! BAM! BAM! BAM!
KIRKMAN & SCOTT
CRINKLE!
TUG! TUG!
SCRUNCH!
Honey
SOPAPILLA CHIPS
CRINKLE! SXKXX!
RUSTLE! CRKKK!
R-R-R-I-I-I-P!!
Honey
THE SNACKIER THE FOOD, THE NOISIER THE PACKAGING.
Honey
SOPAPILLA CHIPS

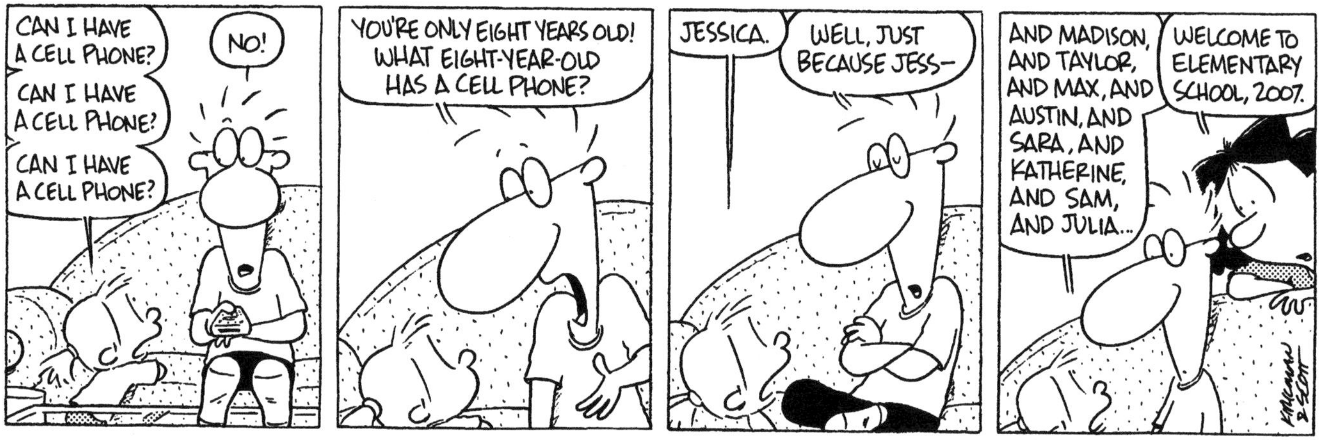
CAN I HAVE A CELL PHONE?
CAN I HAVE A CELL PHONE?
CAN I HAVE A CELL PHONE?
NO!
YOU'RE ONLY EIGHT YEARS OLD! WHAT EIGHT-YEAR-OLD HAS A CELL PHONE?
JESSICA.
WELL, JUST BECAUSE JESS—
AND MADISON, AND TAYLOR, AND MAX, AND AUSTIN, AND SARA, AND KATHERINE, AND SAM, AND JULIA...
WELCOME TO ELEMENTARY SCHOOL, 2007.

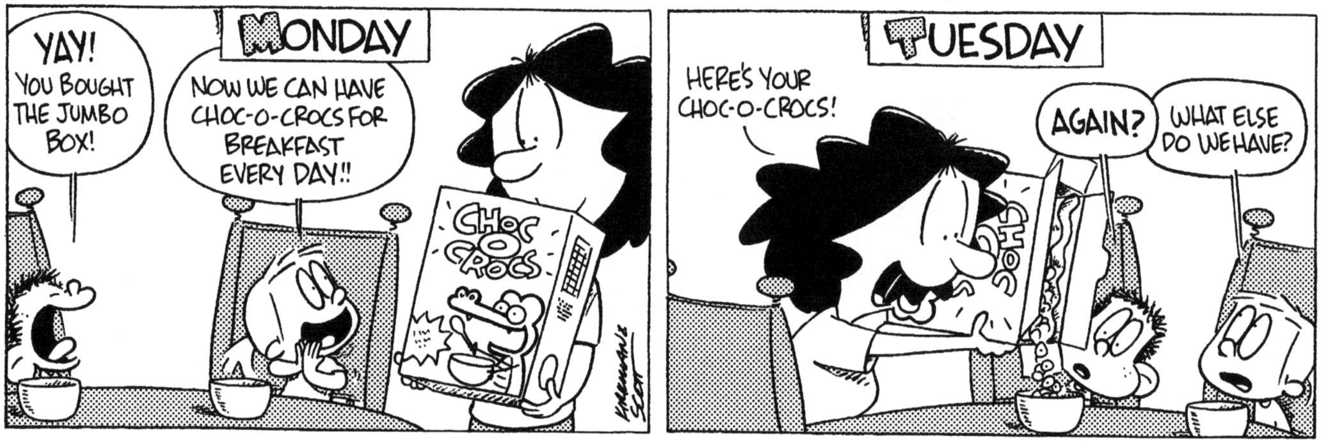
MONDAY
YAY! YOU BOUGHT THE JUMBO BOX!
NOW WE CAN HAVE CHOC-O-CROCS FOR BREAKFAST EVERY DAY!!
CHOC O CROCS
TUESDAY
HERE'S YOUR CHOC-O-CROCS!
AGAIN?
WHAT ELSE DO WE HAVE?

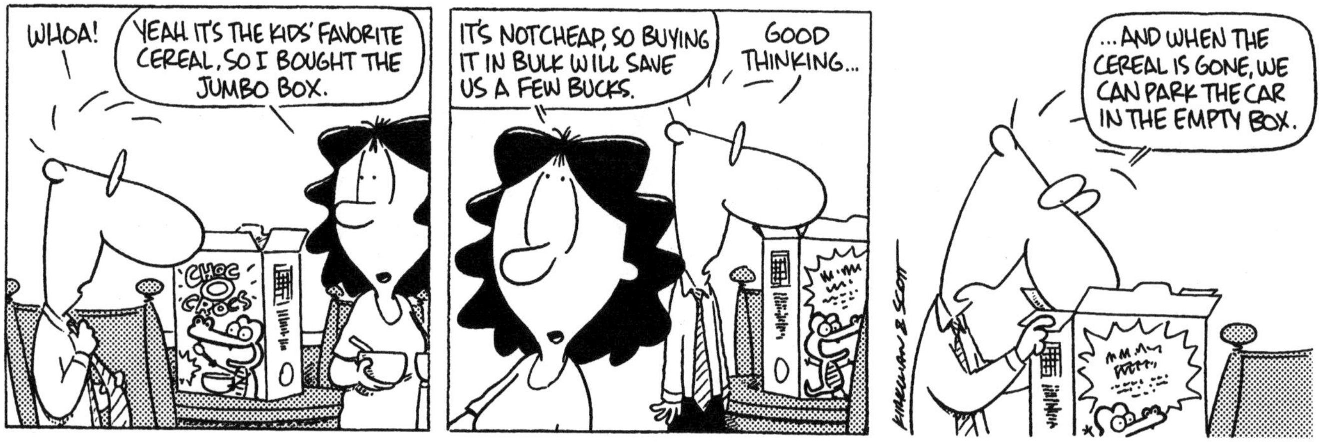
WHOA!
YEAH. IT'S THE KIDS' FAVORITE CEREAL, SO I BOUGHT THE JUMBO BOX.
CHOC O CROCS
IT'S NOT CHEAP, SO BUYING IT IN BULK WILL SAVE US A FEW BUCKS.
GOOD THINKING...
...AND WHEN THE CEREAL IS GONE, WE CAN PARK THE CAR IN THE EMPTY BOX.

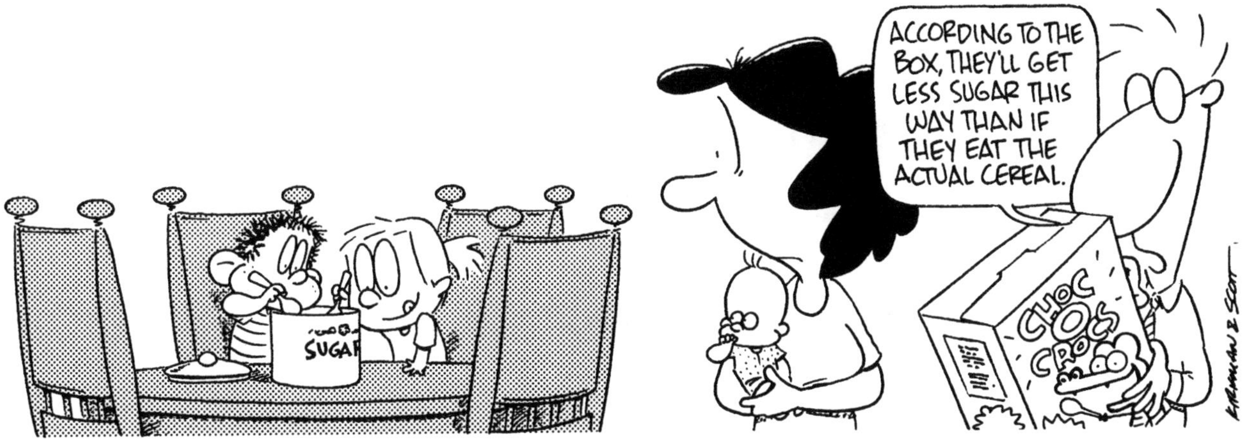
ACCORDING TO THE BOX, THEY'LL GET LESS SUGAR THIS WAY THAN IF THEY EAT THE ACTUAL CEREAL.

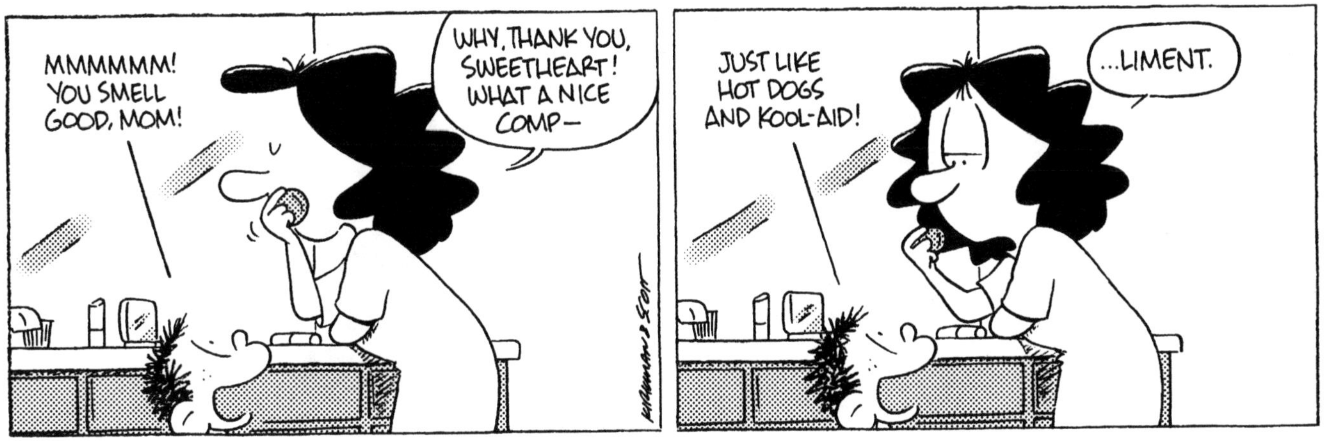
MMMMMM! YOU SMELL GOOD, MOM!
WHY, THANK YOU, SWEETHEART! WHAT A NICE COMP–
JUST LIKE HOT DOGS AND KOOL-AID!
...LIMENT.

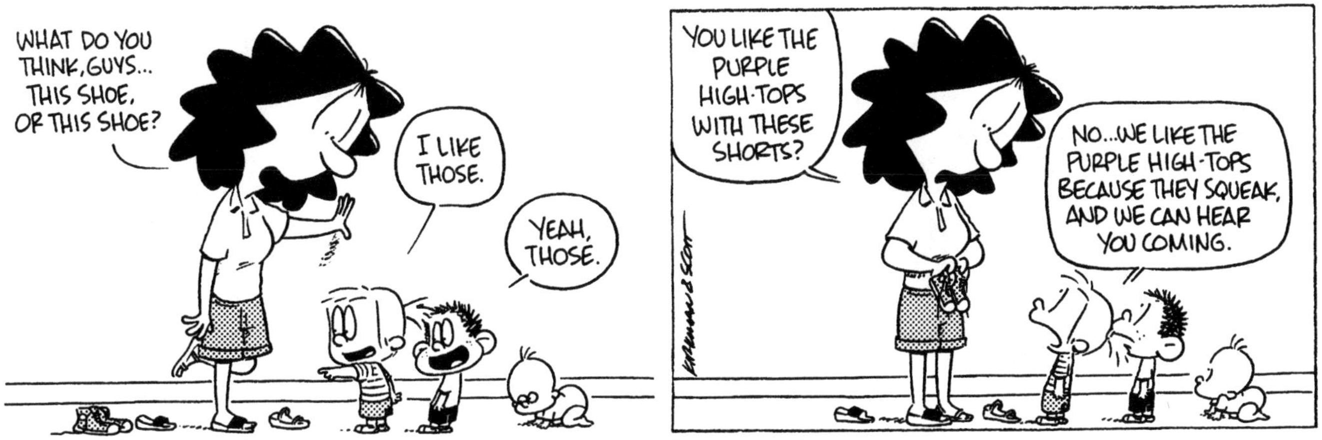
WHAT DO YOU THINK, GUYS... THIS SHOE, OR THIS SHOE?
I LIKE THOSE.
YEAH, THOSE.
YOU LIKE THE PURPLE HIGH-TOPS WITH THESE SHORTS?
NO...WE LIKE THE PURPLE HIGH-TOPS BECAUSE THEY SQUEAK, AND WE CAN HEAR YOU COMING.

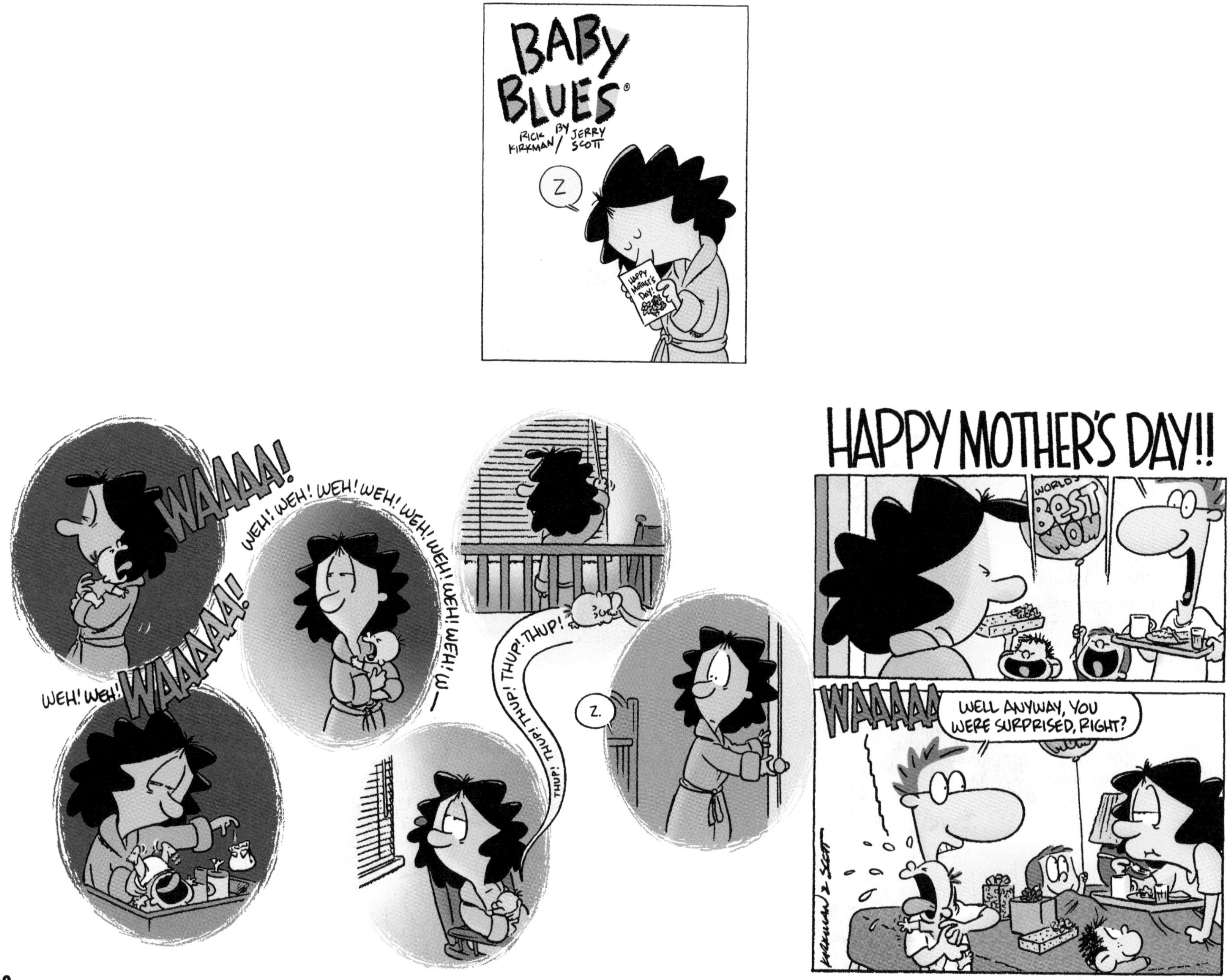

BABY BLUES®
RICK KIRKMAN / BY JERRY SCOTT
Z
HAPPY MOTHER'S DAY!
WAAAAA!
WAAAAAA!
WEH! WEH! WAAAAA
WEH! WEH! WEH! WEH! WEH! WEH! WEH! WEH! WEH! W—
THUP! THUP! THUP! THUP! THUP! THUP!
Z.
HAPPY MOTHER'S DAY!!
WORLD'S BEST MOM
WAAAAA
WELL ANYWAY, YOU WERE SURPRISED, RIGHT?

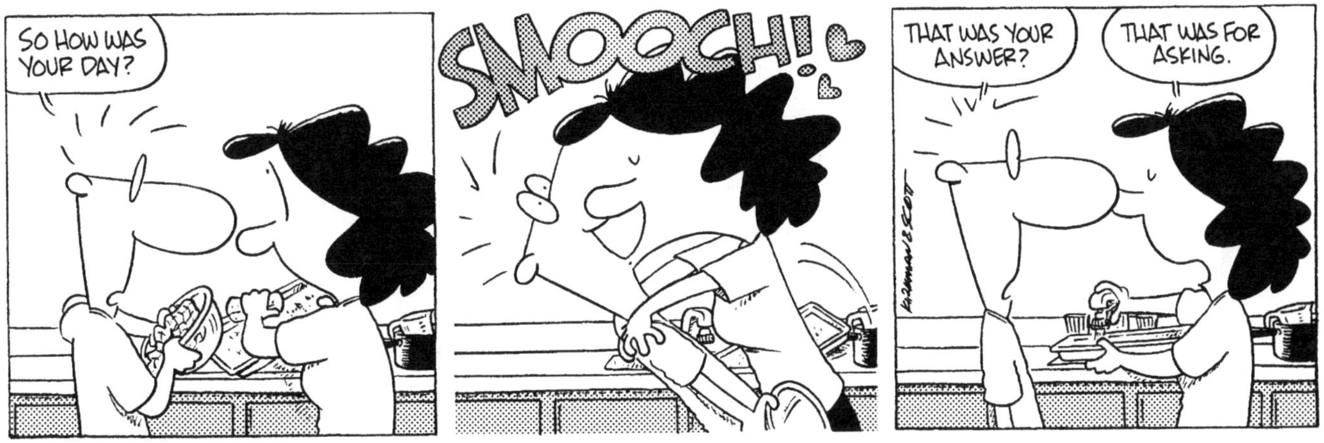
SO HOW WAS YOUR DAY?
SMOOCH!
THAT WAS YOUR ANSWER?
THAT WAS FOR ASKING.
KIRKMAN & SCOTT

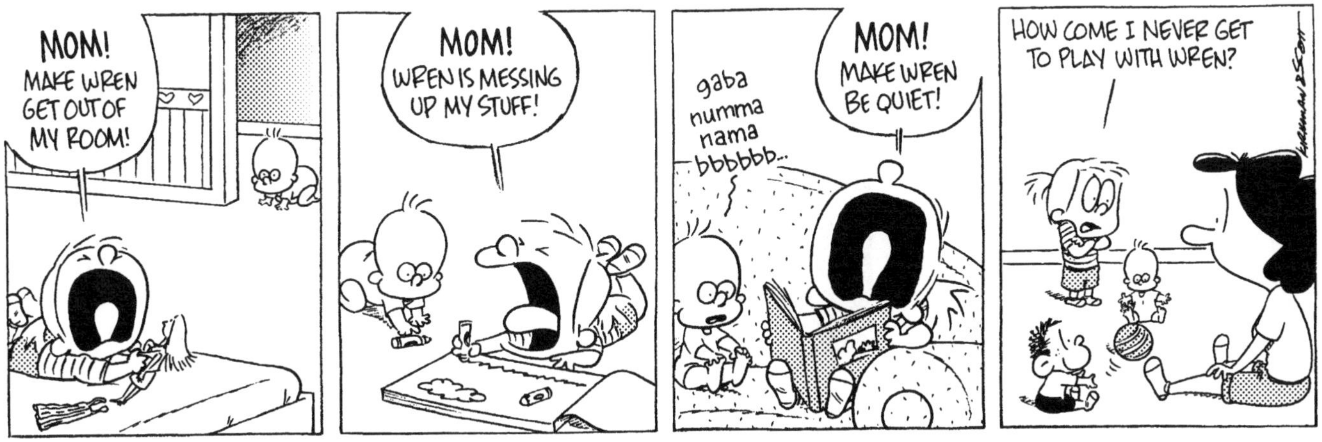
MOM! MAKE WREN GET OUT OF MY ROOM!
MOM! WREN IS MESSING UP MY STUFF!
gaba numma nama bbbbbb..
MOM! MAKE WREN BE QUIET!
HOW COME I NEVER GET TO PLAY WITH WREN?
KIRKMAN & SCOTT

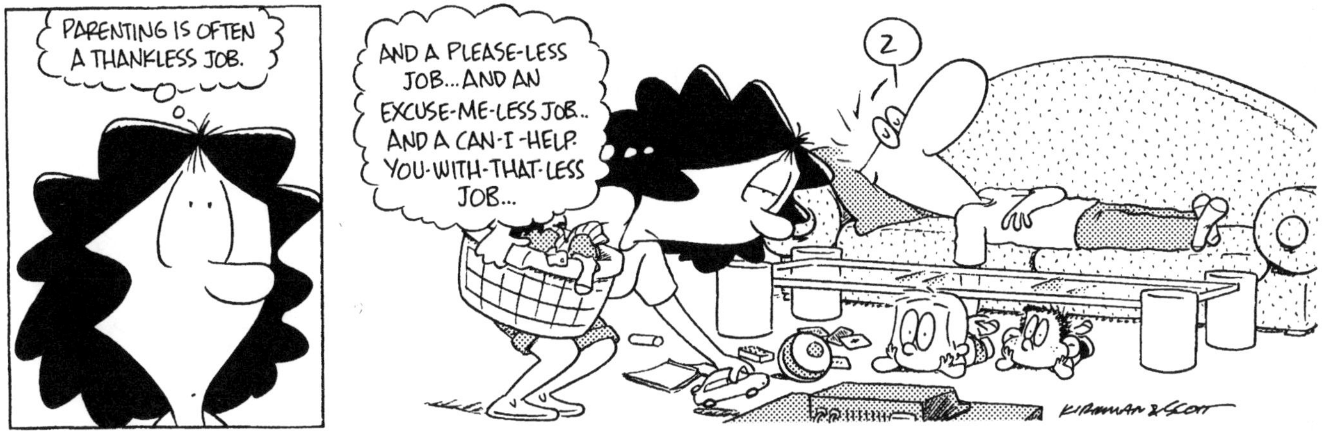
PARENTING IS OFTEN A THANKLESS JOB.
AND A PLEASE-LESS JOB...AND AN EXCUSE-ME-LESS JOB.. AND A CAN-I-HELP-YOU-WITH-THAT-LESS JOB...
Z
KIRKMAN & SCOTT

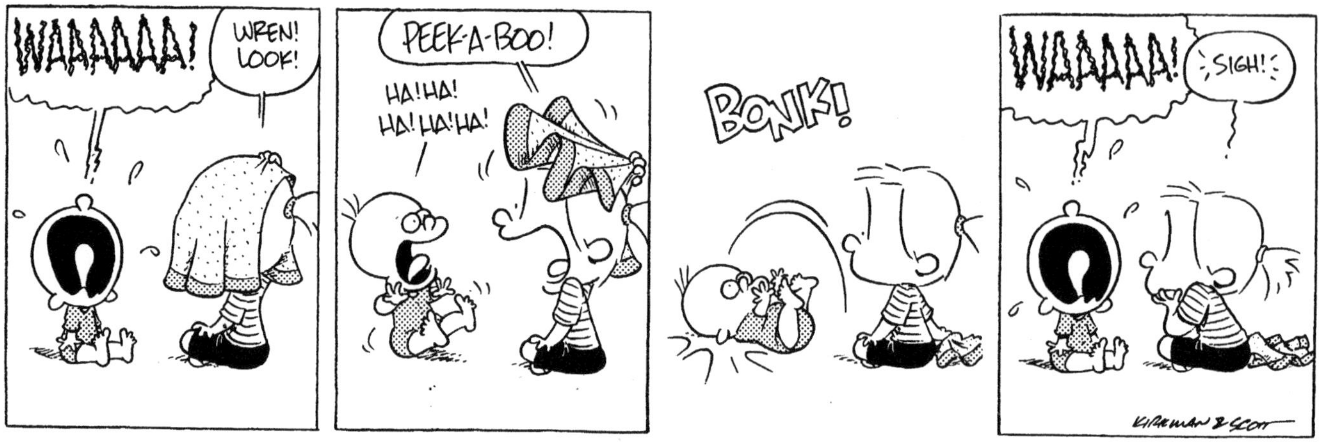
WAAAAAA!
WREN! LOOK!
PEEK-A-BOO!
HA! HA! HA! HA! HA!
BONK!
WAAAAAA!
SIGH!
KIRKMAN & SCOTT

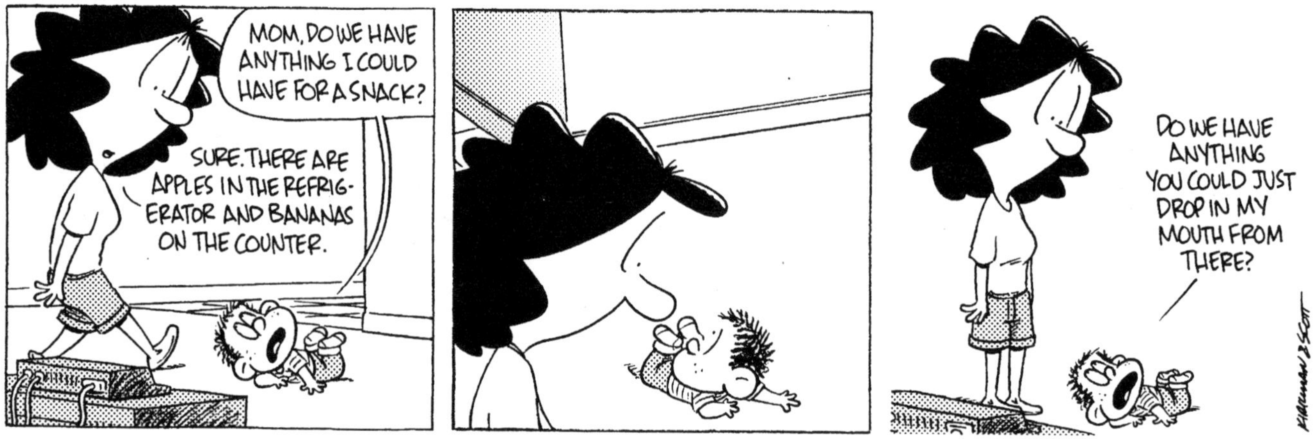
MOM, DO WE HAVE ANYTHING I COULD HAVE FOR A SNACK?
SURE. THERE ARE APPLES IN THE REFRIG-ERATOR AND BANANAS ON THE COUNTER.
DO WE HAVE ANYTHING YOU COULD JUST DROP IN MY MOUTH FROM THERE?
KIRKMAN & SCOTT

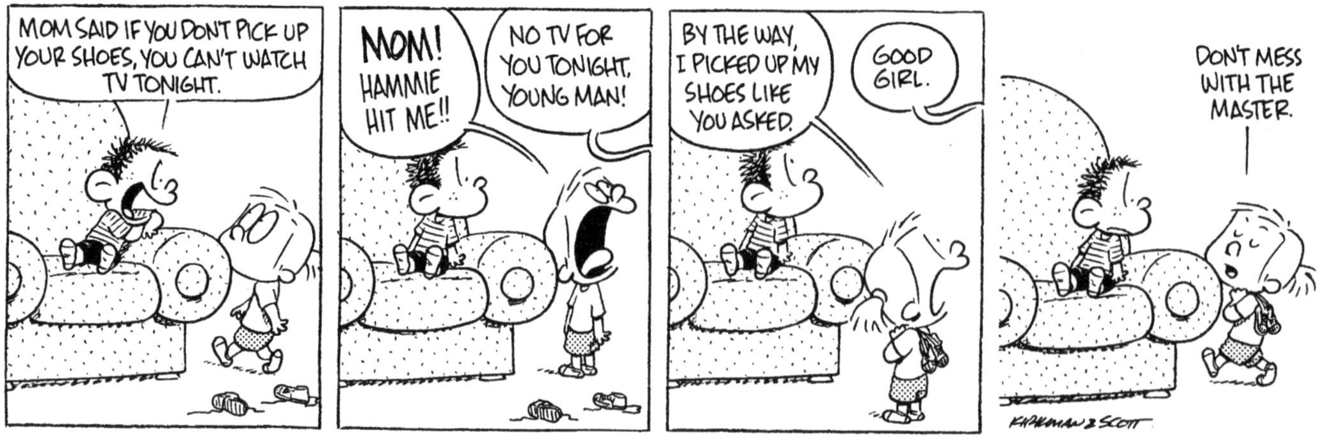
MOM SAID IF YOU DON'T PICK UP YOUR SHOES, YOU CAN'T WATCH TV TONIGHT.
MOM! HAMMIE HIT ME!!
NO TV FOR YOU TONIGHT, YOUNG MAN!
BY THE WAY, I PICKED UP MY SHOES LIKE YOU ASKED.
GOOD GIRL.
DON'T MESS WITH THE MASTER.
KIRKMAN & SCOTT

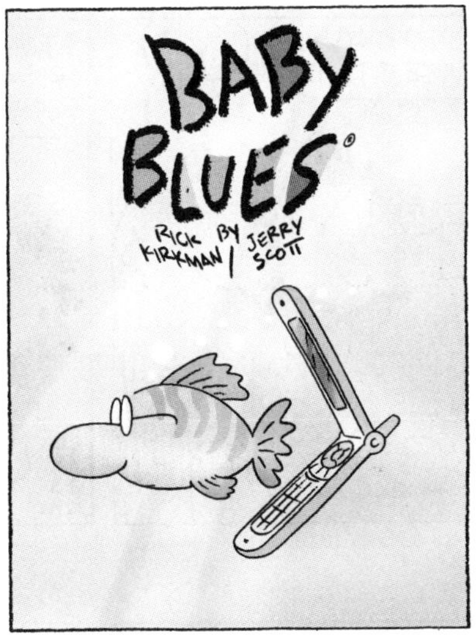
BABY BLUES®
RICK KIRKMAN / BY JERRY SCOTT

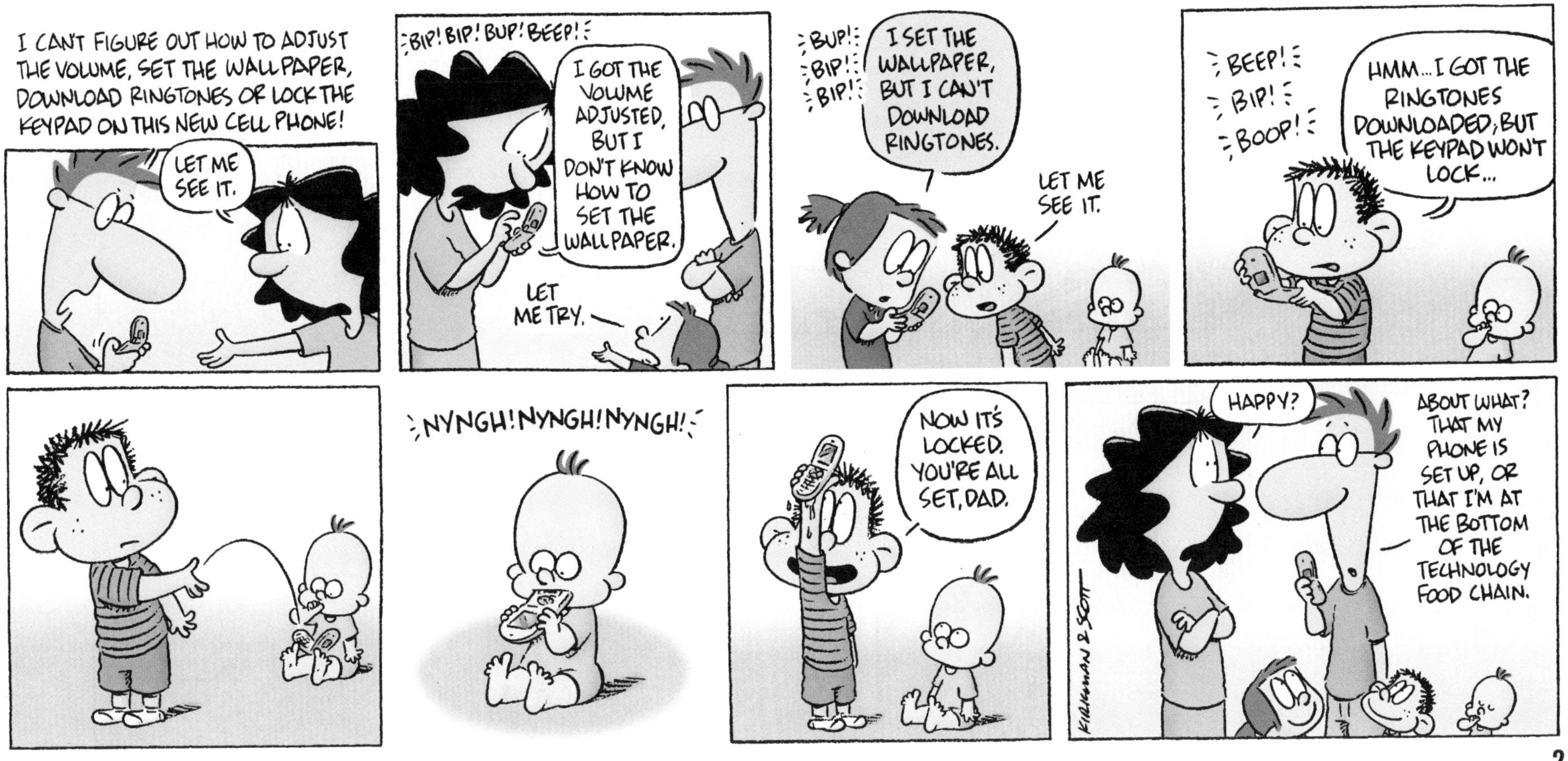
I CAN'T FIGURE OUT HOW TO ADJUST THE VOLUME, SET THE WALLPAPER, DOWNLOAD RINGTONES OR LOCK THE KEYPAD ON THIS NEW CELL PHONE!
LET ME SEE IT.
BIP! BIP! BUP! BEEP!
I GOT THE VOLUME ADJUSTED, BUT I DON'T KNOW HOW TO SET THE WALLPAPER.
LET ME TRY.
BUP! BIP! BIP!
I SET THE WALLPAPER, BUT I CAN'T DOWNLOAD RINGTONES.
LET ME SEE IT.
BEEP! BIP! BOOP!
HMM... I GOT THE RINGTONES DOWNLOADED, BUT THE KEYPAD WON'T LOCK...
NYNGH! NYNGH! NYNGH!
NOW IT'S LOCKED. YOU'RE ALL SET, DAD.
KIRKMAN & SCOTT
HAPPY?
ABOUT WHAT? THAT MY PHONE IS SET UP, OR THAT I'M AT THE BOTTOM OF THE TECHNOLOGY FOOD CHAIN.

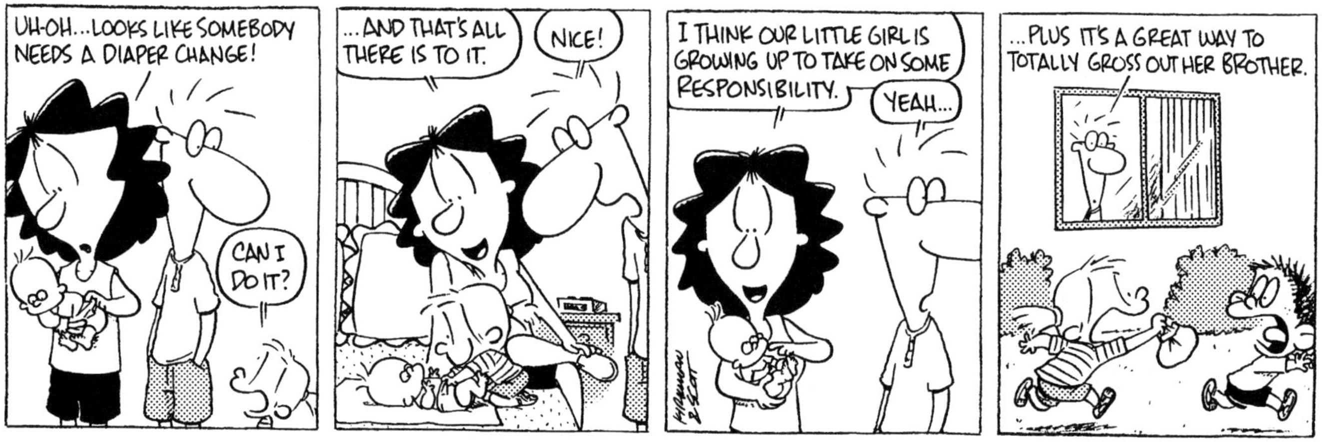
UH-OH... LOOKS LIKE SOMEBODY NEEDS A DIAPER CHANGE!
CAN I DO IT?
...AND THAT'S ALL THERE IS TO IT.
NICE!
I THINK OUR LITTLE GIRL IS GROWING UP TO TAKE ON SOME RESPONSIBILITY.
YEAH...
...PLUS IT'S A GREAT WAY TO TOTALLY GROSS OUT HER BROTHER.

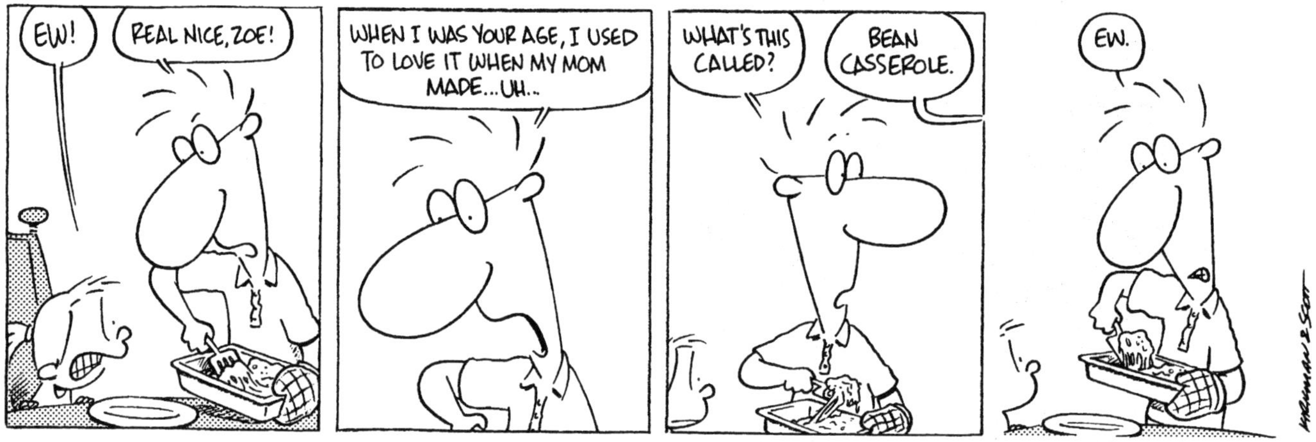
EW!
REAL NICE, ZOE!
WHEN I WAS YOUR AGE, I USED TO LOVE IT WHEN MY MOM MADE... UH...
WHAT'S THIS CALLED?
BEAN CASSEROLE.
EW.

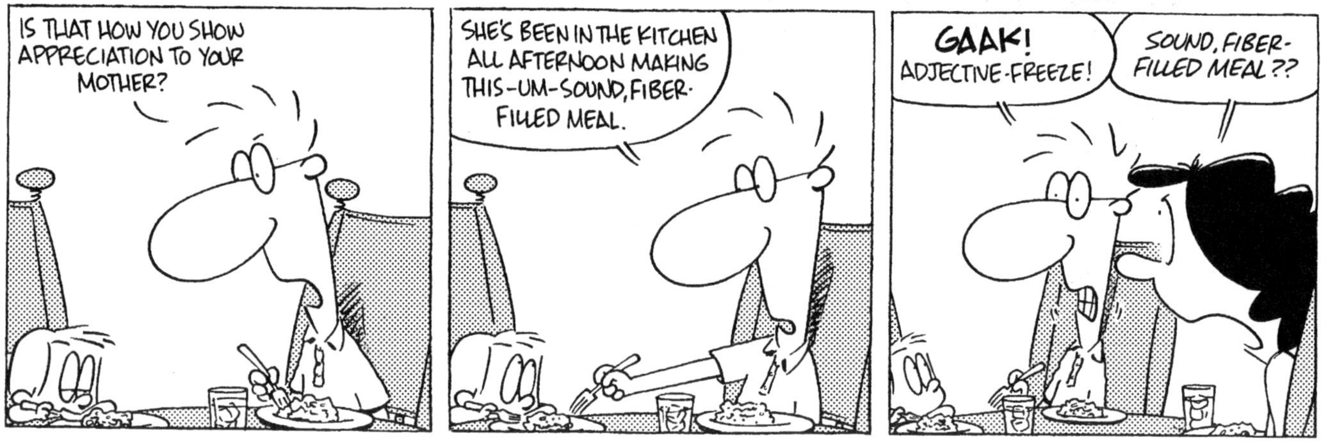
IS THAT HOW YOU SHOW APPRECIATION TO YOUR MOTHER?
SHE'S BEEN IN THE KITCHEN ALL AFTERNOON MAKING THIS-UM-SOUND, FIBER-FILLED MEAL.
GAAK! ADJECTIVE-FREEZE!
SOUND, FIBER-FILLED MEAL??

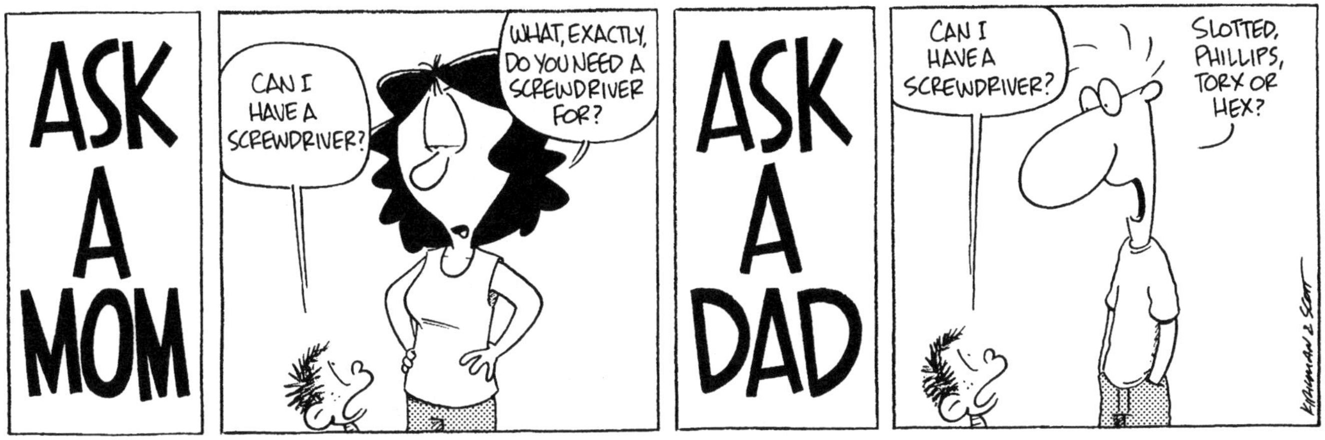
ASK A MOM
CAN I HAVE A SCREWDRIVER?
WHAT, EXACTLY, DO YOU NEED A SCREWDRIVER FOR?
ASK A DAD
CAN I HAVE A SCREWDRIVER?
SLOTTED, PHILLIPS, TORX OR HEX?
KIRKMAN & SCOTT

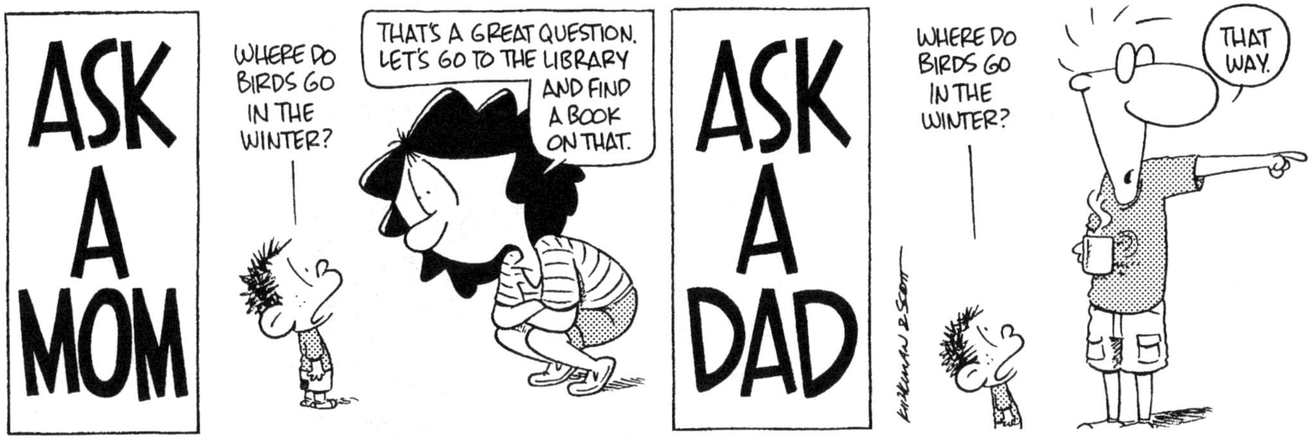
ASK A MOM
WHERE DO BIRDS GO IN THE WINTER?
THAT'S A GREAT QUESTION. LET'S GO TO THE LIBRARY AND FIND A BOOK ON THAT.
KIRKMAN & SCOTT
ASK A DAD
WHERE DO BIRDS GO IN THE WINTER?
THAT WAY.

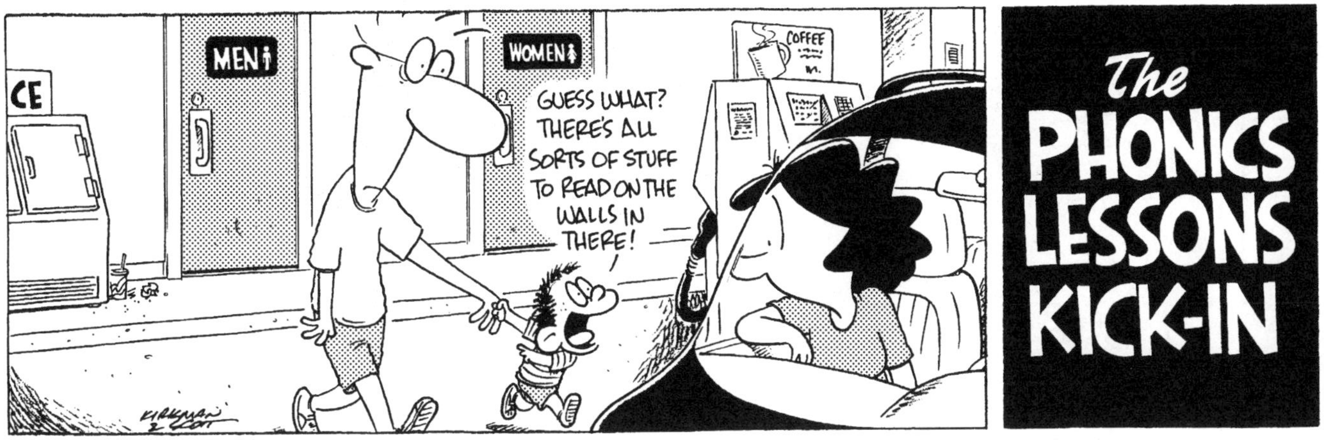
CE
MEN
WOMEN
COFFEE
GUESS WHAT? THERE'S ALL SORTS OF STUFF TO READ ON THE WALLS IN THERE!
KIRKMAN & SCOTT
The PHONICS LESSONS KICK-IN

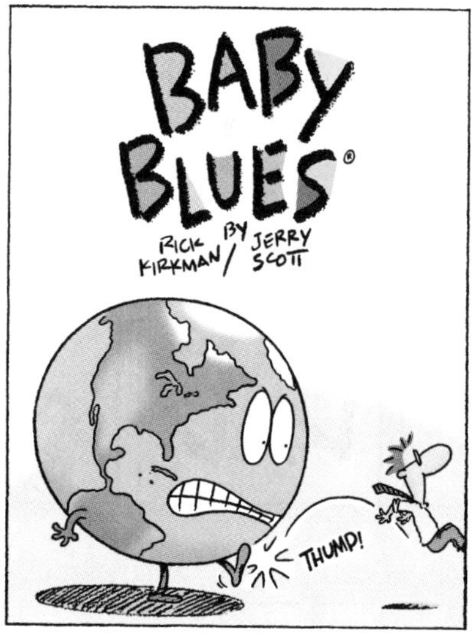
BABY BLUES®
BY RICK KIRKMAN / JERRY SCOTT
THUMP!

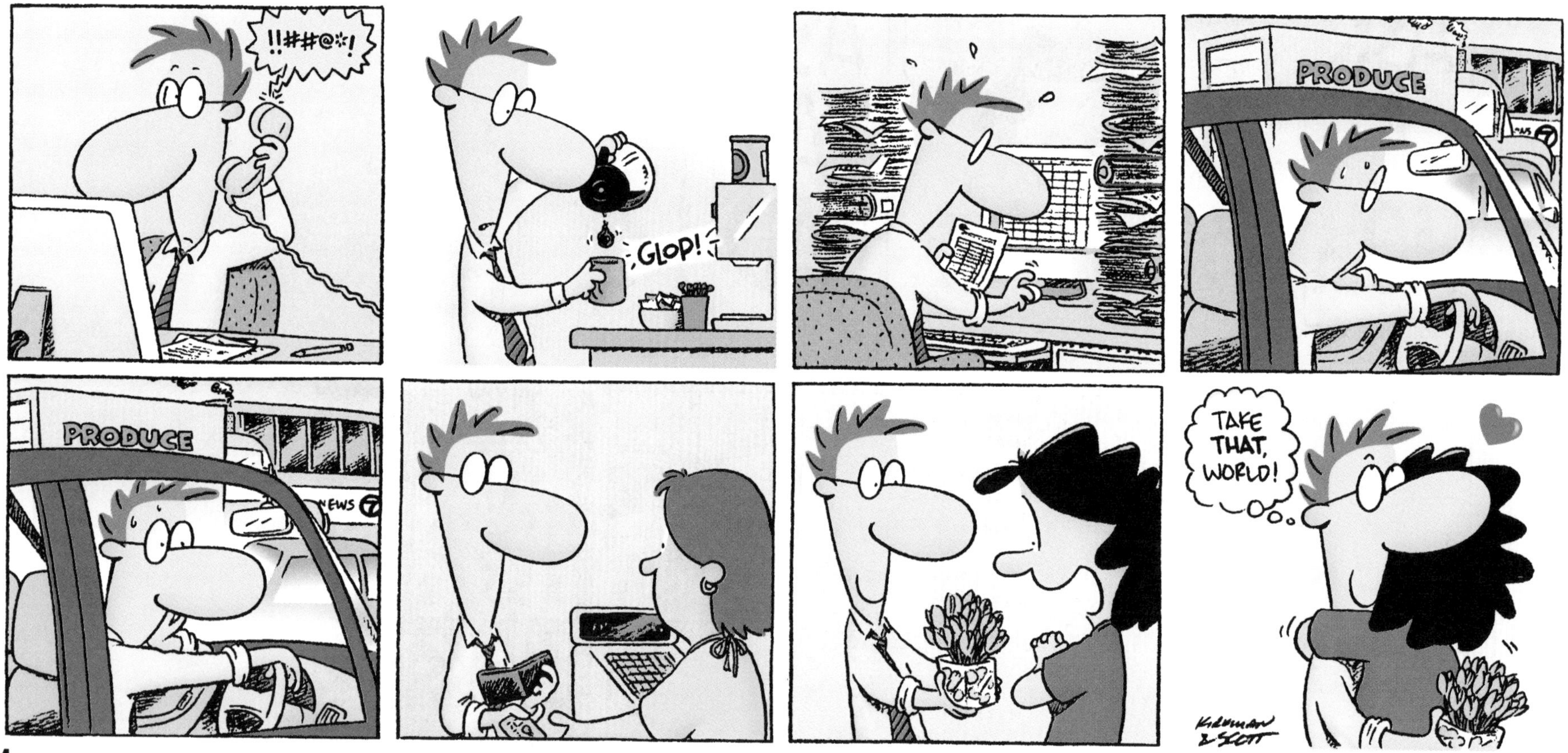
!!##@*!
GLOP!
PRODUCE
PRODUCE
NEWS 7
TAKE THAT, WORLD!
KIRKMAN & SCOTT

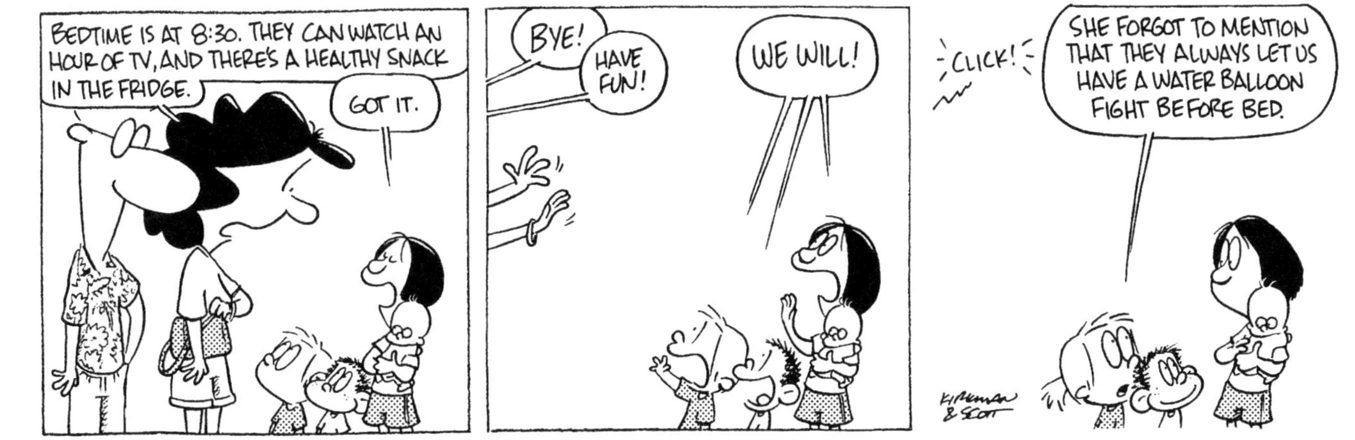
BEDTIME IS AT 8:30. THEY CAN WATCH AN HOUR OF TV, AND THERE'S A HEALTHY SNACK IN THE FRIDGE.
GOT IT.
BYE!
HAVE FUN!
WE WILL!
CLICK!
SHE FORGOT TO MENTION THAT THEY ALWAYS LET US HAVE A WATER BALLOON FIGHT BEFORE BED.
KIRKMAN & SCOTT

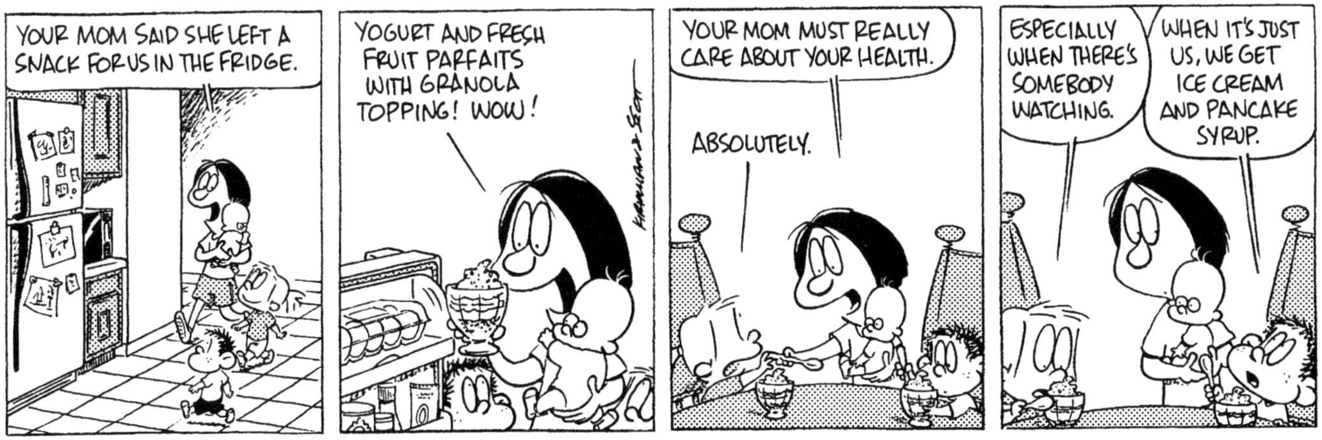
YOUR MOM SAID SHE LEFT A SNACK FOR US IN THE FRIDGE.
YOGURT AND FRESH FRUIT PARFAITS WITH GRANOLA TOPPING! WOW!
KIRKMAN & SCOTT
YOUR MOM MUST REALLY CARE ABOUT YOUR HEALTH.
ABSOLUTELY.
ESPECIALLY WHEN THERE'S SOMEBODY WATCHING.
WHEN IT'S JUST US, WE GET ICE CREAM AND PANCAKE SYRUP.

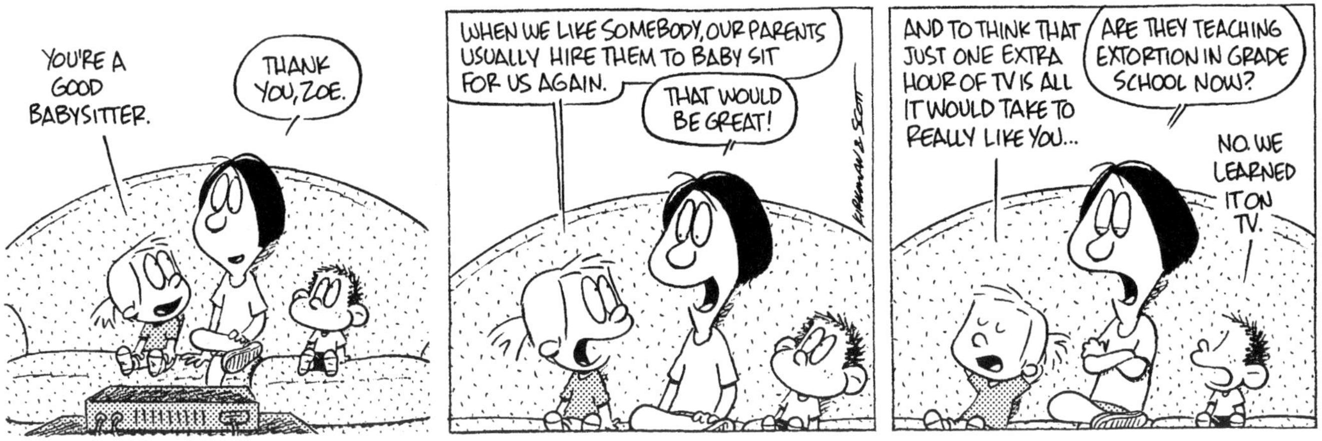
YOU'RE A GOOD BABYSITTER.
THANK YOU, ZOE.
WHEN WE LIKE SOMEBODY, OUR PARENTS USUALLY HIRE THEM TO BABY SIT FOR US AGAIN.
THAT WOULD BE GREAT!
KIRKMAN & SCOTT
AND TO THINK THAT JUST ONE EXTRA HOUR OF TV IS ALL IT WOULD TAKE TO REALLY LIKE YOU...
ARE THEY TEACHING EXTORTION IN GRADE SCHOOL NOW?
NO. WE LEARNED IT ON TV.

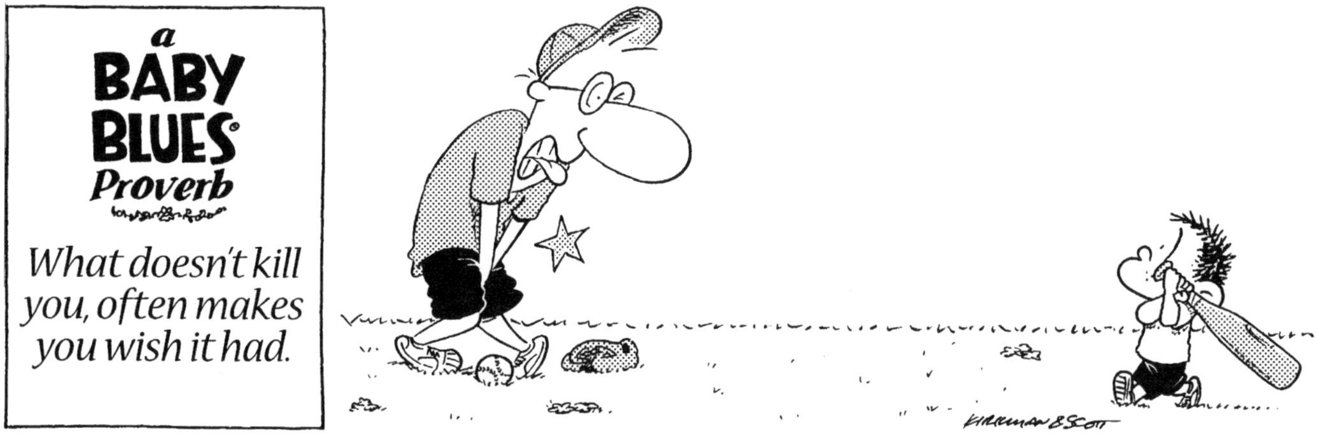
a BABY BLUES® Proverb
What doesn't kill you, often makes you wish it had.
KIRKMAN & SCOTT

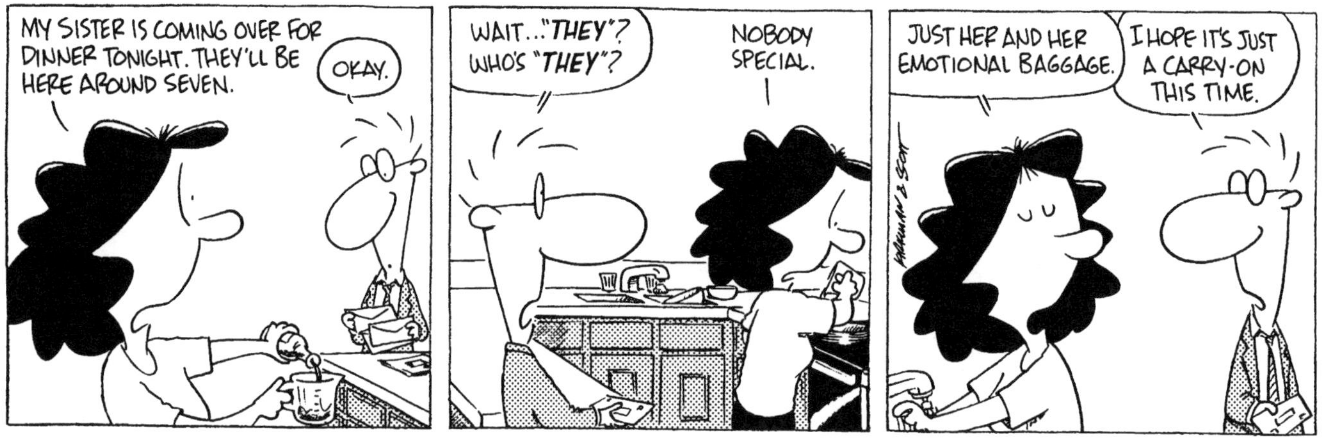
MY SISTER IS COMING OVER FOR DINNER TONIGHT. THEY'LL BE HERE AROUND SEVEN.
OKAY.
WAIT..."THEY"? WHO'S "THEY"?
NOBODY SPECIAL.
JUST HER AND HER EMOTIONAL BAGGAGE.
I HOPE IT'S JUST A CARRY-ON THIS TIME.
KIRKMAN & SCOTT

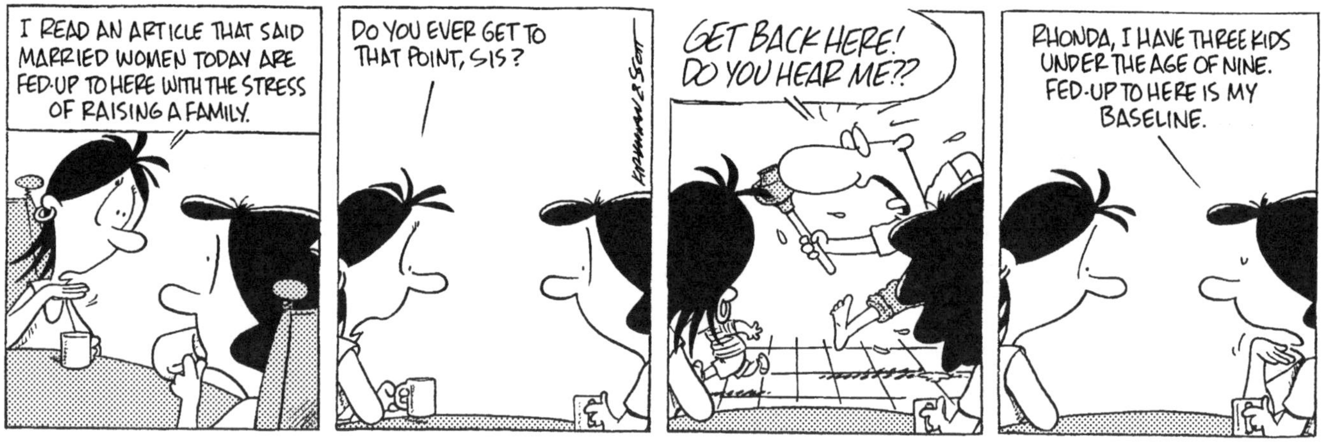
I READ AN ARTICLE THAT SAID MARRIED WOMEN TODAY ARE FED-UP TO HERE WITH THE STRESS OF RAISING A FAMILY.
DO YOU EVER GET TO THAT POINT, SIS?
KIRKMAN & SCOTT
GET BACK HERE! DO YOU HEAR ME??
RHONDA, I HAVE THREE KIDS UNDER THE AGE OF NINE. FED-UP TO HERE IS MY BASELINE.

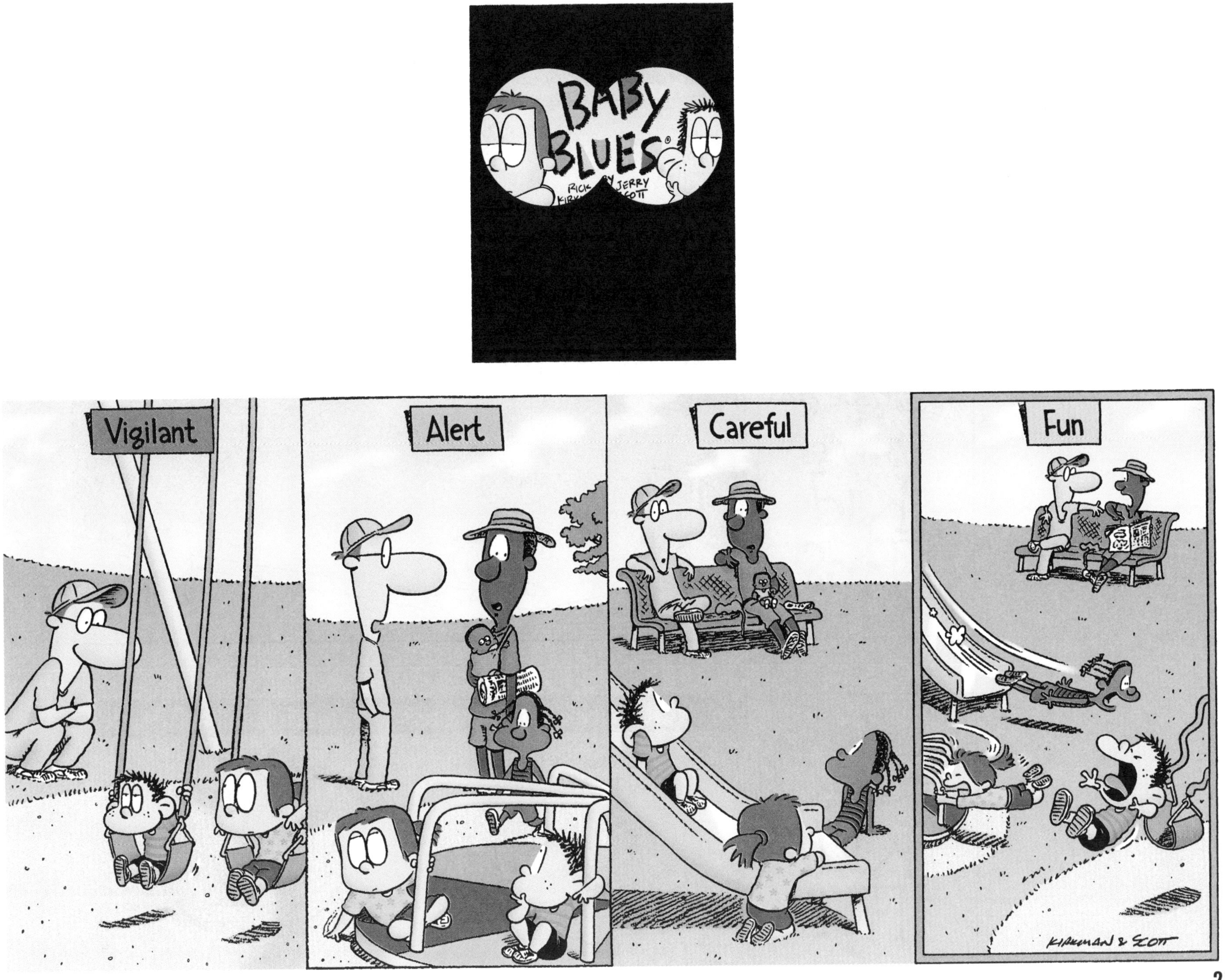
BABY BLUES®
Vigilant
Alert
Careful
Fun
KIRKMAN & SCOTT

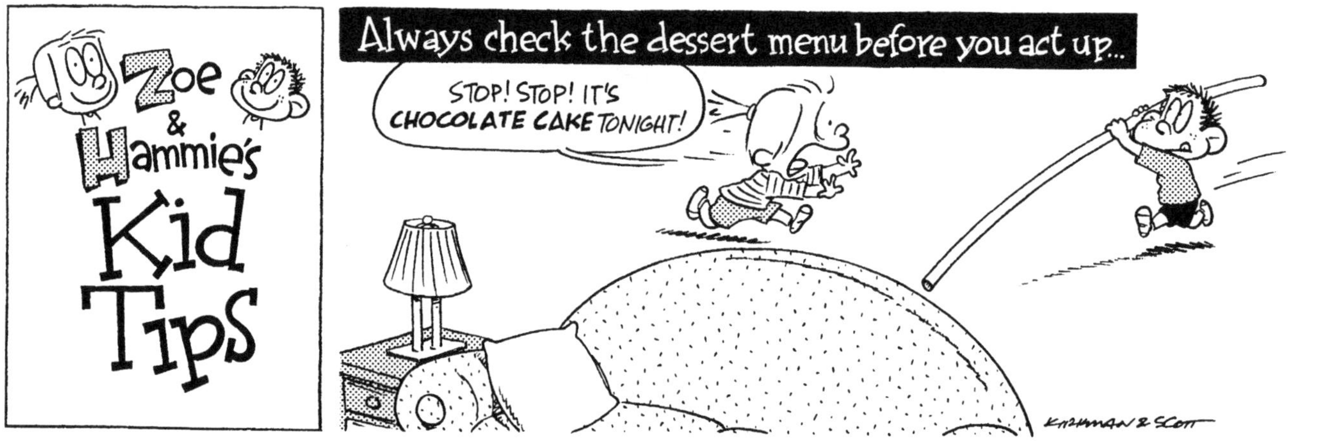
Zoe & Hammie's Kid Tips
Always check the dessert menu before you act up...
STOP! STOP! IT'S CHOCOLATE CAKE TONIGHT!

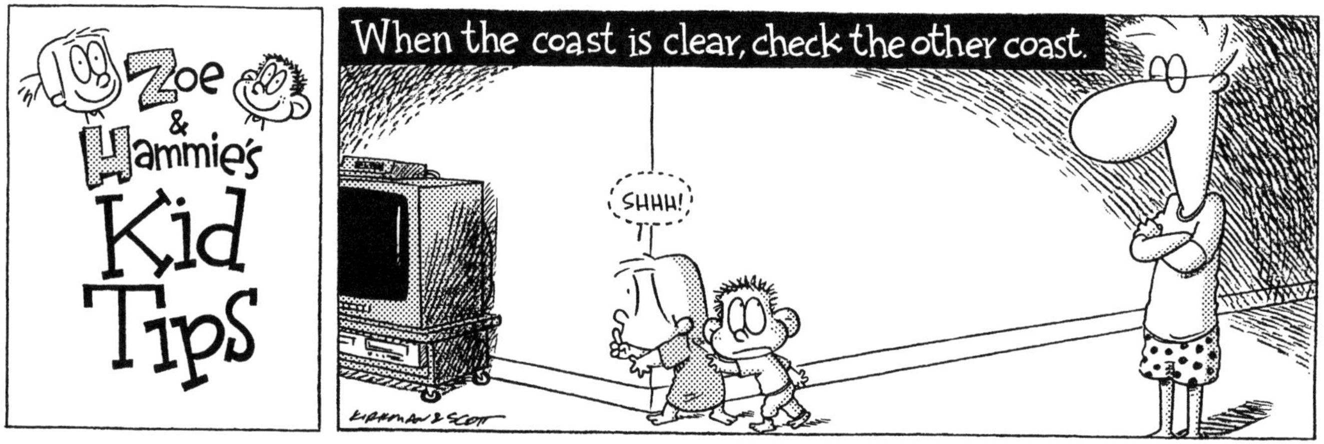
Zoe & Hammie's Kid Tips
When the coast is clear, check the other coast.
SHHH!

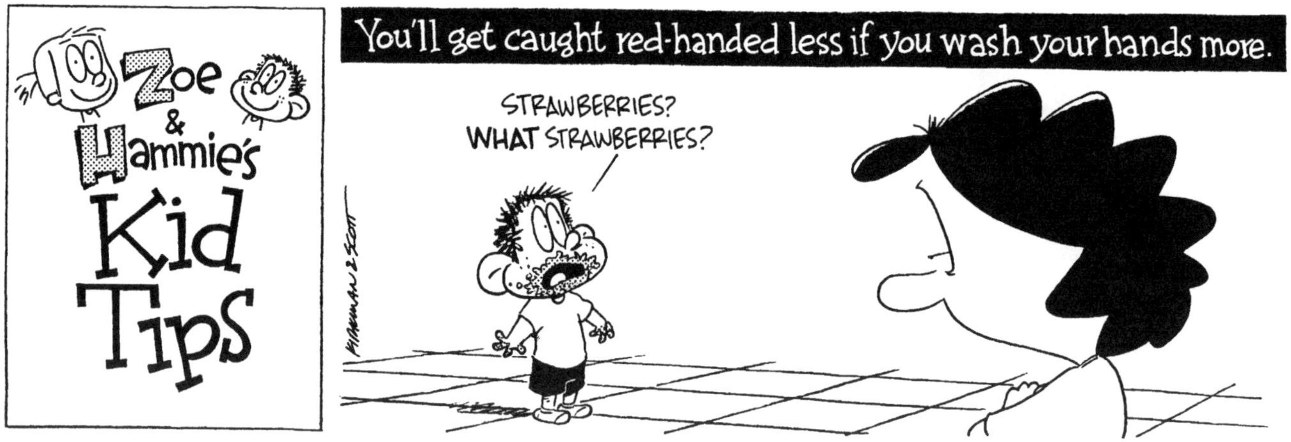
Zoe & Hammie's Kid Tips
You'll get caught red-handed less if you wash your hands more.
STRAWBERRIES? WHAT STRAWBERRIES?

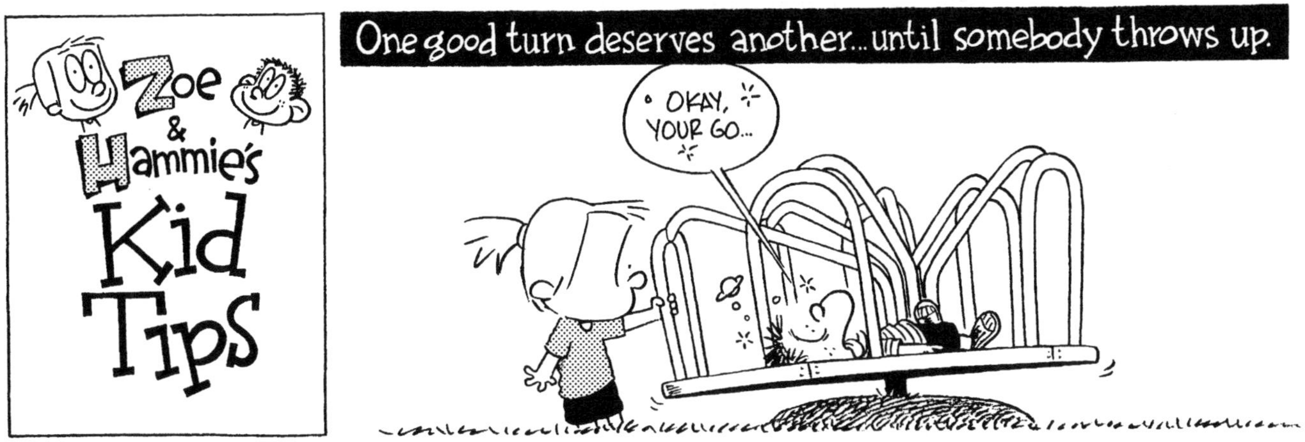
Zoe & Hammie's Kid Tips
One good turn deserves another...until somebody throws up.
OKAY, YOUR GO...

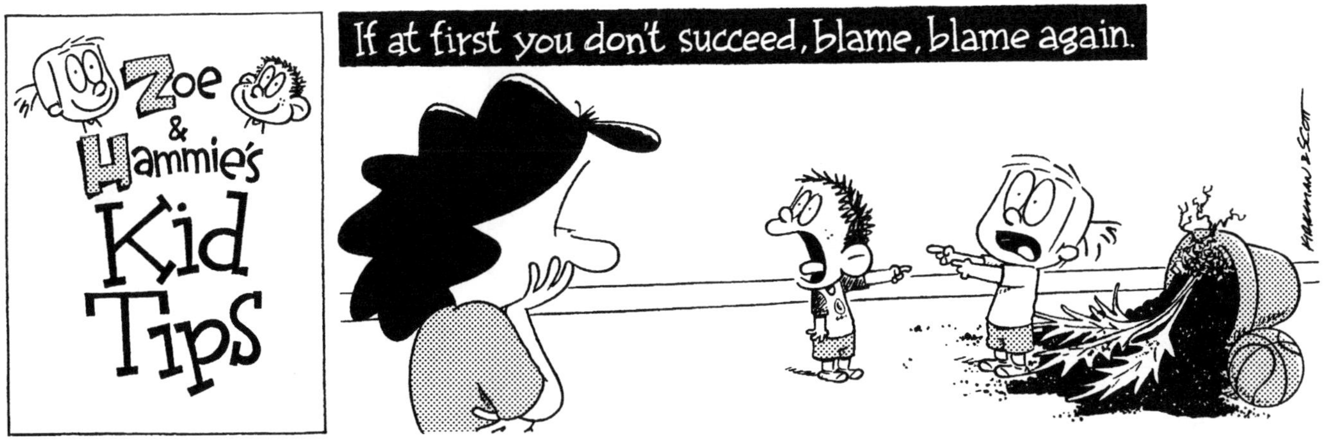
Zoe & Hammie's Kid Tips
If at first you don't succeed, blame, blame again.

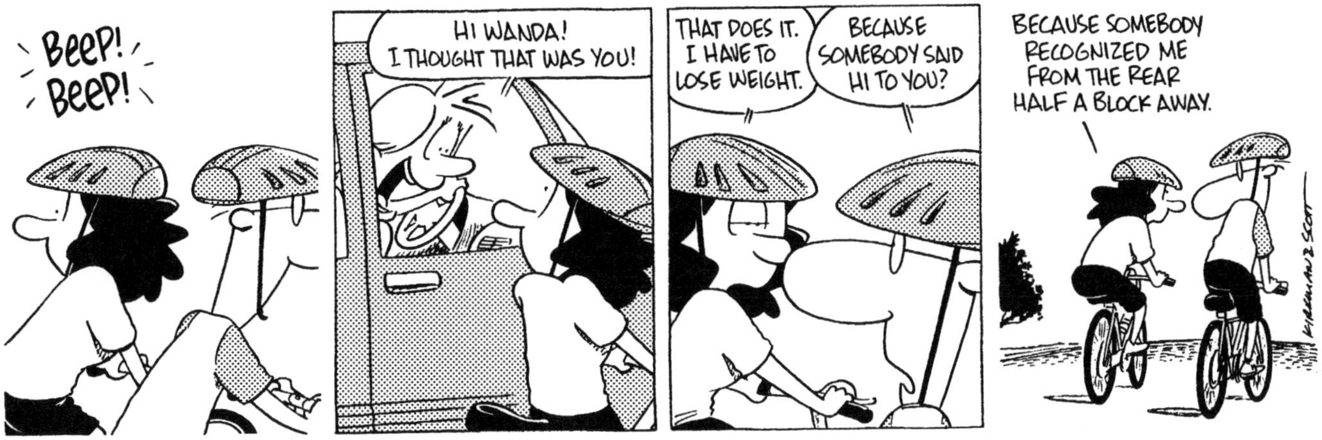
BEEP! BEEP!
HI WANDA! I THOUGHT THAT WAS YOU!
THAT DOES IT. I HAVE TO LOSE WEIGHT.
BECAUSE SOMEBODY SAID HI TO YOU?
BECAUSE SOMEBODY RECOGNIZED ME FROM THE REAR HALF A BLOCK AWAY.

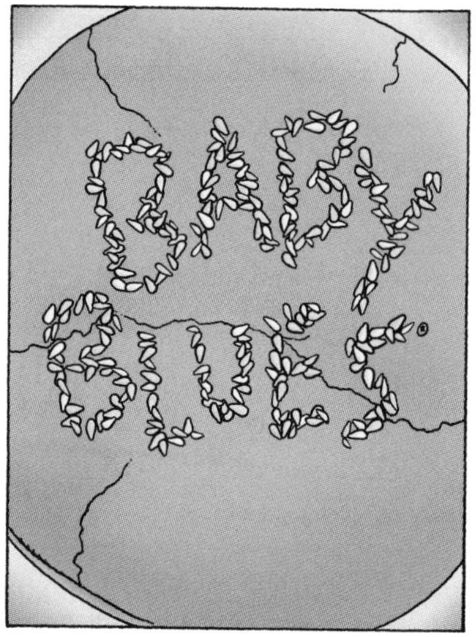
BABY BLUES®

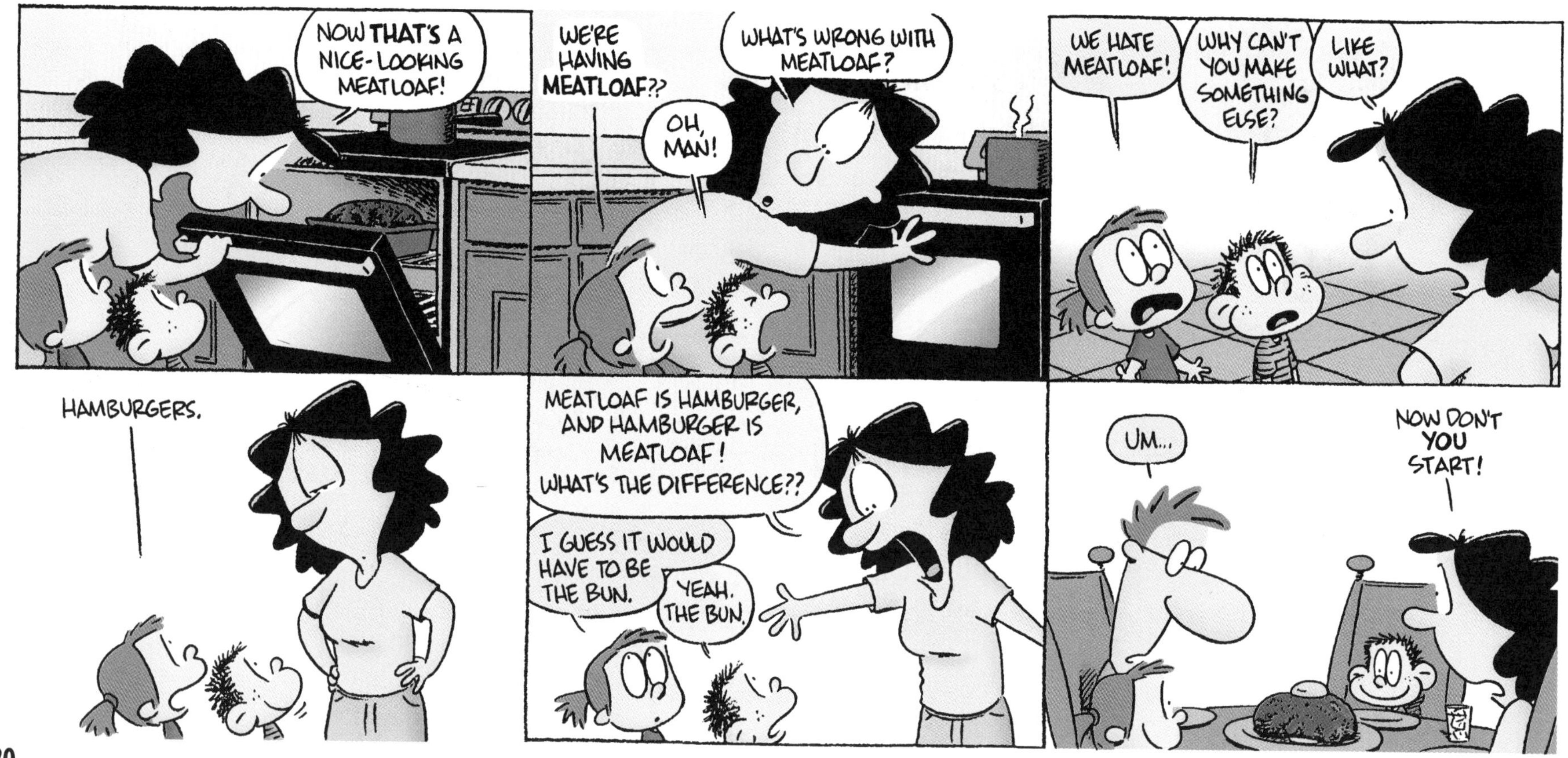
NOW **THAT'S** A NICE-LOOKING MEATLOAF!
WE'RE HAVING **MEATLOAF**??
OH, MAN!
WHAT'S WRONG WITH MEATLOAF?
WE HATE MEATLOAF!
WHY CAN'T YOU MAKE SOMETHING ELSE?
LIKE WHAT?
HAMBURGERS.
MEATLOAF IS HAMBURGER, AND HAMBURGER IS MEATLOAF!
WHAT'S THE DIFFERENCE??
I GUESS IT WOULD HAVE TO BE THE BUN.
YEAH. THE BUN.
UM...
NOW DON'T **YOU** START!

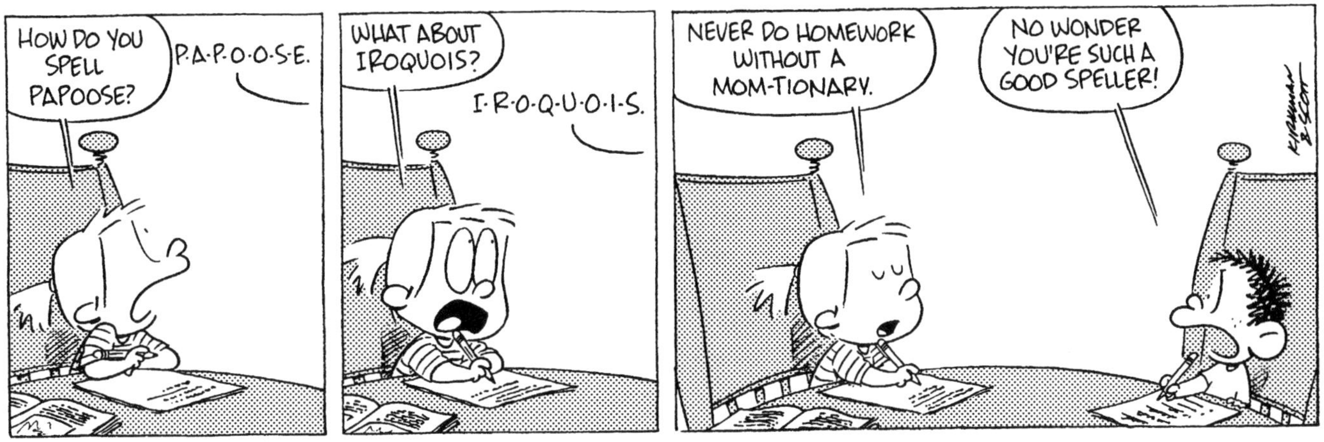
HOW DO YOU SPELL PAPOOSE?
P-A-P-O-O-S-E.
WHAT ABOUT IROQUOIS?
I-R-O-Q-U-O-I-S.
NEVER DO HOMEWORK WITHOUT A MOM-TIONARY.
NO WONDER YOU'RE SUCH A GOOD SPELLER!

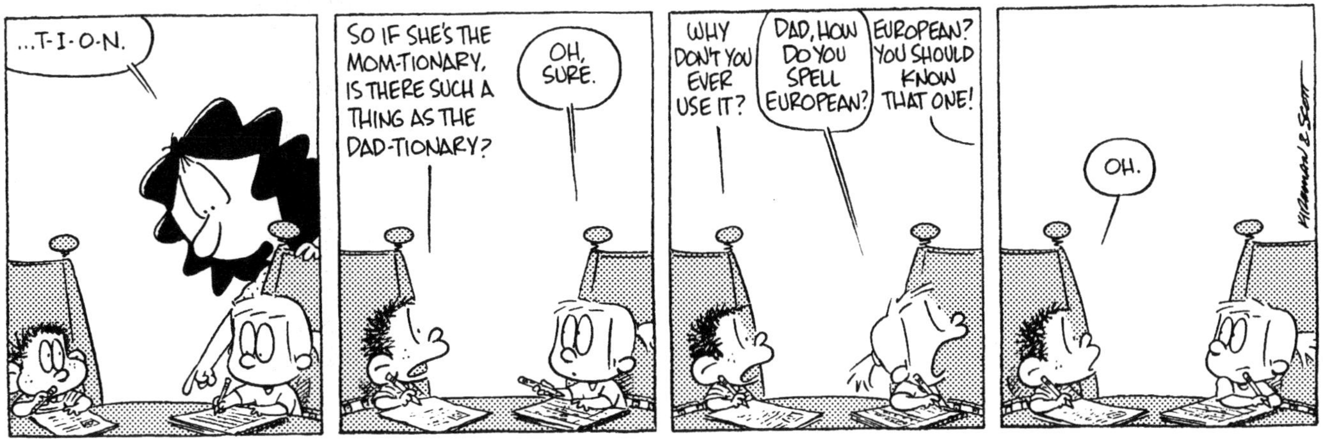
...T-I-O-N.
SO IF SHE'S THE MOM-TIONARY, IS THERE SUCH A THING AS THE DAD-TIONARY?
OH, SURE.
WHY DON'T YOU EVER USE IT?
DAD, HOW DO YOU SPELL EUROPEAN?
EUROPEAN? YOU SHOULD KNOW THAT ONE!
OH.

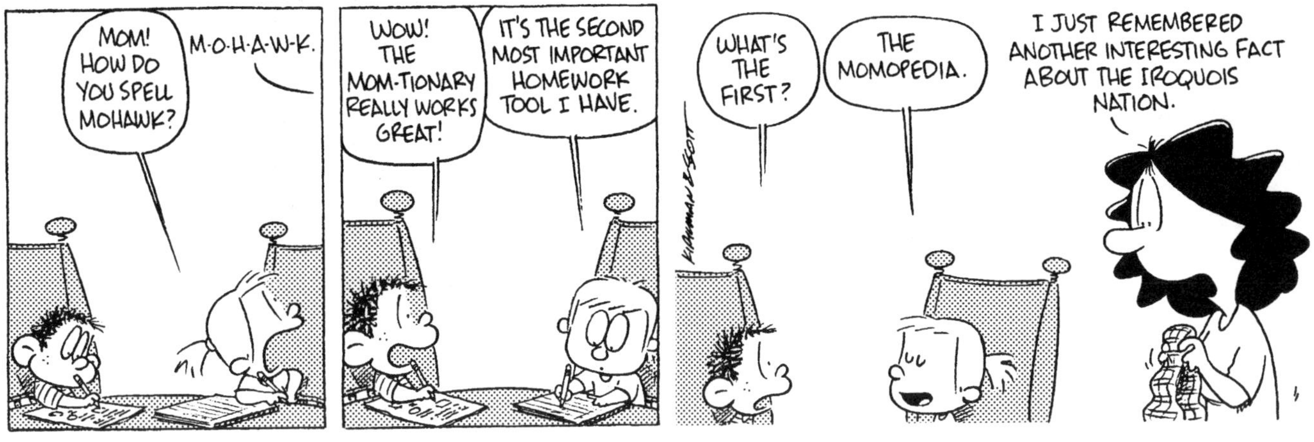
MOM! HOW DO YOU SPELL MOHAWK?
M-O-H-A-W-K.
WOW! THE MOM-TIONARY REALLY WORKS GREAT!
IT'S THE SECOND MOST IMPORTANT HOMEWORK TOOL I HAVE.
WHAT'S THE FIRST?
THE MOMOPEDIA.
I JUST REMEMBERED ANOTHER INTERESTING FACT ABOUT THE IROQUOIS NATION.

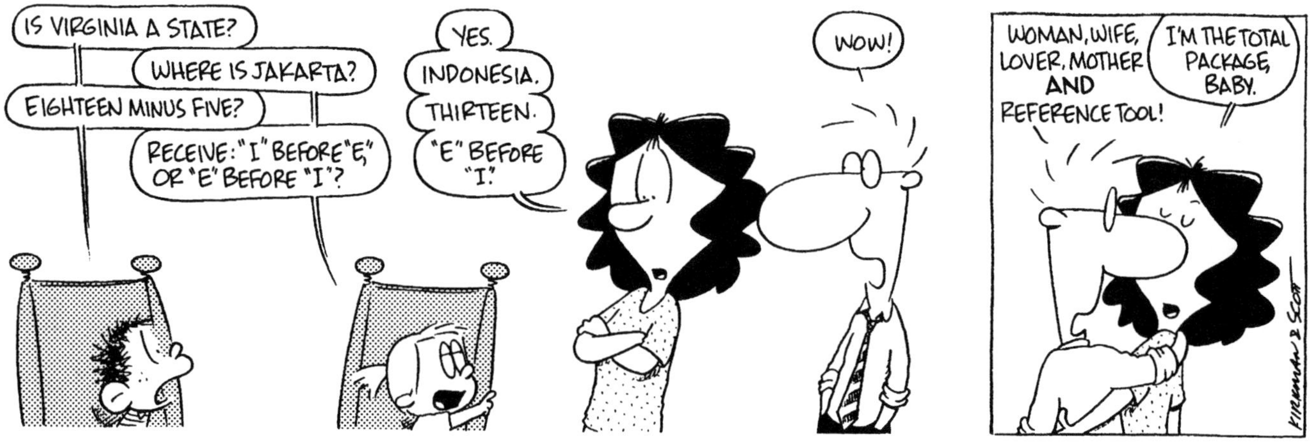
IS VIRGINIA A STATE?
WHERE IS JAKARTA?
EIGHTEEN MINUS FIVE?
RECEIVE: "I" BEFORE "E," OR "E" BEFORE "I"?
YES.
INDONESIA.
THIRTEEN.
"E" BEFORE "I."
WOW!
WOMAN, WIFE, LOVER, MOTHER AND REFERENCE TOOL!
I'M THE TOTAL PACKAGE, BABY.
KIRKMAN & SCOTT

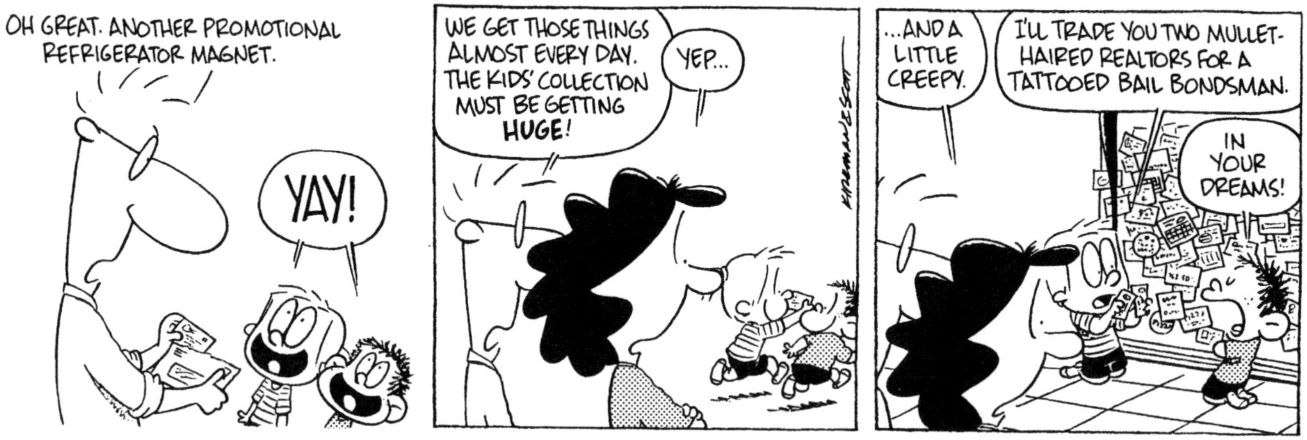
OH GREAT. ANOTHER PROMOTIONAL REFRIGERATOR MAGNET.
YAY!
WE GET THOSE THINGS ALMOST EVERY DAY. THE KIDS' COLLECTION MUST BE GETTING HUGE!
YEP...
KIRKMAN & SCOTT
...AND A LITTLE CREEPY.
I'LL TRADE YOU TWO MULLET-HAIRED REALTORS FOR A TATTOOED BAIL BONDSMAN.
IN YOUR DREAMS!

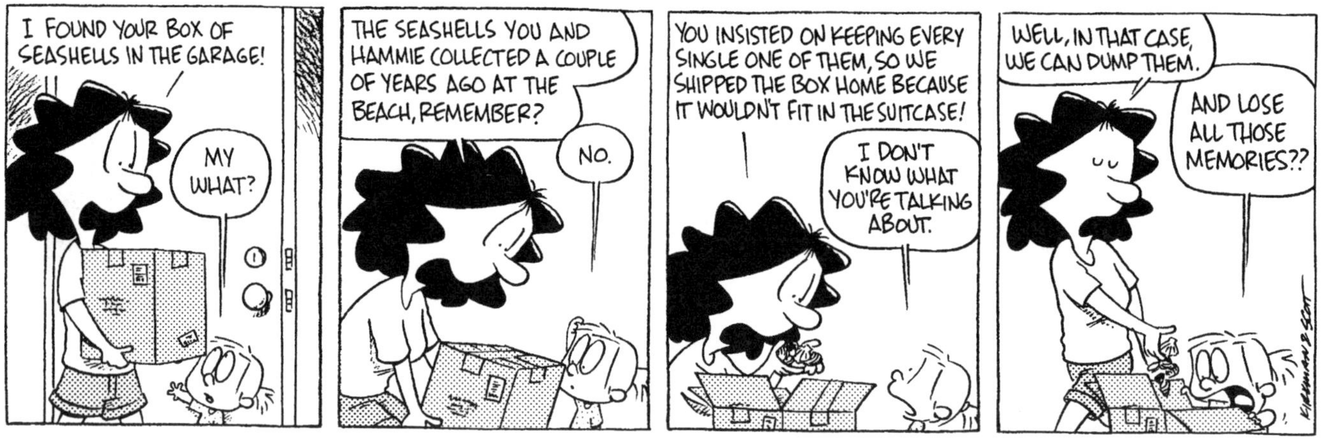
I FOUND YOUR BOX OF SEASHELLS IN THE GARAGE!
MY WHAT?
THE SEASHELLS YOU AND HAMMIE COLLECTED A COUPLE OF YEARS AGO AT THE BEACH, REMEMBER?
NO.
YOU INSISTED ON KEEPING EVERY SINGLE ONE OF THEM, SO WE SHIPPED THE BOX HOME BECAUSE IT WOULDN'T FIT IN THE SUITCASE!
I DON'T KNOW WHAT YOU'RE TALKING ABOUT.
WELL, IN THAT CASE, WE CAN DUMP THEM.
AND LOSE ALL THOSE MEMORIES??
KIRKMAN & SCOTT

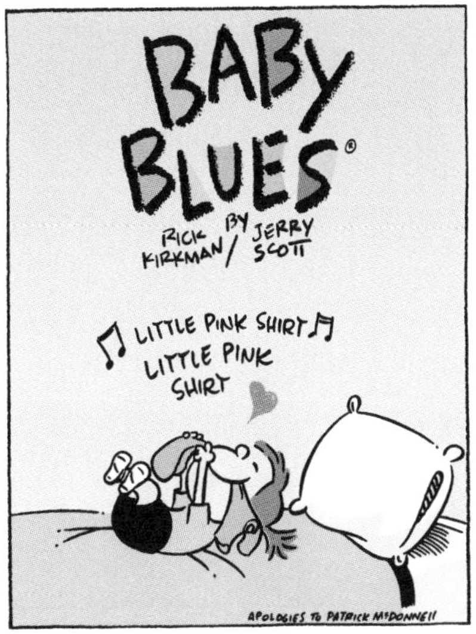
BABY BLUES®
BY RICK KIRKMAN / JERRY SCOTT
♫ LITTLE PINK SHIRT ♫ LITTLE PINK SHIRT
APOLOGIES TO PATRICK McDONNELL

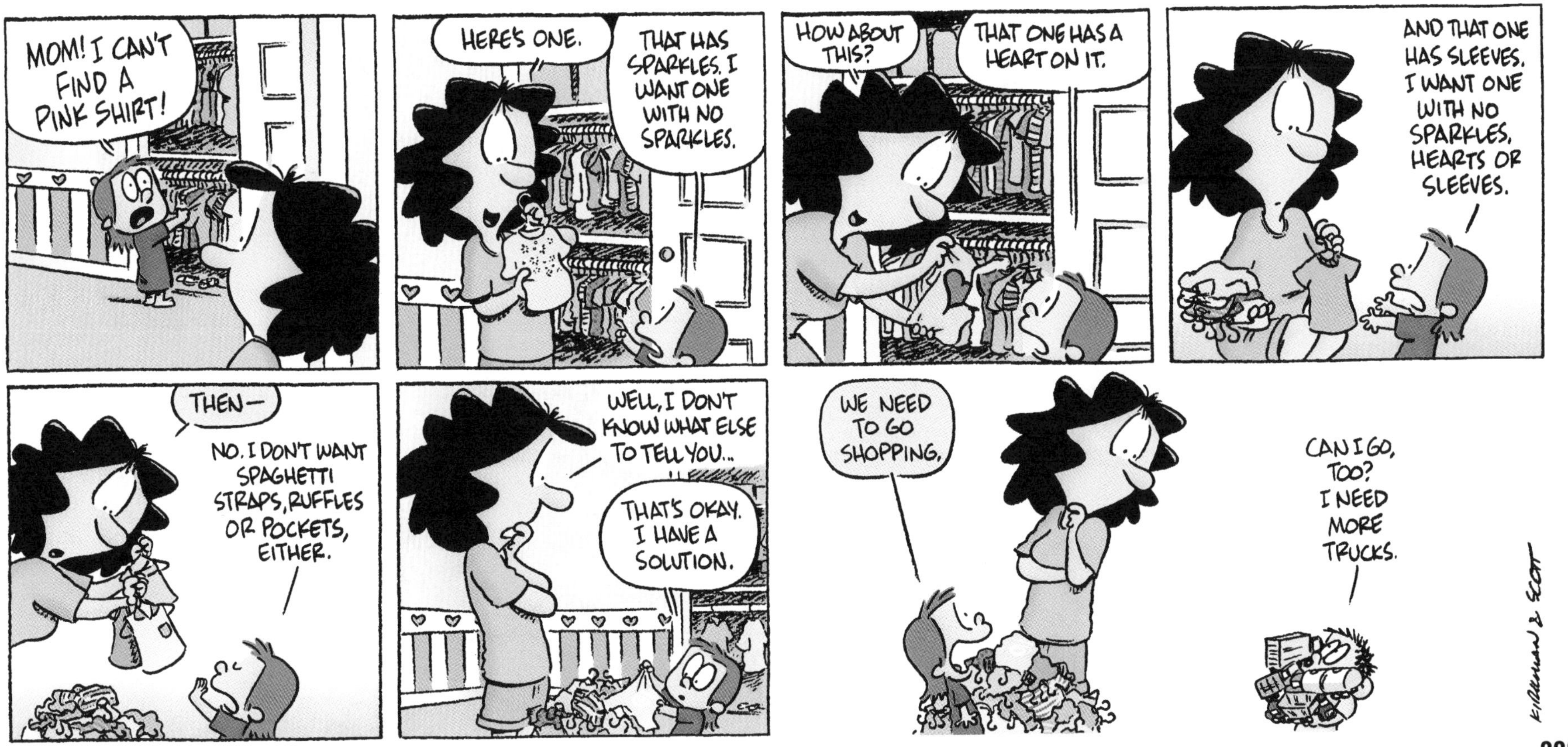
MOM! I CAN'T FIND A PINK SHIRT!
HERE'S ONE.
THAT HAS SPARKLES. I WANT ONE WITH NO SPARKLES.
HOW ABOUT THIS?
THAT ONE HAS A HEART ON IT.
AND THAT ONE HAS SLEEVES. I WANT ONE WITH NO SPARKLES, HEARTS OR SLEEVES.
THEN—
NO. I DON'T WANT SPAGHETTI STRAPS, RUFFLES OR POCKETS, EITHER.
WELL, I DON'T KNOW WHAT ELSE TO TELL YOU...
THAT'S OKAY. I HAVE A SOLUTION.
WE NEED TO GO SHOPPING.
CAN I GO, TOO? I NEED MORE TRUCKS.
KIRKMAN & SCOTT

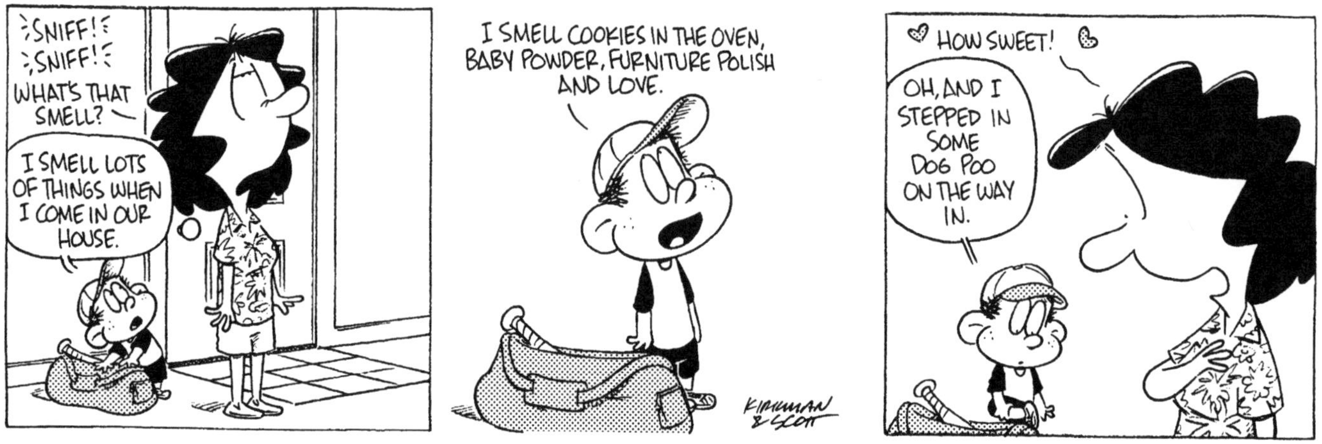
SNIFF! SNIFF!
WHAT'S THAT SMELL?
I SMELL LOTS OF THINGS WHEN I COME IN OUR HOUSE.
I SMELL COOKIES IN THE OVEN, BABY POWDER, FURNITURE POLISH AND LOVE.
KIRKMAN & SCOTT
HOW SWEET!
OH, AND I STEPPED IN SOME DOG POO ON THE WAY IN.

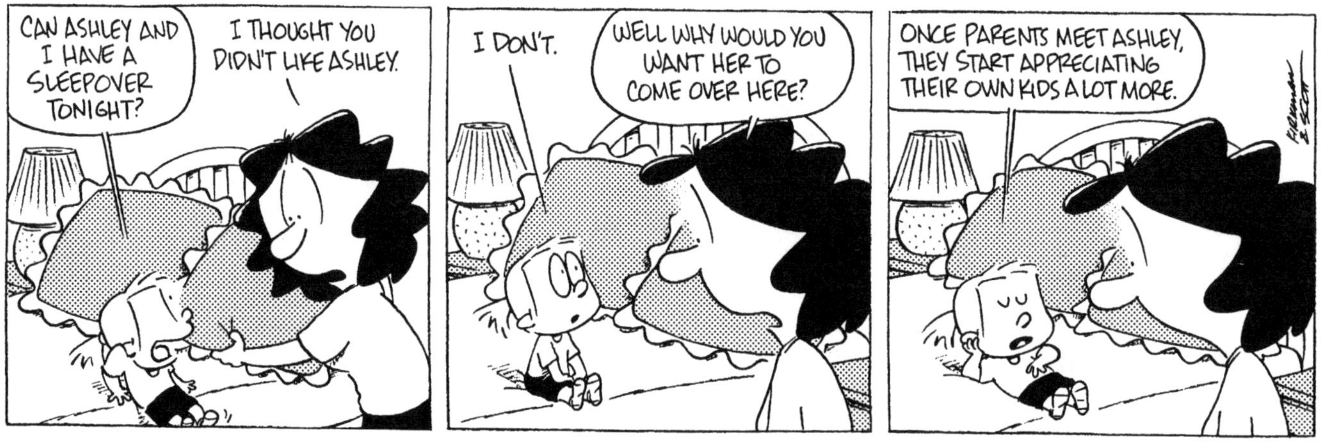
CAN ASHLEY AND I HAVE A SLEEPOVER TONIGHT?
I THOUGHT YOU DIDN'T LIKE ASHLEY.
I DON'T.
WELL WHY WOULD YOU WANT HER TO COME OVER HERE?
ONCE PARENTS MEET ASHLEY, THEY START APPRECIATING THEIR OWN KIDS A LOT MORE.
KIRKMAN & SCOTT

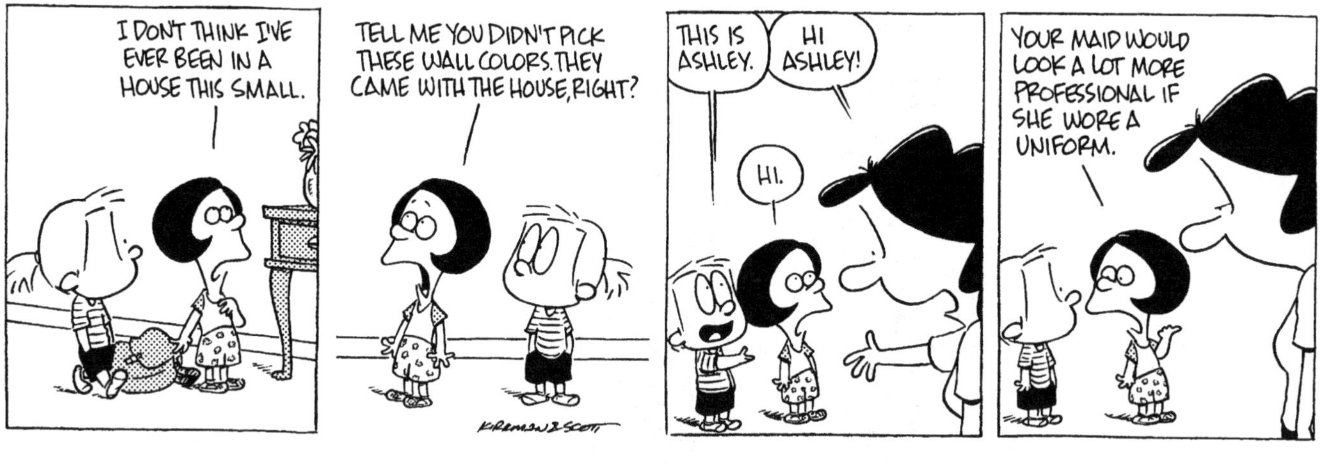
I DON'T THINK I'VE EVER BEEN IN A HOUSE THIS SMALL.
TELL ME YOU DIDN'T PICK THESE WALL COLORS. THEY CAME WITH THE HOUSE, RIGHT?
KIRKMAN & SCOTT
THIS IS ASHLEY.
HI ASHLEY!
HI.
YOUR MAID WOULD LOOK A LOT MORE PROFESSIONAL IF SHE WORE A UNIFORM.

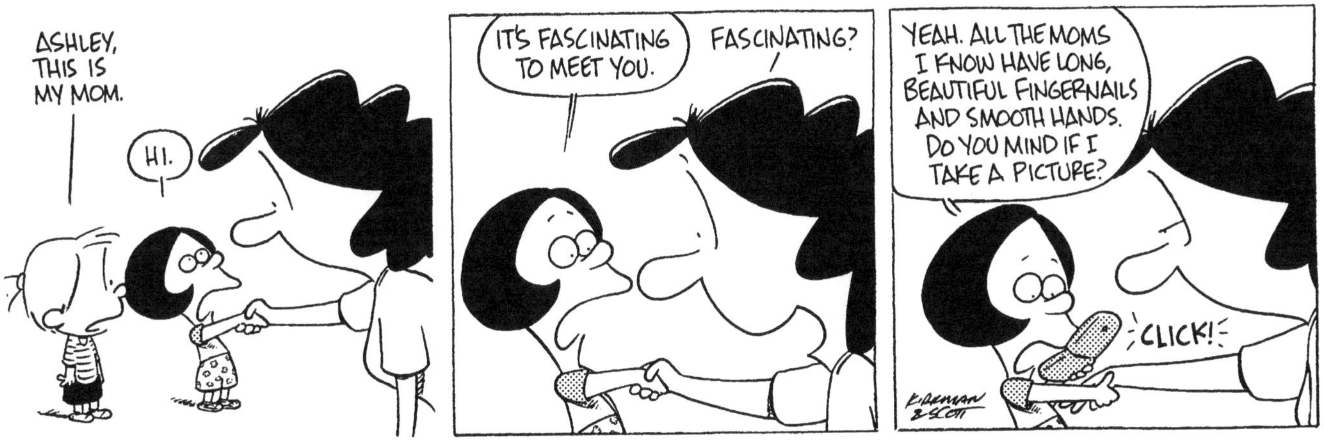
ASHLEY, THIS IS MY MOM.
HI.
IT'S FASCINATING TO MEET YOU.
FASCINATING?
YEAH. ALL THE MOMS I KNOW HAVE LONG, BEAUTIFUL FINGERNAILS AND SMOOTH HANDS. DO YOU MIND IF I TAKE A PICTURE?
CLICK!

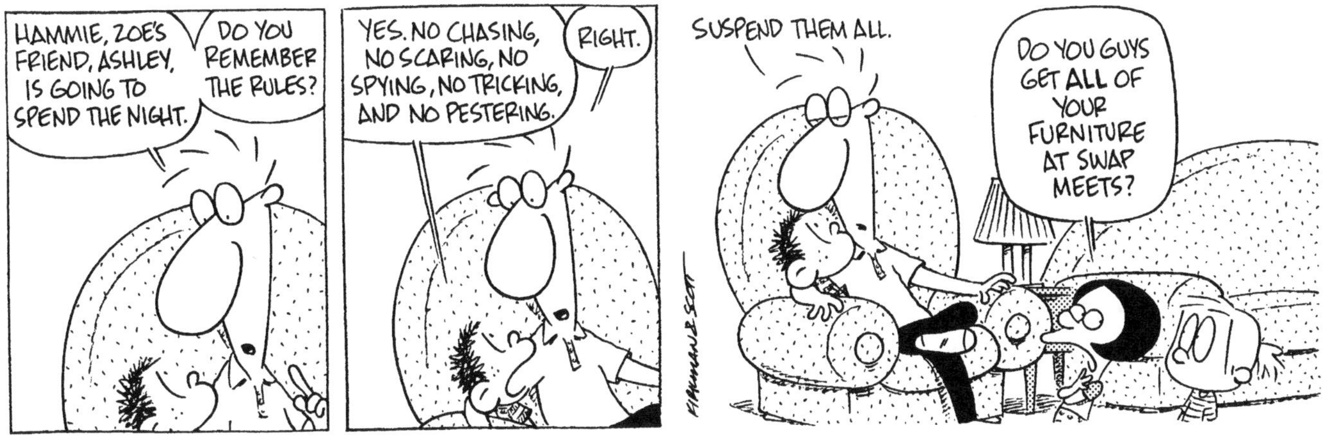
HAMMIE, ZOE'S FRIEND, ASHLEY, IS GOING TO SPEND THE NIGHT.
DO YOU REMEMBER THE RULES?
YES. NO CHASING, NO SCARING, NO SPYING, NO TRICKING, AND NO PESTERING.
RIGHT.
SUSPEND THEM ALL.
DO YOU GUYS GET ALL OF YOUR FURNITURE AT SWAP MEETS?

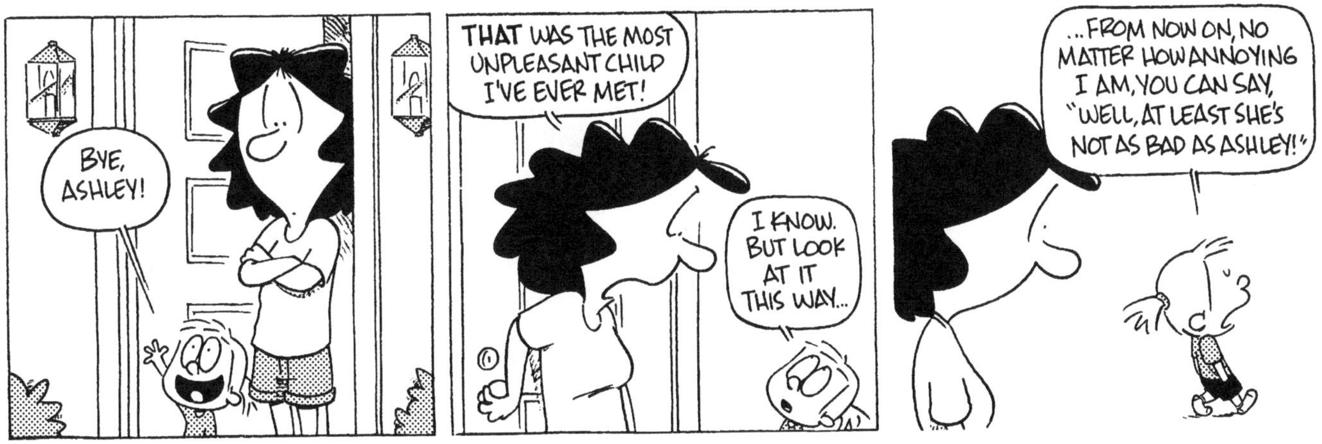
BYE, ASHLEY!
THAT WAS THE MOST UNPLEASANT CHILD I'VE EVER MET!
I KNOW. BUT LOOK AT IT THIS WAY...
...FROM NOW ON, NO MATTER HOW ANNOYING I AM, YOU CAN SAY, "WELL, AT LEAST SHE'S NOT AS BAD AS ASHLEY!"

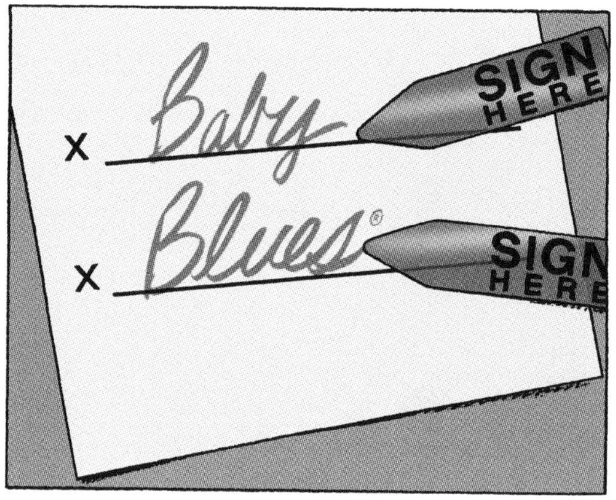
Baby Blues®
SIGN HERE
SIGN HERE

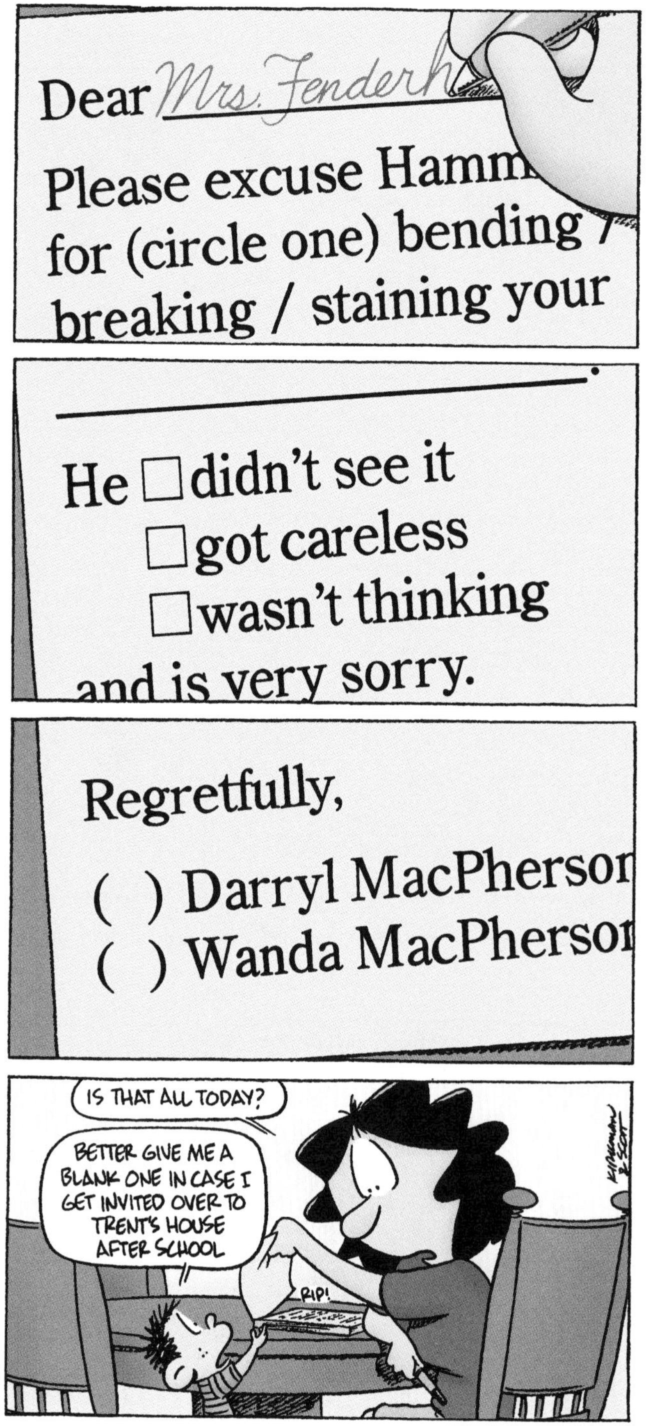
Dear Mrs. Fenderh
Please excuse Hamm
for (circle one) bending /
breaking / staining your
He didn't see it
got careless
wasn't thinking
and is very sorry.
Regretfully,
( ) Darryl MacPherson
( ) Wanda MacPherson
IS THAT ALL TODAY?
BETTER GIVE ME A BLANK ONE IN CASE I GET INVITED OVER TO TRENT'S HOUSE AFTER SCHOOL
RIP!

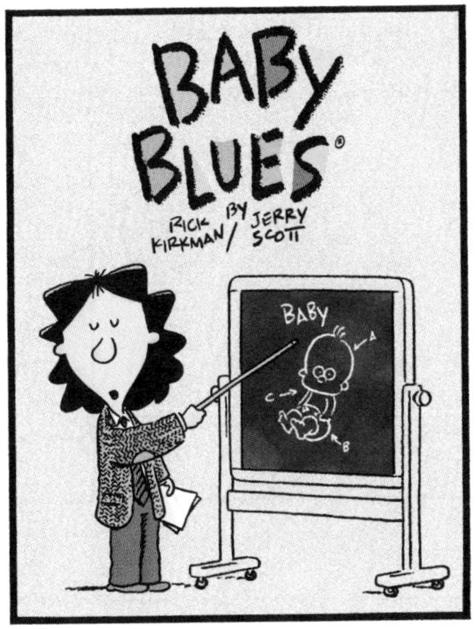
BABY BLUES®
RICK KIRKMAN / BY JERRY SCOTT
BABY

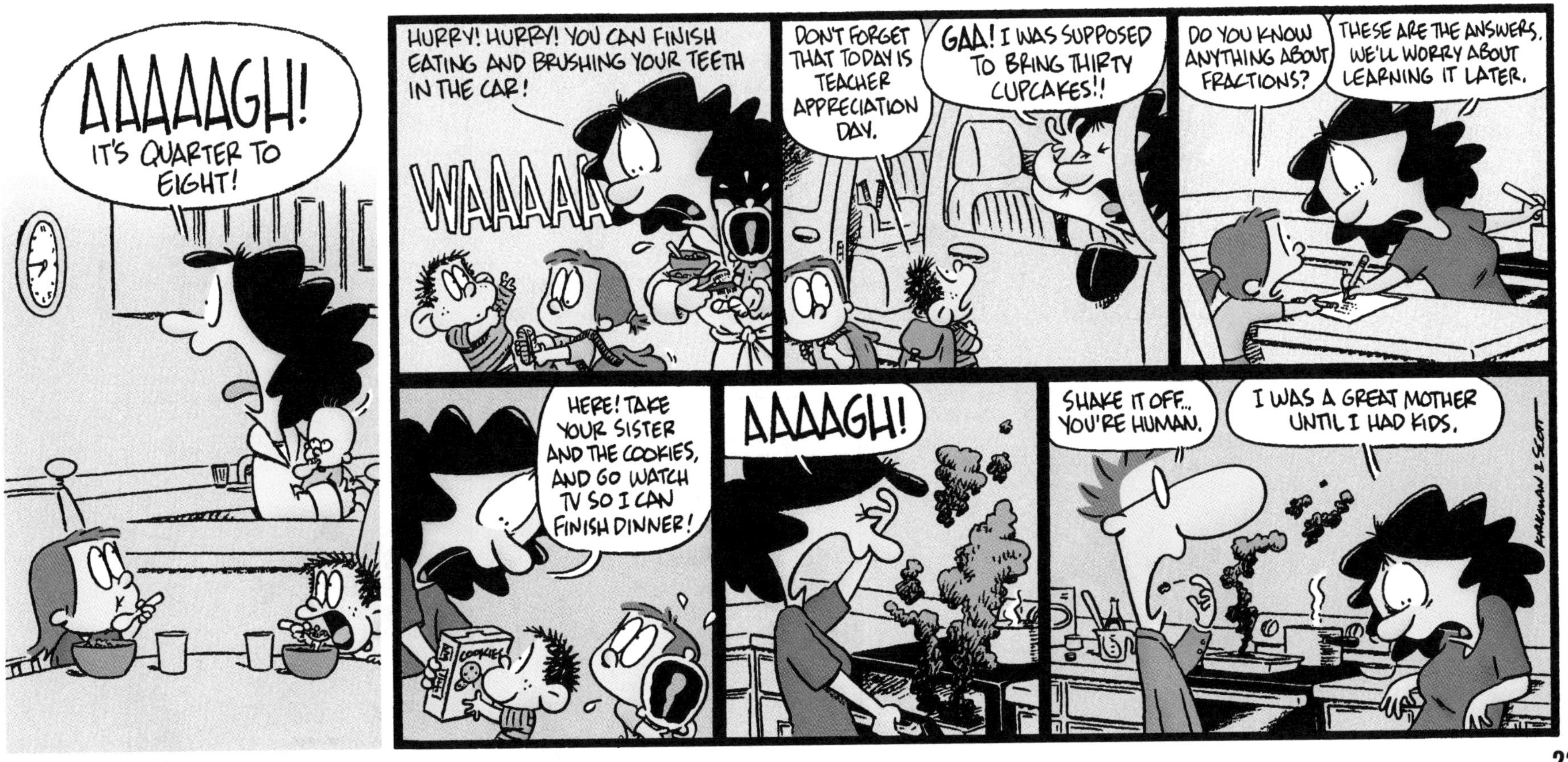
AAAAAGH! IT'S QUARTER TO EIGHT!
HURRY! HURRY! YOU CAN FINISH EATING AND BRUSHING YOUR TEETH IN THE CAR!
WAAAAAA
DON'T FORGET THAT TODAY IS TEACHER APPRECIATION DAY.
GAA! I WAS SUPPOSED TO BRING THIRTY CUPCAKES!!
DO YOU KNOW ANYTHING ABOUT FRACTIONS?
THESE ARE THE ANSWERS. WE'LL WORRY ABOUT LEARNING IT LATER.
HERE! TAKE YOUR SISTER AND THE COOKIES, AND GO WATCH TV SO I CAN FINISH DINNER!
COOKIES
AAAAGH!
SHAKE IT OFF... YOU'RE HUMAN.
I WAS A GREAT MOTHER UNTIL I HAD KIDS.
KIRKMAN & SCOTT

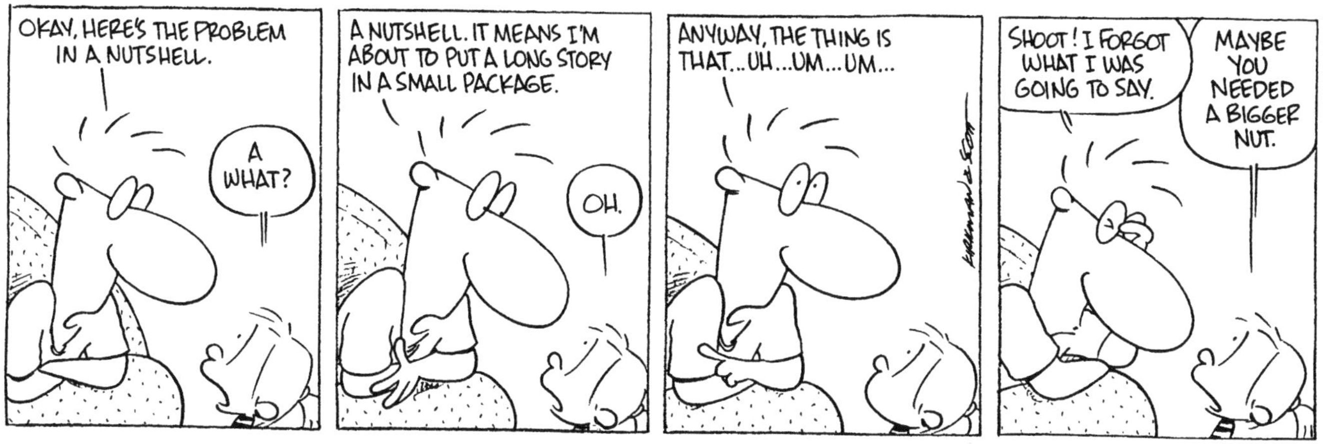
OKAY, HERE'S THE PROBLEM IN A NUTSHELL.
A WHAT?
A NUTSHELL. IT MEANS I'M ABOUT TO PUT A LONG STORY IN A SMALL PACKAGE.
OH.
ANYWAY, THE THING IS THAT...UH...UM...UM...
SHOOT! I FORGOT WHAT I WAS GOING TO SAY.
MAYBE YOU NEEDED A BIGGER NUT.

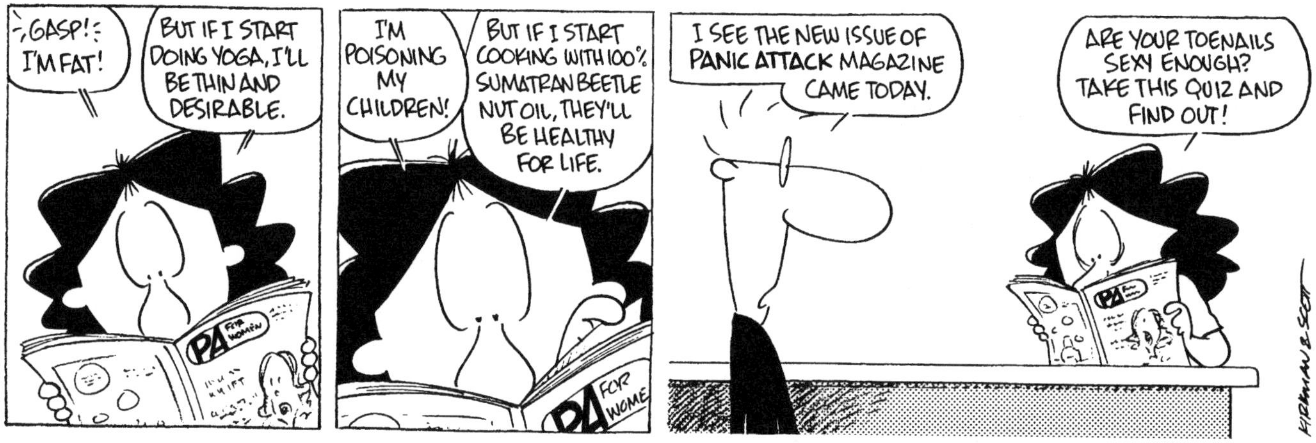
GASP! I'M FAT!
BUT IF I START DOING YOGA, I'LL BE THIN AND DESIRABLE.
I'M POISONING MY CHILDREN!
BUT IF I START COOKING WITH 100% SUMATRAN BEETLE NUT OIL, THEY'LL BE HEALTHY FOR LIFE.
I SEE THE NEW ISSUE OF PANIC ATTACK MAGAZINE CAME TODAY.
ARE YOUR TOENAILS SEXY ENOUGH? TAKE THIS QUIZ AND FIND OUT!

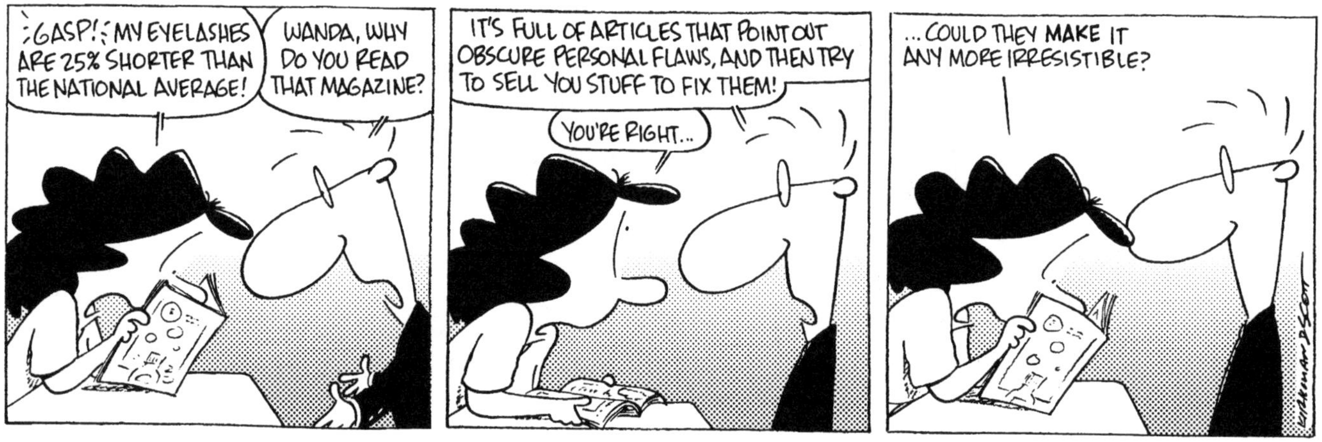
GASP! MY EYELASHES ARE 25% SHORTER THAN THE NATIONAL AVERAGE!
WANDA, WHY DO YOU READ THAT MAGAZINE?
IT'S FULL OF ARTICLES THAT POINT OUT OBSCURE PERSONAL FLAWS, AND THEN TRY TO SELL YOU STUFF TO FIX THEM!
YOU'RE RIGHT...
...COULD THEY MAKE IT ANY MORE IRRESISTIBLE?

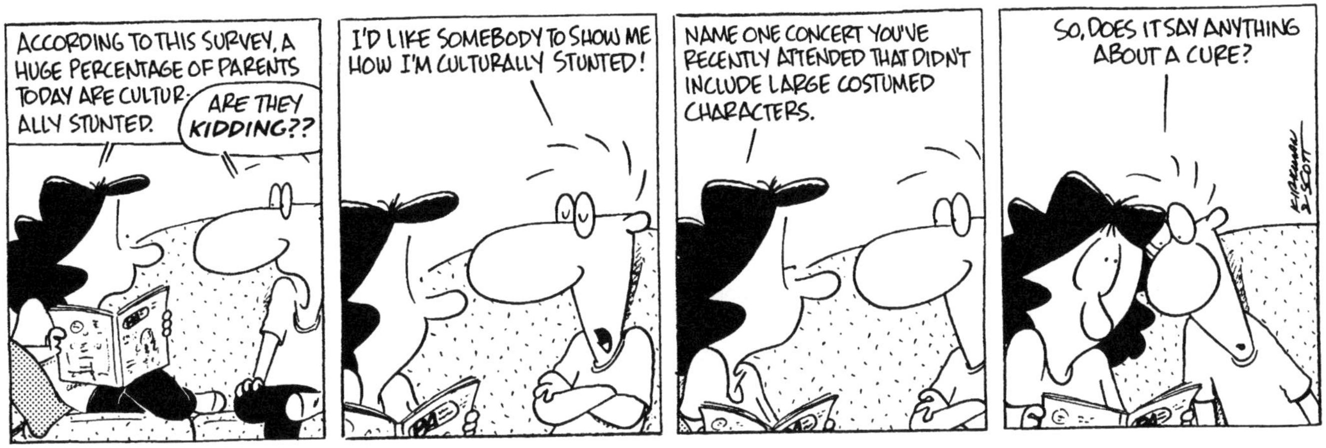
ACCORDING TO THIS SURVEY, A HUGE PERCENTAGE OF PARENTS TODAY ARE CULTURALLY STUNTED.
ARE THEY *KIDDING??*
I'D LIKE SOMEBODY TO SHOW ME HOW I'M CULTURALLY STUNTED!
NAME ONE CONCERT YOU'VE RECENTLY ATTENDED THAT DIDN'T INCLUDE LARGE COSTUMED CHARACTERS.
SO, DOES IT SAY ANYTHING ABOUT A CURE?

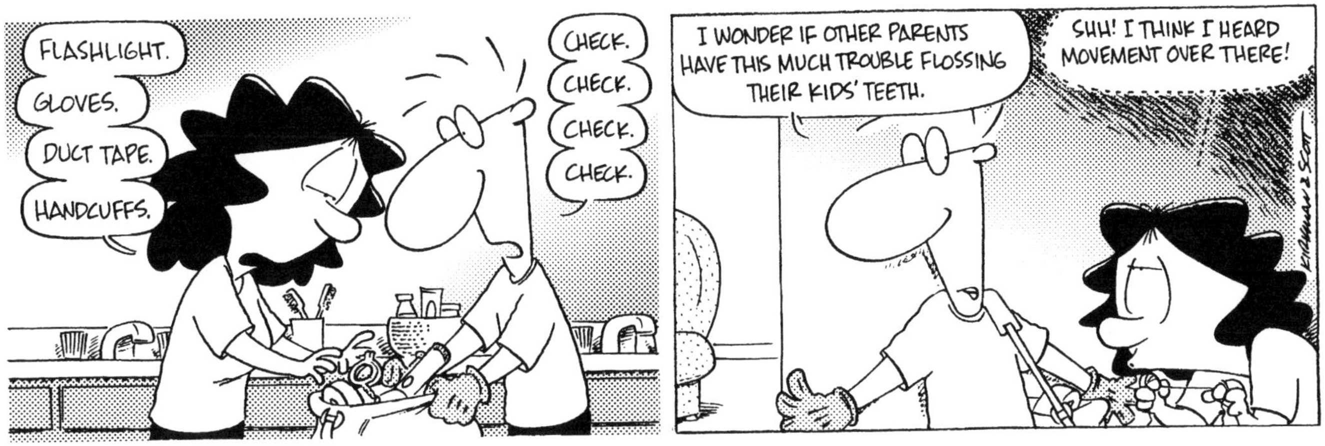
FLASHLIGHT.
CHECK.
GLOVES.
CHECK.
DUCT TAPE.
CHECK.
HANDCUFFS.
CHECK.
I WONDER IF OTHER PARENTS HAVE THIS MUCH TROUBLE FLOSSING THEIR KIDS' TEETH.
SHH! I THINK I HEARD MOVEMENT OVER THERE!

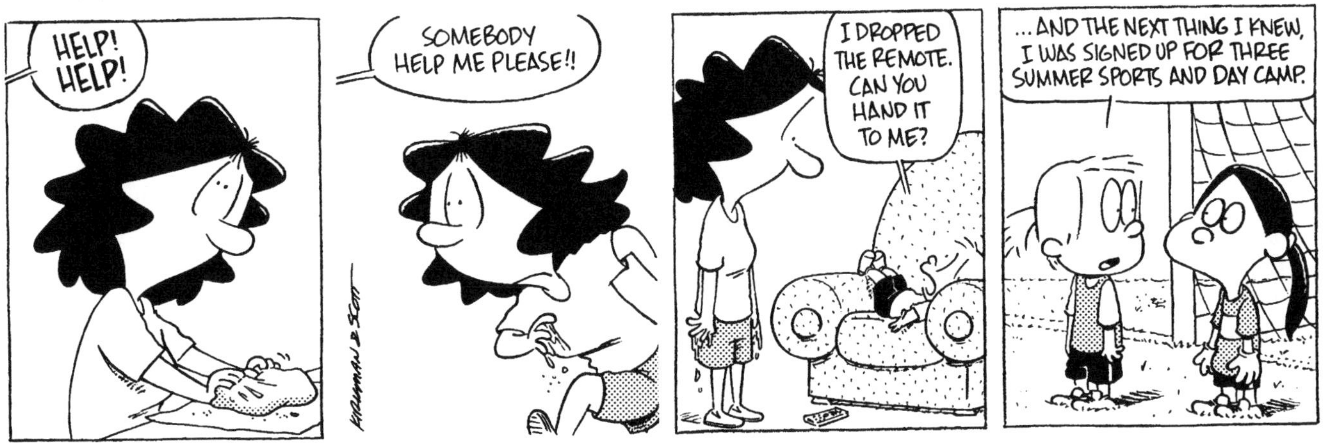
HELP! HELP!
SOMEBODY HELP ME PLEASE!!
I DROPPED THE REMOTE. CAN YOU HAND IT TO ME?
...AND THE NEXT THING I KNEW, I WAS SIGNED UP FOR THREE SUMMER SPORTS AND DAY CAMP.

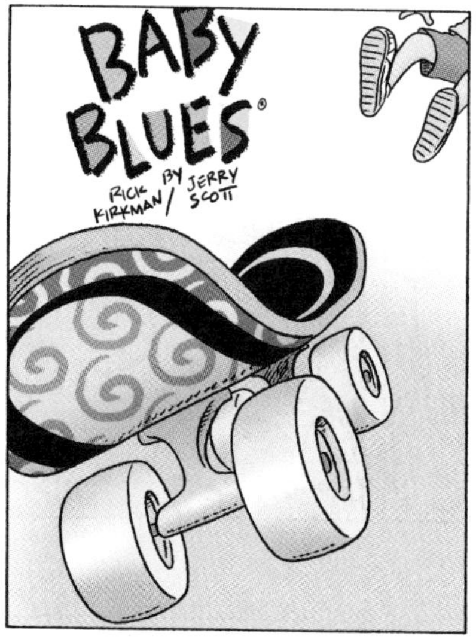
BABY BLUES®
RICK KIRKMAN / BY JERRY SCOTT

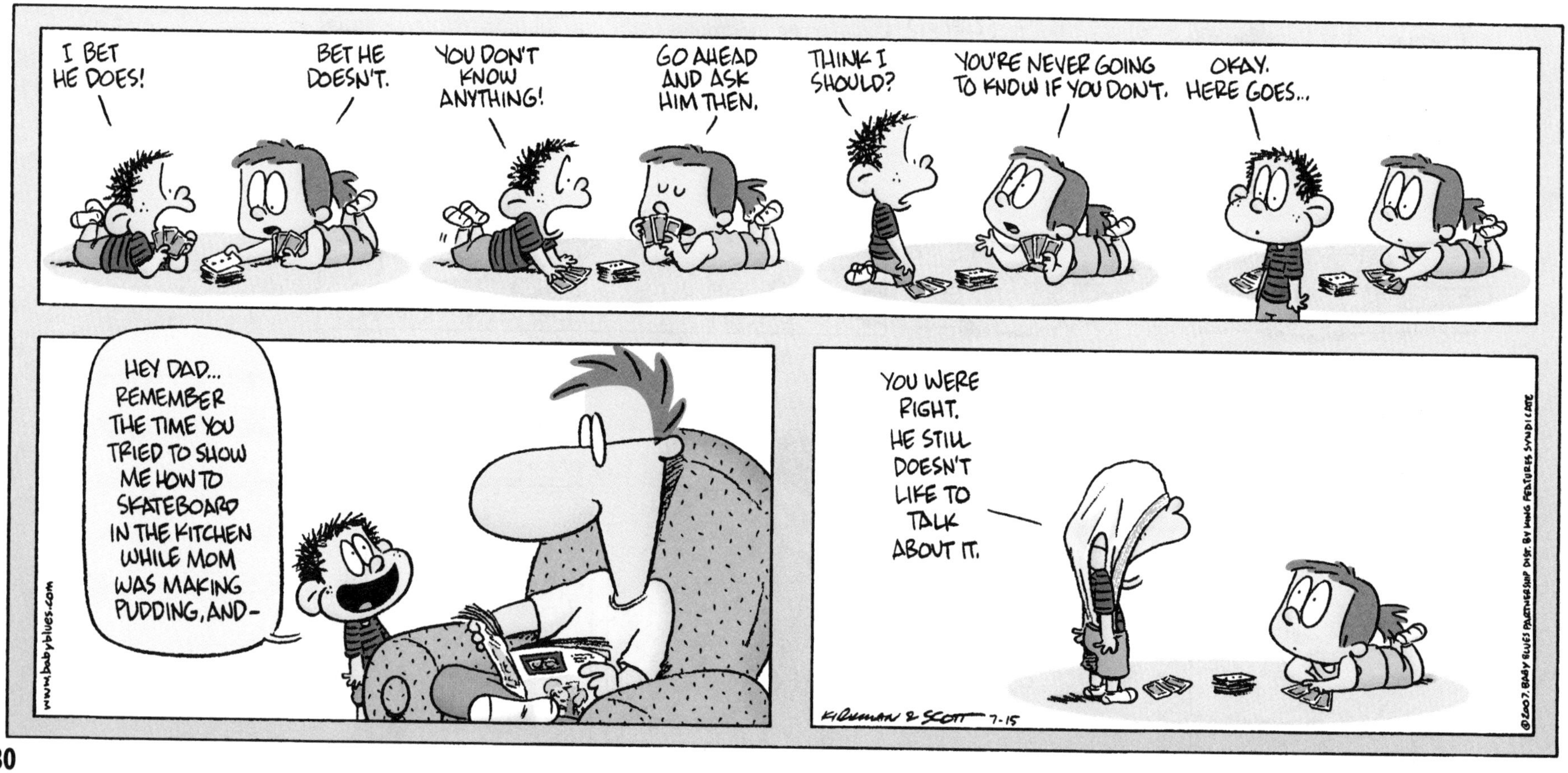
I BET HE DOES!
BET HE DOESN'T.
YOU DON'T KNOW ANYTHING!
GO AHEAD AND ASK HIM THEN.
THINK I SHOULD?
YOU'RE NEVER GOING TO KNOW IF YOU DON'T.
OKAY. HERE GOES...
HEY DAD... REMEMBER THE TIME YOU TRIED TO SHOW ME HOW TO SKATEBOARD IN THE KITCHEN WHILE MOM WAS MAKING PUDDING, AND–
YOU WERE RIGHT. HE STILL DOESN'T LIKE TO TALK ABOUT IT.
www.babyblues.com
KIRKMAN & SCOTT 7-15
© 2007, BABY BLUES PARTNERSHIP DIST. BY KING FEATURES SYNDICATE

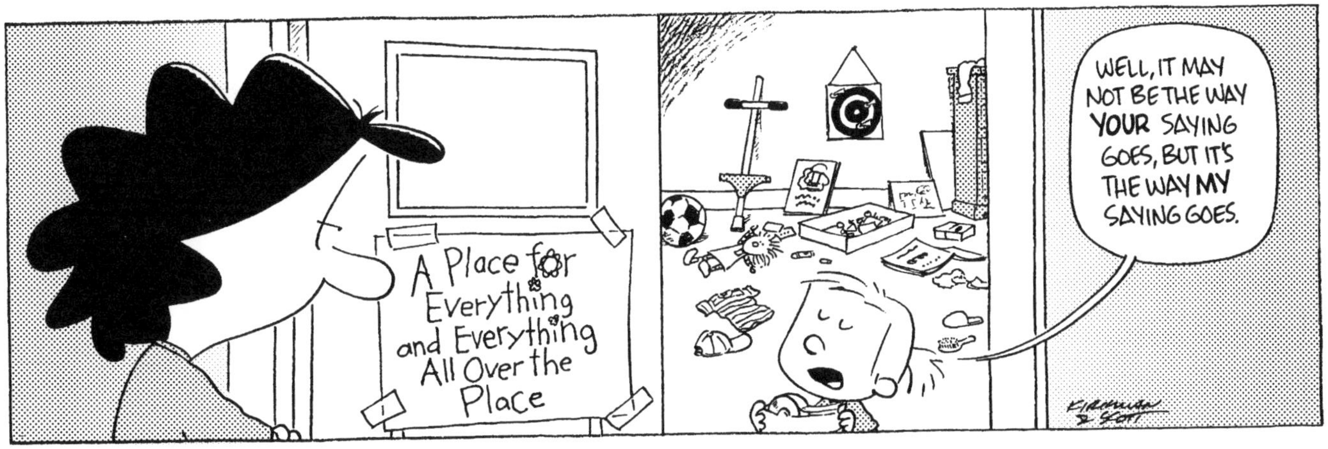
A Place for Everything and Everything All Over the Place
WELL, IT MAY NOT BE THE WAY YOUR SAYING GOES, BUT IT'S THE WAY MY SAYING GOES.
KIRKMAN & SCOTT

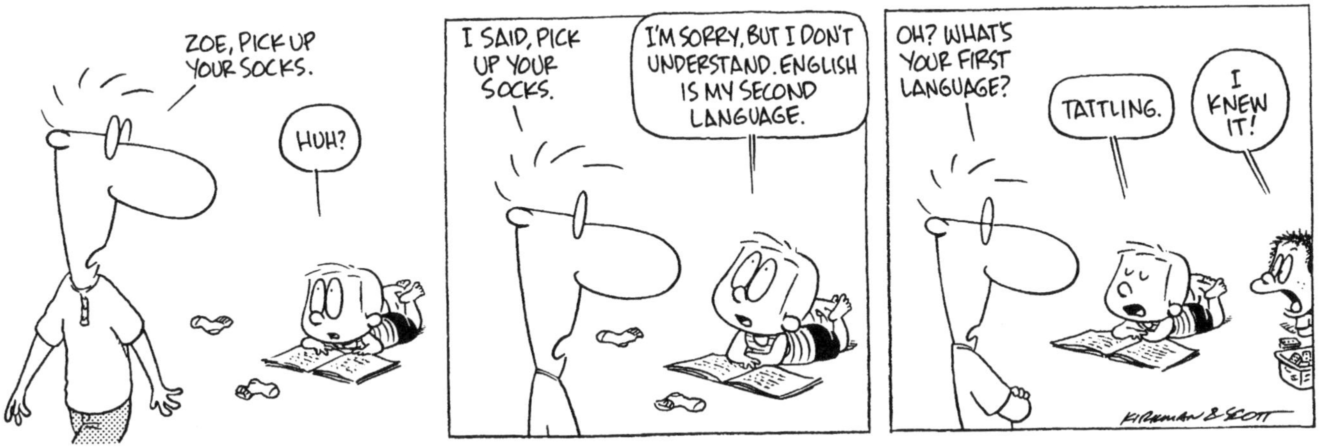
ZOE, PICK UP YOUR SOCKS.
HUH?
I SAID, PICK UP YOUR SOCKS.
I'M SORRY, BUT I DON'T UNDERSTAND. ENGLISH IS MY SECOND LANGUAGE.
OH? WHAT'S YOUR FIRST LANGUAGE?
TATTLING.
I KNEW IT!
KIRKMAN & SCOTT

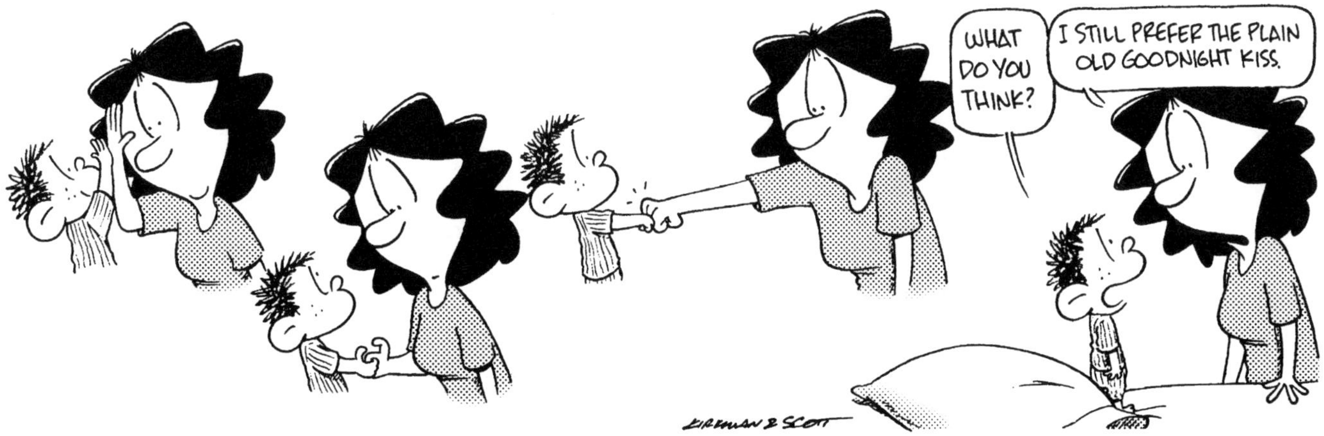
WHAT DO YOU THINK?
I STILL PREFER THE PLAIN OLD GOODNIGHT KISS.
KIRKMAN & SCOTT

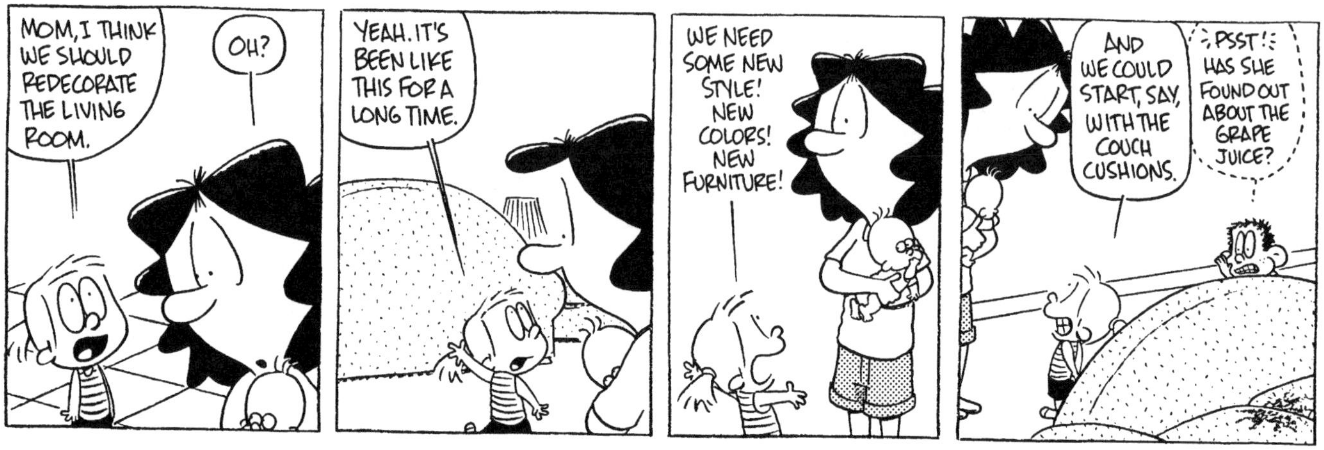
MOM, I THINK WE SHOULD REDECORATE THE LIVING ROOM.
OH?
YEAH. IT'S BEEN LIKE THIS FOR A LONG TIME.
WE NEED SOME NEW STYLE! NEW COLORS! NEW FURNITURE!
AND WE COULD START, SAY, WITH THE COUCH CUSHIONS.
PSST! HAS SHE FOUND OUT ABOUT THE GRAPE JUICE?

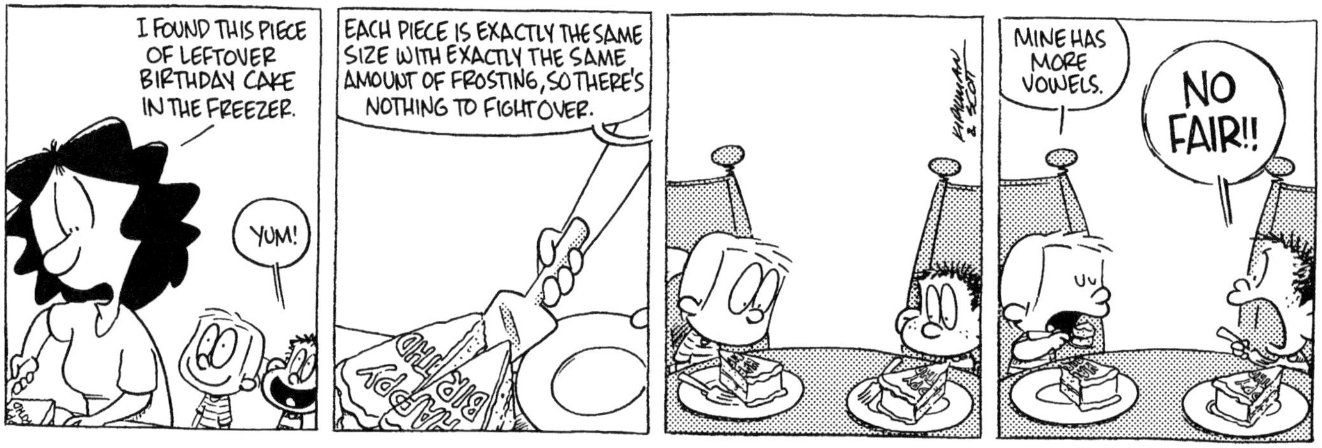
I FOUND THIS PIECE OF LEFTOVER BIRTHDAY CAKE IN THE FREEZER.
YUM!
EACH PIECE IS EXACTLY THE SAME SIZE WITH EXACTLY THE SAME AMOUNT OF FROSTING, SO THERE'S NOTHING TO FIGHT OVER.
MINE HAS MORE VOWELS.
NO FAIR!!

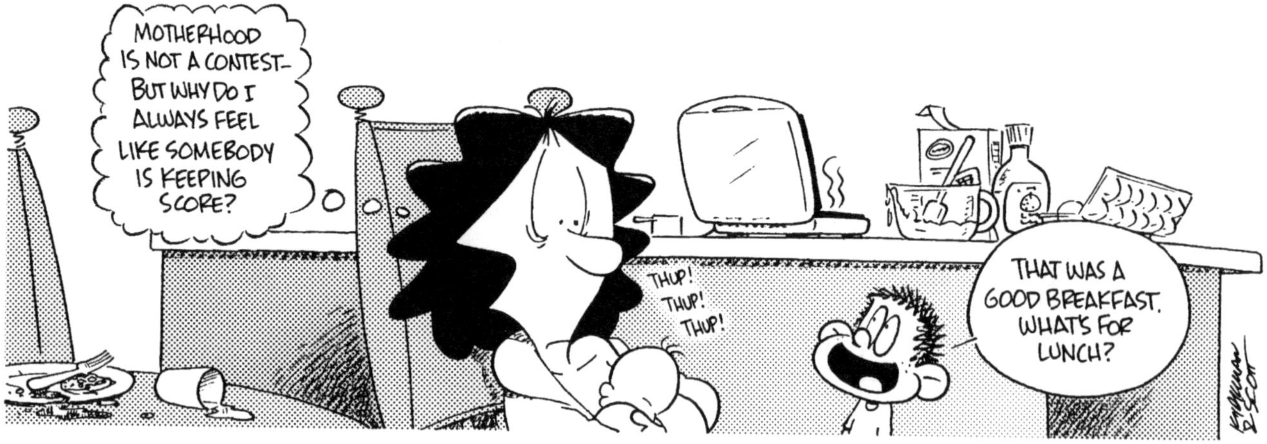
MOTHERHOOD IS NOT A CONTEST- BUT WHY DO I ALWAYS FEEL LIKE SOMEBODY IS KEEPING SCORE?
THUP! THUP! THUP!
THAT WAS A GOOD BREAKFAST. WHAT'S FOR LUNCH?

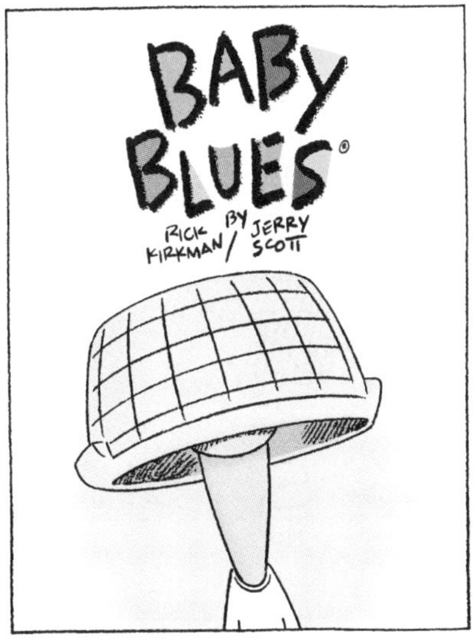

BABY BLUES®
BY RICK KIRKMAN / JERRY SCOTT

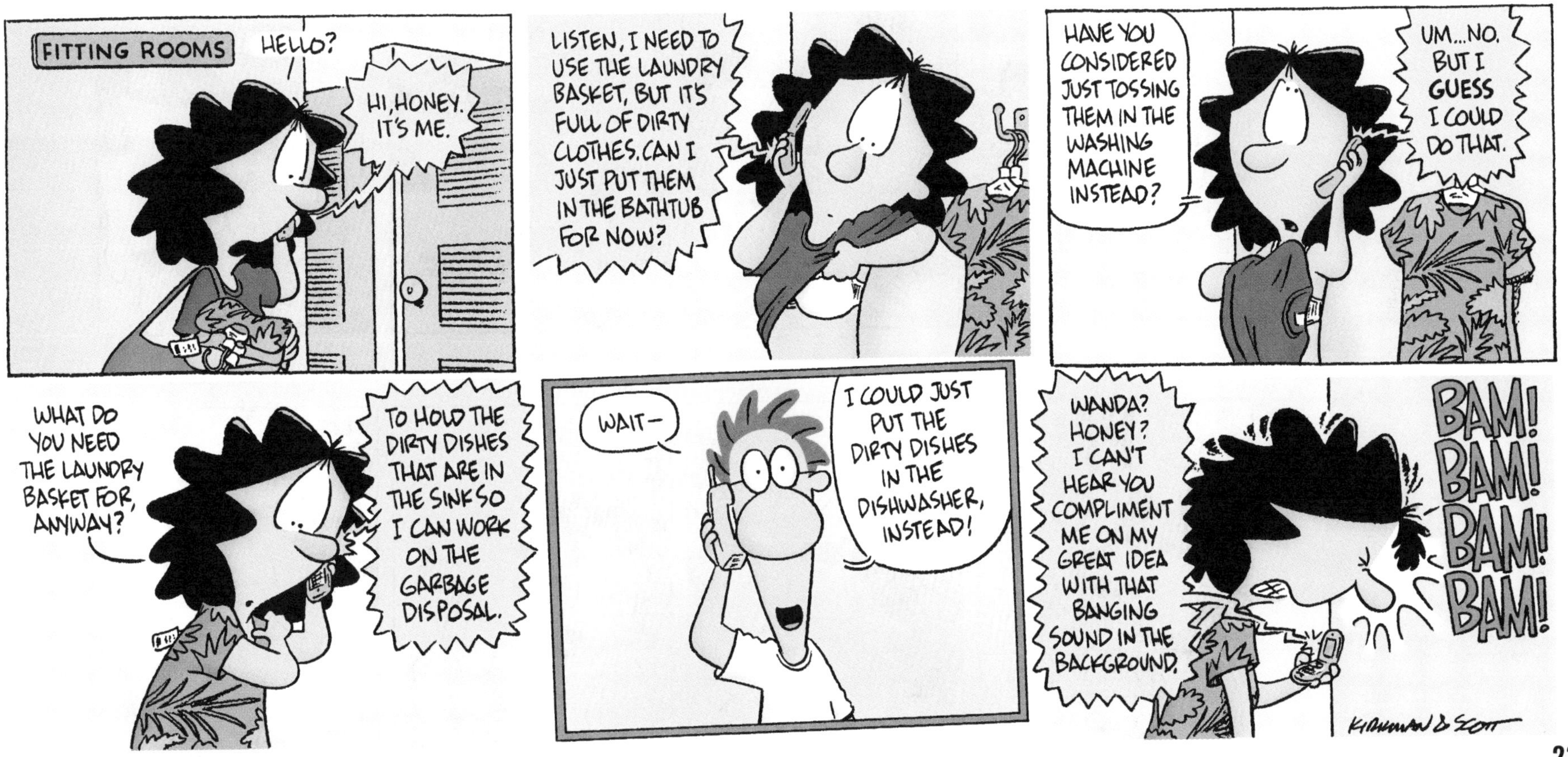

FITTING ROOMS
HELLO?
HI, HONEY. IT'S ME.
LISTEN, I NEED TO USE THE LAUNDRY BASKET, BUT IT'S FULL OF DIRTY CLOTHES. CAN I JUST PUT THEM IN THE BATHTUB FOR NOW?
HAVE YOU CONSIDERED JUST TOSSING THEM IN THE WASHING MACHINE INSTEAD?
UM...NO. BUT I GUESS I COULD DO THAT.
WHAT DO YOU NEED THE LAUNDRY BASKET FOR, ANYWAY?
TO HOLD THE DIRTY DISHES THAT ARE IN THE SINK SO I CAN WORK ON THE GARBAGE DISPOSAL.
WAIT—
I COULD JUST PUT THE DIRTY DISHES IN THE DISHWASHER, INSTEAD!
WANDA? HONEY? I CAN'T HEAR YOU COMPLIMENT ME ON MY GREAT IDEA WITH THAT BANGING SOUND IN THE BACKGROUND.
BAM! BAM! BAM! BAM!
KIRKMAN & SCOTT

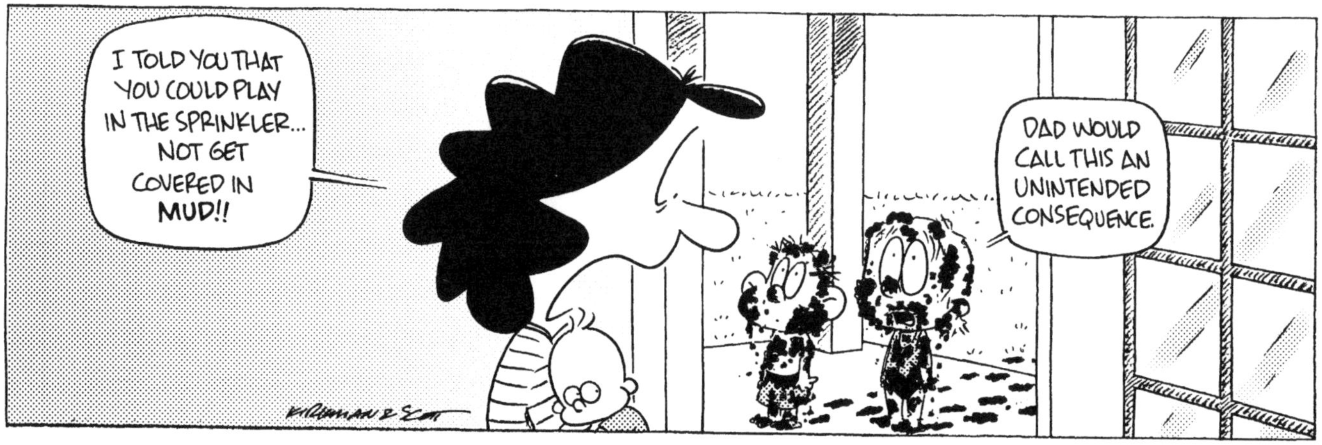
I TOLD YOU THAT YOU COULD PLAY IN THE SPRINKLER... NOT GET COVERED IN **MUD!!**
DAD WOULD CALL THIS AN UNINTENDED CONSEQUENCE.

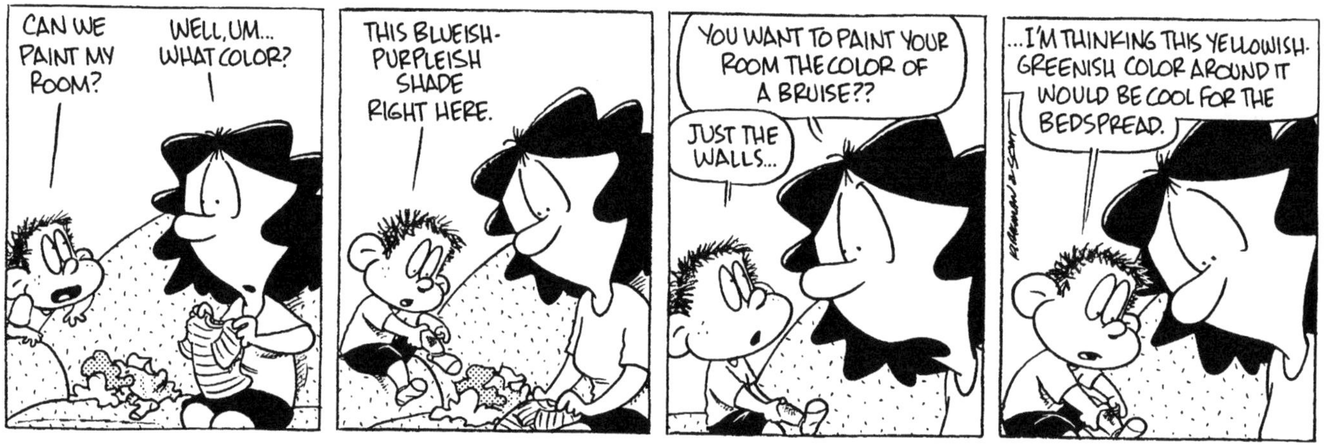
CAN WE PAINT MY ROOM?
WELL, UM... WHAT COLOR?
THIS BLUEISH-PURPLEISH SHADE RIGHT HERE.
YOU WANT TO PAINT YOUR ROOM THE COLOR OF A BRUISE??
JUST THE WALLS...
...I'M THINKING THIS YELLOWISH-GREENISH COLOR AROUND IT WOULD BE COOL FOR THE BEDSPREAD.

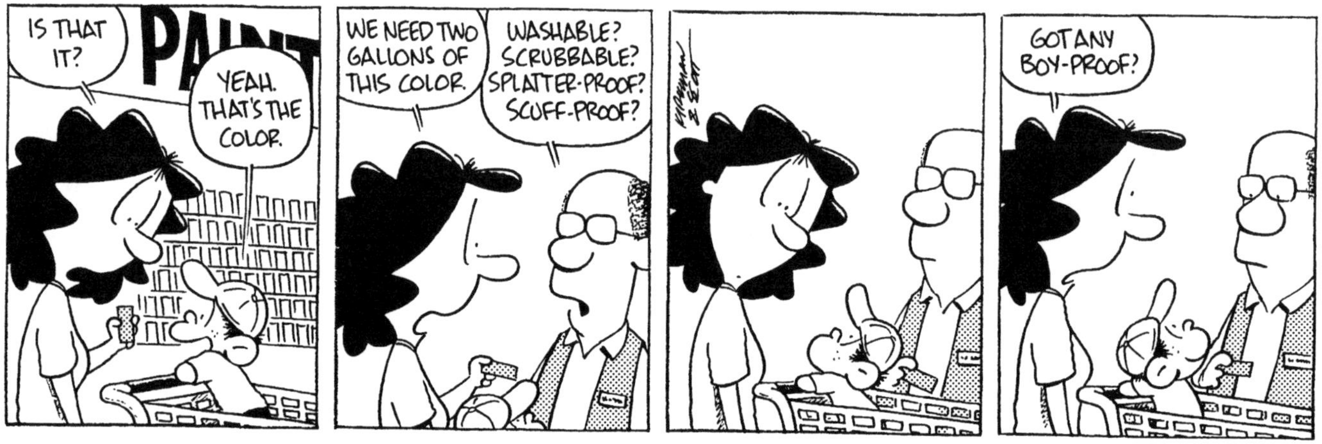
IS THAT IT?
PAINT
YEAH. THAT'S THE COLOR.
WE NEED TWO GALLONS OF THIS COLOR.
WASHABLE? SCRUBBABLE? SPLATTER-PROOF? SCUFF-PROOF?
GOT ANY BOY-PROOF?

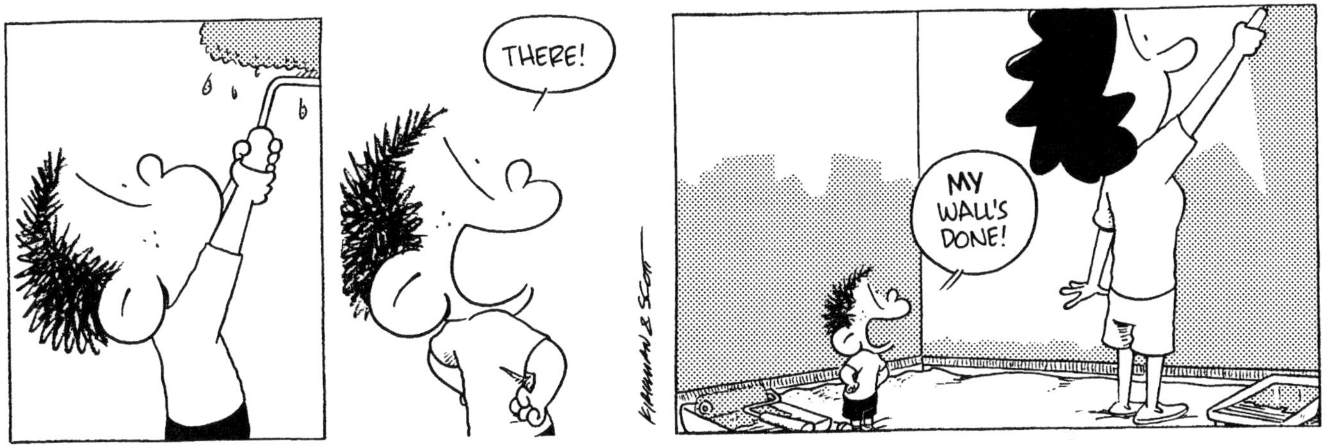
THERE!
MY WALL'S DONE!

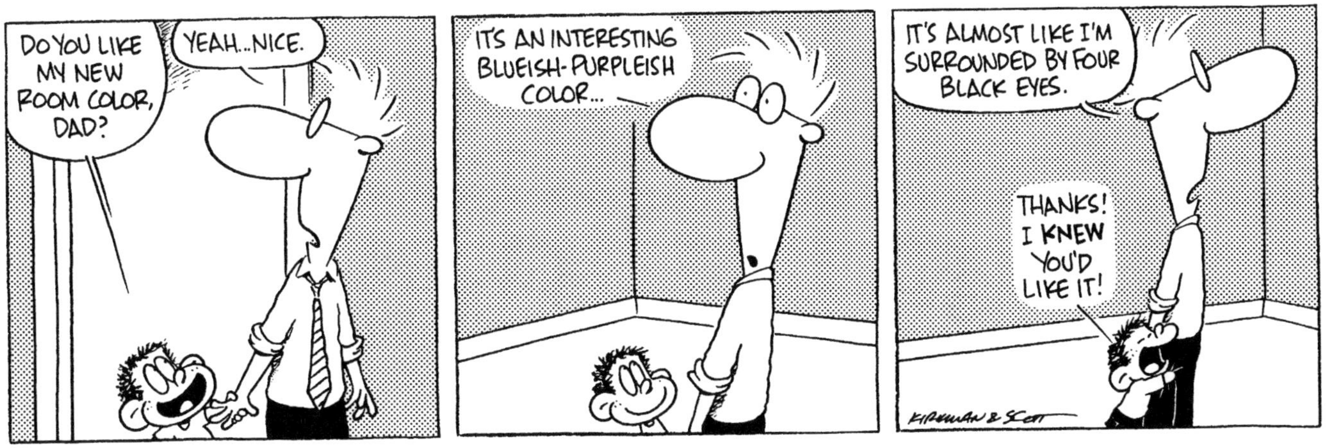
DO YOU LIKE MY NEW ROOM COLOR, DAD?
YEAH...NICE.
IT'S AN INTERESTING BLUEISH-PURPLEISH COLOR...
IT'S ALMOST LIKE I'M SURROUNDED BY FOUR BLACK EYES.
THANKS! I **KNEW** YOU'D LIKE IT!
KIRKMAN & SCOTT

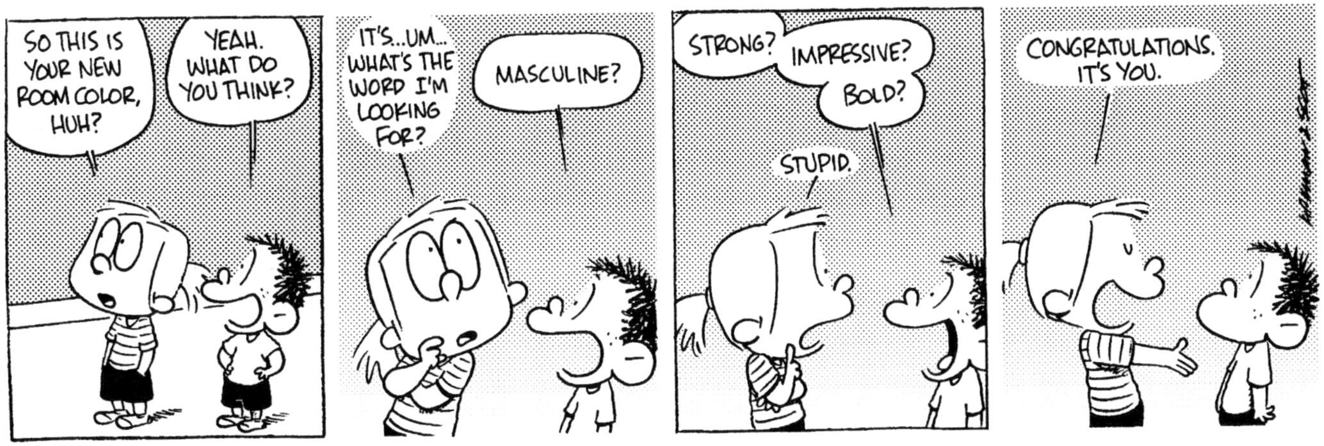
SO THIS IS YOUR NEW ROOM COLOR, HUH?
YEAH. WHAT DO YOU THINK?
IT'S...UM... WHAT'S THE WORD I'M LOOKING FOR?
MASCULINE?
STRONG?
IMPRESSIVE?
BOLD?
STUPID.
CONGRATULATIONS. IT'S YOU.

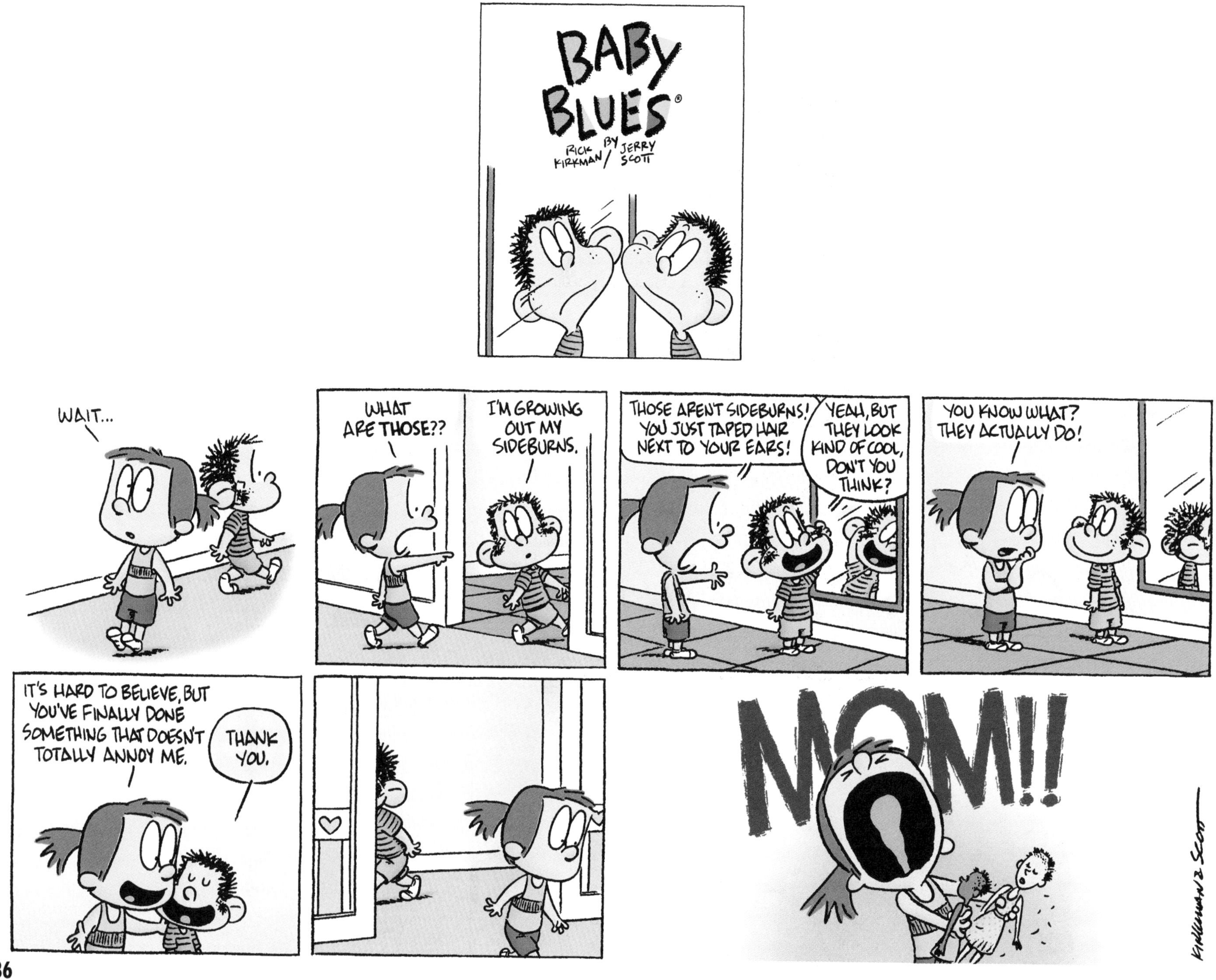
BABY BLUES®
BY RICK KIRKMAN / JERRY SCOTT
WAIT...
WHAT ARE THOSE??
I'M GROWING OUT MY SIDEBURNS.
THOSE AREN'T SIDEBURNS! YOU JUST TAPED HAIR NEXT TO YOUR EARS!
YEAH, BUT THEY LOOK KIND OF COOL, DON'T YOU THINK?
YOU KNOW WHAT? THEY ACTUALLY DO!
IT'S HARD TO BELIEVE, BUT YOU'VE FINALLY DONE SOMETHING THAT DOESN'T TOTALLY ANNOY ME.
THANK YOU.
MOM!!
KIRKMAN & SCOTT

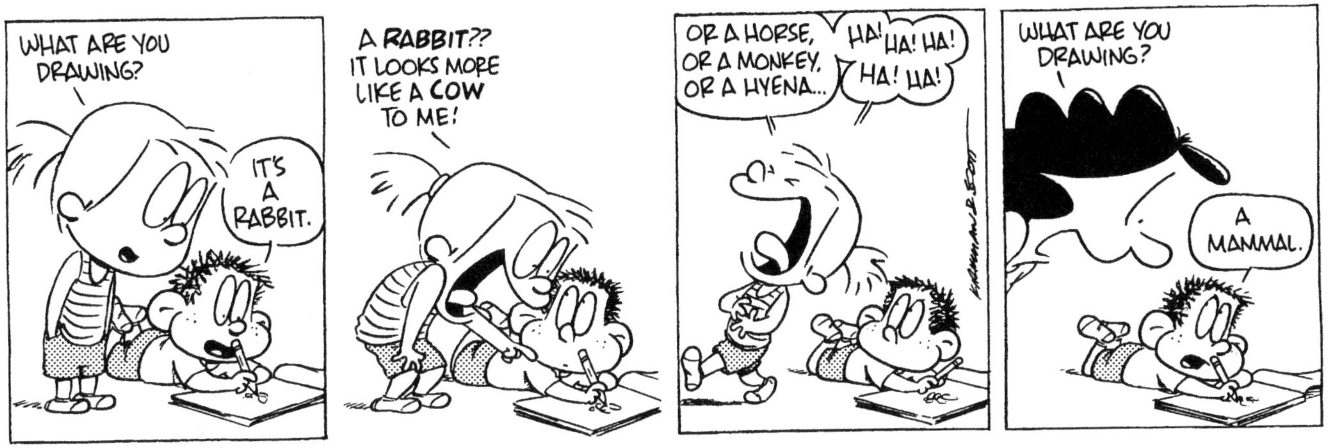
WHAT ARE YOU DRAWING?
IT'S A RABBIT.
A **RABBIT**?? IT LOOKS MORE LIKE A **COW** TO ME!
OR A HORSE, OR A MONKEY, OR A HYENA...
HA! HA! HA! HA! HA!
WHAT ARE YOU DRAWING?
A MAMMAL.

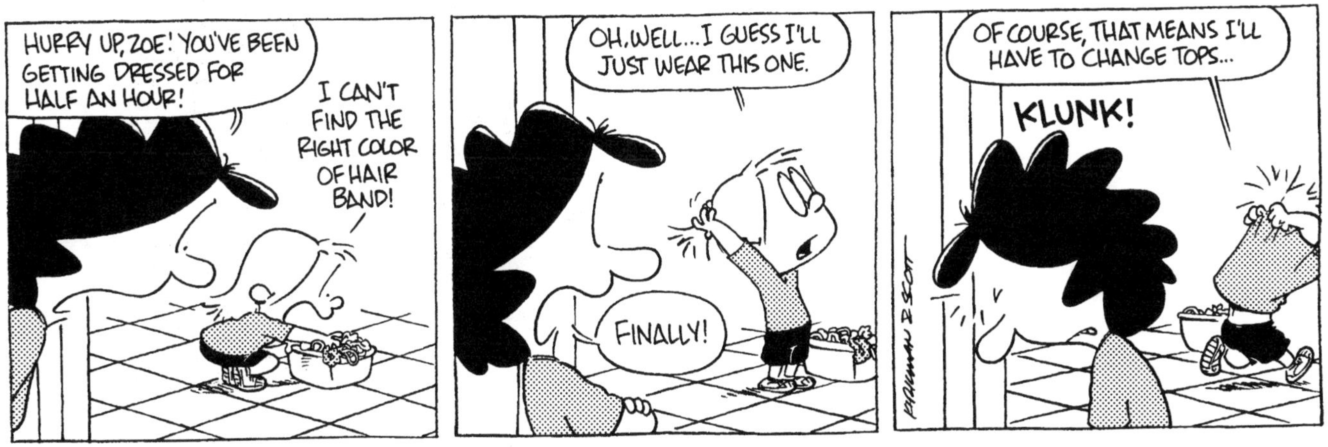
HURRY UP, ZOE! YOU'VE BEEN GETTING DRESSED FOR HALF AN HOUR!
I CAN'T FIND THE RIGHT COLOR OF HAIR BAND!
OH, WELL... I GUESS I'LL JUST WEAR THIS ONE.
FINALLY!
OF COURSE, THAT MEANS I'LL HAVE TO CHANGE TOPS...
KLUNK!

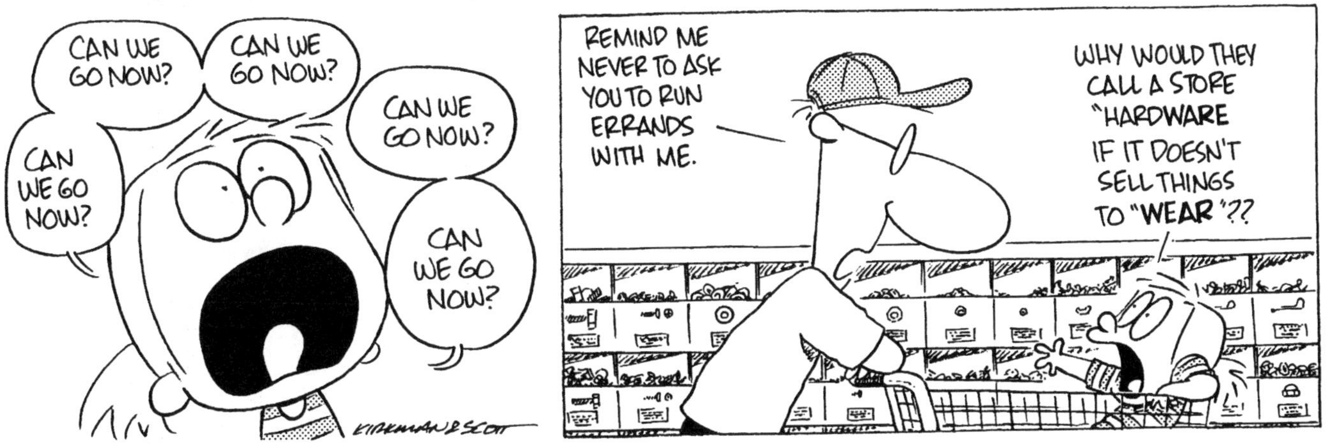
CAN WE GO NOW?
CAN WE GO NOW?
CAN WE GO NOW?
CAN WE GO NOW?
CAN WE GO NOW?
REMIND ME NEVER TO ASK YOU TO RUN ERRANDS WITH ME.
WHY WOULD THEY CALL A STORE "**HARDWARE**" IF IT DOESN'T SELL THINGS TO "**WEAR**"??

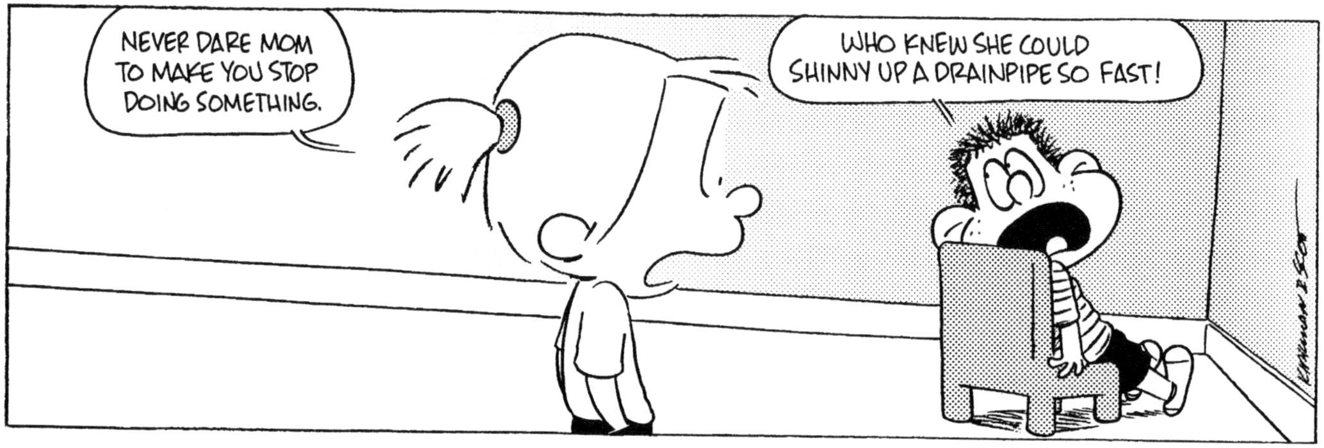
NEVER DARE MOM TO MAKE YOU STOP DOING SOMETHING.
WHO KNEW SHE COULD SHINNY UP A DRAINPIPE SO FAST!

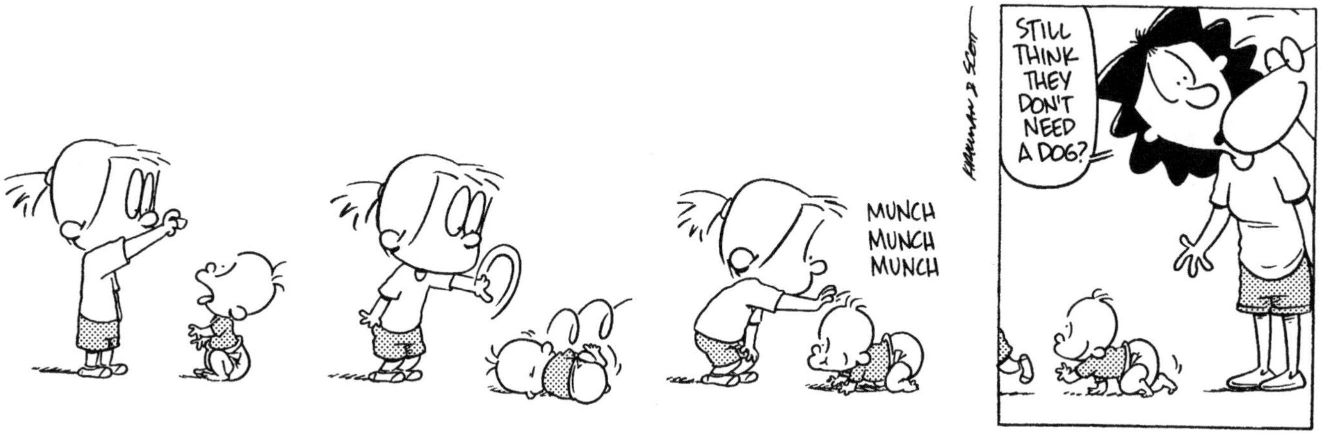
MUNCH MUNCH MUNCH
STILL THINK THEY DON'T NEED A DOG?

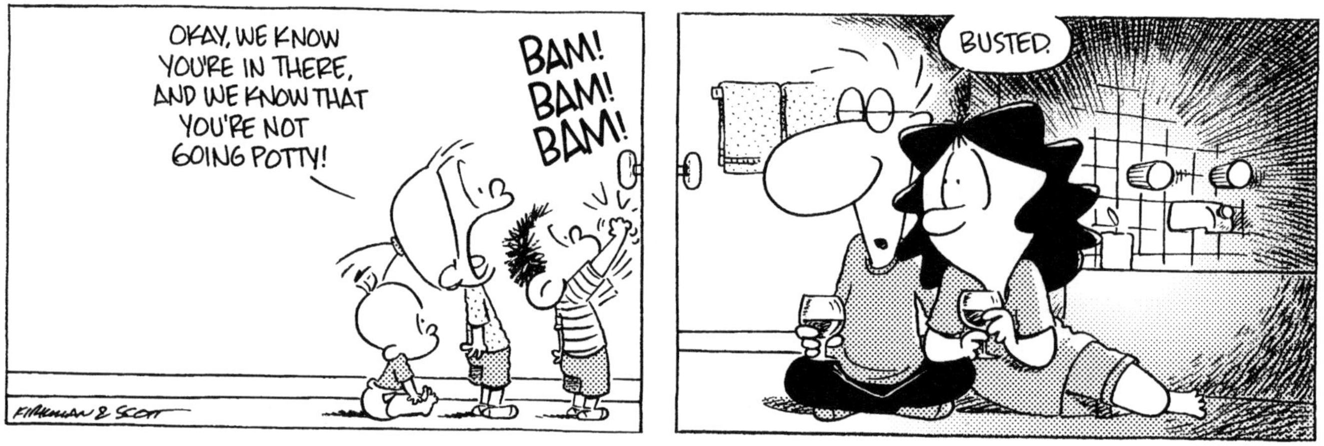
OKAY, WE KNOW YOU'RE IN THERE, AND WE KNOW THAT YOU'RE NOT GOING POTTY!
BAM! BAM! BAM!
BUSTED.

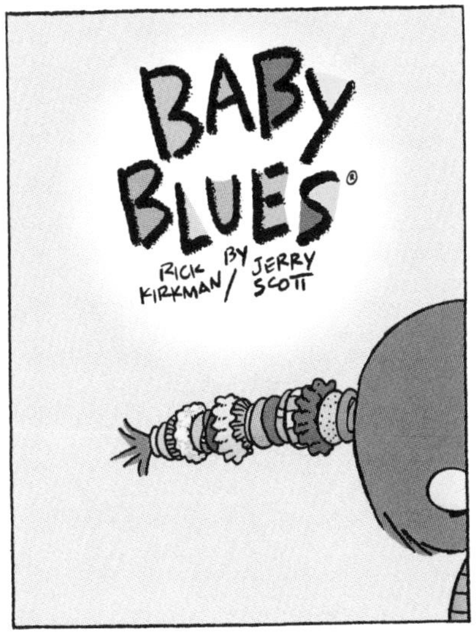
BABY BLUES®
BY RICK KIRKMAN / JERRY SCOTT

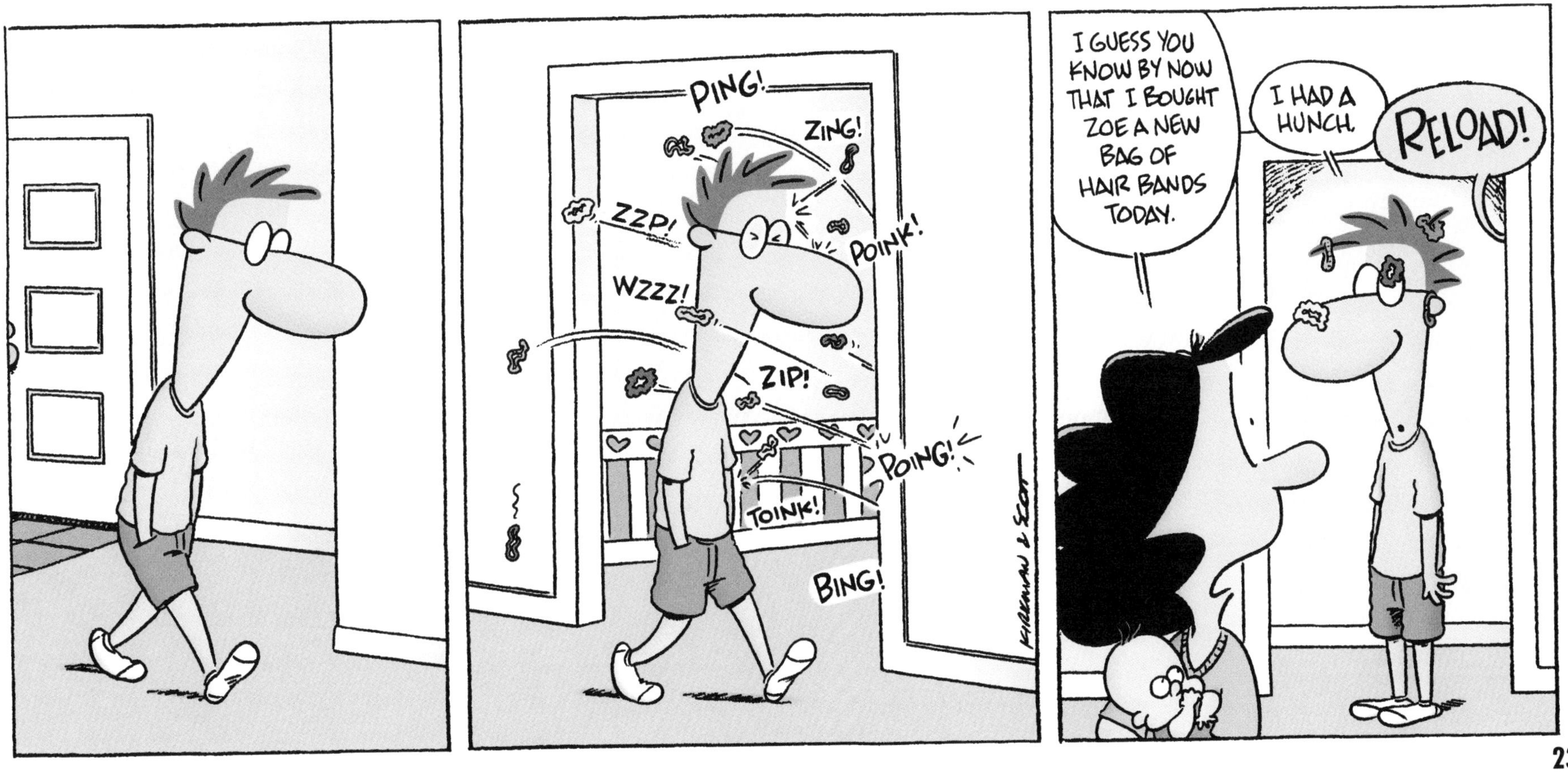
PING!
ZING!
ZZP!
POINK!
WZZZ!
ZIP!
POING!
TOINK!
BING!
KIRKMAN & SCOTT
I GUESS YOU KNOW BY NOW THAT I BOUGHT ZOE A NEW BAG OF HAIR BANDS TODAY.
I HAD A HUNCH.
RELOAD!